SOCIAL ETHICS

MORALITY AND SOCIAL POLICY

SOCIAL ETHICS

MORALITY AND SOCIAL POLICY

THIRD EDITION

Thomas A. Mappes
Frostburg State College

Jane S. Zembaty
University of Dayton

McGRAW-HILL BOOK COMPANY

New York St. Louis San Francisco Auckland Bogotá Hamburg
London Madrid Mexico Milan Montreal New Delhi
Panama Paris São Paulo Singapore Sydney Tokyo Toronto

This book was set in Times Roman by J. M. Post Graphics, Corp.
The editor was Bettina Anderson;
the production supervisor was Joe Campanella;
the cover was designed by Infield + D'Astolfo Associates.
Project supervision was done by The Total Book.
R. R. Donnelley & Sons Company was printer and binder.

SOCIAL ETHICS
Morality and Social Policy

4 5 6 7 8 9 0   DOCDOC   8 9 8

ISBN 0-07-040125-X

Library of Congress Cataloging-in-Publication Data

Mappes, Thomas A.
   Social ethics.

   Includes bibliographies.
      1. Social ethics.   2. United States—Social policy.
   3. United States—Moral conditions.   I. Zembaty,
   Jane S.   II. Title.
   HM216.M27   1987   170   86-10510
   ISBN 0-07-040125-X

ABOUT THE AUTHORS

THOMAS A. MAPPES holds a B.S. in Chemistry from the University of Dayton and a Ph.D. in Philosophy from Georgetown University. He has been teaching in the Department of Philosophy at Frostburg State College since 1973 where he has attained the rank of professor. He is the coauthor of "Is Hume Really a Sceptic about Induction?" (*American Philosophical Quarterly*), and is the coeditor (with Jane S. Zembaty) of *Biomedical Ethics* (McGraw-Hill, 2d ed., 1986). He is a member of the Hume Society and the American Philosophical Association.

JANE S. ZEMBATY holds a B.A. in English from the State University College at Buffalo, New York and a Ph.D. in Philosophy from Georgetown University. She has been teaching ancient Greek philosophy and social philosophy at the University of Dayton since 1975, where she is an associate professor. In addition to *Biomedical Ethics*, her published work includes "Plato's *Timaeus*: Mass and Sortal Terms and Identity through Time in the Phenomenal World" (*Canadian Journal of Philosophy*). She is a member of the Society for Ancient Greek Philosophy and the American Philosophical Association.

CONTENTS

CHAPTER 8   ECONOMIC JUSTICE AND WELFARE   328

CHAPTER 9   WORLD HUNGER   376

PREFACE

Is the death penalty a morally acceptable type of punishment? Is our human interest in eating meat sufficient to justify the way in which we raise and slaughter animals? Do affluent, technologically advanced nations have moral obligations to aid technologically underdeveloped countries? Is society justified in enacting laws that limit individual liberty in sexual matters? Are nuclear deterrence policies that threaten massive nuclear destruction morally acceptable?

The way we answer such moral questions and the social policies we adopt in keeping with our answers will directly affect our lives. It is not surprising, therefore, that discussions of these and other contemporary moral issues often involve rhetorical arguments whose intent is to elicit highly emotional, nonobjective responses. This book is designed to provide material which will encourage an objective study of some contemporary moral problems. To achieve this end, we have developed chapters that bring the central issues into clear focus, while allowing the supporting arguments for widely diverse positions to be presented by those who embrace them.

With the appearance of this third edition, we are confident that *teachability* will continue to be the most salient characteristic of *Social Ethics*. All of the editorial features employed in the first two editions to enhance teachability have been retained in the third. An introduction to each chapter both sets the ethical issues and scans the various positions together with their supporting argumentation. Every selection is prefaced by a headnote that provides both biographical data on the author and a short statement of some of the key points or arguments to be found in the selection. Every selection is followed by questions whose purpose is to elicit further critical analysis and discussion. Finally, each chapter concludes with a short annotated bibliography designed to guide the reader in further research.

We have tried to provide readings that are free of unnecessary technical jargon and yet introduce serious moral argumentation. Further, in order to emphasize the connection of contemporary moral problems with matters of social policy, we have liberally incorporated relevant legal opinions. We have taken substantial editorial license by deleting almost all the numerous citations that usually attend legal writing in order to render the legal opinions maximally readable to the nonlegal eye. Those interested in further legal research can check the appropriate credit lines for the necessary bibliographical data to locate the cases in their original form. We should also note that, where appropriate, both in legal cases and in other readings, we have renumbered footnotes.

We would be remiss not to express our indebtedness to all those whose work is reprinted in these pages. We are also indebted to Joseph C. Kunkel, Patricia A. Johnson, Mark Wicclair, Angelo Bucchino, and Joy Kroeger Mappes for their helpful critical comments. Betty Hume, Lisa Carpenter, and Shelley Drees deserve thanks for their help with manuscript preparation, and we continue to be grateful to the reference librarians at both the University of Dayton and Frostburg State College.

Thomas A. Mappes

Jane S. Zembaty

CHAPTER 1

ABORTION

With the landmark abortion decision of the United States Supreme Court in *Roe v. Wade* (1973), restrictive abortion laws, except under narrowly defined conditions, have been ruled unconstitutional. Thus abortion is *legally* available. The ethical (moral) acceptability of abortion, however, remains a hotly contested issue. This chapter focuses attention on abortion as an ethical issue, that is, on the morality of abortion. In addition, some attention is given to the social policy aspects of abortion.

ABORTION: THE ETHICAL ISSUE

Discussions of the ethical acceptability of abortion often take for granted (1) an awareness of the various kinds of reasons that may be given for having an abortion and (2) a basic acquaintance with the biological development of a human fetus.

1 Reasons for Abortion

Why would a woman have an abortion? The following catalog, not meant to provide an exhaustive survey, is sufficient to indicate that there is a wide range of potential reasons for abortion.

(a) In certain extreme cases, if the fetus is allowed to develop normally and come to term, the mother herself will die.

(b) In other cases it is not the mother's life but her health, physical or mental, that will be severely endangered if the pregnancy is allowed to continue.

(c) There are also cases in which the pregnancy will probably, or surely, produce a severely deformed child.

(**d**) There are others in which the pregnancy is the result of rape or incest.[1]

(**e**) There are instances in which the mother is unmarried and there will be the social stigma of illegitimacy.

(**f**) There are other instances in which having a child, or having another child, will be an unbearable financial burden.

(**g**) Certainly common, and perhaps most common of all, are those instances in which having a child will interfere with the happiness of the woman, or the joint happiness of the parents, or even the joint happiness of a family unit that already includes children. Here there are almost endless possibilities. The woman may desire a professional career. A couple may be content and happy together and feel their relationship would be damaged by the intrusion of a child. Parents may have older children and not feel up to raising another child, etc.

2 The Biological Development of a Human Fetus

During the course of a human pregnancy, in the nine-month period from conception to birth, the product of conception undergoes a continual process of change and development. *Conception* takes place when a male germ cell (the spermatozoon) combines with a female germ cell (the ovum), resulting in a single cell (the single-cell zygote), which embodies the full genetic code, twenty-three pairs of chromosomes. The single-cell zygote soon begins a process of cellular division. The resultant multicell zygote, while continuing to grow and beginning to take shape, proceeds to move through the fallopian tube and then to undergo gradual *implantation* at the uterine wall. The unborn entity is formally designated a zygote up until the time that implantation is complete, almost two weeks after conception. Thereafter, until the end of the eighth week, roughly the point at which brain waves can be detected, the unborn entity is formally designated an *embryo*. It is in this embryonic period that organ systems and other human characteristics begin to undergo noticeable development. From the end of the eighth week until birth, the unborn entity is formally designated a *fetus*. (The term "fetus," however, is commonly used as a general term to designate the unborn entity, whatever its stage of development.) Two other points in the development of the fetus are especially noteworthy as relevant to discussions of abortion. First, somewhere between the twelfth and the sixteenth week *quickening* usually occurs. Quickening is the point at which the mother begins to feel the movements of the fetus. Second, somewhere between the twentieth and the twenty-eighth week the fetus reaches *viability*, the point at which it is capable of surviving outside the womb.

With the facts of fetal development in view, it may be helpful to indicate the various medical techniques of abortion. Early (first trimester) abortions were at one time performed by *dilatation and curettage* (D&C) but are now commonly performed by *uterine aspiration*, also called "suction curettage." The D&C features the stretching

---

[1]The expression "therapeutic abortion" suggests abortion for medical reasons. Accordingly, abortions corresponding to (a), (b), and (c) are usually said to be therapeutic. More problematically, abortions corresponding to (d) have often been identified as therapeutic. Perhaps it is presumed that pregnancies resulting from rape or incest are traumatic, thus a threat to mental health. Or perhaps calling such an abortion "therapeutic" is just a way of indicating that it is thought to be justifiable.

(dilatation) of the cervix and the scraping (curettage) of the inner walls of the uterus. Uterine aspiration simply involves sucking the fetus out of the uterus by means of a tube connected to a suction pump. Later abortions require *dilatation and evacuation* (D&E), *induction techniques,* or *hysterotomy.* In the D&E, which is the abortion procedure commonly used in the early stages of the second trimester, a forceps is used to dismember the fetus within the uterus; the fetal remains are then withdrawn through the cervix. In one commonly employed induction technique, a saline solution injected into the amniotic cavity induces labor, thus expelling the fetus. Another induction technique employs prostaglandins (hormonelike substances) to induce labor. Hysterotomy—in essence a miniature cesarean section—is a major surgical procedure and is uncommonly employed in the United States.

A brief discussion of fetal development together with a cursory survey of various reasons for abortion has prepared the way for a formulation of the ethical issue of abortion in its broadest terms. *Up to what point of fetal development, if any,* and *for what reasons, if any, is abortion ethically acceptable?* Some hold that abortion is *never* ethically acceptable, or at most is acceptable only where abortion is necessary to save the life of the mother. This view is frequently termed the *conservative* view on abortion. Others hold that abortion is *always* ethically acceptable—at any point of fetal development and for any of the standard reasons. This view is frequently termed the *liberal* view on abortion. Still others are anxious to defend more *moderate* views, holding that abortion is ethically acceptable up to a certain point of fetal development *and/or* holding that some reasons provide a sufficient justification for abortion whereas others do not.

THE CONSERVATIVE VIEW AND THE LIBERAL VIEW

The *moral status* of the fetus has been a pivotal issue in discussions of the ethical acceptability of abortion. The concept of moral status is commonly explicated in terms of rights. On this construal, to say that a fetus has moral status is to say that the fetus has rights. What kinds of rights, if any, does the fetus have? Does it have the same rights as more visible humans, and thus *full moral status,* as conservatives typically contend? Does it have no rights, and thus *no (significant) moral status,* as liberals typically contend? (Or perhaps, as some moderates argue, does the fetus have a subsidiary or *partial moral status,* however this is to be conceptualized?) If the fetus has no rights, the liberal is prone to argue, then it does not have any more right to life than a piece of tissue such as an appendix, and an abortion is no more morally objectionable than an appendectomy. If the fetus has the same rights as any other human being, the conservative is prone to argue, then it has the same right to life as the latter, and an abortion, except perhaps when the mother's life is endangered, is as morally objectionable as any other murder.

Discussions of the moral status of the fetus often refer directly to the biological development of the fetus and pose the question: At what point in the continuous development of the fetus do we have a human life? In the context of such discussions, "human" implies full moral status, "nonhuman" implies no (significant) moral status, and any notion of partial moral status is systematically excluded. To distinguish the human from the nonhuman, to "draw the line," and to do so in a nonarbitrary way, is the central matter of concern. The *conservative* on abortion typically holds that the line must be drawn at conception. Usually the conservative argues that conception is the only point at which the line can be nonarbitrarily drawn. Against attempts to draw the line at points such as implantation, quickening, viability, or birth, considerations of continuity in the development of the fetus are pressed. The conservative is sometimes said to employ "slippery-slope arguments," that is, to argue that a line cannot be securely drawn anywhere along the path of fetal development. It is said that the line will inescapably slide back to the point of conception to find objective support. John T. Noonan argues in this fashion as he provides a defense of the conservative view in one of the selections in this chapter.

With regard to "drawing the line," the *liberal* typically contends that the fetus remains nonhuman even in its most advanced stages of development. The liberal, of course, does not mean to deny that a fetus is biologically a human fetus. Rather the claim is that the fetus is not human in any morally significant sense—it has no (significant) moral status. This point is often made in terms of the concept of personhood. Mary Anne Warren, who defends the liberal view on abortion in one of this chapter's selections, argues that the fetus is not a person. She also contends that the fetus bears so little resemblance to a person that it cannot be said to have a significant right to life. It is important to notice that, as Warren analyzes the concept of personhood, even a newborn baby is not a person. This conclusion, as might be expected, prompts Warren to a consideration of the moral justifiability of infanticide, an issue closely related to the problem of abortion.

Though the conservative view on abortion is most commonly predicated on the straightforward contention that the fetus is a person from conception, there are at least two other lines of argument that have been advanced in its defense. One conservative, advancing what might be labeled the "presumption argument," writes:

> In being willing to kill the embryo, we accept responsibility for killing what we must admit *may* be a person. There is some reason to believe it is—namely the *fact* that it is a living, human individual and the inconclusiveness of arguments that try to exclude it from the protected circle of personhood.
> *To be willing to kill what for all we know could be a person is to be willing to kill it if it is a person.* And since we cannot absolutely settle if it is a person except by a metaphysical postulate, for all practical purposes we must hold that to be willing to kill the embryo is to be willing to kill a person.[2]

In accordance with this line of argument, though it may not be possible to show conclusively that the fetus is a person from conception, we must presume that it is. Another line of argument that has been advanced by some conservatives emphasizes the potential rather than the actual personhood of the fetus. Even if the fetus is not a person, it is said, there can be no doubt that it is a potential person. Accordingly, by virtue of its potential personhood, the fetus must be accorded a right to life. Mary

---

[2]Germain Grisez, *Abortion: The Myths, the Realities, and the Arguments* (New York: Corpus Books, 1970), p. 306.

Anne Warren, in response to this line of argument, argues that the potential personhood of the fetus provides no basis for the claim that it has a significant right to life.

MODERATE VIEWS

The conservative and liberal views, as explicated, constitute two extreme poles on the spectrum of ethical views of abortion. Each of the extreme views is marked by a formal simplicity. The conservative proclaims abortion to be immoral, irrespective of the stage of fetal development and irrespective of alleged justifying reasons. The one exception, admitted by some conservatives, is the case in which abortion is necessary to save the life of the mother.[3] The liberal proclaims abortion to be morally acceptable, irrespective of the stage of fetal development.[4] Moreover, there is no need to draw distinctions between those reasons which are sufficient to justify abortion and those which are not. No justification is needed. The *moderate,* in vivid contrast to both the conservative and the liberal, is unwilling to sweepingly condemn or condone abortion. Some abortions are morally justifiable; some are morally objectionable. In some moderate views, the stage of fetal development is a relevant factor in the assessment of the moral acceptability of abortion. In other moderate views, the alleged justifying reason is a relevant factor in the assessment of the moral acceptability of abortion. In still other moderate views, both the stage of fetal development and the alleged justifying reason are relevant factors in the assessment of the moral acceptability of abortion.

Moderate views have been developed in accordance with the following clearly identifiable strategies:

1   Moderation of the Conservative View

One strategy for generating a moderate view presumes the typical conservative contention that the fetus has full moral status from conception. What is denied, however,

---

[3]One especially prominent conservative view is associated with the Roman Catholic Church. In accordance with Catholic moral teaching, the *direct* killing of innocent human life is forbidden. Hence, abortion is forbidden. Even if the mother's life is in danger, perhaps because her heart or kidney function is inadequate, abortion is impermissible. In two special cases, however, procedures resulting in the death of the fetus are allowable. In the case of an ectopic pregnancy, where the developing fetus is lodged in the fallopian tube, the fallopian tube may be removed. In the case of a pregnant woman with a cancerous uterus, the cancerous uterus may be removed. In these cases, the death of the fetus is construed as *indirect* killing, the foreseen but unintended by-product of a surgical procedure designed to protect the life of the mother. If the distinction between direct and indirect killing is a defensible one (and this is a controversial issue), it might still be suggested that the distinction is not rightly applied in the Roman Catholic view of abortion. For example, some critics contend that abortion may be construed as indirect killing, indeed an allowable form of indirect killing, in at least all cases where it is necessary to save the life of the mother. For one helpful exposition and critical analysis of the Roman Catholic position on abortion, see Daniel Callahan, *Abortion: Law, Choice and Morality* (New York: Macmillan, 1970), chap. 12, pp. 409–447.

[4]In considering the liberal contention that abortions are morally acceptable irrespective of the stage of fetal development, we should take note of an ambiguity in the concept of abortion. Does "abortion" refer merely to the termination of a pregnancy in the sense of detaching the fetus from the mother, or does "abortion" entail the death of the fetus as well? Whereas the abortion of a *previable* fetus entails its death, the "abortion" of a *viable* fetus, by means of hysterotomy (a miniature cesarean section), does not entail the death of the fetus and would seem to be tantamount to the birth of a baby. With regard to the "abortion" of a *viable* fetus, liberals can defend the woman's right to detach the fetus from her body without contending that the woman has the right to insist on the death of the child.

is that we must conclude to the moral impermissibility of abortion in *all* cases. In one of this chapter's readings, Jane English attempts to moderate the conservative view in just this way. She argues that certain abortion cases may be assimilated to cases of self-defense. Thus, for English, on the presumption that the fetus from conception has full moral status, some reasons are sufficient to justify abortion whereas others are not.

2 Moderation of the Liberal View

A second strategy for generating a moderate view presumes the liberal contention that the fetus has no (significant) moral status even in the latest stages of pregnancy. What is denied, however, is that we must conclude to the moral permissibility of abortion in *all* cases. It might be said, in accordance with this line of thought, that even though abortion does not violate the rights of the fetus (which is presumed to have no rights), the practice of abortion remains ethically problematic because of its negative social consequences. Such an argument seems especially forceful in the later stages of pregnancy, when the fetus increasingly resembles a newborn infant. It is argued that very late abortions have a brutalizing effect on those involved and, in various ways, lead to the breakdown of attitudes associated with respect for human life. Jane English, in an effort to moderate the liberal view, advances an argument of this general type. Even if the fetus is not a person, she holds, it is gradually becoming increasingly personlike. Appealing to a "coherence of attitudes," she argues that abortion demands more weighty justifying reasons in the later stages of pregnancy than it does in the earlier stages.

3 Moderation in "Drawing the Line"

A third strategy for generating a moderate view, in fact a whole range of moderate views, is associated with "drawing the line" discussions. Whereas the conservative typically draws the line between human (having full moral status) and nonhuman (having no moral status) at conception, and the liberal typically draws that same line at birth (or sometime thereafter), a moderate view may be generated by drawing the line somewhere between these two extremes. For example, the line might be drawn at implantation, at the point where brain activity begins, at quickening, at viability, etc. Whereas drawing the line at implantation would tend to generate a rather "conservative" moderate view, drawing the line at viability would tend to generate a rather "liberal" moderate view. Wherever the line is drawn, it is the burden of any such moderate view to show that the point specified is a nonarbitrary one. Once such a point has been specified, however, it might be argued that abortion is ethically acceptable before that point and ethically unacceptable after that point. Or further stipulations may be added in accordance with strategies (1) and (2) above.

4 Moderation in the Assignment of Moral Status

A fourth strategy for generating a moderate view depends on assigning the fetus some sort of subsidiary or *partial moral status*, an approach taken by Daniel Callahan in one of this chapter's readings. It would seem that anyone who defends a moderate view based on the concept of partial moral status must first of all face the problem of explicating the nature of such partial moral status. A second and closely related problem is that of showing how the interests of those with partial moral status are to be weighed against the interests of those with full moral status.

ABORTION AND SOCIAL POLICY

In the United States, the Supreme Court's decision in *Roe v. Wade* (1973) is at the core of existing social policy on abortion. This case had the effect, for all practical purposes, of legalizing "abortion-on-request." The Court held that it was unconstitutional for a state to have laws prohibiting the abortion of a previable fetus. According to the Court, a woman has a constitutionally guaranteed right to decide to terminate a pregnancy (prior to viability), although a state, for reasons related to maternal health, may restrict the manner and circumstances in which abortions are performed subsequent to the end of the first trimester. The reasoning underlying the Court's holding in *Roe* can be found in the majority opinion reprinted in this chapter.

Since the action of the Court in *Roe* had the practical effect of establishing a woman's legal right to choose whether or not to abort, it was enthusiastically received by "right-to-choose" forces. On the other hand, "right-to-life" forces, committed to the conservative view on the morality of abortion, vehemently denounced the Court for "legalizing murder." In response to *Roe,* right-to-life forces have adopted a number of political strategies. Three of the most significant of these strategies will be discussed here.

For right-to-life forces, the enactment of a constitutional amendment directly overruling *Roe* and banning abortion is the most desirable political outcome. (Less desirable would be the enactment of an amendment allowing Congress and/or each state to decide whether or not to restrict abortion.) The proposed Human Life Amendment, worded so as to declare the personhood of the fetus, is calculated to achieve the legal prohibition of abortion, allowing an exception only when abortion is necessary to save the life of the mother. Right-to-choose forces typically argue that the Human Life Amendment represents an illicit attempt to impose the moral views of one group (conservatives on abortion) on those who have different views. Thus, to some extent, the justifiability of such an amendment is bound up with a much broader question, whether or not it is justifiable to employ the law in an effort to "enforce morality." (Cf. the discussion of the principle of legal moralism in the introduction to Chapter 7.)

Right-to-life forces have been successful in achieving a more limited political aim, the cutoff of Medicaid funding for abortion. Medicaid is a social program designed to provide public funds to pay for the medical care of impoverished people. At issue in *Harris v. McRae,* decided by the Supreme Court in 1980, was the constitutionality of the so-called Hyde Amendment, legislation that had passed Congress with vigorous right-to-life support. The Hyde Amendment, in the version considered by the Court, restricted federal Medicaid funding to (1) cases in which the mother's life is endangered and (2) cases of rape and incest. The Court, in a five-to-four decision, upheld the constitutionality of the Hyde Amendment. According to the Court, a woman's right to an abortion does not entail *the right to have society fund the abortion*. But if there is no constitutional obstacle to the cutoff of Medicaid funding for abortion, it must still be asked if society's refusal to fund the abortions of poor women is an ethically sound social policy. Considerations of social justice are often pressed by those who argue that it is not.

Right-to-life forces have also made efforts to secure the passage of statutes designed (in various ways) to place obstacles in the path of women seeking an abortion. In *Akron v. Akron Center for Reproductive Health* (1983), the Supreme Court considered the constitutionality of a local ordinance of this sort. Although the Court found the Akron ordinance unconstitutional, in a six-to-three decision, Justice Sandra Day O'Connor's *dissenting* opinion explicitly calls for the abandonment of the framework of thought embodied in *Roe v. Wade*. Justice O'Connor's opinion is presented as this chapter's last selection.

Thomas A. Mappes

An Almost Absolute Value in History

John T. Noonan, Jr.

John T. Noonan, Jr., is professor of law at the University of California, Berkeley. His academic interests extend beyond matters of law to philosophical and theological issues, and his intellectual allegiance in this regard is with the Roman Catholic tradition. Among his books are Contraception: A History of Its Treatment by the Catholic Theologians and Canonists *(1965),* Persons and Masks of the Law *(1976), and* A Private Choice: Abortion in America in the Seventies *(1979).*

Noonan, defending the conservative view on abortion, immediately raises the question of how to determine the *humanity* of a being. In an updated version of the traditional theological view he contends that, if a being is conceived by human parents and thereby has a human genetic code, then that being is a *human being.* Conception is the point at which the nonhuman becomes the human. Noonan argues that other alleged criteria of humanity are inadequate. He also argues, primarily through an analysis of probabilities, that his own criterion of humanity is objectively based and nonarbitrary. Finally, Noonan contends, once the humanity of the fetus is recognized, we must judge abortion morally wrong, except in those rare cases where the mother's life is in danger.

The most fundamental question involved in the long history of thought on abortion is: How do you determine the humanity of a being? To phrase the question that way is to put in comprehensive humanistic terms what the theologians either dealt with as

Reprinted by permission of the publishers from John T. Noonan, Jr., ed., *The Morality of Abortion: Legal and Historical Perspectives* (Cambridge, Mass.: Harvard University Press), Copyright © 1970 by the President and Fellows of Harvard College.

an explicitly theological question under the heading of "ensoulment" or dealt with implicitly in their treatment of abortion. The Christian position as it originated did not depend on a narrow theological or philosophical concept. It had no relation to theories of infant baptism. It appealed to no special theory of instantaneous ensoulment. It took the world's view on ensoulment as that view changed from Aristotle to Zacchia. There was, indeed, theological influence affecting the theory of ensoulment finally adopted, and, of course, ensoulment itself was a theological concept, so that the position was always explained in theological terms. But the theological notion of ensoulment could easily be translated into humanistic language by substituting "human" for "rational soul"; the problem of knowing when a man is a man is common to theology and humanism.

If one steps outside the specific categories used by the theologians, the answer they gave can be analyzed as a refusal to discriminate among human beings on the basis of their varying potentialities. Once conceived, the being was recognized as man because he had man's potential. The criterion for humanity, thus, was simple and all-embracing: if you are conceived by human parents, you are human.

The strength of this position may be tested by a review of some of the other distinctions offered in the contemporary controversy over legalizing abortion. Perhaps the most popular distinction is in terms of viability. Before an age of so many months, the fetus is not viable, that is, it cannot be removed from the mother's womb and live apart from her. To that extent, the life of the fetus is absolutely dependent on the life of the mother. This dependence is made the basis of denying recognition to its humanity.

There are difficulties with this distinction. One is that the perfection of artificial incubation may make the fetus viable at any time: it may be removed and artificially sustained. Experiments with animals already show that such a procedure is possible. This hypothetical extreme case relates to an actual difficulty: there is considerable elasticity to the idea of viability. Mere length of life is not an exact measure. The viability of the fetus depends on the extent of its anatomical and functional development. The weight and length of the fetus are better guides to the state of its development than age, but weight and length vary. Moreover, different racial groups have different ages at which their fetuses are viable. Some evidence, for example, suggests that Negro fetuses mature more quickly than white fetuses. If viability is the norm, the standard would vary with race and with many individual circumstances.

The most important objection to this approach is that dependence is not ended by viability. The fetus is still absolutely dependent on someone's care in order to continue existence; indeed a child of one or three or even five years of age is absolutely dependent on another's care for existence; uncared for, the older fetus or the younger child will die as surely as the early fetus detached from the mother. The unsubstantial lessening in dependence at viability does not seem to signify any special acquisition of humanity.

A second distinction has been attempted in terms of experience. A being who has had experience, has lived and suffered, who possesses memories, is more human than one who has not. Humanity depends on formation by experience. The fetus is thus "unformed" in the most basic human sense.

This distinction is not serviceable for the embryo which is already experiencing and reacting. The embryo is responsive to touch after eight weeks and at least at that point is experiencing. At an earlier stage the zygote is certainly alive and responding to its environment. The distinction may also be challenged by the rare case where aphasia has erased adult memory: has it erased humanity? More fundamentally, this distinction leaves even the older fetus or the younger child to be treated as an unformed inhuman thing. Finally, it is not clear why experience as such confers humanity. It could be argued that certain central experiences such as loving or learning are necessary to make a man human. But then human beings who have failed to love or to learn might be excluded from the class called man.

A third distinction is made by appeal to the sentiments of adults. If a fetus dies, the grief of the parents is not the grief they would have for a living child. The fetus is an unnamed "it" till birth, and is not perceived as personality until at least the fourth month of existence when movements in the womb manifest a vigorous presence demanding joyful recognition by the parents.

Yet feeling is notoriously an unsure guide to the humanity of others. Many groups of humans have had difficulty in feeling that persons of another tongue, color, religion, sex, are as human as they. Apart from reactions to alien groups, we mourn the loss of a ten-year-old boy more than the loss of his one-day-old brother or his 90-year-old grandfather. The difference felt and the grief expressed vary with the potentialities extinguished, or the experience wiped out; they do not seem to point to any substantial difference in the humanity of baby, boy, or grandfather.

Distinctions are also made in terms of sensation by the parents. The embryo is felt within the womb only after about the fourth month. The embryo is seen only at birth. What can be neither seen nor felt is different from what is tangible. If the fetus cannot be seen or touched at all, it cannot be perceived as man.

Yet experience shows that sight is even more untrustworthy than feeling in determining humanity. By sight, color became an appropriate index for saying who was a man, and the evil of racial discrimination was given foundation. Nor can touch provide the test; a being confined by sickness, "out of touch" with others, does not thereby seem to lose his humanity. To the extent that touch still has appeal as a criterion, it appears to be a survival of the old English idea of "quickening"—a possible mistranslation of the Latin *animatus* used in the canon law. To that extent touch as a criterion seems to be dependent on the Aristotelian notion of ensoulment, and to fall when this notion is discarded.

Finally, a distinction is sought in social visibility. The fetus is not socially perceived as human. It cannot communicate with others. Thus, both subjectively and objectively, it is not a member of society. As moral rules are rules for the behavior of members of society to each other, they cannot be made for behavior toward what is not yet a member. Excluded from the society of men, the fetus is excluded from the humanity of men.

By force of the argument from the consequences, this distinction is to be rejected. It is more subtle than that founded on an appeal to physical sensation, but it is equally dangerous in its implications. If humanity depends on social recognition, individuals or whole groups may be dehumanized by being denied any status in their society.

Such a fate is fictionally portrayed in *1984* and has actually been the lot of many men in many societies. In the Roman empire, for example, condemnation to slavery meant the practical denial of most human rights; in the Chinese Communist world, landlords have been classified as enemies of the people and so treated as nonpersons by the state. Humanity does not depend on social recognition, though often the failure of society to recognize the prisoner, the alien, the heterodox as human has led to the destruction of human beings. Anyone conceived by a man and a woman is human. Recognition of this condition by society follows a real event in the objective order, however imperfect and halting the recognition. Any attempt to limit humanity to exclude some group runs the risk of furnishing authority and precedent for excluding other groups in the name of the consciousness or perception of the controlling group in the society.

A philosopher may reject the appeal to the humanity of the fetus because he views "humanity" as a secular view of the soul and because he doubts the existence of anything real and objective which can be identified as humanity. One answer to such a philosopher is to ask how he reasons about moral questions without supposing that there is a sense in which he and the others of whom he speaks are human. Whatever group is taken as the society which determines who may be killed is thereby taken as human. A second answer is to ask if he does not believe that there is a right and wrong way of deciding moral questions. If there is such a difference, experience may be appealed to: to decide who is human on the basis of the sentiment of a given society has led to consequences which rational men would characterize as monstrous.

The rejection of the attempted distinctions based on viability and visibility, experience and feeling, may be buttressed by the following considerations: Moral judgments often rest on distinctions, but if the distinctions are not to appear arbitrary fiat, they should relate to some real difference in probabilities. There is a kind of continuity in all life, but the earlier stages of the elements of human life possess tiny probabilities of development. Consider for example, the spermatozoa in any normal ejaculate: There are about 200,000,000 in any single ejaculate, of which one has a chance of developing into a zygote. Consider the oocytes which may become ova: there are 100,000 to 1,000,000 oocytes in a female infant, of which a maximum of 390 are ovulated. But once spermatozoon and ovum meet and the conceptus is formed, such studies as have been made show that roughly in only 20 percent of the cases will spontaneous abortion occur. In other words, the chances are about 4 out of 5 that this new being will develop. At this stage in the life of the being there is a sharp shift in probabilities, an immense jump in potentialities. To make a distinction between the rights of spermatozoa and the rights of the fertilized ovum is to respond to an enormous shift in possibilities. For about twenty days after conception the egg may split to form twins or combine with another egg to form a chimera, but the probability of either event happening is very small.

It may be asked, What does a change in biological probabilities have to do with establishing humanity? The argument from probabilities is not aimed at establishing humanity but at establishing an objective discontinuity which may be taken into account in moral discourse. As life itself is a matter of probabilities, as most moral reasoning is an estimate of probabilities, so it seems in accord with the structure of reality and the nature of moral thought to found a moral judgment on the change in probabilities at conception. The appeal to probabilities is the most commonsensical of arguments, to a greater or smaller degree all of us base our actions on probabilities, and in morals, as in law, prudence and negligence are often measured by the account one has taken of the probabilities. If the chance is 200,000,000 to 1 that the movement in the bushes into which you shoot is a man's, I doubt if many persons would hold you careless in shooting; but if the chances are 4 out of 5 that the movement is a human being's, few would acquit you of blame. Would the argument be different if only one out of ten children conceived came to term? Of course this argument would be different. This argument is an appeal to probabilities that actually exist, not to any and all states of affairs which may be imagined.

The probabilities as they do exist do not show the humanity of the embryo in the sense of a demonstration in logic any more than the probabilities of the movement in the bush being a man demonstrate beyond all doubt that the being is a man. The appeal is a "buttressing" consideration, showing the plausibility of the standard adopted. The argument focuses on the decisional factor in any moral judgment and assumes that part of the business of a moralist is drawing lines. One evidence of the nonarbitrary character of the line drawn is the difference of probabilities on either side of it. If a spermatozoon is destroyed, one destroys a being which had a chance of far less than 1 in 200 million of developing into a reasoning being, possessed of the genetic code, a heart and other organs, and capable of pain. If a fetus is destroyed, one destroys a being already possessed of the genetic code, organs, and sensitivity to pain, and one which had an 80 percent chance of developing further into a baby outside the womb who, in time, would reason.

The positive argument for conception as the decisive moment of humanization is that at conception the new being receives the genetic code. It is this genetic information which determines his characteristics, which is the biological carrier of the possibility of human wisdom, which makes him a self-evolving being. A being with a human genetic code is man.

This review of current controversy over the humanity of the fetus emphasizes what a fundamental question the theologians resolved in asserting the inviolability of the fetus. To regard the fetus as possessed of equal rights with other humans was not, however, to decide every case where abortion might be employed. It did decide the case where the argument was that the fetus should be aborted for its own good. To say a being was human was to say it had a destiny to decide for itself which could not be taken from it by another man's decision. But human beings with equal rights often come in conflict with each other, and some decision must be made as whose claims are to prevail. Cases of conflict involving the fetus are different only in two respects: the total inability of the fetus to speak for itself and the fact that the right of the fetus regularly at stake is the right to life itself.

The approach taken by the theologians to these conflicts was articulated in terms of "direct" and "indirect." Again, to look at what they were doing from outside their categories, they may be said to have been drawing lines or "balancing values." "Direct" and "indirect" are spatial metaphors; "line-drawing" is another. "To weigh" or "to balance" values is a metaphor of a more complicated mathematical sort hinting at the process which goes on in moral judgments. All the metaphors suggest that, in the moral judgments made, comparisons were necessary, that no value completely controlled. The principle of double effect was no doctrine fallen from heaven, but a method of analysis appropriate where two relative values were being compared. In Catholic moral theology, as it developed, life even of the innocent was not taken as an absolute. Judgments on acts affecting life issued from a process of weighing. In the weighing, the fetus was always given a value greater than zero, always a value separate and independent from its parents. This valuation was crucial and fundamental in all Christian thought on the subject and marked it off from any approach which considered that only the parents' interests needed to be considered.

Even with the fetus weighed as human, one interest could be weighed as equal or superior: that of the mother in her own life. The casuists between 1450 and 1895 were willing to weigh this interest as superior. Since 1895, that interest was given decisive weight only in the two special cases of the cancerous uterus and the ectopic pregnancy. In both of these cases the fetus itself had little chance of survival even if the abortion were not performed. As the balance was once struck in favor of the mother whenever her life was endangered, it could be so struck again. The balance reached between 1895 and 1930 attempted prudentially and pastorally to forestall a multitude of exceptions for interests less than life.

The perception of the humanity of the fetus and the weighing of fetal rights against other human rights constituted the work of the moral analysts. But what spirit animated their abstract judgments? For the Christian community it was the injunction of Scripture to love your neighbor as yourself. The fetus as human was a neighbor; his life had parity with one's own. The commandment gave life to what otherwise would have been only rational calculation.

The commandment could be put in humanistic as well as theological terms: Do not injure your fellow man without reason. In these terms, once the humanity of the fetus is perceived, abortion is never right except in self-defense. When life must be taken to save life, reason alone cannot say that a mother must prefer a child's life to her own. With this exception, now of great rarity, abortion violates the rational humanist tenet of the equality of human lives.

For Christians the commandment to love had received a special imprint in that the exemplar proposed of love was the love of the Lord for his disciples. In the light given by this example, self-sacrifice carried to the point of death seemed in the extreme situations not without meaning. In the less extreme cases, preference for one's own interests to the life of another seemed to express cruelty or selfishness irreconcilable with the demands of love.

QUESTIONS

1 Is conception an objectively based and nonarbitrary point at which to draw the line between the human and the nonhuman?

2 If you think that Noonan is wrong in drawing the line at conception, where would you draw the line? How would you answer the charge that the point you specify is an arbitrary one?

3 Consider the following argument: Let it be admitted that the fetus has full moral status from the moment of conception; nevertheless, abortion in the case of rape is morally justifiable because no person (in this case, the fetus) has the right to use another person's body, unless that right has been *freely* extended from the latter to the former. Is this argument successful in its effort to "moderate the conservative view?"

On the Moral and Legal Status of Abortion

Mary Anne Warren

Mary Anne Warren is a philosopher who teaches at San Francisco State University. Feminist-related issues provide one focal point of her philosophical work. Among her published articles are "Secondary Sexism and Quota Hiring," "Do Potential People Have Moral Rights?" and "Is Androgyny the Answer to Sexual Stereotyping?" She is also the author of The Nature of Woman: An Encyclopedia and Guide to the Literature *(1980).*

Warren, defending the liberal view on abortion, promptly distinguishes two senses of the term "human": (1) One is *human in the genetic sense* when one is a member of the biological species *Homo sapiens.* (2) One is *human in the moral sense* when one is a full-fledged member of the moral community. Warren attacks the presupposition underlying Noonan's argument against abortion—that the fetus is human in the moral sense. She contends that the moral community, the set of beings with full and equal moral rights, consists of all and only people (persons). (Thus she takes the concept of personhood to be equivalent to the concept of humanity in the moral sense.) After analyzing the concept of person, she concludes that a fetus is so unlike a person as to have no significant right to life. Nor, she argues, does the fetus's *potential* for being a person provide us any basis for ascribing to it any significant right to life. It follows, she contends, that a woman's right to obtain an abortion is absolute. Abortion is morally justified at any stage of fetal development. It also follows, she contends, that no legislation against abortion can be justified on the grounds of protecting the rights of the fetus. In a concluding postscript, Warren briefly assesses the moral justifiability of infanticide.

The question which we must answer in order to produce a satisfactory solution to the problem of the moral status of abortion is this: How are we to define the moral community, the set of beings with full and equal moral rights, such that we can decide whether a human fetus is a member of this community or not? What sort of entity, exactly, has the inalienable rights to life, liberty, and the pursuit of happiness? Jefferson attributed these rights to all *men,* and it may or may not be fair to suggest that he intended to attribute them *only* to men. Perhaps he ought to have attributed them to all human beings. If so, then we arrive, first, at Noonan's problem of defining what makes a being human, and, second, at the equally vital question which Noonan

Reprinted from *The Monist,* vol. 57, no. 1 (January 1973), with the permission of the author and the publisher. "Postscript on Infanticide" reprinted with permission of the author from Richard Wasserstrom, ed., *Today's Moral Problems* (New York: Macmillan, 1975).

does not consider, namely, What reason is there for identifying the moral community with the set of all human beings, in whatever way we have chosen to define that term?

1 ON THE DEFINITION OF "HUMAN"

One reason why this vital second question is so frequently overlooked in the debate over the moral status of abortion is that the term "human" has two distinct, but not often distinguished, senses. This fact results in a slide of meaning, which serves to conceal the fallaciousness of the traditional argument that since (1) it is wrong to kill innocent human beings, and (2) fetuses are innocent human beings, then (3) it is wrong to kill fetuses. For if "human" is used in the same sense in both (1) and (2) then, whichever of the two senses is meant, one of these premises is question-begging. And if it is used in two different senses then of course the conclusion doesn't follow.

Thus, (1) is a self-evident moral truth,[1] and avoids begging the question about abortion, only if "human being" is used to mean something like "a full-fledged member of the moral community." (It may or may not also be meant to refer exclusively to members of the species *Homo sapiens*.) We may call this the *moral* sense of "human." It is not to be confused with what we will call the *genetic* sense, i.e., the sense in which *any* member of the species is a human being, and no member of any other species could be. If (1) is acceptable only if the moral sense is intended, (2) is non-question-begging only if what is intended is the genetic sense.

In "Deciding Who Is Human," Noonan argues for the classification of fetuses with human beings by pointing to the presence of the full genetic code, and the potential capacity for rational thought.[2] It is clear that what he needs to show, for his version of the traditional argument to be valid, is that fetuses are human in the moral sense, the sense in which it is analytically true that all human beings have full moral rights. But, in the absence of any argument showing that whatever is genetically human is also morally human, and he gives none, nothing more than genetic humanity can be demonstrated by the presence of the human genetic code. And, as we will see, the *potential* capacity for rational thought can at most show that an entity has the potential for *becoming* human in the moral sense.

2 DEFINING THE MORAL COMMUNITY

Can it be established that genetic humanity is sufficient for moral humanity? I think that there are very good reasons for not defining the moral community in this way. I would like to suggest an alternative way of defining the moral community, which I will argue for only to the extent of explaining why it is, or should be, self-evident. The suggestion is simply that the moral community consists of all and only *people,* rather than all and only human beings;[3] and probably the best way of demonstrating

---

[1]Of course, the principle that it is (always) wrong to kill innocent human beings is in need of many other modifications, e.g., that it may be permissible to do so to save a greater number of other innocent human beings, but we may safely ignore these complications here.

[2]John Noonan, "Deciding Who is Human," *Natural Law Forum,* 13 (1968), 135.

[3]From here on, we will use "human" to mean genetically human, since the moral sense seems closely connected to, and perhaps derived from, the assumption that genetic humanity is sufficient for membership in the moral community.

its self-evidence is by considering the concept of personhood, to see what sorts of entity are and are not persons, and what the decision that a being is or is not a person implies about its moral rights.

What characteristics entitle an entity to be considered a person? This is obviously not the place to attempt a complete analysis of the concept of personhood, but we do not need such a fully adequate analysis just to determine whether and why a fetus is or isn't a person. All we need is a rough and approximate list of the most basic criteria of personhood, and some idea of which, or how many, of these an entity must satisfy in order to properly be considered a person.

In searching for such criteria, it is useful to look beyond the set of people with whom we are acquainted, and ask how we would decide whether a totally alien being was a person or not. (For we have no right to assume that genetic humanity is necessary for personhood.) Imagine a space traveler who lands on an unknown planet and encounters a race of beings utterly unlike any he has ever seen or heard of. If he wants to be sure of behaving morally toward these beings, he has to somehow decide whether they are people, and hence have full moral rights, or whether they are the sort of thing which he need not feel guilty about treating as, for example, a source of food.

How should he go about making this decision? If he has some anthropological background, he might look for such things as religion, art, and the manufacturing of tools, weapons, or shelters, since these factors have been used to distinguish our human from our prehuman ancestors, in what seems to be closer to the moral than the genetic sense of "human." And no doubt he would be right to consider the presence of such factors as good evidence that the alien beings were people, and morally human. It would, however, be overly anthropocentric of him to take the absence of these things as adequate evidence that they were not, since we can imagine people who have progressed beyond, or evolved without ever developing, these cultural characteristics.

I suggest that the traits which are most central to the concept of personhood, or humanity in the moral sense, are, very roughly, the following:

1 consciousness (of objects and events external and/or internal to the being), and in particular the capacity to feel pain;

2 reasoning (the *developed* capacity to solve new and relatively complex problems);

3 self-motivated activity (activity which is relatively independent of either genetic or direct external control);

4 the capacity to communicate, by whatever means, messages of an indefinite variety of types, that is, not just with an indefinite number of possible contents, but on indefinitely many possible topics;

5 the presence of self-concepts, and self-awareness, either individual or racial, or both.

Admittedly, there are apt to be a great many problems involved in formulating precise definitions of these criteria, let alone in developing universally valid behavioral criteria for deciding when they apply. But I will assume that both we and our explorer know approximately what (1)–(5) mean, and that he is also able to determine whether or not they apply. How, then, should he use his findings to decide whether or not the alien beings are people? We needn't suppose that an entity must have *all* of these attributes to be properly considered a person; (1) and (2) alone may well be sufficient for personhood, and quite probably (1)–(3) are sufficient. Neither do we need to insist that any one of these criteria is *necessary* for personhood, although once again (1) and (2) look like fairly good candidates for necessary conditions, as does (3), if "activity" is construed so as to include the activity of reasoning.

All we need to claim, to demonstrate that a fetus is not a person, is that any being which satisfies *none* of (1)–(5) is certainly not a person. I consider this claim to be so obvious that I think anyone who denied it, and claimed that a being which satisfied none of (1)–(5) was a person all the same, would thereby demonstrate that he had no notion at all of what a person is—perhaps because he had confused the concept of a person with that of genetic humanity. If the opponents of abortion were to deny the appropriateness of these five criteria, I do not know what further arguments would convince them. We would probably have to admit that our conceptual schemes were indeed irreconcilably different, and that our dispute could not be settled objectively.

I do not expect this to happen, however, since I think that the concept of a person is one which is very nearly universal (to people), and that it is common to both proabortionists and antiabortionists, even though neither group has fully realized the relevance of this concept to the resolution of their dispute. Furthermore, I think that on reflection even the antiabortionists ought to agree not only that (1)–(5) are central to the concept of personhood, but also that it is a part of this concept that all and only people have full moral rights. The concept of a person is in part a moral concept; once we have admitted that x is a person we have recognized, even if we have not agreed to respect, $x's$ right to be treated as a member of the moral community. It is true that the claim that x *is a human being* is more commonly voiced as part of an appeal to treat x decently than is the claim that x is a person, but this is either because "human being" is here used in the sense which implies personhood, or because the genetic and moral senses of "human" have been confused.

Now if (1)–(5) are indeed the primary criteria of personhood, then it is clear that genetic humanity is neither necessary nor sufficient for establishing that an entity is a person. Some human beings are not people, and there may well be people who are not human beings. A man or woman whose consciousness has been permanently obliterated but who remains alive is a human being which is no longer a person; defective human beings, with no appreciable mental capacity, are not and presumably never will be people; and a fetus is a human being which is not yet a person, and which therefore cannot coherently be said to have full moral rights. Citizens of the next century should be prepared to recognize highly advanced, self-aware robots or computers, should such be developed, and intelligent inhabitants of other worlds, should such be found, as people in the fullest sense, and to respect their moral rights. But to ascribe full moral rights to an entity which is not a person is as absurd as to ascribe moral obligations and responsibilities to such an entity.

3 FETAL DEVELOPMENT AND THE RIGHT TO LIFE

Two problems arise in the application of these suggestions for the definition of the moral community to the determination of the precise moral status of a human fetus.

Given that the paradigm example of a person is a normal adult human being, then (1) How like this paradigm, in particular how far advanced since conception, does a human being need to be before it begins to have a right to life by virtue, not of being fully a person as of yet, but of being *like* a person? and (2) To what extent, if any, does the fact that a fetus has the *potential* for becoming a person endow it with some of the same rights? Each of these questions requires some comment.

In answering the first question, we need not attempt a detailed consideration of the moral rights of organisms which are not developed enough, aware enough, intelligent enough, etc., to be considered people, but which resemble people in some respects. It does seem reasonable to suggest that the more like a person, in the relevant respects, a being is, the stronger is the case for regarding it as having a right to life, and indeed the stronger its right to life is. Thus we ought to take seriously the suggestion that, insofar as "the human individual develops biologically in a continuous fashion . . . the rights of a human person might develop in the same way."[4] But we must keep in mind that the attributes which are relevant in determining whether or not an entity is enough like a person to be regarded as having some of the same moral rights are no different from those which are relevant to determining whether or not it is fully a person—i.e., are no different from (1)–(5)—and that being genetically human, or having recognizably human facial and other physical features, or detectable brain activity, or the capacity to survive outside the uterus, are simply not among these relevant attributes.

Thus it is clear that even though a seven- or eight-month fetus has features which make it apt to arouse in us almost the same powerful protective instinct as is commonly aroused by a small infant, nevertheless it is not significantly more personlike than is a very small embryo. It is *somewhat* more personlike; it can apparently feel and respond to pain, and it may even have a rudimentary form of consciousness, insofar as its brain is quite active. Nevertheless, it seems safe to say that it is not fully conscious, in the way that an infant of a few months is, and that it cannot reason, or communicate messages of indefinitely many sorts, does not engage in self-motivated activity, and has no self-awareness. Thus, in the *relevant* respects, a fetus, even a fully developed one, is considerably less personlike than is the average mature mammal, indeed the average fish. And I think that a rational person must conclude that if the right to life of a fetus is to be based upon its resemblance to a person, then it cannot be said to have any more right to life than, let us say, a newborn guppy (which also seems to be capable of feeling pain), and that a right of that magnitude could never override a woman's right to obtain an abortion, at any stage of her pregnancy.

There may, of course, be other arguments in favor of placing legal limits upon the stage of pregnancy in which an abortion may be performed. Given the relative safety of the new techniques of artificially inducing labor during the third trimester, the danger to the woman's life or health is no longer such an argument. Neither is the fact that people tend to respond to the thought of abortion in the later stages of pregnancy with emotional repulsion, since mere emotional responses cannot take the

---

[4]Thomas L. Hayes, "A Biological View," *Commonweal,* 85 (March 17, 1967), 677–78; quoted by Daniel Callahan, in *Abortion: Law, Choice and Morality* (London: Macmillan & Co., 1970).

place of moral reasoning in determining what ought to be permitted. Nor, finally, is the frequently heard argument that legalizing abortion, especially late in the pregnancy, may erode the level of respect for human life, leading, perhaps, to an increase in unjustified euthanasia and other crimes. For this threat, if it is a threat, can be better met by educating people to the kinds of moral distinctions which we are making here than by limiting access to abortion (which limitation may, in its disregard for the rights of women, be just as damaging to the level of respect for human rights).

Thus, since the fact that even a fully developed fetus is not personlike enough to have any significant right to life on the basis of its personlikeness shows that no legal restrictions upon the stage of pregnancy in which an abortion may be performed can be justified on the grounds that we should protect the rights of the older fetus, and since there is no other apparent justification for such restrictions, we may conclude that they are entirely unjustified. Whether or not it would be *indecent* (whatever that means) for a woman in her seventh month to obtain an abortion just to avoid having to postpone a trip to Europe, it would not, in itself, be *immoral,* and therefore it ought to be permitted.

4   POTENTIAL PERSONHOOD AND THE RIGHT TO LIFE

We have seen that a fetus does not resemble a person in any way which can support the claim that it has even some of the same rights. But what about its *potential,* the fact that if nurtured and allowed to develop naturally it will very probably become a person? Doesn't that alone give it at least some right to life? It is hard to deny that the fact that an entity is a potential person is a strong prima facie reason for not destroying it; but we need not conclude from this that a potential person has a right to life, by virtue of that potential. It may be that our feeling that it is better, other things being equal, not to destroy a potential person is better explained by the fact that potential people are still (felt to be) an invaluable resource, not to be lightly squandered. Surely, if every speck of dust were a potential person, we would be much less apt to conclude that every potential person has a right to become actual.

Still, we do not need to insist that a potential person has no right to life whatever. There may well be something immoral, and not just imprudent, about wantonly destroying potential people, when doing so isn't necessary to protect anyone's rights. But even if a potential person does have some prima facie right to life, such a right could not possibly outweigh the right of a woman to obtain an abortion, since the rights of any actual person invariably outweigh those of any potential person, whenever the two conflict. Since this may not be immediately obvious in the case of a human fetus, let us look at another case.

Suppose that our space explorer falls into the hands of an alien culture, whose scientists decide to create a few hundred thousand or more human beings, by breaking his body into its component cells, and using these to create fully developed human beings, with, of course, his genetic code. We may imagine that each of these newly created men will have all of the original man's abilities, skills, knowledge, and so on, and also have an individual self-concept, in short that each of them will be a bona fide (though hardly unique) person. Imagine that the whole project will take only seconds, and that its chances of success are extremely high, and that our explorer knows all of this, and also knows that these people will be treated fairly. I maintain that in such a situation he would have every right to escape if he could, and thus to deprive all of these potential people of their potential lives; for his right to life outweighs all of theirs together, in spite of the fact that they are all genetically human, all innocent, and all have a very high probability of becoming people very soon, if only he refrains from acting.

Indeed, I think he would have a right to escape even if it were not his life which the alien scientists planned to take, but only a year of his freedom, or, indeed, only a day. Nor would he be obligated to stay if he had gotten captured (thus bringing all these people-potentials into existence) because of his own carelessness, or even if he had done so deliberately, knowing the consequences. Regardless of how he got captured, he is not morally obligated to remain in captivity for *any* period of time for the sake of permitting any number of potential people to come into actuality, so great is the margin by which one actual person's right to liberty outweighs whatever right to life even a hundred thousand potential people have. And it seems reasonable to conclude that the rights of a woman will outweigh by a similar margin whatever right to life a fetus may have by virtue of its potential personhood.

Thus, neither a fetus's resemblance to a person, nor its potential for becoming a person provides any basis whatever for the claim that it has any significant right to life. Consequently, a woman's right to protect her health, happiness, freedom, and even her life,[5] by terminating an unwanted pregnancy, will always override whatever right to life it may be appropriate to ascribe to a fetus, even a fully developed one. And thus, in the absence of any overwhelming social need for every possible child, the laws which restrict the right to obtain an abortion, or limit the period of pregnancy during which an abortion may be performed, are a wholly unjustified violation of a woman's most basic moral and constitutional rights.[6]

POSTSCRIPT ON INFANTICIDE

Since the publication of this article, many people have written to point out that my argument appears to justify not only abortion, but infanticide as well. For a newborn infant is not significantly more personlike than an advanced fetus, and consequently it would seem that if the destruction of the latter is permissible so too must be that of the former. Inasmuch as most people, regardless of how they feel about the morality of abortion, consider infanticide a form of murder, this might appear to represent a serious flaw in my argument.

Now, if I am right in holding that it is only people who have a full-fledged right to life, and who can be murdered, and if the criteria of personhood are as I have described them, then it obviously follows that killing a new-born infant isn't murder.

---

[5]That is, insofar as the death rate, for the woman, is higher for childbirth than for early abortion.

[6]My thanks to the following people, who were kind enough to read and criticize an earlier version of this paper: Herbert Gold, Gene Glass, Anne Lauterbach, Judith Thomson, Mary Mothersill, and Timothy Binkley.

It does *not* follow, however, that infanticide is permissible, for two reasons. In the first place, it would be wrong, at least in this country and in this period of history, and other things being equal, to kill a new-born infant, because even if its parents do not want it and would not suffer from its destruction, there are other people who would like to have it, and would, in all probability, be deprived of a great deal of pleasure by its destruction. Thus, infanticide is wrong for reasons analogous to those which make it wrong to wantonly destroy natural resources, or great works of art.

Secondly, most people, at least in this country, value infants and would much prefer that they be preserved, even if foster parents are not immediately available. Most of us would rather be taxed to support orphanages than allow unwanted infants to be destroyed. So long as there are people who want an infant preserved, and who are willing and able to provide the means of caring for it, under reasonably humane conditions, it is *ceteris paribus,* wrong to destroy it.

But, it might be replied, if this argument shows that infanticide is wrong, at least at this time and in this country, doesn't it also show that abortion is wrong? After all, many people value fetuses, are disturbed by their destruction, and would much prefer that they be preserved, even at some cost to themselves. Furthermore, as a potential source of pleasure to some foster family, a fetus is just as valuable as an infant. There is, however, a crucial difference between the two cases: so long as the fetus is unborn, its preservation, contrary to the wishes of the pregnant woman, violates her rights to freedom, happiness, and self-determination. Her rights override the rights of those who would like the fetus preserved, just as if someone's life or limb is threatened by a wild animal, his right to protect himself by destroying the animal overrides the rights of those who would prefer that the animal not be harmed.

The minute the infant is born, however, its preservation no longer violates any of its mother's rights, even if she wants it destroyed, because she is free to put it up for adoption. Consequently, while the moment of birth does not mark any sharp discontinuity in the degree to which an infant possesses the right to life, it does mark the end of its mother's right to determine its fate. Indeed, if abortion could be performed without killing the fetus, she would never possess the right to have the fetus destroyed, for the same reasons that she has no right to have an infant destroyed.

On the other hand, it follows from my argument that when an unwanted or defective infant is born into a society which cannot afford and/or is not willing to care for it, then its destruction is permissible. This conclusion will, no doubt, strike many people as heartless and immoral; but remember that the very existence of people who feel this way, and who are willing and able to provide care for unwanted infants, is reason enough to conclude that they should be preserved.

QUESTIONS

1 Does Warren's analysis effectively undermine Noonan's conservative position on abortion?

2 Does the fetus, even if it is not an *actual* person, have a serious right to life on the grounds that it is a *potential* person?

3 Is a newborn infant a person? In any case, are there any circumstances in which infanticide would be morally permissible?

Abortion Decisions: Personal Morality

Daniel Callahan

Daniel Callahan, a philosopher, is the director of the Institute of Society, Ethics and the Life Sciences, usually called The Hastings Center. His numerous publications reflect an enduring concern with issues in biomedical ethics. He is, for example, the author of Ethics and Population Limitation *(1971) and the coeditor of* Science, Ethics and Medicine *(1976). Callahan's principal work on the subject of abortion is* Abortion: Law, Choice and Morality *(1970), from which this selection is excerpted.*

After declaring himself in support of permissive abortion legislation, Callahan proceeds to defend one kind of moderate view on the problem of the ethical acceptability of abortion. On the issue of the moral status of the fetus, he steers a middle course. He rejects the "tissue" theory, the view that the fetus has negligible moral status, on the grounds that such a theory is out of tune with both the biological evidence and a respect for the sanctity of human life. On the other hand, he contends that the fetus does not qualify as a person and thus rejects the view that the fetus has full moral status. His contention that the fetus is nevertheless an "important and valuable form of human life" can be understood as implying that the fetus has some kind of *partial* moral status.

In Callahan's view, a respect for the sanctity of human life should incline every woman to a strong initial (moral) bias against abortion. Yet, he argues, since a woman has duties to herself, her family, and her society, there may be circumstances in which such duties would override the prima facie duty not to abort. Callahan concludes by criticizing various efforts to dissolve the "moral tension" involved in abortion decisions.

The strength of pluralistic societies lies in the personal freedom they afford individuals. One is free to choose among religious, philosophical, ideological and political creeds; or one can create one's own highly personal, idiosyncratic moral code and view of the universe. Increasingly, the individual is free to ignore the morals, manners and mores of society. The only limitations are upon those actions which seem to present clear and present dangers to the common good, and even there the range of prohibited actions is diminishing as more and more choices are left to personal and private decisions. I have contended that, apart from some regulatory laws, abortion decisions should be left, finally, up to the women themselves. Whatever one may think of the morality of abortion, it cannot be established that it poses a clear and present danger to the common good. Thus society does not have the right decisively to interpose itself between a woman and the abortion she wants. It can only intervene where it can be shown that some of its own interests are at stake *qua* society. Regulatory laws of a minimal kind therefore seem in order, since in a variety of ways already mentioned society will be affected by the number, kind and quality of legal abortions. In short, with a few important stipulations, what I have been urging is tantamount to saying that abortion decisions should be private decisions. It is to accept, in principle, the contention of those who believe that, in a free, pluralistic society, the woman should be allowed to make her own moral choice on abortion and be allowed to implement that choice.

But pluralistic societies also lay a few traps for the unwary. It is not a large psychological step from saying that individuals should be left free to make up their own minds on some crucial moral issues (of which abortion is one) to an adoption of the view that one personal decision is as good as another, that any decision is a good one as long as it is honest or sincere, that a free decision equals a correct decision. However short the psychological step, the logical gap is very large. An absence of cant, hypocrisy and coercion may prepare the way for good personal decisions. But that is only to clean the room, and something must then be put in it. The hazard is that, once cleaned, it will be filled with capriciousness, sentimentality, a thinly disguised conformity to the reigning moral taste, or strongly felt but inadequately analyzed moral opinions. This is a particular danger in affluent pluralistic societies, heavily dominated by popular tastes, communication media and the absence of shared values. Philosophically, the view that all values are equally good and all private moral choices on a par is all but dead; but it still has a strong life at the popular level, where there is a tendency to act as if, once personal freedom is legally and socially achieved, moral questions cease to exist.

A considerable quantity of literature exists in the field of ethics concerned with such problems as subjective and objective values, the meaning and use of ethical principles and moral rules, the role of intentionality. That literature need not be reviewed here. But it is directly to the point to observe that a particular failing of the abortion-on-request literature is that it persistently scants the moral problem of how a woman, if granted the desired legal freedom to make her own decision about abortion, should go about making that decision. Up to a point, this deficiency is understandable. The immediate tactical problem has been to get the laws changed or repealed; that has been the burden of the public struggle, which has concentrated on statutes and legislators rather than on the moral contents and problems of personal decision-making. It is reasonable and legitimate to say that a woman should be left free to make the decision in the light of her own personal values; that is, I believe, the best legal solution. But it leaves totally untouched the question of how, once freedom is achieved, she ought to go about the personal business of forming a coherent, rational, sensitive moral perspective and opinion on abortion. After freedom, what then? Society may have no right to demand that a woman give it good reasons why she should have an abortion before permitting it. But this does not entail that the woman should not, as a morally responsible person, have good reasons to justify her desires or acts in her own eyes.

This is only to say that a solution of the legal problem is not the same as a solution to the moral problem. That the moral struggle is transferred from the public to the private sphere should not be taken to mean that the moral problem has been solved; only its public aspect, under a permissive law or a repeal of all laws, has been dealt with. The personal problem will remain.

Some women will be part of a religious group or ethical tradition which they freely choose and which can offer them something, possibly very much, in the way of helpful moral insight consistent with that tradition. The obvious course in that instance is for them to turn to their tradition to see what it has to offer them on the particular problem of abortion. But what of those who have no tradition to repair to or those who find their tradition wanting on this problem? One way or another, they will have to find some way of developing a set of ethical principles and moral rules to help them act responsibly, to justify their own conduct in their own eyes. To press the problem to a finer point, what ought they to think about as they try to work out their own views on abortion?

Only a few suggestions will be made here, taking the form of arguing for an ethic of personal responsibility which tries, in the process of decision-making, to make itself aware of a number of things. The biological evidence should be considered, just as the problem of methodology must be considered; the philosophical assumptions implicit in different uses of the word "human" need to be considered; a philosophical theory of biological analysis is required; the social consequences of different kinds of analyses and different meanings of the word "human" should be thought through; consistency of meaning and use should be sought to avoid *ad hoc* and arbitrary solutions.

It is my own conviction that the "developmental school" offers the most helpful and illuminating approach to the problem of the beginning of human life, avoiding, on the one hand, a too narrow genetic criterion of human life and, on the other, a too broad and socially dangerous social definition of the "human." Yet the kinds of problems which appear in any attempt to decide upon the beginning of life suggest that no one position can be either proved or disproved from biological evidence alone. It becomes a question of trying to do justice to the evidence while, at the same time, realizing that how the evidence is approached and used will be a function of one's way of looking at reality, one's moral policy, the values and rights one believes need balancing, and the type of questions one thinks need to be asked. At the very least, however, the genetic evidence for the uniqueness of zygotes and embryos (a uniqueness of a different kind than that of the uniqueness of sperm and ova), their potentiality for development into a human person, their early development of human characteristics, their genetic and organic distinctness from the organism of the mother, appear to rule out a treatment even of zygotes, much less the more developed stages of the conceptus, as mere pieces of "tissue," of no human significance or value. The "tissue" theory of the significance of the conceptus can only be made plausible by a systematic disregard of the biological evidence. Moreover, though one may conclude that a conceptus is only potential human life, in the process of continually actualizing its potential through growth and development, a respect for the sanctity of life, with its bias in favor even of undeveloped life, is enough to make the taking of such life a moral problem. There is a choice to be made and it is a moral choice. In the near future, it is likely that some kind of simple, safe abortifacient drug will be developed, which either prevents implantation or destroys the conceptus before it can develop. It will be tempting then to think that the moral dilemma has vanished, but I do not believe it will have.

It is possible to imagine a huge number of situations where a woman could, in good and sensitive conscience, choose abortion as a moral solution to her personal or social difficulties. But, at the very least, the bounds of morality are overstepped when either through a systematic intellectual negligence or a willful choosing of that moral solution most personally convenient, personal choice is deliberately made easy and problem-free. Yet it seems to me that a pressure in that direction is a growing part of the ethos of technological societies; it is easily possible to find people to reassure us that we need have no scruples about the way we act, whether the issue is war, the suppression of rebellion and revolution, discrimination against minorities or the use of technological advances. Pluralism makes possible the achieving of freer, more subtle moral thinking; but it is a possibility constantly endangered by cultural pressures which would simplify or dissolve moral doubts and anguish.

The question of abortion "indications" returns at the level of personal choice. I have contended that the advent of permissive laws should not mean a cessation of efforts to explore the problem of "indications." When a woman asks herself, as she ought, whether her reasons for wanting an abortion are sound reasons—which presumes abortion is a serious enough moral issue to warrant the need to provide oneself with good reasons for choosing it—she will be asking herself about justifiable indications. Thus, transposed from the legal to the personal level, the kinds of concerns adumbrated in the earlier chapters on indications remain fully pertinent. It was argued in those chapters that, with the possible exception of exceedingly rare instances of a direct threat to the physical life of the mother, one cannot speak of general categories of abortion indications as *necessitating* an abortion. In a number of circumstances, abortion may be a wise and justifiable solution to a distressed pregnancy. But when the language of necessity is used, the implication is that no other conceivable alternative is available. It may be granted, willingly enough, that some set of practical circumstances in some (possibly very many) concrete cases may indicate that abortion is the only feasible option open. But these cases cannot readily be determined in advance, and, for that reason, it is necessary to say that no formal indication as such (e.g., a psychiatric indication) entails a necessary, predetermined choice in favor of abortion.

The word "indication" remains the best word, suggesting that a number of given circumstances will bring the possibility or desirability of abortion to the fore. But to escalate the concept of an indication into that of a required procedure is to go too far. Abortion is *one* way to solve the problem of an unwanted or hazardous pregnancy (physically, psychologically, economically or socially), but it is rarely the only way, at least in affluent societies (I would be considerably less certain about making the same statement about poor societies). Even in the most extreme cases—rape, incest, psychosis, for instance—alternatives will usually be available and different choices open. It is not necessarily the end of every woman's chance for a happy, meaningful life to bear an illegitimate child. It is not necessarily the automatic destruction of a family to have a seriously defective child born into it. It is not necessarily the ruination of every family living in overcrowded housing to have still another child. It is not inevitable that every immature woman would become even more so if she bore a child or another child. It is not inevitable that a gravely handicapped child can hope for nothing from life. It is not inevitable that every unwanted child is doomed to misery.

It is not written in the essence of things, as a fixed law of human nature, that a woman cannot come to accept, love and be a good mother to a child who was initially unwanted. Nor is it a fixed law that she could not come to cherish a grossly deformed child. Naturally, these are only generalizations. The point is only that human beings are as a rule flexible, capable of doing more than they sometimes think they can, able to surmount serious dangers and challenges, able to grow and mature, able to transform inauspicious beginnings into satisfactory conclusions. Everything in life, even in procreative and family life, is not fixed in advance; the future is never wholly unalterable.

Yet the problem of personal question-asking must be pushed a step farther. The way the questions are answered will be very much determined by a woman's way of looking at herself and at life. A woman who has decided, as a personal moral policy, that nothing should be allowed to stand in the way of her own happiness, goals and self-interest will have no trouble solving the moral problem. For her, an unwanted pregnancy will, by definition, be a pregnancy to be terminated. But only by a Pickwickian use of words could this form of reasoning be called moral. It would preclude any need to consult the opinion of others, any need to examine the validity of one's own viewpoint, any need to, for instance, ask when human life begins, any need to interrogate oneself in any way, intellectually or morally; will and desire would be king.

Assuming, however, that most women would seek a broader ethical horizon than that of their exclusively personal self-interest, what might they think about when faced with an abortion decision? A respect for the sanctity of human life should, I believe, incline them toward a general and strong bias against abortion. Abortion is an act of killing, the violent, direct destruction of potential human life, already in the process of development. That fact should not be disguised, or glossed over by euphemism and circumlocution. It is not the destruction of a human person—for at no stage of its development does the conceptus fulfill the definition of a person, which implies a developed capacity for reasoning, willing, desiring and relating to others—but it is the destruction of an important and valuable form of human life. Its value and its potentiality are not dependent upon the attitude of the woman toward it; it grows by its own biological dynamism and has a genetic and morphological potential distinct from that of the woman. It has its own distinctive and individual future. If contraception and abortion are both seen as forms of birth limitation, they are distinctly different acts; the former precludes the possibility of a conceptus being formed, while the latter stops a conceptus already in existence from developing. The bias implied by the principle of the sanctity of human life is toward the protection of all forms of human life, especially, in ordinary circumstances, the protection of the right to life. That right should be accorded even to doubtful life; its existence should not be wholly dependent upon the personal self-interest of the woman.

Yet she has her own rights as well, and her own set of responsibilities to those around her; that is why she may have to choose abortion. In extreme situations of overpopulation, she may also have a responsibility for the survival of the species or of a people. In many circumstances, then, a decision in favor of abortion—one which overrides the right to life of that potential human being she carries within—can be a responsible moral decision, worthy neither of the condemnation of others nor of self-condemnation. But the bias of the principle of the sanctity of life is against a routine, unthinking employment of abortion; it bends over backwards not to take life and gives the benefit of the doubt to life. It does not seek to diminish the range of responsibility toward life—potential or actual—but to extend it. It does not seek the narrowest definition of life, but the widest and the richest. It is mindful of individual possibility, on the one hand, and of a destructive human tendency, on the other, to exclude from the category of "the human" or deny rights to those beings whose existence is or could prove burdensome to others.

The language used to describe abortion will have an important bearing on the sensitivities and imagination of those women who must make abortion decisions. Abortion can be talked about in the language of medical technology and technique—as, say, "a therapeutic procedure involving the emptying of the uterine contents." That language is neutral, clinical, unemotional. Or abortion can be talked about in the emotive language of relieving woman from suffering, or meeting the need for freedom among women, or saving a nation from a devastating overpopulation. Both kinds of language have their place, for abortion has more than one result and meaning and abortion can legitimately be talked about in more than one way. What is objectionable is a conscious manipulation of language to incite an irrational emotional response, to allay doubts or to mislead the imagination. Particularly misleading is one commonly employed mixture of rhetorical modes by advocates of abortion on request. That is the use of a detached, clinical language to describe the actual operation itself combined with an emotive rhetoric to evoke the personal and social goods which an abortion can bring about. Thus, when every effort is made to suggest that emotion and feeling are perfectly appropriate to describe the social and personal goals of abortion, but that a clinical language only is appropriate when the actual technique and medical objective of an abortion is described, then the moral imagination is being misled.

Any human act can be described in impersonal, technological language, just as any act can be described in emotive language. What is wanted is an equity in the language. It is fair enough and to the point to say that in many circumstances abortion will save a woman's health or her family. It only becomes misleading when the act itself, as distinguished from its therapeutic goal, is talked about in an entirely different way. For, abortion is not just an "emptying of the uterine contents." It is also an act of killing; there will be no abortion unless the conceptus is killed (or its further existence made impossible, which amounts to the same thing). If it is appropriate to evoke the imagination and elicit sympathy for those women in a distressed pregnancy who could be helped by abortion, it is no less appropriate to evoke the imagination about what actually occurs in an abortion "procedure."

Imagination should also come into play at another point. It is often argued by proponents of abortion that there is no need for a woman ever to take any chances in a distressed pregnancy, particularly in the instance of an otherwise healthy woman who, if she has an abortion on one occasion, could simply get pregnant again on another, more auspicious occasion. This might be termed the "replacement theory" of abortion indications: since fetus "x" can be replaced by fetus "y," then there is no reason why a woman should have any scruples about such a replacement. This way of conceiving the choices effectively dissolves them; it becomes important only to know whether a woman can get pregnant again when she wants to. But this strategy can be employed only at the price of convincing oneself that there is no difference whatever among embryos or fetuses, that they all have exactly the same potentiality. But even the sketchiest knowledge of the genetic uniqueness of each conceptus (save in the instance of monozygotic twins), and thus the different genetic potentialities of each, should raise doubts on that point. Yet, having said that, I would not want to deny that the possibility of a further pregnancy could have an important bearing on the moral reasoning of a woman whose present pregnancy was threatening. If, out of a sense of responsibility toward her present children or her present life situation, a woman decided that an abortion was the wisest, most moral course, then the possibility that she could become pregnant later, when these responsibilities would be less pressing, would be a pertinent consideration.

The goal of these remarks is to keep alive in the consciences of women who have an abortion choice a moral tension; and it is to hope that they will be willing to bear the pain and the uncertainty of having to make a moral choice. It is the automatic, unthinking and unimaginative personal solution of abortion questions which women themselves should be extremely wary of, either for or against an abortion. A woman can, with little trouble, find both people and books to reassure her that there is no problem about abortion at all; or people and books to convince her that she would be a moral monster if she chose abortion. A woman can choose in advance the views she will listen to and thus have her predispositions confirmed. Yet a willingness to keep alive a moral tension, and to be wary of precipitous solutions, presupposes two things. First, that the woman herself wants to do what is right, realizing that what is right may not always be that which is most convenient, most easy or most immediately apt to solve a pressing problem. It is simply not the case that what one wants to do, or would like to do, or is predisposed to do is necessarily the right thing to do. A willingness seriously to entertain that moral perception—which, of course, does not in itself imply a decision for or against an abortion—is one sign of moral seriousness.

Second, moral seriousness presupposes one is concerned with the protection and furthering of life. This means that, out of respect for human life, one bends over backwards not to eliminate human life, not to desensitize oneself to the meaning and value of potential life, not to seek definitions of the "human" which serve one's self-interest only. A desire to respect human life in all of its forms means, therefore, that one voluntarily imposes upon oneself a pressure against the taking of life; that one demands of oneself serious reasons for doing so, even in the case of a very early embryo; that one use not only the mind but also the imagination when a decision is being made; that one seeks not to evade the moral issues but to face them; that one searches out the alternatives and conscientiously entertains them before turning to abortion. A bias in favor of the sanctity of human life in all of its forms would include a bias against abortion on the part of women; it would be the last rather than the first choice when unwanted pregnancies occurred. It would be an act to be avoided if at all possible.

A bias of this kind, voluntarily imposed by a woman upon herself, would not trap her; for it is also part of a respect for the dignity of life to leave the way open for an abortion when other reasonable choices are not available. For she also has duties toward herself, her family and her society. There can be good reasons for taking the life even of a very late fetus; once that also is seen and seen as a counterpoise in particular cases to the general bias against the taking of potential life, the way is open to choose abortion. The bias of the moral policy implies the need for moral rules which seek to preserve life. But, as a policy which leaves room for choice—rather than entailing a fixed set of rules—it is open to flexible interpretation when the circumstances point to the wisdom of taking exception to the normal ordering of the rules in particular cases. Yet, in that case, one is not genuinely taking exception to the rules. More accurately, one would be deciding that, for the preservation or furtherance of other values or rights—species-rights, person-rights—a choice in favor of abortion would be serving the sanctity of life. That there would be, in that case, conflict between rights, with one set of rights set aside (reluctantly) to serve another set, goes without saying. A subversion of the principle occurs when it is made out that there is no conflict and thus nothing to decide.

QUESTIONS

1 Does Callahan's analysis effectively undermine both Noonan's conservative position and Warren's liberal position on abortion?

2 Consider an abortion that is secured for each of the following reasons: (1) to preserve the physical health of the mother, (2) to preserve the mental health of the mother, (3) to prevent the birth of a severely deformed child, (4) to eliminate the product of rape, (5) to prevent the birth of an illegitimate child, (6) to preserve the life-style of the mother. According to Callahan, the fetus is neither a "person" nor a "piece of tissue." Reasoning from this moderate point of view, in which of the above cases would abortion be morally justifiable?

Abortion and the Concept of a Person

Jane English

Jane English (1947–1978) was a philosopher whose life came to a tragic end, at the age of thirty-one, in a mountain-climbing accident on the Matterhorn. She had taught at the University of North Carolina, Chapel Hill, and had published such articles as "Justice between Generations" and "Sex Equality in Sports." She was also the editor of Sex Equality *(1977) and the coeditor of* Feminism and Philosophy *(1977).*

Reprinted with permission of the publisher from the *Canadian Journal of Philosophy,* vol. 5, no. 2 (October 1975), pp. 233–243.

English begins by arguing that one of the central issues in the abortion debate, whether a fetus is a person, cannot be decisively resolved. However, she contends, whether we presume that the fetus is or is not a person, we must arrive at a moderate stance on the problem of abortion. In an effort to moderate the *conservative* view, English argues that it is unwarranted to conclude, from the presumption that the fetus is a person, that abortion is always morally impermissible. Reasoning on the basis of a self-defense model, she finds abortion morally permissible in many cases. In an effort to moderate the *liberal* view, English argues that it is unwarranted to conclude, from the presumption that the fetus is not a person, that abortion is always morally permissible. Even if the fetus is not a person, she argues, the similarity between a fetus and a baby is sufficient to make abortion problematic in the later stages of pregnancy.

The abortion debate rages on. Yet the two most popular positions seem to be clearly mistaken. Conservatives maintain that a human life begins at conception and that therefore abortion must be wrong because it is murder. But not all killings of humans are murders. Most notably, self defense may justify even the killing of an innocent person.

Liberals, on the other hand, are just as mistaken in their argument that since a fetus does not become a person until birth, a woman may do whatever she pleases in and to her own body. First, you cannot do as you please with your own body if it affects other people adversely.[1] Second, if a fetus is not a person, that does not imply that you can do to it anything you wish. Animals, for example, are not persons, yet to kill or torture them for no reason at all is wrong.

At the center of the storm has been the issue of just when it is between ovulation and adulthood that a person appears on the scene. Conservatives draw the line at conception, liberals at birth. In this paper I first examine our concept of a person and conclude that no single criterion can capture the concept of a person and no sharp line can be drawn. Next I argue that if a fetus is a person, abortion is still justifiable in many cases; and if a fetus is not a person, killing it is still wrong in many cases. To a large extent, these two solutions are in agreement. I conclude that our concept of a person cannot and need not bear the weight that the abortion controversy has thrust upon it.

I

The several factions in the abortion argument have drawn battle lines around various proposed criteria for determining what is and what is not a person. For example, Mary Anne Warren[2] lists five features (capacities for reasoning, self-awareness, complex communication, etc.) as her criteria for personhood and argues for the permissibility

---

[1]We also have paternalistic laws which keep us from harming our own bodies even when no one else is affected. Ironically, antiabortion laws were originally designed to protect pregnant women from a dangerous but tempting procedure.
[2]Mary Anne Warren, "On the Moral and Legal Status of Abortion," *Monist 57* (1973), p. 55.

of abortion because a fetus falls outside this concept. Baruch Brody[3] uses brain waves. Michael Tooley[4] picks having-a-concept-of-self as his criterion and concludes that infanticide and abortion are justifiable, while the killing of adult animals is not. On the other side, Paul Ramsey[5] claims a certain gene structure is the defining characteristic. John Noonan[6] prefers conceived-of-humans and presents counterexamples to various other candidate criteria. For instance, he argues against viability as the criterion because the newborn and infirm would then be non-persons, since they cannot live without the aid of others. He rejects any criterion that calls upon the sorts of sentiments a being can evoke in adults on the grounds that this would allow us to exclude other races as non-persons if we could just view them sufficiently unsentimentally.

These approaches are typical: foes of abortion propose sufficient conditions for personhood which fetuses satisfy, while friends of abortion counter with necessary conditions for personhood which fetuses lack. But these both presuppose that the concept of a person can be captured in a strait jacket of necessary and/or sufficient conditions.[7] Rather, "person" is a cluster of features, of which rationality, having a self concept and being conceived of humans are only part.

What is typical of persons? Within our concept of a person we include, first, certain biological factors: descended from humans, having a certain genetic makeup, having a head, hands, arms, eyes, capable of locomotion, breathing, eating, sleeping. There are psychological factors: sentience, perception, having a concept of self and of one's own interests and desires, the ability to use tools, the ability to use language or symbol systems, the ability to joke, to be angry, to doubt. There are rationality factors: the ability to reason and draw conclusions, the ability to generalize and to learn from past experience, the ability to sacrifice present interests for greater gains in the future. There are social factors: the ability to work in groups and respond to peer pressures, the ability to recognize and consider as valuable the interests of others, seeing oneself as one among "other minds," the ability to sympathize, encourage, love, the ability to evoke from others the responses of sympathy, encouragement, love, the ability to work with others for mutual advantage. Then there are legal factors: being subject to the law and protected by it, having the ability to sue and enter contracts, being counted in the census, having a name and citizenship, the ability to own property, inherit, and so forth.

Now the point is not that this list is incomplete, or that you can find counterinstances to each of its points. People typically exhibit rationality, for instance, but someone who was irrational would not thereby fail to qualify as a person. On the other hand, something could exhibit the majority of these features and still fail to be a person, as

---

[3]Baruch Brody, "Fetal Humanity and the Theory of Essentialism," in Robert Baker and Frederick Elliston, eds., *Philosophy and Sex* (Buffalo, N.Y., 1975).

[4]Michael Tooley, "Abortion and Infanticide," *Philosophy and Public Affairs* 2 (1971).

[5]Paul Ramsey, "The Morality of Abortion," in James Rachels, ed., *Moral Problems* (New York, 1971).

[6]John Noonan, "Abortion and the Catholic Church: A Summary History," *Natural Law Forum* 12 (1967), pp. 125–131.

[7]Wittgenstein has argued against the possibility of so capturing the concept of a game, *Philosophical Investigations* (New York, 1958), §66–71.

an advanced robot might. There is no single core of necessary and sufficient features which we can draw upon with the assurance that they constitute what really makes a person; there are only features that are more or less typical.

This is not to say that no necessary or sufficient conditions can be given. Being alive is a necessary condition for being a person, and being a U.S. Senator is sufficient. But rather than falling inside a sufficient condition or outside a necessary one, a fetus lies in the penumbra region where our concept of a person is not so simple. For this reason I think a conclusive answer to the question whether a fetus is a person is unattainable.

Here we might note a family of simple fallacies that proceed by stating a necessary condition for personhood and showing that a fetus has that characteristic. This is a form of the fallacy of affirming the consequent. For example, some have mistakenly reasoned from the premise that a fetus is human (after all, it is a human fetus rather than, say, a canine fetus), to the conclusion that it is *a* human. Adding an equivocation on "being," we get the fallacious argument that since a fetus is something both living and human, it is a human being.

Nonetheless, it does seem clear that a fetus has very few of the above family of characteristics, whereas a newborn baby exhibits a much larger proportion of them— and a two-year-old has even more. Note that one traditional anti-abortion argument has centered on pointing out the many ways in which a fetus resembles a baby. They emphasize its development ("It already has ten fingers. . . . ") without mentioning its dissimilarities to adults (it still has gills and a tail). They also try to evoke the sort of sympathy on our part that we only feel toward other persons ("Never to laugh . . . or feel the sunshine?"). This all seems to be a relevant way to argue, since its purpose is to persuade us that a fetus satisfies so many of the important features on the list that it ought to be treated as a person. Also note that a fetus near the time of birth satisfies many more of these factors than a fetus in the early months of development. This could provide reason for making distinctions among the different stages of pregnancy, as the U.S. Supreme Court has done.[8]

Historically, the time at which a person has been said to come into existence has varied widely. Muslims date personhood from fourteen days after conception. Some medievals followed Aristotle in placing ensoulment at forty days after conception for a male fetus and eighty days for a female fetus.[9] In European common law since the Seventeenth Century, abortion was considered the killing of a person only after quickening, the time when a pregnant woman first feels the fetus move on its own. Nor is this variety of opinions surprising. Biologically, a human being develops gradually. We shouldn't expect there to be any specific time or sharp dividing point when a person appears on the scene.

---

[8]Not because the fetus is partly a person and so has some of the rights of persons, but rather because of the rights of person-like non-persons. This I discuss in part III below.

[9]Aristotle himself was concerned, however, with the different question of when the soul takes form. For historical data, see Jimmye Kimmey, "How the Abortion Laws Happened," *Ms.* 1 (April, 1973), pp. 48ff, and John Noonan, *loc. cit.*

For these reasons I believe our concept of a person is not sharp or decisive enough to bear the weight of a solution to the abortion controversy. To use it to solve that problem is to clarify *obscurum per obscurius*.

II

Next let us consider what follows if a fetus is a person after all. Judith Jarvis Thomson's landmark article, "A Defense of Abortion,"[10] correctly points out that some additional argumentation is needed at this point in the conservative argument to bridge the gap between the premise that a fetus is an innocent person and the conclusion that killing it is always wrong. To arrive at this conclusion, we would need the additional premise that killing an innocent person is always wrong. But killing an innocent person is sometimes permissible, most notably in self defense. Some examples may help draw out our intuitions or ordinary judgments about self defense.

Suppose a mad scientist, for instance, hypnotized innocent people to jump out of the bushes and attack innocent passers-by with knives. If you are so attacked, we agree you have a right to kill the attacker in self defense, if killing him is the only way to protect your life or to save yourself from serious injury. It does not seem to matter here that the attacker is not malicious but himself an innocent pawn, for your killing of him is not done in a spirit of retribution but only in self defense.

How severe an injury may you inflict in self defense? In part this depends upon the severity of the injury to be avoided: you may not shoot someone merely to avoid having your clothes torn. This might lead one to the mistaken conclusion that the defense may only equal the threatened injury in severity; that to avoid death you may kill, but to avoid a black eye you may only inflict a black eye or the equivalent. Rather, our laws and customs seem to say that you may create an injury somewhat, but not enormously, greater than the injury to be avoided. To fend off an attack whose outcome would be as serious as rape, a severe beating or the loss of a finger, you may shoot; to avoid having your clothes torn, you may blacken an eye.

Aside from this, the injury you may inflict should only be the minimum necessary to deter or incapacitate the attacker. Even if you know he intends to kill you, you are not justified in shooting him if you could equally well save yourself by the simple expedient of running away. Self defense is for the purpose of avoiding harms rather than equalizing harms.

Some cases of pregnancy present a parallel situation. Though the fetus is itself innocent, it may pose a threat to the pregnant woman's well-being, life prospects or health, mental or physical. If the pregnancy presents a slight threat to her interests, it seems self defense cannot justify abortion. But if the threat is on a par with a serious beating or the loss of a finger, she may kill the fetus that poses such a threat, even if it is an innocent person. If a lesser harm to the fetus could have the same defensive effect, killing it would not be justified. It is unfortunate that the only way to free the woman from the pregnancy entails the death of the fetus (except in very late stages

---

[10]J. J. Thomson, "A Defense of Abortion," *Philosophy and Public Affairs* 1 (1971).

of pregnancy). Thus a self defense model supports Thomson's point that the woman has a right only to be freed from the fetus, not a right to demand its death.[11]

The self defense model is most helpful when we take the pregnant woman's point of view. In the pre-Thomson literature, abortion is often framed as a question for a third party: do you, a doctor, have a right to choose between the life of the woman and that of the fetus? Some have claimed that if you were a passer-by who witnessed a struggle between the innocent hypnotized attacker and his equally innocent victim, you would have no reason to kill either in defense of the other. They have concluded that the self defense model implies that a woman may attempt to abort herself, but that a doctor should not assist her. I think the position of the third party is somewhat more complex. We do feel some inclination to intervene on behalf of the victim rather than the attacker, other things equal. But if both parties are innocent, other factors come into consideration. You would rush to the aid of your husband whether he was attacker or attackee. If a hypnotized famous violinist were attacking a skid row bum, we would try to save the individual who is of more value to society. These considerations would tend to support abortion in some cases.

But suppose you are a frail senior citizen who wishes to avoid being knifed by one of these innocent hypnotics, so you have hired a bodyguard to accompany you. If you are attacked, it is clear we believe that the bodyguard, acting as your agent, has a right to kill the attacker to save you from a serious beating. Your rights of self defense are transferred to your agent. I suggest that we should similarly view the doctor as the pregnant woman's agent in carrying out a defense she is physically incapable of accomplishing herself.

Thanks to modern technology, the cases are rare in which pregnancy poses as clear a threat to a woman's bodily health as an attacker brandishing a switchblade. How does self defense fare when more subtle, complex and long-range harms are involved?

To consider a somewhat fanciful example, suppose you are a highly trained surgeon when you are kidnapped by the hypnotic attacker. He says he does not intend to harm you but to take you back to the mad scientist who, it turns out, plans to hypnotize you to have a permanent mental block against all your knowledge of medicine. This would automatically destroy your career which would in turn have a serious adverse impact on your family, your personal relationships and your happiness. It seems to me that if the only way you can avoid this outcome is to shoot the innocent attacker, you are justified in so doing. You are defending yourself from a drastic injury to your life prospects. I think it is no exaggeration to claim that unwanted pregnancies (most obviously among teenagers) often have such adverse life-long consequences as the surgeon's loss of livelihood.

Several parallels arise between various views on abortion and the self defense model. Let's suppose further that these hypnotized attackers only operate at night, so that it is well known that they can be avoided completely by the considerable inconvenience of never leaving your house after dark. One view is that since you could stay home at night, therefore if you go out and are selected by one of these hypnotized people,

---

[11]*Ibid.*, p. 52.

you have no right to defend yourself. This parallels the view that abstinence is the only acceptable way to avoid pregnancy. Others might hold that you ought to take along some defense such as Mace which will deter the hypnotized person without killing him, but that if this defense fails, you are obliged to submit to the resulting injury, no matter how severe it is. This parallels the view that contraception is all right but abortion is always wrong, even in cases of contraceptive failure.

A third view is that you may kill the hypnotized person only if he will actually kill you, but not if he will only injure you. This is like the position that abortion is permissible only if it is required to save a woman's life. Finally we have the view that it is all right to kill the attacker, even if only to avoid a very slight inconvenience to yourself and even if you knowingly walked down the very street where all these incidents have been taking place without taking along any Mace or protective escort. If we assume that a fetus is a person, this is the analogue of the view that abortion is always justifiable, "on demand."

The self defense model allows us to see an important difference that exists between abortion and infanticide, even if a fetus is a person from conception. Many have argued that the only way to justify abortion without justifying infanticide would be to find some characteristic of personhood that is acquired at birth. Michael Tooley, for one, claims infanticide is justifiable because the really significant characteristics of person are acquired some time after birth. But all such approaches look to characteristics of the developing human and ignore the relation between the fetus and the woman. What if, after birth, the presence of an infant or the need to support it posed a grave threat to the woman's sanity or life prospects? She could escape this threat by the simple expedient of running away. So a solution that does not entail the death of the infant is available. Before birth, such solutions are not available because of the biological dependence of the fetus on the woman. Birth is the crucial point not because of any characteristics the fetus gains, but because after birth the woman can defend herself by a means less drastic than killing the infant. Hence self defense can be used to justify abortion without necessarily thereby justifying infanticide.

III

On the other hand, supposing a fetus is not after all a person, would abortion always be morally permissible? Some opponents of abortion seem worried that if a fetus is not a full-fledged person, then we are justified in treating it in any way at all. However, this does not follow. Non-persons do get some consideration in our moral code, though of course they do not have the same rights as persons have (and in general they do not have moral responsibilities), and though their interests may be overridden by the interests of persons. Still, we cannot just treat them in any way at all.

Treatment of animals is a case in point. It is wrong to torture dogs for fun or to kill wild birds for no reason at all. It is wrong Period, even though dogs and birds do not have the same rights persons do. However, few people think it is wrong to use dogs as experimental animals, causing them considerable suffering in some cases, provided that the resulting research will probably bring discoveries of great benefit to people. And most of us think it all right to kill birds for food or to protect our crops.

People's rights are different from the consideration we give to animals, then, for it is wrong to experiment on people, even if others might later benefit a great deal as a result of their suffering. You might volunteer to be a subject, but this would be supererogatory; you certainly have a right to refuse to be a medical guinea pig.

But how do we decide what you may or may not do to non-persons? This is a difficult problem, one for which I believe no adequate account exists. You do not want to say, for instance, that torturing dogs is all right whenever the sum of its effects on people is good—when it doesn't warp the sensibilities of the torturer so much that he mistreats people. If that were the case, it would be all right to torture dogs if you did it in private, or if the torturer lived on a desert island or died soon afterward, so that his actions had no effect on people. This is an inadequate account, because whatever moral consideration animals get, it has to be indefeasible, too. It will have to be a general proscription of certain actions, not merely a weighing of the impact on people on a case-by-case basis.

Rather, we need to distinguish two levels on which consequences of actions can be taken into account in moral reasoning. The traditional objections to Utilitarianism focus on the fact that it operates solely on the first level, taking all the consequences into account in particular cases only. Thus Utilitarianism is open to "desert island" and "lifeboat" counterexamples because these cases are rigged to make the consequences of actions severely limited.

Rawls' theory could be described as a teleological sort of theory, but with teleology operating on a higher level.[12] In choosing the principles to regulate society from the original position, his hypothetical choosers make their decision on the basis of the total consequences of various systems. Furthermore, they are constrained to choose a general set of rules which people can readily learn and apply. An ethical theory must operate by generating a set of sympathies and attitudes toward others which reinforces the functioning of that set of moral principles. Our prohibition against killing people operates by means of certain moral sentiments including sympathy, compassion and guilt. But if these attitudes are to form a coherent set, they carry us further: we tend to perform supererogatory actions, and we tend to feel similar compassion toward person-like non-persons.

It is crucial that psychological facts play a role here. Our psychological constitution makes it the case that for our ethical theory to work, it must prohibit certain treatment of non-persons which are significantly person-like. If our moral rules allowed people to treat some person-like non-persons in ways we do not want people to be treated, this would undermine the system of sympathies and attitudes that makes the ethical system work. For this reason, we would choose in the original position to make mistreatment of some sorts of animals wrong in general (not just wrong in the cases with public impact), even though animals are not themselves parties in the original position. Thus it makes sense that it is those animals whose appearance and behavior are most like those of people that get the most consideration in our moral scheme.

---

[12]John Rawls, *A Theory of Justice* (Cambridge, Mass., 1971), §3–4.

It is because of "coherence of attitudes," I think, that the similarity of a fetus to a baby is very significant. A fetus one week before birth is so much like a newborn baby in our psychological space that we cannot allow any cavalier treatment of the former while expecting full sympathy and nurturative support for the latter. Thus, I think that anti-abortion forces are indeed giving their strongest arguments when they point to the similarities between a fetus and a baby, and when they try to evoke our emotional attachment to and sympathy for the fetus. An early horror story from New York about nurses who were expected to alternate between caring for six-week pre-mature infants and disposing of viable 24-week aborted fetuses is just that—a horror story. These beings are so much alike that no one can be asked to draw a distinction and treat them so very differently.

Remember, however, that in the early weeks after conception, a fetus is very much unlike a person. It is hard to develop these feelings for a set of genes which doesn't yet have a head, hands, beating heart, response to touch or the ability to move by itself. Thus it seems to me that the alleged "slippery slope" between conception and birth is not so very slippery. In the early stages of pregnancy, abortion can hardly be compared to murder for psychological reasons, but in the latest stages it is psycho-logically akin to murder.

Another source of similarity is the bodily continuity between fetus and adult. Bodies play a surprisingly central role in our attitudes toward persons. One has only to think of the philosophical literature on how far physical identity suffices for personal identity or Wittgenstein's remark that the best picture of the human soul is the human body. Even after death, when all agree the body is no longer a person, we still observe elaborate customs of respect for the human body; like people who torture dogs, nec-rophiliacs are not to be trusted with people.[13] So it is appropriate that we show respect to a fetus as the body continuous with the body of a person. This is a degree of resemblance to persons that animals cannot rival.

Michael Tooley also utilizes a parallel with animals. He claims that it is always permissible to drown newborn kittens and draws conclusions about infanticide.[14] But it is only permissible to drown kittens when their survival would cause some hardship. Perhaps it would be a burden to feed and house six more cats or to find other homes for them. The alternative of letting them starve produces even more suffering than the drowning. Since the kittens get their rights second-hand, so to speak, *via* the need for coherence in our attitudes, their interests are often overridden by the interests of full-fledged persons. But if their survival would be no inconvenience to people at all, then it is wrong to drown them, *contra* Tooley.

Tooley's conclusions about abortion are wrong for the same reason. Even if a fetus is not a person, abortion is not always permissible, because of the resemblance of a fetus to a person. I agree with Thomson that it would be wrong for a woman who is seven months pregnant to have an abortion just to avoid having to postpone a trip to Europe. In the early months of pregnancy when the fetus hardly resembles a baby at

---

[13]On the other hand, if they can be trusted with people, then our moral customs are mistaken. It all depends on the facts of psychology.

[14]*Op. cit.*, pp. 40, 60–61.

all, then, abortion is permissible whenever it is in the interests of the pregnant woman or her family. The reasons would only need to outweigh the pain and inconvenience of the abortion itself. In the middle months, when the fetus comes to resemble a person, abortion would be justifiable only when the continuation of the pregnancy or the birth of the child would cause harms—physical, psychological, economic or social—to the woman. In the late months of pregnancy, even on our current assumption that a fetus is not a person, abortion seems to be wrong except to save a woman from significant injury or death.

The Supreme Court has recognized similar gradations in the alleged slippery slope stretching between conception and birth. To this point, the present paper has been a discussion of the moral status of abortion only, not its legal status. In view of the great physical, financial and sometimes psychological costs of abortion, perhaps the legal arrangement most compatible with the proposed moral solution would be the absence of restrictions, that is, so-called abortion "on demand."

So I conclude, first, that application of our concept of a person will not suffice to settle the abortion issue. After all, the biological development of a human being is gradual. Second, whether a fetus is a person or not, abortion is justifiable early in pregnancy to avoid modest harms and seldom justifiable late in pregnancy except to avoid significant injury or death.[15]

QUESTIONS

1 Is English successful in her effort to moderate both the conservative view and the liberal view on abortion?
2 Is the following a justifiable criticism? In moderating the conservative view, English winds up with a rather "conservative" moderate view, whereas in moderating the liberal view, she winds up with a rather "liberal" moderate view. Therefore, she is not successful in showing that the problem of abortion can be effectively resolved without first establishing whether or not the fetus is a person.

Majority Opinion in *Roe v. Wade*

Justice Harry A. Blackmun

Harry A. Blackmun, associate justice of the United States Supreme Court, is a graduate of Harvard University Law School. After some fifteen years in private practice he became legal counsel to the Mayo Clinic (1950–1959). Justice Blackmun also served as United States circuit judge (1959–1970) before his appointment in 1970 to the Supreme Court.

[15]I am deeply indebted to Larry Crocker and Arthur Kuflik for their constructive comments.

United States Supreme Court. 410 U.S. 113 (1973).

In this case, a pregnant single woman, suing under the fictitious name of Jane Roe, challenged the constitutionality of the existing Texas criminal abortion law.
According to the Texas Penal Code, the performance of an abortion, except to save the life of the mother, constituted a crime that was punishable by a prison sentence of two to five years. At the time this case was finally resolved by the Supreme Court, abortion legislation varied widely from state to state. Some states, principally New York, had already legalized abortion on demand. Most other states, however, had legalized various forms of therapeutic abortion but had retained some measure of restrictive abortion legislation.

Justice Blackmun, writing an opinion concurred in by six other justices, argues that a woman's decision to terminate a pregnancy is encompassed by a *right to privacy*—but only up to a certain point in the development of the fetus. As the right to privacy is not an absolute right, it must yield at some point to the state's legitimate interests. Justice Blackmun contends that the state has a legitimate interest in protecting the health of the mother and that this interest becomes compelling at approximately the end of the first trimester in the development of the fetus. He also contends that the state has a legitimate interest in protecting potential life and that this interest becomes compelling at the point of viability.

It is . . . apparent that at common law, at the time of the adoption of our Constitution, and throughout the major portion of the 19th century, abortion was viewed with less disfavor than under most American statutes currently in effect. Phrasing it another way, a woman enjoyed a substantially broader right to terminate a pregnancy than she does in most States today. At least with respect to the early stage of pregnancy, and very possibly without such a limitation, the opportunity to make this choice was present in this country well into the 19th century. Even later, the law continued for some time to treat less punitively an abortion procured in early pregnancy. . . .

Three reasons have been advanced to explain historically the enactment of criminal abortion laws in the 19th century and to justify their continued existence.

It has been argued occasionally that these laws were the product of a Victorian social concern to discourage illicit sexual conduct. Texas, however, does not advance this justification in the present case, and it appears that no court or commentator has taken the argument seriously. . . .

A second reason is concerned with abortion as a medical procedure. When most criminal abortion laws were first enacted, the procedure was a hazardous one for the woman. This was particularly true prior to the development of antisepsis. Antiseptic techniques, of course, were based on discoveries by Lister, Pasteur, and others first announced in 1867, but were not generally accepted and employed until about the turn of the century. Abortion mortality was high. Even after 1900, and perhaps until as late as the development of antibiotics in the 1940's, standard modern techniques such as dilatation and curettage were not nearly so safe as they are today. Thus it has been argued that a State's real concern in enacting a criminal abortion law was to protect the pregnant woman, that is, to restrain her from submitting to a procedure that placed her life in serious jeopardy.

Modern medical techniques have altered this situation. Appellants and various *amici* refer to medical data indicating that abortion in early pregnancy, that is, prior to the end of first trimester, although not without its risk, is now relatively safe. Mortality rates for women undergoing early abortions, where the procedure is legal, appear to be as low as or lower than the rates for normal childbirth. Consequently, any interest of the State in protecting the woman from an inherently hazardous procedure, except when it would be equally dangerous for her to forgo it, has largely disappeared. Of course, important state interests in the area of health and medical standards do remain. The State has a legitimate interest in seeing to it that abortion, like any other medical procedure, is performed under circumstances that insure maximum safety for the patient. This interest obviously extends at least to the performing physician and his staff, to the facilities involved, to the availability of after-care, and to adequate provision for any complication or emergency that might arise. The prevalence of high mortality rates at illegal "abortion mills" strengthens, rather than weakens, the State's interest in regulating the conditions under which abortions are performed. Moreover, the risk to the woman increases as her pregnancy continues. Thus the State retains a definite interest in protecting the woman's own health and safety when an abortion is performed at a late stage of pregnancy.

The third reason is the State's interest—some phrase it in terms of duty—in protecting prenatal life. Some of the argument for this justification rests on the theory that a new human life is present from the moment of conception. The State's interest and general obligation to protect life then extends, it is argued, to prenatal life. Only when the life of the pregnant mother herself is at stake, balanced against the life she carries within her, should the interest of the embryo or fetus not prevail. Logically, of course, a legitimate state interest in this area need not stand or fall on acceptance of the belief that life begins at conception or at some other point prior to live birth. In assessing the State's interest, recognition may be given to the less rigid claim that as long as at least *potential* life is involved, the State may assert interests beyond the protection of the pregnant woman alone.

Parties challenging state abortion laws have sharply disputed in some courts the contention that a purpose of these laws, when enacted, was to protect prenatal life. Pointing to the absence of legislative history to support the contention, they claim that most state laws were designed solely to protect the woman. Because medical advances have lessened this concern, at least with respect to abortion in early pregnancy, they argue that with respect to such abortions the laws can no longer be justified by any state interest. There is some scholarly support for this view of original purpose. The few state courts called upon to interpret their laws in the late 19th and early 20th centuries did focus on the State's interest in protecting the woman's health rather than in preserving the embryo and fetus. . . .

The Constitution does not explicitly mention any right of privacy. In a line of decisions, however, going back perhaps as far as *Union Pacific R. Co. v. Botsford* (1891), the Court has recognized that a right of personal privacy, or a guarantee of certain areas or zones of privacy, does exist under the Constitution. In varying contexts the Court or individual Justices have indeed found at least the roots of that right in the First Amendment, . . . in the Fourth and Fifth Amendments . . . in the penumbras of the Bill of Rights . . . in the Ninth Amendment . . . or in the concept of liberty guaranteed by the first section of the Fourteenth Amendment. . . . These decisions make it clear that only personal rights that can be deemed "fundamental" or "implicit in the concept of ordered liberty," . . . are included in this guarantee of personal privacy. They also make it clear that the right has some extension to activities relating to marriage, . . . procreation, . . . contraception, . . . family relationships, . . . and child rearing and education. . . .

This right of privacy, whether it be founded in the Fourteenth Amendment's concept of personal liberty and restrictions upon state action, as we feel it is, or, as the District Court determined, in the Ninth Amendment's reservation of rights to the people, is broad enough to encompass a woman's decision whether or not to terminate her pregnancy. . . .

. . . [A]ppellants and some *amici* argue that the woman's right is absolute and that she is entitled to terminate her pregnancy at whatever time, in whatever way, and for whatever reason she alone chooses. With this we do not agree. Appellants' arguments that Texas either has no valid interest at all in regulating the abortion decision, or no interest strong enough to support any limitation upon the woman's sole determination, is unpersuasive. The Court's decisions recognizing a right of privacy also acknowledge that some state regulation in areas protected by that right is appropriate. As noted above, a state may properly assert important interests in safe-guarding health, in maintaining medical standards, and in protecting potential life. At some point in pregnancy, these respective interests become sufficiently compelling to sustain regulation of the factors that govern the abortion decision. The privacy right involved, therefore, cannot be said to be absolute. . . .

We therefore conclude that the right of personal privacy includes the abortion decision, but that this right is not unqualified and must be considered against important state interests in regulation.

We note that those federal and state courts that have recently considered abortion law challenges have reached the same conclusion. . . .

Although the results are divided, most of these courts have agreed that the right of privacy, however based, is broad enough to cover the abortion decision; that the right, nonetheless, is not absolute and is subject to some limitations; and that at some point the state interests as to protection of health, medical standards, and prenatal life, become dominant. We agree with this approach. . . .

The appellee and certain *amici* argue that the fetus is a "person" within the language and meaning of the Fourteenth Amendment. In support of this they outline at length and in detail the well-known facts of fetal development. If this suggestion of personhood is established, the appellant's case, of course, collapses, for the fetus' right to life is then guaranteed specifically by the Amendment. The appellant conceded as much on reargument. On the other hand, the appellee conceded on reargument that no case could be cited that holds that a fetus is a person within the meaning of the Fourteenth Amendment. . . .

All this, together with our observation, *supra,* that throughout the major portion of the 19th century prevailing legal abortion practices were far freer than they are today, persuades us that the word "person," as used in the Fourteenth Amendment, does not include the unborn. . . . Indeed, our decision in *United States v. Vuitch* (1971) inferentially is to the same effect, for we there would not have indulged in statutory interpretation favorable to abortion in specified circumstances if the necessary consequence was the termination of life entitled to Fourteenth Amendment protection.

. . . As we have intimated above, it is reasonable and appropriate for a State to decide that at some point in time another interest, that of health of the mother or that of potential human life, becomes significantly involved. The woman's privacy is no longer sole and any right of privacy she possesses must be measured accordingly.

Texas urges that, apart from the Fourteenth Amendment, life begins at conception and is present throughout pregnancy, and that, therefore, the State has a compelling interest in protecting that life from and after conception. We need not resolve the difficult question of when life begins. When those trained in the respective disciplines of medicine, philosophy, and theology are unable to arrive at any consensus, the judiciary, at this point in the development of man's knowledge, is not in a position to speculate as to the answer.

It should be sufficient to note briefly the wide divergence of thinking on this most sensitive and difficult question. There has always been strong support for the view that life does not begin until live birth. This was the belief of the Stoics. It appears to be the predominant, though not the unanimous, attitude of the Jewish faith. It may be taken to represent also the position of a large segment of the Protestant community, insofar as that can be ascertained; organized groups that have taken a formal position on the abortion issue have generally regarded abortion as a matter for the conscience of the individual and her family. As we have noted, the common law found greater significance in quickening. Physicians and their scientific colleagues have regarded that event with less interest and have tended to focus either upon conception or upon live birth or upon the interim point at which the fetus becomes "viable," that is, potentially able to live outside the mother's womb, albeit with artificial aid. Viability is usually placed at about seven months (28 weeks) but may occur earlier, even at 24 weeks. . . .

In areas other than criminal abortion the law has been reluctant to endorse any theory that life, as we recognize it, begins before live birth or to accord legal rights to the unborn except in narrowly defined situations and except when the rights are contingent upon live birth. . . . In short, the unborn have never been recognized in the law as persons in the whole sense.

In view of all this, we do not agree that, by adopting one theory of life, Texas may override the rights of the pregnant woman that are at stake. We repeat, however, that the State does have an important and legitimate interest in preserving and protecting the health of the pregnant woman, whether she be a resident of the State or a nonresident who seeks medical consultation and treatment there, and that it has still *another* important and legitimate interest in protecting the potentiality of human life. These interests are separate and distinct. Each grows in substantiality as the woman approaches term and, at a point during pregnancy, each becomes "compelling."

With respect to the State's important and legitimate interest in the health of the mother, the "compelling" point, in the light of present medical knowledge, is at approximately the end of the first trimester. This is so because of the now established medical fact . . . that until the end of the first trimester mortality in abortion is less than mortality in normal childbirth. It follows that, from and after this point, a State may regulate the abortion procedure to the extent that the regulation reasonably relates to the preservation and protection of maternal health. Examples of permissible state regulation in this area are requirements as to the qualifications of the person who is to perform the abortion; as to the licensure of that person; as to the facility in which the procedure is to be performed, that is, whether it must be a hospital or may be a clinic or some other place of less-than-hospital status; as to the licensing of the facility; and the like.

This means, on the other hand, that, for the period of pregnancy prior to this "compelling" point, the attending physician, in consultation with his patient, is free to determine, without regulation by the State, that in his medical judgment the patient's pregnancy should be terminated. If that decision is reached, the judgment may be effectuated by an abortion free of interference by the State.

With respect to the State's important and legitimate interest in potential life, the "compelling" point is at viability. This is so because the fetus then presumably has the capability of meaningful life outside the mother's womb. State regulation protective of fetal life after viability thus has both logical and biological justifications. If the State is interested in protecting fetal life after viability, it may go so far as to proscribe abortion during that period except when it is necessary to preserve the life or health of the mother. . . .

To summarize and repeat:

1. A state criminal abortion statute of the current Texas type, that excepts from criminality only a *life saving* procedure on behalf of the mother, without regard to pregnancy stage and without recognition of the other interests involved, is violative of the Due Process Clause of the Fourteenth Amendment.

(a) For the stage prior to approximately the end of the first trimester, the abortion decision and its effectuation must be left to the medical judgment of the pregnant woman's attending physician.

(b) For the stage subsequent to approximately the end of the first trimester, the State, in promoting its interest in the health of the mother, may, if it chooses, regulate the abortion procedure in ways that are reasonably related to maternal health.

(c) For the stage subsequent to viability the State, in promoting its interest in the potentiality of human life, may, if it chooses, regulate, and even proscribe, abortion except where it is necessary, in appropriate medical judgment, for the preservation of the life or health of the mother.

2. The State may define the term "physician," as it has been employed [here], to mean only a physician currently licensed by the State, and may proscribe any abortion by a person who is not a physician as so defined.

. . . The decision leaves the State free to place increasing restrictions on abortion as the period of pregnancy lengthens, so long as those restrictions are tailored to the recognized state interests. The decision vindicates the right of the physician to administer medical treatment according to his professional judgment up to the points where important state interests provide compelling justifications for intervention. Up to those points the abortion decision in all its aspects is inherently, and primarily, a medical decision, and basic responsibility for it must rest with the physician. If an individual practitioner abuses the privilege of exercising proper medical judgment, the usual remedies, judicial and intraprofessional, are available. . . .

QUESTIONS

1 Justice Blackmun contends that the state's legitimate interest in protecting the health of the mother becomes *compelling* at the end of the first trimester. Does the Court's choice of this particular point as "compelling" have any substantial justification, or is the choice fundamentally arbitrary?

2 Justice Blackmun contends that the state's legitimate interest in protecting potential life becomes *compelling* at the point of viability. Does the Court's choice of this particular point as "compelling" have any substantial justification, or is the choice fundamentally arbitrary?

3 Justice Blackmun *explicitly* disavows entering into philosophical speculation on the problem of the beginning of human life. To what extent could it be said that he *implicitly* takes a philosophical position on this problem?

Dissenting Opinion in *Akron v. Akron Center for Reproductive Health*

Justice Sandra Day O'Connor

Sandra Day O'Connor, a graduate of Stanford University Law School, is associate justice of the United States Supreme Court. Before becoming judge of Maricopa County Superior Court in 1975, she was Arizona assistant attorney general (1965–1969) and Arizona state senator (1969–1975). She was serving on the Arizona Court of Appeals when, in 1981, she became the first woman ever appointed to the Supreme Court.

At issue in this case was the constitutionality of an Akron (Ohio) city ordinance that had been designed in an effort to place obstacles in the path of women seeking an abortion. The most important provisions of the ordinance were: (1) the requirement that any abortion subsequent to the first trimester be performed in a hospital (as opposed to a clinic); (2) the requirement that the attending physician (as opposed to other trained personnel) personally inform the patient of a host of particulars concerning fetal development, the emotional and physical risks of

abortion, etc., "in order to insure . . . truly informed consent"; (3) the requirement
that a physician not perform an abortion until 24 hours after a consent form had
been signed by the pregnant woman. In a six-to-three decision, the Court
reaffirmed *Roe v. Wade* and declared each of the ordinance's provisions to be
unconstitutional. The court called attention to the additional financial burdens
created by provisions (1) and (3) in invalidating them. Although endorsing the
importance of informed consent, the Court emphasized two defects in provision (2).
First, "the information required is designed not to inform the woman's consent but
rather to persuade her to withhold it altogether." Second, a physician may
legitimately delegate the counseling task to another qualified individual.

In her dissenting opinion, Justice O'Connor directly attacks the "trimester"
framework of *Roe v. Wade*. In her view, the *Roe* framework, since it is tied to the
changing state of medical technology, is "on a collision course with itself." She
also insists that state interests in maternal health and in the protection of potential
life exist *throughout* pregnancy; she rejects the idea that there is a "compelling"
point for each of these interests.

In *Roe v. Wade* (1973), the Court held that the "right of privacy . . . founded in the
Fourteenth Amendment's concept of personal liberty and restrictions upon state action . . . is broad enough to encompass a woman's decision whether or not to terminate
her pregnancy." The parties in [this case] have not asked the Court to re-examine the
validity of that holding and the court below did not address it. Accordingly, the Court
does not re-examine its previous holding. Nonetheless, it is apparent from the Court's
opinion that neither sound constitutional theory nor our need to decide cases based on
the application of neutral principles can accommodate an analytical framework that
varies according to the "stages" of pregnancy, where those stages, and their concomitant
standards of review, differ according to the level of medical technology available when
a particular challenge to state regulation occurs. The Court's analysis of the Akron
regulations is inconsistent both with the methods of analysis employed in previous
cases dealing with abortion, and with the Court's approach to fundamental rights in
other areas.

Our recent cases indicate that a regulation imposed on "a lawful abortion 'is
not unconstitutional unless it unduly burdens the right to seek an abortion.' " In my
view, this "unduly burdensome" standard should be applied to the challenged regulations throughout the entire pregnancy without reference to the particular "stage" of
pregnancy involved. If the particular regulation does not "unduly burden[]" the fundamental right, then our evaluation of that regulation is limited to our determination
that the regulation rationally relates to a legitimate state purpose. Irrespective of what
we may believe is wise or prudent policy in this difficult area, "the Constitution does
not constitute us as 'Platonic Guardians' nor does it vest in this Court the authority
to strike down laws because they do not meet our standards of desirable social policy,
'wisdom,' or 'common sense.' "

United States Supreme Court. 462 U.S. 416 (1983).

I

The trimester or "three-stage" approach adopted by the Court in *Roe,* and, in a modified form, employed by the Court to analyze the state regulations in [this case], cannot be supported as a legitimate or useful framework for accommodating the woman's right and the State's interests. The decision of the Court today graphically illustrates why the trimester approach is a completely unworkable method of accommodating the conflicting personal rights and compelling state interests that are involved in the abortion context.

As the Court indicates today, the State's compelling interest in maternal health changes as medical technology changes, and any health regulation must not "depart from accepted medical practice." In applying this standard, the Court holds that "the safety of second-trimester abortions has increased dramatically" since 1973, when *Roe* was decided. Although a regulation such as one requiring that all second-trimester abortions be performed in hospitals "had strong support" in 1973 "as a reasonable health regulation," this regulation can no longer stand because, according to the Court's diligent research into medical and scientific literature, the dilation and evacuation procedure (D&E), used in 1973 only for first-trimester abortions, "is now widely and successfully used for second-trimester abortions." Further, the medical literature relied on by the Court indicates that the D&E procedure may be performed in an appropriate non-hospital setting for "at least . . . the early weeks of the second trimester. . . . " The Court then chooses the period of 16 weeks of gestation as that point at which D&E procedures may be performed safely in a non-hospital setting, and thereby invalidates the Akron hospitalization regulation.

It is not difficult to see that despite the Court's purported adherence to the trimester approach adopted in *Roe,* the lines drawn in that decision have now been "blurred" because of what the Court accepts as technological advancement in the safety of abortion procedure. The State may no longer rely on a "bright line" that separates permissible from impermissible regulation, and it is no longer free to consider the second trimester as a unit and weigh the risks posed by all abortion procedures throughout that trimester. Rather, the State must continuously and conscientiously study contemporary medical and scientific literature in order to determine whether the effect of a particular regulation is to "depart from accepted medical practice" insofar as particular procedures and particular periods within the trimester are concerned. Assuming that legislative bodies are able to engage in this exacting task, it is difficult to believe that our Constitution *requires* that they do it as a prelude to protecting the health of their citizens. It is even more difficult to believe that this Court, without the resources available to those bodies entrusted with making legislative choices, believes itself competent to make these inquiries and to revise these standards every time the American College of Obstetricians and Gynecologists (ACOG) or similar group revises its views about what is and what is not appropriate medical procedure in this area. Indeed, the ACOG standards on which the Court relies were changed in 1982 after trial in the present cases. Before ACOG changed its standards in 1982, it recommended that all mid-trimester abortions be performed in a hospital. As today's decision indicates, medical technology is changing, and this change will necessitate our continued functioning as the nation's "*ex officio* medical board with powers to approve or disapprove medical and operative practices and standards throughout the United States."

Just as improvements in medical technology inevitably will move *forward* the point at which the State may regulate for reasons of maternal health, different technological improvements will move *backward* the point of viability at which the State may proscribe abortions except when necessary to preserve the life and health of the mother.

In 1973, viability before 28 weeks was considered unusual. . . . However, recent studies have demonstrated increasingly earlier fetal viability. It is certainly reasonable to believe that fetal viability in the first trimester of pregnancy may be possible in the not too distant future. Indeed, the Court has explicitly acknowledged that *Roe* left the point of viability "flexible for anticipated advancements in medical skill. [W]e recognized in *Roe* that viability was a matter of medical judgment, skill, and technical ability, and we preserved the flexibility of the term."

The *Roe* framework, then, is clearly on a collision course with itself. As the medical risks of various abortion procedures decrease, the point at which the State may regulate for reasons of maternal health is moved further forward to actual childbirth. As medical science becomes better able to provide for the separate existence of the fetus, the point of viability is moved further back toward conception. Moreover, it is clear that the trimester approach violates the fundamental aspiration of judicial decision making through the application of neutral principles "sufficiently absolute to give them roots throughout the community and continuity over significant periods of time. . . . " The *Roe* framework is inherently tied to the state of medical technology that exists whenever particular litigation ensues. Although legislatures are better suited to make the necessary factual judgments in this area, the Court's framework forces legislatures, as a matter of constitutional law, to speculate about what constitutes "accepted medical practice" at any given time. Without the necessary expertise or ability, courts must then pretend to act as science review boards and examine those legislative judgments.

The Court adheres to the *Roe* framework because the doctrine of *stare decisis* "demands respect in a society governed by the rule of law." Although respect for *stare decisis* cannot be challenged, "this Court's considered practice [is] not to apply *stare decisis* as rigidly in constitutional as in nonconstitutional cases." Although we must be mindful of the "desirability of continuity of decision in constitutional questions . . . when convinced of former error, this Court has never felt constrained to follow precedent. In constitutional questions, when correction depends on amendment and not upon legislative action this Court throughout its history has freely exercised its power to reexamine the basis of its constitutional decisions."

Even assuming that there is a fundamental right to terminate pregnancy in some situations, there is no justification in law or logic for the trimester framework adopted in *Roe* and employed by the Court today on the basis of *stare decisis*. For the reasons stated above, that framework is clearly an unworkable means of balancing the fundamental right and the compelling state interests that are indisputably implicated.

II

The Court in *Roe* correctly realized that the State has important interests "in the areas of health and medical standards" and that "[t]he State has a legitimate interest in seeing to it that abortion, like any other medical procedure, is performed under circumstances that insure maximum safety for the patient." The Court also recognized that the State has "*another* important and legitimate interest in protecting the potentiality of human life." I agree completely that the State has these interests, but in my view, the point at which these interests become compelling does not depend on the trimester of pregnancy. Rather, these interests are present *throughout* pregnancy.

This Court has never failed to recognize that "a State may properly assert important interests in safeguarding health [and] in maintaining medical standards." *Roe*. It cannot be doubted that as long as a state statute is within "the bounds of reason and [does not] assume[] the character of a merely arbitrary fiat . . . [then] [t]he State . . . must decide upon measures that are needful for the protection of its people . . . ." "There is nothing in the United States Constitution which limits the State's power to require that medical procedures be done safely. . . ." "The mode and procedure of medical diagnostic procedures is not the business of judges." Under the *Roe* framework, however, the state interest in maternal health cannot become compelling until the onset of the second trimester of pregnancy because "until the end of the first trimester mortality in abortion may be less than mortality in normal childbirth." *Roe*. Before the second trimester, the decision to perform an abortion "must be left to the medical judgment of the pregnant woman's attending physician." *Roe*.

The fallacy inherent in the *Roe* framework is apparent: just because the State has a compelling interest in ensuring maternal safety once an abortion may be more dangerous than childbirth, it simply does not follow that the State has *no* interest before that point that justifies state regulation to ensure that first-trimester abortions are performed as safely as possible.

The state interest in potential human life is likewise extant throughout pregnancy. In *Roe,* the Court held that although the State had an important and legitimate interest in protecting potential life, that interest could not become compelling until the point at which the fetus was viable. The difficulty with this analysis is clear: *potential* life is no less potential in the first weeks of pregnancy than it is at viability or afterward. At any stage in pregnancy, there is the *potential* for human life. Although the Court refused to "resolve the difficult question of when life begins," the Court chose the point of viability—when the fetus is *capable* of life independent of its mother—to permit the complete proscription of abortion. The choice of viability as the point at which the state interest in *potential* life becomes compelling is no less arbitrary than choosing any point before viability or any point afterward. Accordingly, I believe that the State's interest in protecting potential human life exists throughout the pregnancy. . . .

QUESTIONS

1 Can the *Roe* framework be defended against Justice O'Connor's criticisms?
2 What would be the basic elements of an ideal social policy on abortion? Why?

SUGGESTED ADDITIONAL READINGS FOR CHAPTER ONE

ARMSTRONG, ROBERT L.: "The Right to Life." *Journal of Social Philosophy*, vol. 8, January 1977, pp. 13–19. Armstrong develops an interesting and somewhat distinctive moderate view on the morality of abortion. Though fetuses are not actual persons, he contends, they may be said to have a right to life on the basis of their potential personhood, but *only if* they have what he calls "real or serious" potentiality.

BRODY, BARUCH: "On the Humanity of the Foetus." In Robert L. Perkins, ed., *Abortion: Pro and Con*. Cambridge, Mass.: Schenkman, 1974, pp. 69–90. Brody critically examines the various proposals for "drawing the line" on the humanity of the fetus, ultimately suggesting that the most defensible view would draw the line at the point where fetal brain activity begins.

ENGELHARDT, H. TRISTRAM, JR.: "The Ontology of Abortion." *Ethics*, vol. 84, April 1974, pp. 217–234. Engelhardt focuses attention on the issue of "whether or to what extent the fetus is a person." He argues that, strictly speaking, a human person is not present until the later stages of infancy. However, he finds the point of viability significant in that, with viability, an infant can play the social role of "child" and thus be treated "as if it were a person."

FEINBERG, JOEL: "Abortion." In Tom Regan, ed., *Matters of Life and Death*. New York: Random House, 1980, pp. 183–217. In this long essay, Feinberg analyzes the strengths and weaknesses of alternative views about the moral status of the fetus. He also considers the extent to which abortion is morally justifiable *if* it is granted that the fetus is a person.

FEINBERG, JOEL, ed.: *The Problem of Abortion*, 2d ed. Belmont, Calif.: Wadsworth, 1984. This excellent anthology features a wide range of articles on the moral justifiability of abortion.

GRISEZ, GERMAIN: *Abortion: The Myths, The Realities, and the Arguments*. New York: Corpus Books, 1970. Early chapters of this long book provide discussions of a number of factual and historical aspects of abortion. Grisez's conservative view on the morality of abortion appears in Chapter 6, "Ethical Arguments." Chapter 7, also notable, is entitled "Toward a Sound Public Policy."

HUMBER, JAMES M.: "Abortion: The Avoidable Moral Dilemma." *Journal of Value Inquiry*, vol. 9, Winter 1975, pp. 282–302. Humber, defending the conservative view on the morality of abortion, examines and rejects what he identifies as the major defenses of abortion. He also contends that proabortion arguments are typically so poor that they can only be viewed as "after-the-fact-rationalizations."

LANGERAK, EDWARD A.: "Abortion: Listening to the Middle." *Hastings Center Report*, vol. 9, October 1979, pp. 24–28. Langerak suggests a theoretical framework for a moderate view that incorporates two "widely shared beliefs": (1) that there is something about the fetus *itself* that makes abortion morally problematic and (2) that late abortions are significantly more problematic than early abortions.

ROSS, STEVEN L.: "Abortion and the Death of the Fetus." *Philosophy and Public Affairs*, vol. 11, Summer 1982, pp. 232–245. Ross draws a distinction between abortion as the termination of pregnancy and abortion as the termination of the life of the fetus. He proceeds to defend abortion in the latter sense, insisting that it is justifiable for a woman to desire not only the termination of pregnancy but also the death of the fetus.

THOMSON, JUDITH JARVIS: "A Defense of Abortion." *Philosophy and Public Affairs*, vol. 1, Fall 1971, pp. 47–66. In this widely discussed article, Thomson attempts to "moderate the conservative view." For the sake of argument, she grants the premise that the fetus (from conception) is a person. Still, she argues, under certain conditions abortion remains morally permissible.

TOOLEY, MICHAEL: *Abortion and Infanticide*. New York: Oxford, 1983. In this long book, Tooley defends the liberal view on the morality of abortion. He insists that the question of the morality of abortion cannot be satisfactorily resolved "in isolation from the questions of the morality of infanticide and of the killing of nonhuman animals."

CHAPTER 2

EUTHANASIA

Questions about the morality of euthanasia are not new but they are debated with a new intensity in contemporary times. Recent advances in biomedical technology have made it possible to prolong human life in ways undreamed of by past generations. As a result, it is not unusual to find individuals who have lived a long and useful life now permanently incapable of functioning in any recognizably human fashion. Biological life continues; but some find it tempting to say that human life, in any meaningful sense, has ceased. In one case the patient is in an irreversible coma, reduced to a vegetative existence. In another case the patient's personality has completely deteriorated. In still another case the patient alternates inescapably between excruciating pain and drug-induced stupor. In each of these cases, the quality of human life has deteriorated. There is no longer any capacity for creative employment, intellectual pursuits, or the cultivation of interpersonal relationships. In short, in each of these three cases life seems to have been rendered meaningless in the sense that the individual has lost all capacity for normal human satisfactions. In the first case there is simply no consciousness, which is a necessary condition for deriving satisfaction. In the second case consciousness has been dulled to such an extent that there is no longer any capacity for satisfaction. In the third case excruciating pain and sedation combine to undercut the possibility of satisfaction.

At the other end of the spectrum of life, we are confronted with the severely defective newborn child. In some tragic cases, a child seems to have no significant potential for meaningful human life. For example, an *anencephalic* child, one born with a partial or total absence of the brain, has no prospect for human life as we know it. Biomedical technology is sometimes sufficient to sustain or at least temporarily prolong the life of a severely defective newborn, depending on the particular nature of the child's medical condition, but one question commands attention: Is the child better off dead?

Religious people pray and nonreligious people hope that death will come quickly to themselves or to loved ones who are in the midst of terminal illnesses and forced to endure pain and/or indignity. The same attitudes often prevail in the face of severely defective newborns. The prevalence of these attitudes seems to support the view, however sad, that some human beings, by virtue of their medical condition, are better off dead. But if it is true that someone is better off dead, then mercy is on the side of death, and the issue of euthanasia comes to the fore. Euthanasia, in its various forms, is the focal point of discussion in this chapter.

THE MORAL JUSTIFIABILITY OF EUTHANASIA

Discussions of the moral justifiability of euthanasia often involve distinctions which are themselves controversial. Such distinctions include that between *ordinary* and *extraordinary* means of prolonging life, that between *killing* and *allowing to die,* and that between *active* and *passive* euthanasia. Indeed, the very concept of euthanasia is controversial. In accordance with a "narrow construal of euthanasia," euthanasia is equivalent to mercy *killing.* In this view, if a physician administers a lethal dose of a drug (on grounds of mercy), this act is a paradigm of euthanasia. If, on the other hand, a physician allows the patient to die by ceasing to employ "extraordinary means" (such as a respirator), this does not count as euthanasia. J. Gay-Williams in this chapter adopts a narrow construal of euthanasia. In contrast, on a "broad construal of euthanasia," the category of euthanasia encompasses both killing and allowing to die (on grounds of mercy). Those who adopt a broad construal of euthanasia often distinguish between active euthanasia, i.e., killing, and passive euthanasia, i.e., allowing to die. Though there seem to be clear cases of killing (e.g., the lethal dose) and clear cases of allowing to die (e.g., withdrawing a respirator), there are more troublesome cases as well. Suppose a physician administers pain medication with the knowledge that the patient's life will be shortened as a result. A case of killing? Suppose a physician discontinues "ordinary means" of treatment? A case of allowing to die? Sometimes it is even said that *withdrawing* extraordinary means of life support is active ("pulling the plug!") in a way that *withholding* extraordinary means is not. And at a time when coronary bypass surgery and hemodialysis treatments are almost routine medical procedures, just what distinguishes ordinary means from extraordinary ones? Cost? Availability? The age of the patient? The condition of the patient? In a reading in this chapter, Joanne Lynn and James F. Childress suggest that determining whether a treatment is ordinary or extraordinary in a particular case depends on an assessment of its likely benefits in light of the burdens accompanying the treatment. On their analysis, simply providing nutrition might in some cases constitute extraordinary treatment.

There is one further distinction, itself relatively uncontroversial, that is prominent in discussions of euthanasia. *Voluntary* euthanasia proceeds with the (informed) consent of the person involved. *Involuntary* euthanasia proceeds without the consent of the individual involved because the individual is *incapable* of (informed) consent.[1] The possibility of involuntary euthanasia arises, for example, in the case of comatose adults, such as the much-discussed Karen Ann Quinlan.[2] It also arises in the case of individuals who are not comatose but who are considered *incompetent,* such as Earle N. Spring, whose case is included in this chapter. Another prominent variety of involuntary euthanasia involves severely defective newborns. When the voluntary/involuntary distinction is combined with the active/passive distinction, four types of euthanasia result: (1) active voluntary euthanasia, (2) passive voluntary euthanasia, (3) active involuntary euthanasia, and (4) passive involuntary euthanasia.

A very common view on the morality of euthanasia, so common that it might justifiably be termed the "standard view," may be explicated as follows: Withholding or withdrawing extraordinary means of life support is morally acceptable (under certain specifiable conditions), but mercy killing is never morally acceptable. Those who operate in accordance with the narrow conception of euthanasia would express the standard view by saying that withholding or withdrawing extraordinary means of life support is morally acceptable, but euthanasia is never morally acceptable. J. Gay-Williams expresses the standard view in just this way in this chapter. Those who operate in accordance with the broad conception of euthanasia would express the standard view by saying that *passive euthanasia* is morally acceptable (under certain specifiable conditions), but *active euthanasia* is never morally acceptable. The standard view, as officially endorsed by the American Medical Association (AMA), is vigorously attacked by James Rachels in one of this chapter's readings. Thomas D. Sullivan accuses Rachels of misconstruing the sense behind the standard view. Sullivan offers

---

[1] Is is often suggested that competent adults make a "living will" to express their wishes with regard to the treatment they would desire, should they become incompetent. In this way, it is thought, individual autonomy is fostered and others (e.g., physicians and family) can be relieved of the responsibility for making involuntary euthanasia decisions. One well-known example of a "living will" has been promulgated by the Euthanasia Educational Council. Addressed to all those who may be concerned, the statement reads as follows:

> Death is as much a reality as birth, growth, maturity and old age—it is the one certainty of life. If the times comes when I,_____, can no longer take part in decisions for my own future, let this statement stand as an expression of my wishes, while I am still of sound mind.
>
> If the situation should arise in which there is no reasonable expectation of my recovery from physical or mental disability, I request that I be allowed to die and not be kept alive by artificial means or "heroic measures." I do not fear death itself as much as the indignities of deterioration, dependence and hopeless pain. I, therefore, ask that medication be mercifully administered to me to alleviate suffering even though this may hasten the moment of death.
>
> This request is made after careful consideration. I hope you who care for me will feel morally bound to follow its mandate. I recognize that this appears to place a heavy responsibility upon you, but it is with the intention of relieving you of such responsibility and of placing it upon myself in accordance with my strong convictions, that this statement is made.

[2] In the Quinlan case, Joseph Quinlan, the father of comatose twenty-one-year-old Karen Ann Quinlan, sought to be appointed guardian of the person and property of his daughter. As guardian, he would then authorize the discontinuance of the mechanical respirator that was thought to be sustaining the vital life processes of his daughter. Judge Muir of the Superior Court of New Jersey decided against the request of Joseph Quinlan. *In re Quinlan,* 137 N.J. Super 227 (1975). Justice Hughes of the Supreme Court of New Jersey overturned the lower-court decision. *In re Quinlan,* 70 N.J. 10,335 A. 2d 647 (1976). When the respirator was finally withdrawn, Karen Ann Quinlan proved capable of breathing on her own. She remained alive in a "persistent vegetative state" for about ten years.

a defense of the standard view. Rachels, in turn, criticizes Sullivan's reliance on the distinction between intentional and nonintentional terminations of life and the distinction between ordinary and extraordinary means of life support.

The withholding or withdrawing of extraordinary means of life support in the case of terminally ill patients is surely an established part of medical practice, as reflected in the AMA's official endorsement of the standard view. Moreover, several religious traditions explicitly acknowledge the morality of this practice. In addition, it is widely believed that a patient has the moral (and legal) right to refuse treatment, a right that would encompass the refusal of extraordinary means of life support. Thus, despite any difficulties that might be involved in specifying what counts as "extraordinary means" of life support, there is a substantial body of opinion, perhaps something close to a consensus view, maintaining the moral legitimacy of withholding or withdrawing extraordinary means of life support in the case of terminally ill patients. There is no such consensus view on the morality of mercy killing, which will be referred to here as "active euthanasia."

Those who argue for the moral legitimacy of active euthanasia emphasize considerations of humaneness. In the case of *voluntary* active euthanasia, the humanitarian appeal is often conjoined with an appeal to the primacy of individual freedom. Thus the case for the morality of voluntary active euthanasia incorporates two basic arguments: (1) It is cruel and inhumane to refuse the plea of a terminally ill person that his or her life be mercifully ended to avoid future suffering and indignity. (2) Individuals should be free to do as they choose as long as their actions do not result in harm to others. Since no one is harmed by terminally ill patients undergoing active euthanasia, their freedom to have their lives ended in this fashion should not be infringed.

Those who argue against the moral legitimacy of active euthanasia (in both its voluntary and involuntary forms) rest their case on one or both of the following strategies of argument: (1) They appeal to some "sanctity of life" principle to the effect that the intentional termination of (innocent) human life is always immoral. Sullivan advances this sort of argument in his defense of the standard view. (2) They advance arguments based on considerations of utility. On a *utilitarian view of morality,* actions and social policies should be judged right or wrong solely on the basis of their tendency to produce good or bad consequences. According to the *principle of utility,* that action or social practice is morally correct which in the circumstances will tend to produce the greatest possible balance of good over evil for members of the group affected. Opponents of active euthanasia advancing utilitarian arguments bring out the possible bad consequences of adopting active euthanasia as a social policy. Among the predicted bad consequences are premature deaths resulting from misdiagnosis and a lessening of respect for human life that might have extremely damaging consequences for society. This second sort of argument recurs in discussions of the legalization of active euthanasia.

THE LEGALIZATION OF EUTHANASIA

In recent years a mass of so-called euthanasia legislation has been proposed in the various state legislatures. Most of these legislative proposals have been advanced to establish an individual's right to some form of passive rather than active euthanasia, but even this apparently undramatic sort of legislation has often met with much opposition. Some people oppose passive euthanasia legislation because of the difficulties inherent in trying to define crucial phrases such as "meaningless life," "natural death," "extraordinary means," "heroic measures," and so forth. Others, although supporting the spirit of the proposed legislation, nevertheless argue that it is unnecessary because there is already a generally recognized right to refuse even lifesaving treatment. Still others are worried that the legalization of passive euthanasia would lead to the legalization of active euthanasia.

Active euthanasia is illegal in all fifty states, yet the more dramatic euthanasia proposals would seek to legalize active euthanasia, specifically in its *voluntary* form. There are some who consider active euthanasia in any form intrinsically immoral (sometimes on overtly religious grounds) and thus are opposed to the legalization of voluntary active euthanasia. Others, however, see nothing intrinsically wrong with individual acts of voluntary active euthanasia, but still stand opposed to any systematic social policy that would permit voluntary active euthanasia. Arguments made in this vein have a utilitarian character, emphasizing the undesirable consequences that might attend the legalization of voluntary active euthanasia. It is said that the law will be commonly abused and that patients will needlessly die when mistakenly thought to be incurably ill. Most important, it is said, the legalization of voluntary active euthanasia will lead to disrespect for the sanctity of human life. This latter argument, usually identified as a "wedge argument," has several versions. One version runs like this: The legalization of voluntary active euthanasia will lead to the legalization of *involuntary* active euthanasia and thus the "mercy killing" not only of irreversibly comatose patients but also of the senile, the deformed, and perhaps eventually the politically undesirable.

Those who support the legalization of voluntary active euthanasia argue that prohibitive laws are cruel and inhumane. Moreover, they typically conjoin this consideration with an appeal to personal liberty. Since persons who voluntarily choose to undergo active euthanasia harm no one, it is argued, prohibitive laws unjustifiably deprive individuals of liberty. Those who support the legalization of voluntary active euthanasia recognize that some bad consequences may result from such legislation. However, they seek to establish that potential dangers are minimal.

Thomas A. Mappes and Jane S. Zembaty

The Wrongfulness of Euthanasia

J. Gay-Williams

J. Gay-Williams has requested that no biographical information be provided here.

Gay-Williams, who adopts a narrow construal of euthanasia, defines it as "intentionally taking the life of a presumably hopeless person." He refuses to use the expression "passive euthanasia" to describe actions that are labeled in this way by those who adopt a broad construal of euthanasia. Gay-Williams does not consider these latter actions morally unacceptable, but he does consider all actions falling in the category of euthanasia (as he defines it) morally unacceptable. (Thus, in effect, he defends the standard view on the morality of euthanasia.) He is opposed to euthanasia for three reasons: (1) It violates the natural inclination to preserve life and, therefore, goes against nature; (2) euthanasia may work against our own interest if we practice it or allow it to be practiced on us; and (3) accepting euthanasia as a practice may result in certain undesirable long-term consequences.

My impression is that euthanasia—the idea, if not the practice—is slowly gaining acceptance within our society. Cynics might attribute this to an increasing tendency to devalue human life, but I do not believe this is the major factor. The acceptance is much more likely to be the result of unthinking sympathy and benevolence. Well-publicized, tragic stories like that of Karen Quinlan elicit from us deep feelings of compassion. We think to ourselves, "She and her family would be better off if she were dead." It is an easy step from this very human response to the view that if someone (and others) would be better off dead, then it must be all right to kill that person.[1] Although I respect the compassion that leads to this conclusion, I believe the conclusion is wrong. I want to show that euthanasia is wrong. It is inherently wrong, but it is also wrong judged from the standpoints of self-interest and of practical effects.

Before presenting my arguments to support this claim, it would be well to define "euthanasia." An essential aspect of euthanasia is that it involves taking a human life, either one's own or that of another. Also, the person whose life is taken must be someone who is believed to be suffering from some disease or injury from which recovery cannot reasonably be expected. Finally, the action must be deliberate and intentional. Thus, euthanasia is intentionally taking the life of a presumably hopeless person. Whether the life is one's own or that of another, the taking of it is still euthanasia.

It is important to be clear about the deliberate and intentional aspect of the killing. If a hopeless person is given an injection of the wrong drug by mistake and this causes his death, this is wrongful killing but not euthanasia. The killing cannot be the result of accident. Furthermore, if the person is given an injection of a drug that is believed to be necessary to treat his disease or better his condition and the person dies as a result, then this is neither wrongful killing nor euthanasia. The intention was to make the patient well, not kill him. Similarly, when a patient's condition is such that it is

From Ronald Munson, *Intervention and Reflection: Basic Issues in Medical Ethics.* Copyright © 1979 by Wadsworth Publishing Company, Inc., Belmont, California 94002. Reprinted by permission of the publisher.

[1]For a sophisticated defense of this position see Philippa Foot, "Euthanasia," *Philosophy and Public Affairs,* vol. 6 (1977), pp. 85–112. Foot does not endorse the radical conclusion that euthanasia, voluntary and involuntary, is always right.

not reasonable to hope that any medical procedures or treatments will save his life, a failure to implement the procedures or treatments is not euthanasia. If the person dies, this will be as a result of his injuries or disease and not because of his failure to receive treatment.

The failure to continue treatment after it has been realized that the patient has little chance of benefitting from it has been characterized by some as "passive euthanasia." This phrase is misleading and mistaken.[2] In such cases, the person involved is not killed (the first essential aspect of euthanasia), nor is the death of the person intended by the withholding of additional treatment (the third essential aspect of euthanasia). The aim may be to spare the person additional and unjustifiable pain, to save him from the indignities of hopeless manipulations, and to avoid increasing the financial and emotional burden on his family. When I buy a pencil it is so that I can use it to write, not to contribute to an increase in the gross national product. This may be the unintended consequence of my action, but it is not the aim of my action. So it is with failing to continue the treatment of a dying person. I intend his death no more than I intend to reduce the GNP by not using medical supplies. His is an unintended dying, and so-called "passive euthanasia" is not euthanasia at all.

1 THE ARGUMENT FROM NATURE

Every human being has a natural inclination to continue living.Our reflexes and responses fit us to fight attackers, flee wild animals, and dodge out of the way of trucks. In our daily lives we exercise the caution and care necessary to protect ourselves. Our bodies are similarly structured for survival right down to the molecular level. When we are cut, our capillaries seal shut, our blood clots, and fibrogen is produced to start the process of healing the wound. When we are invaded by bacteria, antibodies are produced to fight against the alien organisms, and their remains are swept out of the body by special cells designed for clean-up work.

Euthanasia does violence to this natural goal of survival. It is literally acting against nature because all the processes of nature are bent towards the end of bodily survival. Euthanasia defeats these subtle mechanisms in a way that, in a particular case, disease and injury might not.

It is possible, but not necessary, to make an appeal to revealed religion in this connection.[3] Man as trustee of his body acts against God, its rightful possessor, when he takes his own life. He also violates the commandment to hold life sacred and never to take it without just and compelling cause. But since this appeal will persuade only those who are prepared to accept that religion has access to revealed truths, I shall not employ this line of argument.

It is enough, I believe, to recognize that the organization of the human body and

---

[2]James Rachels rejects the distinction between active and passive euthanasia as morally irrelevant in his "Active and Passive Euthanasia," *New England Journal of Medicine,* vol. 292, pp. 78–80. But see the criticism by Foot, pp. 100–103.

[3]For a defense of this view see J. V. Sullivan, "The Immorality of Euthanasia," in Marvin Kohl, ed., *Beneficent Euthanasia* (Buffalo, New York: Prometheus Books, 1975), pp. 34–44.

our patterns of behavioral responses make the continuation of life a natural goal. By reason alone, then, we can recognize that euthanasia sets us against our own nature.[4] Furthermore, in doing so, euthanasia does violence to our dignity. Our dignity comes from seeking our ends. When one of our goals is survival, and actions are taken that eliminate that goal, then our natural dignity suffers. Unlike animals, we are conscious through reason of our nature and our ends. Euthanasia involves acting as if this dual nature—inclination towards survival and awareness of this as an end—did not exist. Thus, euthanasia denies our basic human character and requires that we regard ourselves or others as something less than fully human.

2 THE ARGUMENT FROM SELF-INTEREST

The above arguments are, I believe, sufficient to show that euthanasia is inherently wrong. But there are reasons for considering it wrong when judged by standards other than reason. Because death is final and irreversible, euthanasia contains within it the possibility that we will work against our own interest if we practice it or allow it to be practiced on us.

Contemporary medicine has high standards of excellence and a proven record of accomplishment, but it does not possess perfect and complete knowledge. A mistaken diagnosis is possible, and so is a mistaken prognosis. Consequently, we may believe that we are dying of a disease when, as a matter of fact, we may not be. We may think that we have no hope of recovery when, as a matter of fact, our chances are quite good. In such circumstances, if euthanasia were permitted, we would die needlessly. Death is final and the chance of error too great to approve the practice of euthanasia.

Also, there is always the possibility that an experimental procedure or a hitherto untried technique will pull us through. We should at least keep this option open, but euthanasia closes it off. Furthermore, spontaneous remission does occur in many cases. For no apparent reason, a patient simply recovers when those all around him, including his physicians, expected him to die. Euthanasia would just guarantee their expectations and leave no room for the "miraculous" recoveries that frequently occur.

Finally, knowing that we can take our life at any time (or ask another to take it) might well incline us to give up too easily. The will to live is strong in all of us, but it can be weakened by pain and suffering and feelings of hopelessness. If during a bad time we allow ourselves to be killed, we never have a chance to reconsider. Recovery from a serious illness requires that we fight for it, and anything that weakens our determination by suggesting that there is an easy way out is ultimately against our own interest. Also, we may be inclined towards euthanasia because of our concern for others. If we see our sickness and suffering as an emotional and financial burden

---

[4]This point is made by Ray V. McIntyre in "Voluntary Euthanasia: The Ultimate Perversion," *Medical Counterpoint*, vol. 2, pp. 26–29.

on our family, we may feel that to leave our life is to make their lives easier.[5] The very presence of the possibility of euthanasia may keep us from surviving when we might.

3 THE ARGUMENT FROM PRACTICAL EFFECTS

Doctors and nurses are, for the most part, totally committed to saving lives. A life lost is, for them, almost a personal failure, an insult to their skills and knowledge. Euthanasia as a practice might well alter this. It could have a corrupting influence so that in any case that is severe doctors and nurses might not try hard enough to save the patient. They might decide that the patient would simply be "better off dead" and take the steps necessary to make that come about. This attitude could then carry over to their dealings with patients less seriously ill. The result would be an overall decline in the quality of medical care.

Finally, euthanasia as a policy is a slippery slope. A person apparently hopelessly ill may be allowed to take his own life. Then he may be permitted to deputize others to do it for him should he no longer be able to act. The judgment of others then becomes the ruling factor. Already at this point euthanasia is not personal and voluntary, for others are acting "on behalf of" the patient as they see fit. This may well incline them to act on behalf of other patients who have not authorized them to exercise their judgment. It is only a short step, then, from voluntary euthanasia (self-inflicted or authorized), to directed euthanasia administered to a patient who has given no authorization, to involuntary euthanasia conducted as part of a social policy.[6] Recently many psychiatrists and sociologists have argued that we define as "mental illness" those forms of behavior that we disapprove of.[7] This gives us license then to lock up those who display the behavior. The category of the "hopelessly ill" provides the possibility of even worse abuse. Embedded in a social policy, it would give society or its representatives the authority to eliminate all those who might be considered too "ill" to function normally any longer. The dangers of euthanasia are too great to all to run the risk of approving it in any form. The first slippery step may well lead to a serious and harmful fall.

I hope that I have succeeded in showing why the benevolence that inclines us to give approval of euthanasia is misplaced. Euthanasia is inherently wrong because it violates the nature and dignity of human beings. But even those who are not convinced by this must be persuaded that the potential personal and social dangers inherent in euthanasia are sufficient to forbid our approving it either as a personal practice or as a public policy.

Suffering is surely a terrible thing, and we have a clear duty to comfort those in need and to ease their suffering when we can. But suffering is also a natural part of

---

[5]See McIntyre, p. 28.

[6]See Sullivan, "Immorality of Euthanasia," pp. 34–44, for a fuller argument in support of this view.

[7]See, for example, Thomas S. Szasz, *The Myth of Mental Illness,* rev. ed. (New York: Harper & Row, 1974).

life with values for the individual and for others that we should not overlook. We may legitimately seek for others and for ourselves an easeful death, as Arthur Dyck has pointed out.[8] Euthanasia, however, is not just an easeful death. It is a wrongful death. Euthanasia is not just dying. It is killing.

QUESTIONS

1 What is euthanasia? Is it always morally wrong?
2 Gay-Williams contends that "euthanasia as a policy is a slippery slope." Is the slippery-slope argument developed by Gay-Williams a substantial argument or a rhetorical "scare tactic" as it is sometimes alleged to be?

Active and Passive Euthanasia

James Rachels

James Rachels is professor of philosophy at the University of Alabama in Birmingham. Specializing in ethics, he is the author of such articles as "Why Privacy is Important," "On Moral Absolutism," and "Can Ethics Provide Answers?" He is also the editor of Moral Problems: A Collection of Philosophical Essays *(1971, 3d ed., 1979) and* Understanding Moral Philosophy *(1976).*

Rachels identifies the standard (conventional) view on the morality of euthanasia as the doctrine which permits passive euthanasia but rejects active euthanasia. He then argues that the conventional doctrine may be challenged for four reasons. First, active euthanasia is in many cases more humane than passive euthanasia. Second, the conventional doctrine leads to decisions concerning life and death on irrelevant grounds. Third, the doctrine rests on a distinction between killing and letting die that itself has no moral importance. Fourth, the most common arguments in favor of the doctrine are invalid.

The distinction between active and passive euthanasia is thought to be crucial for medical ethics. The idea is that it is permissible, at least in some cases, to withhold treatment and allow a patient to die, but it is never permissible to take any direct action designed to kill the patient. This doctrine seems to be accepted by most doctors, and it is endorsed in a statement adopted by the House of Delegates of the American Medical Association on December 4, 1973:

---

[8]Arthur Dyck, "Beneficent Euthanasia and Benemortasia," Kohl, *op. cit.*, pp. 117–129.

Reprinted by permission from *The New England Journal of Medicine*, vol. 292, no. 2 (Jan. 9, 1975), pp. 78–80.

The intentional termination of the life of one human being by another—mercy killing—is contrary to that for which the medical profession stands and is contrary to the policy of the American Medical Association.

The cessation of the employment of extraordinary means to prolong the life of the body when there is irrefutable evidence that biological death is imminent is the decision of the patient and/or his immediate family. The advice and judgment of the physician should be freely available to the patient and/or his immediate family.

However, a strong case can be made against this doctrine. In what follows, I will set out some of the relevant arguments, and urge doctors to reconsider their views on this matter.

To begin with a familiar type of situation, a patient who is dying of incurable cancer of the throat is in terrible pain, which can no longer be satisfactorily alleviated. He is certain to die within a few days, even if present treatment is continued, but he does not want to go on living for those days since the pain is unbearable. So he asks the doctor for an end to it, and his family joins in the request.

Suppose the doctor agrees to withhold treatment, as the conventional doctrine says he may. The justification for his doing so is that the patient is in terrible agony, and since he is going to die anyway, it would be wrong to prolong his suffering needlessly. But now notice this. If one simply withholds treatment, it may take the patient longer to die, and so he may suffer more than he would if more direct action were taken and a lethal injection given. This fact provides strong reason for thinking that, once the initial decision not to prolong his agony has been made, active euthanasia is actually preferable to passive euthanasia, rather than the reverse. To say otherwise is to endorse the option that leads to more suffering rather than less, and is contrary to the human-itarian impulse that prompts the decision not to prolong his life in the first place.

Part of my point is that the process of being "allowed to die" can be relatively slow and painful, whereas being given a lethal injection is relatively quick and painless. Let me give a different sort of example. In the United States about one in 600 babies is born with Down's syndrome. Most of these babies are otherwise healthy—that is, with only the usual pediatric care, they will proceed to an otherwise normal infancy. Some, however, are born with congenital defects such as intestinal obstructions that require operations if they are to live. Sometimes, the parents and the doctor will decide not to operate, and let the infant die. Anthony Shaw describes what happens then:

> . . . When surgery is denied [the doctor] must try to keep the infant from suffering while natural forces sap the baby's life away. As a surgeon whose natural inclination is to use the scalpel to fight off death, standing by and watching a salvageable baby die is the most emotionally exhausting experience I know. It is easy at a conference, in a theoretical dis-cussion, to decide that such infants should be allowed to die. It is altogether different to stand by in the nursery and watch as dehydration and infection wither a tiny being over hours and days. This is a terrible ordeal for me and the hospital staff—much more so than for the parents who never set foot in the nursery.[1]

I can understand why some people are opposed to all euthanasia, and insist that such

[1]A. Shaw: "Doctor, Do We Have a Choice?" *The New York Times Magazine,* Jan. 30, 1972, p. 54.

infants must be allowed to live. I think I can also understand why other people favor destroying these babies quickly and painlessly. But why should anyone favor letting "dehydration and infection wither a tiny being over hours and days?" The doctrine that says that a baby may be allowed to dehydrate and wither, but may not be given an injection that would end its life without suffering, seems so patently cruel as to require no further refutation. The strong language is not intended to offend, but only to put the point in the clearest possible way.

My second argument is that the conventional doctrine leads to decisions concerning life and death made on irrelevant grounds.

Consider again the case of the infants with Down's syndrome who need operations for congenital defects unrelated to the syndrome to live. Sometimes, there is no operation, and the baby dies, but when there is no such defect, the baby lives on. Now, an operation such as that to remove an intestinal obstruction is not prohibitively difficult. The reason why such operations are not performed in these cases is, clearly, that the child has Down's syndrome and the parents and doctor judge that because of that fact it is better for the child to die.

But notice that this situation is absurd, no matter what view one takes of the lives and potentials of such babies. If the life of such an infant is worth preserving, what does it matter if it needs a simple operation? Or, if one thinks it better that such a baby should not live on, what difference does it make that it happens to have an unobstructed intestinal tract? In either case, the matter of life and death is being decided on irrelevant grounds. It is the Down's syndrome, and not the intestines, that is the issue. The matter should be decided, if at all, on that basis, and not be allowed to depend on the essentially irrelevant question of whether the intestinal tract is blocked.

What makes this situation possible, of course, is the idea that when there is an intestinal blockage, one can "let the baby die," but when there is no such defect there is nothing that can be done, for one must not "kill" it. The fact that this idea leads to such results as deciding life or death on irrelevant grounds is another good reason why the doctrine should be rejected.

One reason why so many people think that there is an important moral difference between active and passive euthanasia is that they think killing someone is morally worse than letting someone die. But is it? Is killing, in itself, worse than letting die? To investigate this issue, two cases may be considered that are exactly alike except that one involves killing whereas the other involves letting someone die. Then, it can be asked whether this difference makes any difference to the moral assessments. It is important that the cases be exactly alike, except for this one difference, since otherwise one cannot be confident that it is this difference and not some other that accounts for any variation in the assessments of the two cases. So, let us consider this pair of cases:

In the first, Smith stands to gain a large inheritance if anything should happen to his six-year-old cousin. One evening while the child is taking his bath, Smith sneaks into the bathroom and drowns the child, and then arranges things so that it will look like an accident.

In the second, Jones also stands to gain if anything should happen to his six-year-old cousin. Like Smith, Jones sneaks in planning to drown the child in his bath. However, just as he enters the bathroom Jones sees the child slip and hit his head, and fall face down in the water. Jones is delighted; he stands by, ready to push the child's head back under if it is necessary, but it is not necessary. With only a little thrashing about the child drowns all by himself, "accidentally," as Jones watches and does nothing.

Now Smith killed the child, whereas Jones "merely" let the child die. That is the only difference between them. Did either man behave better, from a moral point of view? If the difference between killing and letting die were in itself a morally important matter, one should say that Jones's behavior was less reprehensible than Smith's. But does one really want to say that? I think not. In the first place, both men acted from the same motive, personal gain, and both had exactly the same end in view when they acted. It may be inferred from Smith's conduct that he is a bad man, although that judgment may be withdrawn or modified if certain further facts are learned about him— for example, that he is mentally deranged. But would not the very same thing be inferred about Jones from his conduct? And would not the same further considerations also be relevant to any modification of this judgment? Moreover, suppose Jones pleaded, in his own defense, "After all, I didn't do anything except just stand there and watch the child drown. I didn't kill him; I only let him die." Again, if letting die were in itself less bad than killing, this defense should have at least some weight. But it does not. Such a "defense" can only be regarded as a grotesque perversion of moral reasoning. Morally speaking, it is no defense at all.

Now, it may be pointed out, quite properly, that the cases of euthanasia with which doctors are concerned are not like this at all. They do not involve personal gain or the destruction of normally healthy children. Doctors are concerned only with cases in which the patient's life is of no further use to him, or in which the patient's life has become or will soon become a terrible burden. However, the point is the same in these cases: the bare difference between killing and letting die does not, in itself, make a moral difference. If a doctor lets a patient die, for humane reasons, he is in the same moral position as if he had given the patient a lethal injection for humane reasons. If his decision was wrong—if, for example, the patient's illness was in fact curable— the decision would be equally regrettable no matter which method was used to carry it out. And if the doctor's decision was the right one, the method used is not in itself important.

The AMA policy statement isolates the crucial issue very well; the crucial issue is "the intentional termination of the life of one human being by another." But after identifying this issue, and forbidding "mercy killing," the statement goes on to deny that the cessation of treatment is the intentional termination of a life. This is where the mistake comes in, for what is the cessation of treatment, in these circumstances, if it is not "the intentional termination of the life of one human being by another?" Of course, it is exactly that, and if it were not, there would be no point to it.

Many people will find this judgment hard to accept. One reason, I think, is that it is very easy to conflate the question of whether killing is, in itself, worse than letting die, with the very different question of whether most actual cases of killing are more reprehensible than most actual cases of letting die. Most actual cases of killing are clearly terrible (think, for example, of all the murders reported in the newspapers), and one hears of such cases every day. On the other hand, one hardly ever hears of a case of letting die, except for the actions of doctors who are motivated by humanitarian reasons. So one learns to think of killing in a much worse light than of letting die. But this does not mean that there is something about killing that makes it in itself worse than letting die, for it is not the bare difference between killing and letting die that makes the difference in these cases. Rather, the other factors—the murderer's motive of personal gain, for example, contrasted with the doctor's humanitarian motivation—account for different reactions to the different cases.

I have argued that killing is not in itself any worse than letting die; if my contention is right, it follows that active euthanasia is not any worse than passive euthanasia. What arguments can be given on the other side? The most common, I believe, is the following:

"The important difference between active and passive euthanasia is that, in passive euthanasia, the doctor does not do anything to bring about the patient's death. The doctor does nothing, and the patient dies of whatever ills already afflict him. In active euthanasia, however, the doctor does something to bring about the patient's death: he kills him. The doctor who gives the patient with cancer a lethal injection has himself caused his patient's death; whereas if he merely ceases treatment, the cancer is the cause of the death."

A number of points need to be made here. The first is that it is not exactly correct to say that in passive euthanasia the doctor does nothing, for he does do one thing that is very important: he lets the patient die. "Letting someone die" is certainly different, in some respects, from other types of action—mainly in that it is a kind of action that one may perform by way of not performing certain other actions. For example, one may let a patient die by way of not giving medication, just as one may insult someone by way of not shaking his hand. But for any purpose of moral assessment, it is a type of action nonetheless. The decision to let a patient die is subject to moral appraisal in the same way that a decision to kill him would be subject to moral appraisal: it may be assessed as wise or unwise, compassionate or sadistic, right or wrong. If a doctor deliberately let a patient die who was suffering from a routinely curable illness, the doctor would certainly be to blame for what he had done, just as he would be to blame if he had needlessly killed the patient. Charges against him would then be appropriate. If so, it would be no defense at all for him to insist that he didn't "do anything." He would have done something very serious indeed, for he let his patient die.

Fixing the cause of death may be very important from a legal point of view, for it may determine whether criminal charges are brought against the doctor. But I do not think that this notion can be used to show a moral difference between active and passive euthanasia. The reason why it is considered bad to be the cause of someone's death is that death is regarded as a great evil—and so it is. However, if it has been decided that euthanasia—even passive euthanasia—is desirable in a given case, it has also been decided that in this instance death is no greater an evil than the patient's continued existence. And if this is true, the usual reason for not wanting to be the cause of someone's death simply does not apply.

Finally, doctors may think that all of this is only of academic interest—the sort of thing that philosophers may worry about but that has no practical bearing on their own work. After all, doctors must be concerned about the legal consequences of what they do, and active euthanasia is clearly forbidden by the law. But even so, doctors should also be concerned with the fact that the law is forcing upon them a moral doctrine that may well be indefensible, and has a considerable effect on their practices. Of course, most doctors are not now in the position of being coerced in this matter, for they do not regard themselves as merely going along with what the law requires. Rather, in statements such as the AMA policy statement that I have quoted, they are endorsing this doctrine as a central point of medical ethics. In that statement, active euthanasia is condemned not merely as illegal but as "contrary to that for which the medical profession stands," whereas passive euthanasia is approved. However, the preceding considerations suggest that there is really no moral difference between the two, considered in themselves (there may be important moral differences in some cases in their *consequences,* but, as I pointed out, these differences may make active euthanasia, and not passive euthanasia, the morally preferable option). So, whereas doctors may have to discriminate between active and passive euthanasia to satisfy the law, they should not do any more than that. In particular, they should not give the distinction any added authority and weight by writing it into official statements of medical ethics.

QUESTIONS

1 If you were a physician, what would you do when the parents of a baby with Down's syndrome and an intestinal obstruction decided against surgery? Would you let the baby slowly die from dehydration and starvation, or would you take some active step to end the baby's life? Would you take the case to court to force the surgery? How would you justify your decision?
2 Can you rewrite the two paragraphs Rachels cites from the AMA statement so that your version of the statement avoids Rachels's criticisms?
3 Active euthanasia is illegal in all fifty states. Should it be legalized under specified conditions?

Active and Passive Euthanasia: An Impertinent Distinction?

Thomas D. Sullivan

Thomas D. Sullivan is professor of philosophy at the College of St. Thomas in St. Paul, Minnesota. Primarily specializing in logic and metaphysics, he is the author of "Between Thoughts and Things: The Status of Meaning" and the coauthor of "Diffusiveness of Intention Principle: A Counter-Example." He is also the author of an article on abortion, "In Defense of Total Regard."

Sullivan, responding directly to Rachels, offers a defense of the standard (traditional) view on the morality of euthanasia. Sullivan charges Rachels with misconstruing the sense behind the traditional view. On Sullivan's analysis, the traditional view is not dependent on the distinction between killing and letting die. Rather, it simply forbids the *intentional* termination of life, whether by killing or letting die. The cessation of *extraordinary* means, he maintains, is morally permissible because, though death is foreseen, it need not be intended.

Because of recent advances in medical technology, it is today possible to save or prolong the lives of many persons who in an earlier era would have quickly perished. Unhappily, however, it often is impossible to do so without committing the patient and his or her family to a future filled with sorrows. Modern methods of neurosurgery can successfully close the opening at the base of the spine of a baby born with severe myelomeningocoele, but do nothing to relieve the paralysis that afflicts it from the waist down or to remedy the patient's incontinence of stool and urine. Antibiotics and skin grafts can spare the life of a victim of severe and massive burns, but fail to eliminate the immobilizing contractions of arms and legs, the extreme pain, and the hideous disfigurement of the face. It is not surprising, therefore, that physicians and moralists in increasing number recommend that assistance should not be given to such patients, and that some have even begun to advocate the deliberate hastening of death by medical means, provided informed consent has been given by the appropriate parties.

The latter recommendation consciously and directly conflicts with what might be called the "traditional" view of the physician's role. The traditional view, as articulated, for example, by the House of Delegates of the American Medical Association in 1973, declared:

> The intentional termination of the life of one human being by another—mercy killing—is contrary to that for which the medical profession stands and is contrary to the policy of the American Medical Association.
>
> The cessation of the employment of extra-ordinary means to prolong the life of the body when there is irrefutable evidence that biological death is imminent is the decision of the patient and/or his immediate family. The advice and judgment of the physician should be freely available to the patient and/or his immediate family.

Basically this view involves two points: (1) that is is impermissible for the doctor or anyone else to terminate intentionally the life of a patient, but (2) that it is permissible in some cases to cease the employment of "extraordinary means" of preserving life, even though the death of the patient is a foreseeable consequence.

Does this position really make sense? Recent criticism charges that it does not. The heart of the complaint is that the traditional view arbitrarily rules out all cases of intentionally acting to terminate life, but permits what is in fact the moral equivalent, letting patients die. This accusation has been clearly articulated by James Rachels in a widely-read article that appeared in a recent issue of the *New England Journal of Medicine,* entitled "Active and Passive Euthanasia."[1] By "active euthanasia" Rachels seems to mean *doing something* to bring about a patient's death, and by "passive euthanasia," not doing anything, i.e., just letting the patient die. Referring to the A.M.A. statement, Rachels sees the traditional position as always forbidding active

From *Human Life Review,* vol. III, no. 3 (Summer 1977), pp. 40–46. Reprinted with permission from The Human Life Foundation, Inc., 150 East 35th Street, New York, NY 10016.

[1]*The New England Journal of Medicine,* vol. 292 (Jan. 9, 1975), pp. 78–80. [Reprinted, this volume, pp. 60–65.]

euthanasia, but permitting passive euthanasia. Yet, he argues, passive euthanasia may be in some cases morally indistinguishable from active euthanasia, and in other cases even worse. To make his point he asks his readers to consider the case of a Down's syndrome baby with an intestinal obstruction that easily could be remedied through routine surgery. Rachels comments:

> I can understand why some people are opposed to all euthanasia, and insist that such infants must be allowed to live. I think I can also understand why other people favor destroying these babies quickly and painlessly. But why should anyone favor letting 'dehydration and infection wither a tiny being over hours and days?' The doctrine that says that a baby may be allowed to dehydrate and wither, but may not be given an injection that would end its life without suffering, seems so patently cruel as to require no further refutation.[2]

Rachels' point is that decisions such as the one he describes as "patently cruel" arise out of a misconceived moral distinction between active and passive euthanasia, which in turn rests upon a distinction between killing and letting die that itself has no moral importance.

> One reason why so many people think that there is an important moral difference between active and passive euthanasia is that they think killing someone is morally worse than letting someone die. But is it? . . . To investigate this issue, two cases may be considered that are exactly alike except that one involves killing whereas the other involves letting someone die. Then, it can be asked whether this difference makes any difference to the moral assessments. . . .
>
> In the first, Smith stands to gain a large inheritance if anything should happen to his six-year-old cousin. One evening while the child is taking his bath, Smith sneaks into the bathroom and drowns the child, and then arranges things so that it will look like an accident.
>
> In the second, Jones also stands to gain if anything should happen to his six-year-old cousin. Like Smith, Jones sneaks in planning to drown the child in his bath. However, just as he enters the bathroom Jones sees the child slip and hit his head, and fall face down in the water. Jones is delighted; he stands by, ready to push the child's head back under if it is necessary, but it is not necessary. With only a little thrashing about the child drowns all by himself, "accidentally," as Jones watches and does nothing.[3]

Rachels observes that Smith killed the child, whereas Jones "merely" let the child die. If there's an important moral distinction between killing and letting die, then, we should say that Jones' behavior from a moral point of view is less reprehensible than Smith's. But while the law might draw some distinctions here, it seems clear that the acts of Jones and Smith are not different in any important way, or, if there is a difference, Jones' action is even worse.

In essence, then, the objection to the position adopted by the A.M.A. of Rachels and those who argue like him is that it endorses a highly questionable moral distinction between killing and letting die, which, if accepted, leads to indefensible medical decisions. Nowhere does Rachels quite come out and say that he favors active euthanasia in some cases, but the implication is clear. Nearly everyone holds that it is

[2]*Ibid.*, pp. 78–79. [This volume, pp. 61–62.]
[3]*Ibid.*, p. 79. [This volume, pp. 62–63.]

sometimes pointless to prolong the process of dying and that in those cases it is morally permissible to let a patient die even though a few hours or days could be salvaged by procedures that would also increase the agonies of the dying. But if it is impossible to defend a general distinction between letting people die and acting to terminate their lives directly, then it would seem that active euthanasia also may be morally permissible.

Now what shall we make of all this? It *is* cruel to stand by and watch a Down's baby die an agonizing death when a simple operation would remove the intestinal obstruction, but to offer the excuse that in failing to operate we didn't *do* anything to bring about death is an example of moral evasiveness comparable to the excuse Jones would offer for his action of "merely" letting his cousin die. Furthermore, it is true that if someone is trying to bring about the death of another human being, then it makes little difference from the moral point of view if his purpose is achieved by action or by malevolent omission, as in the cases of Jones and Smith.

But if we acknowledge this, are we obliged to give up the traditional view expressed by the A.M.A. statement? Of course not. To begin with, we are hardly obliged to assume the Jones-like role Rachels assigns the defender of the traditional view. We have the option of operating on the Down's baby and saving its life. Rachels mentions that possibility only to hurry past it as if that is not what his opposition would do. But, of course, that is precisely the course of action most defenders of the traditional position would choose.

Secondly, while it may be that the reason some rather confused people give for upholding the traditional view is that they think killing someone is always worse than letting them die, nobody who gives the matter much thought puts it that way. Rather they say that killing someone is clearly morally worse than not killing them, and killing them can be done by acting to bring about their death or by refusing ordinary means to keep them alive in order to bring about the same goal.

What I am suggesting is that Rachels' objections leave the position he sets out to criticize untouched. It is worth noting that the jargon of active and passive euthanasia—and it is jargon—does not appear in the resolution. Nor does the resolution state or imply the distinction Rachels attacks, a distinction that puts a moral premium on overt behavior—moving or not moving one's parts—while totally ignoring the intentions of the agent. That no such distinction is being drawn seems clear from the fact that the A.M.A. resolution speaks approvingly of ceasing to use extra-ordinary means in certain cases, and such withdrawals might easily involve bodily movement, for example unplugging an oxygen machine.

In addition to saddling his opposition with an indefensible distinction it doesn't make, Rachels proceeds to ignore one that it does make—one that is crucial to a just interpretation of the view. Recall the A.M.A. allows the withdrawal of what it calls extra-ordinary means of preserving life; clearly the contrast here is with ordinary means. Though in its short statement those expressions are not defined, the definition Paul Ramsey refers to as standard in his book, *The Patient as Person,* seems to fit.

> Ordinary means of preserving life are all medicines, treatments, and operations, which offer a reasonable hope of benefit for the patient and which can be obtained and used without excessive expense, pain, and other inconveniences.

Extra-ordinary means of preserving life are all those medicines, treatments, and operations which cannot be obtained without excessive expense, pain, or other inconvenience, or which, if used, would not offer a reasonable hope of benefit.[4]

Now with this distinction in mind, we can see how the traditional view differs from the position Rachels mistakes for it. The traditional view is that the intentional termination of human life is impermissible, irrespective of whether this goal is brought about by action or inaction. Is the action or refraining *aimed* at producing a death? Is the termination of life *sought, chosen or planned?* Is the intention deadly? If so, the act or omission is wrong.

But we all know it is entirely possible that the unwillingness of a physician to use extra-ordinary means for preserving life may be prompted not by a determination to bring about death, but by other motives. For example, he may realize that further treatment may offer little hope of reversing the dying process and/or be excruciating, as in the case when a massively necrotic bowel condition in a neonate is out of control. The doctor who does what he can to comfort the infant but does not submit it to further treatment or surgery may foresee that the decision will hasten death, but it certainly doesn't follow from that fact that he intends to bring about its death. It is, after all, entirely possible to foresee that something will come about as a result of one's conduct without intending the consequence or side effect. If I drive downtown, I can foresee that I'll wear out my tires a little, but I don't drive downtown with the intention of wearing out my tires. And if I choose to forego my exercises for a few days, I may think that as a result my physical condition will deteriorate a little, but I don't omit my exercise with a view to running myself down. And if you have to fill a position and select Green, who is better qualified for the post than her rival Brown, you needn't appoint Mrs. Green with the intention of hurting Mr. Brown, though you may foresee that Mr. Brown will feel hurt. And if a country extends its general education programs to its illiterate masses, it is predictable the suicide rate will go up, but even if the public officials are aware of this fact, it doesn't follow that they initiate the program with a view to making the suicide rate go up. In general, then, it is not the case that all the foreseeable consequences and side effects of our conduct are necessarily intended. And it is because the physician's withdrawal of extra-ordinary means can be otherwise motivated than by a desire to bring about the predictable death of the patient that such action cannot categorically be ruled out as wrong.

But the refusal to use ordinary means is an altogether different matter. After all, what is the point of refusing assistance which offers reasonable hope of benefit to the patient without involving excessive pain or other inconvenience? How could it be plausibly maintained that the refusal is not motivated by a desire to bring about the death of the patient? The traditional position, therefore, rules out not only direct actions to bring about death, such as giving a patient a lethal injection, but malevolent omissions as well, such as not providing minimum care for the newborn.

The reason the A.M.A. position sounds so silly when one listens to arguments

---

[4]Paul Ramsey, *The Patient As Person* (New Haven and London: Yale University Press, 1970), p. 122. Ramsey abbreviates the definition first given by Gerald Kelly, S. J., *Medico-Moral Problems* (St. Louis, Mo.: The Catholic Hospital Association, 1958), p. 129.

such as Rachels' is that he slights the distinction between ordinary and extra-ordinary means and then drums on cases where *ordinary* means are refused. The impression is thereby conveyed that the traditional doctrine sanctions omissions that are morally indistinguishable in a substantive way from direct killings, but then incomprehensibly refuses to permit quick and painless termination of life. If the traditional doctrine would approve of Jones' standing by with a grin on his face while his young cousin drowned in a tub, or letting a Down's baby wither and die when ordinary means are available to preserve its life, it would indeed be difficult to see how anyone could defend it. But so to conceive the traditional doctrine is simply to misunderstand it. It is not a doctrine that rests on some supposed distinction between "active" and "passive euthanasia," whatever those words are supposed to mean, nor on a distinction between moving and not moving our bodies. It is simply a prohibition against intentional killing, which includes both direct actions and malevolent omissions.

To summarize—the traditional position represented by the A.M.A. statement is not incoherent. It acknowledges, or more accurately, insists upon the fact that withholding ordinary means to sustain life may be tantamount to killing. The traditional position can be made to appear incoherent only by imposing upon it a crude idea of killing held by none of its more articulate advocates.

Thus the criticism of Rachels and other reformers, misapprehending its target, leaves the traditional position untouched. That position is simply a prohibition of murder. And it is good to remember, as C. S. Lewis once pointed out:

> No man, perhaps, ever at first described to himself the act he was about to do as Murder, or Adultery, or Fraud, or Treachery. . . . And when he hears it so described by other men he is (in a way) sincerely shocked and surprised. Those others "don't understand." If they knew what it had really been like for him, they would not use those crude "stock" names. With a wink or a titter, or a cloud of muddy emotion, the thing has slipped into his will as something not very extraordinary, something of which, rightly understood in all of his peculiar circumstances, he may even feel proud.[5]

I fully realize that there are times when those who have the noble duty to tend the sick and the dying are deeply moved by the sufferings of their patients, especially of the very young and the very old, and desperately wish they could do more than comfort and companion them. Then, perhaps, it seems that universal moral principles are mere abstractions having little to do with the agony of the dying. But of course we do not see best when our eyes are filled with tears.

QUESTIONS

1 Is Sullivan correct in holding that the traditional position is "simply a prohibition of murder"?

2 Is the traditional view dependent on the distinction between killing and letting die (contra Sullivan)?

3 Would it be morally wrong for a physician to withdraw "extraordinary means" *with the explicit intention* of bringing about the death of a terminally ill patient who is in great pain? Would it always be morally wrong for a physician to withdraw "ordinary" means?

---

[5]C. S. Lewis, *A Preface to Paradise Lost* (London and New York: Oxford University Press, 1970), p. 126.

More Impertinent Distinctions and a Defense of Active Euthanasia

James Rachels

A biographical sketch of James Rachels is found on p. 60.

This selection falls into two major sections. In the first major section, Rachels responds to Sullivan; in the second, he develops arguments in support of the moral justifiability of active euthanasia. Rachels makes a new departure in responding to Sullivan. He presents two additional arguments against the standard (traditional) view on the morality of euthanasia. Rachels contends, first, that the traditional view is mistaken because it depends on an indefensible distinction between intentional and nonintentional terminations of life. Next he contends that the traditional view is mistaken because it depends on an indefensible distinction between ordinary and extraordinary means of treatment. Rachels's defense of active euthanasia rests on two arguments—the argument from mercy and the argument from the golden rule.

Many thinkers, including almost all orthodox Catholics, believe that euthanasia is immoral. They oppose killing patients in any circumstances whatever. However, they think it is all right, in some special circumstances, to allow patients to die by with-holding treatment. The American Medical Association's policy statement on mercy killing supports this traditional view. In my paper "Active and Passive Euthanasia"[1] I argued, against the traditional view, that there is in fact no moral difference between killing and letting die—if one is permissible, then so is the other.

Professor Sullivan[2] does not dispute my argument; instead he dismisses it as irrelevant. The traditional doctrine, he says, does not appeal to or depend on the distinction between killing and letting die. Therefore, arguments against that distinction "leave the traditional position untouched."

Is my argument really irrelevant? I don't see how it can be. As Sullivan himself points out,

> Nearly everyone holds that it is sometimes pointless to prolong the process of dying and that in those cases it is morally permissible to let a patient die even though a few hours or days could be salvaged by procedures that would also increase the agonies of the dying. But if it is impossible to defend a general distinction between letting people die and acting to terminate their lives directly, then it would seem that active euthanasia also may be morally permissible.(67–68)

Reprinted from Thomas A. Mappes and Jane S. Zembaty, eds., *Biomedical Ethics* (New York: McGraw-Hill, 1981), pp. 355–359. Copyright © 1978 by James Rachels. Also from Tom Regan, ed., *Matters of Life and Death: New Introductory Essays in Moral Philsophy.* Copyright © 1980 by Random House, Inc. Reprinted by permission of Random House, Inc.

[1]"Active and Passive Euthanasia," *The New England Journal of Medicine*, vol. 292 (Jan. 9, 1975), pp. 78–80. [Reprinted, this volume, pp. 60–65.]
[2]"Active and Passive Euthanasia: An Impertinent Distinction?" *The Human Life Review*, vol. III (1977), pp. 40–46. Parenthetical references in the text are to this article [as reprinted in this volume, pp. 65–70.]

But traditionalists like Professor Sullivan hold that active euthanasia—the direct killing of patients—is *not* morally permissible; so, if my argument is sound, their view must be mistaken. I cannot agree, then, that my argument "leaves the traditional position untouched."

However, I shall not press this point. Instead I shall present some further arguments against the traditional position, concentrating on those elements of the position which Professor Sullivan himself thinks most important. According to him, what is important is, first, that we should never *intentionally* terminate the life of a patient, either by action or omission, and second, that we may cease or omit treatment of a patient, knowing that this will result in death, only if the means of treatment involved are *extraordinary*.

INTENTIONAL AND NONINTENTIONAL TERMINATION OF LIFE

We can, of course, distinguish between what a person does and the intention with which he does it. But what is the significance of this distinction for ethics?

> The traditional view [says Sullivan] is that the intentional termination of human life is impermissible, irrespective of whether this goal is brought about by action or inaction. Is the action or refraining *aimed at* producing a death? Is the termination of life *sought, chosen or planned?* Is the intention deadly? If so, the act or omission is wrong.(69)

Thus on the traditional view there is a very definite sort of moral relation between act and intention. An act which is otherwise permissible may become impermissible if it is accompanied by a bad intention. The intention makes the act wrong.

There is reason to think that this view of the relation between act and intention is mistaken. Consider the following example. Jack visits his sick and lonely grandmother, and entertains her for the afternoon. He loves her and his only intention is to cheer her up. Jill also visits the grandmother, and provides an afternoon's cheer. But Jill's concern is that the old lady will soon be making her will; Jill wants to be included among the heirs. Jack also knows that his visit might influence the making of the will, in his favor, but that is no part of his plan. Thus Jack and Jill do the very same thing—they both spend an afternoon cheering up their sick grandmother—and what they do may lead to the same consequences, namely influencing the will. But their intentions are quite different.

Jack's intention was honorable and Jill's was not. Could we say on that account that what Jack did was right, but what Jill did was wrong? No; for Jack and Jill did the very same thing, and if they did the same thing, we cannot say that one acted rightly and the other wrongly.[3] Consistency requires that we assess similar actions

---

[3]It might be objected that they did not "do the same thing," for Jill manipulated and deceived her grandmother, while Jack did not. If their actions are described in this way, then it may seem that "what Jill did" was wrong, while "what Jack did" was not. However, this description of what Jill did incorporates her intention into the description of the act. In the present context we must keep the act and the intention separate, in order to discuss the relation between them. If they *cannot* be held separate, then the traditional view makes no sense.

similarly. Thus if we are trying to evaluate their *actions,* we must say about one what we say about the other.

However, if we are trying to assess Jack's *character,* or Jill's, things are very different. Even though their actions were similar, Jack seems admirable for what he did, while Jill does not. What Jill did—comforting an elderly sick relative—was a morally good thing, but we would not think well of her for it since she was only scheming after the old lady's money. Jack, on the other hand, did a good thing *and* he did it with an admirable intention. Thus we think well, not only of what Jack did, but of Jack.

The traditional view, as presented by Professor Sullivan, says that the intention with which an act is done is relevant to determining whether the act is right. The example of Jack and Jill suggests that, on the contrary, the intention is not relevant to deciding whether the *act* is right or wrong, but instead it is relevant to assessing the character of the person who does the act, which is very different.

Now let us turn to an example that concerns more important matters of life and death. This example is adapted from one used by Sullivan himself (69). A massively necrotic bowel condition in a neonate is out of control. Dr. White realizes that further treatment offers little hope of reversing the dying process and will only increase the suffering; so, he does not submit the infant to further treatment—even though he knows that this decision will hasten death. However, Dr. White does not seek, choose, or plan that death, so it is not part of his intention that the baby dies.

Dr. Black is faced with a similar case. A massively necrotic bowel condition in a neonate is out of control. He realizes that further treatment offers little hope of saving the baby and will only increase its suffering. He decides that it is better for the baby to die a bit sooner than to go on suffering pointlessly; so, with the intention of letting the baby die, he ceases treatment.

According to the traditional position, Dr. White's action was acceptable, but Dr. Black acted wrongly. However, this assessment faces the same problem we encountered before. Dr. White and Dr. Black did *the very same thing:* their handling of the cases was identical. Both doctors ceased treatment, knowing that the baby would die sooner, and both did so because they regarded continued treatment as pointless, given the infants' prospects. So how could one's action be acceptable and the other's not? There was, of course, a subtle difference in their *attitudes* toward what they did. Dr. Black said to himself, "I want this baby to die now, rather than later, so that it won't suffer more; so I won't continue the treatment." A defender of the traditional view might choose to condemn Dr. Black for this, and say that his character is defective (although I would not say that); but the traditionalist should not say that Dr. Black's *action* was wrong on that account, at least not if he wants to go on saying that Dr. White's action was right. A pure heart cannot make a wrong act right; neither can an impure heart make a right act wrong. As in the case of Jack and Jill, the intention is relevant, not to determining the rightness of actions, but to assessing the character of the people who act.

There is a general lesson to be learned here. The rightness or wrongness of an act is determined by the reasons for or against it. Suppose you are trying to decide, in this example, whether treatment should be continued. What are the reasons for and against this course of action? On the one hand, if treatment is ceased the baby will die very soon. On the other hand, the baby will die eventually anyway, even if treatment is continued. It has no chance of growing up. Moreover, if its life is prolonged, its suffering will be prolonged as well, and the medical resources used will be unavailable to others who would have a better chance of a satisfactory cure. In light of all this, you may well decide against continued treatment. But notice that there is no mention here of anybody's intentions. The intention you would have, if you decided to cease treatment, is not one of the things you need to consider. It is not among the reasons either for or against the action. That is why it is irrelevant to determining whether the action is right.

In short, a person's intention is relevant to an assessment of his character. The fact that a person intended so-and-so by his action may be a reason for thinking him a good or a bad person. But the intention is not relevant to determining whether the act itself is morally right. The rightness of the act must be decided on the basis of the objective reasons for or against it. It is permissible to let the baby die, in Sullivan's example, because of the facts about the baby's condition and its prospects—not because of anything having to do with anyone's intentions. Thus the traditional view is mistaken on this point.

ORDINARY AND EXTRAORDINARY MEANS OF TREATMENT

The American Medical Association policy statement says that life-sustaining treatment may sometimes be stopped if the means of treatment are "extraordinary"; the implication is that "ordinary" means of treatment may not be withheld. The distinction between ordinary and extraordinary treatments is crucial to orthodox Catholic thought in this area, and Professor Sullivan reemphasizes its importance: he says that, while a physician may sometimes rightly refuse to use extraordinary means to prolong life, "the refusal to use ordinary means is an altogether different matter."(69)

However, upon reflection it is clear that it is sometimes permissible to omit even very ordinary sorts of treatments.

> Suppose that a diabetic patient long accustomed to self-administration of insulin falls victim to terminal cancer, or suppose that a terminal cancer patient suddenly develops diabetes. Is he in the first case obliged to continue, and in the second case obliged to begin, insulin treatment and die painfully of cancer, or in either or both cases may the patient choose rather to pass into diabetic coma and an earlier death?. . . What of the conscious patient suffering from painful incurable disease who suddenly gets pneumonia? Or an old man slowly deteriorating who from simply being inactive and recumbent gets pneumonia: Are we to use antibiotics in a likely successful attack upon this disease which from time immemorial has been called "the old man's friend"? [4]

These examples are provided by Paul Ramsey, a leading theological ethicist. Even so conservative a thinker as Ramsey is sympathetic with the idea that, in such cases, life-prolonging treatment is not mandatory: the insulin and the antibiotics need not be used.

[4]*The Patient as Person* (New Haven: Yale University Press, 1970), pp. 115–116.

Yet surely insulin and antibiotics are "ordinary" treatments by today's medical standards. They are common, easily administered, and cheap. There is nothing exotic about them. So it appears that the distinction between ordinary and extraordinary means does not have the significance traditionally attributed to it.

But what of the *definitions* of "ordinary" and "extraordinary" means which Sullivan provides? Quoting Ramsey, he says that

> Ordinary means of preserving life are all medicines, treatments, and operations, which offer a reasonable hope of benefit for the patient and which can be obtained and used without excessive expense, pain, and other inconveniences.
>
> Extra-ordinary means of preserving life are all those medicines, treatments, and operations which cannot be obtained without excessive expense, pain, or other inconvenience, or which, if used, would not offer a reasonable hope of benefit.(68–69)

Do these definitions provide us with a useful distinction—one that can be used in determining when a treatment is mandatory and when it is not?

The first thing to notice is the way the word "excessive" functions in these definitions. It is said that a treatment is extraordinary if it cannot be obtained without *excessive* expense or pain. But when is an expense "excessive"? Is a cost of $10,000 excessive? If it would save the life of a young woman and restore her to perfect health, $10,000 does not seem excessive. But if it would only prolong the life of Ramsey's cancer-stricken diabetic a short while, perhaps $10,000 is excessive. The point is not merely that what is excessive changes from case to case. The point is that what is excessive *depends on* whether it would be a good thing for the life in question to be prolonged.

Second, we should notice the use of the word "benefit" in the definitions. It is said that ordinary treatments offer a reasonable hope of *benefit* for the patient; and that treatments are extraordinary if they will not benefit the patient. But how do we tell if a treatment will benefit the patient? Remember that we are talking about life-prolonging treatments; the "benefit," if any, is the continuation of life. Whether continued life is a benefit depends on the details of the particular case. For a person with a painful terminal illness, a temporarily continued life may not be a benefit. For a person in irreversible coma, such as Karen Quinlan, continued biological existence is almost certainly not a benefit. On the other hand, for a person who can be cured and resume a normal life, life-sustaining treatment definitely is a benefit. Again, the point is that in order to decide whether life-sustaining treatment is a benefit we must *first* decide whether it would be a good thing for the life in question to be prolonged.

Therefore, these definitions do not mark out a distinction that can be used to help us decide when treatment may be omitted. We cannot by using the definitions identify which treatments are extraordinary, and then use that information to determine whether the treatment may be omitted. For the definitions require that we must *already* have decided the moral questions of life and death *before* we can answer the question of which treatments are extraordinary!

We are brought, then, to this conclusion about the distinction between ordinary and extraordinary means. If we apply the distinction in a straightforward, commonsense way, the traditional doctrine is false, for it is clear that it is sometimes permissible to omit ordinary treatments. On the other hand, if we define the terms as suggested by Ramsey and Sullivan, the distinction is useless in practical decision-making. In either case, the distinction provides no help in formulating an acceptable ethic of letting die.

To summarize what has been said so far, the distinction between killing and letting die has no moral importance; on that Professor Sullivan and I agree. He, however, contends that the distinctions between intentional and nonintentional termination of life, and ordinary and extraordinary means, must be at the heart of a correct moral view. I believe that the arguments given above refute this view. Those distinctions are no better than the first one. The traditional view is mistaken.

In my original paper I did not argue in favor of active euthanasia. I merely argued that active and passive euthanasia are equivalent: *if* one is acceptable, so is the other. However, Professor Sullivan correctly inferred that I do endorse active euthanasia. I believe that it is morally justified in some instances and that at least two strong arguments support this position. The first is the argument from mercy; the second is the argument from the golden rule.

THE ARGUMENT FROM MERCY

Preliminary Statement of the Argument

The single most powerful argument in support of euthanasia is the argument from mercy. It is also an exceptionally simple argument, at least in its main idea, which makes one uncomplicated point. Terminal patients sometimes suffer pain so horrible that it is beyond the comprehension of those who have not actually experienced it. Their suffering can be so terrible that we do not like even to read about it or think about it; we recoil even from the descriptions of such agony. The argument from mercy says: Euthanasia is justified because it provides an end to *that*.

The great Irish satirist Jonathan Swift took eight years to die, while, in the words of Joseph Fletcher, "His mind crumbled to pieces."[5] At times the pain in his blinded eyes was so intense he had to be restrained from tearing them out with his own hands. Knives and other potential instruments of suicide had to be kept from him. For the last three years of his life, he could do nothing but sit and drool; and when he finally died it was only after convulsions that lasted thirty-six hours.

Swift died in 1745. Since then, doctors have learned how to eliminate much of the pain that accompanies terminal illness, but the victory has been far from complete. So, here is a more modern example.

Stewart Alsop was a respected journalist who died in 1975 of a rare form of cancer. Before he died, he wrote movingly of his experiences as a terminal patient. Although he had not thought much about euthanasia before, he came to approve of it after rooming briefly with someone he called Jack:

> The third night that I roomed with Jack in our tiny double room in the solid-tumor ward of the cancer clinic of the National Institutes of Health in Bethesda, Md., a terrible thought occurred to me.

[5]*Morals and Medicine* (Boston: Beacon Press, 1960), p. 174.

Jack had a melanoma in his belly, a malignant solid tumor that the doctors guessed was about the size of a softball. The cancer had started a few months before with a small tumor in his left shoulder, and there had been several operations since. The doctors planned to remove the softball-sized tumor, but they knew Jack would soon die. The cancer had metastasized—it had spread beyond control.

Jack was good-looking, about 28, and brave. He was in constant pain, and his doctor had prescribed an intravenous shot of a synthetic opiate—a pain-killer, or analgesic—every four hours. His wife spent many of the daylight hours with him, and she would sit or lie on his bed and pat him all over, as one pats a child, only more methodically, and this seemed to help control the pain. But at night, when his pretty wife had left (wives cannot stay overnight at the NIH clinic) and darkness fell, the pain would attack without pity.

At the prescribed hour, a nurse would give Jack a shot of the synthetic analgesic, and this would control the pain for perhaps two hours or a bit more. Then he would begin to moan, or whimper, very low, as though he didn't want to wake me. Then he would begin to howl, like a dog.

When this happened, either he or I would ring for a nurse, and ask for a pain-killer. She would give him some codeine or the like by mouth, but it never did any real good—it affected him no more than half an aspirin might affect a man who had just broken his arm. Always the nurse would explain as encouragingly as she could that there was not long to go before the next intravenous shot—"Only about 50 minutes now." And always poor Jack's whimpers and howls would become more loud and frequent until at last the blessed relief came.

The third night of this routine, the terrible thought occurred to me: "If Jack were a dog," I thought, "what would be done with him?" The answer was obvious: the pound, and chloroform. No human being with a spark of pity could let a living thing suffer so, to no good end.[6]

The NIH clinic is, of course, one of the most modern and best-equipped hospitals we have. Jack's suffering was not the result of poor treatment in some backward rural facility; it was the inevitable product of his disease, which medical science was powerless to prevent.

I have quoted Alsop at length not for the sake of indulging in gory details but to give a clear idea of the kind of suffering we are talking about. We should not gloss over these facts with euphemistic language, or squeamishly avert our eyes from them. For only by keeping them firmly and vividly in mind can we appreciate the full force of the argument from mercy: If a person prefers—and even begs for—death as the only alternative to lingering on *in this kind of torment,* only to die anyway after a while, then surely it is not immoral to help this person die sooner. As Alsop put it, "No human being with a spark of pity could let a living thing suffer so, to no good end."

The Utilitarian Version of the Argument

In connection with this argument, the utilitarians should be mentioned. They argue that actions and social policies should be judged right or wrong *exclusively* according

---

[6]"The Right to Die with Dignity," *Good Housekeeping,* August 1974, pp. 69, 130.

to whether they cause happiness or misery; and they argue that when judged by this standard, euthanasia turns out to be morally acceptable. The utilitarian argument may be elaborated as follows:

1 Any action or social policy is morally right if it serves to increase the amount of happiness in the world or to decrease the amount of misery. Conversely, an action or social policy is morally wrong if it serves to decrease happiness or to increase misery.

2 The policy of killing, at their own request, hopelessly ill patients who are suffering great pain, would decrease the amount of misery in the world. (An example could be Alsop's friend Jack.)

3 Therefore, such a policy would be morally right.

The first premise of this argument, (1), states the Principle of Utility, which is the basic utilitarian assumption. Today most philosophers think that this principle is wrong, because they think that the promotion of happiness and the avoidance of misery are not the *only* morally important things. Happiness, they say, is only one among many values that should be promoted: freedom, justice, and a respect for people's rights are also important. To take one example: People *might* be happier if there were no freedom of religion; for, if everyone adhered to the same religious beliefs, there would be greater harmony among people. There would be no unhappiness caused within families by Jewish girls marrying Catholic boys, and so forth. Moreover, if people were brainwashed well enough, no one would mind not having freedom of choice. Thus happiness would be increased. But, the argument continues, even if happiness *could* be increased this way, it would not be right to deny people freedom of religion, because people have a right to make their own choices. Therefore, the first premise of the utilitarian argument is unacceptable.

There is a related difficulty for utilitarianism, which connects more directly with the topic of euthanasia. Suppose a person is leading a miserable life—full of more unhappiness than happiness—but does *not* want to die. This person thinks that a miserable life is better than none at all. Now I assume that we would all agree that the person should not be killed; that would be plain, unjustifiable murder. Yet it *would* decrease the amount of misery in the world if we killed this person—it would lead to an increase in the balance of happiness over unhappiness—and so it is hard to see how, on strictly utilitarian grounds, it could be wrong. Again, the Principle of Utility seems to be an inadequate guide for determining right and wrong. So we are on shaky ground if we rely on *this* version of the argument from mercy for a defense of euthanasia.

Doing What Is in Everyone's Best Interests

Although the foregoing utilitarian argument is faulty, it is nevertheless based on a sound idea. For even if the promotion of happiness and avoidance of misery are not the *only* morally important things, they are still very important. So, when an action or a social policy would decrease misery, that is *a* very strong reason in its favor. In the cases of voluntary euthanasia we are now considering, great suffering is eliminated, and since the patient requests it, there is no question of violating individual rights.

That is why, regardless of the difficulties of the Principle of Utility, the utilitarian version of the argument still retains considerable force.

I want now to present a somewhat different version of the argument from mercy, which is inspired by utilitarianism but which avoids the difficulties of the foregoing version by not making the Principle of Utility a premise of the argument. I believe that the following argument is sound and proves that active euthanasia *can* be justified:

1 If an action promotes the best interests of *everyone* concerned, and violates *no one's* rights, then that action is morally acceptable.

2 In at least some cases, active euthanasia promotes the best interests of everyone concerned and violates no one's rights.

3 Therefore, in at least some cases active euthanasia is morally acceptable.

It would have been in everyone's best interests if active euthanasia had been employed in the case of Stewart Alsop's friend, Jack. First, and most important, it would have been in Jack's own interests, since it would have provided him with an easier, better death, without pain. (Who among us would choose Jack's death, if we had a choice, rather than a quick painless death?) Second, it would have been in the best interests of Jack's wife. Her misery, helplessly watching him suffer, must have been almost equal to his. Third, the hospital staff's best interests would have been served, since if Jack's dying had not been prolonged, they could have turned their attention to other patients whom they could have helped. Fourth, other patients would have benefited since medical resources would no longer have been used in the sad, pointless maintenance of Jack's physical existence. Finally, if Jack himself requested to be killed, the act would not have violated his rights. Considering all this, how can active euthanasia in this case be wrong? How can it be wrong to do an action that is merciful, that benefits everyone concerned, and that violates no one's rights?

THE ARGUMENT FROM THE GOLDEN RULE

"Do unto others as you would have them do unto you" is one of the oldest and most familiar moral maxims. Stated in just that way, it is not a very good maxim: Suppose a sexual pervert started treating others as he would like to be treated himself; we might not be happy with the results. Nevertheless, the basic idea behind the golden rule is a good one. The basic idea is that moral rules apply impartially to everyone alike; therefore, you cannot say that you are justified in treating someone else in a certain way unless you are willing to admit that that person would also be justified in treating *you* in that way if your positions were reversed.

Kant and the Golden Rule

The great German philosopher Immanuel Kant (1724–1804) incorporated the basic idea of the Golden Rule into his system of ethics. Kant argued that we should act only on rules that we are willing to have applied universally; that is, we should behave as we would be willing to have *everyone* behave. He held that there is one supreme principle of morality, which he called "the Categorical Imperative." The Categorical Imperative says:

> Act only according to that maxim by which you can at the same time will that it should become a universal law.[7]

Let us discuss what this means. When we are trying to decide whether we ought to do a certain action, we must first ask what general rule or principle we would be following if we did it. Then, we ask whether we would be willing for everyone to follow that rule, in similar circumstances. (This determines whether "the maxim of the act"—the rule we would be following—can be "willed" to be "a universal law.") If we would not be willing for the rule to be followed universally, then we should not follow it ourselves. Thus, if we are not willing for others to apply the rule to *us,* we ought not apply it to *them.*

In the eighteenth chapter of St. Matthew's gospel there is a story that perfectly illustrates this point. A man is owed money by another, who cannot pay, and so he has the debtor thrown into prison. But he himself owes money to the king and begs that *his* debt be forgiven. At first the king forgives the debt. However, when the king hears how this man has treated the one who owed him, he changes his mind and "delivers him unto the tormentors" until he can pay. The moral is clear: If you do not think that others should apply the rule "Don't forgive debts!" to *you,* then you should not apply it to others.

The application of all this to the question of euthanasia is fairly obvious. Each of us is going to die someday, although most of us do not know when or how. But suppose you were told that you would die in one of two ways, and you were asked to choose between them. First, you could die quietly, and without pain, from a fatal injection. Or second, you could choose to die of an affliction so painful that for several days before death you would be reduced to howling like a dog, with your family standing by helplessly, trying to comfort you, but going through its own psychological hell. It is hard to believe that any sane person, when confronted by these possibilities, would choose to have a rule applied that would force upon him or her the second option. And if we would not want such a rule, which excludes euthanasia, applied to us, then we should not apply such a rule to others.

Implications for Christians

There is a considerable irony here. Kant [himself] was personally opposed to active euthanasia, yet his own Categorical Imperative seems to sanction it. The larger irony, however, is for those in the Christian Church who have for centuries opposed active euthanasia. According to the New Testament accounts, Jesus himself promulgated the Golden Rule as the supreme moral principle—"This is the Law and the Prophets," he said. But if this is the supreme principle of morality, then how can active euthanasia be always wrong? If I would have it done to me, how can it be wrong for me to do likewise to others?

R. M. Hare has made this point with great force. A Christian as well as a leading

---

[7]*Foundations of the Metaphysics of Morals,* p. 422.

contemporary moral philosopher, Hare has long argued that "universalizability" is one of the central characteristics of moral judgment. ('Universalizability' is the name he gives to the basic idea embodied in both the Golden Rule and the Categorical Imperative. It means that a moral judgment must conform to universal principles, which apply to everyone alike, if it is to be acceptable.) In an article called "Euthanasia: A Christian View," Hare argues that Christians, if they took Christ's teachings about the Golden Rule seriously, would not think that euthanasia is always wrong. He gives this (true) example:

> The driver of a petrol lorry [i.e., a gas truck] was in an accident in which his tanker overturned and immediately caught fire. He himself was trapped in the cab and could not be freed. He therefore besought the bystanders to kill him by hitting him on the head, so that he would not roast to death. I think that somebody did this, but I do not know what happened in court afterwards.
>
> Now will you please all ask yourselves, as I have many times asked myself, what you wish that men should do to you if you were in the situation of that driver. I cannot believe that anybody who considered the matter seriously, as if he himself were going to be in that situation and had now to give instructions as to what rule the bystanders should follow, would say that the rule should be one ruling out euthanasia absolutely.[8]

We might note that *active* euthanasia is the only option here; the concept of passive euthanasia, in these circumstances, has no application. . . .

Professor Sullivan finds my position pernicious. In his penultimate paragraph he says that the traditional doctrine "is simply a prohibition of murder," and that those of us who think otherwise are confused, teary-eyed sentimentalists. But the traditional doctrine is not that. It is a muddle of indefensible claims, backed by tradition but not by reason.

QUESTIONS

1 Rachels asks, "How can it be wrong to do an action that is merciful, that benefits everyone concerned, and that violates no one's rights?" If you think that it can be wrong to perform such an action, what arguments would you offer against Rachels's argument from mercy?
2 Some people offer the following argument against euthanasia: It is always possible that a patient has been misdiagnosed or that a cure may be found for an apparently terminal illness; therefore, we can *never* be certain that a patient's condition is hopeless. Is this conclusion true? If so, does it lead to the further conclusion that euthanasia is morally wrong?

Opinion in the *Matter of Earle N. Spring*

Judge Christopher J. Armstrong

Christopher J. Armstrong is a graduate of Yale University Law School. He was admitted to the bar in 1961 and appointed to the lifetime position of associate justice of the Massachusetts Appeals Court in 1972.

[8]*Philosophic Exchange* (Brockport, New York), II:I (Summer 1975), p. 45.

In January of 1979, the son and wife of Earle N. Spring petitioned a probate court for legal authorization to discontinue his life-prolonging medical treatment. (The son had earlier been appointed temporary guardian of his father, who was declared legally incompetent.) At that time Earle N. Spring, born in 1901, was suffering from "end-stage kidney disease" which required him to undergo hemodialysis three days a week, five hours a day. He was also diagnosed as suffering from "chronic organic brain syndrome or senility" and was completely confused and disoriented. Both the kidney disease and the senility were considered permanent and irreversible, and there was no prospect of a medical breakthrough that would provide a cure for either disease. The prognosis was that, without the dialysis treatment, Spring would die; with it he might survive for months or even years.

The probate court judge appointed a guardian for Spring, and the guardian opposed the cessation of treatment. The judge, however, rendered a judgment authorizing the discontinuance of further life-prolonging treatment. In response, the court-appointed guardian appealed the judgment to the Massachusetts Appeals Court. The higher court, whose reasoning appears here in the opinion of Judge Armstrong, upheld the judgment of the lower court. Though further legal moves were made by the court-appointed guardian, Spring died in April of 1980, more than a year after the initial petition was filed and prior to any final legal resolution.

Judge Armstrong affirms an individual's right to refuse life-prolonging treatment, barring some overriding state interest. If the individual is *legally incompetent*, however, the problem is to determine whether the incompetent person, if competent, would want life-prolonging treatment to be discontinued. Taking into account a host of factual considerations, Judge Armstrong affirms the finding of the probate court judge: Earle N. Spring, if competent, would wish to discontinue dialysis treatments. Judge Armstrong insists throughout that the judgment of Spring's family should be accorded substantial weight in determining what choice Spring, if competent, would make.

The general parameters of our law applicable to the giving or withholding of medical treatment in cases of incompetency were recently spelled out in *Superintendent of Belchertown State Sch. v. Saikewicz* (1977). . . .

The *Saikewicz* case held that a person does not through incompetency lose his right to be "free from nonconsensual invasion of his bodily integrity"; that "the substantive rights of the competent and the incompetent person are the same in regard to the right to decline potentially life-prolonging treatment"; and that the conceptual mechanism by which the right of the incompetent person to refuse medical treatment is to be effectuated is the doctrine of "substituted judgment," by which is meant the judgment that the incompetent person would himself make in the circumstances if he were competent to do so. "[T]he goal is to determine with as much accuracy as possible the wants and needs of the individual involved."

By the terms of this framework, the present case pivots on the finding made by the judge that, in these circumstances, the ward would wish to have the dialysis treatments discontinued. This finding did not rest on any expression of such an intention by the

Massachusetts Appeals Court. Adv. Sh. (1979) 2469.

ward, and the guardian contended in the trial court that, absent such an expression of intent by the ward when he was competent, such a finding could not appropriately be made. The judge correctly rejected that contention: carried to a conclusion, it would largely stifle the very rights of privacy and personal dignity which the *Saikewicz* case sought to secure for incompetent persons. The essence of that case is that when a person becomes incompetent to formulate a lucid judgment he is not thereby stripped of the right of choice enjoyed by others in the making of treatment decisions. An expression of opinion by the patient when competent would obviously be of great assistance, especially where the expression indicates a contemplation or understanding of the circumstances later obtaining; but the right secured by the *Saikewicz* case is not conditioned on the patient's having had the presence of mind to formulate such an expression of his wishes when competent.

The judge's finding that the ward would wish to have dialysis terminated appears to have been determined in the light of eight subsidiary considerations: (1) the fact that he had led an active, robust, independent life; (2) the fact that he has fallen into a pitiable state of physical dependence and mental incapacity; (3) the fact that no improvement can be expected in his physical or mental condition, but only further deterioration; (4) the fact that dialysis treatments exact a significant toll in terms of frequency and duration of treatments and uncomfortable side effects; (5) the fact that the ward has no understanding of the nature and purpose of his treatments and cannot cooperate and does not reliably acquiesce in their administration; (6) the fact that his wife and son, with whom the ward had and has a very close relationship, feel that it would be his wish not to continue with dialysis in the present circumstances; (7) the fact that it is their wish that dialysis not be administered; and (8) the fact that the attending physician recommends against a continuation of dialysis treatments in these circumstances. We hold that, in light of these considerations, the judge's general finding that the ward would wish not to submit to further dialysis treatments was warranted by the evidence. . . .

Certain of the listed considerations require discussion. The guardian ad litem contends that the ward's condition of mental incapacity may not be appropriately taken into account without violating the principle stated in the *Saikewicz* case, that the "supposed ability of [the patient]. . . to appreciate or experience life has no place in the decision. . . ." We think that the guardian's contention involves a misapplication of that principle. In context, the court was making the important points that "the value of life under the law [has] no relation to intelligence or social position" and that the State's interest in the preservation of life is no less in the case of a profoundly mentally retarded person such as Joseph Saikewicz than it is in the case of one more gifted. That principle is of particular significance in applying the balancing test between the various State interests in the preservation of life and the interest of the individual "in avoiding significant, nonconsensual invasion of his bodily integrity." But a patient's mental condition will in certain circumstances be a relevant factor in determining whether he would elect, if competent to do so, to undergo an intrusive life-saving or life-prolonging treatment. "[T]he decision in cases such as this should be that which would be made by the incompetent person, if that person were competent, but taking into account the present and future incompetency of the individual as one of the factors which would necessarily enter into the decision-making process of the competent person." That statement seems fully in accord with common experience; it is hardly unusual to hear people observe that they would not wish to cling to life for long after their mental faculties have been taken from them. That point of view would not have been relevant in the case of Joseph Saikewicz, for he had known no other condition; but it can be appropriately considered in the case of one who has been reduced in a short time from a state of physical and mental vigor to one of total and irreversible dependence and incompetency, when the evidence generally suggests that that state of incompetency would be a factor which the patient would himself take into account in making a treatment decision if he were able to do so.

Another factor which should be touched on is the role of the family and the recommendation of the attending physician in applying the substituted judgment test. . . . It is evident that we are dealing with a close-knit family unit, with a long history of mutual love, concern and support. In such circumstances the decision of the family, particularly where that decision is in accord with the recommendation of the attending physician, is of particular importance, both as evidence of the decision the patient himself would make in the circumstances and, at a later stage of analysis, as a factor lending added weight to the patient's interest in privacy and personal dignity in the face of any countervailing State interests.

Probably the strongest factor which would, standing by itself, tend towards a contrary determination of the ward's wishes is the fact that, at a time when he was mentally competent (although subject to some degree of impairment), he himself consented to, or at least acquiesced in, the initiation of dialysis treatments. But conditions were different at that time. The ward could then understand the necessity for the treatments and the accompanying discomfort and cooperate in their administration. When the treatments were initiated, it was hoped that they would restore the ward's ability to enjoy a relatively normal existence, subject of course to the burden of lengthy and uncomfortable treatments far from home three times a week, but otherwise permitting him the pleasures of life with his family in familiar and comfortable surroundings. Unfortunately, this hope did not and cannot materialize; he is, and must remain, institutionalized, heavily sedated to restrain his hostile impulses, uncooperative towards his arduous maintenance program, insensible of his family and his situation. There now obtains a very different set of circumstances from those in which the decision to undertake dialysis was made; whether the present circumstances would influence the ward to make a different decision is obviously a question not of law but of fact, one which the trier of fact is in a position superior to that of an appellate court to resolve. . . .

It is thus established as a fact that it would be the ward's wish, if competent, to discontinue dialysis treatments. But because the ward is an incompetent person, towards whom the State stands in the relation of parens patriae, his "wish," as thus determined, is not necessarily decisive of the case. The general rule is that "[t]he constitutional right to privacy . . . is an expression of the sensitivity of individual free choice and self-determination as fundamental constituents of life. The value of life as so perceived is lessened not by a decision to refuse treatment, but by the failure to allow a competent human being the right of choice." . . . Where there is no occasion for State intervention in the treatment decision, "[t]he law protects [the patient's] right to make [his] own decision to accept or reject treatment, whether that decision is wise or unwise."

But the case law in this area recognizes several situations in which the State may intrude on an individual's freedom to consent or not consent, as he wishes, to medical treatment, and require that his right to refuse medical treatment be weighed in the balance against various countervailing State interests. . . .

[The] countervailing interests of the State . . .cannot overcome the right of private choice in the circumstances presented. The policy against suicide and the protection of innocent third parties are of no relevance. The ethics of the medical profession do not present a conflict: the doctor who is treating the ward supports the family's view that further treatment is inappropriate. The general State interest in the preservation of life—most weighty where the patient, properly treated, can return to reasonable health, without great suffering, and a decision to avoid treatment would be aberrational—carries far less weight where the patient is approaching the end of his normal life span, where his afflictions are incapacitating, and where the best that medicine can offer is an extension of suffering. Such a case presents instead the recurrent and always difficult ethical problem: To what extent should aggressive medical treatments be administered to preserve life after life itself, for reasons beyond anyone's control, has become irreversibly burdensome?

The law does not furnish an answer to that question. It leaves the answer to the person whose life is involved, if that person is competent to make the decision for himself. Where the person is incompetent, the law intervenes, not to displace the traditional role of family and the attending physician in weighing that question, but to protect the rights of the incompetent person by determining, as best it can, what his wish would be, and ensuring that that wish is carried out if it does not violate the policy of the State or the ethics of the medical profession. If the patient is fortunate enough to have close family, as does the ward in this case, and where they and the attending physician are at one in recommending a course of treatment, or non-treatment, as that which is in the best interests of the patient and which they feel he would choose, the law should and, we think, does accord their judgment substantial weight not only in determining what course of action the patient would himself choose in the circumstances if he were able to do so, but also in determining the appropriate resolution of conflicting interests. . . .

QUESTIONS

1 What kinds of considerations should be taken into account in deciding whether to discontinue the use of respirators or other life-sustaining apparatus or treatment? (a) The age of the patient? (b) The social responsibilities of the patient? (c) The need of others for the equipment? (d) The length of time the patient may live without the treatment or equipment? (e) The quality of the life the patient is living? Can you suggest any other possible considerations?

2 Who should decide when the use of life-sustaining treatment should be discontinued? The patients? The physicians? A hospital ethics committee? The immediate family? The courts?

Must Patients Always Be Given Food and Water?

Joanne Lynn and James F. Childress

Joanne Lynn, M.D., is on the staff of the division of geriatric medicine at George Washington University. She also served as assistant director on the staff of the President's Commission for the Study of Ethical Problems in Medicine and Biomedical and Behavioral Research. James F. Childress is Commonwealth Professor of Religious Studies and also professor of medical education at the University of Virginia. He is the author of Priorities in Biomedical Ethics *(1981) and* Who Should Decide? *(1982) and the coauthor of* Principles of Biomedical Ethics *(1979).*

Lynn and Childress confront the following question: Is it ever permissible to withhold or withdraw nutrition and hydration from a patient? Their special concern is with decision making in the case of an incompetent patient. In their view, it is *not obligatory* to provide medical nutrition and hydration whenever (1) the treatment would be futile, (2) there is no possibility of patient benefit, or (3) the burden created by the treatment would be disproportionate to the benefit provided. After explicating these matters, Lynn and Childress identify and reject a number of arguments that could be directed against their position.

Many people die from the lack of food or water. For some, this lack is the result of poverty or famine, but for others it is the result of disease or deliberate decision. In the past, malnutrition and dehydration must have accompanied nearly every death that followed an illness of more than a few days. Most dying patients do not eat much on their own, and nothing could be done for them until the first flexible tubing for instilling food or other liquid into the stomach was developed about a hundred years ago. Even then, the procedure was so scarce, so costly in physician and nursing time, and so poorly tolerated that it was used only for patients who clearly could benefit. With the advent of more reliable and efficient procedures in the past few decades, these conditions can be corrected or ameliorated in nearly every patient who would otherwise be malnourished or dehydrated. In fact, intravenous lines and nasogastric tubes have become common images of hospital care.

Providing adequate nutrition and fluids is a high priority for most patients, both because they suffer directly from inadequacies and because these deficiencies hinder their ability to overcome other diseases. But are there some patients who need not receive these treatments? This question has become a prominent public policy issue in a number of recent cases. In May 1981, in Danville, Illinois, the parents and the physician of newborn conjoined twins with shared abdominal organs decided not to feed these children. Feeding and other treatments were given after court intervention, though a grand jury refused to indict the parents.[1] Later that year, two physicians in

---

Reprinted with permission of the authors and the publisher from *Hastings Center Report,* vol. 13 (October 1983), pp. 17–21.

[1]John A. Robertson, "Dilemma in Danville," *The Hastings Center Report* 11 (October 1981), 5–8.

Los Angeles discontinued intravenous nutrition to a patient who had severe brain damage after an episode involving loss of oxygen following routine surgery. Murder charges were brought, but the hearing judge dismissed the charges at a preliminary hearing. On appeal, the charges were reinstated and remanded for trial.[2]

In April 1982, a Bloomington, Indiana, infant who had tracheoesophageal fistula and Down syndrome was not treated or fed, and he died after two courts ruled that the decision was proper but before all appeals could be heard.[3] When the federal government then moved to ensure that such infants would be fed in the future,[4] the Surgeon General, Dr. C. Everett Koop, initially stated that there is never adequate reason to deny nutrition and fluids to a newborn infant.

While these cases were before the public, the nephew of Claire Conroy, an elderly incompetent woman with several serious medical problems, petitioned a New Jersey court for authority to discontinue her nasogastric tube feedings. Although the inter-mediate appeals court has reversed the ruling,[5] the trial court held that he had this authority since the evidence indicated that the patient would not have wanted such treatment and that its value to her was doubtful.

In all these dramatic cases and in many more that go unnoticed, the decision is made to deliberately withhold food or fluid known to be necessary for the life of the patient. Such decisions are unsettling. There is now widespread consensus that some-times a patient is best served by not undertaking or continuing certain treatments that would sustain life, especially if these entail substantial suffering. But food and water are so central to an array of human emotions that it is almost impossible to consider them with the same emotional detachment that one might feel toward a respirator or a dialysis machine.

Nevertheless, the question remains: should it ever be permissible to withhold or withdraw food and nutrition? The answer in any real case should acknowledge the psychological contiguity between feeding and loving and between nutritional satisfac-tion and emotional satisfaction. Yet this acknowledgment does not resolve the core question.

Some have held that it is intrinsically wrong not to feed another. The philosopher G.E.M. Anscombe contends: "For wilful starvation there can be no excuse. The same can't be said quite without qualification about failing to operate or to adopt some

[2]T. Rohrlich, "2 Doctors Face Murder Charges in Patient's Death," L. A. *Times*, August 19, 1982, A-1; Jonathan Kirsch, "A Death at Kaiser Hospital," *California* 7 (1982), 79ff; Magistrate's findings, *California v. Barber and Nejdl*, No. A 925586, Los Angeles Mun. Ct. Cal., (March 9, 1983); Superior Court of California, County of Los Angeles, *California v. Barber and Nejdl*, No. AO 25586, tentative decision May 5, 1983.

[3]*In re Infant Doe*, No. GU 8204-00 (Cir. Ct. Monroe County, Ind., April 12, 1982), writ of mandamus dismissed sub nom. *State ex rel. Infant Doe v. Baker*, No. 482 S140 (Indiana Supreme Ct. May 27, 1982).

[4]Office of the Secretary, Department of Health and Human Services, "Nondiscrimination on the Basis of Handicap," *Federal Register* 48 (1983), 9630-32. [Interim final rule modifying 45 C.F.R. # 84.61]. See Judge Gerhard Gesell's decision, *American Academy of Pediatrics v. Heckler*, No. 83-0774, U.S. District Court, D.C., April 24, 1983; and also George J. Annas, "Disconnecting the Baby Doe Hotline," *The Hastings Center Report* 13 (June 1983), 14–16.

[5]*In re Claire C. Conroy*, Sup Ct NJ (Chancery Div-Essex Co. No. P-19083E) February 2, 1983; *In re Claire C. Conroy*, Sup Ct NJ (Appellate Div. No. 4-2483-82T1) July 8, 1983.

courses of treatment."[6] But the moral issues are more complex than Anscombe's comment suggests. Does correcting nutritional deficiencies always improve patients' well-being? What should be our reflective moral response to withholding or withdrawing nutrition? What moral principles are relevant to our reflections? What medical facts about ways of providing nutrition are relevant? And what policies should be adopted by the society, hospitals, and medical and other health care professionals?

In our effort to find answers to these questions, we will concentrate upon the care of patients who are incompetent to make choices for themselves. Patients who are competent to determine the course of their therapy may refuse any and all interventions proposed by others, as long as their refusals do not seriously harm or impose unfair burdens upon others. A competent patient's decision regarding whether or not to accept the provision of food and water by medical means such as tube feeding or intravenous alimentation is unlikely to raise questions of harm or burden to others.

What then should guide those who must decide about nutrition for a patient who cannot decide? As a start, consider the standard by which other medical decisions are made: one should decide as the incompetent person would have if he or she were competent, when that is possible to determine, and advance that person's interests in a more generalized sense when individual preferences cannot be known.

THE MEDICAL PROCEDURES

There is no reason to apply a different standard to feeding and hydration. Surely, when one inserts a feeding tube, or creates a gastrostomy opening, or inserts a needle into a vein, one intends to benefit the patient. Ideally, one should provide what the patient believes to be of benefit, but at least the effect should be beneficial in the opinions of surrogates and caregivers.

Thus, the question becomes: is it ever in the patient's interest to become malnourished and dehydrated, rather than to receive treatment? Posing the question so starkly points to our need to know what is entailed in treating these conditions and what benefits the treatments offer.

The medical interventions that provide food and fluids are of two basic types. First, liquids can be delivered by a tube that is inserted into a functioning gastrointestinal tract, most commonly through the nose and esophagus into the stomach or through a surgical incision in the abdominal wall and directly into the stomach. The liquids used can be specially prepared solutions of nutrients or a blenderized version of an ordinary diet. The nasogastric tube is cheap; it may lead to pneumonia and often annoys the patient and family, sometimes even requiring that the patient be restrained to prevent its removal.

Creating a gastrostomy is usually a simple surgical procedure, and, once the wound is healed, care is very simple. Since it is out of sight, it is aesthetically more acceptable and restraints are needed less often. Also, the gastrostomy creates no additional risk

---

[6]G. E. M. Anscombe, "Ethical Problems in the Management of Some Severely Handicapped Children: Commentary 2," *Journal of Medical Ethics* 7 (1981), 117–124, at 122.

of pneumonia. However, while elimination of a nasogastric tube requires only removing the tube, a gastrostomy is fairly permanent, and can be closed only by surgery.

The second type of medical intervention is intravenous feeding and hydration, which also has two major forms. The ordinary hospital or peripheral IV, in which fluid is delivered directly to the bloodstream through a small needle, is useful only for temporary efforts to improve hydration and electrolyte concentrations. One cannot provide a balanced diet through the veins in the limbs: to do that requires a central line, or a special catheter placed into one of the major veins in the chest. The latter procedure is much more risky and vulnerable to infections and technical errors, and it is much more costly than any of the other procedures. Both forms of intravenous nutrition and hydration commonly require restraining the patient, cause minor infections and other ill effects, and are costly, especially since they ordinarily require the patient to be in a hospital.

None of these procedures, then, is ideal; each entails some distress, some medical limitations, and some costs. When may a procedure be foregone that might improve nutrition and hydration for a given patient? Only when the procedure and the resulting improvement in nutrition and hydration do not offer the patient a net benefit over what he or she would otherwise have faced.

Are there such circumstances? We believe that there are; but they are few and limited to the following three kinds of situations: 1. The procedures that would be required are so unlikely to achieve improved nutritional and fluid levels that they could be correctly considered futile; 2. The improvement in nutritional and fluid balance, though achievable, could be of no benefit to the patient; 3. The burdens of receiving the treatment may outweigh the benefit.

WHEN FOOD AND WATER MAY BE WITHHELD

Futile Treatment Sometimes even providing "food and water" to a patient becomes a monumental task. Consider a patient with a severe clotting deficiency and a nearly total body burn. Gaining access to the central veins is likely to cause hemorrhage or infection, nasogastric tube placement may be quite painful, and there may be no skin to which to suture the stomach for a gastrostomy tube. Or consider a patient with severe congestive heart failure who develops cancer of the stomach with a fistula that delivers food from the stomach to the colon without passing through the intestine and being absorbed. Feeding the patient may be possible, but little is absorbed. Intravenous feeding cannot be tolerated because the fluid would be too much for the weakened heart. Or consider the infant with infarction of all but a short segment of bowel. Again, the infant can be fed, but little if anything is absorbed. Intravenous methods can be used, but only for a short time (weeks or months) until their complications, including thrombosis, hemorrhage, infections, and malnutrition, cause death.

In these circumstances, the patient is going to die soon, no matter what is done. The ineffective efforts to provide nutrition and hydration may well directly cause suffering that offers no counterbalancing benefit for the patient. Although the procedures might be tried, especially if the competent patient wanted them or the incompetent patient's surrogate had reason to believe that this incompetent patient would have wanted them, they cannot be considered obligatory. To hold that a patient must be subjected to this predictably futile sort of intervention just because protein balance is negative or the blood serum is concentrated is to lose sight of the moral warrant for medical care and to reduce the patient to an array of measurable variables.

No Possibility of Benefit Some patients can be reliably diagnosed to have permanently lost consciousness. This unusual group of patients includes those with anencephaly, persistent vegetative state, and some preterminal comas. In these cases, it is very difficult to discern how any medical intervention can benefit or harm the patient. These patients cannot and never will be able to experience any of the events occurring in the world or in their bodies. When the diagnosis is exceedingly clear, we sustain their lives vigorously mainly for their loved ones and the community at large.

While these considerations probably indicate that continued artificial feeding is best in most cases, there may be some cases in which the family and the caregivers are convinced that artificial feeding is offensive and unreasonable. In such cases, there seems to be no adequate reason to claim that withholding food and water violates any obligations that these parties or the general society have with regard to permanently unconscious patients. Thus, if the parents of an anencephalic infant or of a patient like Karen Quinlan in a persistent vegetative state feel strongly that no medical procedures should be applied to provide nutrition and hydration, and the caregivers are willing to comply, there should be no barrier in law or public policy to thwart the plan.[7]

Disproportionate Burden The most difficult cases are those in which normal nutritional status or fluid balance could be restored, but only with a severe burden for the patient. In these cases, the treatment is futile in a broader sense—the patient will not actually benefit from the improved nutrition and hydration. A patient who is competent can decide the relative merits of the treatment being provided, knowing the probable consequences, and weighing the merits of life under various sets of constrained circumstances. But a surrogate decision maker for a patient who is incompetent to decide will have a difficult task. When the situation is irremediably ambiguous, erring on the side of continued life and improved nutrition and hydration seems the less grievous error. But are there situations that would warrant a determination that this patient, whose nutrition and hydration could surely be improved, is not thereby well served?

Though they are rare, we believe there are such cases. The treatments entailed are not benign. Their effects are far short of ideal. Furthermore, many of the patients most likely to have inadequate food and fluid intake are also likely to suffer the most serious side effects of these therapies.

Patients who are allowed to die without artificial hydration and nutrition may well die more comfortably than patients who receive conventional amounts of intravenous

---

[7]The President's Commission for the Study of Ethical Problems in Medicine and Biomedical and Behavioral Research, *Deciding to Forego Life-Sustaining Treatment* (Washington, D. C.: Government Printing Office, 1982), pp. 171–96.

hydration.[8] Terminal pulmonary edema, nausea, and mental confusion are more likely when patients have been treated to maintain fluid and nutrition until close to the time of death.

Thus, those patients whose "need" for artificial nutrition and hydration arises only near the time of death may be harmed by its provision. It is not at all clear that they receive any benefit in having a slightly prolonged life, and it does seem reasonable to allow a surrogate to decide that, for this patient at this time, slight prolongation of life is not warranted if it involves measures that will probably increase the patient's suffering as he or she dies.

Even patients who might live much longer might not be well served by artificial means to provide fluid and food. Such patients might include those with fairly severe dementia for whom the restraints required could be a constant source of fear, discomfort, and struggle. For such a patient, sedation to tolerate the feeding mechanisms might preclude any of the pleasant experiences that might otherwise have been available. Thus, a decision not to intervene, except perhaps briefly to ascertain that there are no treatable causes, might allow such a patient to live out a shorter life with fair freedom of movement and freedom from fear, while a decision to maintain artificial nutrition and hydration might consign the patient to end his or her life in unremitting anguish. If this were the case a surrogate decision maker would seem to be well justified in refusing the treatment.

INAPPROPRIATE MORAL CONSTRAINTS

Four considerations are frequently proposed as moral constraints on foregoing medical feeding and hydration. We find none of these to dictate that artificial nutrition and hydration must always be provided.

The Obligation to Provide "Ordinary" Care Debates about appropriate medical treatment are often couched in terms of "ordinary" and "extraordinary" means of treatment. Historically, this distinction emerged in the Roman Catholic tradition to differentiate optional treatment from treatment that was obligatory for medical professionals to offer and for patients to accept. These terms also appear in many secular contexts, such as court decisions and medical codes. The recent debates about ordinary and extraordinary means of treatment have been interminable and often unfruitful, in part because of a lack of clarity about what the terms mean. Do they represent the premises of an argument or the conclusion, and what features of a situation are relevant to the categorization as "ordinary" or "extraordinary"?

Several criteria have been implicit in debates about ordinary and extraordinary means of treatment; some of them may be relevant to determining whether and which treatments are obligatory and which are optional. Treatments have been distinguished according to their simplicity (simple/complex), their naturalness (natural/artificial), their customariness (usual/unusual), their invasiveness (noninvasive/invasive), their

---

[8]Joyce V. Zerwekh, "The Dehydration Question," *Nursing 83* (January 1983), 47–51, with comments by Judith R. Brown and Marion B. Dolan.

chance of success (reasonable chance/futile), their balance of benefits and burdens (proportionate/disproportionate), and their expense (inexpensive/costly). Each set of paired terms or phrases in the parentheses suggests a continuum: as the treatment moves from the first of the paired terms to the second, it is said to become less obligatory and more optional.

However, when these various criteria, widely used in discussions about medical treatment, are carefully examined, most of them are not morally relevant in distinguishing optional from obligatory medical treatments. For example, if a rare, complex, artificial, and invasive treatment offers a patient a reasonable chance of nearly painless cure, then one would have to offer a substantial justification not to provide that treatment to an incompetent patient.

What matters, then, in determining whether to provide a treatment to an incompetent patient is not a prior determination that this treatment is "ordinary" per se, but rather a determination that this treatment is likely to provide this patient benefits that are sufficient to make it worthwhile to endure the burdens that accompany the treatment. To this end, some of the considerations listed above are relevant: whether a treatment is likely to succeed is an obvious example. But such considerations taken in isolation are not conclusive. Rather, the surrogate decision maker is obliged to assess the desirability to this patient of each of the options presented, including nontreatment. For most people at most times, this assessment would lead to a clear obligation to provide food and fluids.

But sometimes, as we have indicated, providing food and fluids through medical interventions may fail to benefit and may even harm some patients. Then the treatment cannot be said to be obligatory, no matter how usual and simple its provision may be. If "ordinary" and "extraordinary" are used to convey the conclusion about the obligation to treat, providing nutrition and fluids would have become, in these cases, "extraordinary." Since this phrasing is misleading, it is probably better to use "proportionate" and "disproportionate," as the Vatican now suggests,[9] or "obligatory" and "optional."

Obviously, providing nutrition and hydration may sometimes be necessary to keep patients comfortable while they are dying even though it may temporarily prolong their dying. In such cases, food and fluids constitute warranted palliative care. But in other cases, such as a patient in a deep and irreversible coma, nutrition and hydration do not appear to be needed or helpful, except perhaps to comfort the staff and family. And sometimes the interventions needed for nutrition and hydration are so burdensome that they are harmful and best not utilized.

The Obligation to Continue Treatments Once Started   Once having started a mode of treatment, many caregivers find it very difficult to discontinue it. While this strongly felt difference between the ease of withholding a treatment and the difficulty of withdrawing it provides a psychological explanation of certain actions, it does not justify them. It sometimes even leads to a thoroughly irrational decision process. For example, in caring for a dying, comatose patient, many physicians apparently find it harder to

---

[9]The Sacred Congregation for the Doctrine of the Faith, *Declaration on Euthanasia*, Vatican City, May 5, 1980.

stop a functioning peripheral IV than not to restart one that has infiltrated (that is, has broken through the blood vessel and is leaking fluid into surrounding tissue), especially if the only way to reestablish an IV would be to insert a central line into the heart or to do a cutdown (make an incision to gain access to the deep large blood vessels).

What factors might make withdrawing medical treatment morally worse than withholding it? Withdrawing a treatment seems to be an action, which, when it is likely to end in death, initially seems more serious than an omission that ends in death. However, this view is fraught with errors. Withdrawing is not always an act: failing to put the next infusion into a tube could be correctly described as an omission, for example. Even when withdrawing is an act, it may well be morally correct and even morally obligatory. Discontinuing intravenous lines in a patient now permanently unconscious in accord with that patient's well-informed advance directive would certainly be such a case. Futhermore, the caregiver's obligation to serve the patient's interests through both acts and omissions rules out the exculpation that accompanies omissions in the usual course of social life. An omission that is not warranted by the patient's interests is culpable.

Sometimes initiating a treatment creates expectations in the minds of caregivers, patients, and family that the treatment will be continued indefinitely or until the patient is cured. Such expectations may provide a reason to continue the treatment as a way to keep a promise. However, as with all promises, caregivers could be very careful when initiating a treatment to explain the indications for its discontinuation, and they could modify preconceptions with continuing reevaluation and education during treatment. Though all patients are entitled to expect the continuation of care in the patient's best interests, they are not and should not be entitled to the continuation of a particular mode of care.

Accepting the distinction between withholding and withdrawing medical treatment as morally significant also has a very unfortunate implication: caregivers may become unduly reluctant to begin some treatments precisely because they fear that they will be locked into continuing treatments that are no longer of value to the patient. For example, the physician who had been unwilling to stop the respirator while the infant, Andrew Stinson, died over several months is reportedly "less eager to attach babies to respirators now."[10] But if it were easier to ignore malnutrition and dehydration and to withhold treatments for these problems than to discontinue the same treatments when they have become especially burdensome and insufficiently beneficial for this patient, then the incentives would be perverse. Once a treatment has been tried, it is often much clearer whether it is of value to this patient, and the decision to stop it can be made more reliably.

The same considerations should apply to starting as to stopping a treatment, and whatever assessment warrants withholding should also warrant withdrawing.

The Obligation to Avoid Being the Unambiguous Cause of Death Many physicians will agree with all that we have said and still refuse to allow a choice to forego food and fluid because such a course seems to be a "death sentence." In this view

---

[10]Robert and Peggy Stinson, *The Long Dying of Baby Andrew* (Boston: Little, Brown and Company, 1983), p. 355.

death seems to be more certain from malnutrition and dehydration than from foregoing other forms of medical therapy. This implies that it is acceptable to act in ways that are likely to cause death, as in not operating on a gangrenous leg, only if there remains a chance that the patient will survive. This is a comforting formulation for caregivers, to be sure, since they can thereby avoid feeling the full weight of the responsibility for the time and manner of a patient's death. However, it is not a persuasive moral argument.

First, in appropriate cases discontinuing certain medical treatments is generally accepted despite the fact that death is as certain as with nonfeeding. Dialysis in a patient without kidney function or transfusions in a patient with severe aplastic anemia are obvious examples. The dying that awaits such patients often is not greatly different from dying of dehydration and malnutrition.

Second, the certainty of a generally undesirable outcome such as death is always relevant to a decision, but it does not foreclose the possibility that this course is better than others available to this patient. Ambiguity and uncertainty are so common in medical decision making that caregivers are tempted to use them in distancing themselves from direct responsibility. However, caregivers are in fact responsible for the time and manner of death for many patients. Their distaste for this fact should not constrain otherwise morally justified decisions.

The Obligation to Provide Symbolically Significant Treatment One of the most common arguments for always providing nutrition and hydration is that it symbolizes, expresses, or conveys the essence of care and compassion. Some actions not only aim at goals, they also express values. Such expressive actions should not simply be viewed as means to ends; they should also be viewed in light of what they communicate. From this perspective food and water are not only goods that preserve life and provide comfort; they are also symbols of care and compassion. To withhold or withdraw them—to "starve" a patient—can never express or convey care.

Why is providing food and water a central symbol of care and compassion? Feeding is the first response of the community to the needs of newborns and remains a central mode of nurture and comfort. Eating is associated with social interchange and community, and providing food for someone else is a way to create and maintain bonds of sharing and expressing concern. Furthermore, even the relatively low levels of hunger and thirst that most people have experienced are decidedly uncomfortable, and the common image of severe malnutrition or dehydration is one of unremitting agony. Thus, people are rightly eager to provide food and water. Such provision is essential to minimally tolerable existence and a powerful symbol of our concern for each other.

However, *medical* nutrition and hydration, we have argued, may not always provide net benefits to patients. Medical procedures to provide nutrition and hydration are more similar to other medical procedures than to typical human ways of providing nutrition and hydration, for example, a sip of water. It should be possible to evaluate their benefits and burdens, as we evaluate any other medical procedure. Of course, if family, friends, and caregivers feel that such procedures affirm important values even when they do not benefit the patient, their feelings should not be ignored. We do not contend that there is an obligation to withhold or to withdraw such procedures (unless consideration of the patient's advance directives or current best interest unambiguously dictates that conclusion); we only contend that nutrition and hydration may be foregone in some cases.

The symbolic connection between care and nutrition or hydration adds useful caution to decision making. If decision makers worry over withholding or withdrawing medical nutrition and hydration, they may inquire more seriously into the circumstances that putatively justify their decisions. This is generally salutary for health care decision making. The critical inquiry may well yield the sad but justified conclusion that the patient will be served best by not using medical procedures to provide food and fluids.

A LIMITED CONCLUSION

Our conclusion—that patients or their surrogates, in close collaboration with their physicians and other caregivers and with careful assessment of the relevant information, can correctly decide to forego the provision of medical treatments intended to correct malnutrition and dehydration in some circumstances—is quite limited. Concentrating on incompetent patients, we have argued that in most cases such patients will be best served by providing nutrition and fluids. Thus, there should be a presumption in favor of providing nutrition and fluids as part of the broader presumption to provide means that prolong life. But this presumption may be rebutted in particular cases.

We do not have enough information to be able to determine with clarity and conviction whether withholding or withdrawing nutrition and hydration was justified in the cases that have occasioned public concern, though it seems likely that the Danville and Bloomington babies should have been fed and that Claire Conroy should not.

It is never sufficient to rule out "starvation" categorically. The question is whether the obligation to act in the patient's best interests was discharged by withholding or withdrawing particular medical treatments. All we have claimed is that nutrition and hydration by medical means need not always be provided. Sometimes they may not be in accord with the patient's wishes or interests. Medical nutrition and hydration do not appear to be distinguishable in any morally relevant way from other life-sustaining medical treatments that may on occasion be withheld or withdrawn.

QUESTIONS

1 If you were a surrogate decision maker, are there circumstances in which you would authorize the discontinuance of medical nutrition and hydration? In particular, would you authorize the discontinuance of such treatment for a patient in a persistent vegetative state?
2 Lynn and Childress dismiss a number of considerations as "inappropriate moral constraints" on the forgoing of medical nutrition and hydration. Can any of these constraints be defended as appropriate?

SUGGESTED ADDITIONAL READINGS FOR CHAPTER 2

BEAUCHAMP, TOM L., and SEYMOUR PERLIN, eds.: *Ethical Issues in Death and Dying.* Englewood Cliffs, N.J.: Prentice-Hall, 1978. Chapter 4 of this book is entitled "Euthanasia and Natural Death." It includes subsections on "The Quinlan Case" and "Natural Death and Living Wills." Also noteworthy, in "A Reply to Rachels on Active and Passive Euthanasia" (pp. 246–258), Beauchamp suggests that rule-utilitarian considerations may provide a basis for defending the moral significance of the distinction between active and passive euthanasia.

DOWNING, A. B., ed.: *Euthanasia and the Right to Death: The Case for Voluntary Euthanasia*. New York: Humanities Press; London: Peter Owen, 1969. This collection of euthanasia articles is written from many perspectives—philosophical, humanitarian, sociological, legal, and medical. Especially noteworthy is an article by Antony Flew, "The Principle of Euthanasia." Flew constructs "a general moral case for the establishment of a legal right" to voluntary (active) euthanasia.

DUFF, RAYMOND S., and A. G. M. CAMPBELL: "Moral and Ethical Dilemmas in the Special-Care Nursery." *New England Journal of Medicine,* vol. 289, Oct. 25, 1973, pp. 890–894. This article, a frequent reference point in ethical discussions of the treatment of defective newborns, provides helpful descriptions of the ethical attitudes and actual practices associated with one hospital's special-care nursery. Duff and Campbell make clear that in actual practice some infants are allowed to die.

GRISEZ, GERMAIN, and JOSEPH BOYLE: *Life and Death with Liberty and Justice*. Notre Dame, Ind.: University of Notre Dame Press, 1979. Grisez and Boyle distinguish jurisprudential questions concerning euthanasia from ethical ones and devote most of the book to the former. In addition to euthanasia as such, they discuss assisted and unassisted suicide, the definition of death, killing in war and self-defense, and other related topics.

KOHL, MARVIN, ed.: *Beneficent Euthanasia*. Buffalo, N.Y.: Prometheus Books, 1975. This anthology includes a number of excellent articles on the moral aspects of euthanasia. Also included are articles that provide statements of various religious positions on euthanasia. Other articles address the medical and legal aspects of euthanasia.

MAPPES, THOMAS A. and JANE S. ZEMBATY, eds.: *Biomedical Ethics,* 2d ed. New York: McGraw-Hill, 1986. Chapter 8 of this anthology includes helpful material in subsections entitled "Euthanasia and the Definition of Death," "The Legalization of Voluntary (Active) Euthanasia," and "The Treatment of Defective Newborns."

PRESIDENT'S COMMISSION FOR THE STUDY OF ETHICAL PROBLEMS IN MEDICINE AND BIOMEDICAL AND BEHAVIORAL RESEARCH: *Deciding to Forego Life-Sustaining Treatment*. 1983. This valuable document provides a broad-based discussion of decision making regarding life-sustaining treatment.

STEINBOCK, BONNIE, ed.: *Killing and Letting Die*. Englewood Cliffs, N.J.: Prentice-Hall, 1980. This anthology provides a wealth of material on the killing/letting die distinction.

TRAMMELL, RICHARD L.: "Euthanasia and the Law." *Journal of Social Philosophy,* vol. 9, January 1978, pp. 14–18, Trammell contends that the legalization of voluntary positive (i.e., active) euthanasia would probably not "result in overall positive utility for the class of people eligible to choose." He emphasizes the unwelcome pressures that would be created by legalization.

VEATCH, ROBERT M.: *Death, Dying, and the Biological Revolution: Our Last Quest for Responsibility*. New Haven, Conn.: Yale University Press, 1976. Two chapters of this book are especially notable in the context of euthanasia discussions. Chapter 3 considers many of the prominent conceptual difficulties. Chapter 5 considers various public policy options. Chapters 1 and 2 are of related interest; they provide an extensive discussion of the definition of death.

WEIR, ROBERT F.: *Selective Nontreatment of Handicapped Newborns: Moral Dilemmas in Neonatal Medicine*. New York: Oxford University Press, 1984. Weir surveys and critically analyzes a wide range of views (advanced by various pediatricians, attorneys, and ethicists) on the subject of selective nontreatment. He then presents and defends an overall policy for the guidance of decision making in this area.

CHAPTER 3

THE DEATH PENALTY

Strong convictions are firmly entrenched on both sides of the death penalty controversy. From one side, we hear in forceful tones that "murderers deserve to die." We are also told, not infrequently by those in law enforcement, that society simply cannot do without the death penalty: "Without the death penalty to deter potential criminals, serious crime will run rampant." From the other side of the controversy, in tones of equal conviction, we are told that the death penalty is a cruel and barbarous practice, effectively serving no purpose that could not be equally well served by a more humane punishment. "How long," it is asked, "must we indulge this uncivilized and pointless lust for revenge?" In the face of such strongly held but opposed views, each of us is invited to confront an important ethical issue, the morality of the death penalty. Before approaching the death penalty in its ethical dimensions, however, it may prove helpful to briefly discuss its constitutional dimensions. Many of the considerations raised in discussions of the constitutionality of the death penalty parallel those raised in discussions of its morality.

THE CONSTITUTIONALITY OF THE DEATH PENALTY

The Eighth Amendment to the Constitution of the United States explicitly prohibits the infliction of "cruel and unusual" punishment. If the death penalty is a cruel and unusual punishment, it is unconstitutional. But is it cruel and unusual? In a landmark case, *Furman v. Georgia* (1972), the Supreme Court ruled that the death penalty was unconstitutional *as then administered*. The Court did not comprehensively rule, however, that the death penalty was unconstitutional *by its very nature*. Indeed, subsequent developments in the Court have made clear that the death penalty, when administered under certain circumstances, is not unconstitutional.

The decision reached in *Furman* was by a mere five-to-four majority. There was a basic divergence of viewpoint among those who voted with the majority. Both Justice Marshall and Justice Brennan argued straightforwardly that the death penalty is a cruel and unusual punishment *by its very nature*. From this perspective it would not matter how much the procedures of its administration might be modified. It would still remain a cruel and unusual punishment. Among the reasons advanced to support this contention, two are especially noteworthy. (1) The death penalty is excessive in the sense of being unnecessary; lesser penalties are capable of serving the desired legislative purpose. (2) The death penalty is abhorrent to currently existing moral values.

The other three justices (Douglas, White, and Stewart) who voted with the majority did not commit themselves to the position that the death penalty is unconstitutional *by its very nature*. Leaving this underlying issue unresolved, they simply advanced the more guarded contention that the death penalty was unconstitutional *as then administered*. In their view, the death penalty was unconstitutional primarily because it was being administered in an arbitrary and capricious manner. The essence of their argument can be reconstructed in the following way. The death penalty in its contemporary setting is, as a common matter of course, inflicted at the discretion of a jury (or sometimes a judge). The absence of explicit standards to govern the decision between life and death allows a wide range of unchecked prejudice to operate freely under the heading of "discretion." For example, "discretion" seems to render blacks more prone than whites to the death penalty. Such standardless discretion violates not only the Eighth Amendment but also the Fourteenth Amendment, which guarantees "due process of law."

As matters developed in the wake of *Furman*, it was the Court's objection to *standardless discretion* that provided an opening for the many individual states still anxious to retain the death penalty as a viable component of their legal systems. These states were faced with the challenge of devising procedures for inflicting the death penalty which would not be open to the charge of standardless discretion. Two such approaches gained prominence. (1) Some states (e.g., North Carolina) moved to dissolve the objection of standardless discretion by simply making the death penalty *mandatory* for certain crimes. (2) Other states (e.g., Georgia) took an equally obvious approach to avoid the charge of standardless discretion. It consisted in the effort to establish standards that would provide guidance for the jury (or the judge) in deciding between life and death.

Subsequent developments have made clear that the second approach is constitutionally acceptable whereas the first is not. In *Woodson v. North Carolina* (1976), the Court ruled (though by a mere five-to-four majority) that mandatory death sentences are unconstitutional. In *Gregg v. Georgia* (1976), however, the Court ruled (with only Justice Marshall and Justice Brennan dissenting) that the death penalty is not unconstitutional when imposed at the discretion of a jury for the *crime of murder*,[1] so long

---

[1]In *Gregg,* the Supreme Court considered only the constitutionality of imposing the death penalty for the *crime of murder*. In *Coker v. Georgia* (1977), 433 U.S. 584, the Court subsequently considered the constitutionality of imposing the death penalty for the *crime of rape*. Holding death to be a "grossly disproportionate" punishment for the crime of rape, the Court declared such an employment of the death penalty unconstitutional.

as appropriate safeguards are provided against any arbitrary or capricious imposition. Most important, there must be explicit standards established for the guidance of jury deliberations. The attitude of the Court in this regard is made clear by Justices Stewart, Powell, and Stevens in their opinion in *Gregg v. Georgia* (1976), which appears in this chapter. Also appearing in this chapter is the dissenting opinion of Justice Marshall.

THE ETHICAL ISSUE

In any discussion of the morality of the death penalty, it is important to remember that the death penalty is a kind of punishment. Indeed, it is normally thought to be the most serious kind of punishment, hence the term "*capital* punishment." Most philosophers agree that punishment in general (as contrasted with capital punishment in particular) is a morally justified social practice. For one thing, however uneasy we might feel about inflicting harm on another person, it is hard to visualize a complex society managing to survive without an established legal system of punishment. However, to say that most philosophers agree that punishment in general is a morally justified social practice is not to say that there are no dissenters from this view. Some argue that it is possible to structure society in ways that would not necessitate commitment to a legal system of punishment as we know it. For example, might it not be that undesirable social behavior could be adequately kept in check by therapeutic treatment rather than by traditional kinds of punishment? Such a system would certainly have the advantage of being more humane, but it seems doubtful that present therapeutic techniques are adequate to the task. Perhaps future advances in the behavioral sciences will render such an alternative more plausible. If so, it may be that one day the whole practice of (nontherapeutic) punishment will have to be rejected on moral grounds. Still, for now, there is widespread agreement on the moral defensibility of punishment as an overall social practice. What stands out as an open and hotly debated ethical issue is whether or not the death penalty, as a distinctive kind of punishment, ought to continue to play a role in our legal system of punishment.

Those in favor of retaining the death penalty are commonly called "retentionists." Retentionists differ among themselves regarding the kinds of cases in which they find it appropriate to employ the death penalty. They also differ among themselves regarding the supporting arguments they find acceptable. But anyone who supports the retention of the death penalty—for employment in whatever kinds of cases and for whatever reason—is by definition a retentionist. Those in favor of abolishing the death penalty are commonly called "abolitionists." Abolitionists, by definition, refuse to support any employment of the death penalty. Like the retentionists, however, they differ among themselves concerning the supporting arguments they find acceptable.

There is one extreme, and not widely embraced, abolitionist line of thought. It is based on the belief that the sanctity of human life demands absolute nonviolence. On this view, killing of any kind, for any reason, is always and everywhere morally wrong. No one has the right to take a human life, not in self-defense, not in war, not in any circumstance. Thus, since the death penalty obviously involves a kind of killing, it is a morally unacceptable form of punishment and must be abolished. This general view, which is associated with the Quakers and other pacifists, has struck most moral philosophers as implausible. Can we really think that killing, when it is the only course that will save oneself from an unprovoked violent assault, is morally wrong? Can we really think that it would be morally wrong to kill a terrorist if that were the *only* possible way of stopping him or her from exploding a bomb in the midst of a kindergarten class? The defender of absolute nonviolence is sometimes inclined to argue at this point that violence will only breed violence. There may indeed be much truth in this claim. Still, most people would reject the view that such a claim adequately supports the contention that *all* killing is morally wrong, and if *some* killing is morally acceptable, perhaps the death penalty itself is morally acceptable. What arguments can be made on its behalf?

RETENTIONIST ARGUMENTS

Broadly speaking, arguments for the retention of the death penalty usually emphasize either (1) considerations of *justice* or (2) considerations of *social utility*. Those who emphasize considerations of justice typically develop their case along the following line: When the moral order is upset by the commission of some offense, it is only right that the disorder be rectified by punishment equal in intensity to the seriousness of the offense. This view is reflected in remarks such as "The scales of justice demand retribution" and "The offender must pay for the crime." Along this line, the philosopher Immanuel Kant (1724–1804) is famous for his unequivocal defense of the principle of retaliation. According to this principle, punishment is to be inflicted in a measure that will equalize the offense. And when the offense is murder, *only* capital punishment is sufficient to equalize it.

In one of this chapter's readings, Burton M. Leiser defends the retention of the death penalty on grounds of retributive justice. Hugo Adam Bedau, a prominent abolitionist, provides a contrasting point of view. Emphasizing the difficulties associated with interpreting and applying the principle of "a life for a life," Bedau argues that considerations of retributive justice cannot effectively support the retention of the death penalty.

Although the demand for retribution continues to play a prominent role in the overall case for the death penalty, many retentionists (and obviously abolitionists as well) have come to feel quite uneasy with the notion of imposing the death penalty "because the wrongdoer deserves it." Perhaps, at least to some extent, this uneasiness has been provoked by our growing awareness of the way in which social conditions, such as ghetto living, seem to spawn criminal activity. If so, then it seems we have arrived at a point of intersection with a venerable philosophical problem, the problem of "freedom and determinism."

Since considerations of social utility are commonly advanced in defense of the practice of punishment in general, it is not surprising to find that they are also commonly advanced in defense of retaining the death penalty. Utilitarianism, as a distinct school of moral philosophy, locates the primary justification of punishment in its social utility. Utilitarians acknowledge that punishment consists in the infliction of evil on another person, but they hold that such evil is far outweighed by the future benefits that will accrue to society. Imprisonment, for example, might lead to such socially desirable effects as (1) *rehabilitation* of the criminal, (2) *incapacitation,* whereby we achieve temporary or permanent protection from the imprisoned criminal, and (3) *deterrence* of other potential criminals. When utilitarian considerations are recruited in support of the retention of the *death* penalty, it is clear that rehabilitation of the criminal can play no part in the case. But retentionists do frequently promote considerations of incapacitation and deterrence.

Accordingly, retentionists often appeal to considerations of incapacitation and argue that the death penalty is the only effective way to protect society from certain *violence-prone and irreformable* criminals. (Notice that an important difficulty here would be finding effective criteria for the recognition of those criminals who are truly "violence-prone and irreformable.") Life imprisonment, it is said, cannot assure society of the needed protection, because criminals such as these pose an imminent threat even to their prison guards and fellow inmates. Furthermore, escape is always possible. In one of this chapter's readings, Sidney Hook relies on considerations of incapacitation in defending the retention of the death penalty for employment in the case of certain twice-guilty murderers.

Many retentionists think, however, that the strongest case for the death penalty can be made not on grounds of protecting society from convicted criminals but rather on grounds of deterring potential criminals. Because of the intense fear that most people have of death, it is argued, the death penalty functions as a uniquely effective deterrent to serious crime. When this argument appears, the debate between retentionists and abolitionists focuses totally on a factual issue. Is the death penalty indeed a more substantial deterrent than life imprisonment? Facts and figures often seem to dominate this particular aspect of the debate, and it is by no means easy to discern the true state of affairs. One retentionist argument, advanced by Ernest van den Haag in this chapter, takes as its starting point our very uncertainty. If we are unsure whether or not the death penalty is a uniquely effective deterrent, he argues, we are morally obliged to risk needlessly eradicating the lives of convicted murderers rather than risking the lives of innocent people who might becomes future murder victims.

ABOLITIONIST ARGUMENTS

What can be said of the abolitionist case against the death penalty? Most abolitionists do not care to argue the extreme position, already discussed, of absolute nonviolence, yet they often do want to commit themselves seriously to the "sanctity of human life." They emphasize the inherent worth and dignity of each individual and insist that the taking of a human life, while perhaps sometimes morally permissible, is a very serious matter and not to be permitted in the absence of weighty overriding reasons. At face value, they argue, the death penalty is cruel and inhumane; and since retentionists have not succeeded in advancing substantial reasons in its defense, it must be judged a morally unacceptable practice. Against retentionist arguments based on retribution as a demand of justice, abolitionists frequently argue that the "demand of justice" is nothing but a mask for a barbarous vengeance. Against retentionist arguments based on considerations of social utility, they simply argue that other more humane punishments will serve equally well. Indeed, in the last selection of this chapter, Hugo Adam

Bedau contends that any complete account of utilitarian considerations would probably favor abolition of the death penalty.

In addition to advancing a number of direct arguments against retentionist arguments, abolitionists also prominently incorporate into their overall case the following consideration. It is impossible to guarantee that mistakes will not be made in the administration of punishment. But this factor is especially important in the case of the death penalty, because only *capital* punishment is irrevocable. Thus only the death penalty eradicates the possibility of compensating an innocent person wrongly punished.

Thomas A. Mappes

Opinion in *Gregg v. Georgia*

**Justices
Potter Stewart,
Lewis F. Powell, Jr.,
and John Paul Stevens**

Potter Stewart (1915–1985) was associate justice of the United States Supreme Court. Lewis F. Powell, Jr. and John Paul Stevens continue to serve as associate judges of the Court. Justice Stewart, a graduate of Yale University Law School, spent some years in private practice, served as judge of the United States Court of Appeals, Sixth Circuit (1954–1958), and served on the Supreme Court from 1958 to 1981. Justice Powell, LL.B (Washington and Lee), LL. M (Harvard), practiced law in Richmond, Virginia, for nearly forty years prior to his appointment in 1971 to the Supreme Court. Justice Stevens, a graduate of Northwestern University School of Law, spent a number of years in private practice, served as judge of the United States Court of Appeals, Seventh Circuit (1970–1975), and was appointed to the Supreme Court in 1975.

The State of Georgia reacted to the Court's decision in *Furman v. Georgia* (1972) by drafting a death penalty statute calculated to avoid the Court's objection to "standardless discretion." Georgia's approach, in contrast to the approach of those states that made the death penalty mandatory for certain crimes, embodied an effort to specify standards that would guide a jury (or a judge) in deciding between the death penalty and life imprisonment. In this case, with only Justice Marshall and Justice Brennan dissenting, the Court upheld the constitutionality of imposing the death penalty for the crime of murder under the law of Georgia.

Justices Stewart, Powell, and Stevens initially consider the contention that the death penalty for the crime of murder is, under all circumstances, "cruel and unusual" punishment, thus unconstitutional. On their analysis, a punishment is "cruel and unusual" if it fails to accord with "evolving standards of decency."

United States Supreme Court. 428 U.S. 153 (1976).

Moreover, even if a punishment does accord with contemporary values, it must still be judged "cruel and unusual" if it fails to accord with the "dignity of man," the "basic concept underlying the Eighth Amendment." They take this second stipulation to rule out "excessive" punishment, identified as (1) that which involves the unnecessary and wanton infliction of pain or (2) that which is grossly out of proportion to the severity of the crime. In the light of these considerations, Justices Stewart, Powell, and Stevens argue that the imposition of the death penalty for the crime of murder does not invariably violate the Constitution. They contend that legislative developments since *Furman* have made clear that the death penalty is acceptable to contemporary society. Moreover, they contend, the death penalty is not invariably "excessive": (1) It may properly be considered necessary to achieve two principal social purposes—retribution and deterrence. (2) When the death penalty is imposed for the crime of murder, it may properly be considered not disproportionate to the severity of the crime.

Turning their attention to the death sentence imposed under the law of Georgia in this case, Justices Stewart, Powell, and Stevens maintain that a carefully drafted statute, ensuring "that the sentencing authority is given adequate information and guidance," makes it possible to avoid imposing the death penalty in an arbitrary or capricious manner. The revised Georgia statutory system under which Gregg was sentenced to death, they conclude, does not violate the Constitution.

The issue in this case is whether the imposition of the sentence of death for the crime of murder under the law of Georgia violates the Eighth and Fourteenth Amendments.

I

The petitioner, Troy Gregg, was charged with committing armed robbery and murder. In accordance with Georgia procedure in capital cases, the trial was in two stages, a guilt stage and a sentencing stage. . . .

. . . The jury found the petitioner guilty of two counts of armed robbery and two counts of murder.

At the penalty stage, which took place before the same jury, . . . the trial judge instructed the jury that it could recommend either a death sentence or a life prison sentence on each count. . . . The jury returned verdicts of death on each count.

The Supreme Court of Georgia affirmed the convictions and the imposition of the death sentences for murder. . . . The death sentences imposed for armed robbery, however, were vacated on the grounds that the death penalty had rarely been imposed in Georgia for that offense. . . .

II

. . . The Georgia statute, as amended after our decision in *Furman v. Georgia* (1972), retains the death penalty for six categories of crime: murder, kidnaping for ransom or where the victim is harmed, armed robbery, rape, treason, and aircraft hijacking. . . .

III

We address initially the basic contention that the punishment of death for the crime of murder is, under all circumstances, "cruel and unusual" in violation of the Eighth and Fourteenth Amendments of the Constitution. In Part IV of this opinion, we will consider the sentence of death imposed under the Georgia statutes at issue in this case.

The Court on a number of occasions has both assumed and asserted the constitutionality of capital punishment. In several cases that assumption provided a necessary foundation for the decision, as the Court was asked to decide whether a particular method of carrying out a capital sentence would be allowed to stand under the Eighth Amendment. But until *Furman v. Georgia* (1972), the Court never confronted squarely the fundamental claim that the punishment of death always, regardless of the enormity of the offense or the procedure followed in imposing the sentence, is cruel and unusual punishment in violation of the Constitution. Although this issue was presented and addressed in *Furman,* it was not resolved by the Court. Four Justices would have held that capital punishment is not unconstitutional *per se;* two justices would have reached the opposite conclusion; and three Justices, while agreeing that the statutes then before the Court were invalid as applied, left open the question whether such punishment may ever be imposed. We now hold that the punishment of death does not invariably violate the Constitution.

A

The history of the prohibition of "cruel and unusual" punishment already has been reviewed at length. The phrase first appeared in the English Bill of Rights of 1689, which was drafted by Parliament at the accession of William and Mary. The English version appears to have been directed against punishments unauthorized by statute and beyond the jurisdiction of the sentencing court, as well as those disproportionate to the offense involved. The American draftsmen, who adopted the English phrasing in drafting the Eighth Amendment, were primarily concerned, however, with proscribing "tortures" and other "barbarous" methods of punishment.

In the earliest cases raising Eighth Amendment claims, the Court focused on particular methods of execution to determine whether they were too cruel to pass constitutional muster. The constitutionality of the sentence of death itself was not at issue, and the criterion used to evaluate the mode of execution was its similarity to "torture" and other "barbarous" methods. . . .

But the Court has not confined the prohibition embodied in the Eighth Amendment to "barbarous" methods that were generally outlawed in the 18th century. Instead, the Amendment has been interpreted in a flexible and dynamic manner. The Court early recognized that a "principle to be vital must be capable of wider application than the mischief which gave it birth." Thus the Clause forbidding "cruel and unusual" punishments "is not fastened to the obsolete but may acquire meaning as public opinion becomes enlightened by a humane justice." . . .

It is clear from the foregoing precedents that the Eighth Amendment has not been regarded as a static concept. As Mr. Chief Justice Warren said, in an oftquoted phrase, "[t]he Amendment must draw its meaning from the evolving standards of decency that mark the progress of a maturing society." Thus, as assessment of contemporary values concerning the infliction of a challenged sanction is relevant to the application of the Eighth Amendment. As we develop below more fully, this assessment does not call for a subjective judgment. It requires, rather, that we look to objective indicia that reflect the public attitude toward a given sanction.

But our cases also make clear that public perceptions of standards of decency with respect to criminal sanctions are not conclusive. A penalty also must accord with "the dignity of man," which is the "basic concept underlying the Eighth Amendment." This means, at least, that the punishment not be "excessive." When a form of punishment in the abstract (in this case, whether capital punishment may ever be imposed as a sanction for murder) rather than in the particular (the propriety of death as a penalty to be applied to a specific defendent for a specific crime) is under consideration, the inquiry into "excessiveness" has two aspects. First, the punishment must not involve the unnecessary and wanton infliction of pain. Second, the punishment must not be grossly out of proportion to the severity of the crime.

B

Of course, the requirements of the Eighth Amendment must be applied with an awareness of the limited role to be played by the courts. This does not mean that judges have no role to play, for the Eighth Amendment is a restraint upon the exercise of legislative power. . . .

But, while we have an obligation to insure that constitutional bounds are not overreached, we may not act as judges as we might as legislators. . . .

Therefore, in assessing a punishment selected by a democratically elected legislature against the constitutional measure, we presume its validity. We may not require the legislature to select the least severe penalty possible so long as the penalty selected is not cruelly inhumane or disproportionate to the crime involved. And a heavy burden rests on those who would attack the judgment of the representatives of the people.

This is true in part because the constitutional test is intertwined with an assessment of contemporary standards and the legislative judgment weighs heavily in ascertaining such standards. "[I]n a democratic society legislatures, not courts, are constituted to respond to the will and consequently the moral values of the people."

The deference we owe to the decisions of the state legislatures under our federal system is enhanced where the specification of punishments is concerned, for "these are peculiarly questions of legislative policy." Caution is necessary lest this Court become, "under the aegis of the Cruel and Unusual Punishment Clause, the ultimate arbiter of the standards of criminal responsibility . . . throughout the country." A decision that a given punishment is impermissible under the Eighth Amendment cannot be reversed short of a constitutional amendment. The ability of the people to express their preference through the normal democratic processes, as well as through ballot referenda, is shut off. Revisions cannot be made in the light of further experience.

C

In the discussion to this point we have sought to identify the principles and considerations that guide a court in addressing an Eighth Amendment claim. We now consider specifically whether the sentence of death for the crime of murder is a *per se* violation of the Eighth and Fourteenth Amendments to the Constitution. We note first that history and precedent strongly support a negative answer to this question.

The imposition of the death penalty for the crime of murder has a long history of acceptance both in the United States and in England. . . .

It is apparent from the text of the Constitution itself that the existence of capital punishment was accepted by the Framers. At the time the Eighth Amendment was ratified, capital punishment was a common sanction in every State. Indeed, the First Congress of the United States enacted legislation providing death as the penalty for specified crimes. . . .

For nearly two centuries, this Court, repeatedly and often expressly, has recognized that capital punishment is not invalid *per se*. . . .

Four years ago, the petitioners in *Furman* and its companion cases predicated their argument primarily upon the asserted proposition that standards of decency had evolved to the point where capital punishment no longer could be tolerated. The petitioners in those cases said, in effect, that the evolutionary process had come to an end, and that standards of decency required that the Eighth Amendment be construed finally as prohibiting capital punishment for any crime regardless of its depravity and impact on society. This view was accepted by two Justices. Three other Justices were unwilling to go so far; focusing on the procedures by which convicted defendants were selected for the death penalty rather than on the actual punishment inflicted, they joined in the conclusion that the statutes before the Court were constitutionally invalid.

The petitioners in the capital cases before the Court today renew the "standards of decency" argument, but developments during the four years since *Furman* have undercut substantially the assumptions upon which their argument rested. Despite the continuing debate, dating back to the 19th century, over the morality and utility of capital punishment, it is now evident that a large proportion of American society continues to regard it as an appropriate and necessary criminal sanction.

The most marked indication of society's endorsement of the death penalty for murder is the legislative response to *Furman*. The legislatures of at least 35 States have enacted new statutes that provide for the death penalty for at least some crimes that result in the death of another person. And the Congress of the United States, in 1974, enacted a statute providing the death penalty for aircraft piracy that results in death. These recently adopted statutes have attempted to address the concerns expressed by the Court in *Furman* primarily (i) by specifying the factors to be weighed and the procedures to be followed in deciding when to impose a capital sentence, or (ii) by making the death penalty mandatory for specified crimes. But all of the post-*Furman* statutes make clear that capital punishment itself has not been rejected by the elected representatives of the people. . . .

The jury also is a significant and reliable objective index of contemporary values because it is so directly involved. The Court has said that "one of the most important functions any jury can perform in making . . . a selection [between life imprisonment and death for a defendant convicted in a capital case] is to maintain a link between contemporary community values and the penal system." It may be true that evolving standards have influenced juries in recent decades to be more discriminating in imposing the sentence of death. But the relative infrequency of jury verdicts imposing the death sentence does not indicate rejection of capital punishment *per se*. Rather, the reluctance of juries in many cases to impose the sentence may well reflect the humane feeling that this most irrevocable of sanctions should be reversed for a small number of extreme cases. Indeed, the actions of juries in many States since *Furman* are fully compatible with the legislative judgments, reflected in the new statutes, as to the continued utility and necessity of capital punishment in appropriate cases. At the close of 1974 at least 254 persons had been sentenced to death since *Furman,* and by the end of March 1976, more than 460 persons were subject to death sentences.

As we have seen, however, the Eighth Amendment demands more than that a challenged punishment be acceptable to contemporary society. The Court also must ask whether it comports with the basic concept of human dignity at the core of the Amendment. Although we cannot "invalidate a category of penalties because we deem less severe penalties adequate to serve the ends of penology," the sanction imposed cannot be so totally without penological justification that it results in the gratuitous infliction of suffering.

The death penalty is said to serve two principal social purposes: retribution and deterrence of capital crimes by prospective offenders.[1]

In part, capital punishment is an expression of society's moral outrage at particularly offensive conduct. This function may be unappealing to many, but it is essential in an ordered society that asks its citizens to rely on legal processes rather than self-help to vindicate their wrongs.

> The instinct of retribution is part of the nature of man, and channeling that instinct in the administration of criminal justice serves an important purpose in promoting the stability of a society governed by law. When people begin to believe that organized society is unwilling or unable to impose upon criminal offenders the punishment they "deserve," then there are sown the seeds of anarchy—of self-help, vigilante justice, and lynch law. *Furman v. Georgia* (Stewart, J., concurring).

"Retribution is no longer the dominant objective of the criminal law," but neither is it a forbidden objective nor one inconsistent with our respect for the dignity of men. Indeed, the decision that capital punishment may be the appropriate sanction in extreme cases is an expression of the community's belief that certain crimes are themselves so grievous an affront to humanity that the only adequate response may be the penalty of death.

---

[1] Another purpose that has been discussed is the incapacitation of dangerous criminals and the consequent prevention of crimes that they may otherwise commit in the future.

Statistical attempts to evaluate the worth of the death penalty as a deterrent to crimes by potential offenders have occasioned a great deal of debate. The results simply have been inconclusive. . . .

Although some of the studies suggest that the death penalty may not function as a significantly greater deterrent than lesser penalties, there is no convincing empirical evidence either supporting or refuting this view. We may nevertheless assume safely that there are murderers, such as those who act in passion, for whom the threat of death has little or no deterrent effect. But for many others, the death penalty undoubtedly is a significant deterrent. There are carefully contemplated murders, such as murder for hire, where the possible penalty of death may well enter into the cold calculus that precedes the decision to act. And there are some categories of murder, such as murder by a life prisoner, where other sanctions may not be adequate.

The value of capital punishment as a deterrent of crime is a complex factual issue the resolution of which properly rests with the legislatures, which can evaluate the results of statistical studies in terms of their own local conditions and with a flexibility of approach that is not available to the courts. Indeed, many of the post-*Furman* statutes reflect just such a responsible effort to define those crimes and those criminals for which capital punishment is most probably an effective deterrent.

In sum, we cannot say that the judgment of the Georgia Legislature that capital punishment may be necessary in some cases is clearly wrong. Considerations of federalism, as well as respect for the ability of a legislature to evaluate, in terms of its particular State, the moral consensus concerning the death penalty and its social utility as a sanction, require us to conclude, in the absence of more convincing evidence, that the infliction of death as a punishment for murder is not without justification and thus is not unconstitutionally severe.

Finally, we must consider whether the punishment of death is disproportionate in relation to the crime for which it is imposed. There is no question that death as a punishment is unique in its severity and irrevocability. When a defendant's life is at stake, the Court has been particularly sensitive to insure that every safeguard is observed. But we are concerned here only with the imposition of capital punishment for the crime of murder, and when a life has been taken deliberately by the offender,[2] we cannot say that the punishment is invariably disproportionate to the crime. It is an extreme sanction, suitable to the most extreme of crimes.

We hold that the death penalty is not a form of punishment that may never be imposed, regardless of the circumstances of the offense, regardless of the character of the offender, and regardless of the procedure followed in reaching the decision to impose it.

---

[2]We do not address here the question whether the taking of the criminal's life is a proportionate sanction where no victim has been deprived of life—for example, when capital punishment is imposed for rape, kidnaping, or armed robbery that does not result in the death of any human being.

IV

We now consider whether Georgia may impose the death penalty on the petitioner in this case.

A

While *Furman* did not hold that the infliction of the death penalty *per se* violates the Constitution's ban on cruel and unusual punishments, it did recognize that the penalty of death is different in kind from any other punishment imposed under our system of criminal justice. Because of the uniqueness of the death penalty, *Furman* held that it could not be imposed under sentencing procedures that created a substantial risk that it would be inflicted in an arbitrary and capricious manner. . . .

Furman mandates that where discretion is afforded a sentencing body on a matter so grave as the determination of whether a human life should be taken or spared, that discretion must be suitably directed and limited so as to minimize the risk of wholly arbitrary and capricious action.

It is certainly not a novel proposition that discretion in the area of sentencing be exercised in an informed manner. We have long recognized that "[f]or the determination of sentences, justice generally requires . . . that there be taken into account the circumstances of the offense together with the character and propensities of the offender." . . .

Jury sentencing has been considered desirable in capital cases in order "to maintain a link between contemporary community values and the penal system—a link without which the determination of punishment could hardly reflect 'the evolving standards of decency that mark the progress of a maturing society.' " But it creates special problems. Much of the information that is relevant to the sentencing decision may have no relevance to the question of guilt, or may even be extremely prejudicial to a fair determination of that question. This problem, however, is scarcely insurmountable. Those who have studied the question suggest that a bifurcated procedure—one in which the question of sentence is not considered until the determination of guilt has been made—is the best answer. . . . When a human life is at stake and when the jury must have information prejudicial to the question of guilt but relevant to the question of penalty in order to impose a rational sentence, a bifurcated system is more likely to ensure elimination of the constitutional deficiencies identified in *Furman*.

But the provision of relevant information under fair procedural rules is not alone sufficient to guarantee that the information will be properly used in the imposition of punishment, especially if sentencing is performed by a jury. Since the members of a jury will have had little, if any, previous experience in sentencing, they are unlikely to be skilled in dealing with the information they are given. To the extent that this problem is inherent in jury sentencing, it may not be totally correctible. It seems clear, however, that the problem will be alleviated if the jury is given guidance regarding the factors about the crime and the defendant that the State, representing organized society, deems particularly relevant to the sentencing decision. . . .

While some have suggested that standards to guide a capital jury's sentencing deliberations are impossible to formulate, the fact is that such standards have been developed. When the drafters of the Model Penal Code faced this problem, they concluded "that it is within the realm of possibility to point to the main circumstances of aggravation and of mitigation that should be weighed *and weighed against each other* when they are presented in a concrete case."[3] While such standards are by necessity somewhat general, they do provide guidance to the sentencing authority and thereby reduce the likelihood that it will impose a sentence that fairly can be called capricious or arbitrary. Where the sentencing authority is required to specify the factors it relied upon in reaching its decision, the further safeguard of meaningful appellate review is available to ensure that death sentences are not imposed capriciously or in a freakish manner.

In summary, the concerns expressed in *Furman* that the penalty of death not be imposed in an arbitrary or capricious manner can be met by a carefully drafted statute that ensures that the sentencing authority is given adequate information and guidance. As a general proposition these concerns are best met by a system that provides for a bifurcated proceeding at which the sentencing authority is apprised of the information relevant to the imposition of sentence and provided with standards to guide its use of the information.

We do not intend to suggest that only the above-described procedures would be permissible under *Furman* or that any sentencing system constructed along these

---

[3]The Model Penal Code proposes the following standards: "(3) Aggravating Circumstances.

"(a) The murder was committed by a convict under sentence of imprisonment.

"(b) The defendant was previously convicted of another murder or of a felony involving the use or threat of violence to the person.

"(c) At the time the murder was committed the defendant also committed another murder.

"(d) The defendant knowingly created a great risk of death to many persons.

"(e) The murder was committed while the defendant was engaged or was an accomplice in the commission of, or an attempt to commit, or flight after committing or attempting to commit robbery, rape or deviate sexual intercourse by force or threat of force, arson, burglary or kidnapping.

"(f) The murder was committed for the purpose of avoiding or preventing a lawful arrest or effecting an escape from lawful custody.

"(g) The murder was committed for pecuniary gain.

"(h) The murder was especially heinous, atrocious or cruel, manifesting exceptional depravity.

"(4) Mitigating Circumstances.

"(a) The defendant has no significant history of prior criminal activity.

"(b) The murder was committed while the defendant was under the influence of extreme mental or emotional disturbance.

"(c) The victim was a participant in the defendant's homicidal conduct or consented to the homicidal act.

"(d) The murder was committed under circumstances which the defendant believed to provide a moral justification or extenuation for his conduct.

"(e) The defendant was an accomplice in a murder committed by another person and his participation in the homicidal act was relatively minor.

"(f) The defendant acted under duress or under the domination of another person.

"(g) At the time of the murder, the capacity of the defendant to appreciate the criminality [wrongfulness] of his conduct or to conform his conduct to the requirements of law was impaired as a result of mental disease or defect or intoxication.

"(h) The youth of the defendant at the time of the crime." ALI Model Penal Code § 210.6 (Proposed Official Draft 1962).

general lines would inevitably satisfy the concerns of *Furman,* for each distinct system must be examined on an individual basis. Rather, we have embarked upon this general exposition to make clear that it is possible to construct capital-sentencing systems capable of meeting *Furman's* constitutional concerns.

B

We now turn to consideration of the constitutionality of Georgia's capital-sentencing procedures. In the wake of *Furman,* Georgia amended its capital punishment statute, but chose not to narrow the scope of its murder provisions. Thus, now as before *Furman,* in Georgia "[a] person commits murder when he unlawfully and with malice aforethought, either express or implied, causes the death of another human being." All persons convicted of murder "shall be punished by death or by imprisonment for life."

Georgia did act, however, to narrow the class of murderers subject to capital punishment by specifying 10 statutory aggravating circumstances, one of which must be found by the jury to exist beyond a reasonable doubt before a death sentence can ever be imposed. In addition, the jury is authorized to consider any other appropriate aggravating or mitigating circumstances. The jury is not required to find any mitigating circumstance in order to make a recommendation of mercy that is binding on the trial court, but it must find a *statutory* aggravating circumstance before recommending a sentence of death.

These procedures require the jury to consider the circumstances of the crime and the criminal before it recommends sentence. No longer can a Georgia jury do as Furman's jury did: reach a finding of the defendant's guilt and then, without guidance or direction, decide whether he should live or die. Instead, the jury's attention is directed to the specific circumstances of the crime: Was it committed in the course of another capital felony? Was it committed for money? Was it committed upon a peace officer or judicial officer? Was it committed in a particularly heinous way or in a manner that endangered the lives of many persons? In addition, the jury's attention is focused on the characteristics of the person who committed the crime: Does he have a record of prior convictions for capital offenses? Are there any special facts about this defendant that mitigate against imposing capital punishment (*e.g.,* his youth, the extent of his cooperation with the police, his emotional state at the time of the crime). As a result, while some jury discretion still exists, "the discretion to be exercised is controlled by clear and objective standards so as to produce non-discriminatory application."

As an important additional safeguard against arbitrariness and caprice, the Georgia statutory scheme provides for automatic appeal of all death sentences to the State's Supreme Court. That court is required by statute to review each sentence of death and determine whether it was imposed under the influence of passion or prejudice, whether the evidence supports the jury's finding of a statutory aggravating circumstance, and whether the sentence is disproportionate compared to those sentences imposed in similar cases.

In short, Georgia's new sentencing procedures require as a prerequisite to the imposition of the death penalty, specific jury findings as to the circumstances of the crime or the character of the defendant. Moreover, to guard further against a situation comparable to that presented in *Furman,* the Supreme Court of Georgia compares each death sentence with the sentences imposed on similarly situated defendants to ensure that the sentence of death in a particular case is not disproportionate. On their face these procedures seem to satisfy the concerns of *Furman.* No longer should there be "no meaningful basis for distinguishing the few cases in which [the death penalty] is imposed from the many cases in which it is not." . . .

V

The basic concern of *Furman* centered on those defendants who were being condemned to death capriciously and arbitrarily. Under the procedures before the Court in that case, sentencing authorities were not directed to give attention to the nature or circumstances of the crime committed or to the character or record of the defendant. Left unguided, juries imposed the death sentence in a way that could only be called freakish. The new Georgia sentencing procedures, by contrast, focus the jury's attention on the particularized nature of the crime and the particularized characteristics of the individual defendant. While the jury is permitted to consider any aggravating or mitigating circumstances, it must find and identify at least one statutory aggravating factor before it may impose a penalty of death. In this way the jury's discretion is channeled. No longer can a jury wantonly and freakishly impose the death sentence; it is always circumscribed by the legislative guidelines. In addition, the review function of the Supreme Court of Georgia affords additional assurance that the concerns that prompted our decision in *Furman* are not present to any significant degree in the Georgia procedure applied here.

For the reasons expressed in this opinion, we hold that the statutory system under which Gregg was sentenced to death does not violate the Constitution. Accordingly, the judgment of the Georgia Supreme Court is affirmed.

QUESTIONS

1 With regard to the imposition of the death penalty for the crime of murder, Justices Stewart, Powell, and Stevens write, "we cannot say that the punishment is invariably disproportionate to the crime." The Georgia statute under which Gregg was sentenced, however, retained the death penalty not only for the crime of murder but also for "kidnaping for ransom or where the victim is harmed, armed robbery, rape, treason, and aircraft hijacking." In your view, is the death penalty a disproportionate punishment for such crimes?

2 In footnote 3, we find a set of proposed model standards for the guidance of a jury in deciding whether a murderer warrants the death penalty or some lesser penalty, typically life imprisonment. Is the proposed set of aggravating circumstances (those whose presence should incline a jury toward the death penalty) defensible and complete? Is the proposed set of mitigating circumstances (those whose presence should incline a jury away from the death penalty) defensible and complete?

Dissenting Opinion in *Gregg V. Georgia*

Justice Thurgood Marshall

Thurgood Marshall, associate justice of the United States Supreme Court, is the first black ever to be appointed to the Supreme Court. Much of his distinguished private career was given over to providing legal counsel for groups dedicated to the advancement of civil rights. Justice Marshall also served as United States circuit judge (1961–1965) and United States solicitor general (1965–1967), before his appointment in 1967 to the Supreme Court.

Justice Marshall reaffirms the conclusion he had reached in *Furman v. Georgia* (1972): The death penalty is unconstitutional for two individually sufficient reasons. (1) It is excessive. (2) The American people, if fully informed, would consider it morally unacceptable. He insists that his conclusion in *Furman* has not been undercut by subsequent developments. Despite the fact that legislative activity since *Furman* would seem to indicate that the American people do not consider the death penalty morally unacceptable, Justice Marshall continues to maintain that the citizenry, *if fully informed,* would consider it morally unacceptable. At any rate, he maintains, the death penalty is unconstitutional because it is excessive, i.e., unnecessary to accomplish a legitimate legislative purpose. Neither deterrence nor retribution, the principal purposes asserted by Justices Stewart, Powell, and Stevens, can sustain the death penalty as nonexcessive in Justice Marshall's view. Since the available evidence does not show the death penalty to be a more effective deterrent than life imprisonment, he contends, the death penalty is not necessary to promote the goal of deterrence. Moreover, the death penalty is unnecessary to "further any legitimate notion of retribution." According to Justice Marshall, the notion that a murderer "deserves" death constitutes a denial of the wrongdoer's dignity and worth and thus is fundamentally at odds with the Eighth Amendment.

In *Furman v. Georgia* (1972) (concurring opinion), I set forth at some length my views on the basic issue presented to the Court in [this case]. The death penalty, I concluded, is a cruel and unusual punishment prohibited by the Eighth and Fourteenth Amendments. That continues to be my view.

I have no intention of retracing the "long and tedious journey" that led to my conclusion in *Furman*. My sole purposes here are to consider the suggestion that my conclusion in *Furman* has been undercut by developments since then, and briefly to evaluate the basis for my Brethren's holding that the extinction of life is a permissible form of punishment under the Cruel and Unusual Punishments Clause.

In *Furman* I concluded that the death penalty is constitutionally invalid for two reasons. First, the death penalty is excessive. And second, the American people, fully informed as to the purposes of the death penalty and its liabilities, would in my view reject it as morally unacceptable.

United States Supreme Court. 428 U.S. 153 (1976).

Since the decision in *Furman,* the legislatures of 35 States have enacted new statutes authorizing the imposition of the death sentence for certain crimes, and Congress has enacted a law providing the death penalty for air piracy resulting in death. I would be less than candid if I did not acknowledge that these developments have a significant bearing on a realistic assessment of the moral acceptability of the death penalty to the American people. But if the constitutionality of the death penalty turns, as I have urged, on the opinion of an *informed* citizenry, then even the enactment of new death statutes cannot be viewed as conclusive. In *Furman,* I observed that the American people are largely unaware of the information critical to a judgment on the morality of the death penalty, and concluded that if they were better informed they would consider it shocking, unjust, and unacceptable. A recent study, conducted after the enactment of the post-*Furman* statutes, has confirmed that the American people know little about the death penalty, and that the opinions of an informed public would differ significantly from those of a public unaware of the consequences and effects of the death penalty.

Even assuming, however, that the post-*Furman* enactment of statutes authorizing the death penalty renders the prediction of the views of an informed citizenry an uncertain basis for a constitutional decision, the enactment of those statutes has no bearing whatsoever on the conclusion that the death penalty is unconstitutional because it is excessive. An excessive penalty is invalid under the Cruel and Unusual Punishments Clause "even though popular sentiment may favor" it. The inquiry here, then, is simply whether the death penalty is necessary to accomplish the legitimate legislative purposes in punishment, or whether a less severe penalty—life imprisonment—would do as well.

The two purposes that sustain the death penalty as nonexcessive in the Court's view are general deterrence and retribution. In *Furman,* I canvassed the relevant data on the deterrent effect of capital punishment. The state of knowledge at that point, after literally centuries of debate, was summarized as follows by a United Nations Committee:

> "It is generally agreed between the retentionists and abolitionists, whatever their opinions about the validity of comparative studies of deterrence, that the data which now exist show no correlation between the existence of capital punishment and lower rates of capital crime."

The available evidence, I concluded in *Furman,* was convincing that "capital punishment is not necessary as a deterrent to crime in our society." . . .

. . . The evidence I reviewed in *Furman* remains convincing, in my view, that "capital punishment is not necessary as a deterrent to crime in our society." The justification for the death penalty must be found elsewhere.

The other principal purpose said to be served by the death penalty is retribution. The notion that retribution can serve as a moral justification for the sanction of death finds credence in the opinion of my Brothers STEWART, POWELL, and STEVENS. . . . It is this notion that I find to be the most disturbing aspect of today's unfortunate [decision].

The concept of retribution is a multifaceted one, and any discussion of its role in the criminal law must be undertaken with caution. On one level, it can be said that the notion of retribution or reprobation is the basis of our insistence that only those who have broken the law be punished, and in this sense the notion is quite obviously central to a just system of criminal sanctions. But our recognition that retribution plays a crucial role in determining who may be punished by no means requires approval of retribution as a general justification for punishment. It is the question whether retribution can provide a moral justification for punishment—in particular, capital punishment—that we must consider.

My Brothers STEWART, POWELL, and STEVENS offer the following explanation of the retributive justification for capital punishment:

> The instinct for retribution is part of the nature of man, and channeling that instinct in the administration of criminal justice serves an important purpose in promoting the stability of a society governed by law. When people begin to believe that organized society is unwilling or unable to impose upon criminal offenders the punishment they "deserve," then there are sown the seeds of anarchy—of self-help, vigilante justice, and lynch law.

This statement is wholly inadequate to justify the death penalty. As my Brother BRENNAN stated in *Furman,* "[t]here is no evidence whatever that utilization of imprisonment rather than death encourages private blood feuds and other disorders." It simply defies belief to suggest that the death penalty is necessary to prevent the American people from taking the law into their own hands.

In a related vein, it may be suggested that the expression of moral outrage through the imposition of the death penalty serves to reinforce basic moral values—that it marks some crimes as particularly offensive and therefore to be avoided. The argument is akin to a deterrence argument, but differs in that it contemplates the individual's shrinking from antisocial conduct, not because he fears punishment, but because he has been told in the strongest possible way that the conduct is wrong. This contention, like the previous one, provides no support for the death penalty. It is inconceivable that any individual concerned about conforming his conduct to what society says is "right" would fail to realize that murder is "wrong" if the penalty were simply life imprisonment.

The foregoing contentions—that society's expression of moral outrage through the imposition of the death penalty pre-empts the citizenry from taking the law into its own hands and reinforces moral values—are not retributive in the purest sense. They are essentially utilitarian in that they portray the death penalty as valuable because of its beneficial results. These justifications for the death penalty are inadequate because the penalty is, quite clearly I think, not necessary to the accomplishment of those results.

There remains for consideration, however, what might be termed the purely retributive justification for the death penalty—that the death penalty is appropriate, not because of its beneficial effect on society, but because the taking of the murderer's life is itself morally good. Some of the language of the opinion of my Brothers STEWART, POWELL, and STEVENS . . . appears positively to embrace this notion of retribution for its own sake as a justification for capital punishment. They state:

> [T]he decision that capital punishment may be the appropriate sanction in extreme cases is an expression of the community's belief that certain crimes are themselves so grievous an affront to humanity that the only adequate response may be the penalty of death.

They then quote with approval from Lord Justice Denning's remarks before the British Royal Commission on Capital Punishment:

> The truth is that some crimes are so outrageous that society insists on adequate punishment, because the wrong-doer deserves it, irrespective of whether it is a deterrent or not.

Of course, it may be that these statements are intended as no more than observations as to the popular demands that it is thought must be responded to in order to prevent anarchy. But the implication of the statements appears to me to be quite different— namely, that society's judgment that the murderer "deserves" death must be respected not simply because the preservation of order requires it, but because it is appropriate that society make the judgment and carry it out. It is this latter notion, in particular, that I consider to be fundamentally at odds with the Eighth Amendment. The mere fact that the community demands the murderer's life in return for the evil he has done cannot sustain the death penalty, for as JUSTICES STEWART, POWELL, and STEVENS remind us, "the Eighth Amendment demands more than that a challenged punishment be acceptable to contemporary society." To be sustained under the Eighth Amendment, the death penalty must "compor[t] with the basic concept of human dignity at the core of the Amendment;" the objective in imposing it must be "[consistent] with our respect for the dignity of [other] men." Under these standards, the taking of life "because the wrongdoer deserves it" surely must fail, for such a punishment has as its very basis the total denial of the wrongdoer's dignity and worth.

The death penalty, unnecessary to promote the goal of deterrence or to further any legitimate notion of retribution, is an excessive penalty forbidden by the Eighth and Fourteenth Amendments. I respectfully dissent from the Court's judgment upholding the [sentence] of death imposed upon the [petitioner in this case].

QUESTIONS

1 Is Justice Marshall correct in claiming that the American people, *if fully informed* about the death penalty, would consider it morally unacceptable?
2 Is the death penalty, as Justice Marshall claims, "unnecessary to promote the goal of deterrence or to further any legitimate notion of retribution"?

Retribution and the Limits of Capital Punishment

Burton M. Leiser

Burton M. Leiser is professor of philosophy at Pace University. He is the author of Custom, Law, and Morality *(1969) and* Liberty, Justice, and Morals *(2d ed., 1979), as well as the editor of* Values in Conflict *(1981). In addition to his work in philosophy, Leiser has published articles in the fields of biblical criticism, religion, and archaeology.*

Leiser, a retentionist, responds rather directly to Justice Marshall's contention that imposing the death penalty "because the wrongdoer deserves it" constitutes a denial of the wrongdoer's dignity and worth. Far from this being the case, Leiser contends, to impose the death penalty on grounds of retributive justice is to recognize and affirm the wrongdoer's worth and dignity as a human being who is accountable for his or her action. He proceeds to identify those crimes for which the death penalty is an appropriate punishment. According to Leiser, the death penalty is an appropriate punishment for certain kinds of murder but not for others. He also contends that the death penalty is an appropriate punishment for such serious crimes as terrorism, treason, kidnapping, and airplane hijacking.

RETRIBUTION

In his dissent in *Gregg v. Georgia,* Justice Marshall said that "it simply defies belief to suggest that the death penalty is necessary to prevent the American people from taking the law into their hands." He went on to assert that Lord Denning's contention that some crimes are so outrageous as to deserve the death penalty, regardless of its deterrent effects, is at odds with the Eighth Amendment. "The mere fact that the community demands the murderer's life for the evil he has done," he said, "cannot sustain the death penalty," for

> the Eighth Amendment demands more than that a challenged punishment be acceptable to contemporary society. To be sustained under the Eighth Amendment, the death penalty must [comport] with the basic concept of human dignity at the core of the Amendment; the objective in imposing it must be [consistent] with our respect for the dignity of [other] men. Under these standards, the taking of life "because the wrongdoer deserves it" surely must fail, for such a punishment has as its very basis the total denial of the wrongdoer's dignity and worth. The death penalty, unnecessary to promote the goal of deterrence or to further any legitimate notion of retribution, is an excessive penalty forbidden by the Eighth and Fourteenth Amendments.

But retributive justice does not deny the wrongdoer's worth and dignity. It assumes it, and makes no sense at all unless the wrongdoer is regarded as a human being capable of making his own decisions, acting upon his own volition, and deserving moral praise or blame for what he does. The death penalty is the ultimate condemnation, morally and legally, of a person who has, through his actions, demonstrated his utter contempt for human worth and dignity and for the most fundamental rules of human society. It is precisely because of a nation's belief in the dignity and worth of those who live under the protection of its laws and because of its adherence to the principle that human life is sacred that it may choose to employ the death penalty against those who have demonstrated their disregard of those principles. . . .

THE LIMITS OF CAPITAL PUNISHMENT

The death penalty has historically been employed for such diverse offenses as murder, espionage, treason, kidnapping, rape, arson, robbery, burglary, and theft. Except for the most serious crimes, it is now agreed that lesser penalties are sufficient.

The distinction between first- and second-degree murder [does] not permit fine lines to be drawn between (for example) murder for hire and the killing of a husband by his jealous wife. Most murders committed in the United States are of a domestic nature—spouses or other close relatives becoming involved in angry scenes that end in homicide. Such crimes, usually committed in the heat of a momentary passion, seem inappropriate for the supreme penalty. Although they are premeditated in the legal sense (for it takes no more than an instant for a person to form the intent that is necessary for the legal test to be satisfied), there seems to be a great difference between such crimes and those committed out of desire for personal gain or for political motives, between a crime committed in an instant of overwrought emotion and one carefully charted and planned in advance. It is reasonable, therefore, to suggest that the vast majority of murders not be regarded as capital crimes, because the penalty may be disproportionate to the crime committed and because people caught up in such momentarily overwhelming passions are not likely to be deterred by thoughts of the possible consequences of their actions.

Only the most heinous offenses against the state and against individual persons seem to deserve the ultimate penalty. If the claim that life is sacred has any meaning at all, it must be that no man may deliberately cause another to lose his life without some compelling justification.

Such a justification appears to exist when individuals or groups employ wanton violence against others in order to achieve their ends, whatever those ends might be. However appealing the cause, however noble the motives, the deliberate, systematic destruction of innocent human beings is one of the gravest crimes any person can commit and may justify the imposition of the harshest available penalty, consistent with principles of humanity, decency, and compassion. Some penalties, such as prolonged torture, may in fact be worse than death, but civilized societies reject them as being too barbarous, too brutal, and too dehumanizing to those who must carry them out.

Perpetrators of such crimes as genocide (the deliberate extermination of entire peoples, racial, religious, or ethnic groups) clearly deserve a penalty no less severe than death. Those who perpetrate major war crimes, crimes against peace, or crimes against humanity, deliberately and without justification plunging nations into violent conflicts that entail widespread bloodshed or causing needless suffering on a vast scale, deserve nothing less than the penalty of death.

Because of the reckless manner in which they endanger the lives of innocent citizens and their clear intention to take human lives on a massive scale in order to achieve their ends, terrorists should be subject to the death penalty—particularly because no other penalty is likely to serve as a deterrent to potential terrorists.

Major crimes against the peace, security, and integrity of the state constitute particularly heinous offenses, for they shake the very foundations upon which civilization rests and endanger the lives, the liberties, and the fundamental rights of all the people who depend upon the state for protection. Treason, espionage, and sabotage, particularly during times of great danger (as in time of war), ought to be punishable by death.

Murder for personal gain and murder committed in the course of the commission of a felony that is being committed for personal gain or out of a reckless disregard for the lives or fundamental rights and interests of potential victims ought to be punishable by death.

Murder committed by a person who is serving a life sentence ought to be punishable by death, both because of the enormity of the crime and because no other penalty is likely to deter such crimes.

Any murder that is committed in a particularly vile, wanton, or malicious way ought to be punishable by death.

One of the principal justifications for the state's existence is the protection it offers those who come under its jurisdiction against violations of their fundamental rights. Those who are entrusted with the responsibility for carrying out the duties of administering the state's functions, enforcing its laws, and seeing that justice is done carry an onerous burden and are particularly likely to become the targets of hostile, malicious, or rebellious individuals or groups. Their special vulnerability entitles them to special protection. Hence, any person guilty of murdering a policeman, a fireman, a judge, a governor, a president, a lawmaker, or any other person holding a comparable position while that person is carrying out his official duties or because of the office he holds has struck at the very heart of government and thus at the foundations upon which the state and civilized society depend. The gravity of such a crime warrants imposition of the death penalty.

Because the threat of death is inherent in every act of kidnapping and airplane hijacking—for without such a threat the holding of a hostage would not have the terrorizing effect the perpetrator desires in order to achieve his aim of extorting money or political concessions from those to whom his threats are delivered—those who perpetrate such crimes may appropriately be subject to capital punishment.

But those who commit homicide in a momentary fit of anger or passion, in contrast to those who carefully plan acts as well as those who commit homicide under excusing or mitigating circumstances, may either be fully excused or given some lesser penalty.

From the fact that some persons who bring about the deaths of fellow humans do so under conditions that just and humane men would consider sufficient to justify either complete exculpation or penalties less than death, it does not follow that all of them do. If guilt is clearly established beyond a reasonable doubt under circumstances that guarantee a reasonable opportunity for the defendant to confront his accusers, to cross-examine witnesses, to present his case with the assistance of professional counsel, and in general to enjoy the benefits of due process of law; if in addition he has been given the protection of laws that prevent the use of torture to extract confessions and is provided immunity against self-incrimination; if those who are authorized to pass judgment find there were no excusing or mitigating circumstances; if he is found to have committed a wanton, brutal, callous murder or some other crime that is subversive of the very foundations of an ordered society; and if, finally, the representatives of the people, exercising the people's sovereign authority, have prescribed death as the penalty for that crime; then the judge and jury are fully justified in imposing that penalty, and the proper authorities are justified in carrying it out.

QUESTIONS

1 Does the imposition of the death penalty on retributive grounds, "because the wrongdoer deserves it," constitute a denial of the wrongdoer's dignity and worth?

2 Under what conditions, if any, does murder warrant the death penalty? Are there any other crimes which warrant the death penalty?

Capital Punishment and Retributive Justice

Hugo Adam Bedau

Hugo Adam Bedau is professor of philosophy at Tufts University in Medford, Massachusetts. A past president of the American League to Abolish Capital Punishment, he has been for many years a prominent spokesperson for the abolitionist movement in the United States. He is the editor of The Death Penalty in America *(3d ed., 1982), the coeditor of* Capital Punishment in the United States *(1976), and the author of* The Courts, the Constitution, and Capital Punishment *(1977). Bedau has written extensively in the areas of social, political, and legal philosophy.*

Setting aside all considerations of social defense, Bedau argues that considerations of retributive justice do not effectively support the retention of the death penalty. After dismissing one principle of retributive justice (that crime should be punished) as neutral to the controversy over the death penalty, he focuses attention on a second principle of retributive justice (that the severity of a punishment should be proportional to the gravity of the offense). Though Bedau endorses this latter principle as an important principle of retributive justice, he contends that it need not be understood as implying the view that "the punishment of death best fits the crime of murder." Indeed, he argues, any literal-minded acceptance of the principle of retaliation (*lex talionis*, usually expressed as "a life for a life") is indefensible. In his view, not only is the abstract principle of "a life for a life" notoriously difficult to interpret and apply, it plays virtually no role in our actual system of criminal justice. At any rate, he contends, the principle of "a life for a life" will not suffice as an adequate basis for the retention of the death penalty. Bedau concludes with a discussion of the moral import of the fact that the death penalty is prone to be administered in an unfair (arbitrary or discriminatory) fashion. In the light of such administrative realities, he contends, the retention of the death penalty "does not enhance respect for human life; it cheapens and degrades it."

. . . There are two leading principles of retributive justice relevant to the capital-punishment controversy. One is the principle that crimes should be punished. The other is the principle that the severity of a punishment should be proportional to the gravity of the offense. (A corollary to the latter principle is the judgment that nothing so fits the crime of murder as the punishment of death.) Although these principles do not seem to stem from any concern over the worth, value, dignity, or rights of persons, they are moral principles of recognized weight and no discussion of the morality of capital punishment would be complete without them. Leaving aside all questions of social defense, how strong a case for capital punishment can be made on the basis of these principles? How reliable and persuasive are these principles themselves?

CRIME MUST BE PUNISHED

Given [a general rationale for punishment], there cannot be any dispute over this principle. In embracing it, of course, we are not automatically making a fetish of "law and order," in the sense that we would be if we thought that the most important single thing society can do with its resources is to punish crimes. In addition, this principle is not likely to be in dispute between proponents and opponents of the death penalty. Only those who completely oppose punishment for murder and other erstwhile capital crimes would appear to disregard this principle. Even defenders of the death penalty must admit that putting a convicted murderer in prison for years is a punishment of that criminal. The principle that crime must be punished is neutral to our controversy, because both sides acknowledge it and comply with it.

It is the other principle of retributive justice that seems to be a decisive one. Under the principle of retaliation, *lex talionis,* it must always have seemed that murderers ought to be put to death. Proponents of the death penalty, with rare exceptions, have insisted on this point, and it seems that even opponents of the death penalty must give it grudging assent. The strategy for opponents of the death penalty is to show either (a) that this principle is not really a principle of justice after all, or (b) that although it is, other principles outweigh or cancel its dictates. As we shall see, both these objections have merit.

IS MURDER ALONE TO BE PUNISHED BY DEATH?

Let us recall, first, that not even the Biblical world limited the death penalty to the punishment of murder. Many other nonhomicidal crimes also carried this penalty (e.g., kidnapping, witchcraft, cursing one's parents). In our own recent history, persons have been executed for aggravated assault, rape, kidnapping, armed robbery, sabotage, and espionage. It is not possible to defend any of these executions (not to mention some of the more bizarre capital statutes, like the one in Georgia that used to provide an optional death penalty for desecration of a grave) on grounds of just retribution. This entails that either such executions are not justified or that they are justified on some ground other than retribution. In actual practice, few if any defenders of the death penalty have ever been willing to rest their case entirely on the moral principle of just retribution as formulated in terms of "a life for a life." Kant seems to have been a conspicuous exception. Most defenders of the death penalty have implied by their willingness to use executions to defend limb and property, as well as life, that they did not place much value on the lives of criminals when compared to the value of both lives and things belonging to innocent citizens.

ARE ALL MURDERS TO BE PUNISHED BY DEATH?

Our society for several centuries has endeavored to confine the death penalty to some criminal homicides. Even Kant took a casual attitude toward a mother's killing of her illegitimate child. ("A child born into the world outside marriage is outside the law . . . , and consequently it is also outside the protection of the law.")[1] In our society, the development nearly 200 years ago of the distinction between first- and second-degree murder was an attempt to narrow the class of criminal homicides deserving of the death penalty. Yet those dead owing to manslaughter, or to any kind of unintentional, accidental, unpremeditated, unavoidable, unmalicious killing are just as dead as the victims of the most ghastly murder. Both the law in practice and moral reflection show how difficult it is to identify all and only the criminal homicides that are appropriately punished by death (assuming that any are). Individual judges and juries differ in the conclusions they reach. The history of capital punishment for homicides reveals continual efforts, uniformly unsuccessful, to identify before the fact those homicides for which the slayer should die. Benjamin Cardozo, a justice of the United States Supreme Court fifty years ago, said of the distinction between degrees of murder that it was

> . . . so obscure that no jury hearing it for the first time can fairly be expected to assimilate and understand it. I am not at all sure that I understand it myself after trying to apply it for many years and after diligent study of what has been written in the books. Upon the basis of this fine distinction with its obscure and mystifying psychology, scores of men have gone to their death.[2]

Similar skepticism has been registered on the reliability and rationality of death-penalty statutes that give the trial court the discretion to sentence to prison or to death. As Justice John Marshall Harlan of the Supreme Court observed a decade ago,

> Those who have come to grips with the hard task of actually attempting to draft means of channeling capital sentencing discretion have confirmed the lesson taught by history. . . . To identify before the fact those characteristics of criminal homicide and their perpetrators which call for the death penalty, and to express these characteristics in language which can be fairly understood and applied by the sentencing authority, appear to be tasks which are beyond present human ability.[3]

The abstract principle that the punishment of death best fits the crime of murder turns out to be extremely difficult to interpret and apply.

---

[1]Immanuel Kant, *The Metaphysical Elements of Justice* (1797), tr. John Ladd, p. 106.
[2]Benjamin Cardozo, "What Medicine Can Do for Law" (1928), reprinted in Margaret E. Hall, ed., *Selected Writings of Benjamin Nathan Cardozo* (1947), p. 204.
[3]*McGautha v. California*, 402 U.S. 183 (1971), at p. 204.

If we look at the matter from the standpoint of the actual practice of criminal justice, we can only conclude that "a life for a life" plays little or no role whatever. Plea bargaining (by means of which one of the persons involved in a crime agrees to accept a lesser sentence in exchange for testifying against the others to enable the prosecutor to get them all convicted), even where murder is concerned, is widespread. Studies of criminal justice reveal that what the courts (trial or appellate) decide on a given day is first-degree murder suitably punished by death in a given jurisdiction could just as well be decided in a neighboring jurisdiction on another day either as second-degree murder or as first-degree murder but without the death penalty. The factors that influence prosecutors in determining the charge under which they will prose-cute go far beyond the simple principle of "a life for a life." Nor can it be objected that these facts show that our society does not care about justice. To put it suc-cinctly, either justice in punishment does not consist of retribution, because there are other principles of justice; or there are other moral considerations besides justice that must be honored; or retributive justice is not adequately expressed in the idea of "a life for a life."

IS DEATH SUFFICIENTLY RETRIBUTIVE?

Given the reality of horrible and vicious crimes, one must consider whether there is not a quality of unthinking arbitrariness in advocating capital punishment for murder as the retributively just punishment. Why does death in the electric chair or the gas chamber or before a firing squad or on a gallows meet the requirements of retributive justice? When one thinks of the savage, brutal, wanton character of so many murders, how can retributive justice be served by anything less than equally savage methods of execution for the murderer? From a retributive point of view, the oft-heard exclamation, "Death is too good for him!" has a certain truth. Yet few defenders of the death penalty are willing to embrace this consequence of their own doctrine.

The reason they do not and should not is that, if they did, they would be stooping to the methods and thus to the squalor of the murderer. Where criminals set the limits of just methods of punishment, as they will do if we attempt to give exact and literal implementation to *lex talionis,* society will find itself descending to the cruelties and savagery that criminals employ. But society would be deliberately authorizing such acts, in the cool light of reason, and not (as is often true of vicious criminals) im-pulsively or in hatred and anger or with an insane or unbalanced mind. Moral restraints, in short, prohibit us from trying to make executions perfectly retributive. Once we grant the role of these restraints, the principle of "a life for a life" itself has been qualified and no longer suffices to justify the execution of murderers.

Other considerations take us in a different direction. Few murders, outside television and movie scripts, involve anything like an execution. An execution, after all, begins with a solemn pronouncement of the death sentence from a judge, is followed by long detention in maximum security awaiting the date of execution, various appeals, perhaps a final sanity hearing, and then "the last mile" to the execution chamber itself. As the French writer Albert Camus remarked,

For there to be an equivalence, the death penalty would have to punish a criminal who had warned his victim of the date at which he would inflict a horrible death on him and who, from that moment onward, had confined him at his mercy for months. Such a monster is not encountered in private life.[4]

DIFFERENTIAL SEVERITY DOES NOT REQUIRE EXECUTIONS

What, then, emerges from our examination of retributive justice and the death penalty? If retributive justice is thought to consist in *lex talionis,* all one can say is that this principle has never exercised more than a crude and indirect effect on the actual punishments meted out. Other principles interfere with a literal and single-minded application of this one. Some murders seem improperly punished by death at all; other murders would require methods of execution too horrible to inflict; in still other cases any possible execution is too deliberate and monstrous given the nature of the motivation culminating in the murder. Proponents of the death penalty rarely confine themselves to reliance on this principle of just retribution and nothing else, since they rarely confine themselves to supporting the death penalty only for all murders.

But retributive justice need not be thought to consist of *lex talionis.* One may reject that principle as too crude and still embrace the retributive principle that the severity of punishments should be graded according to the gravity of the offense. Even though one need not claim that life imprisonment (or any kind of punishment other than death) "fits" the crime of murder, one can claim that this punishment is the proper one for murder. To do this, the schedule of punishments accepted by society must be arranged so that this mode of imprisonment is the most severe penalty used. Opponents of the death penalty need not reject this principle of retributive justice, even though they must reject a literal *lex talionis.*

EQUAL JUSTICE AND CAPITAL PUNISHMENT

During the past generation, the strongest practical objection to the death penalty has been the inequities with which it has been applied. As Supreme Court Justice William O. Douglas once observed, "One searches our chronicles in vain for the execution of any member of the affluent strata of this society."[5] One does not search our chronicles in vain for the crime of murder committed by the affluent. Every study of the death penalty for rape has confirmed that black male rapists (especially where the victim is a white female) are far more likely to be sentenced to death (and executed) than white male rapists. Half of all those under death sentence during 1976 and 1977 were black, and nearly half of all those executed since 1930 were black. All the sociological evidence points to the conclusion that the death penalty is the poor man's justice; as the current street saying has it, "Those without the capital get the punishment."

Let us suppose that the factual basis for such a criticism is sound. What follows

---

[4]Albert Camus, *Resistance, Rebellion, and Death* (1961), p. 199.
[5]*Furman v. Georgia,* 408 U.S. 238 (1972), at pp. 251–252.

for the morality of capital punishment? Many defenders of the death penalty have been quick to point out that since there is nothing intrinsic about the crime of murder or rape that dictates that only the poor or racial-minority males will commit it, and since there is nothing overtly racist about the statutes that authorize the death penalty for murder or rape, it is hardly a fault in the idea of capital punishment if in practice it falls with unfair impact on the poor and the black. There is, in short, nothing in the death penalty that requires it to be applied unfairly and with arbitrary or discriminatory results. It is at worst a fault in the system of administering criminal justice (and some, who dispute the facts cited above, would deny even this).

Presumably, both proponents and opponents of capital punishment would concede that it is a fundamental dictate of justice that a punishment should not be unfairly—inequitably or unevenly—enforced and applied. They should also be able to agree that when the punishment in question is the extremely severe one of death, then the requirement to be fair in using such a punishment becomes even more stringent. Thus, there should be no dispute in the death penalty controversy over these principles of justice. The dispute begins as soon as one attempts to connect these principles with the actual use of this punishment.

In this country, many critics of the death penalty have argued, we would long ago have got rid of it entirely if it had been a condition of its use that it be applied equally and fairly. In the words of the attorneys who argued against the death penalty in the Supreme Court during 1972, "It is a freakish aberration, a random extreme act of violence, visibly arbitrary and discriminatory—a penalty reserved for unusual application because, if it were usually used, it would affront univerally shared standards of public decency."[6] It is difficult to dispute this judgment, when one considers that there have been in the United States during the past fifty years about half a million criminal homicides but only about 4,000 executions (all but 50 of which were of men).

We can look at these statistics in another way to illustrate the same point. If we could be assured that the 4,000 persons executed were the worst of the worst, repeated offenders without exception, the most dangerous murderers in captivity—the ones who had killed more than once and were likely to kill again, and the least likely to be confined in prison without imminent danger to other inmates and the staff—then one might accept half a million murders and a few thousand executions with a sense that rough justice had been done. But the truth is otherwise. Persons are sentenced to death and executed not because they have been found to be uncontrollably violent, hopelessly poor parole and release risks, or for other reasons. Instead, they are executed for entirely different reasons. They have a poor defense at trial; they have no funds to bring sympathetic witnesses to court; they are immigrants or strangers in the community where they were tried; the prosecuting attorney wants the publicity that goes with "sending a killer to the chair"; they have inexperienced or overworked counsel at trial; there are no funds for an appeal or for a transcript of the trial record; they are members

---

[6]NAACP Legal Defense and Educational Fund, Brief for Petitioner in *Aikens v. California*, O.T. 1971, No.68-5027, reprinted in Philip English Mackey, ed., *Voices Against Death: American Opposition to Capital Punishment*, 1787–1975 (1975), p. 288.

of a despised racial minority. In short, the actual study of why particular persons have been sentenced to death and executed does not show any careful winnowing of the worst from the bad. It shows that the executed were usually the unlucky victims of prejudice and discrimination, the losers in an arbitrary lottery that could just as well have spared them as killed them, the victims of the disadvantages that almost always go with poverty. A system like this does not enhance respect for human life; it cheapens and degrades it. However heinous murder and other crimes are, the system of capital punishment does not compensate for or erase those crimes. It only tends to add new injuries of its own to the catalogue of our inhumanity to each other.

QUESTIONS

1 To what extent, if at all, should the principle of "a life for a life" be incorporated in our system of criminal justice?

2 Does the retention of the death penalty enhance respect for human life or, as Bedau claims, does it cheapen and degrade it?

The Death Sentence

Sidney Hook

Sidney Hook is now, after some forty years of teaching philosophy at New York University, professor emeritus. Much of his philosophical work has centered on various aspects of human freedom, often as related to social, political, and legal issues. His numerous publications include Political Power and Personal Freedom *(1959),* The Paradoxes of Freedom *(1962), and* The Place of Religion in a Free Society *(1968).*

Hook supports the retention of the death penalty for employment in two diverse cases. (1) Some criminal defendants, when sentenced to life imprisonment, may in fact prefer death. Their preference should be honored. (2) Some convicted murderers, having served one prison sentence, murder again. When such twice-guilty murderers are found to be sane, and when there is a reasonable probability that they will attempt to murder again, the death penalty should be imposed. In arguing for both (1) and (2), Hook attempts to turn humanitarian considerations, usually part of the abolitionist case, against the abolitionist. To resist (1), he argues, is to treat the convicted criminal in an inhumane way. Similarly, to resist (2) involves a posture of inhumanity. Do we not care about the lives of the murderer's future victims?

Reprinted by permission of the author from "The Death Sentence," in Hugo Adam Bedau, ed., *The Death Penalty in America,* rev. ed. (Garden City, N.Y.: Doubleday, 1967).

Since I am not a fanatic or absolutist, I do not wish to go on record as being categorically opposed to the death sentence in all circumstances. I should like to recognize two exceptions. A defendant convicted of murder and sentenced to life should be permitted to choose the death sentence instead. Not so long ago a defendant sentenced to life imprisonment made this request and was rebuked by the judge for his impertinence. I can see no valid grounds for denying such a request out of hand. It may sometimes be denied, particularly if a way can be found to make the defendant labor for the benefit of the dependents of his victim as is done is some European countries. Unless such considerations are present, I do not see on what reasonable ground the request can be denied, particularly by those who believe in capital punishment. Once they argue that life imprisonment is either a more effective deterrent or more justly punitive, they have abandoned their position.

In passing, I should state that I am in favor of permitting *any* criminal defendant, sentenced to life imprisonment, the right to choose death. I can understand why certain jurists, who believe that the defendant wants thereby to cheat the state out of its mode of punishment, should be indignant at the idea. They are usually the ones who believe that even the attempt at suicide should be deemed a crime—in effect saying to the unfortunate person that if he doesn't succeed in his act of suicide, the state will punish him for it. But I am baffled to understand why the absolute abolitionist, dripping with treacly humanitarianism, should oppose this proposal. I have heard some people actually oppose capital punishment in certain cases on the ground that: "Death is too good for the vile wretch! Let him live and suffer to the end of his days." But the absolute abolitionist should be the last person in the world to oppose the wish of the lifer, who regards this form of punishment as torture worse than death, to leave our world.

My second class of exceptions consists of those who having been sentenced once to prison for premeditated murder, murder again. In these particular cases we have evidence that imprisonment is not a sufficient deterrent for the individual in question. If the evidence shows that the prisoner is so psychologically constituted that, without being insane, the fact that he can kill again with impunity may lead to further murderous behavior, the court should have the discretionary power to pass the death sentence if the criminal is found guilty of a second murder.

In saying that the death sentence should be *discretionary* in cases where a man has killed more than once, I am *not* saying that a murderer who murders again is more deserving of death than the murderer who murders once. Bluebeard was not twelve times more deserving of death when he was finally caught. I am saying simply this: that in a sub-class of murderers, i.e., those who murder several times, there may be a special group of sane murderers who, knowing that they will not be executed, will not hesitate to kill again and again. For *them* the argument from deterrence is obviously valid. Those who say that there must be no exceptions to the abolition of capital punishment cannot rule out the existence of such cases on *a priori* grounds. If they admit that there is a reasonable probability that such murderers will murder again or attempt to murder again, a probability which usually grows with the number of repeated murders, and still insist they would *never* approve of capital punishment, I would conclude that they are indifferent to the lives of the human beings doomed, on their position, to be victims. What fancies itself as a humanitarian attitude is sometimes an expression of sentimentalism. The reverse coin of sentimentalism is often cruelty.

Our charity for all human beings must not deprive us of our common sense. Nor should our charity be less for the future or potential victims of the murderer than for the murderer himself. There are crimes in this world which are, like acts of nature, beyond the power of men to anticipate or control. But not all or most crimes are of this character. So long as human beings are responsible and educable, they will respond to praise and blame and punishment. It is hard to imagine it but even Hitler and Stalin were once infants. Once you *can* imagine them as infants, however, it is hard to believe that they were already monsters in their cradles. Every confirmed criminal was once an amateur. The existence of confirmed criminals testifies to the defects of our education—where they can be reformed—and of our penology—where they cannot. That is why we are under the moral obligation to be intelligent about crime and punishment. Intelligence should teach us that the best educational and penological system is the one which prevents crimes rather than punishes them; the next best is one which punishes crime in such a way as to prevent it from happening again.

QUESTIONS

1 If you were condemned to life imprisonment, assuming no possibility of parole, would you prefer life or death?
2 With regard to his contention that a criminal sentenced to life imprisonment ought to be able to choose the death penalty instead, Hook has been accused of defending not the institution of capital punishment but a different institution, a sophisticated form of "supervised suicide." Is this a valid criticism?
3 Can the death penalty be defended, at least in some cases, solely on the grounds that it is necessary to incapacitate a dangerous convicted criminal? Or is life imprisonment sufficient to achieve this aim?

Deterrence and Uncertainty

Ernest van den Haag

Ernest van den Haag is professor of jurisprudence and public policy at Fordham University. For many years, van den Haag maintained a private practice in psychoanalysis. He is the author of such works as The Fabric of Society *(1957),* Political Violence and Civil Disobedience *(1972), and* Punishing Criminals: Concerning a Very Old and Painful Question *(1975).*

Reprinted with permission of the publisher from the *Journal of Criminal Law, Criminology and Police Science,* vol. 60, no. 2 (1969).

The retentionist argument advanced by van den Haag is based on our uncertainty concerning the deterrent effect of the death penalty (whether or not it is a uniquely effective deterrent). According to his analysis, if we retain the death penalty, we run the risk of needlessly eradicating the lives of convicted murderers; perhaps the death penalty is *not* a uniquely effective deterrent. On the other hand, if we abolish the death penalty, we run the risk of innocent people becoming future murder victims; perhaps the death penalty *is* a uniquely effective deterrent. Faced with such uncertainty, van den Haag maintains, it is our moral obligation to retain the death penalty. "We have no right to risk additional future victims of murder for the sake of sparing convicted murderers."

. . . If we do not know whether the death penalty will deter others [in a uniquely effective way], we are confronted with two uncertainties. If we impose the death penalty, and achieve no deterrent effect thereby, the life of a convicted murderer has been expended in vain (from a deterrent viewpoint). There is a net loss. If we impose the death sentence and thereby deter some future murderers, we spared the lives of some future victims (the prospective murderers gain too; they are spared punishment because they were deterred). In this case, the death penalty has led to a net gain, unless the life of a convicted murderer is valued more highly than that of the unknown victim, or victims (and the non-imprisonment of the deterred non-murderer).

The calculation can be turned around, of course. The absence of the death penalty may harm no one and therefore produce a gain—the life of the convicted murderer. Or it may kill future victims of murderers who could have been deterred, and thus produce a loss—their life.

To be sure, we must risk something certain—the death (or life) of the convicted man, for something uncertain—the death (or life) of the victims of murderers who may be deterred. This is in the nature of uncertainty—when we invest, or gamble, we risk the money we have for an uncertain gain. Many human actions, most commitments—including marriage and crime—share this characteristic with the deterrent purpose of any penalization, and with its rehabilitative purpose (and even with the protective).

More proof is demanded for the deterrent effect of the death penalty than is demanded for the deterrent effect of other penalties. This is not justified by the absence of other utilitarian purposes such as protection and rehabilitation; they involve no less uncertainty than deterrence.[1]

Irrevocability may support a demand for some reason to expect more deterrence than revocable penalties might produce, but not a demand for more proof of deterrence, as has been pointed out above. The reason for expecting more deterrence lies in the

---

[1]Rehabilitation or protection are of minor importance in our actual penal system (though not in our theory). We confine many people who do not need rehabilitation and against whom we do not need protection (e.g., the exasperated husband who killed his wife); we release many unrehabilitated offenders against whom protection is needed. Certainly rehabilitation and protection are not, and deterrence is, the main actual function of legal punishment, if we disregard nonutilitarian purposes.

greater severity, the terrifying effect inherent in finality. Since it seems more important to spare victims than to spare murderers, the burden of proving that the greater severity inherent in irrevocability adds nothing to deterrence lies on those who oppose capital punishment. Proponents of the death penalty need show only that there is no more uncertainty about it than about greater severity in general.

The demand that the death penalty be proved more deterrent than alternatives can not be satisfied any more than the demand that six years in prison be proved to be more deterrent than three. But the uncertainty which confronts us favors the death penalty as long as by imposing it we might save future victims of murder. This effect is as plausible as the general idea that penalties have deterrent effects which increase with their severity. Though we have no proof of the positive deterrence of the penalty, we also have no proof of zero, or negative effectiveness. I believe we have no right to risk additional future victims of murder for the sake of sparing convicted murderers; on the contrary, our moral obligation is to risk the possible ineffectiveness of executions. However rationalized, the opposite view appears to be motivated by the simple fact that executions are more subjected to social control than murder. However, this applies to all penalties and does not argue for the abolition of any.

QUESTIONS

1 If we are unsure whether or not the death penalty is a uniquely effective deterrent, does our uncertainty favor retention, abolition, or neither?

2 Is the life of a convicted murderer worth as much as the life of a potential murder victim?

Capital Punishment and Social Defense

Hugo Adam Bedau

A biographical sketch of Hugo Adam Bedau is found on page 120.

As the starting point of his effort to determine whether considerations of social defense can effectively support the retention of the death penalty, Bedau distinguishes between preventing and deterring crime. The death penalty *prevents crime* to the extent that a murderer who would have committed subsequent crimes is permanently incapacitated; it *deters crime* to the extent that other would-be murderers are frightened off by the example of the execution. In his view, not much of a case can be made for the retention of the death penalty based on considerations of crime prevention. With regard to deterrence, Bedau reads the available evidence as indicating that "the deterrence achieved by the death penalty for murder is not measurably greater than the deterrence achieved by long-term imprisonment." Accordingly, he contends, the retention of the death penalty cannot effectively be defended on the basis that it is a uniquely effective deterrent. After pointing out that the retention of the death penalty is attended by a number of social costs, he suggests that an extensive cost/benefit analysis would likely favor abolition of the death penalty. But what would follow regarding the morality of the death penalty, Bedau asks, *if* the death penalty were known to be a uniquely effective method of social defense? Even in the face of such knowledge, he maintains, there might still be other factual considerations ("costs") in the light of which opposition to the death penalty would remain morally responsible.

PREVENTING CRIME *VERSUS* DETERRING CRIME

The analogy [that may be drawn] between capital punishment and self-defense requires us to face squarely the empirical questions surrounding the preventive and deterrent effects of the death penalty. Let us distinguish first between preventing and deterring crime. Executing a murderer in the name of punishment can be seen as a crime-*preventive* measure just to the extent it is reasonable to believe that if the murderer had not been executed he or she would have committed other crimes (including, but not necessarily confined to, murder). Executing a murderer can be seen as a crime *deterrent* just to the extent it is reasonable to believe that by the example of the execution other persons are frightened off from committing murder. Any punishment can be a crime preventive without being a crime deterrent, and it can be a deterrent without being a preventive. It can also be both or neither. Prevention and deterrence are theoretically independent because they operate by different methods. Crimes can be prevented by taking guns out of the hands of criminals, by putting criminals behind bars, by alerting the public to be less careless and less prone to victimization, and so forth. Crimes can be deterred only by making would-be criminals frightened of being arrested, convicted, and punished for crimes—that is, making persons overcome their desire to commit crimes by a stronger desire to avoid the risk of being caught and punished.

THE DEATH PENALTY AS A CRIME PREVENTIVE

Capital punishment is unusual among penalties because its preventive effects limit its deterrent effects. The death penalty can never deter the executed person from further crimes. At most, it can prevent him or her from committing them. Popular discussions of the death penalty are frequently confused and misleading because they so often involve the assumption that the death penalty is a perfect and infallible deterrent so far as the executed criminal is concerned, whereas nothing of the sort is true. It is even an exaggeration to think that in any given case of execution the death penalty has proved to be an infallible crime preventive. What is obviously true is that once a person has been executed, it is physically impossible for him or her to commit any further crimes. But this does not prove that by executing a murderer society has in

From Tom Regan, ed., *Matters of Life and Death: New Introductory Essays in Moral Philosophy.* Copyright © 1980 by Random House, Inc. Reprinted by permission of Random House, Inc.

fact prevented any crimes. To prove this, one would need to know what crimes the executed criminal would have committed if he or she had not been executed and had been punished only in some less severe way (e.g., by imprisonment).

What is the evidence that the death penalty is an effective crime preventive? From the study of imprisonment, and parole and release records, it is clear that in general, if the murderers and other criminals who have been executed are like the murderers who were convicted but not executed, then (a) executing all convicted murderers would have prevented few crimes, but not many murders (less than one convicted murderer in a hundred commits another murder); and (b) convicted murderers, whether inside prison or outside after release, have at least as good a record of no further criminal activity as does any other class of convicted felon.

These facts show that the general public tends to overrate the danger and threat to public safety constituted by the failure to execute every murderer who is caught and convicted. While one would be in error to say that there is no risk such criminals will repeat their crimes—or similar ones—if they are not executed, one would be equally in error to say that by executing every convicted murderer we know that many horrible crimes will never be committed. All we know is that a few such crimes will never be committed; we do not know how many or by whom they would have been committed. (Obviously, if we did we could have prevented them.) This is the nub of the problem. There is no way to know in advance which if any of the incarcerated or released murderers will kill again. It is useful in this connection to remember that the only way to guarantee that no horrible crimes ever occur is to execute *everyone* who might conceivably commit such a crime. Similarly, the only way to guarantee that no convicted murderer ever commits another murder is to execute them all. No society has ever done this, and for 200 years our society has been moving steadily in the opposite direction.

These considerations show that our society has implicitly adopted an attitude toward the risk of murder rather like the attitude it has adopted toward the risk of fatality from other sources, such as automobile accidents, lung cancer, or drowning. Since no one knows when or where or upon whom any of these lethal events will befall, it would be too great an invasion of freedom to undertake the severe restrictions that alone would suffice to prevent any of them from occurring. It is better to take the risks and keep our freedom than to try to eliminate the risks altogether and lose our freedom in the process. Hence, we have lifeguards at the beach, but swimming is not totally prohibited; smokers are warned, but cigarettes are still legally sold; pedestrians may be given the right of way in a crosswalk, but marginally competent drivers are still allowed to operate motor vehicles. Some risk is therefore imposed on the innocent; in the name of our right to freedom, our other rights are not protected by society at all costs.

THE DEATH PENALTY AS A CRIME DETERRENT

Determining whether the death penalty is an effective deterrent is even more difficult than determining its effectiveness as a crime preventive. In general, our knowledge about how penalties deter crimes and whether in fact they do—whom they deter, from which crimes, and under what conditions—is distressingly inexact. Most people never-theless are convinced that punishments do deter, and that the more severe a punishment is the better it will deter. For more than a generation, social scientists have studied the question of whether the death penalty is a deterrent and of whether it is a better deterrent than the alternative of imprisonment. Their verdict, while not unanimous, is fairly clear. Whatever may be true about the deterrence of lesser crimes by other penalties, the deterrence achieved by the death penalty for murder is not measurably greater than the deterrence achieved by long-term imprisonment. In the nature of the case, the evidence is quite indirect. No one can identify for certain any crimes that did not occur because the would-be offender was deterred by the threat of the death penalty and that would not have been deterred by a lesser threat. Likewise, no one can identify any crimes that did occur because the offender was not deterred by the threat of prison even though he would have been deterred by the threat of death. Nevertheless, such evidence as we have fails to show that the more severe penalty (death) is really a better deterrent than the less severe penalty (imprisonment) for such crimes as murder.

If the conclusion stated above is correct, and the death penalty and long-term imprisonment are equally effective (or ineffective) as deterrents to murder, then the argument for the death penalty on grounds of deterrence is seriously weakened. [An important moral principle] comes into play and requires us to reject the death penalty on moral grounds. This is the principle that unless there is a good reason for choosing a more rather than a less severe punishment for a crime, the less severe penalty is to be preferred. This principle obviously commends itself to anyone who values human life and who concedes that, all other things being equal, less pain and suffering is always better than more. Human life is valued in part to the degree that it is free of pain, suffering, misery, and frustration, and in particular that it is free of such ex-periences when they serve no purpose. If the death penalty is not a more effective deterrent than imprisonment, then its greater severity than imprisonment is gratuitous, purposeless suffering and deprivation.

A COST/BENEFIT ANALYSIS OF THE DEATH PENALTY

A full study of the costs and benefits involved in the practice of capital punishment would not be confined solely to the question of whether it is a better deterrent or preventive of murder than imprisonment. Any thoroughgoing utilitarian approach to the death-penalty controversy would need to examine carefully other costs and benefits as well, because maximizing the balance of social benefits over social costs is the sole criterion of right and wrong according to utilitarianism. Let us consider, therefore, some of the other costs and benefits to be calculated. Clinical psychologists have presented evidence to suggest that the death penalty actually incites some persons of unstable mind to murder others, either because they are afraid to take their own lives and hope that society will punish them for murder by putting them to death, or because they fancy that they, too, are killing with justification analogously to the justified killing involved in capital punishment. If such evidence is sound, capital punishment can serve as a counterpreventive or an incitement to murder, and these incited murders become part of its social cost. Imprisonment, however, has not been known to incite any murders or other crimes of violence in a comparable fashion. (A possible exception might be found in the imprisonment of terrorists, which has inspired other terrorists to take hostages as part of a scheme to force the authorities to release their imprisoned comrades.) The risks of executing the innocent are also part of the social cost. The historical record is replete with innocent persons indicted, convicted, sentenced, and occasionally legally executed for crimes they did not commit, not to mention the guilty persons unfairly convicted, sentenced to death, and executed on the strength of perjured testimony, fraudulent evidence, subornation of jurors, and other violations of the civil rights and liberties of the accused. Nor is this all. The high costs of a capital trial, of the inevitable appeals, the costly methods of custody most prisons adopt for convicts on "death row," are among the straightforward economic costs that the death penalty incurs. No scientifically valid cost/benefit analysis of capital punishment has ever been conducted, and it is impossible to predict exactly what such a study would show. Nevertheless, based on such evidence as we do have, it is quite possible that a study of this sort would favor abolition of all death penalties rather than their retention.

WHAT IF EXECUTIONS DID DETER?

From the moral point of view, it is quite important to determine what one should think about capital punishment if the evidence clearly showed that the death penalty is a distinctly superior method of social defense by comparison with less severe alternatives. Kantian moralists . . . would have no use for such knowledge, because their entire case for the morality of the death penalty rests on the way it is thought to provide just retribution, not on the way it is thought to provide social defense. For a utilitarian, however, such knowledge would be conclusive. Those who follow Locke's reasoning would also be gratified, because they defend the morality of the death penalty both on the ground that it is retributively just and on the ground that it provides needed social defense.

What about the opponents of the death penalty, however? To oppose the death penalty in the face of incontestable evidence that it is an effective method of social defense seems to violate the moral principle that where grave risks are to be run, it is better that they be run by the guilty than by the innocent. Consider in this connection an imaginary world in which by executing a murderer the victim is invariably restored to life, whole and intact, as though the murder had never occurred. In such a miraculous world, it is hard to see how anyone could oppose the death penalty on moral grounds. Why shouldn't a murderer die if that will infallibly bring the victim back to life? What could possibly be morally wrong with taking the murderer's life under such conditions? It would turn the death penalty into an instrument of perfect restitution, and it would give a new and better meaning to *lex talionis,* "a life for a life." The whole idea is fanciful, of course, but it shows better than anything else how opposition to the death penalty cannot be both moral and wholly unconditional. If opposition to the death penalty is to be morally responsible, then it must be conceded that there are conditions (however unlikely) under which that opposition should cease.

But even if the death penalty were known to be a uniquely effective social defense, we could still imagine conditions under which it would be reasonable to oppose it. Suppose that in addition to being a slightly better preventive and deterrent than imprisonment, executions also have a slight incitive effect (so that for every ten murders an execution prevents or deters, it also incites another murder). Suppose also that the administration of criminal justice in capital cases is inefficient, unequal, and tends to secure convictions of murderers who least "deserve" to be sentenced to death (including some death sentences and a few executions of the innocent). Under such conditions, it would still be reasonable to oppose the death penalty, because on the facts supposed more (or not fewer) innocent lives are being threatened and lost by using the death penalty than would be risked by abolishing it. It is important to remember throughout our evaluation of the deterrence controversy that we cannot ever apply the principle . . . that advises us to risk the lives of the guilty in order to save the lives of the innocent. Instead, the most we can do is weigh the risk for the general public against the execution of those who are *found* guilty by an imperfect system of criminal justice. These hypothetical factual assumptions illustrate the contingencies upon which the morality of opposition to the death penalty rests. And not only the morality of opposition; the morality of any defense of the death penalty rests on the same contingencies. This should help us understand why, in resolving the morality of capital punishment one way or the other, it is so important to know, as well as we can, whether the death penalty really does deter, prevent, or incite crime, whether the innocent really are ever executed, and whether any of these things are likely to occur in the future.

HOW MANY GUILTY LIVES IS ONE INNOCENT LIFE WORTH?

The great unanswered question that utilitarians must face concerns the level of social defense that executions should be expected to achieve before it is justifiable to carry them out. Consider three possible situations: (1) At the level of a hundred executions per year, each additional execution of a convicted murderer reduces the number of murder victims by ten. (2) Executing every convicted murderer reduces the number of murders to 5,000 victims annually, whereas executing only one out of ten reduces the number to 5,001. (3) Executing every convicted murderer reduces the murder rate no more than does executing one in a hundred and no more than a random pattern of executions does.

Many people contemplating situation (1) would regard this as a reasonable trade-off: The execution of each further guilty person saves the lives of ten innocent ones. (In fact, situation (1) or something like it may be taken as a description of what most of those who defend the death penalty on grounds of social defense believe is true.) But suppose that, instead of saving 10 lives, the number dropped to 0.5, i.e., one victim avoided for each two additional executions. Would that be a reasonable price to pay? We are on the road toward the situation described in situation (2), where a drastic 90 percent reduction in the number of persons executed causes the level of social defense to drop by only 0.0002 percent. Would it be worth it to execute so many more murderers at the cost of such a slight decrease in social defense? How many guilty lives is one innocent life worth? In situation (3), of course, there is no basis for executing all convicted murderers, since there is no gain in social defense to show for each additional murderer executed after the first out of each hundred murderers has been executed. How, then, should we determine which out of each hundred convicted murderers is the unlucky one to be put to death?

It may be possible, under a complete and thoroughgoing cost/benefit analysis of the death penalty, to answer such questions. But an appeal merely to the moral principle that if lives are to be risked then let it be the lives of the guilty rather than the lives of the innocent will not suffice. (We have already noticed, in [the previous section], that this abstract principle is of little use in the actual administration of criminal justice, because the police and the courts do not deal with the guilty as such but only with those *judged* guilty.) Nor will it suffice to agree that society deserves all the crime prevention and deterrence it can get by inflicting severe punishments. These principles are consistent with too many different policies. They are too vague by themselves to resolve the choice on grounds of social defense when confronted with hypothetical situations like those proposed above.

Since no adequate cost/benefit analysis of the death penalty exists, there is no way to resolve these questions from this standpoint at the present time. Moreover, it can be argued that we cannot have such an analysis without already establishing in some way or other the relative value of innocent lives versus guilty lives. Far from being a product of a cost/benefit analysis, this comparative evaluation of lives would have to be brought into any such analysis. Without it, no cost/benefit analysis can get off the ground. Finally, it must be noted that we have no knowledge at present that begins to approximate anything like the situation described above in (1), whereas it appears from the evidence we do have that we achieve about the same deterrent and preventive effects whether we punish murder by death or by imprisonment. Therefore, something like the situation in (2) or in (3) may be correct. If so, this shows that the choice between the two policies of capital punishment and life imprisonment for murder will probably have to be made on some basis other than social defense; on that basis the two policies are equivalent and therefore equally acceptable.

QUESTIONS

1 Are there any good reasons for believing that the death penalty is a uniquely effective deterrent?
2 Is Bedau correct in thinking that an extensive cost/benefit analysis of the death penalty would favor abolition?

SUGGESTED ADDITIONAL READINGS FOR CHAPTER 3

BEDAU, HUGO ADAM, ed.: *The Death Penalty in America*, 3d ed. New York: Oxford, 1982. This sourcebook provides a wealth of factual material relevant to the death penalty controversy. It also incorporates essays by both retentionists and abolitionists.

————, and C. M. PIERCE, eds.: *Capital Punishment in the United States*. New York: AMS Press, 1976. There is an extensive literature in social science dealing with the many factual issues associated with the death penalty controversy. This particular collection of material draws exclusively on that literature and provides a helpful point of entry to it.

BERNS, WALTER: *For Capital Punishment.* New York: Basic Books, 1979. In this book, which provides a broadly ranging discussion of issues relevant to the death penalty controversy, Berns insists that capital punishment can be effectively defended on grounds of retribution.

BLACK, CHARLES L., JR.: *Capital Punishment: The Inevitability of Caprice and Mistake.* New York: Norton, 1974. Black, in this short and most readable book, argues for abolition on the grounds that it is virtually impossible to eliminate arbitrariness and mistake from the numerous decisions that lead to the imposition of the death penalty.

CONWAY, DAVID A.: "Capital Punishment and Deterrence: Some Considerations in Dialogue Form." *Philosophy and Public Affairs,* vol. 3, Summer 1974, pp. 431–443. Conway provides a lively dialogue between a retentionist (who supports the death penalty on grounds of deterrence) and an abolitionist. Of special interest is the abolitionist's reaction to the line of argument advanced by Ernest van den Haag in this chapter.

DAVIS, MICHAEL: "Death, Deterrence, and the Method of Common Sense." *Social Theory and Practice,* vol. 7, Summer 1981, pp. 145–177. Davis argues that common sense is sufficient to establish the claim that death is the most effective deterrent. For other reasons, however, he is unwilling to endorse retention of the death penalty.

EZORSKY, GERTRUDE, ed.: *Philosophical Perspectives on Punishment.* Albany: State University of New York Press, 1972. This book is an excellent anthology on a wide range of general philosophical questions concerning punishment. There is a small section on capital punishment.

GOLDBERG, STEVEN: "On Capital Punishment." *Ethics,* vol. 85, October 1974, pp. 67–74. Goldberg, ultimately sympathetic to retentionism, focuses on the difficulties involved in the factual question of whether or not the death penalty is a uniquely effective deterrent. An extensively revised version of this article appears under the title: "Does Capital Punishment Deter?" in Richard A. Wasserstrom, ed., *Today's Moral Problems,* 2d ed. New York: Macmillan, 1979, pp. 538–551.

MC CAFFERTY, JAMES, A., ed.: *Capital Punishment.* New York: Lieber-Atherton, 1972. This general anthology is especially useful because it includes several position papers that reflect the views (both retentionist and abolitionist) taken by people who are directly involved in the administration of criminal justice.

MURPHY, JEFFRIE G.: *Punishment and Rehabilitation,* 2d ed. Belmont, Calif.: Wadsworth, 1985. This anthology provides a set of helpful readings on the philosophical aspects of punishment. Some explicit attention is paid to capital punishment.

VAN DEN HAAG, ERNEST and JOHN P. CONRAD: *The Death Penalty: A Debate.* New York: Plenum, 1983. Van den Haag (a retentionist) and Conrad (an abolitionist) touch on all aspects of the death penalty controversy as they develop their respective cases and critically respond to each other's arguments.

CHAPTER 4

SEX ROLES AND SEXUAL EQUALITY

Prior to the emergence of contemporary feminism in the United States in the late 1960s and early 1970s, various legal measures explicitly prohibiting certain sexually discriminatory employment practices had already been enacted. Despite such legislation, however, women's earning power had remained much less than that of men, and sexual discrimination was commonplace in the economic sphere. After nearly two decades of contemporary feminist protest, women's economic status has changed very little. As recent U.S. Department of Labor statistics show, the earnings gap between men and women is very wide. The weekly median wage of full-time male workers in 1982 was $371, and that of full-time female workers was $241. These statistics also reveal that women continue to be clustered in the lowest-paid occupations and to be underrepresented in the highest ones.[1] It is obvious that many people still believe that certain jobs are more appropriate for women (e.g., nursing, clerical work) and others more appropriate for men (e.g., construction work, engineering). It is equally obvious that what is traditionally labeled "women's work" usually involves more menial chores, less respect, and less recognition than "men's work."

The fact that female-headed households in the United States are more likely to be poor than male-headed households is related to this traditional sexual division of labor and to the lower value attributed to women's work. Linked to traditional views about the appropriateness of a sexual division of labor are views about sex roles in general. It is not surprising, therefore, that much of the contemporary discussion of the sexual inequalities in our society focuses on the legitimacy of sex roles. Thus the central

---

[1]Earl F. Mellor, "Investigating the Difference in Weekly Earnings of Women and Men," *Monthly Labor Review,* vol. 107 (June 1984), pp. 17–28.

question in this chapter can be expressed as follows: Are sex roles morally justifiable or does morality require their abolition? If abolition is the correct answer, then additional questions arise about just what people in a society without sex roles would be and should be like. All these questions presuppose, of course, that a human society without sex roles is possible, but even that assumption is sometimes challenged.

THE PRINCIPLE OF EQUALITY

One way to determine the morality of a social practice is to assess it by the "principle of equality." According to that principle, equals should be treated as equals and unequals should be treated unequally, in proportion to their differences. This is sometimes called the "formal principle of justice." But what constitutes equality or inequality? In what ways must two individuals be alike before we can claim that they should receive the same treatment? In what ways must two individuals differ before we can claim that they should be accorded unequal treatment?

The usual way of answering these questions is to say that the differences between individuals must be relevant to the treatment in question. When a particular kind of employment is at issue, for example, it would seem that what is relevant is having the appropriate ability or skill. If Joe Smith and John Doe both apply for a job as lifeguard, a difference in their religious beliefs seems to have no bearing on which of them should get the job. But if Joe is a nonswimmer and John an Olympic swimming champion, that difference between them *is relevant* to the treatment they should receive in this case. On this line of reasoning, sex may be relevant when a wet nurse is being hired. But it is not relevant when a choice is being made between competing accountants, although mathematical ability is relevant. Note what has just been claimed: Sex is *not* a relevant characteristic when an accountant is being hired. If a qualified woman accountant is told that she cannot apply for an accounting position simply because of her sex, she is not receiving the same treatment as male accountants whose applications are accepted. When this happens, the principle of equality is clearly violated.

The discussion so far has focused on that part of the principle of equality which states that equals should be treated equally. But some unequal treatment is also in keeping with the principle of equality. Young children, for example, cannot be given the same rights and responsibilities as adults. A five-year-old cannot be expected to take on responsibilities such as voting or signing binding contracts. This kind of unequal treatment of young children and adults is consistent with the principle of equality, since young children differ from adults in relevant respects. They are incapable of exercising the rational capacities needed to assume certain responsibilities. To sum up, both institutional practices that treat equals equally and those that treat unequals unequally, in proportion to their differences, are morally correct according to the principle of equality. But when equals are treated unequally, the principle is clearly violated.

SEX ROLES AND THE PRINCIPLE OF EQUALITY

Are sex roles in keeping with the principle of equality? Before discussing this question, it is necessary to consider just what sex roles are. Two ideas are central in the conception of sex roles relevant to this chapter's concerns. *First,* to say that there are sex roles is to say that women and men are expected to develop different psychological characteristics and to behave in different ways, especially, perhaps, to perform different functions. Women may be expected to be nurturing mothers, for example, while men may be expected to be family breadwinners. Women may be expected to have feminine psychological traits such as gentleness, and men may be expected to have masculine traits such as aggressiveness. These different psychological traits are also expected to manifest themselves in appropriate behaviors, including the work that members of each sex perform. *Second,* it is important to note that sex roles, as understood here, carry with them patterns of expectations and standards of performance as well as various systems of reward and punishment that serve to encourage, support, and, perhaps, even enforce the appropriate behavior. In raising questions about the morality of sex roles in relation to the principle of equality, our primary concern is with the morality of the myriad number of social practices that treat men and women differently in order to direct them into and keep them in their "appropriate" roles—practices that work against those who deviate from the expected patterns of behavior.

Femininity and masculinity, as traditionally understood, may also be conceived of as sex roles. Notice that "masculinity" and "femininity" are not synonymous with "male" and "female." Some males/men do in fact exhibit traits considered feminine, and some females/women exhibit traits considered masculine. Thus it is useful to make a distinction between *sex* and *gender*. Sex can be understood as a biological concept. There are chromosomal differences between men and women and related anatomical differences. In contrast, gender—femininity and masculinity—can be understood as a psychological/behavioral concept. In our society, the words "gender" and "sex" are often used interchangeably, of course. In the *Rostker v. Goldberg* opinion excerpted in this chapter, for example, the expression "gender-based" is used as if it were synonymous with "sex-based," but such use obscures the difference between the two concepts. Some people, of course, see a necessary connection between sex and gender. Men are by nature masculine, they hold, and women feminine. One of the questions raised when sex roles are discussed, however, is whether women should be socialized to be feminine and men to be masculine. This question makes sense only if there is no necessary connection between being biologically male and having masculine traits or between being biologically female and having feminine traits. When questions about the relation between sex, gender, and socialization are raised, it is important to keep in mind the second component in the conception of sex roles presented above. If genders are sex roles, then there are systems of reward and punishment that function to support femininity in women and masculinity in men and discourage the reverse. Thus we are faced with the question of whether systems of reward and punishment that function in this way are in keeping with the principle of equality.

Some defenders of sex roles see them as consistent with the principle of equality. In their view, there are important differences between the sexes that justify the claim that sex *should* be used as a criterion for according unequal political, economic, and social treatment to the sexes. Consider the kinds of things that people often say: "No woman should ever be President of the United States. Women are too emotional for the job." "Women can't manage other women." Or consider this remark made to a woman student: "We expect women who come here to be competent, good students, but we don't expect them to be brilliant or original."[2] Note what all these examples have in common. The sex of an individual is seen as relevant when the individual's capacity to perform certain tasks is being judged. Sex is considered relevant because differences in sex are believed to be naturally correlated with differences in psychological characteristics, including differences in cognitive capacity, and these psychological differences are assumed to be relevant to the professional roles in question. Perhaps the overall argument can best be summarized as follows: There are psychological differences between the sexes and these are relevant to job performance. Furthermore, these differences are natural ones; that is, they are genetically caused. Therefore, some of the unequal treatment accorded women is in keeping with the principle of equality because women *by their very nature* are unequal to men in relevant ways.

Much that is written by those who argue for the abolition of sex roles focuses on the *factual claims* used to support the above argument. Sometimes the existence of sexually related psychological differences is denied. The claim here is that even though we believe, for example, that most women are passive and most men aggressive, these beliefs are incorrect. Culturally engrained erroneous beliefs about male and female psychological differences lead us to dismiss the counterevidence (the many atypical cases we encounter) as "mere" exceptions to the rule. At other times, the following argument is made: Even if it is true that women are more passive and men more aggressive on the average, or men more inclined to abstract thought than women on the average, this does not prove that there are *natural* differences between the sexes relevant to sex roles. Rather, it is because society differentiates between male and female roles and trains individuals to conform to these roles that the sexes tend to develop different psychological characteristics. If there are in fact psychological differences between the sexes, then the differences are artificial and not natural. It is the traditional unequal treatment accorded to the sexes by educational and other socializing institutions that causes any psychological differences between them that might be relevant in denying women access to the most authoritative, best paid, and most prestigious positions in society. Thus, society's unequal treatment of the sexes is not based on any natural inequality between them. Rather, it is the unequal treatment of the sexes that produces the artificial psychological differences whose existence is supposed to justify the further unequal economic, social, and educational treatment of the sexes.

Some philosophers detach themselves from the whole discussion of the *causes* of the assumed psychological differences between men and women and focus on a different question: Even if there are psychological differences between the sexes (natural or socially induced) such that women *on the average* are more emotional and more passive than men as well as less capable *on the average* of abstract thought, is it morally correct to deny systematically some roles to *all* women simply because many

[2]Quoted in a statement made by Ann Sutherland Harris to the Congressional Hearings on Equal Rights in Education and Employment. This statement is included in Catharine R. Simpson, ed., *Discrimination Against Women: Congressional Hearings on Equal Rights in Education and Employment* (New York: Bowker, 1973), p. 399.

women are incapable of filling them? According to the principle of equality, social practices resulting in the systematic exclusion of all the members of a group are not justified when the relevant differences are not universal. The principle of equality requires that each person be judged simply on the basis of individual merit and not on the basis of the "average" makeup of that person's sexual group. On this line of argument, any unequal treatment would be sanctioned by the principle of equality only if the relevant differences between the sexes were universal and not statistical.

OTHER ARGUMENTS FOR AND AGAINST SEX ROLES

Some defenders of sex roles ignore or downplay the significance of the principle of equality. These proponents of unequal treatment begin by arguing that natural differences between the sexes make *most* women relevantly different from most men. On the basis of this claim, further claims are made. For example, Steven Goldberg, in a reading in this chapter, maintains that hormonal differences between the sexes are responsible for differences in their aggression level. As a result, high-status positions in society will inevitably be dominated by men. Even if some women are capable of competing with men, he continues, women on the whole will be better off in the long run if direct competition between the sexes is minimized. Others using this approach argue in a similar consequentialist vein. They give their own accounts of sexual differences. They then maintain that it is in the best interest of women, or in the best interest of society as a whole, to establish social institutions that will sustain and perpetuate sex roles, even if enforcing them violates the principle of equality in individual cases and limits the freedom of individuals to develop any chosen personality or interest. Joyce Trebilcot, in her first article in this chapter, analyzes and evaluates claims of this general type.

One line of argument advanced for the abolition of sex roles focuses not on the issue of equality but on the issue of freedom. Sex roles are seen as morally unacceptable because they restrict freedom and opportunity. Janice Moulton and Francine Rainone in this chapter reject this line of argument and maintain that sex roles as they presently exist are morally unacceptable for a different reason—they reinforce a sexual division of labor that functions to keep women subordinate to men. Think of the information given earlier about the difference between the median wage of men and that of women. Much of this difference can be attributed to the fact, also noted earlier, that jobs considered "women's work" generally pay much less than jobs considered "men's work." What could justify sex roles if they do in fact function to keep women subordinate to men and to perpetuate such gross differences in earning power? In making their case, Moulton and Rainone do not discuss the principle of equality. Implicit in their argument, however, is the belief that there are no relevant differences between men and women that could justify sex roles that perpetuate the subordination and inferior economic status of women. At the same time, they leave open the possibility that sex roles that do not disadvantage one sex in relation to the other might be morally acceptable. Worthy of consideration, then, is the question: What sorts of sex roles, if any, would be in keeping with the principle of equality and other moral principles?

ANDROGYNY AND THE ABOLITION OF SEX ROLES

Suppose sex roles, including the old gender stereotypes, are abandoned. What alternatives should we adopt? Should all women be trained to be physically aggressive, for example? Should all men be trained to express their affections more freely than the traditional model would allow? The word "androgynous" is often used to describe the personality type that should replace the old masculine and feminine models. Formed from the Greek words for "man"(*andros*) and "woman" (*gyne*), the word connotes a personality containing all the positive characteristics traditionally called masculine as well as those traditionally called feminine. Does this mean that social institutions should mold people on this new model to the greatest extent possible? Or should these institutions simply encourage individuals to develop the personalities and interests with which they are most comfortable, even if some people would end up with one-sided personalities and interests? In the second Trebilcot selection in this chapter, she considers both alternatives in an effort to determine which approach is morally most desirable. Critics of any androgynous approach to human personality sometimes express concern about its impact on the sexual attraction that presently exists between men and women. In this chapter's final reading Robert G. Pielke addresses this concern and argues that androgyny may even enhance human sexuality.

Jane S. Zembaty

Majority Opinion in *Rostker v. Goldberg*

Justice William H. Rehnquist

William H. Rehnquist, associate justice of the United States Supreme Court, is a graduate of Stanford University Law School. In 1969, after spending some years in private practice, he became assistant attorney general, Office of Legal Counsel in the United States Department of Justice. Justice Rehnquist was appointed to the Supreme Court in 1972.

The Military Selective Service Act (MSSA) authorizes the President of the United States to require men, but not women, to register for possible military conscription. Registration for the draft was discontinued in 1975 by Presidential Proclamation. In 1980, President Carter, thinking it necessary to reactivate the registration process, asked Congress to allocate appropriate funds. He also recommended that Congress amend MSSA to permit the registration and conscription of women as well as men. Congress agreed that it was necessary to reactivate the registration process but refused to amend MSSA to permit the registration of women and allocated only the funds necessary to register men. After the president ordered the registration of specified groups of young men, several men challenged MSSA's constitutionality. A three-judge District Court ruled that MSSA's gender-based discrimination violated the Due Process Clause of the Fifth Amendment. Appeal was made to the Supreme Court which reversed the lower court's ruling.

Justice Rehnquist, writing the majority opinion, argues that Congress acted well within its constitutional authority when it authorized the registration of men, but not women, under MSSA. He accepts Congress's contention that the purpose of any future draft would be to increase the number of combat troops. Since women unlike men are not eligible for combat, women and men are not similarly situated with respect to a possible draft. Thus MSSA's gender-based classification is constitutionally acceptable. Granting that the argument for registering women is based on considerations of equity, the Court nonetheless holds that Congress was within its rights in focusing not on equity but on military need.

This case is quite different from several of the gender-based discrimination cases we have considered in that, despite appellees' assertions, Congress did not act "unthinkingly" or "reflexively and not for any considered reason." The question of registering women for the draft not only received considerable national attention and was the subject of wide-ranging public debate, but also was extensively considered by Congress in hearings, floor debate, and in committee. . . .

Congress determined that any future draft, which would be facilitated by the registration scheme, would be characterized by a need for combat troops. The Senate Report explained, in a specific finding later adopted by both Houses, that "[i]f mobilization were to be ordered in a wartime scenario, the primary manpower need would be for combat replacements." S. Rep. No. 96-826, p. 160 (1980). . . . The purpose of registration, therefore, was to prepare for a draft *of combat troops*.

Women as a group, however, unlike men as a group, are not eligible for combat. The restrictions on the participation of women in combat in the Navy and Air Force are statutory. Under 10 U.S.C. § 6015 (1976 ed., Supp. III), "women may not be assigned to duty on vessels or in aircraft that are engaged in combat missions," and under 10 U.S.C. § 8549 female members of the Air Force "may not be assigned to duty in aircraft engaged in combat missions." The Army and Marine Corps preclude the use of women in combat as a matter of established policy. Congress specifically recognized and endorsed the exclusion of women from combat in exempting women from registration. In the words of the Senate Report:

> The principle that women should not intentionally and routinely engage in combat is fundamental, and enjoys wide support among our people. It is universally supported by military leaders who have testified before the Committee. . . . Current law and policy exclude women from being assigned to combat in our military forces, and the Committee reaffirms this policy." S. Rep. No. 96-826, p. 157. . . .

The President expressed his intent to continue the current military policy precluding women from combat, and appellees present their argument concerning registration against the background of such restrictions on the use of women in combat. We must

United States Supreme Court. 453 U.S. 57 (1981).

examine appellees' constitutional claim concerning registration with these combat restrictions firmly in mind.

The existence of the combat restrictions clearly indicates the basis for Congress' decision to exempt women from registration. The purpose of registration was to prepare for a draft of combat troops. Since women are excluded from combat, Congress concluded that they would not be needed in the event of a draft, and therefore decided not to register them. Again turning to the Senate Report:

> "In the Committee's view, the starting point for any discussion of the appropriateness of registering women for the draft is the question of the proper role of women in combat. . . . The policy precluding the use of women in combat is, in the Committee's view, the most important reason for not including women in a registration system." S. Rep. No. 96-826, p. 157.

The District Court stressed that the military need for women was irrelevant to the issue of their registration. As that court put it: "Congress could not constitutionally require registration under the MSSA of only black citizens or only white citizens, or single out any political or religious group simply because those groups contain sufficient persons to fill the needs of the Selective Service System." 509 F. Supp., at 596. This reasoning is beside the point. The reason women are exempt from registration is not because military needs can be met by drafting men. This is not a case of Congress arbitrarily choosing to burden one of two similarly situated groups, such as would be the case with an all-black or all-white, or an all-Catholic or all-Lutheran, or an all-Republican or all-Democratic registration. Men and women, because of the combat restrictions on women, are simply not similarly situated for purposes of a draft or registration for a draft.

Congress' decision to authorize the registration of only men, therefore, does not violate the Due Process Clause. The exemption of women from registration is not only sufficiently but also closely related to Congress' purpose in authorizing registration. The fact that Congress and the Executive have decided that women should not serve in combat fully justifies Congress in not authorizing their registration, since the purpose of registration is to develop a pool of potential combat troops. As was the case in *Schlesinger v. Ballard,* "the gender classification is not invidious, but rather realistically reflects the fact that the sexes are not similarly situated" in this case. *Michael M. Superior Court of Sonoma County* (1981) (plurality opinion). The Constitution requires that Congress treat similarly situated persons similarly, not that it engage in gestures of superficial equality.

In holding the MSSA constitutionally invalid the District Court relied heavily on the President's decision to seek authority to register women and the testimony of members of the Executive Branch and the military in support of that decision. As stated by the administration's witnesses before Congress, however, the President's "decision to ask for authority to register women is based on equity." House Hearings 7 (statement of Assistant Secretary of Defense Pirie and Director of Selective Service System Rostker). . . . The Senate Report, evaluating the testimony before the Committee, recognized that "[t]he argument for registration and induction of women . . . is not based on military necessity, but on considerations of equity." S. Rep. No. 96-826, p. 158 (1980). Congress was certainly entitled, in the exercise of its constitutional powers to raise and regulate armies and navies, to focus on the question of military need rather than "equity." As Senator Nunn of the Senate Armed Services Committee put it:

> "Our committee went into very great detail. We found that there was no military necessity cited by any witnesses for the registration of females.
>
> "The main point that those who favored the registration of females made was that they were in favor of this because of the equality issue, which is, of course, a legitimate view. But as far as military necessity, and that is what we are primarily, I hope, considering in the overall registration bill, there is no military necessity for this." 126 Cong. Rec. 13893 (1980).

Although the military experts who testified in favor of registering women uniformly opposed the actual drafting of women, there was testimony that in the event of a draft of 650,000 the military could absorb some 80,000 female inductees. The 80,000 would be used to fill noncombat positions, freeing men to go to the front. In relying on this testimony in striking down the MSSA, the District Court palpably exceeded its authority when it ignored Congress' considered response to this line of reasoning.

In the first place, assuming that a small number of women could be drafted for noncombat roles, Congress simply did not consider it worth the added burdens of including women in draft and registration plans. "It has been suggested that all women be registered, but only a handful actually be inducted in an emergency. The Committee finds this a confused and ultimately unsatisfactory solution." S. Rep. No. 96-826, *supra,* at 158. As the Senate Committee recognized a year before, "training would be needlessly burdened by women recruits who could not be used in combat." S. Rep. No. 96-226, p. 9 (1979). See also S. Rep. No. 96-826, *supra,* at 159 ("Other administrative problems such as housing and different treatment with regard to dependency, hardship and physical standards would also exist"). It is not for this Court to dismiss such problems as insignificant in the context of military preparedness and the exigencies of a future mobilization.

Congress also concluded that whatever the need for women for noncombat roles during mobilization, whether 80,000 or less, it could be met by volunteers. . . .

Most significantly, Congress determined that staffing noncombat positions with women during a mobilization would be positively detrimental to the important goal of military flexibility.

> ". . . [T]here are other military reasons that preclude very large numbers of women from serving. Military flexibility requires that a commander be able to move units or ships quickly. Units or ships not located at the front or not previously scheduled for the front nevertheless must be able to move into action if necessary. In peace and war, significant rotation of personnel is necessary. We should not divide the military into two groups—one in permanent combat and one in permanent support. Large numbers of non-combat positions must be available to which combat troops can return for duty before being redeployed." S. Rep. No. 96-826, *supra,* at 158.

In sum, Congress carefully evaluated the testimony that 80,000 women conscripts could be usefully employed in the event of a draft and rejected it in the permissible exercise of its constitutional responsibility. . . .

In light of the foregoing, we conclude that Congress acted well within its constitutional authority when it authorized the registration of men, and not women, under the Military Selective Service Act. The decision of the District Court holding otherwise is accordingly

Reversed.

QUESTIONS

1 The exclusion of women from combat positions was not challenged in this case. Are there any morally good grounds for excluding women from what some consider a fundamental civic obligation?
2 Women can and do perform many important tasks in the military and military testimony at the Senate Hearings on MSSA included the following comment: "[W]omen should be required to register . . . in order for us to have an inventory of what the available strength is within the military qualified pool within the country." In light of this, should women, too, be required to register for the draft?

The Inevitability of Patriarchy

Steven Goldberg

Steven Goldberg teaches in the department of sociology at City College of the City University of New York. He is the only nonmedical fellow of the American Academy of Psychiatry and Neurology. Goldberg's articles include "Is Astrology a Science?" and "What Is Normal? Logical Aspects of the Question of Homosexual Behavior."

Goldberg defends the nonegalitarianism found in a patriarchy. He attacks the following basic assumption made by John Stuart Mill and other feminists: There is no natural difference between the sexes which makes a male-dominated society inevitable. Goldberg claims that there is such a difference—a hormonal one. Owing to hormonal differences, males are inherently more aggressive than females. This greater aggressiveness assures male domination of the high-status roles in society.

Moreover, Goldberg argues, if society does not socialize women away from competing with men, then most women will be condemned to failure and unhappiness. Given the innate aggression advantage of men over women, consider what would happen if society did not socialize women against competing with men for society's high-status positions. Some women would be aggressive enough to succeed. The vast majority would be failures, however, socialized to desire high-status positions but incapable of attaining them.

Adapted from pp. 49, 51, 63, 81, 93, 105–109, 166–168 in *The Inevitability of Patriarchy* by Steven Goldberg. Copyright © 1973 by Steven Goldberg. By permission of William Morrow & Company.

The view of man and woman in society that implicitly underlies all of the arguments of the feminists is this: there is nothing inherent in the nature of human beings or of society that necessitates that any role or task (save those requiring great strength or the ability to give birth) be associated with one sex or the other,[1] there is no natural order of things decreeing that dyadic and social authority must be associated with men, nor is there any reason why it must be men who rule in every society. Patriarchy, matriarchy, and "equiarchy" are all equally possible and—while every society may invoke "the natural order of things" to justify its particular system—all the expectations we have of men and women are culturally determined and have nothing to do with any sort of basic male or female nature.[2]

There is nothing internally contradictory in such a hypothesis; indeed, it is an ideal place from which to begin an empirical investigation into the nature of man, woman, and society. However, the feminist does not use this as a heuristic first step but unquestioningly accepts it as true. . . .

Given the *seemingly* unlimited plasticity of human beings and the *seemingly* endless variety of their societal institutions, the universality of an institution alerts the objective investigator to the possibility that there is an underlying factor engendering universality and that, if this factor is inseparable from the general nature of society or of human biology, the institution, or some equivalent institutional channel for meeting the requirements of this factor may be inevitable. . . .

The only biological hypothesis included in this book states that those individuals whose male anatomy leads to a social identification as "male" have hormonal systems which generate a greater capacity for "aggression" (or a lower threshold for the release of "aggression"—for our purposes this is the same thing) than those individuals whose female anatomy leads to a social identification as "female" and that socialization and institutions conform to the reality of hormonal sexual differentiation and to the

---

[1]*It is time that we realized that the whole structure of male and female personality is entirely imposed by social conditioning.* All the possible traits of human personality have in this conditioning been *arbitrarily* assigned into two categories; thus aggression is masculine, passivity feminine. . . ." [Emphasis added]. (Kate Millett, *Barnard Alumnae.* Spring, 1970, p. 28.) This statement expresses the assumption which underpins all of Dr. Millett's *Sexual Politics* (New York: Doubleday, 1970).

[2]The best presentation of the feminist assumption is unquestionably John Stuart Mill's *The Subjection of Women.* As an impassioned plea for women's rights Mill's essay is both moving and illuminating. As an attempt to explain the etiology of sexually differentiated behavior and institutions it is indefensible. One is tempted, given the fact that the author of the essay was Mill, to ascribe its inadequacies to the fact that little of the relevant anthropological evidence, and none of the relevant hormonal evidence, was available at the time. But the weakness of Mill's analysis is attributable even more to the fallacious reasoning that his preconceived conclusions demanded. For example, Mill argues that we can have no conception of the limits of possibility imposed by innate sexual differences, or even of whether such limits exist, because no society has been composed of one sex; thus he does not even attempt to explain why the conceptions of male and female held by his society are not reversed in any other society. Similarly Mill attempts to dismiss the possibility of the determinativeness of innate sexual differences by invoking the irrelevant fact that slave owners defended slavery with the invocation of physiological racial differences that do not exist; this fact is correct, of course, but it casts no more doubt on the likelihood that innate sexual differences are determinative to sexual differences in behavior and institutions than it does on the certainty that physiology is determinative to the ability to give birth. Mill's reasoning has been accepted without question by modern feminist writers.

statistical reality of the "aggression advantage" which males derive from their hormonal systems. . . .

The thesis put forth here is that the hormonal renders the social inevitable. . . .

I believe that in the past we have been looking in the wrong direction for the answer to the question of why every society rewards male roles with higher status than it does female roles (even when the male tasks in one society are the female tasks in another). While it is true that men are always in the positions of authority from which status tends to be defined, male roles are not given high status primarily *because* men fill these roles; men fill these roles because their biological aggression "advantage" can be manifested *in any non-child related area rewarded by high status in any society.* (Again: the line of reasoning used in this book demonstrates only that the biological factors we discuss would make the social institutions we discuss inevitable and does not preclude the existence of other forces also leading in the same direction; there may be a biologically based tendency for women to prefer male leadership, but there need not be for male attainment of leadership and high-status roles to be inevitable.) . . . This aggression "advantage" can be most manifested and can most enable men to reap status rewards *not* in those relatively homogeneous, collectivist primitive societies in which both male and female must play similar economic roles if the society is to survive or in the monarchy (which guarantees an occasional female leader); this biological factor will be given freest play in the complex, relatively individualistic, bureaucratic, democratic society which, of necessity, must emphasize organizational authority and in which social mobility is relatively free of traditional barriers to advancement. There were more female heads of state in the first two-thirds of the sixteenth century than in the first two-thirds of the twentieth.

The mechanisms involved here are easily seen if we examine any roles that males have attained by channeling their aggression toward such attainment. We will assume for now that equivalent women could *perform* the tasks of roles as well as men if they could attain the roles.[3] Here we can speak of the corporation president, the union leader, the governor, the chairman of an association, or any other role or position for which aggression is a precondition for attainment. Now the environmentalist and the feminist will say that the fact that all such roles are nearly always filled by men is attributable not to male aggression but to the fact that women have not been allowed to enter the competitive race to attain these positions, that they have been told that these positions are in male areas, and that girls are socialized away from competing with boys in general. Women *are* socialized in this way, but again we must ask why.

---

[3]I assume this for the present in order to demonstrate that these will be male roles even if women can *perform* these roles as well as men when they can attain them. It should be pointed out, however, that the line between attainment and performance is not always clear in a bureaucratic society or in leadership in any society; much of the *performance* of an executive or leader concerns his ability to maintain the authority which his position gives him. Therefore, it is possible that the greater innate male aggression, particularly when opposed to the lesser innate female aggression, leads to *performance* by the male which is superior to that of the female. This does not, of course, mean that the male at any level of the hierarchy has an advantage over the exceptional woman who was aggressive enough to attain a comparable position, but it might indicate that men in general have an innate advantage over women in general which is relevant to the *performance* of bureaucratic and leadership roles.

If innate male aggression has nothing to do with male attainment of positions of authority and status in the political, academic, scientific, or financial spheres, if aggression has nothing to do with the reasons why *every* society socializes girls away from those areas which are given high status and away from competition in general, then why is it never the *girls* in any society who are socialized toward these areas, why is it never the nonbiological roles played by women that have high status, why is it always boys who are told to compete, and why do women never "force" men into the low-status, nonmaternal roles that women play in every society?

These questions pose no problem if we acknowledge a male aggression that enables men to attain any nonbiological role given high status by any society. For one need merely consider the result of society's *not* socializing women away from competitions with men, from its *not* directing girls toward roles women are more capable of playing than are men or roles with status low enough that men will not strive for them. No doubt some women would be aggressive enough to succeed in competitions with men and there would be considerably more women in high-status positions than there are now. But most women would lose in such competitive struggles with men (because men have the aggression advantage) and so most women would be forced to live adult lives as failures in areas in which the society had *wanted them to succeed*. It is women, far more than men, who would never allow a situation in which girls were socialized in such a way that the vast majority of them were doomed to adult lifetimes of failure to live up to their own expectations. Now I have no doubt that there is a biological factor that gives women the desire to emphasize maternal and nurturance roles, but the point here is that we can accept the feminist assumption that there is no female propensity of this sort and still see that a society must socialize women away from roles that men will attain through their aggression. For if women did not develop an alternative set of criteria for success their sense of their own competence would suffer intolerably. It is undeniable that the resulting different values and expectations that are attached to men and women will tend to work against the aggressive woman while they work for the man who is no more aggressive. But this is the unavoidable result of the fact that most men are more aggressive than most women so that this woman, who is as aggressive as the average man, but more aggressive than most women, is an exception. Furthermore, even if the sense of competence of each sex did not necessitate society's attaching to each sex values and expectations based on those qualities possessed by each sex, observation of the majority of each sex by the population would "automatically" lead to these values and expectations being attached to men and women.

SOCIALIZATION'S CONFORMATION TO BIOLOGICAL REALITY

Socialization is the process by which society prepares children for adulthood. The way in which its goals conform to the reality of biology is seen quite clearly when we consider the method in which testosterone generates male aggression (testosterone's serially developing nature). Preadolescent boys and girls have roughly equal testosterone levels, yet young boys are far more aggressive than young girls. Eva Figes has used this observation to dismiss incorrectly the possibility of a hormone-aggression association.[4] Now it is quite probable that the boy is more aggressive than the girl for a purely biological reason. . . . There is evidence of male-female differences in the behavior of infants shortly after birth (when differential socialization is not a plausible explanation of such differences). The fetal alteration of the boy's brain by the testosterone that was generated by his testes has probably left him far more sensitive to the aggression-related properties of the testosterone that is present during boyhood than the girl, who did not receive such alteration. But let us for the moment assume that this is not the case. This does not at all reduce the importance of the hormonal factor. For even if the boy is more aggressive than the girl only because the society allows him to be, the boy's socialization still flows from society's acknowledging biological reality. Let us consider what would happen if girls have the same innate aggression as boys and if a society did not socialize girls away from aggressive competitions. Perhaps half of the third-grade baseball team would be female. As many girls as boys would frame their expectations in masculine values and girls would develop not their feminine abilities but their masculine ones. During adolescence, however, the same assertion of the male chromosomal program that causes the boys to grow beards raises their testosterone level, and their potential for aggression, to a level far above that of the adolescent woman. If society did not teach young girls that beating boys at competitions was unfeminine (behavior inappropriate for a woman), if it did not socialize them away from the political and economic areas in which aggression leads to attainment, these girls would grow into adulthood with self-images based not on succeeding in areas for which biology has left them better prepared than men, but on competitions that most women could not win. If women did not develop feminine qualities as girls (assuming that such qualities do not spring automatically from female biology) then they would be forced to deal with the world in the aggressive terms of men. They would lose every source of power their feminine abilities now give them and they would gain nothing. . . .

The most crucial of the feminist fallacies involves the confusion of cause and function. We need not involve ourselves in a detailed discussion of causation here; a simple example should suffice. A jockey is small because biology made him that way. There may be an element of feedback here in that the jockey might well weigh more if society did not reward his weighing as little as possible, but the causation involved in the determination of his physical characteristics is certainly primarily biological. The function that his size plays in society, its manifestation in his role of jockey, is not biological, but society's putting his size to use. Likewise, the economic functions that sexual differentiation requires do not cause the differentiation. The biological element of male aggression will manifest itself in any economic system. . . . Because the social and economic must conform to the biological, we can change any variable and patriarchy will not be diminished. Political rule is male whether the institutions relevant to private property, control of the means of production, and class stratification

---

[4]Eva Figes, *Patriarchal Attitudes* (Greenwich, Conn.: Fawcett World, 1971), p. 8.

are as minimally present as is possible or as advanced as is found in any society. It is male whether a society is patrilineal, matrilineal, or bilateral; patrilocal, matrilocal, or neolocal; white, black, or heterogeneous; racist, separatist, or equalitarian; primitive, preindustrial, or technological; Shintoist, Catholic, or Zoroastrian; monarchical, totalitarian, or democratic; Spartan, Quaker, or Bourbon; ascetic, hedonist, or libertine. It makes no difference whether a society has a value system that specifically forbids women from entering areas of authority or, like Communist China, an ideological and political commitment to equal distribution of authority positions. One cannot "disprove" the inevitability of biological factors manifesting themselves by demonstrating the function that they serve in a political or economic system. No system could operate that did not conform to, and utilize, the reality that constitutes it. In short, . . . reasoning that concludes that men rule because of the nature of the political-economic system . . . ignores the reality that the possible varieties of political-economic systems are limited by, and must conform to, the nature of man.

QUESTIONS

1 Are social practices that accord unequal treatment to the sexes justified?
2 In *Sex Equality* (Englewood Cliffs, N.J.: Prentice Hall), p. 196, Jane English argues that the following reasoning parallels Goldberg's. "Height is determined by hormones and genes. In virtually all societies, the tall dominate over the short. Even if ten percent of the population were exceptions, this would be irrelevant. Therefore, we should condition short children to accept the dominance of the tall and not to strive for positions of power and leadership." English claims that if this conclusion does not follow from the premises about height, then Goldberg's conclusion does not follow from his analogous claims about sex. Is English correct?

Sex Roles: The Argument From Nature

Joyce Trebilcot

Joyce Trebilcot is associate professor of philosophy at Washington University at St. Louis. Specializing in ethics and feminism, Trebilcot helped to establish a women's studies program at Washington University which she now coordinates. She is the editor of Mothering: Essays in Feminist Theory *(1984). Her articles include "Aprudentialism" and "Taking Responsibility for Sexuality."*

Trebilcot examines and evaluates three arguments frequently given to support the claim that natural psychological differences between the sexes are relevant in deciding whether some roles in society should be assigned on the basis of sex. (1) The argument from inevitability. Since the alleged psychological differences between the sexes and the concomitant differences in behavior are inevitable, society will inevitably be structured to enforce sex roles. Therefore, sex roles are inevitable. (2) The argument from well-being. Because there are natural psychological differences between the sexes, members of each sex will be happier in certain roles than in others; the roles tending to promote happiness will differ according to sex. Thus, society should encourage individuals to make the right role choices so that happiness will be maximized. (3) The argument from efficiency. If there are natural differences in the capacities of the sexes to perform specified tasks, then, for the sake of efficiency, these tasks should be assigned to the sex with the greatest innate ability to perform them.

I am concerned here with the normative question of whether, in an ideal society, certain roles should be assigned to females and others to males. In discussions of this issue, a great deal of attention is given to the claim that there are natural psychological differences between the sexes. Those who hold that at least some roles should be sex roles generally base their view primarily on an appeal to such natural differences, while many of those advocating a society without sex roles argue either that the sexes do not differ in innate psychological traits or that there is no evidence that they do.[1] In this paper I argue that whether there are natural psychological differences between females and males has little bearing on the issue of whether society should reserve certain roles for females and others for males.

Let me begin by saying something about the claim that there are natural psychological differences between the sexes. The issue we are dealing with arises, of course, because there are biological differences among human beings which are bases for designating some as females and others as males. Now it is held by some that, in addition to biological differences between the sexes, there are also natural differences in temperament, interests, abilities, and the like. In this paper I am concerned only with arguments which appeal to these psychological differences as bases of sex roles. Thus, I exclude, for example, arguments that the role of jockey should be female because women are smaller than men or that boxers should be male because men are more muscular than women. Nor do I discuss arguments which appeal directly to the reproductive functions peculiar to each sex. If the physiological processes of gestation or of depositing sperm in a vagina are, apart from any psychological correlates they may have, bases for sex roles, these roles are outside the scope of the present discussion.

It should be noted, however, that virtually all those who hold that there are natural psychological differences between the sexes assume that these differences are determined primarily by differences in biology. According to one hypothesis, natural psychological differences between the sexes are due at least in part to differences between female and male nervous systems. As the male fetus develops in the womb, the testes

Reprinted from *Ethics,* vol. 85, no. 3 (April 1975), pp. 249–255, by permission of the University of Chicago Press. Copyright © 1975 by The University of Chicago.

[1]For support of sex roles, see, for example, Aristotle, *Politics,* book 1; and Erik Erikson, "Womanhood and the Inner Space," *Identity: Youth and Crisis* (New York: W. W. Norton & Co. 1968). Arguments against sex roles may be found, for example, in J. S. Mill, "The Subjection of Women," in Alice S. Rossi, ed., *Essays on Sex Equality: John Stuart Mill and Harriet Taylor Mill* (Chicago: University of Chicago Press, 1970); and Naomi Weisstein, "Psychology Constructs the Female," in Vivian Gornick and Barbara K. Moran, eds., *Women in Sexist Society* (New York: Basic Books, 1971).

secrete a hormone which is held to influence the growth of the central nervous system. The female fetus does not produce this hormone, nor is there an analogous female hormone which is significant at this stage. Hence it is suggested that female and male brains differ in structure, that this difference is due to the prenatal influence of testicular hormone and that the difference in brains is the basis of some later differences in behavior.[2]

A second view about the origin of allegedly natural psychological differences between the sexes, a view not incompatible with the first, is psychoanalytical. It conceives of feminine or masculine behavior as, in part, the individual's response to bodily structure. On this view, one's more or less unconscious experience of one's own body (and in some versions, of the bodies of others) is a major factor in producing sex-specific personality traits. The classic theories of this kind are, of course, Freud's; penis envy and the castration complex are supposed to arise largely from perceptions of differences between female and male bodies. Other writers make much of the analogies between genitals and genders: the uterus is passive and receptive, and so are females; penises are active and penetrating, and so are males.[3] But here we are concerned not with the etiology of allegedly natural differences between the sexes but rather with the question of whether such differences, if they exist, are grounds for holding that there should be sex roles.

That a certain psychological disposition is natural only to one sex is generally taken to mean in part that members of that sex are more likely to have the disposition, or to have it to a greater degree, than persons of the other sex. The situation is thought to be similar to that of height. In a given population, females are on the average shorter than males, but some females are taller than some males, as suggested by figure 1.

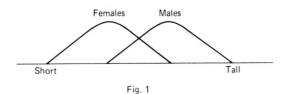

Females   Males

Short   Tall

Fig. 1

The shortest members of the population are all females, and the tallest are all males, but there is an area of overlap. For psychological traits, it is usually assumed that there is some degree of overlap and that the degree of overlap is different for different characteristics. Because of the difficulty of identifying natural psychological characteristics, we have of course little or no data as to the actual distribution of such traits.

[2]See John Money and Anke A. Ehrhardt, *Man and Woman, Boy and Girl* (Baltimore: Johns Hopkins Press, 1972).

[3]For Freud, see, for example, "Some Psychological Consequences of the Anatomical Distinctions between the Sexes," in James Strachey, ed., "Sigmund Freud: Collected Papers (New York: Basic Books, 1959), 5:186–97. See also Karl Stern, *The Flight from Woman* (New York: Farrar, Straus & Giroux, 1965), chap. 2; and Erikson.

I shall not undertake here to define the concept of role, but examples include voter, librarian, wife, president. A broad concept of role might also comprise, for example, being a joker, a person who walks gracefully, a compassionate person. The genders, femininity and masculinity, may also be conceived as roles. On this view, each of the gender roles includes a number of more specific sex roles, some of which may be essential to it. For example, the concept of femininity may be construed in such a way that it is necessary to raise a child in order to be fully feminine, while other feminine roles—teacher, nurse, charity worker—are not essential to gender. In the arguments discussed below, the focus is on sex roles rather than genders, but, on the assumption that the genders are roles, much of what is said applies, *mutatis mutandis,* to them.

A sex role is a role performed only or primarily by persons of a particular sex. Now if this is all we mean by "sex role," the problem of whether there should be sex roles must be dealt with as two separate issues: "Are sex roles a good thing?" and "Should society enforce sex roles?" One might argue, for example, that sex roles have value but that, even so, the demands of individual autonomy and freedom are such that societal institutions and practices should not enforce correlations between roles and sex. But the debate over sex roles is of course mainly a discussion about the second question, whether society should enforce these correlations. The judgment that there should be sex roles is generally taken to mean not just that sex-exclusive roles are a good thing, but that society should promote such exclusivity.

In view of this, I use the term "sex role" in such a way that to ask whether there should be sex roles is to ask whether society should direct women into certain roles and away from others, and similarly for men. A role is a sex role then (or perhaps an "institutionalized sex role") only if it is performed exclusively or primarily by persons of a particular sex *and* societal factors tend to encourage this correlation. These factors may be of various kinds. Parents guide children into what are taken to be sex-appropriate roles. Schools direct students into occupations according to sex. Marriage customs prescribe different roles for females and males. Employers and unions may refuse to consider applications from persons of the "wrong" sex. The media carry tales of the happiness of those who conform and the suffering of the others. The law sometimes penalizes deviators. Individuals may ridicule and condemn role crossing and smile on conformity. Societal sanctions such as these are essential to the notion of sex role employed here.

I turn now to a discussion of the three major ways the claim that there are natural psychological differences between the sexes is held to be relevant to the issue of whether there should be sex roles.

1   INEVITABILITY

It is sometimes held that if there are innate psychological differences between females and males, sex roles are inevitable. The point of this argument is not, of course, to urge that there should be sex roles, but rather to show that the normative question is out of place, that there will be sex roles, whatever we decide. The argument assumes first that the alleged natural differences between the sexes are inevitable; but if such differences are inevitable, differences in behavior are inevitable; and if differences in behavior are inevitable, society will inevitably be structured so as to enforce role differences according to sex. Thus, sex roles are inevitable.

For the purpose of this discussion, let us accept the claim that natural psychological differences are inevitable. We assume that there are such differences and ignore the possibility of their being altered, for example, by evolutionary change or direct biological intervention. Let us also accept the second claim, that behavioral differences are inevitable. Behavioral differences could perhaps be eliminated even given the assumption of natural differences in disposition (for example, those with no natural inclination to a certain kind of behavior might nevertheless learn it), but let us waive this point. We assume then that behavioral differences, and hence also role differences, between the sexes are inevitable. Does it follow that there must be sex roles, that is, that the institutions and practices of society must enforce correlations between roles and sex?

Surely not. Indeed, such sanctions would be pointless. Why bother to direct women into some roles and men into others if the pattern occurs regardless of the nature of society? Mill makes the point elegantly in *The Subjection of Women:* "The anxiety of mankind to interfere in behalf of nature, for fear lest nature should not succeed in effecting its purpose, is an altogether unnecessary solicitude."[4]

It may be objected that if correlations between sex and roles are inevitable, societal sanctions enforcing these correlations will develop because people will expect the sexes to perform different roles and these expectations will lead to behavior which encourages their fulfillment. This can happen, of course, but it is surely not inevitable. One need not act so as to bring about what one expects.

Indeed, there could be a society in which it is held that there are inevitable correlations between roles and sex but institutionalization of these correlations is deliberately avoided. What is inevitable is presumably not, for example, that every woman will perform a certain role and no man will perform it, but rather that most women will perform the role and most men will not. For any individual, then, a particular role may not be inevitable. Now suppose it is a value in the society in question that people should be free to choose roles according to their individual needs and interests. But then there should not be sanctions enforcing correlations between roles and sex, for such sanctions tend to force some individuals into roles for which they have no natural inclination and which they might otherwise choose against.

I conclude then that, even granting the assumptions that natural psychological differences, and therefore role differences, between the sexes are inevitable, it does not follow that there must be sanctions enforcing correlations between roles and sex. Indeed, if individual freedom is valued, those who vary from the statistical norm should not be required to conform to it.

[4]Mill, p. 154.

2 WELL-BEING

The argument from well-being begins with the claim that, because of natural psychological differences between the sexes, members of each sex are happier in certain roles than in others, and the roles which tend to promote happiness are different for each sex. It is also held that if all roles are equally available to everyone regardless of sex, some individuals will choose against their own well-being. Hence, the argument concludes, for the sake of maximizing well-being there should be sex roles: society should encourage individuals to make "correct" role choices.

Suppose that women, on the average, are more compassionate than men. Suppose also that there are two sets of roles, "female" and "male," and that because of the natural compassion of women, women are happier in female than in male roles. Now if females and males overlap with respect to compassion, some men have as much natural compassion as some women, so they too will be happier in female than in male roles. Thus, the first premise of the argument from well-being should read: Suppose that, because of natural psychological differences between the sexes, *most* women are happier in female roles and *most* men in male roles. The argument continues: If all roles are equally available to everyone, some of the women who would be happier in female roles will choose against their own well-being, and similarly for men.

Now if the conclusion that there should be sex roles is to be based on these premises, another assumption must be added—that the loss of potential well-being resulting from societally produced adoption of unsuitable roles by individuals in the overlapping areas of the distibution is *less* than the loss that would result from "mistaken" free choices if there were no sex roles. With sex roles, some individuals who would be happier in roles assigned to the other sex perform roles assigned to their own sex, and so there is a loss of potential happiness. Without sex roles, some individuals, we assume, choose against their own well-being. But surely we are not now in a position to compare the two systems with respect to the number of mismatches produced. Hence the additional premise required for the argument, that overall well-being is greater with sex roles than without them, is entirely unsupported.

Even if we grant, then, that because of innate psychological differences between the sexes members of each sex achieve greater well-being in some roles than in others, the argument from well-being does not support the conclusion that there should be sex roles. In our present state of knowledge, there is no reason to suppose that a sex role system which makes no discriminations within a sex would produce fewer mismatches between individuals and roles than a system in which all roles are open equally to both sexes.

3 EFFICIENCY

If there are natural differences between the sexes in the capacity to perform socially valuable tasks, then, it is sometimes argued, efficiency is served if these tasks are assigned to the sex with the greatest innate ability for them. Suppose, for example, that females are naturally better than males at learning foreign languages. This means that, if everything else is equal and females and males are given the same training in a foreign language, females, on the average, will achieve a higher level of skill than males. Now suppose that society needs interpreters and translators and that in order to have such a job one must complete a special training program whose only purpose is to provide persons for these roles. Clearly, efficiency is served if only individuals with a good deal of natural ability are selected for training, for the time and effort required to bring them to a given level of proficiency is less than that required for the less talented. But suppose that the innate ability in question is normally distributed within each sex and that the sexes overlap (see fig. 2). If we assume that a sufficient

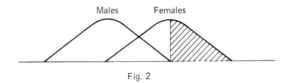

Fig. 2

number of candidates can be recruited by considering only persons in the shaded area, they are the only ones who should be eligible. There are no men in this group. Hence, although screening is necessary in order to exclude nontalented women, it would be inefficient even to consider men, for it is known that no man is as talented as the talented women. In the interest of efficiency, then, the occupational roles of interpreter and translator should be sex roles; men should be denied access to these roles but women who are interested in them, especially talented women, should be encouraged to pursue them.

This argument is sound. That is, if we grant the factual assumptions and suppose also that efficiency for the society we are concerned with has some value, the argument from efficiency provides one reason for holding that some roles should be sex roles. This conclusion of course is only prima facie. In order to determine whether there should be sex roles, one would have to weigh efficiency, together with other reasons for such roles, against reasons for holding that there should not be sex roles. The reasons against sex roles are very strong. They are couched in terms of individual rights—in terms of liberty, justice, equality of opportunity. Efficiency by itself does not outweigh these moral values. Nevertheless, the appeal to nature, if true, combined with an appeal to the value of efficiency, does provide one reason for the view that there should be sex roles.

The arguments I have discussed here are not the only ones which appeal to natural psychological differences between the sexes in defense of sex roles, but these three arguments—from inevitability, well-being, and efficiency—are, I believe, the most common and the most plausible ones. The argument from efficiency alone, among them, provides a reason—albeit a rather weak reason—for thinking that there should be sex roles. I suggest, therefore, that the issue of natural psychological differences between women and men does not deserve the central place it is given, both traditionally and currently, in the literature on this topic.

It is frequently pointed out that the argument from nature functions as a cover, as a myth to make patriarchy palatable to both women and men. Insofar as this is so, it is surely worthwhile exploring and exposing the myth. But of course most of those who use the argument from nature take it seriously and literally, and this is the spirit in which I have dealt with it. Considering the argument in this way, I conclude that whether there should be sex roles does not depend primarily on whether there are innate psychological differences between the sexes. The question is, after all, not what women and men naturally are, but what kind of society is morally justifiable. In order to answer this question, we must appeal to the notions of justice, equality, and liberty. It is these moral concepts, not the empirical issue of sex differences, which should have pride of place in the philosophical discussion of sex roles.

QUESTIONS

1 Summarize Trebilcot's criticisms of the arguments based on appeals to well-being and inevitability. Are her criticisms well-taken?
2 If there are innate psychological differences between the sexes, should society enforce sex roles?
3 If there are innate psychological sexual differences, should society attempt to minimize such differences?

Women's Work and Sex Roles

Janice Moulton and Francine Rainone

Janice Moulton is visiting assistant professor at Smith College. Her specializations are feminism, linguistics, and philosophical methodology. Moulton is co-author of The Organization of Language *(1981) and her articles include "Education and Sports: A Reply to 'Justice and Gender in School Sports.' " Francine Rainone has taught philosophy at the University of Colorado and at Colby Sawyer College, where she also headed Women's Studies. She and Moulton are coauthors of another, related article, "Sex roles and the Sexual Division of Labor."*

Moulton and Rainone argue that there is something wrong with sex roles as they presently exist. However, they criticize and reject the claim that sex roles are wrong *because* they restrict freedom and opportunity. The authors argue that *all* roles restrict freedom in some ways and yet roles are essential to our freedom. On their analysis sex roles as they presently exist in most societies are morally indefensible because they reinforce a sexual division of labor that functions to subordinate women. Moulton and Rainone conclude by considering alternative strategies for reducing the subordination of women to men.

Janice Moulton and Francine Rainone, "Women's Work and Sex Roles," in Carol C. Gould, ed., *Beyond Domination: New Perspectives on Women and Philosophy* (Totowa, N.J.: Rowman & Allanheld, 1984), pp. 189–203.

Most contemporary feminist critics maintain that sex roles ought to be abolished. Their argument is that sex roles restrict freedom and opportunity, and if they were abolished individual freedom would be enhanced and opportunities made more equal. On this view the interests of males as well as females would be served by such a change. We agree that much of what are called sex roles should be changed. But we consider this argument for their abolition to be inadequate because it neither tells us why women in particular are disadvantaged by sex roles, nor does it give a correct account of what is wrong with sex roles. In this essay we will argue that the problem is not that sex roles restrict freedom; rather the problem is that sex roles reinforce the sexual division of labor (SDL) that functions in most existing societies to subordinate women.

The concept of "role" is used quite widely—and very loosely—in contemporary social science. The more specific concept of a "sex role" is equally widespread: every college student who has taken an introductory sociology or psychology class can discuss roles and sex roles. Some have argued that these concepts are hopelessly inexact and foster confused thinking about the way society actually functions. We do not wish to enter into that debate here. Instead, we hope to show that theorists who criticize current sex roles base their criticisms on the wrong grounds. They do not understand what is really wrong with sex roles.

By focusing on sex roles one can easily lose sight of the main problem: subordination. Even if women freely choose their sex roles, these roles are still wrong whenever they subordinate women to men. We believe that sex roles and subordination are in principle independent; only under certain social conditions are sex roles pernicious.[1] Whether or not sex roles are pernicious depends on how they affect the total structure of society. When sex roles are used to effect the subordination of women, to prevent women from having an equal share in the distribution of social resources, they should be changed. On the restricts-freedom view of sex roles, sex roles are intrinsically wrong: because sex roles restrict the freedom of individuals to do certain things they are wrong. In the next section we challenge this claim, arguing that many roles that do restrict freedom are not wrong.

ALL ROLES RESTRICT FREEDOM

Dictionaries define a role as a part, an office, a duty, or a function. In addition to roles that people assume are roles that people just have, sometimes by choice and sometimes not. There are actors' roles and advisory roles, personal and professional roles, child, parent, and adult roles. The term "role" is used so broadly that nearly any pattern of behavior or function in a group or system can be called a role.

It is not sufficient for a behavior pattern or function to exist in a society for it to be a role; there must be expectations or standards about the behavior for it to be a role. It might even be said that social roles are characterized more by expectations and standards than by what people actually do. The expectations might be so unrealistic or impossible that no one, or hardly anyone, could ever meet them, but the role would still be characterized by the expectations and not by its fulfillment. For example, very few ballerinas in the world achieve the perfection of Makarova, yet her flawless performances help set the standards for that role. To give a different kind of example, it is almost impossible to be an ideal father, as that role is currently defined. Ideal fathers work long hours to provide the maximum in material benefits for their children, yet they are also supposed to spend long hours playing with and caring for their children. These two demands are incompatible, but they may still form the basis of our expectations of fathers.

On the other hand, people might follow a pattern of behavior or perform a function with no concomitant expectations or standards, which consequently would not be a role. For example, we all, in exhaling carbon dioxide, perform a function, but there are no expectations or standards about such behavior. We are not enjoined to exhale deeply near plants nor expected to produce certain amounts of carbon dioxide. Exhaling carbon dioxide is a pattern of behavior and a function, but it is not a social role.

Where there are expectations and standards in a society, rewards and penalties will be given according to how well people conform to the behavior patterns set by those expectations and standards. Some penalties may be merely the withholding of desired rewards, while in other cases social and legal sanctions may exist for ensuring conformity. The restrictions on freedom and opportunity that these penalties produce have been the subject of debate in previous discussions of sex roles.

It is certainly true that sex roles limit individual freedom and opportunity, but so do roles other than sex roles. One must be qualified to fill certain roles. The law restricts who may fill some roles and determines penalities for playing disallowed roles. Immigrants cannot be President; convicted felons cannot legally be gun owners. Freedom and opportunity are restricted because having one role can prevent a person from having another. Just as society tells us that men are not supposed to act like women, it also tells us that adults are not supposed to act like children and that lawyers are not supposed to dress like rock stars. One cannot simultaneously take a vow of silence and be on a debating team, have two nine-to-five jobs, be a boxer and a concert pianist, nor be a member of a city council and live in another city.

So sex roles are not alone in imposing limitations. The arguments used against sex roles will apply to any roles whatever: roles in general impose limitations on the people in them, and roles come with expectations about conduct, style, behavior, and so on, incurring sanctions when the expectations are not met.

Yet someone might argue that the sanctions imposed on sex role violators are particularly unfair; that while the severe sanctions imposed on felons and other disrupters of the social order are appropriate, those imposed on people who do not or cannot live up to sex role expectations are unjust. The argument might be that sanctions and restrictions arising from roles freely chosen are justified, but since sex roles are certainly not freely chosen, sex role restrictions are not fair.

This argument does not recognize that a great many occupations and social roles are not freely chosen, but rather are determined by economic necessity, social pressures, or ignorance about alternatives. And many of the roles that are chosen are done so with little information about the actual requirements of the roles. For example, all the roles involved in public entertainment attract many people, but most aspiring performers usually overlook the actual working conditions—low pay, job insecurity, long periods on the road. Influences such as early childhood experience (e.g., exposure, or lack of exposure, to team sports, musical training, or role models) often determine one's roles in later life. It is not clear, for example, that Wanda Landowska's being a harpsichordist was any more freely chosen than was her being a woman. Distinguishing acceptable roles from sex roles cannot be done on the assumption that the first are all freely chosen.

Let us emphasize this conclusion. The claim is that sex roles are unjust because they are not freely chosen. Nevertheless, many roles that most of us would allow to be unobjectionable, fair, and perhaps even beneficial to their holders are not freely chosen. Many factors interfere with free choice: ignorance, economic and social pressures, lack of ability. Yet the roles themselves might be rewarding, enriching, even desirable, and not at all unjust. Therefore it cannot be lack of free choice that makes sex roles unjust. It must be something else.

Many feminist critics argue that sex roles are wrong because they are assigned from birth rather than chosen. But we also do not choose whether we will be tall or short, attractive or ugly; and many roles depend on such attributes. Some might object that this analogy is faulty. It is true that one's height cannot be chosen any more than one's sex. But height materially disqualifies a person from fulfilling certain social roles, while sex does not, because it is not a relevant characteristic for fulfilling any social role. The answer to this objection is that *no* characteristic is relevant to the performance of a role if one is willing to change society and/or develop new technology. Short people could be basketball players with other short basketball players, or if gym shoes were designed to propel their wearers several feet into the air. Wealth would not be a relevant characteristic of potential political officeholders if campaigns were funded solely by public money. So the question is not what *is* relevant, but what *ought* to count as relevant. We do not believe that sex ought to be a relevant characteristic for the performance of social roles. But we are arguing against the claim that it ought not to be relevant *because* making it relevant limits women's freedom of choice. Let us examine the concept of freedom of choice and how it applies to this issue.

In the ordinary sense of free choice, someone chooses freely if s/he has alternatives, knows what the alternatives are, and chooses among them on the basis of preference rather than as a result of coercion. Unfortunately, it is very difficult to know what counts as coercion. Moreover, after enough coercion, people tend to have certain preferences. The feminist concern about sex role stereotyping in early education stems from this realization. But is it sensible to say, for example, that a 35-year-old woman is coerced into wearing make-up because of influences on her during her childhood and adolescence? And if not, can we say she freely chooses to wear make-up? Even if we could resolve these issues, the argument would still be unconvincing, for two reasons.

First, not all coercion is bad. In fact, education could hardly proceed without it. Children are coerced into learning many rules and types of behavior that curtail their freedom of choice about what sort of adults they become, in ways that we approve of. So proponents of this argument need to distinguish between acceptable and unacceptable coercion. Second, this argument cannot tell us why women are more severely disadvantaged by sex roles, because it ignores the issue of power and domination.

Boys are as coerced as girls to learn their socially determined role. A strong case can be made that men have *less* freedom to choose their sex roles and less latitude of behavior within them. Yet the sex roles of women attract more concern about injustice. This indicates that the real issue about sex roles is not freedom of choice, but the other effects of sex roles on their bearers. The real issue concerns the respective positions of women and men in the distribution of social resources, which result from sex roles. The central effect of sex roles is the perpetuation of a worldwide SDL in which:

> women are one-third of the world's formal labor force, and do four-fifths of all "informal" work, but receive only 10 percent of the world's income and own less than 1 percent of the world's property.[2]

The fact that sex roles reinforce the SDL, and thereby perpetuate the subordination of women to men, is what makes sex roles wrong. Even if it were true that many housewives had more freedom of choice in their daily lives than their husbands, this would not change the feminist problems with the position of housewives. The issue of whether men or women have more freedom to choose their social roles, or even whether they have any freedom at all, does not address the problem with sex roles. In sum, the free-choice argument is inadequate because it is based on a vague concept of free choice, and because it fails to confront the issues of power and domination.

One could try to distinguish sex roles from acceptable roles by claiming that the acceptable roles are restrictions on occupational roles, while sex roles are restrictions on persons. Restrictions on occupational roles include training and licensing requirements and rules in games and sports, and they are justified by the purpose they serve. But restrictions on persons as persons are not justified. This argument ignores the extent to which sex roles *are* job roles and how important that is for this issue. Let us consider it nonetheless. It claims that sex roles serve no purpose. But don't they? One can claim they tell people how to "play the game," if nothing else, and serve at least as much purpose as any other game. Or one can argue that they tell people what to expect of others. Perhaps they add stability to a culture. In a world where economic and political roles may fluctuate greatly, sex roles can provide a focus for one's self-identity because they are stable. So sex roles may serve a purpose just as some other roles do. This does not mean that their purpose cannot be served some other way, just as the purposes served by many other roles can be served in other ways. But it does mean that lack of purpose is not a reason for eliminating sex roles.

In addition, restrictions on occupations are, like sex-role restrictions, also restrictions on persons, namely the persons who have those jobs and who must do certain things, and the persons who do not have those jobs and therefore are not allowed to do certain things. A person not accepted to medical or dental school can never legally prescribe certain drugs; that is a restriction on that person whether or not she or he wanted to prescribe drugs. So sex roles do not appear to be significantly different from occupational roles after all.

Suppose one argues that the degree of severity of the sanctions and restrictions makes sex roles wrong. The trouble with sex roles, one might say, is that there are only two, and the social cost of nonconformity is very great. To show that this is true, one would have to show that the social cost of disobeying sex role expectations was greater than that of not living up to other standards and stereotypes. And it is not clear that this is true. It would seem, for example, that the social cost of breaking the law, of being poor or illiterate in an industrialized society, of being handicapped, old, or naive is greater than the social cost of being unmasculine or unfeminine (however they are characterized). One might contradict this by pointing out the threats of violence, the ostracism, or the fear of being locked up or left unprotected that come with sex role nonconformity. Yet felons, the mentally handicapped, and others have the same problems. The sanctions for sex role violations are not essentially different from the sanctions for other role violations. We may think sex role sanctions are worse than other sanctions because we think that they are wrong *and* can be corrected.

ROLES AREN'T WRONG

Freedom cannot be used to distinguish sex roles from other, acceptable roles. But instead of looking elsewhere to find out what is wrong with sex roles, we might conclude that all roles are wrong—that to guarantee individual freedom there should be no roles at all. We are going to argue that this second alternative is mistaken as well. We shall claim that roles are essential to our freedom because they provide information about what to expect when we make decisions, and that only with roles are informed choices possible. On our view, a society without roles would be impossible; roles could neither be abolished nor ignored when we act.

Suppose there were no roles. How then could we decide what specific activities to undertake, what is worth training for, or whether some activities will be rewarded well in the future? If there were no roles, there would be no expectations about patterns of behavior and functions and therefore no reason to believe that a person's current actions or situation are part of, or prerequisites for, particular future actions or situations. We could not require an education, apprenticeship, or practice to prepare an individual to become an X (driver, teacher, scuba diver) because that would amount to a role restriction. And if we went to school, served an apprenticeship, or practiced with the aim of becoming an X in this society-without-roles, we would be deluded. If there were no roles, no one would be able to gain an advantage by special training to fulfill some X, for that would restrict the people who had not trained to be Xs. We could not say that something was done well or ill because that would impose sanctions, restrictions on the way something was done; it would show that we had standards and expectations about doing X well. Work done toward a goal produces expectations that can, and very often will, be exhibited by rewards for some and punishments for others. If there were no roles, we could never decide between occupations or hobbies on the grounds that one appeared to involve more interesting activities, or more material rewards, or attracted more praise or respect than another, for all these attributes are part of the rewards and punishments that are supposed to be eliminated. If we chose occupations based on knowledge or beliefs of what we would do in those jobs, we would be using role expectations to make our decisions. Surely such a society without roles is both undesirable and impossible. Different sorts of things to do will always require training for some and produce expectations about performance, with praise for success and penalties for failure.

Consider the following analogy. Our theories and beliefs about the world affect our perceptions by restricting what we perceive, so that we see things one way and not another. But this restriction is what allows us to understand and make sense of the world, by organizing our experience and relating it to other knowledge. Similarly, roles constitute restrictions. They limit our freedom so that some choices are possible and others are not. But in so doing, roles provide information about the future—what behavior is possible, how behaviors are related, what treatment to expect from others. And this information is essential for making choices. If we had no theories and beliefs we would have no coherent perceptions at all, and if we had no roles in our society we would have no reason for making choices. The limitations that roles produce do restrict freedom, but without roles there would be no reason for freedom.

If our arguments so far are correct, we have established that all roles limit freedom and opportunity, but that this does not prove them unjustified. In fact, a world without roles would be impossible. This does not mean that every particular role is justified; far from it. But it does mean that to show what is wrong with sex roles we must show something other than that they limit freedom.

WHAT IS REALLY WRONG WITH SEX ROLES?

We have argued against the contention that the wrongness of sex roles is simply that they restrict individual freedom and opportunity. On this view there could be sex roles and sexual divisions of labor that are not at all morally objectionable. If we want to find out what is wrong with sex roles, we should look at their particular effects. For example, roles that can be characterized as women's roles are given fewer rewards, less respect, more menial chores, and less recognition than those that can be characterized as male roles. In this section we are going to claim that what *is* wrong with sex roles is that they provide the rationale, and even the idealogy, for a sexual division of labor that subordinates women to men.

We have to show that sex roles do function to give women their subordinate status in society, and that alternative explanations for the subordinate status of females are inadequate. And to do that we have to discuss more specifically what sex roles are.

To say that there are sex roles is to say that females perform and/or are expected to perform functions different from those of males. In some societies (ancient Greece and 20th-century Arab countries, for example) sex roles dictate that one sex does the shopping and that the other sex does the cooking. In other societies one sex is expected to do both the shopping and the cooking, and the other sex, neither. In our society, women are expected to raise children, and men are expected to repair cars, but not the other way around. Another part of our sex roles is that women are expected to earn less money than, and be shorter and younger than, their sexual partners.

There is no universal agreement about what each sex ought to do, and no single view about what sex roles are. We will consider two main versions of sex roles and show how they work together to promote women's subordination. There are "modern" versions that tell us what each sex's primary roles ought to be, but do not rule out the possibility that they can do other things as well, and "traditional" versions that specifically rule out certain roles for either sex. Someone might have a modern version of women's roles and a traditional version of men's roles, or vice versa. In fact, most people probably hold some combination of the two.

The modern version of female sex roles can be divided again into two, somewhat inconsistent, but nevertheless often held, requirements. The primary responsibility for a woman on this view is either to be a successful wife and mother, or to be attractive to men in general. Within this view may be a wide range of views about what counts as successful or attractive. The modern version of women's roles does not directly subordinate women to men, although it does assume that women's nature and value are given mainly in terms of their relationships with and acceptability to men. It is the one that is promoted in current advertising and suggests that women can be nuclear physicists, professional athletes, or workers on the Alaskan pipeline, as long as their jobs do not interfere with their roles as wives and mothers or with their attractiveness.

According to the modern version of sex roles, nothing in principle prevents women from doing other things, as long as they do not violate their primary roles. Success as a traditional wife and mother, however, requires considerable work in caring for a husband and teaching and caring for children. The work that wives and mothers do is unpaid and has low prestige, and this work leaves less time for other work. Since being a wife and mother is supposed to come first no matter what one's other work, problems with marriage or children are often blamed on the other roles, and a woman will be expected to curtail those other roles, making them subordinate to her job as a wife and mother, which is subordinate to the interests of her husband and/or children.

One might argue that the primary fault of this version of sex roles is that it is deceptive, a bit of false advertising. Being a wife and mother is touted as a desirable role, when in fact the working conditions are likely to be pretty poor. But this is not the whole problem. Even if the unpaid, low-prestige duties were made clear, the assignment or requirement of unpaid low-prestige duties to women is wrong. Would work-saving appliances and paid homemaking be a solution? (Of course, such suggestions would not help poor families, who could not afford the homemaker's salary and the appliances.) Suppose that housework were paid for from outside the family and independent of the earnings and evaluation of the others in the family who are employed outside. Poorly paid males might, if they married wisely, have excellent housekeepers with high salaries. But if such an institution were a reality, it is hard to believe that only wives or women would be housekeepers. Competition would arise, and skilled, professional housekeepers would want employment in the best home environments, not necessarily their own. Even for affluent families, the problem would remain that the woman's role is supposed to be that of a subordinate.

Let us consider the other requirement for the modern version of female roles. Sexual attractiveness is determined by the approval or disapproval of men. This may not seem different from many other roles where success is dependent on others—those of colleague, employer, or supervisor, for example. The important difference, however, is that this particular role relegates women *as a group* to a position subject to the approval of men, and hence to a lower status.

Couldn't one argue that this version of female roles has a parallel version for males and therefore does not subordinate one to the other? After all, many boys and unattached men feel that their success depends on female approval. Teenage boys and girls may both be particularly unhappy because they feel dependent on approval by the other sex. It seems to them that they will be failures if they are not appreciated by the other sex, despite their other accomplishments. Yet if male and female dependence on sexual approval were exactly parallel, there would be no difference in their status. But males *can* become respected and appreciated for their other accomplishments and be attractive to females as a *result of* their other accomplishments. In contrast, the primary way for females to be attractive to males is to be pretty. Simone de Beauvoir has pointed out that women are expected to wear a variety of clothing, keep up with fashion changes, and wear cosmetics and elaborate hair styles, and that all this leaves women with much less time (as well as less money) to pursue their other roles.[3] The expectation that they accomplish this in addition to other roles handicaps women in competition with men and contributes to their lesser status. In addition, being attractive to males is often considered a disqualification for some professional roles and/or an invitation to sexual harassment, which can make functioning in the other roles very difficult.[4] Another significant problem is that much physical labor, although well paid, is not thought appropriate for women. Physical strength is usually cited as the problem, but women can operate forklifts and many other power tools as well as men. The real problem seems to be that the work clothes, hard hats, sweat, and dirt involved in these jobs are not considered "feminine."

These modern versions of sex roles indirectly create and support a dominance hierarchy that places women on lower levels because they are women. Being successful as a wife and mother requires one to be subordinate to men and spend a great part of one's life doing unpaid, low-prestige work with less time available for well-paid, high-prestige work. Being attractive to men also requires considerable time taken away from other work, as well as being subordinate to the opinions and preferences of men in one's primary role. Still, the modern versions allow some latitude, and even though they place serious restrictions on women's ability to achieve other goals, it is possible on these views to play some other roles and still be a sex role success.

Since women do much more than fill the roles of wives and mothers or be sexually attractive, one could not say that men were dominant over women in general, or that sex roles supported this dominance, if women were not subordinate to men in their other roles. After all, they might be peers, colleagues, and even supervisors in their other roles. The subordination of someone in one role might only be one side of the story. Women might be subordinate to men in some roles and dominant over men in others. This is where the traditional version of sex roles complements the modern version, designating certain jobs as suitable for males and other jobs as suitable for females. Far fewer jobs are considered traditionally suitable for females, and they are concentrated at the lower ends of scales of pay, power, and prestige. So the more than 40 percent of the workforce that is female is crowded into a very small number of occupations. These occupations—nursing, clerical, secretarial, teaching (at the lower levels), domestic service, textile and electronic industries, food service jobs—pay little and/or require work largely under the supervision of men (nursing and secretarial work are clear examples of the latter).

The usual argument for a sexual divison of labor is that women are more suited for certain jobs and men for others. On this view, the function of the division of labor is economic efficiency, and the lower status is a side effect. It may be unfortunate, so the argument goes, that what women are suited for is not worth much, just as it is unfortunate that what mentally handicapped people are suited for is not worth much, but that's the way it is.

But let us look at some of the *activities* of the low-prestige, female-assigned occupations and compare them with those of some of the high-prestige, male-assigned occupations. If this division of labor *were* based on economic efficiency we would expect the actual work done to be of very different sorts. The skills and abilities required for female work ought to be different in kind from the skills and abilities required for male work. But are they really so different? It is expected that a woman can follow an intricate pattern for a dress or jacket, while reading a blueprint for a building or a road is thought inappropriate for her. Yet both activities require much the same skills: following a graphic representation, keeping note of dimensions and materials, and translating a two-dimensional outline into a three-dimensional object. The concepts dealt with by computer scientists might be thought more easily understood by males than females, yet at least two well-known books on computer programming explain the basic principles in terms of an analogy with knitting patterns.[5] We expect women to clean up the various excretions of babies and care for the diseased and dying, but morticians who do the same washing and dressing of the dead are almost always men. Women office workers are expected to manage switchboards, typewriters hooked to computers, photo-duplicating machinery, and dictaphones. Women homemakers may operate food processors, floor waxers, microwave ovens, sewing machines, and other machinery. But women are not supposed to be good at operating lathes, radial arm saws, or engine-tuning equipment (except during wartime). Women assemble most of the electronic equipment produced in this country, but electronic technicians are expected to be men. This list could go on, giving more evidence that there is no clear division between the activities that women are expected to perform at low or no pay and those that men are expected to perform.

Perhaps one might think that the assignment of women to subordinate positions is just a side-effect of the beliefs in different abilities of men and women. Women are assigned to the jobs that are less important for the society or to the jobs that do not require much training, because they are thought to be less important themselves or less able. However, it is easy to find examples to show that the importance of a job and the training required for it do not determine the status of the job when women's work is at issue. For example, women are responsible for creating the future citizens of the society and for the socialization and early cognitive training of these children, and for a society not much could be more important. Nurses, social workers, and school teachers receive more education and training than plumbers and garage mechanics, but are usually paid less. And female office workers usually come to their jobs with more of the relevant skills than do male office workers. So it does not look as if women are relegated to occupations that in fact deserve less prestige, but rather that those occupations have less prestige and pay because they are filled by women.

Furthermore, even if it were true that the subjugation of women were a secondary effect of other factors that determined job status, or a secondary effect of an interaction of haphazard factors, objecting to the sexual division of labor because it subordinates women would be no less appropriate. One does not have to attribute a motive or purpose to a social structure to condemn its ill effects. Since sex roles are not based on the activities themselves, since women's jobs are not distinguished from men's jobs by amount of training or other incidental properties, and since the difference in salaries, status, and other benefits between women's and men's jobs cannot be explained in terms of training or importance to society, we can conclude that the main function of the sexual division of labor supported by sex roles is to keep women subordinate to men.

CHANGING WOMEN'S WORK

It looks like the next approach ought to be to reduce the sexual division of labor. With this problem in mind, it has been argued that sex roles ought to be abolished.

In this chapter we have argued that sex roles are not wrong because they restrict freedom; all roles restrict freedom by directing our choices and providing frameworks for future action. If there were no such restrictions, making decisions would be like operating in a world without other physical objects: there would be no obstructions to movement, but also no reason to move in one direction rather than another, no reference points to guide our movements, and so no reason to move at all.

But sex roles *are* wrong because they foster the subordination of women to men. And we've considered the various ways different views of sex roles do this. Note that we have not claimed that sex roles or a sexual division of labor are necessarily wrong. They do subordinate women, but there could be sex roles or a sexual division of labor in which neither sex were subordinate. And this difference allows us to consider alternative strategies for changing this wrongness. No matter how well-trained or how necessary to society the work is, if it is characteristically done by women it is rewarded far less than work traditionally done by men. In the United States, for every dollar a man earns, a woman earns 59 cents. The average American woman with some college education will earn less in a full-time job than a man with less than seven years of schooling. In attempts to alter these inequities, many have argued for equal pay. This is an important and necessary step, but it is not enough because most women and men work at different sorts of jobs. Sixty percent of all working women are crowded into a few, predominantly female, professions—clerks, salespeople, waitresses, and hairdressers. Only 1 percent of all registered apprentices are female; 97.6 percent of all secretaries are female. And of course most of the work traditionally done by women is unpaid. So although equal pay for people with the same job classification is important, it will not end the subordination of women.

Another approach is the attempt to obtain for women equal pay for work of comparable value. On this approach, evaluation criteria are developed that attempt to measure the value of work in terms that are neutral with respect to the specific jobs. For example, truck drivers and secretaries would be assessed differently, and wages for "women's work" would rise dramatically. This is an innovative and important strategy for improving women's position in society. If it worked, it could equalize men's and women's salaries, and that would be a great step toward equality. But questions can be raised about its overall efficacy.

But would the actual outcome be the expected one? First, the strategy could backfire. Because of the higher status of men, identical accomplishments by men and women tend to be perceived differently.[6] So the criteria developed might result in *lowering* women's wages.

Second, it will be difficult to compare solidly female jobs with other jobs. For example, wages for child care might not rise at all. As more women move into a primarily male occupation, hierarchies and status differences could be created where there were none before, so that women would continue to have lower status than men in that profession.

Third, this strategy would leave women in the same subordinate positions in the job hierarchy they now occupy—female secretaries would still work for male management trainees—and therefore would leave them exposed to much of the same exploitation they now confront. Despite increased numbers of women entering the paid work force, women continue to have only token representation, if at all, in the highest ranks of highest status positions.

Fourth, nothing can be done to equalize the division of reproductive work, short of ceasing it altogether. We might acknowledge that making babies is a form of work that should be valued and rewarded like other forms of production. But this might not change the actual value accorded such work.

Last, this strategy would tend to reinforce the SDL, making it more difficult to challenge the notion that women and men are different "by nature." And this could make it even harder for women in this society to rise to the real positions of power, which are at the top of the hierarchy.

A dilemma confronts feminist organizers. To create sexual equality, women need to gain control of social resources. They cannot do this without doing "men's work." Men's work in the institutions by means of which social resources are controlled (for example, banks and governmental agencies) is based on a hierarchical power structure of domination and exploitation. Working in these institutions requires acting in accordance with these values, at least to some extent. But acting in accordance with these values strengthens the bases of oppression rather than weakening them.

To try to reduce the subordination of women by placing them in positions formerly reserved for men is to accept the value and status already accorded such positions. But perhaps we could do as much or more by questioning these values and trying to change the working conditions that support them. For example, what in the structure of office organization and job conceptions makes secretaries more subordinate to the people they type for than grocers and car salespeople are to the people they sell to?

What kind of fringe benefits, tax deductions, promotion opportunities, etc., that add to the status of men's work are not available for women's work? Does unionization or some other factor determine the larger salaries for construction workers than for nurses? Professional child-care centers and home appliances can relieve the work required for women's family roles, but do they improve the status and dignity of these roles—and if not, what else would?

This essay is just a preliminary to raising these questions, but we hope it leads to the consideration of other alternatives to remedy the subordination of women beyond trying to minimize the distinctions between women's work and men's work.

NOTES

1 See Eleanor Leacock, *Myths of Male Dominance: Collected Articles* (New York: Monthly Review Press, 1982); and Peggy Sanday, *Female Power and Male Dominance: On the Origins of Sexual Inequality* (Cambridge: Cambridge University Press, 1981), for discussions of societies that have sex roles based on SDL, but in which women are not oppressed.

2 Lisa Leghorn and Katherine Parker, *Woman's Worth: Sexual Economics and the World of Women* (Boston: Routledge and Kegan Paul, 1981), p. 14.

3 Simone de Beauvoir, *The Second Sex* (New York: Alfred A. Knopf, 1953).

4 We do not mean to imply that only "attractive" women are subject to sexual harassment. In *Sexual Shakedown* (New York: Warner, 1980), Lin Farley argues convincingly that the sexual division of labor is sustained largely by male sexual harassment.

5 Margaret Boden, *Artificial Intelligence and Natural Man* (New York: Basic Books, 1977), pp. 9–12; Douglas Hofstadter, *Gödel, Escher, Bach,* (New York: Vintage Books, 1979): pp. 149–50.

6 For documentation of this phenonmenon, see Phillip Goldberg, *Transactions* (April 1968): 28–30. Other works on this subject both criticize and support the original claim.

QUESTIONS

1 Do you agree with Moulton and Rainone that the modern version of women's roles assumes that women's nature and value are given mainly in terms of their relationships with and acceptability to men? If yes, is there anything wrong with this assumption?

2 Moulton and Rainone reject the "comparable value" approach to improving women's economic status. Is their reasoning sound?

Two Forms of Androgynism

Joyce Trebilcot

A biographical sketch of Joyce Trebilcot is found on page 152.

Trebilcot sees two opposing tendencies in the positions of those who advocate androgyny and relates these opposing tendencies to two versions of androgynism.

One version of androgynism, which she labels *monoandrogynism,* holds that every individual should develop all the positive characteristics traditionally associated with both male and female roles. On this view, there is one ideal type that every "healthy person" should exemplify. The second version of androgynism, *polyandrogynism,* requires only that people be free to adopt any morally acceptable psychological characteristics and social roles which are in keeping with their wishes and inclinations, unbound by any stereotypical social expectations. Whereas polyandrogynism emphasizes freedom of choice, monoandrogynism limits individuals insofar as it prescribes one type of personality as the ideal one. Trebilcot attempts to determine which of these two versions of androgynism is more acceptable. She opts for the provisional adoption of polyandrogyny on the basis of arguments from freedom and from universal value.

Traditional concepts of women and men, of what we are and should be as females and males, of the implications of sex for our relationships to one another and for our places in society, are not acceptable. But what models, if any, should we adopt to replace them? In this paper I consider just two of the alternatives discussed in recent literature—two versions of androgynism.

In discussing these two views I follow the convention of distinguishing between sex (female and male) and gender (feminine and masculine). Sex is biological, whereas gender is psychosocial. Thus, for example, a person who is biologically female may be—in terms of psychological characteristics or social roles—feminine or masculine, or both.

Although what counts as feminine and masculine varies among societies and over time, I use these terms here to refer to the gender concepts traditionally dominant in our own society. Femininity, on this traditional view, has nurturing as its core: it centers on the image of woman as mother, as provider of food, warmth, and emotional sustenance. Masculinity focuses on mastery: it comprises the notion of man struggling to overcome obstacles, to control nature, and also the notion of man as patriarch or leader in society and the family.

The first form of androgynism to be discussed here takes the word "androgyny" literally, so to speak. In this word the Greek roots for man *(andros)* and woman *(gynē)* exist side by side. According to the first form of androgynism, both feminine and masculine characteristics should exist "side by side" in every individual: each woman and man should develop personality traits and engage in activities traditionally assigned to only one sex. Because this view postulates a single ideal for everyone, I call it monoandrogynism, or, for brevity, *M.*

Monoandrogynism, insofar as it advocates shared roles, is now official policy in a number of countries. For example, the Swedish government presented a report to the United Nations in 1968 specifying that in Sweden, "every individual, regardless of

Reprinted with permission of the publisher from the *Journal of Social Philosophy,* vol. VIII, no. 1 (January 1977), pp. 4–8.

sex, shall have the same practical opportunities not only for education and employment but also fundamentally the same responsibility for his or her own financial support as well as shared responsibility for child upbringing and housework."[1]

Closer to home, Jessie Bernard, in her discussion of women's roles, distinguishes the one-role view, according to which woman's place is in the home; the two-role pattern, which prescribes a combination of the traditional housewife-mother functions and work outside the home; and what she calls the "shared-role ideology" which holds "that children should have the care of both parents, that all who benefit from the services supplied in the household should contribute to them, and that both partners should share in supporting the household."[2]

Caroline Bird in her chapter "The Androgynous Life" writes with approval of role-sharing. She also suggests that the ideal person "combines characteristics usually attributed to men with characteristics usually attributed to women."[3] The psychological dimension of M is stressed by Judith M. Bardwick. In her essay "Androgyny and Humanistic Goals, or Goodbye, Cardboard People," she discusses a view according to which the ideal or "healthy" person would have traits of both genders. "We would then expect," she says, "both nurturance and competence, openness and objectivity, compassion and competitiveness from both women and men, as individuals, according to what they were doing."[4]

The work of these and other writers provides the basis for a normative theory, M, which prescribes a single ideal for everyone: the person who is, in both psychological characteristics and social roles, both feminine and masculine.

The second form of androgynism shares with the first the principle that biological sex should not be a basis for judgments about the appropriateness of gender characteristics. It differs from the first, however, in that it advocates not a single ideal but rather a variety of options including "pure" femininity and masculinity as well as any combination of the two. According to this view, all alternatives with respect to gender should be equally available to and equally approved for everyone, regardless of sex. Thus, for example, a female might acceptably develop as a completely feminine sort of person, as both feminine and masculine in any proportion, or as wholly masculine. Because this view prescribes a variety of acceptable models, I call it polyandrogynism, or P.[5]

[1]Official Report to the United Nations on the Status of Women in Sweden, 1968. Quoted in Rita Liljeström, "The Swedish Model," in Georgene H. Seward and Robert C. Williamson, eds., *Sex Roles in Changing Society* (New York: Randon House, 1970), p. 200.

[2]Jessie Bernard, *Women and the Public Interest* (Chicago: Aldine, 1971); and idem, *The Future of Marriage* (New York: Bantam Books, 1972). The quotation is from the latter book, p. 279.

[3]Caroline Bird, *Born Female* (New York: Pocket Books, 1968), p. xi.

[4]Judith M. Bardwick, "Androgyny and Humanistic Goals, or Goodbye, Cardboard People," in Mary Louise McBee and Kathryn A. Blake, eds., *The American Woman: Who Will She Be?* (Beverly Hills, Calif.: Glencoe Press, 1974), p. 61.

[5]"Monoandrogynism" and "polyandrogynism" are perhaps not very happy terms, but I have been unable to find alternatives which are both descriptive and non-question-begging. In an earlier version of this paper I used "A₁" and "A₂" but these labels are not as perspicuous as "M" and "P." Mary Anne Warren in "The Ideal of Androgyny" (unpublished) refers to "the strong thesis" and "the weak thesis," but this terminology tends to prejudice judgment as to which view is preferable. Hence, I use "M" and "P."

Constantina Safilios-Rothschild supports *P* in her recent book *Women and Social Policy*. In this work she makes a variety of policy recommendations aimed at bringing about the liberation of both sexes. Liberation requires, she says, that individuals live "according to their wishes, inclinations, potentials, abilities, and needs rather than according to the prevailing stereotypes about sex roles and sex-appropriate modes of thought and behavior." Some persons, she adds, "might *choose* to behave according to their sex's stereotypic . . . patterns. But some women and some men may *choose*, if they are so inclined, to take options in some or all of the life sectors now limited to the opposite sex."[6]

Carolyn Heilbrun's work also suggests *P*. In *Toward a Recognition of Androgyny* she writes, "The ideal toward which I believe we should move is best described by the term 'androgyny.' This ancient Greek word . . . defines a condition under which the characteristics of the sexes, and the human impulses expressed by men and women, are not rigidly assigned. Androgyny seeks to liberate the individual from the confines of the appropriate." Androgyny suggests, Heilbrun says, "a full range of experience open to individuals who may, as women, be aggressive, as men, tender; it suggests a spectrum upon which human beings choose their places without regard to propriety or custom."[7]

This second form of androgynism focuses on a variety of options rather than on the single model of the part-woman/part-man (that is, of the androgyne in the classic sense). It is appropriate, however, to extend the term "androgynism" to apply to it; for, like *M*, it seeks to break the connection between sex and gender.

For both forms of androgynism, the postulated ideals are best construed so as to exclude aspects of traditional gender concepts which are morally objectionable. Femininity should not be taken to include, for example, weakness, foolishness, or incompetence. Similarly, tendencies such as those to authoritarianism and violence should be eliminated from the concept of masculinity. Most importantly, aspects of the gender concepts which prescribe female submissiveness and male domination (over women and over other men) must, on moral grounds, be excluded from both the single ideal advocated by *M* and the range of options recommended by *P*.

Either form of androgyny may, in the long run, lead to major changes in human attributes. It is often suggested that the androgyne is a person who is feminine part of the time and masculine part of the time. But such compartmentalization might be expected to break down, so that the feminine and masculine qualities would influence one another and be modified. Imagine a person who is at the same time and in the same respect both nurturant and mastery-oriented, emotional and rational, cooperative and competitive, and so on. I shall not undertake here to speculate on whether this is possible, or, if it is, on how such qualities might combine. The point is just that androgyny in the long run may lead to an integrating of femininity and masculinity that will yield new attributes, new kinds of personalities. The androgyne at this extreme

---

[6]Constantina Safilios-Rothschild, *Women and Social Policy* (Englewood Cliffs, N.J.: Prentice-Hall 1974), p. 7; emphasis hers.

[7]Carolyn Heilbrun, *Toward a Recognition of Androgyny* (New York: Harper & Row, 1973), pp. 7–8.

would perhaps be not part feminine and part masculine, but neither feminine nor masculine, a person in whom the genders disappear.

I turn now to the question of which of these two forms of androgynism is more acceptable. I am not concerned here to evaluate these positions in relation to other alternatives (for example, to the traditional sexual constitution of society or to matriarchy).[8] For the sake of this discussion, I assume that either *M* or *P* is preferable to any alternative, and that the problem is only to decide between them. Let us first consider this problem not as abstract speculation, and not as a problem for some distant society, but rather as an immediate issue for our own society. The question is then: Which form of androgynism is preferable as a guide to action for us here and now?

Suppose we adopt *M*. Our task then is to provide opportunities, encouragement, and perhaps even incentives for those who are now feminine to be also masculine, and conversely. Suppose, on the other hand, that we adopt *P*. Our task is to create an environment in which, without reference to sex, people choose among all (moral) gender alternatives. How can this best be accomplished? What is required, clearly, is that the deeply-entrenched normative connection between sex and gender be severed. Virtually everyone now, in formulating preferences for the self and in judging the appropriateness of gender characteristics for others, at least on some occasions takes it, consciously or otherwise, that the sex of the individual in question is a relevant consideration: that one is female tends to count in favor of a feminine trait and against a masculine one, and conversely. In order to break this connection, it must be shown that masculinity is acceptable for females and femininity for males. There must, then, be opportunities, encouragement, and perhaps even incentives for gender-crossing. But this is what is required by *M*. Hence, under present conditions, the two forms of androgynism prescribe the same course of action—that is, the promotion of gender-crossing.

The question "Which form of androgynism is preferable here and now?" then, is misconstrued. If one is an androgynist of either sort, what one must do now is seek to break the normative connection between sex and gender by bringing about gender-crossing. However, once the habit of taking sex as a reason for gender evaluation is overcome, or is at least much weaker and less widespread than it is today, then the two forms of androgynism do prescribe different courses of action. In particular, on *M* "pure" gender is condemned, but on *P* it is accepted. Let us consider, then, which version of androgynism is preferable for a hypothetical future society in which femininity and masculinity are no longer normatively associated with sex.

The major argument in favor of *P* is, of course, that because it stipulates a variety of acceptable gender alternatives it provides greater gender freedom than *M*. Now, freedom is a very high priority value, so arguments for *M* must be strong indeed. Let

---

[8]My current view is that we should work for the universal realization of women's values; but that is another paper. (For some arguments against the use of the term "androgyny" in feminist theory, see, for example, Mary Daly, "The Qualitative Leap beyond Patriarchal Religion," *Quest: A Feminist Quarterly*, vol. 1, no. 4 [Spring 1975], pp. 29ff.; and Janice Raymond, "The Illusion of Androgyny," *Quest*, vol. 2, no. 1 [Summer 1975].)

us consider, then, two arguments used to support *M* over *P*—one psychological, one ethical.

The psychological argument holds that in a society which is open with respect to gender, many people are likely to experience anxiety when faced with the need, or opportunity, to choose among different but equally acceptable gender models. Consider the words of Judith M. Bardwick:

> People need guidelines, directions that are agreed upon because they help each individual to know where one ought to go, how one can get there, and how far one is from one's goal. It is easier to sustain frustration that comes from knowing how far you are from your objective or what barriers are in your way than it is to sustain the anxiety that comes from not being sure about what you want to do or what others want you to do. It will be necessary, then, to develop new formulations by which people will guide their lives.[9]

Bardwick says that anxiety "comes from not being sure about what you want to do or what others want you to do." But in a society of the sort proposed by *P*, the notion that one should seek to please others in deciding among gender models would be rejected; ideally "what others want you to do" in such a society is to make your own decisions. Of course there is still the problem of not being sure about what *you* want to do. Presumably, under *P*, people would provide one another with help and support in finding suitable life-styles. Nevertheless, it could be that for some, choosing among alternatives would be anxiety-producing. On the other hand, under *M*, the lack of approved alternatives could produce frustration. Hence, the argument from anxiety should be paired with an argument from frustration. In *M*, socialization is designed to make everyone androgynous (in ways similar, perhaps, to those which have traditionally produced exclusive femininity and masculinity in our own society), and frustration is part of the cost. In *P*, socialization is directed toward enabling people to perceive, evaluate, and choose among alternatives, and there is a risk of anxiety. We are not now in a position to decide whether the frustration or the anxiety is worse, for there are no data on the numbers of people likely to suffer these emotions nor on the extent of the harm that they are likely to do. Hence, neither the argument from anxiety nor the argument from frustration is of any help in deciding between the two forms of androgynism.

I turn now to a more persuasive argument for *M*, one which claims that androgyny has universal value. This argument supports *M* not, as the argument from anxiety does, because *M* prescribes some norm or other, but rather because of the content of the norm. The argument holds that both traditional genders include qualities that have human value, qualities that it would be good for everyone to have. Among the elements of femininity, candidates for universal value are openness and responsiveness to needs and feelings, and being gentle, tender, intuitive, sensitive, expressive, considerate, cooperative, compassionate. Masculine qualities appealed to in this connection include being logical, rational, objective, efficient, responsible, independent, courageous. It

---

[9]Bardwick, *op. cit.*, p. 50.

is claimed, then, that there are some aspects of both genders (not necessarily all or only the ones I have mentioned) which are desirable for everyone, which we should value both in ourselves and in one another. But if there are aspects of femininity and masculinity which are valuable in this way—which are, as we might call them, virtues—they are *human* virtues, and are desirable for everyone. If Smith is a better person for being compassionate or courageous, then so is Jones, and never mind the sex of Smith or Jones. Hence, the argument concludes, the world envisioned by M, in which everyone or nearly everyone is both feminine and masculine, is one in which life for everyone is more rewarding than the world advocated by P, in which some people are of only one gender; therefore we should undertake to bring about M.

The argument claims, then, that both genders embody traits that it would be valuable for everyone to have. But how is this claim to be tested? Let us adopt the view that to say that something is valuable for everyone is, roughly, to say that if everyone were unbiased, well-informed, and thinking and feeling clearly, everyone would, in fact, value it. As things are now, it is difficult or impossible to predict what everyone would value under such conditions. But there is an alternative. We can seek to establish conditions in which people do make unbiased, informed, etc., choices, and see whether they then value both feminine and masculine traits.

But this reminds us, of course, of the program of P. P does not guarantee clear thought and emotional sensitivity, but it does propose an environment in which people are informed about all gender options and are unbiased with respect to them. If, in this context, all or most people, when they are thinking clearly, etc., tend to prefer, for themselves and others, both feminine and masculine virtues, we will have evidence to support the claim that androgyny has universal value. (In this case, P is likely to change into M.) On the other hand, if "pure" gender is preferred by many, we should be skeptical of the claim that androgyny has universal value. (In this case we should probably seek to preserve P.) It appears, then, that in order to discover whether M is preferable to P, we should seek to bring about P.

In summary, we have noted the argument from freedom, which supports P; arguments from anxiety and frustration, which are indecisive; and the argument from universal value, whose analysis suggests the provisional adoption of P. As far as I know, there are no additional major arguments which can plausibly be presented now for either side of the issue. Given, then, the problem of deciding between M and P without reference to other alternatives, my tentative conclusion is that because of the great value of freedom, and because in an atmosphere of gender-freedom we will be in a good position to evaluate the major argument for M (that is, the argument from the universal value of androgyny), P is preferable to M.

Of course all we have assumed about the specific nature of the hypothetical society for which we are making this judgment is that the connection between sex and gender would be absent, as would be the unacceptable components of traditional gender concepts, particularly dominance and submission. It might be, then, that particular social conditions would constitute grounds for supporting M rather than P. For example, if the society in question were hierarchical with leadership roles tightly held by the predominantly masculine individuals, and if leaders with feminine characteristics were more likely to bring about changes of significant value (for example, eliminating war or oppression), it could reasonably be argued that *M,* in which everyone, including leaders, has both feminine and masculine characteristics, would be preferable to *P.* But such conditions are only speculative now.

QUESTIONS

1 Trebilcot wants everyone to have the opportunity to develop into an *autonomous* individual. In your view, what characteristics are essential components of the autonomous personality?
2 In "Trebilcot on Androgynism" (*Journal of Social Philosophy,* 10 [May 1979], pp. 1–4) Mark Timmons and Wayne Wasserman argue that monoandrogyny is the ideal toward which all individuals should strive. In their view, it is this ideal which "most closely resembles our conception of the ideal *autonomous* moral agent," and, as such, should be adopted by our society as a universal ideal. Do you agree with Timmons and Wasserman? If yes, what arguments would you offer to counter those of Trebilcot?

Are Androgyny and Sexuality Compatible?

Robert G. Pielke

Robert G. Pielke is associate professor of philosophy and religious studies at George Mason University. He specializes in social and political philosophy, ethical theory, and normative ethics. Pielke's published work includes "Recent Science Fiction and the Problem of Evil."

Pielke challenges an objection that is sometimes made against androgyny: Androgyny should not be adopted as a social ideal because it is incompatible with sexuality. Proponents of this objection see an androgynous society as one in which all individuals have the same psychological characteristics and take this to be incompatible with sexual attraction. Working with Trebilcot's distinction between monoandrogyny (M) and polyandrogyny (P), Pielke begins by clarifying the concept of androgyny. On his analysis, although both M and P would exclude certain character traits, each would allow a genuine choice among some combinations. Thus, all kinds of personality differences would still exist. After briefly discussing the concept of sexuality, Pielke concludes by arguing that androgyny is not only compatible with sexuality, it may actually enhance it.

Proponents of androgyny as a social ideal must respond to a number of serious and challenging objections. Among them are the claims that androgyny would be detrimental to mental health,[1] that it would covertly endorse a traditional and therefore

Robert G. Pielke, "Are Androgyny and Sexuality Compatible?" in Mary Vetterling-Braggin, ed., *"Femininity," "Masculinity," and "Androgyny": A Modern Philosophical Discussion* (Totowa, N.J.: Rowman & Allanheld, 1982), pp. 187–196.

sexist heterosexuality[2] and further, that it would actually require universal masculinization.[3] The literature abounds with discussions on these and related topics. An
unspoken, and perhaps even unconscious, objection however, is a fear that androgyny
would in some way be incompatible with sexuality, and it is this objection which I
intend to explore in what follows. To my knowledge, no advocate of androgyny has
attempted to do this, yet I feel that it just might be the underlying basis for most, if
not all, of the other objections. If this fear is the fundamental problem, a satisfactory
response would inevitably make androgyny a much more attractive style of life.

My initial intuition is that the fear of androgyny being incompatible with sexuality
is completely unfounded, and that on the contrary androgynous people would enjoy
a quantitative and qualitative enhancement of their sexuality. In order to see whether
this would in fact be the case, it will first be necessary to clarify the concept of
androgyny itself as far as it is possible. Then, after a brief characterization of sexuality,
the precise nature of the fear will have to be examined and shown to be groundless.
It should then be apparent that androgyny is not only compatible with sexuality but
is also likely to enhance it significantly.

I

Androgyny is an exceedingly tricky concept for its literal meaning continues to raise
questions. A mixture of male and female traits (*andros* means man and *gyne* means
woman) tells us nothing about how those traits are to be mixed, their desirable proportions, if all traits are equally valuable, whether a variety of mixtures is possible,
or even if these traits are psychological, behavioral, physiological, or all three. Clearly,
the first task for anyone discussing androgyny is to specify precisely what meaning
the term is to have. Fortunately, a consensus is emerging so that debates about the
merits of androgyny need not become fruitlessly stalled at this preliminary stage. The
distinction drawn by Joyce Trebilcot between monoandrogyny and polyandrogyny, for
example, has advanced the meaning of androgyny considerably,[4] and I plan to make
use of this distinction in describing how I understand the term.

Trebilcot's first category, monoandrogyny (M), is understood by advocates as a
single ideal for everyone. Monoandrogynous people would thus adopt most of the
psychological characteristics and social roles which have been traditionally assigned
to both masculine *and* feminine genders.[5] These hitherto bifurcated traits would thus
exist simultaneously in the very same person. What comes immediately to mind is the
term "unisex," most often used pejoratively. There are, however, quite a few people
who seem to consider this desirable, at least according to Trebilcot. Her second
category, polyandrogyny (P), derives from the proposal that "not a single ideal but
rather a variety of options including 'pure' femininity and masculinity as well as any
combination of the two" be available regardless of a person's biological sex.[6] Again,
there are a number of supporters for this as a social ideal.

The underlying connection between the two, as she rightly points out, is an attempt
to break the connection between sex and gender. This means bringing into play a
fundamental moral principle, namely, "that biological sex should not be a basis for
judgments about the appropriateness of gender characteristics."[7] It seems to me that

proponents of androgyny (whatever its meaning) *must* affirm this in some way, otherwise their efforts would involve self-contradiction. A second, more specific, moral principle is also brought into play by Trebilcot, but this one is *not* logically entailed by either M or P. It is the notion that gender traits which are morally objectionable ought to be "excluded from both the single ideal advocated by M and the range of options recommended by P."[8] Now, as it happens, I agree with her on this, but she has provided no argument for this moral assertion; neither has she given any basis for judging which traits are objectionable and which are not. Although this might first appear to be a trivial objection, it is by no means obvious (to everyone) which traits are morally desirable and which are not. Some, such as courage and nurturance have a positive connotation. But others, such as aggressiveness and modesty, are questionable. Conceivably, advocates of androgyny could propose combinations of traits which would offend nearly everyone's moral sensibilties.

I strongly feel that there *are* independent moral arguments for ruling out such offensive traits as submissiveness, foolishness, incompetence, and weakness for women, and dominance, authoritarianism, and violence for men (the very ones Trebilcot mentions). I don't feel that it is necessary to develop them here, for others have done so at length elsewhere. Suffice it to say that an advocate of androgyny must specify and provide a defense for which traits are morally acceptable options (P), or which ones can legitimately be used in constructing a single ideal (M). But regardless of what moral norm is used to exclude offensive traits, it must be applied universally so as to avoid arbitrariness. Thus if a trait is desirable it ought to be adopted, if it is undesirable, it ought to be discouraged, but if it is *neither,* it ought to be up to the individual as to whether to adopt it or not. This triple distinction between right, wrong, and obligatory (often overlooked in ethical disputes) allows the freedom of choice argument implicit in P as well as the argument from virtue implicit in M. The task is simplified considerably, however, when M and P are examined more closely. For they turn out to be pretty much the same, if not identical, as they are actually dealt with by Trebilcot. Hence the confusing situation will never arise wherein traits found morally acceptable, or even obligatory, for one version of androgyny are not also found acceptable for the other.

Given the norms to break the connection between sex and gender and to exclude offensive traits, one other criterion must be kept in mind: the logical (and perhaps empirical) requirement of consistency or noncontradiction. Together, these three criteria form the necessary preconditions for a single version of androgyny. With regard to the third criterion, it would make no logical or empirical sense to construe as obligatory traits which contradict one another, or even to consider as permissible traits which would conflict with obligatory traits. The most meaningful way to conceptualize obligatory (or desirable) traits is to understand them as virtues (and the undesirable ones as vices). In accordance with the basic norm to break the link between sex and gender, virtues and vices must be seen as *human,* not sex-linked, dispositions. As such, the virtues would necessarily be compatible, since it would clearly be absurd for a moral theory to encourage dispositions which, if acted on, would contradict one another. However, not all traits are either obligatory or forbidden, having more to do with personality than with character. Admittedly, while it is enormously difficult to decide which traits are optional, it should nevertheless be obvious that, whatever they are, they are permissible if and only if they do not conflict with any of the virtues. (Again, the threefold distinction is crucial.) Although Trebilcot seems to recognize the possibility that some traits might not be compatible, she declines to speculate on what practical effects this logical limitation might have.[9] Others, however, have not been so reluctant. Ann Ferguson points out that "as we presently understand these [masculine and feminine] stereotypes, they exclude each other," and she then proceeds to illustrate their logical and empirical incompatibilities.[10] Carrying the point further, Janice Raymond says that "one would not put master and slave language or imagery together to define a free person," clearly pointing out the absurdity of such a proposal.[11]

While there are certainly many other traits which would be disqualified on grounds of inconsistency, it should be rather obvious that neither M nor P can include certain traditionally feminine and masculine gender characteristics (which include virtues and vices as well as other kinds of traits). In other words, when properly understood, androgyny rules out genderization as we have come to know it. Whatever else it might affirm (and this would depend on a moral assessment of character and personality traits), it would reject "pure" femininity and masculinity as well as many combinations of the two. Nevertheless, within certain logical and moral (including nonsexist) limitations, it would still permit a real choice among some combinations.

II

In dealing with the phenomenon of human sexuality, it must be kept in mind that many physiological, psychological, and behavioral factors are involved in a very complex interrelationship. Attempts to understand the phenomenon philosophically have differed, often dramatically, making conceptual clarity difficult, if not impossible. For the purpose of this paper, however, sexuality may be understood simply as a certain kind of desire and/or the behavior intended to satisfy it. Most important is the fact that sexual desire, so specified, is not something which is subject to choice; it is a major component in the struggle of all life-forms to survive. Commonly characterized as a need or an appetite, it functions as a primary motivating force in human life (if not the basic one). Further, while this desire certainly has biological or physiological roots, the objects of desire and the activities undertaken to fulfill it are socially defined. Thus sexual desire is logically and empirically independent of both the objects of desire as well as sexual behavior itself. Consequently, while sexual activity and the choice of objects are open to the varying influences of differing societies and cultures, humans inevitably *will* have sexual desire for *some* object or objects and *will* try to act accordingly (barring physical and/or psychological impairments).

The fear that androgyny would inhibit or even abolish our sexuality is typically expressed in emotive outbursts such as, "if women (or men) were to act like men (or women), then I wouldn't want anything to do with them," or "I can't get turned-on to somebody who looks and behaves like me," or simply "vive la difference!" Implicit in these remarks and others like them is a belief that a sex-based gender differentiation is essential for sexual attraction or desire. The fear is that a society *un*differentiated by gender would somehow result in the permanent inactivity or possibly the destruction of the sex drive itself. After all, so the rhetorical claim seems to go, when the objects of desire are no longer specifically identified, can the desire long remain? Opposing gender traits alone are apparently thought to be responsible for eliciting sexual desire (which is perhaps thought to lie dormant until awakened); so to obviate such differences might destroy the mechanism of arousal itself. Presumably, the sex drive is regarded as totally passive, waiting to be triggered by gender-traits different from those of the agent. If there is no opportunity for this to happen, not only will the drive never be activated, it might actually atrophy. The aphorism, "use it or lose it" only makes sense in this context. (Interestingly enough, there is seemingly no female equivalent for this warning. No doubt this omission stems from the sexist notion that arousal, initiation, intercourse and orgasm have traditionally been understood in a stereotypically masculine fashion.)

Another related fear is that the loss of differentiated sex roles would remove the guidance and direction that such roles provide. Many people perceive this as a distinct threat. In societies where rigid gender differentiation is maintained, all expressions of sexuality are rigorously channeled through sex roles. This includes prescribing who are to be considered desirable partners, how to attract them, how to recognize favorable and unfavorable reactions, what constitutes acceptable and satisfying physical activity, how to perform such activity and for what purposes. Nothing is left to chance; everything is laid out in a pattern to be followed. When confronted with forces as powerful as the sex drive, this affords the individual a great deal of security and comfort. To remove these patterns would, accordingly, cause considerable distress. Without their guidance, the sex drive could not identify a suitable object, know what to do with one or why. As a result, sexuality could be expected to diminish or even die. Again, the underlying assumption seems to be that the sexual drive is passive, awaiting specific gender-traits to trigger it!

In responding to these two related fears, I want to avoid relying on the obvious rejoinder, namely, an analogy to our appetite for food. It would go something like this: even if all food looked and tasted the same, we'd still get hungry and often eat ravenously. But this analogy does as much harm to my case as any good it might do, for it grants a point which androgynists need not and should not grant. It concedes the implicit accusation that everyone would look and act alike if the connection between biological sex and gender (sex roles) were broken. As we have already seen, this is not what proponents of androgyny as M or P actually favor. On the contrary, within certain logical and moral (including nonsexist) parameters, there would be a considerable variety of options available. Even if a wide variety of traits were deemed obligatory (and hence virtuous), there would still be numerous permissible traits which would ensure individuality. Granted, none of them would be tied to biological sex; but if this is used as an objection, it is different from the ones being considered here. No matter how androgyny is initially construed, as long as the three preconditions are met, there would be enormous variations in how people are disposed to look and act.

A better response to these two fears would begin by pointing out that they only make sense in a thoroughly genderized context, one in which biological sex is the basis for gender differentiation. It is obviously the case in such societies that if a "woman" ceases playing her assigned role and instead plays that of a "man" (or some deviant role), most (if not all) "men" would not find her appealing; they've been programmed to find only "women" appealing. The same is true in reverse, of course. However, in a society in which the connection between traits and sex has been broken and there are a variety of morally acceptable role options, the problem of "women" acting like "men" would never arise. There would be no prescribed patterns of sexual expectations, and activities; therefore, the sex drive would not be held to any rigid paths in seeking satisfaction. Anything moral would go! If this kind of situation is considered threatening, then so be it; if androgyny is morally desirable, then any loss of direction and guidance will simply have to be endured. Besides, it is highly questionable if such a loss would occur. What would be abandoned is gender, not morality, and moral guidance would seem to be quite sufficient for countering any putative, psychological threat. So to the extent that both versions of the fear presuppose a "unisex" understanding of androgyny, they are unfounded.

Even more significant is the misconception of sexuality that both assume. The idea that the sex drive is passive, waiting to be activated by gender-traits opposite those of the agent, is naive and based, in all probability, on an antiandrogynous ideology, and not on any kind of evidence. The only evidence that I'm familiar with supports the idea that sexual desire is both logically and empirically independent of a sexual object. The choice of this object may, of course, be culturally determined; but it need not be. Without sex roles to prescribe which objects should be of interest to us, the sex drive would still survive. The object has nothing whatsoever to do with the drive; it has everything to do with its satisfaction, in that *some* object (real or imagined) seems to be needed. But this hardly rules out androgyny as an ideal. Thus to the extent that both versions of the fear assume a passive interpretation of sexual desire, they are, again, unfounded.

Being unfounded, the original claim that sexuality (i.e., sexual desire as well as any activity which would tend to fulfill it) is incompatible with androgyny is clearly false. Furthermore, there is every reason to believe that an androgynous society would actually enhance sexuality, both quantitatively and qualitatively. Since the traditional sex roles (gender) have served to *restrict* the sex drive in every conceivable way, their removal would inevitably serve to encourage a much freer and more abundant sex life than ever before. This being the case, the overall *quality* of sex must similarly increase, just as the unlimited availability of food would enhance our ability to make better judgments about taste. Whether or not this increase in quantity and quality would be desirable is another question, but it's hard to imagine an argument against it. In fact, it should provide a rather convincing argument why androgyny ought to be adopted!

While these fears have been shown to be illusory, there is at least one genuine problem that arises during an attempted transition to androgyny. Those persons who are conscientiously attempting to move beyond gender differentiation, while living in a society with traditional sex-roles, are caught in a particularly difficult situation. They are almost always misunderstood by androgynists and nonandrogynists alike. Traditional societies will simply not permit its members to be perceived as not playing some kind of sex role (even though it might be a deviant sex role, e.g., "butch," "dyke," "queen," or "macho-man"). Most often such people are viewed as transsexuals or, more crassly, "queers." Only another androgynist has the capacity to make an accurate interpretation, but this is certainly no guarantee. When it comes to expressions of sexual interest, for example, there is just no way to be confident whether a sexual overture is androgynous or not. Aside from some obvious types of genderized behavior, an overture by itself gives no clue. Visually inspecting and appreciating another person's body is consistent with any social form.

The fact that such a problem arises, however, is further evidence that androgyny is not incompatible with sexuality. Indeed, the more the problem surfaces, the greater the probability that androgynous individuals are increasing their sexual activities. If this is so, people who have feared androgyny may be persuaded to convert to the androgynous ideal.

NOTES

1 For example, Ronald A. LaTorre, *Sexual Identity* (Chicago: Nelson-Hall, 1979), argues that sexual differentiation is vital for a person's mental health, although such a society need not be sexist (pp. 145–46).

2 For example, Catherine Stimpson, "The Androgyne and the Homosexual," *Women's Studies* 2, no. 2 (1974): 237–47. "It [androgyny] fails to conceptualize the world and to organize phenomena in a new way that leaves 'feminine' and 'masculine' behind" (p. 242).

3 For example, Janice Raymond, "The Illusion of Androgyny," *Quest: A Feminist Quarterly* 2 (Summer 1975): 57–66, defines her ideal society as one of "Integrity," which seeks to go beyond one that is gender-defined. The androgynization of our present society would be no more than its masculinization! (pp. 61–64).

4 Joyce Trebilcot, "Two Forms of Androgynism," in *Feminism and Philosophy,* ed. Mary Vetterling-Braggin, Frederick Elliston, and Jane English (Totowa, N.J.: Littlefield, Adams and Co., 1977), pp. 70–78.

5 Ibid., pp. 71–72.

6 Ibid., p. 72.

7 Ibid.

8 Ibid., p. 73.

9 Ibid.

10 Ann Ferguson, "Androgyny as an Ideal for Human Development," in Vetterling-Braggin, Elliston and English, op. cit., p. 46.

11 Raymond, op. cit., p. 61.

QUESTIONS

1 Would sexuality be enhanced in an androgynous society? What reasons can you give to support your answer?

2 What, if any, are the advantages of an androgynous society? Of a society with rigid gender differentiations?

SUGGESTED ADDITIONAL READINGS FOR CHAPTER 4

FELDBERG, ROSLYN L.: "Comparable Worth: Toward Theory and Practice in the United States." *Signs,* vol. 2, 1984, pp. 311–328. Feldberg first presents a brief history of women's low wages in the United States. She then argues for comparable worth policies as one way of liberating women from poverty and social, economic, and political subordination.

GOULD, CAROL C., ed.: *Beyond Domination: New Perspectives on Women and Philosophy*. Totowa, N.J.: Rowman and Allanheld, 1984. This collection of articles includes a section on sex, gender, and women's identity as well as one on work, personal relations, and political life.

JAGGAR, ALISON M.: *Feminist Politics and Human Nature*. Totowa, N.J.: Rowman & Allanheld, 1983. Jaggar identifies and evaluates four alternative conceptions of women's liberation: liberal feminism, traditional Marxism, radical feminism, and socialist feminism. She argues for the latter. Jaggar's discussion includes an examination of the conceptual connections between the various political philosophies and theories of human nature.

LOWE, MARIAN, and RUTH HUBBARD, eds.: *Woman's Nature: Rationalizations of Inequality*. New York: Pergamon Press, 1983. The authors of the articles in this collection share a common conviction: there is no single myth of woman's nature. Writing from the perspectives of their own disciplines—chemistry, biology, sociology, anthropology, and the history and philosophy of science—they examine some of these myths and their effects on the status of women.

MCMILLAN, CAROL: *Women, Reason and Nature: Some Philosophical Problems with Feminism*. Princeton, N.J.: Princeton University Press, 1982. McMillan argues that feminists and their critics share a common view about the nature of rationality and about the relation between personhood and reason. She argues that this view is mistaken and has led feminists to advocate the "misguided" goals of equality and androgyny.

POSTOW, BETSY C., ed.: *Women, Philosophy, and Sport: A Collection of New Essays*. Metuchen, N.J.: The Scarecrow Press, 1983. Many of the articles in this collection focus on questions of gender and justice in sports.

RESTAK, RICHARD M.: *The Brain: The Last Frontier*. Garden City, N.Y.: Doubleday, 1979. This is a very readable survey of recent attempts to combine brain science with behavioral science to provide a psychological explanation of how the physical functions of the human brain affect language, health, emotion, intelligence, and personality. Restak, a neurologist, discusses the cultural, moral, philosophical, and political implications of the recent psychobiological theories.

VETTERLING-BRAGGIN, MARY, ed.: *"Femininity," "Masculinity," and "Androgyny": A Modern Philosophical Discussion*. Totowa, N.J.: Littlefield, Adams, & Company, 1982. The articles in this collection center on notions of sex and gender, the nature-nurture controversy, and androgyny.

WARREN, MARY ANNE: *The Nature of Woman: An Encyclopedia and Guide to the Literature*, 2 vols. Inverness, Calif.: Edgepress, 1980. This work includes over a thousand entries. The majority of the items cited are written by contemporary American philosophers and social scientists.

CHAPTER 5

DISCRIMINATION AND REVERSE DISCRIMINATION

Before the 1960s and 1970s blatant racial discrimination was a fact of life for many minorities, especially blacks.[1] Many factors, including discrimination in housing, inferior education, and outright denial of access to most nonmenial positions as well as to union membership, kept the majority of blacks in the lowest economic strata of American society. Attempts to justify the unequal treatment accorded blacks rested at times on claims about inherent differences between blacks and members of the preferred groups. Frequently cited were the results of IQ or other psychometric tests purporting to support the claim that blacks by nature did not have the same cognitive abilities or psychological makeup as members of the preferred groups. Claiming that such differences were relevant ones, defenders of racially unequal treatment argued that these practices were just because they were in keeping with the formal principle of justice, the principle of equality, which allows the unequal treatment of unequals.[2] In rebuttal, those who condemned the unequal treatment of blacks argued either that there were no such inherent differences between blacks and others or that, even if there were some kind of cognitive or other psychological differences, they were statistical and not universal.[3] In response to claims about differences in IQ test results among races and ethnic groups, for example, the following reasoning was advanced: (1) IQ tests are culturally biased; they tend to favor middle- and upper-class children, and many blacks come from the lower economic groups; and (2) regardless of the findings about

---

[1]To say this is not to claim that discrimination against blacks and other minorities no longer exists. But before the legislation of the 1960s and 1970s it was both more blatant and less challenged.

[2]The principle of equality is discussed in the introduction to Chapter 4.

[3]The arguments on this issue are analogous to those presented in Chapter 4 regarding sexual differences.

differences among groups, on the individual level many blacks score higher than many whites; and what the principle of equality requires is the equal treatment of equal *individuals*.

There is widespread agreement today that the hiring, housing, and education practices of the past, which routinely disadvantaged blacks, as well as women and other minorities, were morally wrong because they used an irrelevant criterion—race or sex—as a basis for denying individuals equality of treatment. But there is widespread disagreement about the correct answers to the following sorts of questions. Does society owe a debt to groups whose members have been systematically denied employment opportunities in the past? Must it rectify the wrongs resulting from discriminatory quotas that effectively limited the access of blacks and other minorities to the most desirable professions and graduate schools?[4] Just what is society's obligation to those groups whose members have been treated in ways that are grossly inconsistent with the principle of equality? These and related questions are the focal point of discussion in this chapter.

COMPENSATORY JUSTICE AND UTILITY

One possible approach to the issues is to claim that *compensation* is due to groups whose members have been discriminated against in the past. This answer appeals to the "principle of compensatory justice," which states that whenever an injustice has been committed, just compensation or reparation must be made to the injured parties. The principle of compensatory justice is often invoked, for example, when the claim is made that American Indians must be compensated for the past unjust deprivation of land and water rights due to government exploitation. Another possible approach, however, is to deny that the primary issue is compensation or rectification for past injustices. Rather, it is said, the central concern must be the *morally good consequences* to be produced for minority groups and/or society as a whole by measures designed to eliminate the *ongoing effects* of past discrimination. This approach appeals to the "principle of utility," which states that that action or practice is morally correct that on balance will tend to produce better consequences than any alternative when the interests of everyone affected are given equal weight. Various measures have been adopted in keeping with one or both of these approaches including, for example, granting monetary awards to American Indians as compensation for past injustice. The measures that cause the greatest moral controversies, however, are certain hiring, promotion, and admission programs adopted by businesses and educational institutions, primarily in response to government affirmative-action policies. To understand these controversies, it is useful to look briefly at the ways in which the call for affirmative action has been understood and reflected in business and university hiring, promotion, and admission policies.

---

[4]Even though women are not a numerical minority in our society, for purposes of convenience all further references to minorities in this introduction are also references to women (wherever relevant).

AFFIRMATIVE ACTION

Employers have responded to calls for affirmative action in various ways. Some have adopted practices of *passive nondiscrimination* that simply require all decisions about hiring and promotion to disregard race and sex. Note that passive nondiscrimination involves no compensation for past injustices. Nor does it help to undo the ongoing effects of past discrimination. The limitations of this approach are readily apparent, moreover, when we realize the extent to which seniority systems perpetuate old discriminatory patterns. Other employers have adopted measures that more accurately fall under the heading "affirmative" action. Some of these measures involve no more than making every effort to find minority applicants and to ensure that employment and promotion opportunities are highly visible. Here the pool of minority applicants may be enlarged, but no preference is given to minorities when decisions are made about hiring and promotion. Other employers committed to affirmative action have attempted to go further by giving preference to minority applicants. The programs involved, often called "preferential treatment" programs, are the focal point of the moral debate about affirmative-action programs. Preferential treatment programs are of two types. The first type involves hard quotas or specific numerical goals. Such preferential treatment programs specify some set number or proportion of minority applicants who must be hired or promoted. The second type involves neither a hard quota nor a specific numerical goal, but nevertheless does require the preferential treatment of minority applicants.

Institutions of higher learning, such as law and medical schools, have also attempted to establish affirmative-action admissions policies, including preferential treatment programs. Some of these programs have led to landmark lawsuits. A preferential treatment program at the University of Washington Law School, for example, led to the well-known *DeFunis v. Odegaard* case.[5] Another program, at the University of California at Davis Medical School, resulted in the *University of California v. Bakke* case presented in this chapter. The *DeFunis* case illustrates some of the moral perplexities raised by preferential treatment programs as well as the kind of reasoning that is sometimes advanced in their defense.

In the DeFunis case, Marco DeFunis, a nonminority applicant, was denied admission to the University of Washington Law School's first-year law class in 1971. He filed a suit claiming that the Law School's Admissions Committee had treated him unfairly insofar as it had discriminated against him on the basis of race. Preferential treatment that year was accorded to blacks, American Indians, Chicanos, and Filipinos. The Law School had 150 available spaces in its first-year law class. There were 1,601 applicants. In order to enroll 150 students, 275 applicants were offered acceptances. Among the 275 who were accepted there were 37 minority applicants. Of these 37, 18 actually enrolled. The Law School Admission Test (LSAT) scores and Projected Grade Point Averages (PGAs) of almost all these minority applicants were lower than those of some of the rejected nonminority applicants, who were denied admission simply because their PGAs and LSAT scores fell below a certain level. Minority

[5]*DeFunis v. Odegaard,* 82 Wash. 2d 11 (1973).

applicants, however, whose scores fell even below the level of some rejected non-minority applicants were evaluated on the basis of other criteria and then admitted to the school.

The Supreme Court of the State of Washington ruled against DeFunis and argued as follows: (1) Racial classifications are not unconstitutional in themselves. A state university can take race and ethnic background into account when considering applicants. (2) If there is a compelling state interest that can be served only through the use of racial classifications, such use is acceptable. (3) The shortage of minority attorneys, and, therefore, also minority prosecutors, judges, and public officials, constitutes an undeniably compelling state interest. Although the case was appealed to the United States Supreme Court, the Court did not hand down a ruling. Since DeFunis had been attending the Law School while the case was making its way through the courts and was then in his last year, the case was declared moot. The first university preferential treatment case decided by the United States Supreme Court was the Bakke case, mentioned above. The Court ruled in favor of Bakke, declaring Davis's hard quota approach constitutionally unacceptable. The Court also ruled, however, that admissions policies can take race into account when evaluating individual applicants.

PREFERENTIAL TREATMENT: THE ETHICAL DILEMMA

Our primary concern here is not with the legal and constitutional issues raised by cases such as *DeFunis* and *Bakke* but with the ethical dilemma posed by the preferential treatment programs that gave rise to these cases. Consider our earlier discussion of the principle of equality. We said that when two or more individuals compete for the same position, some of their characteristics are relevant to the position in question; other characteristics are not relevant. The principle of equality is violated whenever individuals are denied equal treatment simply on the basis of generally irrelevant characteristics such as sex or race. This is what seems to have happened to DeFunis and Bakke. They were not accorded the same treatment as members of the favored minority groups. The unequal treatment given Bakke and DeFunis is sometimes called "reverse discrimination." This label is used to describe actions or practices that discriminate against an individual or a group, on the basis of some normally irrelevant characteristic, *because* preference is being given to members of previously discriminated-against groups. In keeping with our earlier account of the principle of equality, reverse discrimination certainly seems to be morally wrong. Thus, according to the principle of equality, preferential treatment practices productive of reverse discrimination appear to be morally wrong. However, in keeping with our earlier discussion of the principles of compensatory justice and utility, preferential treatment programs may be justified by one or both of these ethical principles. Thus, according to these principles, practices productive of reverse discrimination may be morally correct. We seem to be faced with a moral dilemma.

One way of approaching this dilemma is to ask whether the injustices suffered by blacks and others in employment and education have made race and sex relevant criteria in these areas today. Some who call for compensatory justice argue that preferential treatment programs are one way of compensating minorities by giving them things that they were unjustly denied in the past. Race and sex under these conditions, they maintain, can be perceived as *morally* relevant criteria, even though they are unrelated to job or school performance. On this approach, the principle of compensatory justice is invoked to justify the relevance of using sexual or racial criteria to distinguish equals from unequals. Both a black and a white male may show promise of having the same ability to perform a job, for example, but the black in addition merits compensation for past wrongs; in this respect the white is not his "equal." A related line of reasoning is advanced by George Sher in this chapter. Sher argues that preferential treatment in employment should be given to individuals who because of certain past privations (e.g., inferior education) were unable to adequately develop the relevant competencies.

Problems are raised for any compensatory approach to preferential treatment programs by several considerations. First, individuals receiving preferential treatment may not have actually suffered any unjust treatment. Sher argues, for example, that not all blacks merit preferential treatment, but only those who have suffered the relevant privations. Furthermore, as Michael E. Levin asks in this chapter, why should the wrongs done to past members of certain groups merit special moral attention and require special treatment for present members of those groups. Individuals have suffered all sorts of wrongs (e.g., theft and murder) that, on Levin's account, may be as bad or worse than the wrong of racial discrimination; yet no one suggests that the descendents of those who were wronged in these other ways must be compensated. Second, individuals who lose out because others receive preferential treatment may themselves have been severely disadvantaged economically and socially. Third, if compensatory justice requires preferential treatment for *individuals who have been treated unjustly in the past,* then race or sex is irrelevant. What is relevant is past unjust treatment, and individuals who have been treated unjustly belong to both sexes and to many different ethnic and racial groups. A different line of attack against the compensatory approach utilizes an infinite regress argument: Suppose we are required to give preference today to individuals belonging to groups that were discriminated against in the past in order to compensate them for past inequality of treatment. Will we be required to give compensatory preferential treatment in the future to members of groups denied equality of treatment by today's compensatory programs? And what about the compensation due to those treated unequally by those future programs? Still another line of attack, advanced by Lisa H. Newton in this chapter, maintains that the use of any criteria other than merit or qualification in hiring or school admission is unjust because these are the *only* morally relevant characteristics.

In response to the above sorts of criticism, defenders of preferential treatment policies make a number of moves. The first major move, made by D. H. M. Brooks in this chapter, challenges Levin's contention that there is nothing about the wrong of past racial discrimination that merits special attention. Brooks distinguishes between individual acts (e.g., fraud and theft) and institutionalized practices such as racial discrimination. On Brooks' account, one of the legacies of past discrimination is an entrenched pattern of discrimination that needs rectification. Preferential treatment programs may be one legitimate way of changing an unfair status quo. The second major move, exemplified by Richard Wasserstrom in this chapter, questions an important presumption underlying many of the attacks on preferential treatment programs—the presumption that the only morally relevant characteristics in hiring and school admittance are "pure qualifications." Wasserstrom and others argue that this presumption itself must be justified in some way, perhaps by a utilitarian appeal to consequences. But if this is the case, Wasserstrom argues, it becomes relevant to consider the morally desirable consequences that preferential treatment programs are designed to bring about. The third major move, which also focuses on consequences, is represented by the kind of reasoning found in the DeFunis case and in the reasoning of those who denied Bakke admission to medical school. Here stress is placed on important social goods that will result from these programs. These goods include the demise of ongoing discrimination and, eventually, greater sexual and racial equality. Some who argue in this way concede that the principle of equality is violated by preferential treatment programs. As a result, some individuals are treated unjustly. Nevertheless, they argue, the good consequences produced by these programs will far outweigh the bad consequences, even though those bad consequences include the injustices resulting from reverse discrimination. The fourth major move, exemplified by Laura M. Purdy in this chapter, maintains that preferential treatment programs are necessary to prevent continued racial and sexual discrimination. Although Purdy's article deals only with women, the kind of agrument she advances has been applied to blacks and others as well. The central claim here is a factual one: subjective elements in the judging process, due to past and present prejudices, result in the systematic downgrading of women's abilities. Without preferential treatment programs that require hiring women who are judged to be less qualified than the top male contenders, women who are equally or more qualified than the latter will not be hired. On this line of reasoning, women will continue to be treated unjustly according to the principle of equality unless institutions are required to hire them even when they *appear* to be less qualified.

Defenders of preferential treatment who utilize the above sorts of arguments must pay special attention to *factual* issues. They must attempt to answer the following kinds of questions: Is racial and sexual discrimination still prevalent in our society? If it is, can we eliminate present discriminatory practices against minority applicants without using quota systems or other preferential treatment measures? Are racist and sexist attitudes so pervasive in our society that mandatory quota systems are required to eliminate continued discrimination against minorities? Are preferential treatment programs necessary to change institutions that perpetuate the results of past injustices? If they are, can only hard quota programs do the job?

Answers to such factual questions are important in evaluating the potential consequences of either adopting or not adopting preferential treatment programs. The answers given may help to determine the answer to the moral question: Are preferential treatment programs based on race and/or sex morally justified in a society with a long history of racial and sexual discrimination?

Jane S. Zembaty

Is Racial Discrimination Special?

Michael E. Levin

Michael E. Levin is professor of philosophy at the City University of New York. His published work includes Metaphysics and the Mind-Body Problem *(1979), "Negative Liberty," "Why Homosexuality is Abnormal," and "Comparable Worth: The Feminist Road to Socialism."*

Levin rejects affirmative action programs involving reverse discrimination. He maintains that the only possible defense of reverse discrimination is that it attempts to rectify the consequences of a past wrong—racial discrimination. He argues, however, that there is nothing about this particular wrong that makes it especially deserving of rectification. Using examples of other sorts of wrong (e.g., theft, murder, and fraud), Levin examines and rejects some of the reasons advanced to support the view that there is something about past racial discrimination that requires special moral attention. Tangentially, he also challenges the view that the *appropriate* way to rectify the wrongs done to blacks in the past is to give present blacks preferential treatment in hiring.

I take "reverse discrimination" to be the policy of favoring members of certain groups (usually racial), in situations in which merit has been at least ideally the criterion, on the grounds that *past* members of these groups have suffered discrimination. I do not include giving someone a job he was denied because *he* was discriminated against, since such redress is justified by ordinary canons of justice, in particular that of giving someone what he is owed. I am referring, rather, to the practice of hiring or admitting a preset number of (e.g.) blacks regardless of whether the blacks so hired have been wronged, and regardless of the qualifications of competing whites. The difference between the two policies is that between restoring a robbery victim's property to him, and hunting up the descendants of robbery victims and giving them goods at the expense of people who themselves robbed no one. I have no quarrel with the former, many quarrels with the latter: I believe reverse discrimination is as ill-advised a course of action as any undertaken by this country in at least a century. It cannot be justified by its social benefits, since experience suggests that the consequences of this policy are proving disastrous. It cannot be justified as giving particular members of the chosen group what they would have gotten if they had not been discriminated against, since by stipulation "affirmative action" goes beyond such an appeal to ordinary ideas of justice and compensation. It penalizes a group of present-day whites—those who are at least as well qualified but passed over—without proof that they have discriminated or directly benefited from discrimination; whites no more responsible for past discrimination than anyone else.

But such frontal assaults on reverse discrimination (or "affirmative action", in bureaucratese) usually accomplish nothing, so I will not attempt one here. I will try

Reprinted with permission of the author and the publisher from the *Journal of Value Inquiry*, vol. 15 (1981), pp. 225–232. Copyright © 1981 Martinus Nijhoff Publishers, The Hague.

instead to focus on a clear-cut issue which is central to the debate but which has, surprisingly, been almost completely ignored. It is this: what is so special about racial discrimination? Let me put the question more exactly. I will be arguing shortly that the only possible defense of reverse discrimination represents it as an attempt to rectify the consequences of past racial discrimination. But why has society selected one kind of wrong—discrimination—as particularly deserving or demanding rectification? Other past wrongs have left their traces—acts of theft, despoliation, fraud, anti-Semitism— yet society has no organized policy of rectifying those wrongs. It surely seems that if the consequences of one kind of wrong should not be allowed to unfold, neither should those of any other. And this is what I want to convince you of: acts of racial discrimination have no morally special status. Important consequences flow from this. For reasons I will propose, it seems to me clear that society—and in particular the employer—has no general standing obligation to block the consequences of past wrongs. So if discriminatory acts are no more deserving of rectification than wrong acts generally, no one is under any obligation at all to rectify them, or to be deprived so that these acts may be rectified.

With these preliminary points as background, let us look at the issue again. I noted that reverse discrimination discriminates against whites in a way which cannot be justified by ordinary notions of justice. Thus, if it is justifiable at all, it must be because we owe something to present-day blacks in some extraordinary sense. And the standard reason offered is that the blacks to be hired today bear the burdens of past discrimination. Had there been no racial discrimination, they would have been able to get those jobs; their qualifications would have been as good as those of the better-qualified whites they are displacing. (It is sometimes added that all whites benefit in some way from past discrimination, so all whites owe blacks something, namely a more advantageous position.) Affirmative action is supposed to rectify the consequences of past discrimination, to draw the sting from acts so bad that their consequences cannot be permitted to unfold.

But if our aim is to undo the consequences of past discrimination, the issue I raised becomes very pressing. If there is nothing morally special about discrimination, nothing which makes it especially deserving of rectification, any policy which treats discrimination as if it were morally special is arbitrary and irrational. Consider: Mr. X, a black of today, is supposedly owed special treatment. But surely if you owe Mr. X special treatment because his ancestors were the target of one wrong—discrimination— it would seem you owe Mr. Y special treatment if his ancestors were the target of some other wrong—theft, say. Racial discrimination is not the *only* wrong that can be committed against someone, and indeed it is far from the worst. I would rather be denied a job because I am Jewish than be murdered. My murderer violates my rights and handicaps my children much more seriously than someone who keeps me out of medical school. So the question is: if I owe Mr. X a job because his ancestors were discriminated against, don't I owe Mr. Y the same if his ancestors were defrauded? I believe the answer must be yes: there is nothing special about acts of discrimination. And even if you think I have misrepresented affirmative action or its rationale, the question and its answer are important. Other justifications for reverse discrimination also tend to treat racial discrimination as somehow special. Indeed, a quarter-century's preoccupation with race has created a sense that racial prejudice is not just a wrong but a sin, an inexpungeable blot on the soul. Whether this attitude is rational is an issue worth considering.

Let me start with a truism. Discrimination deserves to be halted where it exists, and redressed where it can be, because it is *wrong*. Discrimination is worth doing something about because *wrongs* are worth doing something about and discrimination is wrong. Once we grant this, we start to see that there is nothing *sui generis* about discrimination. It competes with other wrongs for righting. And I take it as obvious that some wrongs demand righting more urgently than others. If I pass a negative comment on Jones's tie in private but defame Robinson's ancestry on national television, I had better apologize to Robinson before I do so to Jones. And if I have embezzled the funds of an orphanage, top priority goes to seeing that I give the money back. Finally, if Smith is destitute because I defrauded Smith's father, I had better make amends before I worry about the sons of men I insulted. So: denying a man a job on grounds of color is evidently just one among many ways of wronging him. It is far less egregious than assault or murder.

It is frequently but mistakenly claimed that racial discrimination is special because it involves a group. Certainly, an act of racial discrimination involves a whole group in the sense that it involves treating an individual not in his own right but insofar as he belongs to a group. But racial discrimination is not the only kind of act that is thus group-related. Many wrongs having nothing to do with race are discriminatory in the precise sense that they base the treatment of an individual on membership in a morally irrelevant group. Nepotism is discrimination against nonrelatives. When I make my lazy nephew district manager, I am disqualifying more able competitors because they belong to a group—nonfamily—membership in which should not count in the matter at hand. Discrimination need not be racial: any time you make a moral distinction on morally irrelevant grounds, you discriminate invidiously. In a society in which racial discrimination was unknown but capricious nepotism was the norm, denial of due process on grounds of family would provoke as much indignation as racial discrimination does now.

It would be sheer confusion to argue that acts of racial discrimination are special because they insult a whole race as well as wrong an individual. When I assault you, I assault no one else—and when I discriminate against you, I discriminate against no one else. True, my discrimination may indicate a readiness to discriminate against others and may create widespread anxiety—but my assaulting you may indicate a readiness to assault others and create even greater general anxiety. If I bypass Mr. X because he is black, only Mr. X and his dependents suffer thereby. Perhaps because color is so salient a trait, we tend in uncritical moments to think of the black race as an entity existing in and of itself, above and beyond the particular blacks who make it up. Philosophers call this "reification". We then think that an insult to this reified race is particularly malign, either in itself or because this entity somehow transmits to all blacks the harm done by single acts of discrimination. Some such reasoning must underlie the oft-heard ideas that the harm done to a single black man "hurts blacks everywhere" and that the appointment of a black to the Supreme Court is "a victory for blacks everywhere", remarks which make no literal sense. This tendency to reify is especially pernicious in the context of compensation. Why are we willing to contemplate special treatment for blacks now, when we would not contemplate special treatment for someone whose ancestors were defrauded by a man who left no descendants? Because, I suspect, we think that by benefiting today's black we will apologize for the long-ago insult to the race, and that this apology and benefit will somehow be transmitted back to the blacks who endured the original discrimination. Were this picture accurate, it might justify supposing that past discriminatory acts cast longer shadows than other wrongs. But it is just a myth. A racial grouping no more deserves reification than does the class of people whose ancestors were defrauded. We resist the impulse in the latter case only because the trait in question is not visually salient and has no especially coherent history.

(Some slight sense can be made of "injury to a group", as when we say that a traitor endangers the security of a nation. But even here the harm done is to individuals, the particular citizens. The traitor deserves punishment because of the harm he has done to each citizen, not to "the nation" as a thing apart.)

Perhaps the main reason for thinking of acts of racial discrimination as morally distinctive is that each is an instance of a pattern. My discriminating against Mr. X is part of a self-sustaining pattern of wrongs. And, indeed, we do find wrong acts that together form a pattern more disturbing than each wrong act taken singly: Jack the Ripper's legacy is more appalling than eleven isolated murders. Wrongs seem to be like notes, which have different musical values when part of a melody than when heard in isolation. But this intuition must be carefully assessed. A single wrong act cannot be made *more wrong* because there is some other wrong act which it resembles. If I discriminate against you, my act has a certain amount of wrongness. If I then discriminate against someone else, my previous act against you does not take on more wrongness. This is so even with Jack the Ripper. His murder of the first prostitute did not become *more wrong* when he murdered his second. If he had died before committing his second murder, his first murder would still have been as bad as it actually was. If, say, he owed the family of the first prostitute some compensation for his action, he did not suddenly owe them more after his second. So the fact that acts of discrimination come in groups does not show that a single act of discrimination is any worse, any more deserving of rectification, than it would have been had it occurred alone.

Two factors account for our feeling that patterned wrongs are worse than isolated ones. The first is that the *perpetrator* of a patterned wrong is worse. Jack the Ripper is worse than a man who kills once from passion. But this does not mean that what he did, in each case, is worse than a single act of murder. Similarly, the most we can say of bigotry is that a habitual bigot is worse than a one-shot bigot, not that an act of bigotry is in itself worse than an act of caprice. The second reason patterned wrongs seem especially malign is that they create anxiety through their promise of repetition. Jack the Ripper's actions create more anxiety than eleven unconnected murders because we believe he will strike again. But this shows only that it is especially important to *halt patterns,* be they of murder or discrimination. It does not mean that a particular act in a discriminatory pattern is worse than it would have been in isolation. And it is worth repeating that antidiscrimination laws without benefit of affirmative action suffice to halt patterns of discrimination.

Granted, racial wrongs have gone beyond discrimination in hiring or the use of public facilities, extending all the way to lynching. But to acknowledge this is to bring racial wrongs under independent headings—denial of due process, assault, murder. Lynching Emmet Till was wrong not because Emmet Till was black, but because lynching is murder. So if blacks deserve special treatment because of (say) this country's history of lynching, it is because descendants of murder victims deserve special treatment. But this concedes my point: what was wrong about especially egregious acts of racial discrimination is what is wrong about parallel nonracial acts; and if we treat the former as special, we must treat the latter as special as well. I also deny that past discriminations were special because they were state-approved and in some case state-mandated. State sanction in itself can make no difference. Even if "the state" is an entity over and above its citizens and their legal relations, the wrongness of an act (although not the blameworthiness of an agent) is independent of who performs it. So if discriminating is wrong, it is wrong, and to the same extent, no matter who performs it. Therefore, state-sanctioned past discrimination is no stronger a candidate for rectification than any other discrimination. In any case, even if we did consider state sanction to be morally significant, to be consistent we would have to apply this to all other state-sanctioned wrongs. We would have to say, for example, that we ought to give special treatment now to descendants of people who were harmed under the terms of a statute repealed decades ago. But I take it that no one would support affirmative action for the grandchildren of brewmasters bankrupted by the Volstead Act.

Finally, it has been suggested that grave discriminatory wrongs, such as the lynching of Negroes, were special because done with the intention of intimidating the other members of the terrorized group. Quite so: but again this makes my very point. To call an act of lynching wrong for this reason is to bring it under the umbrella of *intimidation:* a precisely parallel nonracial act of intimidation is just as wrong (although we might have reason to think the perpetrator is not as vicious). Many years ago, unions were in the habit of wrecking restaurants that refused to be unionized as a warning to other restaurants. Even today, Mob enforcers will kill an informer, or a retailer who refuses to pay protection, in order to intimidate other potential informers or defaulters. So if we treat Blacks as special because they belong to a class other members of which were terrorized, so must we treat restauranteurs as special, and indeed all small businessmen in businesses once victimized by the protection racket. And I take it that no one would suggest affirmative action for restauranteurs. Nor will it do to say that this is because today no restauranteur is in danger from union or Mob goons. In fact, a restauranteur is in considerably more danger than a Black. The last lynching occurred in 1954, while union vandalism and criminal extortion are the stuff of today's sensational press.

A subsidiary point. I have so far let pass one peculiarity of affirmative action programs: they award jobs (or placement) to rectify past wrongs. Yet normally when we compensate someone for wrongful deprivation, we give him the equivalent of what he lost, giving him the thing itself only when feasible. If a pianist loses his hands through your negligence, you are not obliged to hire him to do a concert. The whole thrust of his complaint, after all, is that he is no longer competent to undertake such an enterprise. You owe him the money he would have made from concertizing, plus some monetary equivalent of the satisfaction your negligence has cost him. So *even if* past racial discrimination has wrongfully cost Mr. X a job, it does not follow that proper compensation is a job. What he is owed is the job or the monetary equivalent thereof. If the job is unavailable—where this normally includes Mr. X's not being the best-qualified applicant—all he is owed is its monetary equivalent. Why, then, is it assumed without question in so many quarters that if past discrimination has cost present-day blacks jobs, they deserve *jobs* rather than the monetary equivalent of the jobs they would have gotten? Only, I believe, because we think there is something *special* about discrimination, that its consequences deserve amelioration in a way that the consequences of other wrongs do not. Discrimination is so bad that not only must we compensate for it, we must so change the world that things will become as if the wrong had never been. Only by attributing such reasoning can I make sense of the special form "affirmative action" programs invariably take. And if indeed racial discrimination is not especially wrong, such special compensation starts to appear morally arbitrary and even bizarre.

It is obvious that no employer has a general obligation to rectify wrongful acts, to offer extraordinary compensation. I am not speaking, again, of righting wrongs he perpetrates or directly benefits from. I mean that if, as a result of some wrong once done—not necessarily to an ancestor—I am worse off than I would have been, you, an arbitrarily chosen employer, have no obligation whatever to neutralize the consequences of that wrong. No one has any obligation to make me as well off as I would have been had that wrong not been committed. Why? Basically because it is *impossible* to rectify the consequences of all past wrongs. Consider how we might decide on compensatory payments. We trace the world back to the moment at which the wrong was done, suppose the wrong not done, and hypothetically trace forward the history of the world. Where I end up under this hypothetical reconstruction is where I deserve to be. I am owed the net difference between where I am now and where I would have been had the wrong not been done. But for most wrongs, it would take omniscience to say how the world would have turned out had the wrong not been done. If you wanted to make up to me for the theft of my grandfather's watch in 1900, how on Earth do you propose to reckon the position I would have been in had my grandfather's watch not been stolen? I might have been richer by a watch. I might have been poorer—since, being in fact deprived of a watch, I have worked harder than I otherwise would have. I might not have existed—if my grandfather met my grandmother while hunting for his stolen watch. Indeed, if you suppose yourself under a general ameliorative obligation, you will have to calculate simultaneously how well off each and every one of us would have been had all past wrongs not occurred. There is more: I am supposedly owed a certain something, but who owes it to me? Surely not you—you don't owe me *all* of it. Do all employers owe me an equal proportion? Or is their proportion dependent on how much they have benefited from the initial theft? If the latter, how is one to calculate their debt, if the theft was in another country and another century?

Suppose I take it on myself to yield to Mr. X if I am better off than he is because of some past wrong—not to him, necessarily, since I am offering extraordinary compensation. Now surely there is some *other* past wrong which has made *me* worse off than I would otherwise have been, worse off than (say) Mr. Y. So I must drop myself down to make way for Mr. X, but I also deserve a push up beyond Mr. Y. If each of us tried to put himself just where he would be if there had been no past wrongs, we would all be caught in a mad whirl of exchanging positions and privileges with one another. If a full reckoning were in, those who now seem as if they would end up in a better position might end up in a worse one. Take Mr. X, an American black, who we think is worse off than he would have been had there been no slavery. Yet he may now be better off than he would have been had his African ancestors not conquered a neighboring tribe that was then raided by slave traders; had his ancestors respected territorial boundaries, Mr. X might now be a sickly native of Uganda. So unless we quite arbitrarily decide to rectify only some wrongs, we are undertaking a quite impossible task. What about limiting ourselves to rectifying wrongs we know about? But then we should surely try as hard as possible to find out about other wrongs, and trace their consequences. Once again, if we set out on that path, we will find ourselves with obligations that cannot be discharged. And an undischargeable obligation is no obligation at all. Indeed, it is far from obvious that the consequences of discrimination are easier to trace than those of other wrongs. I know victims of theft who have nothing to show for it. Why not benefit them? It is clearer that they are worse off from a past wrong than that an arbitrarily chosen black is.

We must remember that we are all where we are in the competitive and distributional scheme of things because of past wrongs. It may be that we got something in a wrongful way, but those from whom we got it may have gotten it wrongfully in turn. Who knows but that all of us are in this room because of some dirty Hellenic trick on the plains of Marathon. Perhaps we should award Western Civilization to the descendants of Xerxes, or give them its dollar equivalent! Each of us lies on a "competition curve", which graphs jobs against our chances of getting them. These curves are connected: I can't move to a better one without bumping someone else down to a worse. If we try to put each person on the curve he would have occupied had there been no relevant wrongdoing, we will be raising and lowering everybody, sometimes at the same time, with no end in sight. Perhaps God is sufficiently powerful, well-intentioned, and well-informed to put each of us on his proper curve. But no lesser power—not ITT and not HEW—can undertake the task without absurdity.

Since, then, no one has any general rectificatory obligation, and since—as I argued earlier—past discrimination does not stand out from other wrongs as especially demanding righting, I can see no justification at all for reverse discrimination.

I have embedded my main point in a somewhat complex argumentative context. Let me end by highlighting it. While racial discrimination is wrong, it is only one wrong among many and has no special claim on our moral attention. Past discrimination no more deserves extraordinary compensation than many other wrongs. And any employment policy which does treat racial discrimination as special is arbitrary and irrational.

QUESTIONS

1 Do the wrongs done to blacks in the past require rectification? If yes, how should rectification be made? If not, why not?
2 Is there a morally significant difference between the wrong of racial discrimination suffered by blacks and other wrongs such as theft and fraud? If yes, what is the difference?

Why Discrimination Is Especially Wrong

D. H. M. Brooks

D. H. M. Brooks teaches at the University of Capetown, South Africa. His published articles include "When Is Discrimination Discrimination?," "Joint Action," "Individuating Agents," and "Confirmability and Meaningfulness."

Brooks criticizes the arguments advanced by Michael E. Levin. The wrong of racial discrimination, he argues, *is* different in significant ways from wrongs such as murder and fraud. In making his case, Brooks distinguishes between *individual acts* (e.g., murder and fraud) and *institutionalized ongoing discrimination*. Affirmative action, he concludes, may be one legitimate way of rectifying an *entrenched practice* of racial discrimination.

Michael Levin in his "Is Racial Discrimination Special?", *Journal of Value Inquiry* Vol. 15, No. 3, 1981, argues that there is nothing especially wrong with racial discrimination. He does this in the context of reverse discrimination or affirmative action, arguing that only if there is something particularly wrong with racial discrimination, in comparison with wrongs such as theft, fraud or murder, are affirmative action programmes justified. He says, "(I)f I owe Mr. X a job because his ancestors were discriminated against, don't I owe Mr. Y the same if his ancestors were defrauded? I believe the answer must be yes: there is nothing special about acts of discrimination." (pp. 226–227 "Is Racial Discrimination Special?"; all following quotes are from this article). He concludes by saying "While racial discrimination is wrong, it is only one wrong among many and has no special credit on our moral attention. Past discrimination no more deserves extraordinary compensation than many other wrongs. And any employment policy which does treat racial discrimination as special is arbitrary and irrational." (p. 232).

Without wishing to get entangled in the whole issue of affirmative action, I would like to answer Levin's question by pointing out some aspects of the matter which he

Reprinted with permission of the author and the publisher from the *Journal of Value Inquiry,* vol. 17 (1983), pp. 305–312. Copyright © 1983 Martinus Nijhoff Publishers, The Hague.

has overlooked and which provide at least a *prima facie* case for the mounting of compensatory programmes.

Where Levin goes wrong should emerge as I go through his arguments for the ordinary status of racial discrimination. He begins by pointing out that "Racial discrimination is not the only wrong that can be committed against someone, and indeed it is far from the worst. I would rather be denied a job because I am Jewish than be murdered. My murderer violates my rights and handicaps my children much more seriously than someone who keeps me out of medical school." Here and throughout the paper Levin treats racial discrimination as if it were a particular kind of morally wrong act, and as if a society characterised by racial discrimination were simply one where such acts occurred. Fraud can be treated thus. There is no more to fraud than many different fraudulent acts committed from a variety of motives. If in a society no specific acts of a clearly defined sort occur, then there is no fraud in that society. This is not the case with racial discrimination. Suppose that a society fifteen years ago passed a law to the effect that no black person could live or own property in a particular desirable area. At the time of the passing of the legislation no blacks live or own property in this area. After the legislation is passed such is the law-abidingness of the community that no black person even attempts to rent or buy in the designated area. How many acts of discrimination have taken place? Just one, the passing of the bill? Does this mean that the society has been free of racial discrimination for the past ten years? Clearly a discriminatory situation can be in force even though no clear overt acts of discrimination take place. Besides acts of discrimination, discriminatory laws and customs, and the habits and casts of mind of both those who discriminate and those who are discriminated against, will typically go towards constituting the practice of discrimination within a society.

Levin goes on to say that "it is frequently but mistakenly claimed that racial discrimination is special because it involves a group. Certainly, an act of racial discrimination involves a whole group in the sense that it involves treating an individual not in his own right but insofar as he belongs to a group. But racial discrimination is not the only kind of act that is thus group-related. Many wrongs having nothing to do with race are discriminatory in the precise sense that they base treatment of an individual on membership in a morally irrelevant group. Nepotism is discrimination against non-relatives." (p. 227) Levin characterises an act of discrimination correctly as an act of prejudicial treatment of an individual on the grounds that he or she has a morally irrelevant property. He is also correct in saying that this involves a group, namely the group of people who have that morally irrelevant property. So far so good. He, now, unfortunately clouds the issue by using an example where the group of people who have that morally irrelevant property is arbitrary. The class of those who are not closely related to John Smith probably cannot be picked out by any other property. Moreover members of this specific group are only discriminated against on this one occasion by this one person. Even if Smith has a large family and runs a big concern, positions within which are highly sought after and generally filled on nepotic principles, the number of people directly disadvantaged is miniscule compared to the 4,000 million or so people in the group as a whole. Racial discrimination is the opposite pole to such idiosyncratically unfair policies as not hiring anyone taller than oneself or rapidly promoting anyone who has black hair and blue eyes; Only isolated individuals, if any, discriminate against those who do not have black hair and blue eyes; there is no practice of such discrimination. We must distinguish between a consistent practice of picking out members of a single group for prejudicial treatment and isolated cases where decisions are made on morally irrelevant considerations. Nepotism forms a half-way house between these two cases, since, while there can be a practice of nepotism, normally, if there is, each nepotic act will discriminate against a different group and most people will be able to count on some nepotic acts discriminating in their favour.

Levin could now, perhaps, be informed that what is especially wrong with racial discrimination is that it is a consistent practice of prejudicially treating members of a single group because they belong to that group, rather than a number of isolated incidents. Some of his points though seem aimed against exactly this. First he says, "It would be sheer confusion to argue that acts of racial discrimination are special because they insult a whole race as well as wrong an individual. When I assault you, I assault no one else—and when I discriminate against you I discriminate against no one else. True, my discrimination may indicate a readiness to discriminate against others and may create widespread anxiety—but my assaulting you may indicate a readiness to assault others and create even greater general anxiety . . . Perhaps because color is so salient a trait, we tend in uncritical moments to think of the black race as an entity existing in and of itself, above and beyond the particular blacks who make it up. Philosophers call this "reification". We then think that an insult to this reified race is particularly malign either in itself or because this entity somehow transmits to all blacks the harm done by single acts of discrimination . . . this picture . . . is just a myth. A racial grouping no more deserves reification than does the class of people whose ancestors were defrauded. We resist the impulse in the latter case only because the trait in question is not visually salient and has no especially coherent history." (pp. 227–228). A misleading dichotomy is implied here in that Levin seems to suggest that there are only two ways of analysing human groups. Either we have a completely arbitrary collection, like the members of a mathematical set, which may have in common only such an arbitrary and artificial property as *being members of that set,* or we fall into the fallacy of believing that there is some further entity over and above the members of the group. Levin is only too keen to juxtapose a race with the class of people who have been defrauded. The latter class will have very little in common besides their victimhood and what follows from it, viz. their having had some money at some time and perhaps a tendency to gullibility or carelessness with accounts. It should be noted that they have not been wronged *because* they fall into this category. Members of a racial group will normally have far more in common than this. Typically they will share a common language, a common heritage, a feeling that in some sense they all belong together and in the case of groups that are discriminated against, a common experience of injustice. Even if it is fallacious to posit a race as an entity over and above its members, this does not mean that members of a race are no more closely knit than any group of people with a common property. Levin uses the spectre of reification to cast doubt on the meaningfulness of notions to which perfectly good sense can be given. He says, "the oftheard idea that the harm done to a single black man 'hurts blacks everywhere' or that the appointment of a black to the Supreme Court is 'a victory for blacks everywhere' (are) remarks which make no literal sense." (p. 228). It requires little ingenuity to supply ways of interpreting these remarks without relying on the causal efficacy of strange entities. People feel sympathy for others especially when others suffer a misfortune they have suffered or are likely to suffer. Insofar as blacks are likely to be emotionally perturbed on learning of injuries (probably, in context, caused by discriminatory practices) suffered by other blacks, it is not hyperbole to speak of their being injured. Of course other blacks have to hear of it, not be calloused to such wrongs and so forth, but outside the philosophy department these *ceteris paribus* clauses are usually taken as read. Nor is this the only way in which all blacks can be harmed by an injury done to one; for example, all blacks have a chance of being discriminated against in future by a bigot whose racism is learned or reinforced by witnessing a discriminatory action. All blacks can be seen as advantaged by a black Supreme Court appointment, insofar as it may provide a counter-example to those who talk about black inferiority. It can be seen as a victory for all blacks, insofar as all blacks are involved in and support a struggle for full enjoyment of their right as citizens, just as victory in wartime is a victory for all citizens of the country involved in and supporting their country's struggle.

One important difference between people in the group harmed by discrimination and fraud victims, which Levin skims over, is that they are harmed *because* they belong to that group. This is significant for a number of reasons. Normally those who discriminate against members of a group will not give as their reasons that members of the affected group speak a particular language or are of a particular colour, but will claim, in one way or another, that they are dealing with inferior beings. They are different from us, they don't feel things the way we do, they aren't capable, they are used to living like that, they could not cope with our responsibilities and so on; I have cited some of the milder rationalisations. Some of those who discriminate may not justify themselves in this way, but the phenomenon is sufficiently common for those who are discriminated against to be justified in regarding discrimination as insulting and as an affront to their human dignity and to that of all members of their group. This may be met by Levin with the breezy remark, "So what's special about that? Many wrongs are degrading and an affront to human dignity. Consider a homosexual gang rape." There is, I believe, a deeper point here. People have a very strong tendency to form us and them groups. These groups may be formed on the basis of kinship or various similarities between the members, or simply because of some existing competition (consider sports fans). Once these groups have been formed people tend to develop loyalties and affections for their own group and to denigrate the other group. These tendencies are very deeply rooted in our nature. Indeed, the results of socio-biology seem to be that they have an important survival function and serve to explain the biological basis of altruism. We are not at first universally altruistic, nor are we in our practice now. Still group loyalties lead to altruistic behaviour benefitting members of the group. The possession of these loyalties by members of the group enhances the survival chances of the genes of the altruist, through he and his kin getting like altruism from other members of the group. Biological altruism benefits us at the expense of them. Peter Singer documents this in his book, *The Expanding Circle: Ethics and*

Sociobiology (Farrer, Strauss & Giroux, New York, 1981), and argues further that a vital factor in the progress of ethical thought is the gradual expansion of the group to which we owe full ethical duties. We have advanced since the days when Aristotle denied that women and slaves were rational animals, and hence that they had full personhood. Insofar as this is true, we can see that part of the evil of discrimination, however explicable this tendency may be, is that it involves refusing full humanity to another human being. Even murder need not involve this. Refusing something the status of a fully rational ethical subject is a serious matter. Animals lack this status and most of us regard eating, factory farming and experimenting upon animals as justifiable. Even if we are uncomfortable about this, these practices are not as morally abhorrent to us as they would be if performed upon people. Insofar as discrimination is motivated or rationalised by a belief that those discriminated against are not fully human or fully rational or fully responsible, it is something special as compared to other wrongs.

The other argument Levin raises against racial discrimination's being particularly wrong because it is a consistent practice directed against members of a group because they belong to that group, is that a pattern of discrimination does not make discrimination worse. He says, "A single wrong act cannot be made *more wrong* because there is some other wrong act which it resembles. If I discriminate against you, my act has a certain amount of wrongness. If I then discriminate against someone else, my previous act against you does not take on more wrongness. . . . Two factors account for our feeling that patterned wrongs are worse than isolated ones. The first is that the *perpetrator* of a patterned wrong is worse. Jack the Ripper is worse than a man who kills once from passion . . . The second reason patterned wrongs seem especially malign is that they create anxiety through the promise of repetition. Jack the Ripper's actions create more anxiety than eleven unconnected murders because we believe he will strike again." (pp. 228–229). Before commenting on this I will give Levin's two last points; "Granted racial wrongs have gone beyond racial discrimination in hiring or the use of public facilities all the way to lynching. But to acknowledge this is to bring racial wrongs under independent headings—denial of due process, assault, murder. . . . what was wrong about especially egregious acts of racial discrimination is what is wrong about parallel non-racial acts; and if we treat the former as special, we must treat the latter as special as well. I also deny that past discriminations were special because they were state approved and in some case state-mandated. State sanction in itself can make no difference . . . the wrongness of an act . . . is independent of who performs it." (p. 229) "Finally, it has been suggested that grave discriminatory wrongs, such as the lynching of Negroes, were special because done with the intention of intimidating the other members of the terrorised group. Quite so: but again this makes my very point. To call an act of lynching wrong for this reason is to bring it under the umbrella of *intimidation*: a precisely parallel nonracial act of intimidation is just as wrong." (p. 230) Again Levin's primary error is to look at acts of discrimination rather than the practice. He wants it to look like Jack the Ripper having bought the Chief of Police, a few murders, a bit of corruption, but now it's all over and the culprits have been dealt with we can breathe and live easily again. A long standing social practice is not like this. . . . There are sociologically significant groupings of people, like classes, nations, races and generations and there are complex sociological relations between these groupings which cannot in any simple way, be reduced to particular acts of individuals.

To point up the blindnesses of Levin's crudely individualistic model, I will sketch the sort of things which make up an institutionalised, continuing state of discrimination. First of all within a society there are at least two distinguishable groups of people, each of which can be fairly easily distinguished from the other, though there may be borderline cases. One of these groups has effective control of the power in that society. Generally the dominant group will have many advantages at the expense of the less dominant group, they will earn larger salaries, live in pleasanter areas, attend better schools, have greater mobility, greater access to good medical facilities and generally be better off. There will also be mechanisms ensuring that these advantages continue to accrue to the dominant class. The most obvious of these will of course be legal restrictions reserving these goods to the dominant group. Other devices work as well. Even if there are no legal bars or barely legal subterfuges, economic forces and various poverty traps may keep the disadvantaged disadvantaged. Even attitudes of mind may contribute. Theories of the inherent inferiority of the disadvantaged, confirmed in part by their being disadvantaged, may be accepted in one way or another by both groups and contribute to the maintenance of an unfair *status quo*. Habits, attitudes or ways of life, perhaps acquired through living at the bottom of the heap, may keep people there. Those who have little and have little to lose may fail to develop financial responsibility or the puritan work ethic. Those who resent the educational advantages reserved to others may develop traditions of anti-intellectualism. Those who are kicked around may adopt a mantle of subservience. Traits such as these do not help people climb the ladder to success. Another powerful preservative for the *status quo* will be the innumerable acts of discrimination on the part of private individuals which as well as disadvantaging the individuals discriminated against will tend to keep discrimination at large going in many different ways, by *inter alia,* hardening attitudes, confirming prejudices and teaching the young by example. When a society realises that it has such a situation within it a mere barring of discriminatory acts, the solution Levin advocates, may not be enough to cure the evil. Affirmative action is one of the bits of social engineering which has been devised to rectify an entrenched practice of discrimination.

What I have said here may not fully satisfy Levin. It may be that a demonstration that racial discrimination is a wrong of a type such that affirmative action is an appropriate response to it, demands a justification of the practice of affirmative action itself. Underlying Levin's arguments there is also an assumption that only individual people are ethical subjects, that only an individual can be responsible, harmed or compensated. He does not argue for it but we do have strong ethical intuitions in its favour. A full examination of the question would have to consider the principle very carefully and work out exactly what moral status should be accorded to groups and why. This is a big task and this is not the place to undertake it; however I trust that I have shown that there is at least a prima facie case for affirmative action in that there is something especially wrong with racial discrimination.

QUESTIONS

1 Is preferential treatment in employment an appropriate moral response to the wrongs of past racial discrimination?
2 Because of the social and economic effects of past discrimination, are some/many/most blacks at a competitive disadvantage in comparison with some/many/most whites? If yes, what ought to be done about it?

Bakke and Davis: Justice, American Style

Lisa H. Newton

Lisa H. Newton is professor of philosophy at Fairfield University and adjunct professor of philosophy at Sacred Heart University. Her published articles include "Reverse Discrimination as Unjustified," "Collective Responsibility in Health Care," and "Professionalization: The Intractable Plurality of Values."

In this short essay, which first appeared as the nation awaited the decision of the Supreme Court in the Bakke case, Newton focuses on the quota system employed at the University of California Medical School at Davis. She attacks all preferential treatment programs as unjust for the following reasons (the first set appeals to justice; the second set, to consequences): (1) Those candidates who unjustly "lose out" because they do not belong to the preferred group are expected to make "reparations" for "wrongs" they did not commit; strict justice requires that the merit system be strictly applied. (2) The bad effects of quota systems will far outweigh any "social goods" produced.

The use of the special minority quota or "goal" to achieve a desirable racial mix in certain professions might appear to be an attractive solution to the problem of justice posed by generations of racial discrimination.[1] Ultimately, however, the quota solution fails. It puts an intolerable burden of injustice on a system strained by too much of that in the past, and prolongs the terrible stereotypes of inferiority into the indefinite future. It is a serious error to urge this course on the American people.

The quota system, as employed by the University of California's medical school at Davis or any similar institution, is unjust, for all the same reasons that the discrimination it attempts to reverse is unjust.[2] It diminishes the opportunities of some candidates for a social purpose that has nothing to do with them, to make "reparation" for acts they never committed. And "they" are no homogeneous "majority": as Swedish-

Reprinted with permission of the author and the publisher from *National Forum (The Phi Kappa Phi Journal)*, vol. LVIII, no. 1 (Winter 1978), pp. 22–23.

[1] See, for example, *The New York Times* editorial, "Reparation, American Style," June 19, 1977.
[2] See my "Reverse Discrimination as Unjustified," *Ethics* 83:308 (July, 1973).

Americans, Irish-Americans, Americans of Polish or Jewish or Italian descent, they can claim a past history of the same irrational discrimination, poverty and cultural deprivation that now plagues Blacks and Spanish-speaking individuals. In simple justice, all applicants (except, of course, the minority of WASPs!) should have access to a "track" specially constructed for their group, if any do. And none should. The salvation of every minority in America has been strict justice, the merit system strictly applied; the Davis quota system is nothing but a suspension of justice in favor of the most recent minorities, and is flatly unfair to all the others.

The quota system is generally defended by suggesting that a little bit of injustice is far outweighed by the great social good which will follow from it; the argument envisions a fully integrated society where all discrimination will be abolished. Such a result hardly seems likely. Much more likely, if ethnic quotas are legitimated by the Court in the Bakke Case, all the other ethnic minorities will promptly organize to secure special tracks of their own, including minorities which have never previously organized at all. In these days, the advantage of a medical education is sufficiently attractive to make the effort worthwhile. As elsewhere, grave political penalties will be inflicted on legislatures and institutions that attempt to ignore these interest groups. I give Davis, and every other desirable school in the country, one decade from a Supreme Court decision favorable to quotas, to collapse under the sheer administrative weight of the hundreds of special admissions tracks and quotas it will have to maintain.

But the worst effect of the quota system is on the minorities supposedly favored by it. In the past, Blacks were socially stereotyped as less intelligent than whites because disproportionately few Blacks could get into medical school; the stereotype was the result of the very racial discrimination that it attempted to justify. Under any minority quota sytem, ironically, that stereotype would be tragically reinforced. From the day the Court blesses the two-track system of admissions at Davis, the word is out that Black physicians, or those of Spanish or Asian derivation, are less qualified, just a little less qualified, than their "White-Anglo" counterparts, for they did not have to meet as strict a test for admission to medical school. And that judgment will apply, as the quota applies, on the basis of race alone, for we will have no way of knowing which Blacks, Spanish or Asians were admitted in a medical school's regular competition and which were admitted on the "special minority" track. The opportunity to bury their unfavorable ethnic stereotypes by clean and public success in strictly fair competition, an opportunity that our older ethnic groups seized enthusiastically, will be denied to these "special minorities" for yet another century.

In short, there are no gains, for American society or for groups previously disadvantaged by it, in quota systems that attempt reparation by reverse discrimination. The larger moral question of whether we should set aside strict justice for some larger social gain, does not have to be taken up in a case like this one, where procedural injustice produces only substantive harm for all concerned. Blacks, Hispanic and other minority groups which are presently economically disadvantaged will see real progress when, and only when, the American economy expands to make room for more higher status employment for all groups. The economy is not improved in the least by special tracks and quotas for special groups; on the contrary, it is burdened by the enormous weight of the nonproductive administrative procedure required to implement them. No social purpose will be served, and no justice done, by the establishment of such procedural monsters; we should hope that the Supreme Court will see its way clear to abolishing them once and for all.

QUESTIONS

1 Can you specify criteria for determining that a group had been sufficiently discriminated against in the past to warrant preferential treatment in the present?

2 If there were no affirmative action programs, do you believe that the *merit system would be strictly applied* in all hiring, promotions, and school admissions in the United States? If not, would "injustice" be rampant in hiring, etc.?

Opinion in *University of California v. Bakke*

Justice Lewis F. Powell, Jr.

A biographical sketch of Justice Lewis F. Powell, Jr., is found on page 102.

Allen Bakke, a white male, applied for admission to the University of California at Davis Medical School. The school, which had a hard quota preferential treatment admissions policy favoring minority students, had set aside 16 of its 100 places in the first-year class for those students. Admission was denied to Bakke, but it was granted to minority students whose college grade-point averages (GPA) and scores on the Medical College Admission Test (MCAT) were much lower than Bakke's. The trial court ruled that Bakke was a victim of *invidious* racial discrimination, and the Supreme Court of the State of California upheld that decision. The justices of the United States Supreme Court were divided four-to-four on the major issues in the case, with Justice Powell providing the decisive vote. Justice Powell sided with Chief Justice Warren E. Burger, Justice Potter Stewart, Justice William H. Rehnquist, and Justice John Paul Stevens in holding that the admissions program which resulted in Bakke's rejection was unlawful. With them he ruled that Bakke must be admitted to the medical school. But Justice Powell sided with Justice William J. Brennan, Justice Byron R. White, Justice Thurgood Marshall, and Justice Harry A. Blackmun in holding that colleges and universities *can* consider race as a factor in the admissions process.

In this excerpt from Justice Powell's opinion, the Court rejects "quotas" or "goals" drawn on the basis of race or ethnic status and holds that such quotas are not legitimated *simply* by their benign purposes. Justice Powell examines the purported purposes of the special admissions program at Davis to see if the program's racial classification is constitutionally permissible. In its previous rulings the Court had held that in "order to justify the use of a suspect classification a State

United States Supreme Court, 438 U.S. 265 (1978).

must show that its purpose or interest is both constitutionally permissible and substantial, and that its use of the classification is 'necessary . . . to the accomplishment' of its purpose or the safeguarding of its interest." Justice Powell maintains that the Davis program is not constitutionally permissible; but he concludes that other admissions programs, such as Harvard's, which take race into account but treat each applicant as an individual in the admissions process, are constitutionally acceptable.

I

Over the past 30 years, this Court has embarked upon the crucial mission of interpreting the Equal Protection Clause with the view of assuring to all persons "the protection of equal laws," in a Nation confronting a legacy of slavery and racial discrimination. Because the landmark decisions in this area arose in response to the continued exclusion of Negroes from the mainstream of American society, they could be characterized as involving discrimination by the "majority" white race against the Negro minority. But they need not be read as depending upon that characterization for their results. It suffices to say that "[o]ver the years, this Court has consistently repudiated '[d]istinctions between citizens solely because of their ancestry' as being 'odious to a free people whose institutions are founded upon the doctrine of equality.' "

Petitioner urges us to adopt for the first time a more restrictive view of the Equal Protection Clause and hold that discrimination against members of the white "majority" cannot be suspect if its purpose can be characterized as "benign." The clock of our liberties, however, cannot be turned back to 1868. It is far too late to argue that the guarantee of equal protection to *all* persons permits the recognition of special wards entitled to a degree of protection greater than that accorded others. "The Fourteenth Amendment is not directed solely against discrimination due to a 'two-class theory'— that is, based upon differences between 'white' and Negro." . . .

II

We have held that in "order to justify the use of a suspect classification, a State must show that its purpose or interest is both constitutionally permissible and substantial, and that its use of the classification is 'necessary . . . to the accomplishment' of its purpose or the safeguarding of its interest." The special admissions program purports to serve the purposes of: (i) "reducing the historic deficit of traditionally disfavored minorities in medical schools and in the medical profession"; (ii) countering the effects of societal discrimination; (iii) increasing the number of physicians who will practice in communities currently underserved; and (iv) obtaining the educational benefits that flow from an ethnically diverse student body. It is necessary to decide which, if any, of these purposes is substantial enough to support the use of a suspect classification.

A

If petitioner's purpose is to assure within its student body some specified percentage of a particular group merely because of its race or ethnic origin, such a preferential purpose must be rejected not as insubstantial but as facially invalid. Preferring members of any one group for no reason other than race or ethnic origin is discrimination for its own sake. This the Constitution forbids.

B

The State certainly has a legitimate and substantial interest in ameliorating, or eliminating where feasible, the disabling effects of identified discrimination. The line of school desegregation cases, commencing with *Brown v. Board of Education* (1954) attests to the importance of this state goal and the commitment of the judiciary to affirm all lawful means toward its attainment. In the school cases, the States were required by court order to redress the wrongs worked by specific instances of racial discrimination. That goal was far more focused than the remedying of the effects of "societal discrimination," an amorphous concept of injury that may be ageless in its reach into the past.

We have never approved a classification that aids persons perceived as members of relatively victimized groups at the expense of other innocent individuals in the absence of judicial, legislative, or administrative findings of constitutional or statutory violations. After such findings have been made, the governmental interest in preferring members of the injured groups at the expense of others is substantial, since the legal rights of the victims must be vindicated. In such a case, the extent of the injury and the consequent remedy will have been judicially, legislatively, or administratively defined. Also, the remedial action usually remains subject to continuing oversight to assure that it will work the least harm possible to other innocent persons competing for the benefit. Without such findings of constitutional or statutory violations, it cannot be said that the government has any greater interest in helping one individual than in refraining from harming another. Thus, the government has no compelling justification for inflicting such harm.

Petitioner does not purport to have made, and is in no position to make, such findings. Its broad mission is education, not the formulation of any legislative policy or the adjudication of particular claims of illegality. . . . [I]solated segments of our vast governmental structures are not competent to make those decisions, at least in the absence of legislative mandates and legislatively determined criteria. Before relying upon these sorts of findings in establishing a racial classification, a governmental body must have the authority and capability to establish, in the record, that the classification is responsive to identified discrimination. Lacking this capability, petitioner has not carried its burden of justification on this issue.

Hence, the purpose of helping certain groups whom the faculty of the Davis Medical School perceived as victims of "societal discrimination" does not justify a classification that imposes disadvantages upon persons like respondent, who bear no responsibility for whatever harm the beneficiaries of the special admissions program are thought to have suffered. To hold otherwise would be to convert a remedy heretofore reserved for violations of legal rights into a privilege that all institutions throughout the Nation could grant at their pleasure to whatever groups are perceived as victims of societal discrimination. That is a step we have never approved.

C

Petitioner identifies, as another purpose of its program, improving the delivery of heath-care services to communities currently underserved. It may be assumed that in some situations a State's interest in facilitating the health care of its citizens is sufficiently compelling to support the use of a suspect classification. But there is virtually no evidence in the record indicating that petitioner's special admissions program is either needed or geared to promote that goal. The court below addressed this failure of proof:

> "The University concedes it cannot assure that minority doctors who entered under the program, all of whom expressed an 'interest' in practicing in a disadvantaged community, will actually do so. It may be correct to assume that some of them will carry out this intention, and that it is more likely they will practice in minority communities than the average white doctor. Nevertheless, there are more precise and reliable ways to identify applicants who are genuinely interested in the medical problems of minorities than by race. An applicant of whatever race who has demonstrated his concern for disadvantaged minorities in the past and who declares that practice in such a community is his primary professional goal would be more likely to contribute to alleviation of the medical shortage than one who is chosen entirely on the basis of race and disadvantage. In short, there is no empirical data to demonstrate that any one race is more selflessly socially oriented or by contrast that another is more selfishly acquisitive."

Petitioner simply has not carried its burden of demonstrating that it must prefer members of particular ethnic groups over all other individuals in order to promote better health-care delivery to deprived citizens. Indeed, petitioner has not shown that its preferential classification is likely to have any significant effect on the problem.

D

The fourth goal asserted by petitioner is the attainment of a diverse student body. This clearly is a constitutionally permissible goal for an institution of higher education. Academic freedom, though not a specifically enumerated constitutional right, long has been viewed as a special concern of the First Amendment. The freedom of a university to make its own judgments as to education includes the selection of its student body.

Ethnic diversity, however, is only one element in a range of factors a university properly may consider in attaining the goal of a heterogeneous student body. Although a university must have wide discretion in making the sensitive judgments as to who should be admitted, constitutional limitations protecting individual rights may not be disregarded. Respondent urges—and the courts below have held—that petitioner's dual admissions program is a racial classification that impermissibly infringes his rights under the Fourteenth Amendment. As the interest of diversity is compelling in the context of a university's admissions program, the question remains whether the program's racial classification is necessary to promote this interest.

III

A

It may be assumed that the reservation of a specified number of seats in each class for individuals from the preferred ethnic groups would contribute to the attainment of considerable ethnic diversity in the student body. But petitioner's argument that this is the only effective means of serving the interest of diversity is seriously flawed. In a most fundamental sense the argument misconceives the nature of the state interest that would justify consideration of race or ethnic background. It is not an interest in simple ethnic diversity, in which a specified percentage of the student body is in effect guaranteed to be members of selected ethnic groups, with the remaining percentage an undifferentiated aggregation of students. The diversity that furthers a compelling state interest encompasses a far broader array of qualifications and characteristics of which racial or ethnic origin is but a single though important element. Petitioner's special admissions program, focused *solely* on ethnic diversity, would hinder rather than further attainment of genuine diversity.

Nor would the state interest in genuine diversity be served by expanding petitioner's two-track system into a multitrack program with a prescribed number of seats set aside for each identifiable category of applicants. Indeed, it is inconceivable that a university would thus pursue the logic of petitioner's two-track program to the illogical end of insulating each category of applicants with certain desired qualifications from competition with all other applicants.

The experience of other university admissions programs, which take race into account in achieving the educational diversity valued by the First Amendment, demonstrates that the assignment of a fixed number of places to a minority group is not a necessary means toward that end. An illuminating example is found in the Harvard College program:

"In recent years Harvard College has expanded the concept of diversity to include students from disadvantaged economic, racial and ethnic groups. Harvard College now recruits not only Californians or Louisianans but also blacks and Chicanos and other minority students. . . .

"In practice, this new definition of diversity has meant that race has been a factor in some admission decisions. When the Committee on Admissions reviews the large middle group of applicants who are 'admissible' and deemed capable of doing good work in their courses, the race of an applicant may tip the balance in his favor just as geographic origin or a life spent on a farm may tip the balance in other candidates' cases. A farm boy from Idaho can bring something to Harvard College that a Bostonian cannot offer. Similarly, a black student can usually bring something that a white person cannot offer. . . .

"In Harvard college admissions the Committee has not set target-quotas for the number of blacks, or of musicians, football players, physicists or Californians to be admitted in a given year. . . . But that awareness [of the necessity of including more than a token number of black students] does not mean that the Committee sets a minimum number of blacks or of people from west of the Mississippi who are to be admitted. It means only that in choosing among thousands of applicants who are not only 'admissible' academically but have other strong qualities, the Committee, with a number of criteria in mind, pays some attention to distribution among many types and categories of students."

In such an admissions program, race or ethnic background may be deemed a "plus" in a particular applicant's file, yet it does not insulate the individual from comparison with all other candidates for the available seats. The file of a particular black applicant may be examined for his potential contribution to diversity without the factor of race being decisive when compared, for example, with that of an applicant identified as an Italian-American if the latter is thought to exhibit qualities more likely to promote beneficial educational pluralism. Such qualities could include exceptional personal talents, unique work or service experience, leadership potential, maturity, demonstrated compassion, a history of overcoming disadvantage, ability to communicate with the poor, or other qualifications deemed important. In short, an admissions program operated in this way is flexible enough to consider all pertinent elements of diversity in light of the particular qualifications of each applicant, and to place them on the same footing for consideration, although not necessarily according them the same weight. Indeed, the weight attributed to a particular quality may vary from year to year depending upon the "mix" both of the student body and the applicants for the incoming class.

This kind of program treats each applicant as an individual in the admissions process. The applicant who loses out on the last available seat to another candidate receiving a "plus" on the basis of ethnic background will not have been foreclosed from all consideration for that seat simply because he was not the right color or had the wrong surname. It would mean only that his combined qualifications, which may have included similar nonobjective factors, did not outweigh those of the other applicant. His qualifications would have been weighed fairly and competitively, and he would have no basis to complain of unequal treatment under the Fourteenth Amendment.

It has been suggested that an admissions program which considers race only as one factor is simply a subtle and more sophisticated—but no less effective—means of according racial preference than the Davis program. A facial intent to discriminate, however, is evident in petitioner's preference program and not denied in this case. No such facial infirmity exists in an admissions program where race or ethnic background is simply one element—to be weighed fairly against other elements—in the selection process. "A boundary line," as Mr. Justice Frankfurter remarked in another connection, "is none the worse for being narrow." And a court would not assume that a university, professing to employ a facially nondiscriminatory admissions policy, would operate it as a cover for the functional equivalent of a quota system. In short, good faith would be presumed in the absence of a showing to the contrary in the manner permitted by our cases.

B

In summary, it is evident that the Davis special admissions program involves the use of an explicit racial classification never before countenanced by this Court. It tells applicants who are not Negro, Asian, or Chicano that they are totally excluded from a specific percentage of the seats in an entering class. No matter how strong their qualifications, quantitative and extracurricular, including their own potential for contribution to educational diversity, they are never afforded the chance to compete with applicants from the preferred groups for the special admissions seats. At the same time, the preferred applicants have the opportunity to compete for every seat in the class.

The fatal flaw in petitioner's preferential program is its disregard of individual rights as guaranteed by the Fourteenth Amendment. Such rights are not absolute. But when a State's distribution of benefits or imposition of burdens hinges on ancestry or the color of a person's skin or ancestry, that individual is entitled to a demonstration that the challenged classification is necessary to promote a substantial state interest. Petitioner has failed to carry this burden. For this reason, that portion of the California court's judgment holding petitioner's special admissions program invalid under the Fourteenth Amendment must be affirmed.

C

In enjoining petitioner from ever considering the race of any applicant, however, the courts below failed to recognize that the State has a substantial interest that legitimately may be served by a properly devised admissions program involving the competitive consideration of race and ethnic origin. For this reason, so much of the California court's judgment as enjoins petitioner from any consideration of the race of any applicant must be reversed.

QUESTIONS

1 Are there any morally good reasons for having two sets of criteria for judging applicants to institutions of higher learning?
2 Can you suggest any criteria that should be used to distinguish morally acceptable racial classifications from invidious and pernicious ones?

A Defense of Programs of Preferential Treatment

Richard Wasserstrom

Richard Wasserstrom is professor of philosophy at the University of Califoria at Santa Cruz. He is the editor of Morality and the Law *(1970) and* Today's Moral Problems *(3d ed., 1985), and author of* Philosophy and Social Issues: Five Studies *(1980). The last volume includes an*

Reprinted with permission of the author and the publisher from *National Forum (The Phi Kappa Phi Journal)*, vol. LVIII, no. 1 (Winter 1978), pp. 15–18.

essay, "Preferential Treatment," which is a longer, more complete account of his views on the topic discussed here. Wasserstrom's many articles include "On Racism and Sexism" and "War, Nuclear War and Nuclear Deterrence: Some Conceptual and Moral Issues."

In his limited defense of preferential treatment programs, Wasserstrom attacks two arguments frequently used to support the view that no matter what social goods they produce, preferential treatment programs are unfair or unjust. The two arguments at issue are the folllowing: (1) One cannot consistently *condemn as immoral* past racial and sexual discriminatory quotas and exclusions which worked against blacks and women and *support as morally correct* present racial and sexual classifications which discriminate against white males. (2) Preferential treatment programs are wrong because race or sex are irrelevant when decisions are made about university employment and admissions; the only relevant factor is merit or qualification. Against (1) Wasserstrom argues that no inconsistency is involved in holding both views and gives reasons to show that quotas against blacks and women were pernicious whereas quotas favoring them are not. Against (2) he brings out a number of practical and theoretical difficulties faced by its proponents.

Many justifications of programs of preferential treatment depend upon the claim that in one respect or another such programs have good consequences or that they are effective means by which to bring about some desirable end, e.g., an integrated, equalitarian society. I mean by "programs of preferential treatment" to refer to programs such as those at issue in the *Bakke* case—programs which set aside a certain number of places (for example, in a law school) as to which members of minority groups (for example, persons who are non-white or female) who possess certain minimum qualifications (in terms of grades and test scores) may be preferred for admission to those places over some members of the majority group who possess higher qualifications (in terms of grades and test scores).

Many criticisms of programs of preferential treatment claim that such programs, even if effective, are unjustifiable because they are in some important sense unfair or unjust. In this paper I present a limited defense of such programs by showing that two of the chief arguments offered for the unfairness or injustice of these programs do not work in the way or to the degree supposed by critics of these programs.

The first argument is this. Opponents of preferential treatment programs sometimes assert that proponents of these programs are guilty of intellectual inconsistency, if not racism or sexism. For, as is now readily acknowledged, at times past employers, universities, and many other social institutions did have racial or sexual quotas (when they did not practice overt racial or sexual exclusion), and many of those who were most concerned to bring about the eradication of those racial quotas are now untroubled by the new programs which reinstitute them. And this, it is claimed, is inconsistent. If it was wrong to take race or sex into account when blacks and women were the objects of racial and sexual policies and practices of exclusion, then it is wrong to take race or sex into account when the objects of the policies have their race or sex reversed. Simple considerations of intellectual consistency—of what it means to give racism or sexism as a reason for condemning these social policies and practices—require that what was a good reason then is still a good reason now.

The problem with this argument is that despite appearances, there is no inconsistency involved in holding both views. Even if contemporary preferential treatment programs which contain quotas are wrong, they are not wrong for the reasons that made quotas against blacks and women pernicious. The reason why is that the social realities do make an enormous difference. The fundamental evil of programs that discriminated against blacks or women was that these programs were a part of a larger social universe which systematically maintained a network of institutions which unjustifiably concentrated power, authority, and goods in the hands of white male individuals, and which systematically consigned blacks and women to subordinate positions in the society.

Whatever may be wrong with today's affirmative action programs and quota systems, it should be clear that the evil, if any, is just not the same. Racial and sexual minorities do not constitute the dominant social group. Nor is the conception of who is a fully developed member of the moral and social community one of an individual who is either female or black. Quotas which prefer women or blacks do not add to an already relatively overabundant supply of resources and opportunities at the disposal of members of these groups in the way in which the quotas of the past did maintain and augment the overabundant supply of resources and opportunities already available to white males.

The same point can be made in a somewhat different way. Sometimes people say that what was wrong, for example, with the system of racial discrimination in the South was that it took an irrelevant characteristic, namely race, and used it systematically to allocate social benefits and burdens of various sorts. The defect was the irrelevance of the characteristic used—race—for that meant that individuals ended up being treated in a manner that was arbitrary and capricious.

I do not think that was the central flaw at all. Take, for instance, the most hideous of the practices, human slavery. The primary thing that was wrong with the institution was not that the particular individuals who were assigned the place of slaves were assigned there arbitrarily because the assignment was made in virtue of an irrelevant characteristic, their race. Rather, it seems to me that the primary thing that was and is wrong with slavery is the practice itself—the fact of some individuals being able to own other individuals and all that goes with that practice. It would not matter by what criterion individuals were assigned; human slavery would still be wrong. And the same can be said for most if not all of the other discrete practices and institutions which comprised the system of racial discrimination even after human slavery was abolished. The practices were unjustifiable—they were oppressive—and they would have been so no matter how the assignment of victims had been made. What made it worse, still, was that the institutions and the supporting ideology all interlocked to create a system of human oppression whose effects on those living under it were as devastating as they were unjustifiable.

Again, if there is anything wrong with the programs of preferential treatment that have begun to flourish within the past ten years, it should be evident that the social realities in respect to the distribution of resources and opportunities make the difference.

Apart from everything else, there is simply no way in which all of these programs taken together could plausibly be viewed as capable of relegating white males to the kind of genuinely oppressive status characteristically bestowed upon women and blacks by the dominant social institutions and ideology.

The second objection is that preferential treatment programs are wrong because they take race or sex into account rather than the only thing that does matter—that is, an individual's qualifications. What all such programs have in common and what makes them all objectionable, so this argument goes, is that they ignore the persons who are more qualified by bestowing a preference on those who are less qualified in virtue of their being either black or female.

There are, I think, a number of things wrong with this objection based on qualifications, and not the least of them is that we do not live in a society in which there is even the serious pretense of a qualification requirement for many jobs of substantial power and authority. Would anyone claim, for example, that the persons who comprise the judiciary are there because they are the most qualified lawyers or the most qualified persons to be judges? Would anyone claim that Henry Ford II is the head of the Ford Motor Company because he is the most qualified person for the job? Part of what is wrong with even talking about qualifications and merit is that the argument derives some of its force from the erroneous notion that we would have a meritocracy were it not for programs of preferential treatment. In fact, the higher one goes in terms of prestige, power and the like, the less qualifications seem ever to be decisive. It is only for certain jobs and certain places that qualifications are used to do more than establish the possession of certain minimum competencies.

But difficulties such as these to one side, there are theoretical difficulties as well which cut much more deeply into the argument about qualifications. To begin with, it is important to see that there is a serious inconsistency present if the person who favors "pure qualifications" does so on the ground that the most qualified ought to be selected because this promotes maximum efficiency. Let us suppose that the argument is that if we have the most qualified performing the relevant tasks we will get those tasks done in the most economical and efficient manner. There is nothing wrong in principle with arguments based upon the good consequences that will flow from maintaining a social practice in a certain way. But it is inconsistent for the opponent of preferential treatment to attach much weight to qualifications on this ground, because it was an analogous appeal to the good consequences that the opponent of preferential treatment thought was wrong in the first place. That is to say, if the chief thing to be said in favor of strict qualifications and preferring the most qualified is that it is the most efficient way of getting things done, then we are right back to an assessment of the different consequences that will flow from different programs, and we are far removed from the considerations of justice or fairness that were thought to weigh so heavily against these programs.

It is important to note, too, that qualifications—at least in the educational context—are often not connected at all closely with any plausible conception of social effectiveness. To admit the most qualified students to law school, for example—given the way qualifications are now determined—is primarily to admit those who have the greatest chance of scoring the highest grades at law school. This says little about efficiency except perhaps that these students are the easiest for the faculty to teach. However, since we know so little about what constitutes being a good, or even successful lawyer, and even less about the correlation between being a very good law student and being a very good lawyer, we can hardly claim very confidently that the legal system will operate most effectively if we admit only the most qualified students to law school.

To be at all decisive, the argument for qualifications must be that those who are the most qualified deserve to receive the benefits (the job, the place in law school, etc.) because they are the most qualified. The introduction of the concept of desert now makes it an objection as to justice or fairness of the sort promised by the original criticism of the programs. But now the problem is that there is no reason to think that there is any strong sense of "desert" in which it is correct that the most qualified deserve anything.

Let us consider more closely one case, that of preferential treatment in respect to admission to college or graduate school. There is a logical gap in the inference from the claim that a person is most qualified to perform a task, e.g., to be a good student, to the conclusion that he or she deserves to be admitted as a student. Of course, those who deserve to be admitted should be admitted. But why do the most qualified deserve anything? There is simply no necessary connection between academic merit (in the sense of being the most qualified) and deserving to be a member of a student body. Suppose, for instance, that there is only one tennis court in the community. Is it clear that the two best tennis players ought to be the ones permitted to use it? Why not those who were there first? Or those who will enjoy playing the most? Or those who are the worst and, therefore, need the greatest opportunity to practice? Or those who have the chance to play least frequently?

We might, of course, have a rule that says that the best tennis players get to use the court before the others. Under such a rule the best players would deserve the court more than the poorer ones. But that is just to push the inquiry back one stage. Is there any reason to think that we ought to have a rule giving good tennis players such a preference? Indeed, the arguments that might be given for or against such a rule are many and varied. And few if any of the arguments that might support the rule would depend upon a connection between ability and desert.

Someone might reply, however, that the most able students deserve to be admitted to the university because all of their earlier schooling was a kind of competition, with university admission being the prize awarded to the winners. They deserve to be admitted because that is what the rule of the competition provides. In addition, it might be argued, it would be unfair now to exclude them in favor of others, given the reasonable expectations they developed about the way in which their industry and performance would be rewarded. Minority-admission programs, which inevitably prefer some who are less qualified over some who are more qualified, all possess this flaw.

There are several problems with this argument. The most substantial of them is that it is an empirically implausible picture of our social world. Most of what are regarded as the decisive characteristics for higher education have a great deal to do with things over which the individual has neither control nor responsibility: such things as home environment, socioeconomic class of parents, and, of course, the quality of the primary and secondary schools attended. Since individuals do not deserve having had any of these things vis-à-vis other individuals, they do not, for the most part, deserve their qualifications. And since they do not deserve their abilities they do not in any strong sense deserve to be admitted because of their abilities.

To be sure, if there has been a rule which connects, say, performance at high school with admission to college, then there is a weak sense in which those who do well at high school deserve, for that reason alone, to be admitted to college. In addition, if persons have built up or relied upon their reasonable expectations concerning performance and admission, they have a claim to be admitted on this ground as well. But it is certainly not obvious that these claims of desert are any stronger or more compelling than the competing claims based upon the needs of or advantages to women or blacks from programs of preferential treatment. And as I have indicated, all rule-based claims of desert are very weak unless and until the rule which creates the claim is itself shown to be a justified one. Unless one has a strong preference for the status quo, and unless one can defend that preference, the practice within a system of allocating places in a certain way does not go very far at all in showing that that is the right or the just way to allocate those places in the future.

A proponent of programs of preferential treatment is not at all committed to the view that qualifications ought to be wholly irrelevant. He or she can agree that, given the existing structure of any institution, there is probably some minimal set of qualifications without which one cannot participate meaningfully within the institution. In addition, it can be granted that the qualifications of those involved will affect the way the institution works and the way it affects others in the society. And the consequences will vary depending upon the particular institution. But all of this only establishes that qualifications, in this sense, are relevant, not that they are decisive. This is wholly consistent with the claim that race or sex should today also be relevant when it comes to matters such as admission to college or law school. And that is all that any preferential treatment program—even one with the kind of quota used in the *Bakke* case—has ever tried to do.

I have not attempted to establish that programs of preferential treatment are right and desirable. There are empirical issues concerning the consequences of these programs that I have not discussed, and certainly not settled. Nor, for that matter, have I considered the argument that justice may permit, if not require, these programs as a way to provide compensation or reparation for injuries suffered in the recent as well as distant past, or as a way to remove benefits that are undeservedly enjoyed by those of the dominant group. What I have tried to do is show that it is wrong to think that programs of preferential treatment are objectionable in the centrally important sense in which many past and present discriminatory features of our society have been and are racist and sexist. The social realities as to power and opportunity do make a fundamental difference. It is also wrong to think that programs of preferential treatment are in any strong sense either unjust or unprincipled. The case for programs of preferential treatment could, therefore, plausibly rest both on the view that such programs are not unfair to white males (except in the weak, rule-dependent sense described above) and on the view that it is unfair to continue the present set of unjust—often racist and sexist—institutions that comprise the social reality. And the case for these programs could rest as well on the proposition that, given the distribution of power and influence in the United States today, such programs may reasonably be viewed as potentially valuable, effective means by which to achieve admirable and significant social ideals of equality and integration.

QUESTIONS

1 Wasserstrom's tennis court analogy has been severely criticized. Examine the analogy. What are its weaknesses? What are its strengths?

2 What criteria should be used in selecting candidates for professional schools?

Justifying Reverse Discrimination in Employment

George Sher

George Sher is professor of philosophy at the University of Vermont. His philosophical interests include metaphysical and normative issues and the connections between them. Sher's published articles include "Reverse Discrimination, The Future and The Past," "Ancient Wrongs and Modern Rights," and "The U.S. Bishops' Position on Nuclear Deterrence: A Moral Assessment."

Sher first examines and critizes several arguments advanced in support of reverse discrimination. He argues, however, that a reasonable case can be made for reverse discrimination when it is seen as compensation for lost ability to compete on equal terms. Sher gives examples to illustrate four ways in which a person's environment can affect his or her ability to compete. He concludes by arguing the following: (1) Reverse discrimination can only be justified when an individual's present competitive disadvantage is due to an inadequate education or to factors such as an inadequate diet or lack of early intellectual stimulation; (2) It cannot be justified in the case of women as a group because the privations which have affected their ability to compete were of a different kind; and (3) Strictly speaking, it cannot be justified in regard to all blacks, but only in regard to those who are at a competitive disadvantage due to privations of the sort noted in (1). On Sher's account racial (and possibly sexual) boundaries should only be used to suggest roughly which individuals are likely to be at a competitive disadvantage because of past discrimination.

A currently favored way of compensating for past discrimination is to afford preferential treatment to the members of those groups which have been discriminated against in

George Sher, "Justifying Reverse Discrimination in Employment," *Philosophy & Public Affairs* 4, no. 2 (Winter 1975). Copyright © 1975 by Princeton University Press. Reprinted by permission of Princeton University Press.

the past. I propose to examine the rationale behind this practice when it is applied in the area of employment.[1] I want to ask whether, and if so under what conditions, past acts of discrimination against members of a particular group justify the current hiring of a member of that group who is less than the best qualified applicant for a given job. Since I am mainly concerned about exploring the relations between past discrimination and present claims to employment, I shall make the assumption that each applicant is at least minimally competent to perform the job he seeks; this will eliminate the need to consider the claims of those who are to receive the services in question. Whether it is ever justifiable to discriminate in favor of an incompetent applicant, or a less than best qualified applicant for a job such as teaching, in which almost any increase in employee competence brings a real increase in services rendered, will be left to be decided elsewhere. Such questions, which turn on balancing the claim of the less than best qualified applicant against the competing claims of those who are to receive his services, are not as basic as the question of whether the less than best qualified applicant ever *has* a claim to employment.[2]

I

It is sometimes argued, when members of a particular group have been barred from employment of a certain kind, that since this group has in the past received *less* than its fair share of the employment in question, it now deserves to receive *more* by way of compensation.[3] This argument, if sound, has the virtue of showing clearly why preferential treatment should be extended even to those current group members who have not themselves been denied employment: if the point of reverse discrimination is to compensate a wronged *group,* it will presumably hardly matter if those who are preferentially hired were not among the original victims of discrimination. However, the argument's basic presupposition, that groups as opposed to their individual members are the sorts of entities that can be wronged and deserve redress, is itself problematic. Thus the defense of reverse discrimination would only be convincing if it were backed by a further argument showing that groups can indeed be wronged and have deserts

---

[1] I am grateful to Michael Levin, Edward Erwin, and my wife Emily Gordon Sher for helpful discussion of this topic.

[2] In what follows I will have nothing to say about utilitarian justifications of reverse discrimination. There are two reasons for this. First, the winds of utilitarian argumentation blow in too many directions. It is certainly socially beneficial to avoid the desperate actions to which festering resentments may lead— but so too is it socially useful to confirm the validity of qualifications of the traditional sort, to assure those who have amassed such qualifications that "the rules of the game have not been changed in the middle," that accomplishment has not been downgraded in society's eyes. How could these conflicting utilities possibly be measured against one another?

Second and even more important, to rest a defense of reverse discrimination upon utilitarian considerations would be to ignore what is surely the guiding intuition of its proponents, that this treatment is *deserved* where discrimination has been practiced in the past. It is the intuition that reverse discrimination is a matter not (only) of social good but of right which I want to try to elucidate.

[3] This argument, as well as the others I shall consider, presupposes that jobs are (among other things) *goods,* and so ought to be distributed as fairly as possible. This presupposition seems to be amply supported by the sheer economic necessity of earning a living, as well as by the fact that some jobs carry more prestige and are more interesting and pay better than others.

of the relevant sort. No one, as far as I know, has yet produced a powerful argument to this effect, and I am not hopeful about the possibilities. Therefore I shall not try to develop a defense of reverse discrimination along these lines.

Another possible way of connecting past acts of discrimination in hiring with the claims of current group members is to argue that even if these current group members have not (yet) been denied *employment,* their membership in the group makes it very likely that they have been discriminatorily deprived of *other* sorts of goods. It is a commonplace, after all, that people who are forced to do menial and low-paying jobs must often endure corresponding privations in housing, diet, and other areas. These privations are apt to be distributed among young and old alike, and so to afflict even those group members who are still too young to have had their qualifications for employment bypassed. It is, moreover, generally acknowledged by both common sense and law that a person who has been deprived of a certain amount of one sort of good may sometimes reasonably be compensated by an equivalent amount of a good of another sort. (It is this principle, surely, that underlies the legal practice of awarding sums of money to compensate for pain incurred in accidents, damaged reputations, etc.) Given these facts and this principle, it appears that the preferential hiring of current members of discriminated-against groups may be justified as compensation for the *other* sorts of discrimination these individuals are apt to have suffered.

But, although this argument seems more promising than one presupposing group deserts, it surely cannot be accepted as it stands. For one thing, insofar as the point is simply to compensate individuals for the various sorts of privations they have suffered, there is no special reason to use reverse discrimination rather than some other mechanism to effect compensation. There are, moreoever, certain other mechanisms of redress which seem prima facie preferable. It seems, for instance, that it would be most appropriate to compensate for past privations simply by making preferentially available to the discriminated-against individuals equivalent amounts of the very same sorts of goods of which they have been deprived; simple cash settlements would allow a far greater precision in the adjustment of compensation to privation than reverse discriminatory hiring ever could. Insofar as it does not provide any reason to adopt reverse discrimination rather than these prima facie preferable mechanisms of redress, the suggested defense of reverse discrimination is at least incomplete.

Moreover, and even more important, if reverse discrimination is viewed simply as a form of compensation for past privations, there are serious questions about its fairness. Certainly the privations to be compensated for are not the sole responsibility of those individuals whose superior qualifications will have to be bypassed in the reverse discriminatory process. These individuals, if responsible for those privations at all, will at least be no more responsible than others with relevantly similar histories. Yet reverse discrimination will compensate for the privations in question at the expense of these individuals alone. It will have no effect at all upon those other, equally responsible persons whose qualifications are inferior to begin with, who are already entrenched in their jobs, or whose vocations are noncompetitive in nature. Surely it is unfair to distribute the burden of compensation so unequally.

These considerations show, I think, that reverse discriminatory hiring of members of groups that have been denied jobs in the past cannot be justified simply by the fact that each group member has been discriminated against in other areas. If this fact is to enter into the justification of reverse discrimination at all, it must be in some more complicated way.

II

Consider again the sorts of privations that are apt to be distributed among the members of those groups restricted in large part to menial and low-paying jobs. These individuals, we said, are apt to live in substandard homes, to subsist on improper and imbalanced diets, and to receive inadequate educations. Now, it is certainly true that adequate housing, food, and education are goods in and of themselves; a life without them is certainly less pleasant and less full than one with them. But, and crucially, they are also goods in a different sense entirely. It is an obvious and well-documented fact that (at least) the sorts of nourishment and education a person receives as a child will causally affect the sorts of skills and capacities he will have as an adult—including, of course, the very skills which are needed if he is to compete on equal terms for jobs and other goods. Since this is so, a child who is deprived of adequate food and education may lose not only the immediate enjoyments which a comfortable and stimulating environment bring but also the subsequent ability to compete equally for other things of intrinsic value. But to lose this ability to compete is, in essence, to lose one's access to the goods that are being competed for; and this, surely, is itself a privation to be compensated for if possible. It is, I think, the key to an adequate justification of reverse discrimination to see that practice, not as the redressing of *past* privations, but rather as a way of neutralizing the *present* competitive disadvantage *caused* by those past privations and thus as a way of restoring equal access to those goods which society distributes competitively. When reverse discrimination is justified in this way, many of the difficulties besetting the simpler justification of it disappear.

For whenever someone has been irrevocably deprived of a certain good and there are several alternative ways of providing him with an equivalent amount of another good, it will ceteris paribus be preferable to choose whichever substitute comes closest to actually replacing the lost good. It is this principle that makes preferential access to decent housing, food, and education especially desirable as a way of compensating for the experiential impoverishment of a deprived childhood. If, however, we are concerned to compensate not for the experiential poverty, but for the effects of child-hood deprivations, then this principle tells just as heavily for reverse discrimination as the proper form of compensation. If the lost good is just the *ability* to compete on equal terms for first-level goods like desirable jobs, then surely the most appropriate (and so preferable) way of substituting for what has been lost is just to remove the *necessity* of competing on equal terms for these goods—which, of course, is precisely what reverse discrimination does.

When reverse discrimination is viewed as compensation for lost ability to compete on equal terms, a reasonable case can also be made for its fairness. Our doubts about its fairness arose because it seemed to place the entire burden of redress upon those individuals whose superior qualifications are bypassed in the reverse discriminatory process. This seemed wrong because these individuals are, of course, not apt to be

any more responsible for past discrimination than others with relevantly similar histories. But, as we are now in a position to see, this objection misses the point. The crucial fact about these individuals is not that they are more *responsible* for past discrimination than others with relevantly similar histories (in fact, the dirty work may well have been done before any of their generation attained the age of responsibility), but rather that unless reverse discrimination is practiced, they will *benefit* more than the others from its effects on their competitors. They will benefit more because unless they are restrained, they, but not the others, will use their competitive edge to claim jobs which their competitors would otherwise have gotten. Thus, it is only because they stand to *gain* the most from the relevant effects of the *original* discrimination, that the bypassed individuals stand to *lose* the most from *reverse* discrimination. This is surely a valid reply to the charge that reverse discrimination does not distribute the burden of compensation equally.

III

So far, the argument has been that reverse discrimination is justified insofar as it neutralizes competitive disadvantages caused by past privations. This may be correct, but it is also oversimplified. In actuality, there are many ways in which a person's environment may affect his ability to compete; and there may well be logical differences among these ways which affect the degree to which reverse discrimination is called for. Consider, for example, the following cases:

1 An inadequate education prevents someone from acquiring the degree of a certain skill that he would have been able to acquire with a better education.

2 An inadequate diet, lack of early intellectual stimulation, etc., lower an individual's ability, and thus prevent him from acquiring the degree of competence in a skill that he would otherwise have been able to acquire.

3 The likelihood that he will not be able to use a certain skill because he belongs to a group which has been discriminated against in the past leads a person to decide, rationally, not even to try developing that skill.

4 Some aspect of his childhood environment renders an individual incapable of putting forth the sustained effort needed to improve his skills.

These are four different ways in which past privations might adversely affect a person's skills. Ignoring for analytical purposes the fact that privation often works in more than one of these ways at a time, shall we say that reverse discrimination is equally called for in each case?

It might seem that we should say it is, since in each case a difference in the individual's environment would have been accompanied by an increase in his mastery of a certain skill (and, hence, by an improvement in his competitive position with respect to jobs requiring that skill). But this blanket counterfactual formulation conceals several important distinctions. For one thing, it suggests (and our justification of reverse discrimination seems to require) the possibility of giving *just enough* preferential treatment to the disadvantaged individual in each case to restore to him the competitive

position that he would have had, had he not suffered his initial disadvantage. But in fact, this does not seem to be equally possible in all cases. We can roughly calculate the difference that a certain improvement in education or intellectual stimulation would have made in the development of a person's skills if his efforts had been held constant (cases 1 and 2); for achievement is known to be a relatively straightforward compositional function of ability, environmental factors, and effort. We cannot, however, calculate in the same way the difference that improved prospects or environment would have made in degree of *effort* expended; for although effort is affected by environmental factors, it is not a known compositional function of them (or of anything else). Because of this, there would be no way for us to decide how much preferential treatment is just enough to make up for the efforts that a particular disadvantaged individual would have made under happier circumstances.

There is also another problem with (3) and (4). Even if there were a way to afford a disadvantaged person just enough preferential treatment to make up for the efforts he was prevented from making by his environment, it is not clear that he *ought* to be afforded that much preferential treatment. To allow this, after all, would be to concede that the effort he *would* have made under other conditions is worth just as much as the effort that his rival actually *did* make; and this, I think, is implausible. Surely a person who *actually has* labored long and hard to achieve a given degree of a certain skill is more deserving of a job requiring that skill than another who is equal in all other relevant respects, but who merely *would* have worked and achieved the same amount under different conditions. Because actual effort creates desert in a way that merely possible effort does not, reverse discrimination to restore precisely the competitive position that a person would have had if he had not been prevented from working harder would not be desirable even if it were possible.

There is perhaps also a further distinction to be made here. A person who is rationally persuaded by an absence of opportunities not to develop a certain skill (case 3) will typically not undergo any sort of character transformation in the process of making this decision. He will be the same person after his decision as before it, and, most often, the same person without his skill as with it. In cases such as (4), this is less clear. A person who is rendered incapable of effort by his environment does in a sense undergo a character transformation; to become truly incapable of sustained effort is to become a different (and less meritorious) person from the person one would otherwise have been. Because of this (and somewhat paradoxically, since his character change is itself apt to stem from factors beyond his control), such an individual may have less of a claim to reverse discrimination than one whose lack of effort does not flow from even an environmentally induced character fault, but rather from a justified rational decision.[4]

---

[4] A somewhat similar difference might seem to obtain between cases (1) and (2). One's ability to learn is more intimately a part of him than his actual degree of education; hence, someone whose ability to learn is lowered by his environment (case 2) is a changed person in a way in which a person who is merely denied education (case 1) is not. However, one's ability to learn is not a feature of *moral* character in the way ability to exert effort is, and so this difference between (1) and (2) will have little bearing on the degree to which reverse discrimination is called for in these cases.

IV

When reverse discrimination is discussed in a nontheoretical context, it is usually assumed that the people most deserving of such treatment are blacks, members of other ethnic minorities, and women. In this last section, I shall bring the results of the foregoing discussion to bear on this assumption. Doubts will be raised both about the analogy between the claims of blacks and women to reverse discrimination and about the propriety, in absolute terms, of singling out either group as the proper recipient of such treatment.

For many people, the analogy between the claims of blacks and the claims of women to reverse discrimination rests simply upon the undoubted fact that both groups have been discriminatorily denied jobs in the past. But on the account just proposed, past discrimination justifies reverse discrimination only insofar as it has adversely affected the competitive position of present group members. When this standard is invoked, the analogy between the claims of blacks and those of women seems immediately to break down. The exclusion of blacks from good jobs in the past has been only one element in an interlocking pattern of exclusions and often has resulted in a poverty issuing in (and in turn reinforced by) such other privations as inadequate nourishment, housing, and health care, lack of time to provide adequate guidance and intellectual stimulation for the young, dependence on (often inadequate) public education, etc. It is this whole complex of privations that undermines the ability of the young to compete; and it is largely because of its central causal role in this complex that the past unavailability of good jobs for blacks justifies reverse discrimination in their favor now. In the case of women, past discrimination in employment simply has not played the same role. Because children commonly come equipped with both male *and* female parents, the inability of the female parent to get a good job need not, and usually does not, result in a poverty detracting from the quality of the nourishment, education, housing, health, or intellectual stimulation of the female child (and, of course, when such poverty does result, it affects male and female children indifferently). For this reason, the past inaccessibility of good jobs for women does not seem to create for them the same sort of claim on reverse discrimination that its counterpart does for blacks.

Many defenders of reverse discrimination in favor of women would reply at this point that although past discrimination in employment has of course not played the *same* causal role in the case of women which it has in the case of blacks, it has nevertheless played *a* causal role in both cases. In the case of women, the argument runs, that role has been mainly psychological: past discrimination in hiring has led to a scarcity of female "role-models" of suitably high achievement. This lack, together with a culture which in many other ways subtly inculcates the idea that women should not or cannot do the jobs that men do, has in turn made women psychologically less able to do these jobs. This argument is hard to assess fully, since it obviously rests on a complex and problematic psychological claim.[5] The following objections, how-

---

[5]The feminist movement has convincingly documented the ways in which sexual bias is built into the information received by the young; but it is one thing to show that such information is received, and quite another to show how, and to what extent, its reception is causally efficacious.

ever, are surely relevant. First, even if it is granted without question that cultural bias and absence of suitable role-models do have some direct and pervasive effect upon women, it is not clear that this effect must take the form of a reduction of women's *abilities* to do the jobs men do. A more likely outcome would seem to be a reduction of women's *inclinations* to do these jobs—a result whose proper compensation is not preferential treatment of those women who have sought the jobs in question, but rather the encouragement of others to seek those jobs as well. Of course, this disinclination to do these jobs may in turn lead some women not to develop the relevant skills; to the extent that this occurs, the competitive position of these women will indeed be affected, albeit indirectly, by the scarcity of female role-models. Even here, however, the resulting disadvantage will not be comparable to those commonly produced by the poverty syndrome. It will flow solely from lack of effort, and so will be of the sort (cases 3 and 4) that neither calls for nor admits of full equalization by reverse discrimination. Moreover, and conclusively, since there is surely the same dearth of role-models, etc., for blacks as for women, whatever psychological disadvantages accrue to women because of this will beset blacks as well. Since blacks, but not women, must also suffer the privations associated with poverty, it follows that they are the group more deserving of reverse discrimination.

Strictly speaking, however, the account offered here does not allow us to speak this way of *either* group. If the point of reverse discrimination is to compensate for competitive disadvantages caused by past discrimination, it will be justified in favor of only those group members whose abilities have actually been reduced; and it would be most implausible to suppose that *every* black (or *every* woman) has been affected in this way. Blacks from middle-class or affluent backgrounds will surely have escaped many, if not all, of the competitive handicaps besetting those raised under less fortunate circumstances; and if they have, our account provides no reason to practice reverse discrimination in their favor. Again, whites from impoverished backgrounds may suffer many, if not all, of the competitive handicaps besetting their black counterparts; and if they do, the account provides no reason *not* to practice reverse discrimination in their favor. Generally, the proposed account allows us to view racial (and sexual) boundaries only as roughly suggesting which individuals are likely to have been disadvantaged by past discrimination. Anyone who construes these boundaries as playing a different and more decisive role must show us that a different defense of reverse discrimination is plausible.

QUESTIONS

1 Should all individuals (regardless of race or sex) who are at a competitive disadvantage due to an inferior education be given preference in hiring?
2 Are there relevant differences between blacks and women such that even if the former should receive preferential treatment, the latter should not?

In Defense of Hiring Apparently Less Qualified Women

Laura M. Purdy

Laura M. Purdy is associate professor of philosophy at Wells College (Aurora, N.Y.). She has also taught at Cornell University, where she was postdoctoral associate in the Program on Science, Technology, and Society. Specializing in ethics and political philosophy, Purdy has published articles such as "Genetic Diseases: Can Having Children Be Immoral?" and "The Morality of Euthanasia."

Purdy maintains that discrimination against women in academic hiring will end only through the institution of affirmative action programs that require hiring women *perceived* to be less qualified than the leading male contenders. Purdy's arguments are grounded on a factual claim: Women are frequently perceived to be less qualified than they really are because subjective elements in evaluations lead to systematic lowering of women's perceived qualifications. She offers two arguments to support this claim and backs these up by appeal to various studies: (1) Past prejudice biases the evidence and (2) Present prejudice biases perception of the evidence. Purdy ends by considering cases involving women of equal or more promise than their male competitors who nevertheless are not as well qualified as the latter because of stumbling blocks that women do and men do not face as students. In such cases the "qualifications" used as criteria may not be accurate indications of who will be best for the job.

A Man's mind—what there is of it—has always the advantage of being masculine—as the smallest birchtree is of higher kind than the most soaring palm—and even his ignorance is of a sounder quality.

George Elliot, *Middlemarch*, ch. 2

There are relatively few women in academe, and it is reasonable to believe that discrimination—conscious and unconscious, subtle and overt, individual and institutional—is responsible for this state of affairs.[1] Affirmative action programs have been promoted to try to neutralize this discrimination. One form requires academic departments to search actively for female candidates; if a woman with qualifications at least as good as those of the leading male contender is found, she is to be hired.

Does this policy create new and serious injustice, as some contend?[2] If a woman and a man were equally qualified, and one could be sure that prejudice against women played no part in the decision to hire, such a policy would certainly be an imposition

Reprinted with permission of the author and the publisher from the *Journal of Social Philosophy*, vol. 15 (Summer 1984), pp. 26–33.

on the department's freedom to hire the most compatible-seeming colleague. (This is not to say that such an imposition could never be justified: we might, for example, believe that the importance of creating role models for female students justifies some loss of freedom on the part of departments.) However, it is widely conceded that there is prejudice against women among academics, with the result that women are not getting the appointments they deserve. My intent here is to consider how this happens. I will argue that women are often not perceived to be as highly qualified as they really are. Thus when the qualifications of candidates are compared, a woman may not be thought equally (or more highly) qualified, even when she is. Affirmative action programs which require hiring of equally qualified women will therefore be ineffective: the hiring of women perceived to be less qualified is needed if discrimination against women is to cease.

Some people think that the latter course is both unnecessary and unfair. Alan Goldman, for instance, maintains that it is unnecessary because the procedural requirements of good affirmative action programs are sufficient to guarantee equal opportunity. He also believes it to be unfair because it deprives the most successful new Ph.D.'s of their just reward—a good job.[3] I will argue that neither of these claims is true and that there is a good case for hiring women perceived to be less well qualified than their male competitors.

The general difficulty of forming accurate assessments of candidates' merit is well-known, and it is probable that the better candidate has sometimes been taken for the worse. It is reasonable to believe, however, that the subjective elements in evaluations lead to systematic lowering of women's perceived qualifications. I have two arguments for this claim. The first is that past prejudice biases the evidence and the second is that present prejudice biases perception of the evidence. Let us examine each in turn.

Why then may women be better qualified than their records suggest? One principal reason is that many men simply do not take women seriously:

> You might think that the evaluation of a specific performance would be an objective process, judged on characteristics of performance itself rather than on assumptions about the personality or ability of the performer. Yet performance is rarely a totally objective process. Two people may view the same event and interpret it differently. In the same way, it is possible for someone to view two people acting in exactly the same way and yet come to different conclusions about that behavior.[4]

Studies by Rosenthal and Jacobson provide experimental support for this claim. They found that students reported one group of rats to run mazes faster than another identical group, when they had previously been told that the first group was brighter. Ann Sutherland Harris quite plausibly concludes that such studies have important implications for women:

> If male scholars believe that women are intellectually inferior to men—less likely to have original contributions to make, less likely to be logical, and so on—will they not also find the evidence to support their beliefs in the women students in their classes, evidence of a far more sophisticated nature than the speed at which one rat finds its way through a maze? Their motives will be subconscious. Indeed, they will firmly believe that their judgment is rational and objective.[5]

What grounds are there for maintaining that this does not occur whenever women are evaluated? Other studies suggest additional hurdles for women that bias the evidence upon which they are judged. For instance, male students (though not female ones) rate identical course syllabi higher when the professor is said to be a man.[6]

Sociologist Jessie Bernard suggests that bias occurs whether women present accepted ideas or novel ones. In one study, a man and a woman taught classes using the same material. The man engaged the students' interest: he was thought both more biased and more authoritative than the equally competent woman. According to Bernard, she was taken less seriously because she did not "look the part."[7] To support her position that novel ideas are less well received from women than men, Bernard mentions the case of Agnes Pockels, whose discoveries in physics were ignored for years. She cites this as an example of the general inability to see women in "the idea-man or instrumental role. We are simply not used to looking for innovation and originality from women."[8] The consequences of failing to take new ideas seriously may be even more detrimental to women than the failure to be taken seriously as a teacher. Bernard argues: "The importance of priority . . . highlights the importance of followers, or, in the case of science, of the public qualified to judge innovations. If an innovation is not recognized—even if recognition takes the form of rejection and a fight—it is dead."[9]

Additional persuasive evidence that women's ideas are not taken seriously by men comes from a study by Daryl and Sandra Bem, replicating a previous study by Philip Goldberg with women. A number of scholarly articles were submitted to a group of undergraduate men, who were to judge how good they were. Each paper was read by each man, but the paper read by half the students was attributed to a man, that read by the other half, to a woman. The results were striking: the "man's" article was rated higher than the "woman's" in most cases.[10] Does this prejudice continue to operate at more advanced levels?

One significant study showed more papers by women were chosen for presentation at the annual meeting of a national professional organization when they were submitted anonymously.[11] This suggests that whether a woman's work is published or not will also depend more on the reviewers' conception of women than upon the merits of the piece—at least until blind reviewing becomes the rule. Furthermore, there is evidence that even when a woman is recognized as having done a good job at some task, her performance is more likely than a man's to be attributed to factors other than ability. Hence others are less likely to expect future repeated success on her part.[12] And, unsuccessful performance by a male is more likely than that of a female to be attributed to bad luck.[13] Studies have also shown that male applicants for scholarship funds were judged more intelligent and likeable than their female counterparts,[14] and that males were favored over females for study abroad programs.[15] In addition, until very recently, recommendations written for women were more likely to mention personal appearance in an undermining way (as well as marital status) than those written for men.[16] These facts have obvious repercussions for candidates' overall records. Hence if the hypotheses considered so far here are true, then women are systematically undervalued with respect to some of the most widely-used indicators of quality.

Much of this bias could be neutralized if women were able to attract the best faculty as mentors. Bernard stresses the importance of mentors:

> The association of the graduate student with his mentor may make all the difference between success or lack of it in his subsequent career. If a top man takes him under his wing, doors will open for him and he will be in the club. If no one takes him on, he may never arrive professionally. He will not be recommended for the best jobs; he will not be in.[17]

The existence of a first-rate mentor is doubly important for women, if the results of a study by Gail Pheterson, Sara Kiesler, and Philip Goldberg are valid.[18] It suggests that women's performances will be taken seriously if an authority publicly recognizes their worth. This is because it is sometimes difficult to judge quality and in an ambiguous case, sexual stereotypes tend to step in to "help" the viewer decide. But there is no need for this when an individual acknowledged to be an expert has affirmed the value of the work.

Kay Deaux reports that this tendency is particularly evident when the judge has little training in the area to be evaluated. This is presumably not the case when faculties judge candidates within their own discipline. But it is plausible to believe that the uncertain nature of standards and the ambiguous performances in academe—especially in the conflict-ridden humanities—creates some of the same pressures. Bernard provides more support for this hypothesis when, in another context, she comments: "Because there are so few objective criteria for judging the worth of a person and because so much competition is judgmental in nature, academic people depend on recognition from one another to a greater extent than do those in professions where autonomous competition is the rule."[19]

Thus graduate school mentors could help talented women achieve the professional recognition they deserve. Unfortunately women are less likely to enjoy the advantages of a good mentor. The best graduate schools have few women on their faculties and not every such woman will be interested in or capable of helping others advance. The men in such schools, with their poor record of hiring women, appear to be among the most prejudiced against them and hence cannot be counted on for help here.[20] The failure to take women seriously in graduate schools downgrades their apparent quality. This diminishes their chance of obtaining a prestigious post where they will have the opportunity to do significant research; in the current market, it also diminishes the probability that they will find any job in their field.

As if this were not enough, they run the risk of having their already undervalued qualifications devalued again when they are candidates for a position. This conclusion is supported by a study which showed that the same dossier was often ranked higher by academic departments when it was attributed to a man than when it was attributed to a woman.[21] Research on interviews also suggests that both men and women are systematically biased against women.[22]

I have been arguing that women are likely to be more highly qualified than they seem. This fact alone would support a policy of hiring women perceived to be less qualified. However, I think there is another sound argument for such a policy. Women may sometimes be less qualified than their male competitors because as students they faced stumbling-blocks the men did not. Hence some women probably deserve their weak recommendations and dearth of publications because their work is less fully developed and their claims less well supported than a man's might be. This can occur because women's social role often precludes opportunities for informal constructive criticism; it may also be the result of the lack of a mentor to push her to her limits. Finally, a woman is likely to have had to work in a debilitating environment of lowered expectations.[23]

Goldman argues that it would be wrong to hire such a woman if there were a more qualified candidate: " . . . the white male who has successfully met the requirements necessary to attaining maximal competence attains some right to that position. It seems unjust for society to set standards of achievement and then to thwart the expectations of those who have met those standards."[24]

But surely hiring is ultimately intended to produce the best scholar and teacher, not to reward the most successful graduate student. Consequently, if there are grounds for believing that women turn into the former, despite not having been the latter according to the traditional criteria, it is reasonable to hold that they should sometimes be hired anyway. And there are such grounds.

The obstacles encountered by women in academe are well-documented and there is no need to elaborate at length upon them here. What matters is the nature of the person they create. Until very recently, at every stage of schooling, fewer girls than boys continued.[25] There is considerable evidence that women graduate students have higher academic qualifications than their male counterparts.[26] This appears to be because only the very highly qualified get into graduate school.[27] Harris argues that it " . . . is worth remembering that women candidates for graduate school are the survivors of a long sifting process—only the very best of the good students go on to graduate school."[28] A report issued by women at the University of Chicago supports this claim—the grade averages of women students entering graduate school were significantly higher than those of men.[29]

Once there, women have somewhat higher attrition rates than men. But Harris thinks that this is "largely explained by the lack of encouragement and the actual discouragement experienced by women graduate students for their career plans. . . . It is not surprising that some women decide that they are not cut out to be scholars and teachers."[30] She argues that if women were not highly committed, the attrition rate would be much higher: ". . . only the hardiest survive."[31]

In light of all these facts, a temporary policy of hiring women perceived to be less well qualified would be reasonable, to see if the hypothesis that they will bloom is borne out. Such a policy is less risky than it might seem since junior faculty members are on probation and can be fired if they do not start to fulfill their promise.

In conclusion, there are good grounds for at least a trial of the policy I am proposing with regard to hiring in academe, since existing affirmative action programs have not been and cannot be effective.[32] I have tried to show why women may often seem less qualified than they really are, and why they may be more promising than they seem. Unless faculty members take these factors into account, no improvements in the position of women can be expected, for women are likely to seem less worthy of being hired than their male competitors when they are judged in the usual manner. Requiring departments to hire women perceived to be less well qualified may well turn out to be the most efficacious way to force departments to recognize and remedy the situation. It might also have a more generally beneficial side-effect of promoting faculty-members' awareness of their own biases as they struggle to distinguish between truly mediocre women and those merely perceived to be so!

NOTES

1 The general trend continues to be that the more prestigious the post or institution, the fewer women there are to be found. See, for instance, "Status of Female Faculty Members, 1979–80," *The Chronicle of Higher Education*, 29 September 1980.

2 See Alan Goldman, "Affirmative Action," *Philosophy and Public Affairs*, Vol. 5, n. 2 (Winter 1976), 178.

3 Ibid.

4 Kay Deaux, *The Behavior of Women and Men*, (Monterey, Ca.: Brooks/Cole Publishing Co., 1976), p. 24.

5 Ann Sutherland Harris reports this study in "The Second Sex in Academe" in *And Jill Came Tumbling After: Sexism in American Education*, ed. Judith Stacey et al., (New York: 1974), p. 299.

6 Jessie Bernard, *Academic Women*, (New York: Meridian Press, 1965), pp. 255–57. "The 'teachers' were selected by the department as being of about equal competence in communications skills. They were given two written lectures to deliver to sections of Sociology 1. . . . both young people were given the lectures in advance, and they agreed on how to interpret all major points in their presentations, which were to be identical. One spoke to each section and a week later each spoke to the other section" (p. 256).

7 Ibid.

8 Ibid.

9 Ibid.

10 Reported by Deaux, p. 25.

11 This study appeared in "On Campus with Women," March 1977, Association of American Colleges, and was reported in *Ms.*, Vol. 7, n. 5 (November 1978), 87. *Ms.* writes: "In 1973, at the last annual conference held before the policy was initiated, 6.3 percent of the papers selected were from women scholars. In 1975, 17 percent of the papers selected were from women scholars." The organization in question is the Archaeological Institute of America.

12 Veronica F. Nieva and Barbara Gutek, "Sex Effects on Evaluation," *Academy of Management Review*, Vol. 5, n. 2 (1980), p. 267.

13 Ibid., p. 270.

14 Ibid., p. 268.

15 Ibid.

16 Jennie Farley, "Academic Recommendations: Males and Females as Judges and Judged," *AAUP Bulletin*, Vol. 64, n. 2 (May 1978), p. 84.

17 Bernard, p. 140.

18 Reported by Deaux, p. 25.

19 Bernard, p. 193.

20 See Harris, above.

21 L. S. Fidell, "Empirical Verification of Sex Discrimination in Hiring Practices in Psychology," *American Psychologist*, Vol. 60 (1970), 1049–98.

22 Robert L. Dipboye, Richard D. Arvey, and David E. Terpstra, "Sex and Physical Attractiveness of Raters and Applicants as Determinants of Resume Evaluations," *Journal of*

Applied Psychology, Vol. 62, n. 3 (June 1977), p. 288. This study was limited to undergraduate students, however, so it should not be assumed that it can be generalized to the educated population we are concerned with here.

23 Nieva and Gutek, p. 271.

24 Goldman, p. 191.

25 See Harris and Barnard in Stacey et al., pp. 302–5.

26 Harris, pp. 304–5.

27 Ibid.

28 Ibid.

29 Ibid.

30 Ibid.

31 Ibid. My own experience at the prestigious Ivy League institution where I took my Ph.D. was far from encouraging. When I arrived, there were no women faculty members. The class before mine, numbering about 10, contained no women, and I was the only woman in my class of about 10. Twice in my first year I was present in groups addressed by professors as "Gentlemen." One of these occasions was especially fraught with emotion. I and four men gathered at a professor's office to return one of the crucial 4-hour field exams required of first-year students. The professor beamed at us and said, "Well, we'll see how you did, gentlemen!"

32 See *Sex Discrimination in Higher Education,* ed. Jennie Farley, (Ithaca: ILR Publications, 1981).

QUESTIONS

1 Do Purdy's arguments apply to the business world as well? If yes, does it follow that business enterprises should adopt policies that require them to hire and promote women who appear to be less qualified than the top male contenders?

2 Without affirmative action programs would women and blacks continue to be discriminated against in employment? With these programs is discrimination against women and/or blacks and other minorities still common? Rare? Nonexistent?

SUGGESTED ADDITIONAL READINGS FOR CHAPTER 5

BEAUCHAMP, TOM L.: "The Justification of Reverse Discrimination." In William T. Blackstone and Robert Heslep, eds., *Social Justice and Preferential Treatment* (Athens: University of Georgia Press, 1976). Beauchamp offers a utilitarian argument in favor of policies productive of reverse discrimination in hiring. He proffers "factual evidence" to support his claim that such policies are a necessary means to achieve a morally desirable end—the demise of the continued discrimination against women and blacks.

COHEN, MARSHALL, THOMAS NAGEL, and THOMAS SCANLON, eds.: *Equality and Preferential Treatment.* Princeton: Princeton University Press, 1977. This is an excellent collection of articles which, with one exception, originally appeared in different volumes of *Philosophy and Public Affairs.* The authors include Thomas Nagel, George Sher, Ronald Dworkin, Owen M. Fiss, Alan H. Goldman, Judith Jarvis Thomson, and Robert Simon. Ronald Dworkin's article, which was not originally published in *Philosophy and Public Affairs,* is especially interesting insofar as Dworkin compares and contrasts the issues raised by two important legal decisions—the first dealing with a 1945 admittance policy which denied a black man admittance to the University of Texas Law School, the second with a 1971 admissions policy which worked to keep a white male (DeFunis) out of the University of Washington Law School.

EZORSKY, GERTRUDE: "Hiring Women Faculty." *Philosophy and Public Affairs,* vol. 7, Fall 1977, pp. 82–91. Ezorsky contends that neither departmental advertising for women faculty nor requirements for hiring women according to "availability ratio" are sufficient to remedy sex discrimination in college. She suggests that preferential goals are necessary to remedy the situation.

GROSS, BARRY R., ed.: *Reverse Discrimination.* Buffalo, N.Y.: Prometheus Books, 1977. This anthology includes some well-known articles on the topic, including those of Sidney Hook, Lisa H. Newton, Bernard Boxhill, and Alan H. Goldman. The large collection of articles is organized into three sections, labeled "Facts and Polemics," "The Law," and "Value."

HELD, VIRGINIA: "Reasonable Progress and Self-Respect." *The Monist,* vol. 57, January 1973, pp. 12–27. Held focuses on two questions: How long is it reasonable to expect the victims of past discrimination to wait for a redress of their wrongs? What reasonable rate of progress would not involve a loss of self-respect?

KATZNER, LOUIS: "Is the Favoring of Women and Blacks in Employment and Educational Opportunities Justified?" In Joel Feinberg and Hyman Gross, eds., *Philosophy of Law* (Encino, Calif.: Dickenson, 1975), pp. 291–296. Katzner's argument for the justification of reverse discrimination is based on the claim that the obligation to compensate for past wrongs justifies present policies productive of reverse discrimination.

SHER, GEORGE: "Reverse Discrimination, the Future, and the Past." *Ethics,* vol. 90, October 1979, pp. 81–87. Sher analyzes and criticizes some of the "forward-looking arguments" made to support preferential treatment programs.

THALBERG, IRVING: "Justification of Institutional Racism." *Philosophical Forum* (Boston), vol. 3, Winter 1972, pp. 243–264. Thalberg criticizes the arguments of those who oppose the kinds of changes which, on his view, are necessary to equalize the economic and political status of blacks.

WARREN, MARY ANNE: "Secondary Sexism and Quota Hiring." *Philosophy and Public Affairs,* vol. 6, 1977, pp. 240–261. Warren argues that there exist certain discriminatory practices that although not explicitly based on sex, *de facto* discriminate against women. To counter this ongoing discrimination, she contends, minimum numerical quotas for the hiring and promotion of women are necessary.

CHAPTER 6

SEXUAL MORALITY

Individuals are sometimes described as having "loose morals" when their *sexual* behavior is out of line with what is considered morally appropriate. But assessments of morally appropriate sexual behavior vary enormously. Conventionalists consider sex morally appropriate only within the bounds of marriage. Some conventionalists even insist that there are substantial moral restrictions on sex *within marriage;* they are committed to the principle that sexual activity may not take place in a way that cuts off the possibility of procreation. More liberal thinkers espouse various degrees of permissiveness. Some would allow a full and open promiscuity; some would not. Some would allow homosexual behavior; some would not. In this chapter, various views on the topic of sexual morality are investigated.

CONVENTIONAL SEXUAL MORALITY

According to conventional sexual morality, sex is morally legitimate only within the bounds of marriage; nonmarital sex is immoral. The category of *nonmarital sex* is applicable to any sexual relation other than that between marriage partners. Thus it includes sexual relations between single people as well as adulterous sexual relations. Both religious and nonreligious arguments are advanced in support of conventional sexual morality, but our concern here is with the nonreligious arguments that are advanced in its defense.

One common defense of the traditional convention that sex is permissible only within the bounds of marriage is based on considerations of *social utility*. It takes the following form: A stable family life is absolutely essential for the proper raising of children and the consequent welfare of society as a whole. But the limitation of sex to marriage is a necessary condition of forming and maintaining stable family units.

The availability of sex within marriage will reinforce the loving relationship between husband and wife, the *exclusive* availability of sex within marriage will lead most people to get married and to stay married, and the unavailability of extramarital sex will keep the marriage strong. Therefore, the convention that sex is permissible only within the bounds of marriage is solidly based on considerations of social utility.

This argument is attacked in many ways. Sometimes it is argued that stable family units are not really so essential. More commonly, it is argued that the availability of nonmarital sex does not really undercut family life. Whereas adultery might very well undermine a marital relationship, it is argued, premarital sex often prepares one for marriage. At any rate, it is pointed out, people continue to marry even after they have had somewhat free access to sexual relations.

Another prominent defense of conventional sexual morality is intimately bound up with *natural law theory,* an approach to ethics that is historically associated with the medieval philosopher and theologian Thomas Aquinas (1225–1274). The fundamental principle of natural law theory may be expressed in rather rough form as follows: Actions are morally appropriate insofar as they accord with our nature and end as human beings and morally inappropriate insofar as they fail to accord with our nature and end as human beings. With regard to sexual morality, Aquinas argues as follows:

> . . . the emission of semen ought to be so ordered that it will result in both the production of the proper offspring and in the upbringing of this offspring.
>
> It is evident from this that every emission of semen, in such a way that generation cannot follow, is contrary to the good for man. And if this be done deliberately, it must be a sin. Now, I am speaking of a way from which, *in itself,* generation could not result; such would be any emission of semen apart from the natural union of male and female. For which reason, sins of this type are called *contrary to nature.* . . .
>
> Likewise, it must also be contrary to the good for man if the semen be emitted under conditions such that generation could result but the proper upbringing would be prevented. . . .
>
> Now, it is abundantly evident that the female in the human species is not at all able to take care of the upbringing of offspring by herself, since the needs of human life demand many things which cannot be provided by one person alone. Therefore, it is appropriate to human nature that a man remain together with a woman after the generative act, and not leave her immediately to have such relations with another woman, as is the practice with fornicators. . . .
>
> Now, we call this society *matrimony.* Therefore, matrimony is natural for man, and promiscuous performance of the sexual act, outside matrimony, is contrary to man's good. For this reason, it must be a sin.[1]

According to Aquinas, procreation is the natural purpose or end of sexual activity. Accordingly, sexual activity is morally legitimate only when it accords with this fundamental aspect of human nature. Since sex is for the purpose of procreation, and since the proper upbringing of children can occur only within the framework of marriage, nonmarital sex violates the natural law; it is thereby immoral. In this way, then, Aquinas constructs a defense of conventional sexual morality.

[1] Thomas Aquinas, *On the Truth of the Catholic Faith,* Book Three, "Providence," Part II, trans. Vernon J. Bourke (New York: Doubleday, 1956).

Notice, however, that Aquinas is also committed to substantial restrictions on marital sex itself. Since procreation is the natural purpose or end of sexual activity, he contends, any sexual act that cuts off the possibility of procreation is "contrary to nature." It follows that such practices as oral intercourse, anal intercourse, "mutual masturbation," and the use of artificial birth control are illicit, even within marriage. Of course, Aquinas also condemns masturbation and homosexual intercourse as "contrary to nature," but the immorality of these practices can also be understood, on his view, as following from his rejection of nonmarital sex.

One common criticism of Aquinas's point of view on sexual morality centers on his insistence that sexual activity must not frustrate its natural purpose—procreation. Granted, it is said, procreation is in a biological sense the "natural" purpose of sex. Still, the argument goes, it is not clear that sexual activity cannot legitimately serve other important human purposes. Why cannot sex legitimately function as a means for the expression of love? Why, for that matter, cannot sex legitimately function simply as a source of intense (recreational) pleasure?

In contemporary times, Aquinas's point of view on sexual morality is continually reaffirmed in the formal teaching of the Roman Catholic Church. In the 1968 papal encyclical *Humanae Vitae*, artificial birth control is once again identified as immoral, a violation of the natural law: "Each and every marriage act must remain open to the transmission of life."[2] In a more recent Vatican document, reprinted in this chapter, the natural law framework of Aquinas is equally apparent: "The deliberate use of the sexual faculties outside of normal conjugal relations essentially contradicts its finality." "Homosexual acts are disordered by their very nature." "Masturbation is an intrinsically and seriously disordered act."

In one of this chapter's readings, Vincent C. Punzo provides a somewhat distinctive defense of conventional sexual morality. At the core of his argument is the idea of existential integrity. In Punzo's view, existential integrity is compromised whenever sexual intercourse is detached from the framework of commitment that is constitutive of marriage.

THE LIBERAL VIEW

In vivid contrast to conventional sexual morality is an approach that will be referred to here as the *liberal* view of sexual morality. Liberals reject as unfounded the conventionalist claim that nonmarital sex is immoral. They also reject the related claim (made by some conventionalists) that sex is immoral if it cuts off the possibility of procreation. Nor are liberals willing to accept the claim (defended by some nonconventionalists) that *sex without love* is immoral. Yet liberals insist that there are important moral restrictions on sexual activity. In the liberal view, sexual activity (like any other type of human activity) is morally objectionable to the extent that it is incompatible with a justified moral rule or principle. Accordingly, it is argued, the way to construct

---

[2]*Humanae Vitae* (1968), section 11. This encyclical is widely reprinted. See, for example, Robert Baker and Frederick Elliston, eds., *Philosophy and Sex* (Buffalo, N.Y.: Prometheus Books, 1975), pp. 131–149.

a defensible account of sexual morality is simply to work out the implications of relevant moral rules or principles in the area of sexual behavior.

In this vein, since it is widely acknowledged that the infliction of personal harm is morally objectionable, *some* sexual activity may be identified as immoral simply because it involves one person inflicting harm on another. The seduction of a minor who does not even know "what it's all about," for example, is morally objectionable on the grounds that the minor will almost inevitably be psychologically harmed. Rape, of course, is a moral outrage, in no small part because it typically involves the infliction of both physical and psychological harm. Its immorality, however, can also be established by reference to another widely acknowledged (when properly understood) moral principle, roughly the principle that it is wrong for one person to "use" another person.

Since the domain of sexual interaction seems to offer ample opportunity for "using" another person, the concept of using is worthy of special attention in this context. In one of this chapter's selections, Thomas A. Mappes attempts to clarify what he calls the morally significant sense of "using another person." His ultimate aim is to determine the conditions under which someone would be guilty of *sexually* using another person, and the essence of his view is that the sexual using of another person takes place whenever there is a violation of the requirement of *voluntary informed consent* (to sexual interaction). Mappes especially emphasizes both *deception* and *coercion* as mechanisms for the sexual using of another person.

Is nonmarital sex immoral? Is sex that cuts off the possibility of procreation immoral? Is sex without love immoral? According to the liberal, *no* sexual activity is immoral unless some well-established moral rule or principle is transgressed. Does one's sexual activity involve the infliction of harm on another? Does it involve the using of another? Does it involve promise-breaking, another commonly recognized ground of moral condemnation? If the answer to such questions is no, the liberal maintains, then the sexual activity in question is perfectly acceptable from a moral point of view.

According to the liberal, then, we must conclude that nonmarital sex is, in many cases, morally acceptable. Sexual partners may share some degree of mutual affection or love, or they may merely share a mutual desire to attain sexual satisfaction. The sexual interaction may be heterosexual or homosexual. Or there may be no *inter*action at all; the sexual activity may be masturbation. But what about the morality of adultery, an especially noteworthy type of nonmarital sex? As the marriage bond is usually understood, the liberal might respond, there is present in case of adultery a distinctive ground of moral condemnation. To the extent that marriage involves a pledge of sexual exclusivity, as is typically the case, then adulterous behavior seems to involve a serious breaking of trust. However, the liberal would insist, if marriage partners have entered upon a so-called open marriage, with no pledge of sexual exclusivity, then this special ground of moral condemnation evaporates.

If the liberal approach to sexual morality is correct, it is nevertheless important to recognize that a particular sexual involvement could be morally acceptable and yet unwise or imprudent, that is, not in a person's best long-term interests. An individual, for example, might very well decide to steer clear of casual sex, not because it is immoral but because of a conviction (perhaps based on past experience) that it is not productive of personal happiness.

THE SEX WITH LOVE APPROACH

There is one additional point of view on sexual morality that is sufficiently common to warrant explicit recognition. One may, after all, find conventional sexual morality unwarranted and yet be inclined to stop short of granting moral approval to the "promiscuity" that is found morally acceptable on the liberal view. This intermediate point of view can be identified as the *sex with love* approach. Defenders of this approach typically insist that sex without love reduces a humanly significant activity to a merely mechanical performance, which in turn leads to the disintegration (fragmentation) of the human personality. They differ among themselves, however, as to whether the love necessary to warrant a sexual relationship must be an *exclusive* love or whether it may be a *nonexclusive* love. Those who argue that it must be exclusive nevertheless grant that *successive* sexual liaisons are not objectionable. Those who argue that the love may be nonexclusive necessarily presume that a person is capable of simultaneously loving several persons. On their view, even *simultaneous* love affairs are not objectionable. Whether exclusive or nonexclusive love is taken to be the relevant standard, proponents of the sex with love approach usually argue that their view allows for sexual freedom in a way that avoids the alleged dehumanizing effects of mere promiscuity. Where sex and love remain united, it is argued, there is no danger of dehumanization and psychological disintegration. The liberal might respond: If psychological disintegration is a justifiable fear, which can be doubted, such a consideration shows not that sex without love is immoral but only that it is imprudent.

HOMOSEXUALITY, MORALITY, AND THE LAW

Is homosexual behavior immoral? While the advocate of conventional sexual morality vigorously condemns it, the liberal typically maintains that homosexual behavior is no more immoral in itself than heterosexual behavior. There are, however, a substantial number of people who reject conventional sexual morality but nevertheless remain morally opposed to homosexual behavior. Are such people correct in thinking that homosexual behavior is morally problematic in a way that heterosexual behavior is not? A homosexual, in the most generic sense, is a person (male or female) whose dominant sexual preference is for a person of the same sex. In common parlance, however, the term "homosexual" is often taken to designate a male, whereas the term "lesbian" is used to designate a female. It is apparently true that male homosexual behavior occasions a higher degree of societal indignation than female homosexual behavior, but it is implausible to believe that there is any morally relevant difference between the two.

There is no lack of invective against the homosexual and against homosexual behavior. For example, the following comments are often made: (1) "Homosexual behavior is repulsive and highly offensive." (2) "Homosexuality as a way of life is totally given over to promiscuity and is little susceptible of enduring human relationships." (3) "Homosexuals make the streets unsafe for our children." (4) "Homosexuality is a perversion, a sin against nature." (5) "If homosexual behavior is tolerated, the stability of family life will be threatened and the social fabric will be undermined."

It is important to assess the extent to which such claims support the view that homosexual behavior is morally objectionable. With regard to (1), it may in fact be true that many people find homosexual behavior repulsive and offensive, but it is also true that many people find eating liver repulsive and offensive, and no one thinks that this fact establishes the conclusion that eating liver is morally objectionable. With regard to (2), it may be true that homosexuality is typically a promiscuous way of life, but it can be argued that society's attitude toward homosexuality is responsible for making stable homosexual relationships impossible. With regard to (3), it may be true that *some* homosexuals prey upon children, and surely this is morally reprehensible, but still we find ourselves left with the more typical case in which homosexual relations take place between consenting adults.

Arguments (4) and (5), in contrast to the other three, correlate with arguments already identified in our earlier discussion of conventional sexual morality. The "unnaturalness argument" (4), of course, is typically applied not only against homosexual behavior but also against other "perversions," such as masturbation, oral-genital sex practices, etc. In one of this chapter's selections, Burton M. Leiser critically analyzes and rejects the "unnaturalness argument" as it applies to homosexual behavior. Argument (5) is reminiscent of the argument that conventional sexual morality can be firmly based on considerations of *social utility*. Defenders of (5), however, need not be committed to a full-scale rejection of nonmarital sex. Some moral opposition to homosexual behavior derives, it is clear, from those who explicitly reject conventional sexual morality. Whereas nonmarital *heterosexual* behavior does not pose a serious threat to social well-being, they argue, homosexual behavior does pose a serious threat.

One of the central goals of the "gay liberation" movement is to achieve the decriminalization of homosexual behavior *between consenting adults in private*. Presently, however, homosexual behavior (even between consenting adults in private) remains a criminal offense in many states. These states have statutes that are often referred to as sodomy statutes. In the law, "sodomy" is roughly synonymous with "unnatural sex practices" or "crimes against nature." Accordingly, sodomy statutes typically prohibit both oral and anal intercourse, as well as other "crimes against nature," such as bestiality, i.e., sexual intercourse with animals. Though sodomy statutes apply to heterosexuals as well as homosexuals, they are usually enforced only against (male) homosexuals. The constitutionality of sodomy statutes is at issue in a court case presented in this chapter, *Doe v. Commonwealth's Attorney for City of Richmond* (1975). In addition to constitutional questions, sodomy statutes also raise important questions about the wisdom and the ethical justification of laws that criminalize sexual conduct *between consenting adults in private*. For one thing, such laws seem, at least in part, to be designed to "enforce" conventional sexual morality. This is a dimension, however, that is more fully discussed in conjunction with the topic of pornography in Chapter 7.

Thomas A. Mappes

Vatican Declaration on Some Questions of Sexual Ethics

The title of this document is sometimes translated from the Latin as "Declaration on Certain Questions Concerning Sexual Ethics." The document itself was issued by the Sacred Congregation for the Doctrine of the Faith. It was approved by Pope Paul VI and first released for publication on January 15, 1976.

In this declaration, traditional Roman Catholic teaching is explicitly reaffirmed with regard to certain matters of sexual ethics. Both religious arguments (appeals to revealed truth) and philosophical arguments are advanced. (The philosophical arguments are developed within the framework of a natural law theory of ethics.) According to the document, there is an objective and unchanging moral order. Moral principles (including the principles of sexual morality) "have their origin in human nature itself." Accordingly, these principles may be known in two complementary ways: (1) through reason alone, via rational reflection on human nature, or (2) through divine revelation. After briefly explicating the natural law foundation of the traditional view that exercise of the sexual function is appropriate only within the marriage relationship, the document proceeds to reaffirm the immorality of premarital sex, homosexual behavior, and masturbation.

INTRODUCTION

Importance of Sexuality

1. The human person, according to the scientific disciplines of our day, is so deeply influenced by his sexuality that this latter must be regarded as one of the basic factors shaping human life. The person's sex is the source of the biological, psychological and spiritual characteristics which make the person male or female, and thus are extremely important and influential in the maturation and socialization of the individual. It is easy to understand, therefore, why matters pertaining to sex are frequently and openly discussed in books, periodicals, newspapers and other communications media.

Meanwhile, moral corruption is on the increase. One of the most serious signs of this is the boundless exaltation of sex. In addition, with the help of the mass media and the various forms of entertainment, sex has even invaded the field of education and infected the public mind.

In this situation, some educators, teachers and moralists have been able to contribute to a better understanding and vital integration of the special values and qualities proper to each sex. Others, however, have defended views and ways of acting which are in conflict with the true moral requirements of man, and have even opened the door to a licentious hedonism.

The result is that, within a few years' time, teachings, moral norms and habits of life hitherto faithfully preserved have been called into doubt, even by Christians. Many today are asking what they are to regard as true when so many current views are at odds with what they learned from the Church.

Occasion for This Declaration

2. In the face of this intellectual confusion and moral corruption the Church cannot stand by and do nothing. The issue here is too important in the life both of the individual and of contemporary society.[1]

Bishops see each day the ever increasing difficulties of the faithful in acquiring sound moral teaching, especially in sexual matters, and of pastors in effectively explaining that teaching. The bishops know it is their pastoral duty to come to the aid of the faithful in such a serious matter. Indeed, some outstanding documents have been published on the subject by some bishops and some episcopal conferences. But, since erroneous views and the deviations they produce continue to be broadcast everywhere, the Sacred Congregation for the Doctrine of the Faith in accordance with its role in the universal Church[2] and by mandate of the Supreme Pontiff, has thought it necessary to issue this Declaration.

I GENERAL CONSIDERATIONS

The Sources of Moral Knowledge

3. The men of our day are increasingly persuaded that their dignity and calling as human beings requires them to use their minds to discover the values and powers inherent in their nature, to develop these without ceasing and to translate them into action, so that they may make daily greater progress.

When it comes to judgments on moral matters, however, man may not proceed simply as he thinks fit. "Deep within, man detects the law of conscience—a law which is not self-imposed but which holds him to obedience. . . . For man has in his heart a law written by God. To obey it is the very dignity of man; according to it he will be judged."[3]

To us Christians, moreover, God has revealed his plan of salvation and has given us Christ, the Savior and sanctifier, as the supreme and immutable norm of life through his teaching and example. Christ himself has said: "I am the light of the world. No follower of mine shall ever walk in darkness; no, he shall possess the light of life."[4]

The authentic dignity of man cannot be promoted, therefore, except through adherence to the order which is essential to his nature. There is no denying, of course, that in the history of civilization many of the concrete conditions and relationships of human life have changed and will change again in the future but every moral evolution

---

[1]See Vatican II, *Pastoral Constitution on the Church in the World of Today,* no. 47: *Acta Apostolicae Sedis* 58 (1966) 1067 [*The Pope Speaks* XI, 289–290].

[2]See the Apostolic Constitution *Regimini Ecclesiae universae* (August 15, 1967), no. 29: *AAS* 59 (1967) 897 [*TPS* XII, 401–402].

[3]*Pastoral Constitution on the Church in the World of Today,* no. 16: *AAS* 58 (1966) 1037 [*TPS* XI, 268].

[4]*Jn* 8, 12.

and every manner of life must respect the limits set by the immutable principles which are grounded in the constitutive elements and essential relations proper to the human person. These elements and relations are not subject to historical contingency.

The basic principles in question can be grasped by man's reason. They are contained in "the divine law—eternal, objective and universal—whereby God orders, directs and governs the entire universe and all the ways of the human community by a plan conceived in wisdom and love. God has made man a participant in this law, with the result that, under the gentle disposition of divine Providence, he can come to perceive ever more fully the truth that is unchanging."[5] This divine law is something we can know.

The Principles of Morality Are Perennial

4. Wrongly, therefore, do many today deny that either human nature or revealed law furnishes any absolute and changeless norm for particular actions except the general law of love and respect for human dignity. To justify this position, they argue that both the so-called norms of the natural law and the precepts of Sacred Scripture are simply products of a particular human culture and its expressions at a certain point in history.

But divine revelation and, in its own order, natural human wisdom show us genuine exigencies of human nature and, as a direct and necessary consequence, immutable laws which are grounded in the constitutive elements of human nature and show themselves the same in all rational beings.

Furthermore, the Church was established by Christ to be "the pillar and bulwark of truth."[6] With the help of the Holy Spirit she keeps a sleepless watch over the truths of morality and transmits them without falsification. She provides the authentic interpretation not only of the revealed positive law but also of "those principles of the moral order which have their origin in human nature itself"[7] and which relate to man's full development and sanctification. Throughout her history the Church has constantly maintained that certain precepts of the natural law bind immutably and without qualification, and that the violation of them contradicts the spirit and teaching of the Gospel.

The Fundamental Principles of Sexual Morality

5. Since sexual morality has to do with values which are basic to human and Christian life, the general doctrine we have been presenting applies to it. In this area there are principles and norms which the Church has always unhesitatingly transmitted as part

[5]*Declaration on Religious Freedom,* no. 3: *AAS* 58 (1966) 931 [*TPS* XI, 86].

[6]*1 TM* 3, 15.

[7]*Declaration on Religious Freedom,* no. 14: *AAS* 58 (1966) 940 [*TPS* XI, 93]. See also Pius XI, Encyclical *Casti Connubii* (December 31, 1930): *AAS* 22 (1930) 579–580; Pius XII, Address of November 2, 1954 *AAS* 46 (1954) 671–672 [*TPS* 1, 380–381]; John XXIII, Encyclical *Mater et Magistra* (May 25, 1961), no. 239: *AAS* 53 (1961) 457 [*TPS* VII, 388]; Paul VI, Encyclical *Humanae Vitae* (July 25, 1968), no. 4: *AAS* 60 (1968) 483 [*TPS* XIII, 331–332].

of her teaching, however opposed they might be to the mentality and ways of the world. These principles and norms have their origin, not in a particular culture, but in knowledge of the divine law and human nature. Consequently, it is impossible for them to lose their binding force or to be called into doubt on the grounds of cultural change.

These principles guided Vatican Council II when it provided advice and directives for the establishment of the kind of social life in which the equal dignity of man and woman will be respected, even while the differences between them also are preserved.[8]

In speaking of the sexual nature of the human being and of the human generative powers, the Council observes that these are "remarkably superior to those found in lower grades of life."[9] Then it deals in detail with the principles and norms which apply to human sexuality in the married state and are based on the finality of the function proper to marriage.

In this context the Council asserts that the moral goodness of the actions proper to married life, when ordered as man's true dignity requires, "does not depend only on a sincere intention and the evaluating of motives, but must be judged by objective standards. These are drawn from the nature of the human person and of his acts, and have regard for the whole meaning of mutual self-giving and human procreation in the context of true love."[10]

These last words are a brief summation of the Council's teaching (previously set forth at length in the same document[11]) on the finality of the sexual act and on the chief norm governing its morality. It is respect for this finality which guarantees the moral goodness of the act.

The same principle, which the Church derives from divine revelation and from her authentic interpretation of the natural law, is also the source of her traditional teaching that the exercise of the sexual function has its true meaning and is morally good only in legitimate marriage.[12]

Limits of this Declaration

6. It is not the intention of this declaration to treat all abuses of the sexual powers nor to deal with all that is involved in the practice of chastity but rather to recall the Church's norms on certain specific points, since there is a crying need of opposing certain serious errors and deviant forms of behavior.

---

[8]See Vatican II, *Declaration on Christian Education*, nos. 1 and 8: *AAS* 58 (1966) 729–730, 734–736 [*TPS* XI, 201–202, 206–207]; *Pastoral Constitution on the Church in the World of Today*, nos. 29, 60, 67: *AAS* 58 (1966) 1048–1049, 1080–1081, 1088–1089 [*TPS* XI, 276–277, 299–300, 304–305].

[9]*Pastoral Constitution on the Church in the World of Today*, no. 51: *AAS* 58 (1966) 1072 [*TPS* XI, 293].

[10]*Loc. cit.*; see also no. 49: *AAS* 58 (1966) 1069–1070 [*TPS* XI, 291–292].

[11]See *Pastoral Constitution on the Church in the World of Today*, nos. 49–50: *AAS* 58 (1966) 1069–1072 [*TPS* XI, 291–293].

[12]The present Declaration does not review all the moral norms for the use of sex, since they have already been set forth in the encyclicals *Casti Connubii* and *Humanae Vitae*.

II SPECIFIC APPLICATIONS

Premarital Relations

7. Many individuals at the present time are claiming the right to sexual union before marriage, at least when there is a firm intention of marrying and when a love which both partners think of as already conjugal demands this further step which seems to them connatural. They consider this further step justified especially when external circumstances prevent the formal entry into marriage or when intimate union seems necessary if love is to be kept alive.

This view is opposed to the Christian teaching that any human genital act whatsoever may be placed only within the framework of marriage. For, however firm the intention of those who pledge themselves to each other in such premature unions, these unions cannot guarantee the sincerity and fidelity of the relationship between man and woman, and, above all, cannot protect the relationship against the changeableness of desire and determination.

Yet, Christ the Lord willed that the union be a stable one and he restored it to its original condition as founded in the difference between the sexes. "Have you not read that at the beginning the Creator made them male and female and declared, 'For this reason a man shall leave his father and mother and cling to his wife and the two shall become as one'? Thus they are no longer two but one flesh. Therefore, let no man separate what God has joined."[13]

St. Paul is even more explicit when he teaches that if unmarried people or widows cannot be continent, they have no alternative but to enter into a stable marital union: "It is better to marry than to be on fire."[14] For, through marriage the love of the spouses is taken up into the irrevocable love of Christ for his Church,[15] whereas unchaste bodily union[16] defiles the temple of the Holy Spirit which the Christian has become. Fleshly union is illicit, therefore, unless a permanent community of life has been established between man and woman.

Such has always been the Church's understanding of and teaching on the exercise of the sexual function.[17] She finds, moreover, that natural human wisdom and the lessons of history are in profound agreement with her.

Experience teaches that if sexual union is truly to satisfy the requirements of its own finality and of human dignity, love must be safeguarded by the stability marriage gives. These requirements necessitate a contract which is sanctioned and protected by society; the contract gives rise to a new state of life and is of exceptional importance

---

[13]*Mt* 19, 4–6.

[14]*1 Cor* 7, 9.

[15]See *Eph* 5, 25–32.

[16]Extramarital intercourse is expressly condemned in *1 Cor* 5, 1; 6, 9; 7, 2; 10, 8; *Eph* 5, 5–7; *1 Tm* 1, 10; *Heb* 13, 4; there are explicit arguments given in *1 Cor* 6, 12–20.

[17]See Innocent IV, Letter *Sub Catholicae professione* (March 6, 1254) (*DS* 835); Pius II, Letter *Cum sicut accepimus* (November 14, 1459) (*DS* 1367); Decrees of the Holy Office on September 24, 1665 (*DS* 2045) and March 2, 1679 (*DS* 2148); Pius XI, Encyclical *Casti Connubii* (December 31, 1930): *AAS* 22 (1930) 538–539.

for the exclusive union of man and woman as well as for the good of their family and the whole of human society. Premarital relations, on the other hand, most often exclude any prospect of children. Such love claims in vain to be conjugal since it cannot, as it certainly should, grow into a maternal and paternal love; or, if the pair do become parents, it will be to the detriment of the children, who are deprived of a stable environment in which they can grow up in a proper fashion and find the way and means of entering into the larger society of men.

Therefore, the consent of those entering into marriage must be externally manifested, and this in such a way as to render it binding in the eyes of society. The faithful, for their part, must follow the laws of the Church in declaring their marital consent; it is this consent that makes their marriage a sacrament of Christ.

Homosexuality

8. Contrary to the perennial teaching of the Church and the moral sense of the Christian people, some individuals today have, on psychological grounds, begun to judge indulgently or even simply to excuse homosexual relations for certain people.

They make a distinction which has indeed some foundation: between homosexuals whose bent derives from improper education or a failure of sexual maturation or habit or bad example or some similar cause and is only temporary or at least is not incurable; and homosexuals who are permanently such because of some innate drive or a pathological condition which is considered incurable.

The propensity of those in the latter class is—it is argued— so natural that it should be regarded as justifying homosexual relations within a sincere and loving communion of life which is comparable to marriage inasmuch as those involved in it deem it impossible for them to live a solitary life.

Objective Evil of Such Acts

As far as pastoral care is concerned, such homosexuals are certainly to be treated with understanding and encouraged to hope that they can some day overcome their difficulties and their inability to fit into society in a normal fashion. Prudence, too, must be exercised in judging their guilt. However, no pastoral approach may be taken which would consider these individuals morally justified on the grounds that such acts are in accordance with their nature. For, according to the objective moral order homosexual relations are acts deprived of the essential ordination they ought to have.

In Sacred Scripture such acts are condemned as serious deviations and are even considered to be the lamentable effect of rejecting God.[18] This judgment on the part

---

[18]*Rom* 1:24–27: "In consequence, God delivered them up in their lusts to unclean practices; they engaged in the mutual degradation of their bodies, these men who exchanged the truth of God for a lie and worshipped and served the creature rather than the Creator—blessed be he forever, amen! God therefore delivered them to disgraceful passions. Their women exchanged natural intercourse for unnatural, and the men gave up natural intercourse with women and burned with lust for one another. Men did shameful things with men, and thus received in their own persons the penalty for their perversity." See also what St. Paul says of sodomy in *1 Cor* 6, 9;*1 Tm* 1,10.

of the divinely inspired Scriptures does not justify us in saying that all who suffer from this anomaly are guilty of personal sin but it does show that homosexual acts are disordered by their very nature and can never be approved.

Masturbation

9. Frequently today we find doubt or open rejection of the traditional Catholic teaching that masturbation is a serious moral disorder. Psychology and sociology (it is claimed) show that masturbation, especially in adolescents, is a normal phase in the process of sexual maturation and is, therefore, not gravely sinful unless the individual deliberately cultivates a solitary pleasure that is turned in upon itself ("ipsation"). In this last case, the act would be radically opposed to that loving communion between persons of different sexes which (according to some) is the principal goal to be sought in the use of the sexual powers.

This opinion is contrary to the teaching and pastoral practice of the Catholic Church. Whatever be the validity of certain arguments of a biological and philosophical kind which theologians sometimes use, both the magisterium of the Church (following a constant tradition) and the moral sense of the faithful have unhesitatingly asserted that masturbation is an intrinsically and seriously disordered act.[19] The chief reason for this stand is that, whatever the motive, the deliberate use of the sexual faculty outside of normal conjugal relations essentially contradicts its finality. In such an act there is lacking the sexual relationship which the moral order requires, the kind of relationship in which "the whole meaning of mutual self-giving and human procreation" is made concretely real "in the context of true love."[20] Only within such a relationship may the sexual powers be deliberately exercised.

Even if it cannot be established that Sacred Scripture condemns this sin under a specific name, the Church's tradition rightly understands it to be condemned in the New Testament when the latter speaks of "uncleanness" or "unchasteness" or the other vices contrary to chastity and continence.

Sociological research can show the relative frequency of this disorder according to places, types of people and various circumstances which may be taken into account. It thus provides an array of facts. But facts provide no norm for judging the morality of human acts.[21] The frequency of the act here in question is connected with innate human weakness deriving from original sin, but also with the loss of the sense of God, with the moral corruption fostered by the commercialization of vice, with the unbridled

---

[19]See Leo IX, Letter *Ad splendidum nitentes* (1054) (*DS* 687–688); Decree of the Holy Office on March 2, 1679 (*DS* 2149); Pius XII, Addresses of October 8, 1953: *AAS* 45 (1953) 677–678, and May 19, 1956: *AAS* 48 (1956) 472–473.

[20]*Pastoral Constitution on the Church in the World of Today*, no. 51: *AAS* 58 (1966) 1072 [*TPS* XI, 293].

[21]See Paul VI, Apostolic Exhortation *Quinque iam anni* (December 8, 1970): *AAS* 63 (1971) 102 [*TPS* XV, 329]: "If sociological surveys are useful for better discovering the thought patterns of the people of a particular place, the anxieties and needs of those to whom we proclaim the word of God, and also the oppositions made to it by modern reasoning through the widespread notion that outside science there exists no legitimate form of knowledge, still the conclusions drawn from such surveys could not of themselves constitute a determining criterion of truth."

license to be found in so many books and forms of public entertainment and with the forgetfulness of modesty, which is the safeguard of chastity.

In dealing with masturbation, modern psychology provides a number of valid and useful insights which enable us to judge more equitably of moral responsibility. They can also help us understand how adolescent immaturity (sometimes prolonged beyond the adolescent years) or a lack of psychological balance or habits can affect behavior, since they may make an action less deliberate and not always a subjectively serious sin. But the lack of serious responsibility should not be generally presumed; if it is, there is simply a failure to recognize man's ability to act in a moral way.

In the pastoral ministry, in order to reach a balanced judgment in individual cases account must be taken of the overall habitual manner in which the person acts, not only in regard to charity and justice, but also in regard to the care with which he observes the precept of chastity in particular. Special heed must be paid to whether he uses the necessary natural and supernatural helps which Christian asceticism recommends, in the light of long experience, for mastering the passions and attaining virtue. . . .

QUESTIONS

1 Is it plausible to maintain that unchanging moral principles "have their origin in human nature itself"? Is it plausible to maintain this especially with regard to principles of sexual morality?
2 Is masturbation immoral?

Sexual Morality and the Concept of Using Another Person

Thomas A. Mappes

Thomas A. Mappes is professor of philosophy at Frostburg State College, Maryland. He is coeditor of Biomedical Ethics *(2d ed., 1986) and coauthor of "Is Hume Really a Sceptic about Induction?"*

Advocating a liberal approach to sexual morality, Mappes attempts to determine the conditions under which someone would be guilty of *sexually* using another person. On his view, the morally significant sense of "using another person" is best understood in reference to the notion of voluntary informed consent. Accordingly, his central thesis is that one person (A) is guilty of *sexually* using another person (B) "if and only if A intentionally acts in a way that violates the requirement that B's sexual interaction with A be based on B's voluntary informed consent." Mappes emphasizes the importance of deception and coercion as mechanisms for the sexual using of another person, but he also insists that such using can result from "taking advantage of someone's desperate situation."

The central tenet of *conventional* sexual morality is that nonmarital sex is immoral. A somewhat less restrictive sexual ethic holds that *sex without love* is immoral. If neither of these positions is philosophically defensible, and I would contend that neither is, it does not follow that there are no substantive moral restrictions on human sexual interaction. *Any* human interaction, including sexual interaction, may be judged morally objectionable to the extent that it transgresses a justified moral rule or principle. The way to construct a detailed account of sexual morality, it would seem, is simply to work out the implications of relevant moral rules or principles in the area of human sexual interaction.

As one important step in the direction of such an account, I will attempt to work out the implications of an especially relevant moral principle, the principle that it is wrong for one person to use another person. However ambiguous the expression "using another person" may seem to be, there is a determinate and clearly specifiable sense according to which using another person is morally objectionable. Once this morally significant sense of "using another person" is identified and explicated, the concept of using another person can play an important role in the articulation of a defensible account of sexual morality.

I   THE MORALLY SIGNIFICANT SENSE OF "USING ANOTHER PERSON"

Historically, the concept of using another person is associated with the ethical system of Immanuel Kant. According to a fundamental Kantian principle, it is morally wrong for A to use B *merely as a means* (to achieve A's ends). Kant's principle does not rule out A using B as a means, only A using B *merely* as a means, that is, in a way incompatible with respect for B as a person. In the ordinary course of life, it is surely unavoidable (and morally unproblematic) that each of us in numerous ways uses others as a means to achieve our various ends. A college teacher uses students as a means to achieve his or her livelihood. A college student uses instructors as a means of gaining knowledge and skills. Such human interactions, presumably based on the voluntary participation of the respective parties, are quite compatible with the idea of respect for persons. But respect for persons entails that each of us recognize the rightful authority of other persons (as rational beings) to conduct their individual lives as they see fit. We may legitimately recruit others to participate in the satisfaction of our personal ends, but they are used merely as a means whenever we undermine the voluntary or informed character of their consent to interact with us in some desired way. A coerces B at knife point to hand over $200. A uses B merely as a means. If A had requested of B a gift of $200, leaving B free to determine whether or not to make the gift, A would have proceeded in a manner compatible with respect for B as a person. C deceptively rolls back the odometer of a car and thereby manipulates D's decision to buy the car. C uses D merely as a means.

On the basis of these considerations, I would suggest that the morally significant sense of "using another person" is best understood by reference to the notion of *voluntary informed consent*. More specifically, A immorally uses B if and only if A intentionally acts in a way that violates the requirement that B's involvement with A's ends be based on B's voluntary informed consent. If this account is correct, using another person (in the morally significant sense) can arise in at least two important ways: via *coercion,* which is antithetical to voluntary consent, and via *deception,*which undermines the informed character of voluntary consent.

The notion of voluntary informed consent is very prominent in the literature of biomedical ethics and is systematically related to the much emphasized notion of (patient) autonomy. We find in the famous words of Supreme Court Justice Cardozo a ringing affirmation of patient autonomy. "Every human being of adult years and sound mind has a right to determine what shall be done with his own body." Because respect for individual autonomy is an essential part of respect for persons, if medical professionals (and biomedical researchers) are to interact with their patients (and research subjects) in an acceptable way, they must respect individual autonomy. That is, they must respect the self-determination of the patient/subject, the individual's right to determine what shall be done with his or her body. This means that they must not act in a way that violates the requirement of voluntary informed consent. Medical procedures must not be performed without the consent of competent patients; research on human subjects must not be carried out without the consent of the subjects involved. Moreover, consent must be voluntary; coercion undermines individual autonomy. Consent must also be informed; lying or withholding relevant information undercuts rational decision making and thereby undermines individual autonomy.

To further illuminate the concept of using that has been proposed, I will consider in greater detail the matter of research involving human subjects. In the sphere of researcher-subject interaction, just as in the sphere of human sexual interaction, there is ample opportunity for immorally using another person. If a researcher is engaged in a study that involves human subjects, we may presume that the "end" of the researcher is the successful completion of the study. (The researcher may desire this particular end for any number of reasons: the speculative understanding it will provide, the technology it will make possible, the eventual benefit of humankind, increased status in the scientific community, a raise in pay, etc.) The work, let us presume, strictly requires the use (employment) of human research subjects. The researcher, however, immorally uses other people only if he or she intentionally acts in a way that violates the requirement that the participation of research subjects be based on their voluntary informed consent.

Let us assume that in a particular case participation as a research subject involves some rather significant risks. Accordingly, the researcher finds that potential subjects are reluctant to volunteer. At this point, if an unscrupulous researcher is willing to resort to the immoral using of other people (to achieve his or her own ends), two manifest options are available—deception and coercion. By way of deception, the researcher might choose to lie about the risks involved. For example, potential subjects could be explicitly told that there are no significant risks associated with research participation. On the other hand, the researcher could simply withhold a full disclosure of risks. Whether pumped full of false information or simply deprived of relevant information, the potential subject is intentionally deceived in such a way as to be led to a decision that furthers the researcher's ends. In manipulating the decision making process of the potential subject in this way, the researcher is guilty of immorally using another person.

To explain how an unscrupulous researcher might immorally use another person via coercion, it is helpful to distinguish two basic forms of coercion.[1] "Occurrent" coercion involves the use of physical force. "Dispositional" coercion involves the threat of harm. If I am forcibly thrown out of my office by an intruder, I am the victim of occurent coercion. If, on the other hand, I leave my office because an intruder has threatened to shoot me if I do not leave, I am the victim of dispositional coercion. The victim of occurent coercion literally has no choice in what happens. The victim of dispositional coercion, in contrast, does intentionally choose a certain course of action. However, one's choice, in the face of the threat of harm, is less than fully voluntary.

It is perhaps unlikely that even an unscrupulous researcher would resort to any very explicit measure of coercion. Deception, it seems, is less risky. Still, it is well known that Nazi medical experimenters ruthlessly employed coercion. By way of occurent coercion, the Nazis literally forced great numbers of concentration camp victims to participate in experiments that entailed their own death or dismemberment. And if some concentration camp victims "volunteered" to participate in Nazi research to avoid even more unspeakable horrors, clearly we must consider them victims of dispositional coercion. The Nazi researchers, employing coercion, immorally used other human beings with a vengeance.

II DECEPTION AND SEXUAL MORALITY

To this point, I have been concerned to identify and explicate the morally significant sense of "using another person." On the view proposed, A immorally uses B if and only if A intentionally acts in a way that violates the requirement that B's involvement with A's ends be based on B's voluntary informed consent. I will now apply this account to the area of human sexual interaction and explore its implications. For economy of expression in what follows, "using" (and its cognates) is to be understood as referring only to the morally significant sense.

If we presume a state of affairs in which A desires some form of sexual interaction with B, we can say that this desired form of sexual interaction with B is A's end. Thus A sexually *uses* B if and only if A intentionally acts in a way that violates the requirement that B's sexual interaction with A be based on B's voluntary informed consent. It seems clear then that A may sexually use B in at least two distinctive ways, (1) via coercion and (2) via deception. However, before proceeding to discuss deception and then the more problematic case of coercion, one important point must be made. In emphasizing the centrality of coercion and deception as mechanisms for the sexual using of another person, I have in mind sexual interaction with a fully competent adult

---

[1] I follow here an account of coercion developed by Michael D. Bayles in "A Concept of Coercion," in J. Roland Pennock and John W. Chapman, eds., *Coercion: Nomos XIV* (Chicago: Aldine-Atherton, 1972), pp. 16–29.

partner. We should also want to say, I think, that sexual interaction with a child inescapably involves the sexual using of another person. Even if a child "consents" to sexual interaction, he or she is, strictly speaking, incapable of *informed* consent. It's a matter of being *incompetent* to give consent. Similarly, to the extent that a mentally retarded person is rightly considered incompetent, sexual interaction with such a person amounts to the sexual using of that person, unless someone empowered to give "proxy consent" has done so. (In certain circumstances, sexual involvement might be in the best interests of a mentally retarded person.) We can also visualize the case of an otherwise fully competent adult temporarily disordered by drugs or alcohol. To the extent that such a person is rightly regarded as temporarily incompetent, winning his or her "consent" to sexual interaction could culminate in the sexual using of that person.

There are a host of clear cases in which one person sexually uses another precisely because the former employs deception in a way that undermines the informed character of the latter's consent to sexual interaction. Consider this example. One person, A, has decided, as a matter of personal prudence based on past experience, not to become sexually involved outside the confines of a loving relationship. Another person, B, strongly desires a sexual relationship with A but does not love A. B, aware of A's unwillingness to engage in sex without love, professes love for A, thereby hoping to win A's consent to a sexual relationship. B's ploy is successful; A consents. When the smoke clears and A becomes aware of B's deception, it would be both appropriate and natural for A to complain, "I've been used."

In the same vein, here are some other examples. (1) Mr. A is aware that Ms. B will consent to sexual involvement only on the understanding that in time the two will be married. Mr. A has no intention of marrying Ms. B but says that he will. (2) Ms. C has herpes and is well aware that Mr. D will never consent to sex if he knows of her condition. When asked by Mr. D, Ms. C denies that she has herpes. (3). Mr. E knows that Ms. F will not consent to sexual intercourse in the absence of responsible birth control measures. Mr. E tells Ms. F that he has had a vasectomy, which is not the case. (4) Ms. G knows that Mr. H. would not consent to sexual involvement with a married woman. Ms. G is married but tells Mr. H that she is single. (5) Ms. I is well aware that Ms. J is interested in a stable lesbian relationship and will not consent to become sexually involved with someone who is bisexual. Ms. I tells Ms. J that she is exclusively homosexual, whereas the truth is that she is bisexual.

If one person's consent to sex is predicated on false beliefs that have been intentionally and deceptively inculcated by one's sexual partner in an effort to win the former's consent, the resulting sexual interaction involves one person sexually using another. In each of the above cases, one person explicitly *lies* to another. False information is intentionally conveyed to win consent to sexual interaction, and the end result is the sexual using of another person.

As noted earlier, however, lying is not the only form of deception. Under certain circumstances, the simple withholding of information can be considered a form of deception. Accordingly, it is possible to sexually use another person not only by (deceptively) lying about relevant facts but also by (deceptively) not disclosing relevant facts. If A has good reason to believe that B would refuse to consent to sexual interaction should B become aware of certain factual information, and if A withholds disclosure of this information in order to enhance the possibility of gaining B's consent, then, if B does consent, A sexually uses B via deception. One example will suffice. Suppose that Mr. A meets Ms. B in a singles bar. Mr. A realizes immediately that Ms. B is the sister of Ms. C, a woman that Mr. A has been sexually involved with for a long time. Mr. A, knowing that it is very unlikely that Ms. B will consent to sexual interaction if she becomes aware of Mr. A's involvement with her sister, decides not to disclose this information. If Ms. B eventually consents to sexual interaction, since her consent is the product of Mr. A's deception, it is rightly thought that she has been sexually used by him.

III COERCION AND SEXUAL MORALITY

We have considered the case of deception. The present task is to consider the more difficult case of coercion. Whereas deception functions to undermine the *informed* character of voluntary consent (to sexual interaction), coercion either obliterates consent entirely (the case of occurrent coercion) or undermines the voluntariness of consent (the case of dispositional coercion).

Forcible rape is the most conspicuous, and most brutal, way of sexually using another person via coercion.[2] Forcible rape may involve either occurrent coercion or dispositional coercion. A man who rapes a woman by the employment of sheer physical force, by simply overpowering her, employs occurrent coercion. There is literally no sexual *interaction* in such a case; only the rapist performs an action. In no sense does the woman consent to or participate in sexual activity. She has no choice in what takes place, or rather, physical force results in her choice being simply beside the point. The employment of occurent coercion for the purpose of rape "objectifies" the victim in the strongest sense of that term. She is treated like a physical object. One does not interact with physical objects; one acts upon them. In a perfectly ordinary (not the morally significant) sense of the term, we "use" physical objects. But when the victim of rape is treated as if she were a physical object, there we have one of the most vivid examples of the immoral using of another person.

Frequently, forcible rape involves not occurrent coercion (or not *only* occurrent coercion) but dispositional coercion.[3] In dispositional coercion, the relevant factor is not physical force but the threat of harm. The rapist threatens his victim with immediate and serious bodily harm. For example, a man threatens to kill or beat a woman if she resists his sexual demands. She "consents," that is, she submits to his demands. He may demand only passive participation (simply not struggling against him) or he may demand some measure of active participation. Rape that employs dispositional coercion is surely just as wrong as rape that employs occurrent coercion, but there is a notable

[2]Statutory rape, sexual relations with a person under the legal age of consent, can also be construed as the sexual using of another person. In contrast to forcible rape, however, statutory rape need not involve coercion. The victim of statutory rape may freely "consent" to sexual interaction but, at least in the eyes of the law, is deemed incompetent to consent.

[3]A man wrestles a woman to the ground. She is the victim of occurrent coercion. He threatens to beat her unless she submits to his sexual demands. Now she becomes the victim of dispositional coercion.

difference in the mechanism by which the rapist uses his victim in the two cases. With occurrent coercion, the victim's consent is entirely bypassed. With dispositional coercion, the victim's consent is not bypassed. It is coerced. Dispositional coercion undermines the *voluntariness* of consent. The rapist, by employing the threat of immediate and serious bodily harm, may succeed in bending the victim's will. He may gain the victim's "consent." But he uses another person precisely because consent is coerced.

The relevance of occurrent coercion is limited to the case of forcible rape. Dispositional coercion, a notion that also plays an indispensable role in an overall account of forcible rape, now becomes our central concern. Although the threat of immediate and serious bodily harm stands out as the most brutal way of coercing consent to sexual interaction, we must not neglect the employment of other kinds of threats to this same end. There are numerous ways in which one person can effectively harm, and thus effectively threaten, another. Accordingly, for example, consent to sexual interaction might be coerced by threatening to damage someone's reputation. If a person consents to sexual interaction to avoid a threatened harm, then that person has been sexually used (via dispositional coercion). In the face of a threat, of course, it remains possible that a person will refuse to comply with another's sexual demands. It is probably best to describe this sort of situation as a case not of coercion, which entails the *successful* use of threats to gain compliance, but of *attempted* coercion. Of course, the moral fault of an individual emerges with the *attempt* to coerce. A person who attempts murder is morally blameworthy even if the attempt fails. The same is true for someone who fails in an effort to coerce consent to sexual interaction.

Consider now each of the following cases:

Case 1   Mr. Supervisor makes a series of increasingly less subtle sexual overtures to Ms. Employee. These advances are consistently and firmly rejected by Ms. Employee. Eventually, Mr. Supervisor makes it clear that the granting of "sexual favors" is a condition of her continued employment.

Case 2   Ms. Debtor borrowed a substantial sum of money from Mr. Creditor, on the understanding that she would pay it back within one year. In the meantime, Ms. Debtor has become sexually attracted to Mr. Creditor, but he does not share her interest. At the end of the one-year period, Mr. Creditor asks Ms. Debtor to return the money. She says she will be happy to return the money so long as he consents to sexual interaction with her.

Case 3   Mr. Theatregoer has two tickets to the most talked-about play of the season. He is introduced to a woman whom he finds sexually attractive and who shares his interest in the theater. In the course of their conversation, she expresses disappointment that the play everyone is talking about is sold out; she would love to see it. At this point, Mr. Theatregoer suggests that she be his guest at the theater. "Oh, by the way," he says, "I always expect sex from my dates."

Case 4   Ms. Jetsetter is planning a trip to Europe. She has been trying for some time to develop a sexual relationship with a man who has shown little interest in her. She knows, however, that he has always wanted to go to Europe and that it is only lack of money that has deterred him. Ms. Jetsetter proposes that he come along as her traveling companion, all expenses paid, on the express understanding that sex is part of the arrangement.

Cases 1 and 2 involve attempts to sexually use another person whereas cases 3 and 4 do not. To see why this is so, it is essential to introduce a distinction between two kinds of proposals, viz., the distinction between *threats* and *offers*.[4] The logical form of a threat differs from the logical form of an offer in the following way. Threat: "If you *do not* do what I am proposing you do, I will bring about an *undesirable consequence* for you." Offer: "If you *do* what I am proposing you do, I will bring about a *desirable consequence* for you." The person who makes a threat attempts to gain compliance by attaching an undesirable consequence to the alternative of noncompliance. This person attempts to *coerce* consent. The person who makes an offer attempts to gain compliance by attaching a desirable consequence to the alternative of compliance. This person attempts not to coerce but to *induce* consent.

Since threats are morally problematic in a way that offers are not, it is not uncommon for threats to be advanced in the language of offers. Threats are represented as if they were offers. An armed assailant might say, "I'm going to make you an *offer*. If you give me your money, I will allow you to go on living." Though this proposal on the surface has the logical form of an offer, it is in reality a threat. The underlying sense of the proposal is this: "If you do not give me your money, I will kill you." If, in a given case, it is initially unclear whether a certain proposal is to count as a threat or an offer, ask the following question. Does the proposal in question have the effect of making a person *worse off upon noncompliance?* The recipient of an offer, upon noncompliance, *is not worse off* than he or she was before the offer. In contrast, the recipient of a threat, upon noncompliance, *is worse off* than he or she was before the threat. Since the "offer" of our armed assailant has the effect, upon noncompliance, of rendering its recipient worse off (relative to the preproposal situation of the recipient), the recipient is faced with a threat, not an offer.

The most obvious way for a coercer to attach an undesirable consequence to the path of noncompliance is by threatening to render the victim of coercion materially worse off than he or she has heretofore been. Thus a person is threatened with loss of life, bodily injury, damage to property, damage to reputation, etc. It is important to realize, however, that a person can also be effectively coerced by being threatened with the withholding of something (in some cases, what we would call a "benefit") to which the person is entitled. Suppose that A is mired in quicksand and is slowly but surely approaching death. When B happens along, A cries out to B for assistance. All B need do is throw A a rope. B is quite willing to accommodate A, "provided you pay me $100,000 over the next ten years." Is B making A an offer? Hardly! B, we must presume, stands under a moral obligation to come to the aid of a person in serious distress, at least when such assistance entails no significant risk, sacrifice of time, etc. A is entitled to B's assistance. Thus, in reality, B attaches an undesirable consequence to A's noncompliance with the proposal that A pay B $100,000. A is undoubtedly better off that B has happened along, but A is not rendered better off *by B's proposal*. Before B's proposal, A legitimately expected assistance from B, "no

---

[4]My account of this distinction largely derives from Robert Nozick, "Coercion," in Sidney Morgenbesser, Patrick Suppes, and Morton White, eds., *Philosophy, Science, and Method* (New York: St. Martin's Press, 1969), pp. 440–472, and from Michael D. Bayles, "Coercive Offers and Public Benefits," *The Personalist* 55, no. 2 (Spring 1974), 139–144.

strings attached." In attaching a very unwelcome string, B's proposal effectively renders A worse off. What B proposes, then, is not an offer of assistance. Rather, B threatens A with the withholding of something (assistance) that A is entitled to have from B.

Since threats have the effect of rendering a person worse off upon noncompliance, it is ordinarily the case that a person does not welcome (indeed, despises) them. Offers, on the other hand, are ordinarily welcome to a person. Since an offer provides no penalty for noncompliance with a proposal but only an inducement for compliance, there is *in principle* only potential advantage in being confronted with an offer. In real life, of course, there are numerous reasons why a person may be less than enthusiastic about being presented with an offer. Enduring the presentation of trivial offers does not warrant the necessary time and energy expenditures. Offers can be both annoying and offensive; certainly this is true of some sexual offers. A person might also be unsettled by an offer that confronts him or her with a difficult decision. All this, however, is compatible with the fact that an offer is fundamentally welcome to a rational person in the sense that the *content* of an offer necessarily widens the field of opportunity and thus provides, in principle, only potential advantage.

With the distinction between threats and offers clearly in view, it now becomes clear why cases 1 and 2 do indeed involve attempts to sexually use another person whereas cases 3 and 4 do not. Cases 1 and 2 embody threats, whereas cases 3 and 4 embody offers. In case 1, Mr. Supervisor proposes sexual interaction with Ms. Employee and, in an effort to gain compliance, threatens her with the loss of her job. Mr. Supervisor thereby attaches an undesirable consequence to one of Ms. Employee's alternatives, the path of noncompliance. Typical of the threat situation, Mr. Supervisor's proposal has the effect of rendering Ms. Employee worse off upon noncompliance. Mr. Supervisor is attempting via (dispositional) coercion to sexually use Ms. Employee. The situation in case 2 is similar. Ms. Debtor, as *she* might be inclined to say, "offers" to pay Mr. Creditor the money she owes him *if* he consents to sexual interaction with her. In reality, Ms. Debtor is threatening Mr. Creditor, attempting to coerce his consent to sexual interaction, attempting to sexually use him. Though Mr. Creditor is not now in possession of the money Ms. Debtor owes him, he is *entitled* to receive it from her at this time. She threatens to deprive him of something to which he is entitled. Clearly, her proposal has the effect of rendering him worse off upon noncompliance. Before her proposal, he had the legitimate expectation, "no strings attached," of receiving the money in question.

Cases 3 and 4 embody offers; neither involves an attempt to sexually use another person. Mr. Theatregoer simply provides an inducement for the woman he has just met to accept his proposal of sexual interaction. He offers her the opportunity to see the play that everyone is talking about. In attaching a desirable consequence to the alternative of compliance, Mr. Theatregoer in no way threatens or attempts to coerce his potential companion. Typical of the offer situation, his proposal does not have the effect of rendering her worse off upon noncompliance. She now has a new opportunity; if she chooses to forgo this opportunity, she is no worse off. The situation in case 4 is similar. Ms. Jetsetter provides an inducement for a man that she is interested in to accept her proposal of sexual involvement. She offers him the opportunity to see

Europe, without expense, as her traveling companion. Before Ms. Jetsetter's proposal, he had no prospect of a European trip. If he choses to reject her proposal, he is no worse off than he has heretofore been. Ms. Jetsetter's proposal embodies an offer, not a threat. She cannot be accused of attempting to sexually use her potential traveling companion.

Consider now two further cases, 5 and 6, each of which develops in the following way. Professor Highstatus, a man of high academic accomplishment, is sexually attracted to a student in one of his classes. He is very anxious to secure her consent to sexual interaction. Ms. Student, confused and unsettled by his sexual advances, has begun to practice "avoidance behavior." To the extent that it is possible, she goes out of her way to avoid him.

Case 5   Professor Highstatus tells Ms. Student that, though her work is such as to entitle her to a grade of B in the class, she will be assigned a D unless she consents to sexual interaction.

Case 6   Professor Highstatus tells Ms. Student that, though her work is such as to entitle her to a grade of B, she will be assigned an A if she consents to sexual interaction.

It is clear that case 5 involves an attempt to sexually use another person. Case 6, however, at least at face value, does not. In case 5, Professor Highstatus *threatens* to deprive Ms. Student of the grade she deserves. In case 6, he *offers* to assign her a grade that is higher than she deserves. In case 5, Ms. Student would be worse off upon noncompliance with Professor Highstatus' proposal. In case 6, she would not be worse off upon noncompliance with his proposal. In saying that case 6 does not involve an attempt to sexually use another person, it is not being asserted that Professor Highstatus is acting in a morally legitimate fashion. In offering a student a higher grade than she deserves, he is guilty of abusing his institutional authority. He is under an obligation to assign the grades that students earn, as defined by the relevant course standards. In case 6, Professor Highstatus is undoubtedly acting in a morally reprehensible way, but in contrast to case 5, where it is fair to say that he both abuses his institutional authority *and* attempts to sexually use another person, we can plausibly say that in case 6 his moral failure is limited to abuse of his institutional authority.

There remains, however, a suspicion that case 6 might after all embody an attempt to sexually use another person. There is no question that the literal content of what Professor Highstatus conveys to Ms. Student has the logical form of an offer and not a threat. Still, is it not the case that Ms. Student may very well feel threatened? Professor Highstatus, in an effort to secure consent to sexual interaction, has announced that he will assign Ms. Student a higher grade than she deserves. Can she really turn him down without substantial risk? Is he not likely to retaliate? If she spurns him, will he not lower her grade or otherwise make it harder for her to succeed in her academic program? He does, after all, have power over her. Will he use it to her detriment? Surely he is not above abusing his institutional authority to achieve his ends; this much is abundantly clear from his willingness to assign a grade higher than a student deserves.

Is Professor Highstatus naive to the threat that Ms. Student may find implicit in the situation? Perhaps. In such a case, if Ms. Student reluctantly consents to sexual interaction, we may be inclined to say that he has *unwittingly* used her. More likely, Professor Highstatus is well aware of the way in which Ms. Student will perceive his proposal. He knows that threats need not be verbally expressed. Indeed, it may even be the case that he consciously exploits his underground reputation. "Everyone knows what happens to the women who reject Professor Highstatus's little offers." To the extent, then, that Professor Highstatus intends to convey a threat in case 6, he is attempting via coercion to sexually use another person.

Many researchers "have pointed out the fact that the possibility of sanctions for noncooperation is implicit in all sexual advances across authority lines, as between teacher and student."[5] I do not think that this consideration should lead us to the conclusion that a person with an academic appointment is obliged in all circumstances to refrain from attempting to initiate sexual involvement with one of his or her students. Still, since even "good faith" sexual advances may be ambiguous in the eyes of a student, it is an interesting question what precautions an instructor must take to avoid unwittingly coercing a student to consent to sexual interaction.

Much of what has been said about the professor/student relationship in an academic setting can be applied as well to the supervisor/subordinate relationship in an employment setting. A manager who functions within an organizational structure is required to evaluate fairly his or her subordinates according to relevant corporate or institutional standards. An unscrupulous manager, willing to abuse his or her institutional authority in an effort to win the consent of a subordinate to sexual interaction, can advance threats and/or offers related to the managerial task of employee evaluation. An employee whose job performance is entirely satisfactory can be threatened with an unsatisfactory performance rating, perhaps leading to termination. An employee whose job performance is excellent can be threatened with an unfair evaluation, designed to bar the employee from recognition, merit pay, consideration for promotion, etc. Such threats, when made in an effort to coerce employee consent to sexual interaction, clearly embody the attempt to sexually use another person. On the other hand, the manager who (abusing his or her institutional authority) offers to provide an employee with an inflated evaluation as an inducement for consent to sexual interaction does not, at face value, attempt to sexually use another person. Of course, all of the qualifications introduced in the discussion of case 6 above are applicable here as well.

IV THE IDEA OF A COERCIVE OFFER

In section III, I have sketched an overall account of sexually using another person *via coercion*. In this section, I will consider the need for modifications or extensions of the suggested account. As before, certain case studies will serve as points of departure.

Case 7 Ms. Starlet, a glamorous, wealthy, and highly successful model, wants nothing more than to become a movie superstar. Mr. Moviemogul, a famous producer, is very taken with Ms. Starlet's beauty. He invites her to come to his office for a

[5]The National Advisory Council on Women's Educational Programs, *Sexual Harassment: A Report on the Sexual Harassment of Students* (August 1980), p. 12.

screen test. After the screen test, Mr. Moviemogul tells Ms. Starlet that he is prepared to make her a star, on the condition that she agree to sexual involvement with him. Ms. Starlet finds Mr. Moviemogul personally repugnant; she is not at all sexually attracted to him. With great reluctance, she agrees to his proposal.

Has Mr. Moviemogul sexually used Ms. Starlet? No. He has made her an offer that she has accepted, however reluctantly. The situation would be quite different if it were plausible to believe that she was, before acceptance of his proposal, *entitled* to his efforts to make her a star. Then we could read case 7 as amounting to his threatening to deprive her of something to which she was entitled. But what conceivable grounds could be found for the claim that Mr. Moviemogul, before Ms. Starlet's acceptance of his proposal, is under an obligation to make her a star? He does not threaten her; he makes her an offer. Even if there are other good grounds for morally condemning his action, it is a mistake to think that he is guilty of coercing consent.

But some would assert that Mr. Moviemogul's offer, on the grounds that it confronts Ms. Starlet with an overwhelming inducement, is simply an example of a *coercive offer*. The more general claim at issue is that offers are coercive precisely inasmuch as they are extremely enticing or seductive. Though there is an important reality associated with the notion of a coercive offer, a reality that must shortly be confronted, we ought not embrace the view that an offer is coercive merely because it is extremely enticing or seductive. Virginia Held is a leading proponent of the view under attack here. She writes:

> A person unable to spurn an offer may act as unwillingly as a person unable to resist a threat. Consider the distinction between rape and seduction. In one case constraint and threat are operative, in the other inducement and offer. If the degree of inducement is set high enough in the case of seduction, there may seem to be little difference in the extent of coercion involved. In both cases, persons may act against their own wills.[6]

Certainly a rape victim who acquiesces at knife point is forced to act *against her will*. Does Ms. Starlet, however, act against her will? We have said that she consents "with great reluctance" to sexual involvement, but she does not act against her will. She *wants* very much to be a movie star. I might want very much to be thin. She regrets having to become sexually involved with Mr. Moviemogul as a means of achieving what she wants. I might regret very much having to go on a diet to lose weight. If we say that Ms. Starlet acts against her will in case 7, then we must say that I am acting against my will in embracing "with great reluctance" the diet I despise.

A more important line of argument against Held's view can be advanced on the basis of the widely accepted notion that there is a moral presumption against coercion. Held herself embraces this notion and very effectively clarifies it:

> . . . although coercion is not *always* wrong (quite obviously: one coerces the small child not to run across the highway, or the murderer to drop his weapon), there is a presumption against it. . . . This has the standing of a fundamental moral principle. . . .
>
> What can be concluded at the moral level is that we have a *prima facie* obligation not to employ coercion.[7] [all italics hers]

---

[6]Virginia Held, "Coercion and Coercive Offers," in *Coercion: Nomos XIV*, p. 58.
[7]*Ibid.*, pp. 61, 62.

But it would seem that acceptance of the moral presumption against coercion is not compatible with the view that offers become coercive precisely inasmuch as they become extremely enticing or seductive. Suppose you are my neighbor and regularly spend your Saturday afternoon on the golf course. Suppose also that you are a skilled gardener. I am anxious to convince you to do some gardening work for me and it must be done this Saturday. I offer you $100, $200, $300, . . . in an effort to make it worth your while to sacrifice your recreation and undertake my gardening. At some point, my proposal becomes very enticing. Yet, at the same time in no sense is my proposal becoming morally problematic. If my proposal were becoming coercive, surely our moral sense would be aroused.

Though it is surely not true that the extremely enticing character of an offer is sufficient to make it coercive, we need not reach the conclusion that no sense can be made out of the notion of a coercive offer. Indeed, there is an important social reality that the notion of a coercive offer appears to capture, and insight into this reality can be gained by simply taking note of the sort of case that most draws us to the language of "coercive offer." Is it not a case in which the recipient of an offer is in circumstances of genuine need, and acceptance of the offer seems to present the only realistic possibility for alleviating the need? Assuming that this sort of case is the heart of the matter, it seems that we cannot avoid introducing some sort of distinction between *genuine needs* and *mere wants*. Though the philosophical difficulties involved in drawing this distinction are not insignificant, I nevertheless claim that we will not achieve any clarity about the notion of a coercive offer, at least in this context, except in reference to it. Whatever puzzlement we may feel with regard to the host of borderline cases that can be advanced, it is nevertheless true, for example, that I *genuinely need* food and that I *merely want* a backyard tennis court. In the same spirit, I think it can be acknowledged by all that Ms. Starlet, though she *wants* very much to be a star, does not in any relevant sense *need* to be a star. Accordingly, there is little plausibility in thinking that Mr. Moviemogul makes her a coercive offer. The following case, in contrast, can more plausibly be thought to embody a coercive offer.

Case 8 Mr. Troubled is a young widower who is raising his three children. He lives in a small town and believes that it is important for him to stay there so that his children continue to have the emotional support of other family members. But economic times are tough. Mr. Troubled has been laid off from his job and has not been able to find another. His unemployment benefits have ceased and his relatives are in no position to help him financially. If he is unable to come up with the money for his mortgage payments, he will lose his rather modest house. Ms. Opportunistic lives in the same town. Since shortly after the death of Mr. Troubled's wife, she has consistently made sexual overtures in his direction. Mr. Troubled, for his part, does not care for Ms. Opportunistic and has made it clear to her that he is not interested in sexual involvement with her. She, however, is well aware of his present difficulties. To win his consent to a sexual affair, Ms. Opportunistic offers to make mortgage payments for Mr. Troubled on a continuing basis.

Is Ms. Opportunistic attempting to sexually use Mr. Troubled? The correct answer is yes, even though we must first accept the conclusion that her proposal embodies an offer and not a threat. If Ms. Opportunistic were threatening Mr. Troubled, her proposal would have the effect of rendering him worse off upon noncompliance. But this is not the case. If he rejects her proposal, his situation will not worsen; he will simply remain, as before, in circumstances of extreme need. It might be objected at this point that Ms. Opportunistic does in fact threaten Mr. Troubled. She threatens to deprive him of something to which he is entitled, namely, the alleviation of a genuine need. But this approach is defensible only if, before acceptance of her proposal, he is entitled to have his needs alleviated *by her*. And whatever Mr. Troubled and his children are entitled to from their society as a whole—they are perhaps slipping through the "social safety net"—it cannot be plausibly maintained that Mr. Troubled is entitled to have his mortgage payments made *by Ms. Opportunistic*.

Yet, though she does not threaten him, she is attempting to sexually use him. How can this conclusion be reconciled with our overall account of sexually using another person? First of all, I want to suggest that nothing hangs on whether or not we decide to call Ms. Opportunistic's offer "coercive." More important than the label "coercive offer" is an appreciation of the social reality that inclines us to consider the label appropriate. The label most forcefully asserts itself when we reflect on what Mr. Troubled is likely to say after accepting the offer. "I really had no choice." "I didn't want to accept her offer but what could I do? I have my children to think about." Both Mr. Troubled and Ms. Starlet (in our previous case) *reluctantly* consented to sexual interaction, but I think it can be agreed that Ms. Starlet had a choice in a way that Mr. Troubled did not. Mr. Troubled's choice was *severely constrained by his needs,* whereas Ms. Starlet's was not. As for Ms. Opportunistic, it seems that we might describe her approach as in some sense exploiting or taking advantage of Mr. Troubled's desperate situation. It is not so much, as we would say in the case of threats, that she coerces him or his consent, but rather that she achieves her aim of winning consent by taking advantage of the fact that he is already "under coercion," that is, his choice is severely constrained by his need. If we choose to describe what has taken place as a "coercive offer," we should remember that Mr. Troubled is "coerced" (constrained) by his own need or perhaps by preexisting factors in his situation rather than by Ms. Opportunistic or her offer.

Since it is not quite right to say that Ms. Opportunistic is attempting to coerce Mr. Troubled, even if we are prepared to embrace the label "coercive offer," we cannot simply say, as we would say in the case of threats, that she is attempting to sexually use him *via coercion*. The proper account of the way in which Ms. Opportunistic attempts to sexually use Mr. Troubled is somewhat different. Let us say simply that she attempts to sexually use him *by taking advantage of his desperate situation.* The sense behind this distinctive way of sexually using someone is that a person's choice situation can sometimes be subject to such severe prior constraints that the possibility of *voluntary* consent to sexual interaction is precluded. A advances an offer calculated to gain B's reluctant consent to sexual interaction by confronting B, who has no apparent way of alleviating a genuine need, with an opportunity to do so, but makes this opportunity contingent upon consent to sexual interaction. In such a case, should we not say simply that B's need, when coupled with a lack of viable alternatives, results in B being incapable of *voluntarily* accepting A's offer? Thus A, in making an offer which B "cannot refuse," although not coercing B, nevertheless does intentionally act in a way that violates the requirement that B's sexual interaction with A be based upon B's voluntary informed consent. Thus A sexually uses B.

The central claim of this paper is that A sexually uses B if and only if A intentionally acts in a way that violates the requirement that B's sexual interaction with A be based on B's voluntary informed consent. Clearly, deception and coercion are important mechanisms whereby sexual using takes place. But consideration of case 8 has led us to the identification of yet another mechanism. In summary, then, limiting attention to cases of sexual interaction with a fully competent adult partner, A can sexually use B not only (1) by deceiving B or (2) by coercing B but also (3) by taking advantage of B's desperate situation.

QUESTIONS

1 Is there a morally relevant sense of *sexually* using another person that is not captured by reference to the notion of voluntary informed consent?
2 What is promiscuity? Is promiscuity immoral?
3 Is prostitution immoral?

Morality and Human Sexuality

Vincent C. Punzo

Vincent C. Punzo is professor of philosophy at St. Louis University. His published articles include "Reason in Morals" and "Natural Law Ethics: Immediate or Mediated Naturalism." Punzo is also the author of Reflective Naturalism: An Introduction To Moral Philosophy *(1969), from which this selection is excerpted.*

Punzo begins by arguing that there is a morally significant difference between sexual intercourse and other types of human activity. Then, emphasizing the historical aspect of the human self, he constructs an argument against premarital sexual intercourse. Marriage, in his view, is constituted by a mutual and total commitment. Apart from this framework of commitment, he argues, sexual unions are "morally deficient because they lack existential integrity." Although Punzo is essentially a proponent of conventional sexual morality, he understands marriage in such a way that he does not condemn "preceremonial" intercourse. He insists that the commitment constitutive of marriage can exist prior to and apart from any legal or ceremonial formalities.

If one sees man's moral task as being simply that of not harming anyone, that is if one sees this task in purely negative terms, he will certainly not accept the argument to be presented in the following section. However, if one accepts the notion of the morality of aspiration, if one accepts the view that man's moral task involves the positive attempt to live up to what is best in man, to give reality to what he sees to be the perfection of himself as a human subject, the argument may be acceptable.

SEXUALITY AND THE HUMAN SUBJECT

[Prior discussion] has left us with the question as to whether sexual intercourse is a type of activity that is similar to choosing a dinner from a menu. This question is of utmost significance in that one's view of the morality of premarital intercourse seems to depend on the significance that one gives to the sexual encounter in human life. Those such as [John] Wilson and [Eustace] Chesser who see nothing immoral about the premarital character of sexual intercourse seem to see sexual intercourse as being no different from myriad of other purely aesthetic matters. This point is seen in Chesser's questioning of the reason for demanding permanence in the relationship of sexual partners when we do not see such permanence as being important to other human relationships.[1] It is also seen in his asking why we raise a moral issue about premarital coition when two people may engage in it, with the resulting social and psychological consequences being no different than if they had gone to a movie.[2]

Wilson most explicitly makes a case for the view that sexual intercourse does not differ significantly from other human activities. He holds that people think that there is a logical difference between the question "Will you engage in sexual intercourse with me?" and the question, "Will you play tennis with me?" only because they are influenced by the acquisitive character of contemporary society.[3] Granted that the two questions may be identical from the purely formal perspective of logic, the ethician must move beyond this perspective to a consideration of their content. Men and women find themselves involved in many different relationships: for example, as buyer-seller, employer-employee, teacher-student, lawyer-client, and partners or competitors in certain games such as tennis or bridge. Is there any morally significant difference between these relationships and sexual intercourse? We cannot examine all the possible relationships into which a man and woman can enter, but we will consider the employer-employee relationship in order to get some perspective on the distinctive character of the sexual relationship.

A man pays a woman to act as his secretary. What rights does he have over her in such a situation? The woman agrees to work a certain number of hours during the day taking dictation, typing letters, filing reports, arranging appointments and flight schedules, and greeting clients and competitors. In short, we can say that the man has rights to certain of the woman's services or skills. The use of the word "services" may lead some to conclude that this relationship is not significantly different from the relationship between a prostitute and her client in that the prostitute also offers her "services."

It is true that we sometimes speak euphemistically of a prostitute offering her services to a man for a sum of money, but if we are serious about our quest for the difference

---

[1]Eustace Chesser, *Unmarried Love* (New York: Pocket Books, 1965), p. 29.
[2]*Ibid.*, pp. 35–36, see also p. 66.
[3]John Wilson, *Logic and Sexual Morality* (Baltimore, Md.: Penguin Books, 1965). See footnote 1, p. 67.

between the sexual encounter and other types of human relationships, it is necessary to drop euphemisms and face the issue directly. The man and woman who engage in sexual intercourse are giving their bodies, the most intimate physical expression of themselves, over to the other. Unlike the man who plays tennis with a woman, the man who has sexual relations with her has literally entered her. A man and woman engaging in sexual intercourse have united themselves as intimately and as totally as is physically possible for two human beings. Their union is not simply a union of organs, but is as intimate and as total a physical union of two selves as is possible of achievement. Granted the character of this union, it seems strange to imply that there is no need for a man and a woman to give any more thought to the question of whether they should engage in sexual intercourse than to the question of whether they should play tennis.

In opposition to Wilson, I think that it is the acquisitive character of our society that has blinded us to the distinction between the two activities. Wilson's and Chesser's positions seem to imply that exactly the same moral considerations ought to apply to a situation in which a housewife is bartering with a butcher for a few pounds of pork chops and the situation in which two human beings are deciding whether sexual intercourse ought to be an ingredient of their relationship. So long as the butcher does not put his thumb on the scale in the weighing process, so long as he is truthful in stating that the meat is actually pork, so long as the woman pays the proper amount with the proper currency, the trade is perfectly moral. Reflecting on sexual intercourse from the same sort of economic perspective, one can say that so long as the sexual partners are truthful in reporting their freedom from contagious venereal diseases and so long as they are truthful in reporting that they are interested in the activity for the mere pleasure of it or to try out their sexual techniques, there is nothing immoral about such activity. That in the one case pork chops are being exchanged for money whereas in the other the decision concerns the most complete and intimate merging of one's self with another makes no difference to the moral evaluation of the respective cases.

It is not surprising that such a reductionistic outlook should pervade our thinking on sexual matters, since in our society sexuality is used to sell everything from shave cream to underarm deodorants, to soap, to mouthwash, to cigarettes, and to automobiles. Sexuality has come to play so large a role in our commercial lives that it is not surprising that our sexuality should itself come to be treated as a commodity governed by the same moral rules that govern any other economic transaction.

Once sexuality is taken out of this commercial framework, once the character of the sexual encounter is faced directly and squarely, we will come to see that Doctor Mary Calderone has brought out the type of questions that ought to be asked by those contemplating the introduction of sexual intercourse into their relationships: "How many times, and how casually, are you willing to invest a portion of your total self, and to be the custodian of a like investment from the other person, without the sureness of knowing that these investments are being made for keeps?"[4] These questions come out of the recognition that the sexual encounter is a definitive experience, one in which the physical intimacy and merging involves also a merging of the nonphysical di-

---

[4]Mary Steichen Calderone, "The Case for Chastity," *Sex in America,* ed. by Henry Anatole Grunwald (New York: Bantam Books, 1964), p. 147.

mensions of the partners. With these questions, man moves beyond the negative concern with avoiding his or another's physical and psychological harm to the question of what he is making of himself and what he is contributing to the existential formation of his partner as a human subject.

If we are to make a start toward responding to Calderone's questions we must cease talking about human selfhood in abstraction. The human self is an historical as well as a physical being. He is a being who is capable of making at least a portion of his past an object of his consciousness and thus is able to make this past play a conscious role in his present and in his looking toward the future. He is also a being who looks to the future, who faces tomorrow with plans, ideals, hopes, and fears. The very being of a human self involves his past and his movement toward the future. Moreover, the human self is not completely shut off in his own past and future. Men and women are capable of consciously and purposively uniting themselves in a common career and venture. They can commit themselves to sharing the future with another, sharing it in all its aspects—in its fortunes and misfortunes, in its times of happiness and times of tragedy. Within the lives of those who have so committed themselves to each other, sexual intercourse is a way of asserting and confirming the fullness and totality of their mutual commitment.

Unlike those who have made such a commitment and who come together in the sexual act in the fullness of their selfhood, those who engage in premarital sexual unions and who have made no such commitment act as though they can amputate their bodily existence and the most intimate physical expression of their selfhood from their existence as historical beings. Granting that there may be honesty on the verbal level in that two people engaging in premarital intercourse openly state that they are interested only in the pleasure of the activity, the fact remains that such unions are morally deficient because they lack existential integrity in that there is a total merging and union on a physical level, on the one hand, and a conscious decision not to unite any other dimension of themselves, on the other hand. Their sexual union thus involves a "depersonalization" of their bodily existence, an attempt to cut off the most intimate physical expression of their respective selves from their very selfhood. The mutual agreement of premarital sex partners is an agreement to merge with the other not as a self, but as a body which one takes unto oneself, which one possesses in a most intimate and total fashion for one's own pleasure or designs, allowing the other to treat oneself in the same way. It may be true that no physical or psychological harm may result from such unions, but such partners have failed to existentially incorporate human sexuality, which is at the very least the most intimate physical expression of the human self, into the character of this selfhood.

In so far as premarital sexual unions separate the intimate and total physical union that is sexual intercourse from any commitment to the self in his historicity, human sexuality, and consequently the human body, have been fashioned into external things or objects to be handed over totally to someone else, whenever one feels that he can get possession of another's body, which he can use for his own purposes.[5] The human

---

[5]The psychoanalyst Rollo May makes an excellent point in calling attention to the tendency in contemporary society to exploit the human body as if it were only a machine. Rollo May, "The New Puritanism," *Sex in America*, pp. 161–164.

body has thus been treated no differently from the pork chops spoken of previously or from any other object or commodity, which human beings exchange and haggle over in their day-to-day transactions. One hesitates to use the word that might be used to capture the moral value that has been sacrificed in premarital unions because in our day the word has taken on a completely negative meaning at best, and, at worst, it has become a word used by "sophisticates" to mock or deride certain attitudes toward human sexuality. However, because the word "chastity" has been thus abused is no reason to leave it in the hands of those who have misrepresented the human value to which it gives expression.

The chaste person has often been described as one intent on denying his sexuality. The value of chastity as conceived in this section is in direct opposition to this description. It is the unchaste person who is separating himself from his sexuality, who is willing to exchange human bodies as one would exchange money for tickets to a baseball game—honestly and with no commitment of self to self. Against this alienation of one's sexuality from one's self, an alienation that makes ones' sexuality an object, which is to be given to another in exchange for his objectified sexuality, chastity affirms the integrity of the self in his bodily and historical existence. The sexuality of man is seen as an integral part of his subjectivity. Hence, the chaste man rejects depersonalized sexual relations as a reduction of man in his most intimate physical being to the status of an object or pure instrument for another. He asserts that man is a subject and end in himself, not in some trans-temporal, nonphysical world, but in the historical-physical world in which he carries on his moral task and where he finds his fellow man. He will not freely make of himself in his bodily existence a thing to be handed over to another's possession, nor will he ask that another treat his own body in this way. The total physical intimacy of sexual intercourse will be an expression of total union with the other self on all levels of their beings. Seen from this perspective, chastity is one aspect of man's attempt to attain existential integrity, to accept his body as a dimension of his total personality.

In concluding this section, it should be noted that I have tried to make a case against the morality of premarital sexual intercourse even in those cases in which the partners are completely honest with each other. There is reason to question whether the complete honesty, to which those who see nothing immoral in such unions refer, is as a matter of fact actually found very often among premarital sex partners. We may well have been dealing with textbook cases which present these unions in their best light. One may be pardoned for wondering whether sexual intercourse often occurs under the following conditions: "Hello, my name is Josiah. I am interested in having a sexual experience with you. I can assure you that I am good at it and that I have no communicable disease. If it sounds good to you and if you have taken the proper contraceptive precautions, we might have a go at it. Of course, I want to make it clear to you that I am interested only in the sexual experience and that I have no intention of making any long-range commitment to you." If those, who defend the morality of premarital sexual unions so long as they are honestly entered into, think that I have misrepresented what they mean by honesty, then they must specify what they mean by an honest premarital union. . . .

MARRIAGE AS A TOTAL HUMAN COMMITMENT

The preceding argument against the morality of premarital sexual unions was not based on the view that the moral character of marriage rests on a legal certificate or on a legal or religious ceremony. The argument was not directed against "preceremonial" intercourse, but against premarital intercourse. Morally speaking, a man and woman are married when they make the mutual and total commitment to share the problems and prospects of their historical existence in the world. . . .

. . . A total commitment to another means a commitment to him in his historical existence. Such a commitment is not simply a matter of words or of feelings, however strong. It involves a full existential sharing on the part of two beings of the burdens, opportunities, and challenges of their historical existence.

Granted the importance that the character of their commitment to each other plays in determining the moral quality of a couple's sexual encounter, it is clear that there may be nothing immoral in the behavior of couples who engage in sexual intercourse before participating in the marriage ceremony. For example, it is foolish to say that two people who are totally committed to each other and who have made all the arrangements to live this commitment are immoral if they engage in sexual intercourse the night before the marriage ceremony. Admittedly this position can be abused by those who have made a purely verbal commitment, a commitment, which will be carried out in some vague and ill-defined future. At some time or other, they will unite their two lives totally by setting up house together and by actually undertaking the task of meeting the economic, social, legal, medical responsibilities that are involved in living this commitment. Apart from the reference to a vague and amorphous future time when they will share the full responsibility for each other, their commitment presently realizes itself in going to dances, sharing a box of popcorn at Saturday night movies, and sharing their bodies whenever they can do so without taking too great a risk of having the girl become pregnant.

Having acknowledged that the position advanced in this section can be abused by those who would use the word "commitment" to rationalize what is an interest only in the body of the other person, it must be pointed out that neither the ethician nor any other human being can tell two people whether they actually have made the commitment that is marriage or are mistaking a "warm glow" for such a commitment. There comes a time when this issue falls out of the area of moral philosophy and into the area of practical wisdom. . . .

The characterization of marriage as a total commitment between two human beings may lead some to conclude that the marriage ceremony is a wholly superfluous affair. It must be admitted that people may be morally married without having engaged in a marriage ceremony. However, to conclude from this point that the ceremony is totally meaningless is to lose sight of the social character of human beings. The couple contemplating marriage do not exist in a vacuum, although there may be times when they think they do. Their existences reach out beyond their union to include other human beings. By making their commitment a matter of public record, by solemnly expressing it before the law and in the presence of their respective families and friends and, if they are religious people, in the presence of God and one of his ministers, they sink the roots of their commitment more deeply and extensively in the world in which they live, thus taking steps to provide for the future growth of their commitment to each other. The public expression of this commitment makes it more fully and more explicitly a part of a couple's lives and of the world in which they live. . . .

QUESTIONS

1 Could the idea of existential integrity be developed in such a way as to provide a justification for the sex with love approach instead of conventional sexual morality?
2 Punzo says that no one is capable of telling "two people whether they actually have made the commitment that is marriage or are mistaking a 'warm glow' for such a commitment." What factors should a couple consider in attempting to resolve this question?

Homosexuality and the "Unnaturalness Argument"

Burton M. Leiser

A biographical sketch of Burton M. Leiser is found on page 116.

Leiser critiques an argument which is often advanced to show the immorality of homosexual behavior: Homosexual behavior is unnatural and therefore immoral. On Leiser's analysis, an adequate "unnaturalness argument" would have to provide the following: (1) a clearly specified sense of "unnatural" according to which homosexual behavior is rightly identified as unnatural; (2) substantiation for thinking that the unnaturalness of homosexual behavior is linked with the production of harm and is thus a ground of moral condemnation. Leiser analyzes four possible senses that proponents of the argument might attribute to "unnatural." Finding that each suggestion fails to satisfy one or both of the conditions necessary to sustain the argument, he concludes that the argument must be rejected.

[The alleged "unnaturalness" of homosexuality] raises the question of the meaning of *nature, natural,* and similar terms. Theologians and other moralists have said that [homosexual acts] violate the "natural law," and that they are therefore immoral and ought to be prohibited by the state.

The word *nature* has a built-in ambiguity that can lead to serious misunderstandings. When something is said to be "natural" or in conformity with "natural law" or the "law of nature," this may mean either (1) that it is in conformity with the descriptive laws of nature, or (2) that it is not artificial, that man has not imposed his will or his devices upon events or conditions as they exist or would have existed without such interference.

1 THE DESCRIPTIVE LAWS OF NATURE

The laws of nature, as these are understood by the scientist, differ from the laws of man. The former are purely descriptive, whereas the latter are prescriptive. When a scientist says that water boils at 212° Fahrenheit or that the volume of a gas varies directly with the heat that is applied to it and inversely with the pressure, he means merely that as a matter of recorded and observable fact, pure water under standard conditions always boils at precisely 212° Fahrenheit and that as a matter of observed fact, the volume of a gas rises as it is heated and falls as pressure is applied to it. These "laws" merely *describe* the manner in which physical substances *actually behave*. They differ from municipal and federal laws in that they *do not prescribe behavior*. Unlike manmade laws, natural laws are not passed by any legislator or group of legislators; they are not proclaimed or announced; they impose no obligation upon anyone or anything; their "violation" entails no penalty, and there is no reward for "following" them or "abiding by" them. When a scientist says that the air in a tire "obeys" the laws of nature that "govern" gases, he does *not* mean that the air, having been informed that it *ought* to behave in a certain way, behaves appropriately under the right conditions. He means, rather, that as a matter of fact, the air in a tire *will* behave like all other gases. In saying that Boyle's law "governs" the behavior of gases, he means merely that gases do, as a matter of fact, behave in accordance with Boyle's law, and that Boyle's law enables one to predict accurately what will happen to a given quantity of a gas as its pressure is raised; he does *not* mean to suggest that some heavenly voice has proclaimed that all gases should henceforth behave in accordance with the terms of Boyle's law and that a ghostly policeman patrols the world, ready to mete out punishments to any gases that "violate" the heavenly decree. In fact, according to the scientist, it does not make sense to speak of a natural law being violated. For if there were a true exception to a so-called law of nature, the exception would require a change in the description of those phenomena, and the "law" would have been shown to be no law at all. The laws of nature are revised as scientists discover new phenomena that require new refinements in their descriptions of the way things actually happen. In this respect they differ fundamentally from human laws, which are revised periodically by legislators who are not so interested in *describing* human behavior as they are in *prescribing* what human behavior *should* be.

2 THE ARTIFICIAL AS A FORM OF THE UNNATURAL

On occasion when we say that something is not natural, we mean that it is a product of human artifice. My typewriter is not a natural object, in this sense, for the substances of which it is composed have been removed from their natural state—the state in which they existed before men came along—and have been transformed by a series of chemical and physical and mechanical processes into other substances. They have been rearranged into a whole that is quite different from anything found in nature. In short, my typewriter is an artificial object. In this sense, the clothing that I wear as I lecture before my students is not natural, for it has been transformed considerably from the state in which it was found in nature; and my wearing of clothing as I lecture before my students is also not natural, in this sense, for in my natural state, before the application of anything artificial, before any human interference with things as they are, I am quite naked. Human laws, being artificial conventions designed to exercise a degree of control over the natural inclinations and propensities of men, may in this sense be considered to be unnatural.

Now when theologians and moralists speak of homosexuality, contraception, abortion, and other forms of human behavior as being unnatural, and say that for that reason such behavior must be considered to be wrong, in what sense are they using the word *unnatural?* Are they saying that homosexual behavior and the use of contraceptives are contrary to the scientific laws of nature, are they saying that they are artificial forms of behavior, or are they using the terms *natural* and *unnatural* in some third sense?

They cannot mean that homosexual behavior (to stick to the subject presently under discussion) violates the laws of nature in the first sense, for, as we have pointed out, in *that* sense it is impossible to violate the laws of nature. Those laws, being merely descriptive of what actually does happen, would have to *include* homosexual behavior if such behavior does actually take place. Even if the defenders of the theological view that homosexuality is unnatural were to appeal to a statistical analysis by pointing out that such behavior is not normal from a statistical point of view, and therefore not what the laws of nature require, it would be open to their critics to reply that any descriptive law of nature must account for and incorporate all statistical deviations, and that the laws of nature, in this sense, do not *require anything*. These critics might also note that the best statistics available reveal that about half of all American males engage in homosexual activity at some time in their lives, and that a very large percentage of American males have exclusively homosexual relations for a fairly extensive period of time; from which it would follow that such behavior is natural, for them, at any rate, in this sense of the word *natural*.

If those who say that homosexual behavior is unnatural are using the term *unnatural* in the second sense, it is difficult to see why they should be fussing over it. Certainly nothing is intrinsically wrong with going against nature (if that is how it should be put) in this sense. That which is artificial is often far better than what is natural. Artificial homes seem, at any rate, to be more suited to human habitation and more conducive to longer life and better health than caves and other natural shelters. There are distinct advantages to the use of such unnatural (i.e., artificial) amenities as clothes, furniture, and books. Although we may dream of an idyllic return to nature in our more wistful moments, we would soon discover, as Thoreau did in his attempt to escape from the artificiality of civilization, that needles and thread, knives and matches, ploughs and nails, and countless other products of human artifice are essential to human life. We would discover, as Plato pointed out in the *Republic,* that no man can be truly self-sufficient. Some of the by-products of industry are less than desirable; but neither industry itself, nor the products of industry, are intrinsically evil, even though both are unnatural in this sense of the word.

Interference with nature is not evil in itself. Nature, as some writers have put it, must be tamed. In some respects man must look upon it as an enemy to be conquered. If nature were left to its own devices, without the intervention of human artifice, men would be consumed with disease, they would be plagued by insects, they would be chained to the places where they were born with no means of swift communication or transport, and they would suffer the discomforts and the torments of wind and weather and flood and fire with no practical means of combating any of them. Interfering with nature, doing battle with nature, using human will and reason and skill to thwart what might otherwise follow from the conditions that prevail in the world, is a peculiarly human enterprise, one that can hardly be condemned merely because it does what is not natural.

Homosexual behavior can hardly be considered to be unnatural in this sense. There is nothing "artificial" about such behavior. On the contrary, it is quite natural, in this sense, to those who engage in it. And even if it were not, even if it were quite artificial, this is not in itself a ground for condemning it.

It would seem, then, that those who condemn homosexuality as an unnatural form of behavior must mean something else by the word *unnatural,* something not covered by either of the preceding definitions. A third possibility is this:

3 ANYTHING UNCOMMON OR ABNORMAL IS UNNATURAL

If this is what is meant by those who condemn homosexuality on the ground that it is unnatural, it is quite obvious that their condemnation cannot be accepted without further argument. For the fact that a given form of behavior is uncommon provides no justification for condemning it. Playing viola in a string quartet is no doubt an uncommon form of human behavior. I do not know what percentage of the human race engages in such behavior, or what percentage of his life any given violist devotes to such behavior, but I suspect that the number of such people must be very small indeed, and that the total number of manhours spent in such activity would justify our calling that form of activity uncommon, abnormal (in the sense that it is statistically not the kind of thing that people are ordinarily inclined to do), and therefore unnatural, in this sense of the word. Yet there is no reason to suppose that such uncommon, abnormal behavior is, by virtue of its uncommonness, deserving of condemnation or ethically or morally wrong. On the contrary, many forms of behavior are praised precisely because they are so uncommon. Great artists, poets, musicians, and scientists are "abnormal" in this sense; but clearly the world is better off for having them, and it would be absurd to condemn them or their activities for their failure to be common and normal. If homosexual behavior is wrong, then, it must be for some reason other than its "unnaturalness" in this sense of the word.

4 ANY USE OF AN ORGAN OR AN INSTRUMENT THAT IS CONTRARY TO ITS PRINCIPAL PURPOSE OR FUNCTION IS UNNATURAL

Every organ and every instrument—perhaps even every creature—has a function to perform, one for which it is particularly designed. Any use of those instruments and organs that is consonant with their purposes is natural and proper, but any use that is inconsistent with their principal functions is unnatural and improper, and to that extent, evil or harmful. Human teeth, for example, are admirably designed for their principal functions—biting and chewing the kinds of food suitable for human consumption. But they are not particularly well suited for prying the caps from beer bottles. If they are used for the latter purpose, which is not natural to them, they are liable to crack or break under the strain. The abuse of one's teeth leads to their destruction and to a consequent deterioration in one's overall health. If they are used only for their proper function, however, they may continue to serve well for many years. Similarly, a given drug may have a proper function. If used in the furtherance of that end, it can preserve life and restore health. But if it is abused, and employed for purposes for which it was never intended, it may cause serious harm and even death. The natural uses of things are good and proper, but their unnatural uses are bad and harmful.

What we must do, then, is to find the proper use, or the true purpose, of each organ in our bodies. Once we have discovered that, we will know what constitutes the natural use of each organ, and what constitutes an unnatural, abusive, and potentially harmful employment of the various parts of our bodies. If we are rational, we will be careful to confine our behavior to our proper functions and to refrain from unnatural behavior. According to those philosophers who follow this line of reasoning, the way to discover the "proper" use of any organ is to determine what it is peculiarly suited to do. The eye is suited for seeing, the ear for hearing, the nerves for transmitting impulses from one part of the body to another, and so on.

What are the sex organs peculiarly suited to do? Obviously, they are peculiarly suited to enable men and women to reproduce their own kind. No other organ in the body is capable of fulfilling that function. It follows, according to those who follow the natural-law line, that the "proper" or "natural" function of the sex organs is reproduction, and that strictly speaking, any use of those organs for other purposes is unnatural, abusive, potentially harmful, and therefore wrong. The sex organs have been given to us in order to enable us to maintain the continued existence of mankind on this earth. All perversions—including masturbation, homosexual behavior, and heterosexual intercourse that deliberately frustrates the design of the sexual organs—are unnatural and bad. As Pope Pius XI once said, "Private individuals have no other power over the members of their bodies than that which pertains to their natural ends."

But the problem is not so easily resolved. Is it true that every organ has one and only one proper function? A hammer may have been designed to pound nails, and it may perform that particular job best. But it is not sinful to employ a hammer to crack nuts if I have no other more suitable tool immediately available. The hammer, being a relatively versatile tool, may be employed in a number of ways. It has no one "proper" or "natural" function. A woman's eyes are well adapted to seeing, it is true. But they seem also to be well adapted to flirting. Is a woman's use of her eyes for the latter purpose sinful merely because she is not using them, at that moment, for their "primary" purpose of seeing? Our sexual organs are uniquely adapted for procreation, but that is obviously not the only function for which they are adapted. Human beings may—and do—use those organs for a great many other purposes, and it is difficult to see why any *one* use should be considered to be the only proper one. The sex organs, for one thing, seem to be particularly well adapted to give their owners and others intense sensations of pleasure. Unless one believes that pleasure itself is bad, there seems to be little reason to believe that the use of the sex organs for the production of pleasure in oneself or in others is evil. In view of the peculiar design of these organs, with their great concentration of nerve endings, it would seem that they were designed (if they *were* designed) with that very goal in mind, and that their use for such purposes would be no more unnatural than their use for the purpose of procreation.

Nor should we overlook the fact that human sex organs may be and are used to express, in the deepest and most intimate way open to man, the love of one person for another. Even the most ardent opponents of "unfruitful" intercourse admit that sex does serve this function. They have accordingly conceded that a man and his wife may have intercourse even though she is pregnant, or past the age of child bearing, or in the infertile period of her menstrual cycle.

Human beings are remarkably complex and adaptable creatures. Neither they nor their organs can properly be compared to hammers or to other tools. The analogy quickly breaks down. The generalization that a given organ or instrument has one and only one proper function does not hold up, even with regard to the simplest manufactured tools, for, as we have seen, a tool may be used for more than one purpose— less effectively than one especially designed for a given task, perhaps, but "properly" and certainly not *sinfully*. A woman may use her eyes not only to see and to flirt, but also to earn money—if she is, for example, an actress or a model. Though neither of the latter functions seems to have been a part of the original "design," if one may speak sensibly of *design* in this context, of the eye, it is difficult to see why such a use of the eyes of a woman should be considered sinful, perverse, or unnatural. Her sex organs have the unique capacity of producing ova and nurturing human embryos, under the right conditions; but why should any other use of those organs, including their use to bring pleasure to their owner or to someone else, or to manifest love to another person, or even, perhaps, to earn money, be regarded as perverse, sinful, or unnatural? Similarly, a man's sexual organs possess the unique capacity of causing the generation of another human being, but if a man chooses to use them for pleasure, or for the expression of love, or for some other purpose—so long as he does not interfere with the rights of some other person—the fact that his sex organs do have their unique capabilities does not constitute a convincing justification for condemning their other uses as being perverse, sinful, unnatural, or criminal. If a man "perverts" himself by wiggling his ears for the entertainment of his neighbors instead of using them exclusively for their "natural" function of hearing, no one thinks of consigning him to prison. If he abuses his teeth by using them to pull staples from memos—a function for which teeth were clearly not designed—he is not accused of being immoral, degraded, and degenerate. The fact that people *are* condemned for using their sex organs for their own pleasure or profit, or for that of others, may be more revealing about the prejudices and taboos of our society than it is about our perception of the true nature or purpose or "end" (whatever that might be) of our bodies.

To sum up, then, the proposition that any use of an organ that is contrary to its principal purpose or function is unnatural assumes that organs *have* a principal purpose or function, but this may be denied on the ground that the purpose or function of a given organ may vary according to the needs or desires of its owner. It may be denied on the ground that a given organ may have more than one principal purpose or function, and any attempt to call one use or another the only natural one seems to be arbitrary, if not questionbegging. Also, the proposition suggests that what is unnatural is evil or depraved. This goes beyond the pure description of things, and enters into the problem of the evaluation of human behavior, which leads us to the fifth meaning of "natural."

5 THAT WHICH IS NATURAL IS GOOD, AND WHATEVER IS UNNATURAL IS BAD

When one condemns homosexuality or masturbation or the use of contraceptives on the ground that it is unnatural, one implies that whatever is unnatural is bad, wrongful, or perverse. But as we have seen, in some senses of the word, the unnatural (i.e., the artificial) is often very good, whereas that which is natural (i.e., that which has not been subjected to human artifice or improvement) may be very bad indeed. Of course, interference with nature may be bad. Ecologists have made us more aware than we have ever been of the dangers of unplanned and uninformed interference with nature. But this is not to say that *all* interference with nature is bad. Every time a man cuts down a tree to make room for a home for himself, or catches a fish to feed himself or his family, he is interfering with nature. If men did not interfere with nature, they would have no homes, they could eat no fish, and, in fact, they could not survive. What, then, can be meant by those who say that whatever is natural is good and whatever is unnatural is bad? Clearly, they cannot have intended merely to reduce the word *natural* to a synonym of *good, right,* and *proper,* and *unnatural* to a synonym of *evil, wrong, improper, corrupt,* and *depraved.* If that were all they had intended to do, there would be very little to discuss as to whether a given form of behavior might be proper even though it is not in strict conformity with someone's views of what is natural; for *good* and *natural* being synonyms, it would follow inevitably that whatever is good must be natural, and vice versa, by definition. This is certainly not what the opponents of homosexuality have been saying when they claim that homo-sexuality, being unnatural, is evil. For if it were, their claim would be quite empty. They would be saying merely that homosexuality, being evil, is evil—a redundancy that could as easily be reduced to the simpler assertion that homosexuality is evil. This assertion, however, is not an argument. Those who oppose homosexuality and other sexual "perversions" on the ground that they are "unnatural" are saying that there is some objectively identifiable quality in such behavior that is unnatural; and that that quality, once it has been identified by some kind of scientific observation, can be seen to be detrimental to those who engage in such behavior, or to those around them; and that *because* of the harm (physical, mental, moral, or spiritual) that results from engaging in any behavior possessing the attribute of unnaturalness, such behavior must be considered to be wrongful, and should be discouraged by society. "Unnaturalness" and "wrongfulness" are not synonyms, then, but different concepts. The problem with which we are wrestling is that we are unable to find a meaning for *unnatural* that enables us to arrive at the conclusion that homosexuality is unnatural or that if homosexuality is unnatural, it is therefore wrongful behavior. We have examined four common meanings of *natural* and *unnatural,* and have seen that none of them performs the task that it must perform if the advocates of this argument are to prevail. Without some more satisfactory explanation of the connection between the wrongfulness of homosexuality and its alleged unnaturalness, the argument must be rejected.

QUESTIONS

1 Can the "unnaturalness argument" be developed in a way that avoids Leiser's criticisms?
2 Is homosexual behavior immoral? If so, on what grounds?

Majority Opinion in *Doe v. Commonwealth's Attorney for City of Richmond*

Judge Albert V. Bryan

Albert V. Bryan (1899–1984) served as judge of the U.S. Court of Appeals, Fourth Circuit. A graduate of the University of Virginia Law School, he was admitted to the Virginia bar in 1920 and maintained a private practice in Alexandria, Virginia, before becoming a U.S. district judge in 1947.

In this case, two anonymous homosexuals brought an action before a three-judge District Court in Richmond, Virginia. They sought to have the Virginia statute making sodomy a crime declared unconstitutional. In a two-to-one decision, the District Court upheld the constitutionality of the statute. The case was subsequently appealed to the United States Supreme Court, but in 1976, by a vote of six-to-three, the Court refused to hear arguments and summarily affirmed the lower-court ruling. Laws similar to the Virginia statute at issue here presently exist in many states. In the majority opinion of the District Court, Judge Bryan contends that Virginia's sodomy statute, inasmuch as it applies to homosexuals (even those who are *consenting adults* engaged in *private* behavior), is not unconstitutional. The constitutionally guaranteed right of privacy, in his view, is applicable to sexual behavior only within a marriage relationship, not without. Moreover, he insists, a legitimate state interest underlies Virginia's sodomy statute.

United States District Court, E.D. Virginia. 403 F. Supp. 1199 (1975).

Virginia's statute making sodomy a crime is unconstitutional, each of the male plaintiffs aver, when it is applied to his active and regular homosexual relations with another *adult male, consensually* and *in private.* They assert that local State officers threaten them with prosecution for violation of this law, that such enforcement would deny them their Fifth and Fourteenth Ammendments' assurance of due process, the First Ammendment's protection of their rights of freedom of expression, the First and Ninth Amendments' guarantee of privacy, and the Eighth Amendment's forbiddance of cruel and unusual punishments. A declaration of the statute's invalidity in the circumstances is prayed as well as an injunction against its enforcement. Defendants are State prosecuting officials and they take issue with the plaintiffs' conclusions. With no conflict of fact present, the validity of this enactment becomes a question of law.

So far as relevant, the Code of Virginia, 1950, as amended, provides:

> "§ 18. 1–212. Crimes against nature. —If any person shall carnally know in any manner any brute animal, or carnally know any male or female person by the anus or by or with the mouth, or voluntarily submit to such carnal knowledge, he or she shall be guilty of a felony and shall be confined in the penitentiary not less than one year nor more than three years."

Our decision is that on its face and in the circumstances here it is not unconstitutional. No judgment is made upon the wisdom or policy of the statute. It is simply that we cannot say that the statute offends the Bill of Rights or any other of the Amendments and the wisdom or policy is a matter for the State's resolve.

I

Precedents cited to us as *contra* rest exclusively on the precept that the Constitution condemns State legislation that trespasses upon the privacy of the incidents of marriage, upon the sanctity of the home, or upon the nurture of family life. This and only this concern has been the justification for nullification of State regulation in this area. Review of plaintiffs' authorities will reveal these as the principles underlying the referenced decisions.

In *Griswold v. Connecticut* (1965), plaintiffs' chief reliance, the Court has most recently announced its views on the question here. Striking down a State statute forbidding the use of contraceptives, the ruling was put on the right of marital privacy— held to be one of the specific guarantees of the Bill of Rights— and was also put on the sanctity of the home and family. Its thesis is epitomized by the author of the opinion, Mr. Justice Douglas, in his conclusion:

> "We deal with a right of privacy older than the Bill of Rights—older than our political parties, older than our school system. Marriage is a coming together for better or for worse, hopefully enduring and intimate to the degree of being sacred. It is an association that promotes a way of life, not causes; a harmony in living, not political faiths; a bilateral loyalty, not commercial or social projects. Yet it is an association for as noble a purpose as any involved in our prior decisions."

That *Griswold* is premised on the right of privacy and that homosexual intimacy is denunciable by the State is unequivocally demonstrated by Mr. Justice Goldberg in his concurrence in his adoption of Mr. Justice Harlan's dissenting statement in *Poe v. Ullman* (1961):

"Adultery, *homosexuality* and the like are sexual intimacies *which the State forbids*. . . but the intimacy of husband and wife is necessarily an essential and accepted feature of the institution of marriage, an institution which the State not only must allow, but which always and in every age it has fostered and protected. *It is one thing when the State exerts its power either to forbid extramarital sexuality* . . . or to say who may marry, but it is quite another when, having acknowledged a marriage and the intimacies inherent in it, it undertakes to regulate by means of the criminal law the details of that intimacy." (Emphasis added.)

Equally forceful is the succeeding paragraph of Justice Harlan:

"In sum, even though the State has determined that the use of contraceptives is as iniquitous as any act of extra-marital sexual immorality, the intrusion of the whole machinery of the criminal law into the very heart of marital privacy, requiring husband and wife to render account before a criminal tribunal of their uses of that intimacy is surely *a very different thing indeed from punishing those who establish intimacies which the law has always forbidden and which can have no claim to social protection*." (Emphasis added.)

Justice Harlan's words are nonetheless commanding merely because they were written in dissent. To begin with, as heretofore observed, they were authentically approved in *Griswold*. Moreover, he was not differing with the majority there on the merits of the substantive case but only as to the procedural reason of its dismissal. At all events, the Justice's exegesis is that of a jurist of widely acknowledged superior stature and weighty whatever its context.

With his standing, what he had further to say in *Poe v. Ullman* is worthy of high regard. On the plaintiffs' effort presently to shield the practice of homosexuality from State incrimination by according it immunity when committed in private as against public exercise, the Justice said this:

"Indeed to attempt a line between public behavior and that which is purely consensual or solitary would be to withdraw from community concern a range of subjects with which every society in civilized times has found it necessary to deal. The laws regarding marriage which provide both when the sexual powers may be used and the legal and societal context in which children are born and brought up, as well as laws *forbidding adultery, fornication, and homosexual practices which express the negative of the proposition,* confining sexuality to lawful marriage, form a pattern so deeply pressed into the substance of our social life that any Constitutional doctrine in this area must build upon that basis." (Accent added.)

Again:

"Thus, I would not suggest that *adultery, homosexuality, fornication, and incest are immune* from criminal enquiry, *however privately practiced*. So much has been explicitly recognized in acknowledging the State's rightful concern for its people's moral welfare. . . . But not to discriminate between what is involved in this case and either the traditional offenses against good morals or crimes which, though they may be committed anywhere, *happen to have been committed or concealed in the home,* would entirely misconceive the argument that is being made." (Accent added.)

Many states have long had, and still have, statutes and decisional law criminalizing conduct depicted in the Virginia legislation.

II

With no authoritative judicial bar to the proscription of homosexuality—since it is obviously no portion of marriage, home or family life—the next question is whether there is any ground for barring Virginia from branding it as criminal. If a State determines that punishment therefore, even when committed in the home, is appropriate in the promotion of morality and decency, it is not for the courts to say that the State is not free to do so. In short, it is an inquiry addressable only to the State's Legislature.

Furthermore, if the State has the burden of proving that it has a legitimate interest in the subject of the statute or that the statute is rationally supportable, Virginia has completely fulfilled this obligation. Fundamentally, the State action is simply directed to the suppression of crime, whether committed in public or in private. Both instances . . . are within the reach of the police power.

Moreover, to sustain its action, the State is not required to show that moral delinquency actually results from homosexuality. It is enough for upholding the legislation to establish that the conduct is likely to end in a contribution to moral delinquency. Plainly, it would indeed be impractible to prove the actuality of such a consequence, and the law is not so exacting.

If such a prospect or expectation was in the mind of the General Assembly of Virginia, the prophecy proved only too true in the occurrences narrated in *Lovisi v. Slayton* (EDVa. 1973, now on appeal in the Fourth Circuit). The graphic outline by the District Judge there describes just such a sexual orgy as the statute was evidently intended to punish. The Lovisis, a married couple, advertised their wish "to meet people" and in response a man came to Virginia to meet the Lovisis on several occasions. In one instance the three of them participated in acts of fellatio. Photographs of the conduct were taken by a set camera and the acts were witnessed by the wife's daughters, aged 11 and 13. The pictures were carried by them to school.

Although a questionable law is not removed from question by the lapse of any prescriptive period, the longevity of the Virginia statute does testify to the State's interest and its legitimacy. It is not an upstart notion; it has ancestry going back to Judaic and Christian law. The immediate parentage may be readily traced to the Code of Virginia of 1792. All the while the law has been kept alive, as evidenced by periodic amendments, the last in the 1968 Acts of the General Assembly of Virginia.

In sum, we believe that the sodomy statute, so long in force in Virginia, has a rational basis of State interest demonstrably legitimate and mirrored in the cited decisional law of the Supreme Court. Indeed, the Court has treated as free of infirmity a State law with a background similar to the Virginia enactment in suit.

The prayers for a declaratory judgment and an injunction invalidating the sodomy statute will be denied.

QUESTIONS

1 Though he finds the Virginia sodomy statute not unconstitutional, Judge Bryan says, "No judgment is made upon the wisdom or policy of the statute." As a matter of social policy, is such a law well advised?
2 Some states retain statutes making both fornication and adultery criminal actions. As a matter of social policy, would these states be well advised to decriminalize such actions?

Dissenting Opinion in *Doe v. Commonwealth's Attorney for City of Richmond*

Judge Robert R. Merhige, Jr.

Robert R. Merhige, Jr., is judge of the U.S. District Court, Richmond, Virginia. He is a graduate of the University of Richmond Law School, was admitted to the Virginia bar in 1942, and maintained a private practice in Richmond until 1967, when he was appointed judge.

In his dissenting opinion, Judge Merhige rejects Judge Bryan's claim that the right of privacy is applicable to sexual behavior only within a marriage relationship. According to Judge Merhige, the right of privacy is applicable to all sexual behavior (whether heterosexual or homosexual) between consenting adults in private. Accordingly, he contends, state restrictions on private consensual sex acts between adults are justified only if a compelling state interest can validly be asserted. Thus, in his view, since there is no evidence that homosexual acts between consenting adults in private cause socially significant harm, Virginia's sodomy statute is unconstitutional.

. . . Regretfully, . . . my views as to the constitutionality of the statute in question, as it applies to consenting adults acting in the privacy of their homes, [do not conform with those of the majority].

In my view, in the absence of any legitimate interest or rational basis to support the statute's application we must, without regard to our own proclivities and reluctance to judicially bar the state proscription of homosexuality, hold the statute as it applies to the plaintiffs to be violative of their rights under the Due Process Clause of the Fourteenth Amendment to the Constitution of the United States. The Supreme Court decision in *Griswold v. Connecticut* (1965), is, as the majority points out, premised on the right of privacy, but I fear my brothers have misapplied its precedential value through an apparent overadherence to its factual circumstances.

The Supreme Court has consistently held that the Due Process Clause of the Fourteenth Amendment protects the right of individuals to make personal choices, unfettered by arbitrary and purposeless restraints, in the private matters of marriage and pro-

United States District Court, E.D. Virginia. 403 F. Supp. 1199 (1975).

creation. I view those cases as standing for the principle that every individual has a right to be free from unwarranted governmental intrusion into one's decisions on private matters of intimate concern. A mature individual's choice of an adult sexual partner, in the privacy of his or her own home, would appear to me to be a decision of the utmost private and intimate concern. Private consensual sex acts between adults are matters, absent evidence that they are harmful, in which the state has no legitimate interest.

To say, as the majority does, that the right of privacy, which every citizen has, is limited to matters of marital, home or family life is unwarranted under the law. Such a contention places a distinction in marital-nonmarital matters which is inconsistent with current Supreme Court opinions and is unsupportable.

In my view, the reliance of the majority on Mr. Justice Harlan's dissenting statement in *Poe v. Ullman* (1961) is misplaced. An analysis of the cases indicates that in 1965 when *Griswold*, which invalidated a statute prohibiting the use of contraceptives by married couples, was decided, at least three of the Court, relying primarily on Mr. Justice Harlan's dissent in *Poe v. Ullman*, and Mr. Justice Harlan himself, would not have been willing to attach the right of privacy to homosexual conduct. In my view, *Griswold* applied the right of privacy to its particular factual situation. That the right of privacy is not limited to the facts of *Griswold* is demonstrated by later Supreme Court decisions. After *Griswold*, by virtue of *Eisenstadt v. Baird* (1972), the legal viability of a marital-nonmarital distinction in private sexual acts if not eliminated, was at the very least seriously impaired. In *Eisenstadt*, the Court declined to restrict the right of privacy in sexual matters to married couples:

> Yet the marital couple is not an independent entity with a mind and heart of its own, but an association of two individuals each with a separate intellectual and emotional makeup. If the right of privacy means anything, it is the right of the *individual*, married or single, to be free from unwarranted governmental intrusion into matters so fundamentally affecting a person as the decision whether to bear or beget a child.

In significantly diminishing the importance of the marital-nonmarital distinction, the Court to a great extent vitiated any implication that the state can, as suggested by Mr. Justice Harlan in *Poe v. Ullman*, forbid extra-marital sexuality, and such implications are no longer fully accurate.

> It is one thing when the State exerts its power either to forbid extra-marital sexuality altogether, or to say who may marry, but it is quite another when, having acknowledged a marriage and the intimacies inherent in it, it undertakes to regulate by means of the criminal law the details of that intimacy. (Harlan J., dissenting).

Griswold, in its context, applied the right of privacy in sexual matters to the marital relationship. *Eisenstadt*, however, clearly demonstrates that the right to privacy in sexual relationships is not limited to the marital relationship. Both *Roe v. Wade* (1973) and *Eisenstadt* cogently demonstrate that intimate personal decisions or private matters of substantial importance to the well-being of the individuals involved are protected by the Due Process Clause. The right to select consenting adult sexual partners must be considered within this category. The exercise of that right, whether heterosexual or homosexual, should not be proscribed by state regulation absent compelling justification.

This approach does not unqualifiedly sanction personal whim. If the activity in question involves more than one participant, as in the instant case, each must be capable of consenting, and each must in fact consent to the conduct for the right of privacy to attach. For example, if one of the participants in homosexual contact is a minor, or force is used to coerce one of the participants to yield, the right will not attach. Similarly, the right of privacy cannot be extended to protect conduct that takes place in publicly frequented areas. However, if the right of privacy does apply to specific courses of conduct, legitimate state restriction on personal autonomy may be justified only under the compelling state interest test.

Plaintiffs are adults seeking protection from the effects of the statute under attack in order to engage in homosexual relations in private. Viewing the issue as we are bound to, as Mr. Justice Blackmun stated in *Roe v. Wade,* "by constitutional measurement, free of emotion and predilection," it is my view that they are entitled to be protected in their right to privacy by the Due Process Clause.

The defendants, represented by the highest legal officer of the state, made no tender of any evidence which even impliedly demonstrated that homosexuality causes society any significant harm. No effort was made by the defendants to establish either a rational basis or a compelling state interest so as to justify the proscription of § 8.1–212 of the Code of Virginia, presently under attack. To suggest, as defendants do, that the prohibition of homosexual conduct will in some manner encourage new heterosexual marriages and prevent the dissolution of existing ones is unworthy of judicial response. In any event, what we know as men is not forgotten as judges—it is difficult to envision any substantial number of heterosexual marriages being in danger of dissolution because of the private sexual activities of homosexuals.

On the basis of this record one can only conclude that the sole basis of the proscription of homosexuality was what the majority refers to as the promotion of morality and decency. As salutary a legislative goal as this may be, I can find no authority for intrusion by the state into the private dwelling of a citizen. *Stanley v. Georgia* (1969) teaches us that socially condemned activity, excepting that of demonstrable external effect, is and was intended by the Constitution to be beyond the scope of state regulation when conducted within the privacy of the home. "The Constitution extends special safeguards to the privacy of the home. . . ." Whether the guarantee of personal privacy springs from the First, Fourth, Fifth, Ninth, the penumbra of the Bill of Rights, or, as I believe, in the concept of liberty guaranteed by the first section of the Fourteenth Amendment, the Supreme Court has made it clear that fundamental rights of such an intimate facet of an individual's life as sex, absent circumstances warranting intrusion by the state, are to be respected. My brothers, I respectfully suggest, have by today's ruling misinterpreted the issue—the issue centers not around morality or decency, but the constitutional right of privacy.

I respectfully note my dissent.

QUESTIONS

1 Opponents of the decriminalization of sodomy sometimes argue as follows: It is necessary that homosexual behavior, even between consenting adults in private, be considered a criminal offense; toleration of homosexual behavior would lead to long-term consequences disastrous for society. Is this a sound argument?

2 Constitutional considerations aside, would a state be well advised, as a matter of social policy, to decriminalize *all* sexual behavior between consenting adults in private?

SUGGESTED ADDITIONAL READINGS FOR CHAPTER 6

BAKER, ROBERT, and FREDERICK ELLISTON: *Philosophy and Sex,* New Revised Edition. Buffalo, N.Y.: Prometheus, 1984. This anthology contains a number of articles relevant to the topic of sexual morality.

BARNHART, J. E., and MARY ANN BARNHART: "Marital Faithfulness and Unfaithfulness." *Journal of Social Philosophy,* vol. 4, April 1973, pp. 10–15. The Barnharts argue that we should recognize the legitimacy of different marriage styles, including a marriage style that incorporates extramarital sex.

BELLIOTTI, RAYMOND A.: "A Philosophical Analysis of Sexual Ethics." *Journal of Social Philosophy,* vol. 10, September 1979, pp. 8–11. Belliotti contends that sexual interactions have a contractual basis and argues that they are morally objectionable if and only if they involve (1) deception, (2) promise-breaking, or (3) exploitation, that is, treating another *merely* as a means to one's own ends.

BERTOCCI, PETER A.: *Sex, Love, and the Person.* New York: Sheed & Ward, 1967. Bertocci emphasizes considerations of personal development and constructs a defense of conventional sexual morality.

CAMERON, PAUL: "A Case Against Homosexuality." *Human Life Review,* vol. 4, Summer 1978, pp. 17–49. As a psychologist, Cameron introduces empirical data about homosexuality. He contends that homosexuality is an undesirable life-style and argues against the liberalization of social policy (regarding homosexuality).

LEISER, BURTON M.: *Liberty, Justice and Morals,* 2d ed. New York: Macmillan, 1979. Chapter 2 of this book deals with homosexuality. In the course of constructing a case against criminal sanctions, Leiser analyzes the arguments commonly made in support of the condemnation of homosexual behavior.

TAYLOR, RICHARD: *Having Love Affairs.* Buffalo, N.Y., Prometheus, 1982. Taylor rejects the idea that adultery is immoral. He also emphasizes the values served by love affairs and defends their moral legitimacy.

VANNOY, RUSSELL: *Sex Without Love: A Philosophical Exploration.* Buffalo, N.Y.: Prometheus, 1980. Vannoy defends sex without love: "I conclude, therefore, that on the whole, sex with a humanistic non-lover is far preferable to sex with an erotic lover." Both Chapter 1, "Sex with Love vs. Sex without Love" (pp. 7–29), and Chapter 4, "Types of Sexual Philosophy: A Summary" (pp. 118–127), are especially relevant to the topic of sexual morality.

WASSERSTROM, RICHARD: "Is Adultery Immoral?" In Richard Wasserstrom, ed., *Today's Moral Problems,* 2d ed. New York: Macmillan, 1979. This helpful article investigates the various arguments that can plausibly be made in support of the claim that adultery is immoral. Wasserstrom's analysis is especially valuable in focusing attention on the presuppositions of such arguments.

WELLMAN, CARL: *Morals & Ethics.* Glenview, Ill.: Scott, Foresman, 1975. Chapter 5 of this book provides a highly readable analysis of the arguments that may be given for and against the moral acceptability of premarital sex.

WHITELEY, C. H., and W. N. WHITELEY: *Sex and Morals.* New York: Basic Books, 1967. This book as a whole is useful, but Chapter 5, on "Unfruitful Sex," is especially germane. In this chapter, the Whiteleys examine the morality of masturbation, homosexual behavior, and other types of sexual activity that cut off the possibility of procreation.

CHAPTER 7

PORNOGRAPHY AND CENSORSHIP

In 1967, the Congress of the United States, labeling the traffic in obscene and pornographic materials "a matter of national concern," established the Commission on Obscenity and Pornography. This advisory commission, whose members were appointed by the President in January 1968, was charged with initiating a thorough study of obscenity and pornography and, on the basis of such a study, submitting recommendations for the regulation of obscene and pornographic materials. In September 1970 the Commission transmitted its final report to the President and to the Congress. Its fundamental recommendation was that all legislation prohibiting the sale, exhibition, or distribution of sexual materials to *consenting adults* be repealed. However, the Commission recommended the continuation of legislation intended to protect nonconsenting adults from being confronted with sexually explicit material through public displays and unsolicited mailings. It also recommended the continuation of legislation prohibiting the commercial distribution of certain sexual material to juveniles. The Commission based its fundamental recommendation largely, though not exclusively, on its central factual finding: There is no evidence to support the contention that exposure to explicit sexual materials plays a significant role in the causation of either social harms (via antisocial behavior) or individual harms (such as severe emotional disturbance).

The report of the Commission on Obscenity and Pornography was unwelcome in many quarters. To begin with, only twelve of the Commission's eighteen members voted in support of its fundamental recommendation. In fact, the report itself features a substantial minority report that questions the factual findings as well as the recommendations of the Commission. President Richard Nixon contended that the report was completely unsatisfactory. Many members of Congress were also displeased, and there was a substantial public outcry that the conclusions of the Commission were "morally bankrupt." As a result, there has been little movement to implement its fundamental recommendation.[1]

The developments just described encourage us to pose, as the central issue of this chapter, the following ethical question: Is a government justified in limiting the access of consenting adults to pornographic materials?

LIBERTY-LIMITING PRINCIPLES

Laws limiting the access of consenting adults to pornographic materials, like all prohibitive laws, inevitably involve limitation of individual liberty. Accordingly, one way of approaching our central question is to take notice of the kinds of grounds that may be advanced to justify the limitation of individual liberty. Four suggested liberty-limiting principles are especially noteworthy:[2]

1 The harm principle—Individual liberty is justifiably limited to prevent *harm to others*.

2 The principle of legal paternalism—Individual liberty is justifiably limited to prevent *harm to self*.

3 The principle of legal moralism—Individual liberty is justifiably limited to prevent *immoral behavior*.

4 The offense principle—Individual liberty is justifiably limited to prevent *offense to others*.

The *harm principle* is the most widely accepted liberty-limiting principle. Few will dispute that the law is within its proper bounds when it restricts actions whereby one person causes harm to others. (The category of *harm to others* is understood as encompassing not only personal injury but also damage to the general welfare of society.) What remains a lively source of debate is whether any, or all, of the other suggested principles are legitimate liberty-limiting principles. According to John Stuart Mill (1806–1873), only the harm principle is a legitimate liberty-limiting principle. A short excerpt from his famous essay *On Liberty* appears in this chapter. Though Mill need not be read as unsympathetic to the offense principle, he clearly and vigorously rejects both the principle of legal paternalism and the principle of legal moralism.

According to the *principle of legal paternalism,* the law may justifiably be invoked to prevent self-harm, and thus "to protect individuals from themselves." Supporters of this principle think that the law rightfully serves much as a benevolent parent who limits his or her child's liberty in order to save the child from harm. Some, of course, often in the spirit of Mill, hotly contest the legitimacy of the principle of legal paternalism. It is said, for example, that government does not have the right to meddle in the private life of its citizens. Though there is little doubt that there are presently

---

[1]In the spring of 1985, Attorney General Edwin Meese III named an eleven-member commission to *reexamine* the issue of pornography.

[2]Joel Feinberg's discussion of such principles served as a guide for the formulations adopted here. *Social Philosophy* (Englewood Cliffs, N.J.: Prentice-Hall, 1973), chap. 2.

numerous paternalistic features in our legal system, their justifiability remains a disputed issue. The widespread law that requires motorcyclists to wear protective headgear is one apparent example of a paternalistic law.

According to the *principle of legal moralism,* the law may justifiably be invoked to prevent immoral behavior or, as it is often expressed, to "enforce morals." Such things as kidnapping, murder, and fraud are undoubtedly immoral, but there would seem to be no need to appeal to the principle of legal moralism to justify laws against them. An appeal to the harm principle already provides a widely accepted independent justification. As a result, the principle of legal moralism usually comes to the fore only when so-called victimless crimes are under discussion. Is it justifiable to legislate against homosexual relations, gambling, and smoking marijuana simply on the grounds that such activities are thought to be morally unacceptable? There are many such laws, and presumably they are intended to enforce conventional morality, but some people continue to call for their repeal on the grounds that the principle of legal moralism is an unacceptable liberty-limiting principle. To accept the principle of legal moralism, in Mill's words, is tantamount to permitting a "tyranny of the majority."

According to the *offense principle,* the law may justifiably be invoked to prevent "offensive" behavior in public. "Offensive" behavior is understood as behavior that causes shame, embarrassment, discomfort, etc., to be experienced by onlookers. The offense principle, unlike the other principles discussed above, is not ordinarily advanced to justify laws that would limit the access of *consenting* adults to pornographic materials. The offense principle, however, is sometimes advanced to justify laws that protect *nonconsenting* adults from "offensive" displays of pornography.

THE CASE FOR CENSORSHIP

Arguments in support of laws that would limit the access of consenting adults to pornographic materials can conveniently be organized by the liberty-limiting principles on which they are based.

1 Arguments Based on the Harm Principle

It is often alleged that exposure to pornography is a direct cause of crime. It is thought, on this view, that exposure to pornography is a significant casual factor in sex-related crimes such as rape. Defenders of this thesis sometimes argue for their claim by citing examples of persons exposed to pornographic material who subsequently commit sex-related crimes. Such examples, however, fail to establish that the crime, which *follows* exposure to pornography, is a *causal result* of exposure to pornography. Indeed, the Commission on Obscenity and Pornography reported that there is no evidence to support such a causal connection. On the other hand, the Commission's finding on this score continues to be hotly debated. Since the harm principle is a widely accepted liberty-limiting principle, a formidable argument for censorship emerges to the extent that a causal connection between the use of pornography and antisocial behavior can be established.

A second line of argument based on the harm principle emphasizes the alleged disastrous effects of the widespread exposure to pornography on the overall welfare of society. It is said, for example, that society will become obsessed with impersonal expressions of sexuality, that love will disappear, and that children entering such a society will be psychologically deprived. It has even been suggested that unlimited access to pornographic materials might eventually culminate in the total decay of order and civilization. "What is at stake is civilization and humanity, nothing less."[3] According to a closely related line of thought, pornography functions to break down the feelings of shame associated with sex and thereby represents a serious threat to democracy.

> To live together requires rules and a governing of the passions, and those who are without shame will be unruly and unreliable; having lost the ability to restrain themselves by observing the rules they collectively give themselves, they will have to be ruled by others. Tyranny is the natural and inevitable mode of government for the shameless and the self-indulgent who have carried liberty beyond any restraint.[4]

In the face of harm-principle arguments to the effect that widespread exposure to pornography will (in the long run) produce dire consequences for society, two responses are commonly made: (1) The anticipated dire effects will not in fact occur. (2) The anticipated effects are so speculative as not to constitute a "clear and present danger."

2 Arguments Based on the Principle of Legal Paternalism

It is often said that those exposed to pornography will be harmed by such exposure. They will, it is thought, develop or reinforce emotional problems; they will render themselves incapable of love and other human relationships necessary for a happy and satisfying life. In a more abstract and possibly rhetorical version of this argument, it is alleged that frequent exposure to pornography "depersonalizes" or "dehumanizes," and presumably such effects are at least in a broad sense harmful to the individual. Arguments based on the principle of legal paternalism are answered in two ways: (1) The alleged self-harm does not occur. (2) Regardless of the truth or falsity of the claim of self-harm, the principle of legal paternalism is not an acceptable liberty-limiting principle.

3 Arguments Based on the Principle of Legal Moralism

It is frequently claimed that there is a widespread consensus to the effect that pornography is morally repugnant. Inasmuch as the principle of legal moralism seems to allow a community to enforce its moral convictions, it follows that the access of consenting adults to pornographic materials may rightfully be restricted. Arguments thus based on the principle of legal moralism are answered in two ways: (1) The alleged consensus of moral opinion is nonexistent. (2) Regardless of the truth or falsity

[3]Irving Kristol, "Pornography, Obscenity, and the Case for Censorship," *The New York Times Magazine,* March 28, 1971, p. 113.

[4]Walter Berns, "Pornography vs. Democracy: The Case for Censorship," *Public Interest,* vol. 22, Winter 1971, p. 13.

of the claim of an existing moral consensus, the principle of legal moralism is not an acceptable liberty-limiting principle.

The morality of pornography is an important ethical issue in its own right. To some extent, of course, one's moral assessment of pornography will be a function of one's views on sexual morality in general. In one of this chapter's selections, Charles H. Keating, Jr., argues on rather traditional grounds that pornography is clearly immoral. Because Keating takes his view to be the consensus view of society, and because he explicitly endorses the principle of legal moralism, he is a vigorous proponent of censorship.

THE CASE AGAINST CENSORSHIP

The overall case against laws limiting the access of consenting adults to pornographic materials usually takes the following direction: The principle of legal paternalism is an unacceptable liberty-limiting principle; the government has no business meddling in the private affairs of its citizens since such meddling is likely to produce more harm than it prevents. The principle of legal moralism is also an unacceptable liberty-limiting principle; to enforce the moral views of the majority is, in effect, to allow a "tyranny of the majority." A government can rightfully legislate against the private activity of consenting adults only on the grounds that such activity is *harmful to others*. At the present time, however, there is no evidence that the access of consenting adults to pornographic materials presents a "clear and present danger." Thus, censorship is unwarranted.

It is sometimes further argued by opponents of censorship, in conjunction with the claim that pornography has no socially damaging consequences, that it is positively beneficial to those exposed to it and to society as a whole. Here it is said, for example, that exposure to pornography can aid normal sexual development, that it can invigorate sexual relationships, and that it can provide a socially harmless release from sexual tension. Such considerations are developed by G. L. Simons in one of the readings in this chapter.

FEMINISM AND PORNOGRAPHY

In recent years, an important new critique of pornography has arisen from a feminist point of view. In contrast to more traditional critics of pornography, feminists do not ordinarily object to the sexual explicitness that is found in pornography. Rather, their concern is rooted in the fact that pornography typically portrays *women* in a degrading and dehumanizing way. Related to this central concern is a distinction that feminists ordinarily draw between *pornography* (which is morally and socially problematic) and mere *erotica* (which is not).

In one of this chapter's selections, Helen E. Longino defines pornography as "material that explicitly represents or describes degrading and abusive sexual behavior so as to endorse and/or recommend the behavior as described." Because pornography is *injurious* to women in a number of related ways, she maintains, its production and distribution are justifiably subject to control. In essence, then, Longino presents a pro-censorship argument based on the harm principle. However, not all feminists advocate the censorship of pornography. In another of this chapter's selections, Mark R. Wicclair vigorously defends an anticensorship stance within the framework of feminism. He emphasizes the values associated with the principle of freedom of expression and calls attention to the detrimental side effects of censorship. He also maintains, against the pro-censorship feminist, that the connection between pornography and harm to women is too speculative to warrant incurring the social costs of censorship. This claim is in turn contested by Lorenne M. G. Clark in the last reading of this chapter. Clark insists that the harm to women that is produced by pornography is sufficiently direct to warrant its censorship. She also argues that pornography inhibits desirable social progress because it functions to reinforce the disadvantaged position of women.

Thomas A. Mappes

Majority Opinion in *Paris Adult Theatre I v. Slaton*

Chief Justice Warren Burger

Warren Burger is chief justice of the United States Supreme Court. Admitted to the Minnesota bar in 1931, he then spent a number of years in private practice, while simultaneously serving on the faculty of the Mitchell College of Law in St. Paul. Chief Justice Burger also served as assistant attorney general (1953–1956) and as judge of the U.S. Court of Appeals, District of Columbia Circuit (1956–1969). In 1969 he was appointed to the Supreme Court.

The state of Georgia sought an injunction against the showing of two films—*It All Comes Out in the End* and *Magic Mirror*—by the Paris Adult Theatres I and II (Atlanta). The state claimed that the films were obscene under the relevant Georgia standards. The trial court refused to grant the injunction, holding that the showing of the films could be prohibited only if it were proved that they were shown to minors or nonconsenting adults. The Supreme Court of Georgia reversed the decision of the trial court, and the Supreme Court of the United States upheld the reversal, though by a mere five-to-four majority.

In Chief Justice Burger's majority opinion, he argues that there are legitimate state interests at stake in the state regulation of consenting adults' access to obscene material. According to Chief Justice Burger, such interests include the maintenance of a decent society, the tone of commerce in large cities, and "possibly" the public safety. Chief Justice Burger acknowledges that there is no conclusive proof of a connection between obscene material and antisocial behavior, but he nevertheless considers the belief in such a connection to be a reasonable one. In arguing that state regulation of obscene material is constitutionally acceptable, he emphasizes

United States Supreme Court. 413 U.S. 49 (1973).

two points: (1) State regulation of obscene material in no way violates the constitutionally protected right to privacy. (2) State regulation of obscene material is not tantamount to restricting the communication of ideas and thus does not violate the First Amendment.

We categorically disapprove the theory, apparently adopted by the trial judge, that obscene, pornographic films acquire constitutional immunity from state regulation simply because they are exhibited for consenting adults only. This holding was properly rejected by the Georgia Supreme Court. Although we have often pointedly recognized the high importance of the state interest in regulating the exposure of obscene materials to juveniles and unconsenting adults, this Court has never declared these to be the only legitimate state interests permitting regulation of obscene material. The States have a long-recognized legitimate interest in regulating the use of obscene material in local commerce and in all places of public accommodation, as long as these regulations do not run afoul of specific constitutional prohibitions. "In an unbroken series of cases extending over a long stretch of this Court's history, it has been accepted as a postulate that 'the primary requirements of decency may be enforced against obscene publications.' "

In particular, we hold that there are legitimate state interests at stake in stemming the tide of commercialized obscenity, even assuming it is feasible to enforce effective safequards against exposure to juveniles and to the passerby. Rights and interests "other than those of the advocates are involved." These include the interest of the public in the quality of life and the total community environment, the tone of commerce in the great city centers, and, possibly, the public safety itself. The Hill-Link Minority Report of the Commission on Obscenity and Pornography indicates that there is at least an arguable correlation between obscene material and crime. Quite apart from sex crimes, however, there remains one problem of large proportions aptly described by Professor Bickel:

> It concerns the tone of the society, the mode, or to use terms that have perhaps greater currency, the style and quality of life, now and in the future. A man may be entitled to read an obscene book in his room, or expose himself indecently there. . . . We should protect his privacy. But if he demands a right to obtain the books and pictures he wants in the market and to foregather in public places—discreet, if you will, but accessible to all—with others who share his tastes, *then to grant him his right is to affect the world about the rest of us, and to impinge on other privacies.* Even supposing that each of us can, if he wishes, effectively avert the eye and stop the ear (which, in truth, we cannot), what is commonly read and seen and heard and done intrudes upon us all, want it or not.
>
> The Public Interest 25, 25–26 (Winter, 1971). (Emphasis supplied.)

As Chief Justice Warren stated there is a "right of the Nation and of the States to maintain a decent society. . . ."

But, it is argued, there is no scientific data which conclusively demonstrates that exposure to obscene materials adversely affects men and women or their society. It is urged on behalf of the petitioner that, absent such a demonstration, any kind of state regulation is "impermissible." We reject this argument. It is not for us to resolve empirical uncertainties underlying state legislation, save in the exceptional case where that legislation plainly impinges upon rights protected by the Constitution itself. Mr. Justice Brennan, speaking for the Court in *Ginsberg v. New York (1968)*, said "We do not demand of legislatures 'scientifically certain criteria of legislation.' "Although there is no conclusive proof of a connection between antisocial behavior and obscene material, the legislature of Georgia could quite reasonably determine that such a connection does or might exist. . . .

If we accept the unprovable assumption that a complete education requires the reading of certain books, and the well nigh universal belief that good books, plays, and art lift the spirit, improve the mind, enrich the human personality and develop character, can we then say that a state legislature may not act on the corollary assumption that commerce in obscene books, or public exhibitions focused on obscene conduct, have a tendency to exert a corrupting and debasing impact leading to antisocial behavior? "Many of these effects may be intangible and indistinct, but they are nonetheless real." Mr. Justice Cardozo said that all laws in Western civilization are "guided by a robust common sense. . . ." The sum of experience, including that of the past two decades, affords an ample basis for legislatures to conclude that a sensitive, key relationship of human existence, central to family life, community welfare, and the development of human personality, can be debased and distorted by crass commercial exploitation of sex. Nothing in the Constitution prohibits a State from reaching such a conclusion and acting on it legislatively simply because there is no conclusive evidence or empirical data.

It is argued that individual "free will" must govern, even in activities beyond the protection of the First Amendment and other constitutional guarantees of privacy, and that Government cannot legitimately impede an individual's desire to see or acquire obscene plays, movies, and books. We do indeed base our society on certain assumptions that people have the capacity for free choice. Most exercises of individual free choice—those in politics, religion, and expression of ideas—are explicitly protected by the Constitution. Totally unlimited play for free will, however, is not allowed in ours or any other society. We have just noted, for example, that neither the First Amendment nor "free will" precludes States from having "blue sky" laws to regulate what sellers of securities may write or publish about their wares. Such laws are to protect the weak, the uninformed, the unsuspecting, and the gullible from the exercise of their own volition. Nor do modern societies leave disposal of garbage and sewage up to the individual "free will," but impose regulation to protect both public health and the appearance of public places. States are told by some that they must await a "laissez faire" market solution to the obscenity-pornography problem, paradoxically "by people who have never otherwise had a kind word to say for laissez-faire," particularly in solving urban, commercial, and environmental pollution problems.

The States, of course, may follow such a "laissez faire" policy and drop all controls on commercialized obscenity, if that is what they prefer, just as they can ignore consumer protection in the market place, but nothing in the Constitution *compels* the States to do so with regard to matters falling within state jurisdiction. . . .

It is asserted, however, that standards for evaluating state commercial regulations are inapposite in the present context, as state regulation of access by consenting adults to obscene material violates the constitutionally protected right to privacy enjoyed by petitioners' customers. Even assuming that petitioners have vicarious standing to assert potential customers' rights, it is unavailing to compare a theatre, open to the public for a fee, with the private home of *Stanley v. Georgia* (1969) and the marital bedroom of *Griswold v. Connecticut* (1965). This Court, has, on numerous occasions, refused to hold that commercial ventures such as a motion-picture house are "private" for the purpose of civil rights litigation and civil rights statutes. The Civil Rights Act of 1964 specifically defines motion-picture houses and theatres as places of "public accommodation" covered by the Act as operations affecting commerce.

Our prior decisions recognizing a right to privacy guaranteed by the Fourteenth Amendment included "only those personal rights that can be deemed 'fundamental' or 'implicit in the concept of ordered liberty.' " This privacy right encompasses and protects the personal intimacies of the home, the family, marriage, motherhood, procreation, and child rearing. Nothing, however, in this Court's decisions intimates that there is any "fundamental" privacy right "implicit in the concept of ordered liberty" to watch obscene movies in places of public accommodation.

If obscene material unprotected by the First Amendment in itself carried with it a "penumbra" of constitutionally protected privacy, this Court would not have found it necessary to decide *Stanley* on the narrow basis of the "privacy of the home," which was hardly more than a reaffirmation that "a man's home is his castle." Moreover, we have declined to equate the privacy of the home relied on in *Stanley* with a "zone" of "privacy" that follows a distributor or a consumer of obscene materials wherever he goes. The idea of a "privacy" right and a place of public accommodation are, in this context, mutually exclusive. Conduct or depictions of conduct that the state police power can prohibit on a public street does not become automatically protected by the Constitution merely because the conduct is moved to a bar or a "live" theatre stage, any more than a "live" performance of a man and woman locked in a sexual embrace at high noon in Times Square is protected by the Constitution because they simultaneously engage in a valid political dialogue.

It is also argued that the State has no legitimate interest in "control [of] the moral content of a person's thoughts," and we need not quarrel with this. But we reject the claim that the State of Georgia is here attempting to control the minds or thoughts of those who patronize theatres. Preventing unlimited display or distribution of obscene material, which by definition lacks any serious literary, artistic, political, or scientific value as communication, is distinct from a control of reason and the intellect. Where communication of ideas, protected by the First Amendment, is not involved, nor the particular privacy of the home protected by *Stanley*, nor any of the other "areas or zones" of constitutionally protected privacy, the mere fact that, as a consequence, some human "utterances" or "thoughts" may be incidentally affected does not bar the State from acting to protect legitimate state interests. The fantasies of a drug addict are his own and beyond the reach of government, but government regulation of drug sales is not prohibited by the Constitution.

Finally, petitioners argue that conduct which directly involves "consenting adults" only has, for that sole reason, a special claim to constitutional protection. Our Constitution establishes a broad range of conditions on the exercise of power by the states, but for us to say that our Constitution incorporates the proposition that conduct involving consenting adults only is always beyond state regulation, that is a step we are unable to take. Commercial exploitation of depictions, descriptions, or exhibitions of obscene conduct on commercial premises open to the adult public falls within a State's broad power to regulate commerce and protect the public environment. The issue in this context goes beyond whether someone, or even the majority, considers the conduct depicted as "wrong" or "sinful." The States have the power to make a morally neutral judgment that public exhibition of obscene material, or commerce in such material, has a tendency to injure the community as a whole, to endanger the public safety, or to jeopardize in Chief Justice Warren's words, the States' "right . . . to maintain a decent society."

To summarize, we have today reaffirmed the basic holding of *Roth v. United States* (1957) that obscene material has no protection under the First Amendment. We have directed our holdings, not at thoughts or speech, but at depiction and description of specifically defined sexual conduct that States may regulate within limits designed to prevent infringement of First Amendment rights. We have also reaffirmed the holdings of *United States v. Reidel* (1971) and *United States v. Thirty-Seven Photographs* (1971) that commerce in obscene material is unprotected by any constitutional doctrine of privacy. In this case we hold that the States have a legitimate interest in regulating commerce in obscene material and in regulating exhibition of obscene material in places of public accommodation, including so-called "adult" theatres from which minors are excluded. In light of these holdings, nothing precludes the State of Georgia from the regulation of the allegedly obscene materials exhibited in Paris Adult Theatre I or II, provided that the applicable Georgia law, as written or authoritatively interpreted by the Georgia courts, meets the First Amendment standards set forth in *Miller v. California* (1973). . . .

QUESTIONS

1 To what extent, if at all, does the opinion of Chief Justice Burger reveal a commitment to the principle of legal moralism and/or the principle of legal paternalism?
2 Chief Justice Burger contends that state regulation of obscene material is not tantamount to restricting the communication of ideas and thus does not violate the First Amendment. Is this a defensible position?

Dissenting Opinion in *Paris Adult Theatre I v. Slaton*

Justice William Brennan

William Brennan, associate justice of the United States Supreme Court, is a graduate of the Harvard University Law School. He maintained a private law practice in Newark, New Jersey, until 1949. He then served as superior court judge (1949–1950), appellate division judge

United States Supreme Court. 413 U.S. 49 (1973).

(1950–1952), and justice of the Supreme Court of New Jersey (1952–1956). Justice Brennan was appointed to the United States Supreme Court in 1956.

Justice Brennan acknowledges that there may be a class of material—obscene material—that in itself is not protected by the First Amendment guarantee of free speech. He argues, however, that it is impossible to specifically define "obscenity," and, as a result, that state efforts to totally suppress obscene material inevitably lead to the erosion of protected speech, thus infringing on the first Amendment. Likewise, he contends, such state efforts inevitably infringe on the Fourteenth Amendment and generate "costly institutional harms." He analyzes the interests of the state in suppressing obscene material and concludes that such interests are not sufficient to "justify the substantial damage to constitutional rights and to this nation's judicial machinery."

Our experience since *Roth v. United States* (1957) requires us not only to abandon the effort to pick out obscene materials on a case-by-case basis, but also to reconsider a fundamental postulate of *Roth:* that there exists a definable class of sexually oriented expression that may be totally suppressed by the Federal and State Governments. Assuming that such a class of expression does in fact exist, I am forced to conclude that the concept of "obscenity" cannot be defined with sufficient specificity and clarity to provide fair notice to persons who create and distribute sexually oriented materials, to prevent substantial erosion of protected speech as a by-product of the attempt to suppress unprotected speech, and to avoid very costly institutional harms. Given these inevitable side-effects of state efforts to suppress what is assumed to be *unprotected* speech, we must scrutinize with care the state interest that is asserted to justify the suppression. For in the absence of some very substantial interest in suppressing such speech, we can hardly condone the ill-effects that seem to flow inevitably from the effort. . . .

Because we assumed—incorrectly, as experience has proven—that obscenity could be separated from other sexually oriented expression without significant costs either to the First Amendment or to the judicial machinery charged with the task of safe-guarding First Amendment freedoms, we had no occasion in *Roth* to probe the asserted state interest in curtailing unprotected, sexually oriented speech. Yet as we have increasingly come to appreciate the vagueness of the concept of obscenity, we have begun to recognize and articulate the state interests at stake. Significantly, in *Redrup v. New York* (1967), where we set aside findings of obscenity with regard to three sets of material, we pointed out that

> [i]n none of the cases was there a claim that the statute in question reflected a specific and limited state concern for juveniles. In none was there any suggestion of an assault upon individual privacy by publication in a manner so obtrusive as to make it impossible for an unwilling individual to avoid exposure to it. And in none was there evidence of the sort of 'pandering' which the Court found significant in *Ginzburg v. United States* (1966).

The opinions in *Redrup* and *Stanley v. Georgia* (1969) reflected our emerging view that the state interests in protecting children and in protecting unconsenting adults may stand on a different footing from the other asserted state interests. . . .

But whatever the strength of the state interests in protecting juveniles and unconsenting adults from exposure to sexually oriented materials, those interests cannot be asserted in defense of the holding of the Georgia Supreme Court in this case. That court assumed for the purposes of its decision that the films in issue were exhibited only to persons over the age of 21 who viewed them willingly and with prior knowledge of the nature of their contents. And on that assumption the state court held that the films could still be suppressed. The justification for the suppression must be found, therefore, in some independent interest in regulating the reading and viewing habits of consenting adults.

At the outset it should be noted that virtually all of the interests that might be asserted in defense of suppression, laying aside the special interests associated with distribution to juveniles and unconsenting adults, were also posited in *Stanley v. Georgia* where we held that the State could not make the "mere private possession of obscene material a crime." That decision presages the conclusions I reach here today.

In *Stanley* we pointed out that "[t]here appears to be little empirical basis for" the assertion that "exposure to obscene materials may lead to deviant sexual behavior or crimes of sexual violence." In any event, we added that "if the State is only concerned about printed or filmed materials inducing antisocial conduct, we believe that in the context of private consumption of ideas and information we should adhere to the view that '[a]mong free men, the deterrents ordinarily to be applied to prevent crime are education and punishment for violations of the law. . . .' "

Moreover, in *Stanley* we rejected as "wholly inconsistent with the philosophy of the First Amendment," the notion that there is a legitimate state concern in the "control [of] the moral content of a person's thoughts," and we held that a State "cannot constitutionally premise legislation on the desirability of controlling a person's private thoughts." That is not to say, of course, that a State must remain utterly indifferent to—and take no action bearing on—the morality of the community. The traditional description of state police power does embrace the regulation of morals as well as the health, safety, and general welfare of the citizenry. And much legislation—compulsory public education laws, civil rights laws, even the abolition of capital punishment— are grounded at least in part on a concern with the morality of the community. But the State's interest in regulating morality by suppressing obscenity, while often asserted, remains essentially unfocused and ill-defined. And, since the attempt to curtail unprotected speech necessarily spills over into the area of protected speech, the effort to serve this speculative interest through the suppression of obscene material must tread heavily on rights protected by the First Amendment.

In *Roe v. Wade* (1973), we held constitutionally invalid a state abortion law, even though we were aware of

> the sensitive and emotional nature of the abortion controversy, of the vigorous opposing views, even among physicians, and of the deep and seemingly absolute convictions that the subject inspires. One's philosophy, one's experiences, one's exposure to the raw edges of human existence, one's religious training, one's attitudes toward life and family and their values, and the moral standards one establishes and seeks to observe, are all likely to influence and to color one's thinking and conclusions about abortion.

Like the proscription of abortions, the effort to suppress obscenity is predicated on unprovable, although strongly held, assumptions about human behavior, morality, sex, and religion. The existence of these assumptions cannot validate a statute that substantially undermines the guarantees of the First Amendment, any more than the existence of similar assumptions on the issue of abortion can validate a statute that infringes the constitutionally protected privacy interests of a pregnant woman.

If, as the Court today assumes, "a state legislature may . . . act on the . . . assumption that . . . commerce in obscene books, or public exhibitions focused on obscene conduct, have a tendency to exert a corrupting and debasing impact leading to antisocial behavior," then it is hard to see how state-ordered regimentation of our minds can ever be forestalled. For if a State may, in an effort to maintain or create a particular moral tone, prescribe what its citizens cannot read or cannot see, then it would seem to follow that in pursuit of that same objective a State could decree that its citizens must read certain books or must view certain films. However laudable its goal—and that is obviously a question on which reasonable minds may differ—the State cannot proceed by means that violate the Constitution. . . .

Recognizing these principles, we have held that so-called thematic obscenity—obscenity which might persuade the viewer or reader to engage in "obscene" conduct—is not outside the protection of the First Amendment:

> It is contended that the State's action was justified because the motion picture attractively portrays a relationship which is contrary to the moral standards, the religious precepts, and the legal code of its citizenry. This argument misconceives what it is that the Constitution protects. Its guarantee is not confined to the expression of ideas that are conventional or shared by a majority. It protects advocacy of the opinion that adultery may sometimes be proper, no less than advocacy of socialism or the single tax. And in the realm of ideas it protects expression which is eloquent no less than that which is unconvincing. *Kingsley Int'l Pictures Corp. v. Regents* (1959).

Even a legitimate, sharply focused state concern for the morality of the community cannot, in other words, justify an assault on the protections of the First Amendment. Where the state interest in regulation of morality is vague and ill-defined, interference with the guarantees of the First Amendment is even more difficult to justify.

In short, while I cannot say that the interests of the State—apart from the question of juveniles and unconsenting adults—are trivial or nonexistent, I am compelled to conclude that these interests cannot justify the substantial damage to constitutional rights and to this Nation's judicial machinery that inevitably results from state efforts to bar the distribution even of unprotected material to consenting adults. I would hold, therefore, that at least in the absence of distribution to juveniles or obtrusive exposure to unconsenting adults, the First and Fourteenth Amendments prohibit the state and federal governments from attempting wholly to suppress sexually oriented materials on the basis of their allegedly "obscene" contents. Nothing in this approach precludes those governments from taking action to serve what may be strong and legitimate interests through regulation of the manner of distribution of sexually oriented material.

QUESTIONS

1 Is it impossible, as Justice Brennan believes, to specifically define "obscenity," or can a workable definition be advanced and defended?

2 Is "substantial damage to constitutional rights and to this nation's judicial machinery" the inevitable outcome of state efforts to suppress obscene material?

3 To what extent, if at all, does the opinion of Justice Brennan reveal a commitment to the principle of legal moralism?

The Harm Principle

John Stuart Mill

John Stuart Mill (1806–1873) is known primarily as an advocate of utilitarianism. Unlike most contemporary philosophers, Mill was not an academician. He had a successful career with the British East India Company and served one term as a member of Parliament. Mill's most important works include Utilitarianism, On Liberty, *and the feminist classic,* The Subjection of Women.

In this excerpt from his classic work *On Liberty* (1859), Mill contends that society is warranted in restricting individual liberty only if an action is harmful to others, never because an action in one way or another is harmful to the person who performs the action. He clearly rejects both the principle of legal paternalism and the principle of legal moralism. Mill argues on utilitarian grounds for an exclusive adherence to the harm principle, holding that society will be better off by tolerating all expressions of individual liberty that involve no harm to others, rather than by "compelling each to live as seems good to the rest." While alluding to offenses against decency, he makes it clear that certain actions may be exclusively "self-harming" when done in private and yet, when done in public, may constitute an offense against others.

The object of this Essay is to assert one very simple principle, as entitled to govern absolutely the dealings of society with the individual in the way of compulsion and control, whether the means used be physical force in the form of legal penalties, or the moral coercion of public opinion. That principle is, that the sole end for which mankind are warranted, individually or collectively, in interfering with the liberty of action of any of their number, is self-protection. That the only purpose for which power can be rightfully exercised over any member of a civilized community, against his will, is to prevent harm to others. His own good, either physical or moral, is not a sufficient warrant. He cannot rightfully be compelled to do or forbear because it will be better for him to do so, because it will make him happier, because, in the opinions of others, to do so would be wise, or even right. These are good reasons for remonstrating with him, or reasoning with him, or persuading him, or entreating him, but not for compelling him, or visiting him with any evil in case he do otherwise. To

Reprinted from the original edition of *On Liberty* (London, 1859).

justify that, the conduct from which it is desired to deter him, must be calculated to produce evil to some one else. The only part of the conduct of any one, for which he is amenable to society, is that which concerns others. In the part which merely concerns himself, his independence is, of right, absolute. Over himself, over his own body and mind, the individual is sovereign.

It is, perhaps, hardly necessary to say that this doctrine is meant to apply only to human beings in the maturity of their faculties. We are not speaking of children, or of young persons below the age which the law may fix as that of manhood and womanhood. Those who are still in a state to require being taken care of by others, must be protected against their own actions as well as against external injury. . . .

There is a sphere of action in which society, as distinguished from the individual, has, if any, only an indirect interest; comprehending all that portion of a person's life and conduct which affects only himself, or if it also affects others, only with their free, voluntary, and undeceived consent and participation. When I say only himself, I mean directly, and in the first instance: for whatever affects himself, may affect others *through* himself; and the objection which may be grounded on this contingency, will receive consideration in the sequel. This, then, is the appropriate region of human liberty. It comprises, first, the inward domain of consciousness; demanding liberty of conscience, in the most comprehensive sense; liberty of thought and feeling; absolute freedom of opinion and sentiment on all subjects, practical or speculative, scientific, moral, or theological. The liberty of expressing and publishing opinions may seem to fall under a different principle, since it belongs to that part of the conduct of an individual which concerns other people; but, being almost of as much importance as the liberty of thought itself, and resting in great part on the same reasons, is practically inseparable from it. Secondly, the principle requires liberty of tastes and pursuits; of framing the plan of our life to suit our own character; of doing as we like, subject to such consequences as may follow; without impediment from our fellow-creatures, so long as what we do does not harm them, even though they should think our conduct foolish, perverse, or wrong. Thirdly, from this liberty of each individual, follows the liberty, within the same limits, of combination among individuals; freedom to unite, for any purpose not involving harm to others: the persons combining being supposed to be of full age, and not forced or deceived.

No society in which these liberties are not, on the whole, respected, is free, whatever may be its form of government; and none is completely free in which they do not exist absolute and unqualified. The only freedom which deserves the name, is that of pursuing our own good in our own way, so long as we do not attempt to deprive others of theirs, or impede their efforts to obtain it. Each is the proper guardian of his own health, whether bodily, or mental and spiritual. Mankind are greater gainers by suffering each other to live as seems good to themselves, than by compelling each to live as seems good to the rest. . . .

Again, there are many acts which, being directly injurious only to the agents themselves, ought not to be legally interdicted, but which, if done publicly, are a violation of good manners, and coming thus within the category of offences against others, may rightfully be prohibited. Of this kind are offences against decency; on which it is unnecessary to dwell, the rather as they are only connected indirectly with our subject, the objection to publicity being equally strong in the case of many actions not in themselves condemnable, nor supposed to be so. . . .

QUESTIONS

1 Would Mill find permissible laws restricting the access of consenting adults to pornography? Would Mill find permissible laws restricting the access of minors to pornography? Would Mill find permissible laws prohibiting pornographic billboards? Explain.

2 Is it true, as Mill claims, that "Mankind are greater gainers by suffering each other to live as seems good to themselves, than by compelling each to live as seems good to the rest?"

3 Are those who are exposed to pornography themselves harmed by such exposure? If so, is the fact of self-harm sufficient to justify laws that limit the access of consenting adults to pornographic materials?

Pornography and the Public Morality

Charles H. Keating, Jr.

Charles H. Keating, Jr., is a lawyer and businessman now based in Phoenix, Arizona. In 1956, he founded Citizens for Decent Literature, Inc. Keating, who served as a member of the Commission on Obscenity and Pornography, vigorously dissented from the findings of the majority. This short selection is taken from his extensive dissenting statement.

Keating characterizes pornography as a form of prostitution; it provides sexual pleasure for a price. In his view, which he identifies as "the traditional Judeo-Christian ethic," any form of impersonal sexual activity is debasing, a violation of human dignity. The use of pornography is immoral, he contends, because it involves the pursuit of pleasure for its own sake, thereby excluding "the higher purposes and values to which pleasure is attached." In vivid contrast to John Stuart Mill, Keating explicitly endorses the principle of legal moralism. Even if it were admitted that access to pornographic material plays no significant role in the causation of social or individual harms, he insists, antipornography laws are justified. In his view, the need to protect the public morality is not only the historical reason for antipornography laws but also a sufficient justification for them.

. . . I cannot undertake consideration of the subject of pornography without commenting on its underlying philosophical and moral basis.

Reprinted from the "Statement of Charles H. Keating, Jr.," in *The Report of the Commission on Obscenity and Pornography* (Washington, D.C.: U.S. Government Printing Office, 1970).

For those who believe in God, in His absolute supremacy as the Creator and Lawgiver of life, in the dignity and destiny which He has conferred upon the human person, in the moral code that governs sexual activity—for those who believe in these "things," no argument against pornography should be necessary.

Though the meaning of pornography is generally understood, reference is seldom made to the root meaning of the term itself. This seems important to me. The Greeks had a word for it, for many "its." And the Greek word for pornography is highly significant. It comes from two Greek words, in fact: "prostitute" and "write." So, the dictionary defines pornography as "originally a description of prostitutes and their trade."

Pornography is not merely associated in this historical sense with prostitution, but it is actually a form of prostitution because it advertises and advocates "sex for sale," pleasure for a price.

The use of sexual powers is intimately bound up with both love and life, not merely with the momentary satisfaction of desire. Only a person is capable of love, but any of the lower forms of animal life can experience pleasure as a mere sense reaction. A person is much more than a body, and any form of sexual activity which is impersonal, which uses the body alone for pleasure, violates the integrity of the person and thereby reduces him to the level of an irrational and irresponsible animal.

The traditional Judeo-Christian ethic does not condemn pleasure as an evil in itself; it does condemn the pursuit of pleasure for its own sake, as an end rather than a means, deliberately excluding the higher purposes and values to which pleasure is attached. Everybody knows that the appetite for food makes the necessity of eating more palatable, more pleasurable. To eat to live is rational, sound procedure; to live to eat is an abuse of a basically good thing. The same is true of the sex drive. It serves the individual and the common good of the human race, only when it is creative, productive, when it ministers to love and life. When, however, it serves only itself, it becomes a perversion, actually an antisocial force disruptive and eventually destructive of all love and life. Every word by which the organs of sex are designated bears out this statement: genital, generative, reproductive, procreative. Love is always fruitful of lasting good; mere pleasure is of its nature transitory, barren, the only residue likely to be unhappy, remorseful memories. This thought could be amplified and graphically illustrated.

Those who speak in defense of sexual morality are accused of making sex "dirty." It's the other way around. The defenders of pornography are guilty of degrading sex. Marcel Proust, French novelist *(Sodom and Gomorrah),* described the effect of his early reading of erotica upon himself: "Oh stream of hell that undermined my adolescence." Literature is a better reflection of life than is scientific opinion; and I am certain that the testimony of men like Proust could be multiplied if someone took the time to assemble the sources.

No, the state cannot legislate virtue, cannot make moral goodness by merely enacting law; but the state can and does legislate against vices which publicly jeopardize the virtue of people who might prefer to remain virtuous. If it is not the proper function of law to offer citizens such protection, then what is it? . . .

EFFECTS OF PORNOGRAPHY

We should begin by saying the law is clear. The law founded in reason and common sense recognizes obscenity as intrinsically evil and does not demand the "clear and present danger" test so ardently advocated by [Commission on Obscenity and Pornography] Chairman Lockhart and the American Civil Liberties Union. The law, rather, proscribes pornography on the basis of the public good—protecting public health and welfare, public decency, and morality, a condition absolutely essential to the well-being of the nation. . . .

One can consult all the experts he chooses, can write reports, make studies, etc., but the fact that obscenity corrupts lies within the common sense, the reason, and the logic of every man. . . .

If man is affected by his environment, by circumstances of his life, by reading, by instruction, by anything, he is then certainly affected by pornography. The mere nature of pornography makes it impossible for pornography to effect good. Therefore, it must necessarily effect evil. Sexual immorality, more than any other causative factor, historically speaking, is the root cause of the demise of all great nations and all great peoples. (Ref. Toynbee: Moral decay from within destroyed most of the world's great civilizations.) . . .

The Commission majority bases their recommended repeal of all federal and state laws that "prohibit consensual distribution of sexual material to adults" on the statement that "extensive empirical investigation, both by the Commission and by others, provides no evidence that exposure to or use of explicit sexual materials play a significant role in the causation of social or individual harms such as crime, delinquency, sexual or nonsexual deviancy or severe emotional disturbances."

While it is a fact that a significant percentage of nationally recognized psychiatric authorities and many law enforcement officials at all levels of jurisdiction would disagree with that statement, the important point I want to make here is that the reasons for obscenity laws are *not* contained in the statement. Obscenity laws have existed historically in recognition of the need to protect the *public morality*. . . .

I submit that never in the history of modern civilization have we seen more obvious evidence of a decline in public morality than we see today. Venereal disease is at epidemic proportions and literally out of control in many large urban centers—despite medicine. Illegitimacy statistics are skyrocketing—despite the pill and other contraceptive devices—and despite the relatively easy access to abortion. Both of these social statistics reflect a promiscuous attitude toward sex which is no doubt contributed to by many factors—but certainly one factor has to be the deluge of pornography which is screaming at young people from records, motion picture screens, newsstands, the United States mail and their peer groups.

To say that pornography has no effect is patently ridiculous. I submit that if pornography does *not* affect a person—that person has a problem. Pornography is intended to arouse the sexual appetite—one of the most volatile appetites of human nature. Once that appetite is aroused, it will seek satisfaction—and the satisfaction sought—without proper moral restraints—is often reflected in the social statistics discussed above. . . .

In addition to the social problems of venereal disease and illegitimacy, it is also of

the very nature of obscenity to degrade sex and distort the role that sex plays in a normal life. There is no way to measure the terrible effects that pornography has had and is having on marital infidelity that is reflected in divorce statistics, abortions, suicide and other social problems that further reflect the decline in public morality. . . .

QUESTIONS

1 Is pornography immoral?
2 Is there a widespread consensus in American society to the effect that pornography is morally repugnant? If so, is the existence of such a consensus sufficient to justify laws that limit the access of consenting adults to pornographic materials?
3 Is the principle of legal moralism an acceptable liberty-limiting principle?

Is Pornography Beneficial?

G. L. Simons

G. L. Simons, an Englishman, is an author who has written extensively on various aspects of human sexuality. His books include A History of Sex *(1970),* A Place for Pleasure, The History of the Brothel *(1975), and* Pornography without Prejudice *(1972), from which this selection is excerpted.*

Emphasizing that individual liberty is justifiably limited only when there is clear evidence that an activity produces significant harm, Simons constructs a case against censorship. In a more positive vein, he actively defends easy access to pornography. In the first place, he argues, pornography provides pleasure without producing significant harms; moreover, pornography is socially beneficial. Simons cites evidence in support of the view that pornography can aid normal sexual development. He also contends that pornography can provide "sex by proxy" for lonely and deprived people. Finally, he contends, with regard to an especially important aspect of "sex by proxy," it is least plausible to think that the availability of pornography provides release for sexual desires that might otherwise be released through socially harmful behavior.

It is not sufficient, for the objectors' case, that they demonstrate that some harm has flowed from pornography. It would be extremely difficult to show that pornography had *never* had unfortunate consequences, but we should not make too much of this. Harm has flowed from religion, patriotism, alcohol and cigarettes without this fact impelling people to demand abolition. The harm, if established, has to be weighed against a variety of considerations before a decision can be reached as to the propriety of certain laws. Of the British Obscenity Laws the Arts Council Report comments[1] that "the harm would need to be both indisputable and very dire indeed before it could be judged to outweigh the evils and anomalies inherent in the Acts we have been asked to examine."

The onus therefore is upon the anti-pornographers to demonstrate not only that harm is caused by certain types of sexual material but that the harm is considerable: if the first is difficult the second is necessarily more so, and the attempts to date have not been impressive. It is even possible to argue that easily available pornography has a number of benefits. Many people will be familiar with the *catharsis* argument whereby pornography is said to cut down on delinquency by providing would-be criminals with substitute satisfactions. This is considered later but we mention it here to indicate that access to pornography may be socially beneficial in certain instances, and that where this is possible the requirement for anti-pornographers to *justify* their objections must be stressed.

The general conclusion[2] of the U.S. Commission was that no adequate proof had been provided that pornography was harmful to individual or society—"if a case is to be made out against 'pornography' [in 1970] it will have to be made on grounds other than demonstrated effects of a damaging personal or social nature." . . .

The heresy (to some ears) that pornography is harmless is compounded by the even greater impiety that it may be beneficial. Some of us are managing to adjust to the notion that pornography is unlikely to bring down the world in moral ruin, but the idea that it may actually do good is altogether another thing. When we read of Professor Emeritus E. T. Rasmussen, a pioneer of psychological studies in Denmark, and a government adviser, saying that there is a possibility "that pornography can be beneficial," many of us are likely to have *mixed* reactions, to say the least. In fact this thesis can be argued in a number of ways.

The simplest approach is to remark that people enjoy it. This can be seen to be true whether we rely on personal testimony or the most respectable index of all in capitalist society—"preparedness to pay." The appeal that pornography has for many people is hardly in dispute, and in a more sober social climate that would be justification enough. Today we are not quite puritan enough to deny that *pleasure* has a worthwhile place in human life: not many of us object to our food being tasty or our clothes being attractive. It was not always like this. In sterner times it was *de rigueur* to prepare food without spices and to wear the plainest clothes. The cult of puritanism reached its apotheosis in the most fanatical asceticism, where it was fashionable for holy men to wander off into a convenient desert and neglect the body to the point of cultivating its lice as "pearls of God." In such a bizarre philosophy pleasure was not only condemned in its sexual manifestations but in all areas where the body could conceivably take satisfaction. These days we are able to countenance pleasure in most fields but in many instances still the case for *sexual* pleasure has to be argued.

Pleasure is not of course its own justification. If it clearly leads to serious malaise,

---

[1]*The Obscenity Laws,* André Deutsch, 1969, p. 33.
[2]*The Report of the Commission on Obscenity and Pornography,* Part Three, II, Bantam Books, 1970, p. 169.

early death, or the *dis*pleasure of others, then there is something to be said against it. But the serious consequences have to be demonstrated: it is not enough to condemn certain forms of pleasurable experience on the grounds of *possible* ill effect. With such an approach *any* human activity could be censured and freedom would have no place. In short, if something is pleasurable and its bad effects are small or nonexistent then it is to be encouraged: opposition to such a creed should be recognized as an unwholesome antipathy to human potential. Pleasure is a good except where it is harmful (and where the harmfulness is *significant*). . . .

That pornography is enjoyable to many people is the first of the arguments in its favour. In any other field this would be argument enough. It is certainly sufficient to justify many activities that have—unlike a taste for pornography—demonstrably harmful consequences. Only in a sexually neurotic society could a tool for heightening sexual enjoyment be regarded as reprehensible and such as to warrant suppression by law. The position is well summarized[3] in the *first* of the Arts Council's twelve reasons for advocating the repeal of the Obscenity Publications Acts:

> "It is not for the State to prohibit private citizens from choosing what they may or may not enjoy in literature or art unless there were incontrovertible evidence that the result would be injurious to society. There is no such evidence."

A further point is that availability of pornography may *aid,* rather than frustrate normal sexual development. Thus in 1966, for example, the New Jersey Committee for the Right to Read presented the findings of a survey conducted among nearly a thousand psychiatrists and psychologists of that state. Amongst the various personal statements included was the view that "sexually stimulating materials" might help particular people develop a normal sex drive.[4] In similar spirit, Dr. John Money writes[5] that pornography "may encourage normal sexual development and broadmindedness," a view that may not sound well to the anti-pornographers. And even in circumstances where possible dangers of pornography are pointed out conceivable good effects are sometimes acknowledged. In a paper issued[6] by the Danish Forensic Medicine Council it is pointed out that neurotic and sexually shy people may, by reading pornographic descriptions of normal sexual activity, be freed from some of their apprehension regarding sex and may thereby attain a freer and less frustrated attitude to the sexual side of life. . . .

One argument in favour of pornography is that it can serve as a substitute for actual sexual activity involving another person or other people. This argument has two parts, relating as it does to (1) people who fantasize over *socially acceptable* modes of sexual involvement, and (2) people who fantasize over types of sexual activity that would be regarded as illegal or at least immoral. The first type relates to lonely and deprived people who for one reason or another have been unable to form "normal" sexual

---

[3]*The Obscenity Laws,* André Deutsch, 1969, p. 35.

[4]Quoted by Isadore Rubin, "What Should Parents Do About Pornography?" *Sex in the Adolescent Years,* Fontana, 1969, p. 202.

[5]John Money, contribution to "Is Pornography Harmful to Young Children?" *Sex in the Childhood Years,* Fontana, 1971, p. 181–5.

[6]Paper from the Danish Forensic Medicine Council to The Danish Penal Code Council, published in The Penal Code Council Report on Penalty for Pornography, Report No. 435, Copenhagen, 1966, pp. 78–80, and as appendix to *The Obscenity Laws,* pp. 120–4.

contacts with other people; the second type are instances of the much quoted *catharsis* argument.

One writer notes[7] that pornography can serve as a substitute for both the knowledge of which some people have been deprived and the pleasure in sexual experience which they have not enjoyed. One can well imagine men or women too inhibited to secure sexual satisfaction with other adults and where explicit sexual material can alleviate some of their misery. It is facile to remark that such people should seek psychiatric assistance or even "make an effort": the factors that prevent the forming of effective sexual liaisons are just as likely to inhibit any efforts to seek medical or other assistance. Pornography provides *sex by proxy,* and in such usage it can have a clear justification.

It is also possible to imagine circumstances in which men or women—for reasons of illness, travel or bereavement—are unable to seek sexual satisfaction with spouse or other loved one. Pornography can help here too. Again it is easy to suggest that a person abstain from sexual experience, or, if having *permanently* lost a spouse, seek out another partner. Needless to say such advice is often quite impractical—and the alternative to pornography may be prostitution or adultery. Montagu notes that pornography can serve the same purpose as "dirty jokes," allowing a person to discharge harmlessly repressed and unsatisfied sexual desires.

In this spirit, Mercier (1970) is quoted by the U.S. Commission:

> ". . . it is in periods of sexual deprivation—to which the young and the old are far more subject than those in their prime—that males, at any rate, are likely to reap psychological benefit from pornography."

And also Kenneth Tynan (1970):

> "For men on long journeys, geographically cut off from wives and mistresses, pornography can act as a portable memory, a welcome shortcut to remembered bliss, relieving tension without involving disloyalty."

It is difficult to see how anyone could object to the use of pornography in such circumstances, other than on the grounds of a morbid anti-sexuality.

The *catharsis argument* has long been put forward to suggest that availability of pornography will neutralize "aberrant" sexual tendencies and so reduce the incidence of sex crime or clearly immoral behaviour in related fields. (Before evidence is put forward for this thesis it is worth remarking that it should not be necessary to demonstrate a *reduction* in sex crime to justify repeal of the Obscenity Laws. It should be quite sufficient to show that an *increase* in crime will not ensue following repeal. We may even argue that a small increase may be tolerable if other benefits from easy access to pornography could be shown: but it is no part of the present argument to put this latter contention.)

Many psychiatrists and psychologists have favoured the catharsis argument. Chesser, for instance, sees[8] pornography as a form of voyeurism in which—as with sadomasochistic material—the desire to hurt is satisfied passively. If this is so and the

---

[7]Ashley Montagu, "Is Pornography Harmful to Young Children?" *Sex in the Childhood Years,* Fontana, 1971, p. 182.

[8]Eustace Chesser, *The Human Aspects of Sexual Deviation,* Arrow Books, 1971, p. 39.

analogy can be extended we have only to look at the character of the voyeur—generally furtive and clandestine—to realize that we have little to fear from the pornography addict. Where consumers are preoccupied with fantasy there is little danger to the rest of us. Karpman (1959), quoted by the U.S. Commission, notes that people reading "salacious literature" are less likely to become sexual offenders than those who do not since the reading often neutralizes "aberrant sexual interests." Similarly the Kronhausens have argued that "these 'unholy' instruments" may be a safety-valve for the sexual deviate and potential sex offender. And Cairns, Paul and Wishner (1962) have remarked that *obscene materials* provide a way of releasing strong sexual urges without doing harm to others.

It is easy to see the plausibility of this argument. The popularity of all forms of sexual literature—from the superficial, *sexless,* sentimentality of the popular women's magazine to the clearest "hard-core" porn—has demonstrated over the ages the perennial appetite that people have for fantasy. To an extent, a great extent with many single people and frustrated married ones, the fantasy constitutes an important part of the sex-life. The experience may be vicarious and sterile but it self-evidently fills a need for many individuals. If literature, as a *symbol* of reality, can so involve human sensitivities it is highly likely that when the sensitivities are *distorted* for one reason or another the same sublimatory function can occur: the "perverted" or potentially criminal mentality can gain satisfaction, as does the lonely unfortunate, in *sex by proxy*. If we wanted to force the potential sex criminal onto the streets in search of a human victim perhaps we would do well to deny him his sublimatory substitutes: deny him fantasy and he will be forced to go after the real thing. . . .

The importance of this possibility should be fully faced. If a causal connection *does* exist between availability of pornographic material and a *reduction* in the amount of sex crime—and the evidence is wholly consistent with this possibility rather than its converse—then people who deliberately restrict pornography by supporting repressive legislation are prime architects of sexual offences against the individual. The anti-pornographers would do well to note that their anxieties may be driving them into a position the exact opposite of the one they explicitly maintain—their commitment to reduce the amount of sexual delinquency in society.

The most that the anti-pornographers can argue is that at present the evidence is inconclusive. . . . But if the inconclusive character of the data is once admitted then the case for repressive legislation falls at once. For in a *free* society, or one supposedly aiming after freedom, social phenomena are, like individuals, innocent until proven guilty—and an activity will be permitted unless there is clear evidence of its harmful consequences. This point was well put—in the specific connection with pornography— by Bertrand Russell, talking[9] when he was well over 90 to Rupert Crawshay-Williams.

After noting how people beg the question of causation in instances such as the Moors murders (where the murders and the reading of de Sade *may* have a common cause), Russell ("Bertie") said that on the whole he disapproved of sadistic pornography being available. But when Crawshay-Williams put the catharsis view, that such material might provide a harmless release for individuals who otherwise may be dangerous,

---

[9]Rupert Crawshay-Williams, *Russell Remembered,* Oxford University Press, 1970, p. 144.

Russell said at once—"Oh, well, if that's true, then I don't see that there is anything against sadistic pornography. In fact it should be encouraged. . . ." When it was stressed that there was no preponderating evidence either way Russell argued that we should fall back on an overriding principle—"in this case the principle of free speech."

Thus in the absence of evidence of harm we should be permissive. Any other view is totalitarian. . . .

If human enjoyment *per se* is not to be condemned then it is not too rash to say that we *know* pornography does good. We can easily produce our witnesses to testify to experiencing pleasure. If in the face of this—and no other favourable argument— we are unable to demonstrate a countervailing harm, then the case for easy availability of pornography is unassailable. If, in such circumstances, we find some people un- convinced it is futile to seek out further empirical data. Once we commit ourselves to the notion that the evil nature of something is axiomatic we tacitly concede that evidence is largely irrelevant to our position. If pornography never fails to fill us with predictable loathing then statistics on crime, or measured statements by careful specialists, will not be useful: our reactions will stay the same. But in this event we would do well to reflect on what our emotions tell us of our own mentality. . . .

QUESTIONS

1 Is pornography of genuine benefit to society?
2 Consider the following claim: Seeking access to pornographic materials is not in a person's best self-interest because the immediate pleasure that pornography provides is far outweighed by its detrimental impact on the person in the long run. Is this a defensible position?
3 If the access of consenting adults to pornographic materials were left totally unregulated, what would be the long-term impact on the general welfare? Would the results, on balance, be desirable or undesirable?

Pornography, Oppression, and Freedom: A Closer Look

Helen E. Longino

Helen E. Longino is associate professor of philosophy at Mills College. Her research interests are in the philosophy of science and in feminist philosophy; her published articles include "Evidence and Hypothesis," "Scientific Objectivity and the Logics of Science," and "Body, Bias and Behavior."

Longino constructs a case against pornography from a feminist point of view. She begins by defining pornography in such a way as to distinguish it from both erotica

Reprinted with permission of the author from Laura Lederer, ed., *Take Back the Night: Women on Pornography* (New York: William Morrow, 1980). Copyright © by Helen E. Longino.

and moral realism; pornography is "material that explicitly represents or describes degrading and abusive sexual behavior so as to endorse and/or recommend the behavior as described." In Longino's view, pornography is immoral not because it is sexually explicit but because it typically portrays women in a degrading and dehumanizing way. She explicitly identifies a number of related ways in which pornography is injurious to women. Because of pornography's injurious character, she concludes, its production and distribution are justifiably subject to control.

I. INTRODUCTION

The much-touted sexual revolution of the 1960's and 1970's not only freed various modes of sexual behavior from the constraints of social disapproval, but also made possible a flood of pornographic material. According to figures provided by WAVPM (Women Against Violence in Pornography and Media), the number of pornographic magazines available at newsstands has grown from zero in 1953 to forty in 1977, while sales of pornographic films in Los Angeles alone have grown from $15 million in 1969 to $85 million in 1976.[1]

Traditionally, pornography was condemned as immoral because it presented sexually explicit material in a manner designed to appeal to "prurient interests" or a "morbid" interest in nudity and sexuality, material which furthermore lacked any redeeming social value and which exceeded "customary limits of candor." While these phrases, taken from a definition of "obscenity" proposed in the 1954 American Law Institute's *Model Penal Code,*[2] require some criteria of application to eliminate vagueness, it seems that what is objectionable is the explicit description or representation of bodily parts or sexual behavior for the purpose of inducing sexual stimulation or pleasure on the part of the reader or viewer. This kind of objection is part of a sexual ethic that subordinates sex to procreation and condemns all sexual interactions outside of legitimated marriage. It is this code which was the primary target of the sexual revolutionaries in the 1960's, and which has given way in many areas to more open standards of sexual behavior.

One of the beneficial results of the sexual revolution has been a growing acceptance of the distinction between questions of sexual mores and questions of morality. This distinction underlies the old slogan, "Make love, not war," and takes harm to others as the defining characteristic of immorality. What is immoral is behavior which causes injury to or violation of another person or people. Such injury may be physical or it may be psychological. To cause pain to another, to lie to another, to hinder another in the exercise of her or his rights, to exploit another, to degrade another, to misrepresent and slander another are instances of immoral behavior. Masturbation or engaging voluntarily in sexual intercourse with another consenting adult of the same or the other sex, as long as neither injury nor violation of either individual or another is involved, are not immoral. Some sexual behavior is morally objectionable, but not because of

---

[1]*Women Against Violence in Pornography and Media Newspage,* Vol. II, No. 5, June 1978; and Judith Reisman in *Women Against Violence in Pornography and Media Proposal.*
[2]American Law Institute *Model Penal Code,* sec. 251.4.

its sexual character. Thus, adultery is immoral not because it involves sexual intercourse with someone to whom one is not legally married, but because it involves breaking a promise (of sexual and emotional fidelity to one's spouse). Sadistic, abusive, or forced sex is immoral because it injures and violates another.

The detachment of sexual chastity from moral virtue implies that we cannot condemn forms of sexual behavior merely because they strike us as distasteful or subversive of the Protestant work ethic, or because they depart from standards of behavior we have individually adopted. It has thus seemed to imply that no matter how offensive we might find pornography, we must tolerate it in the name of freedom from illegitimate repression. I wish to argue that this is not so, that pornography is immoral because it is harmful to people.

II WHAT IS PORNOGRAPHY?

I define pornography as *verbal or pictorial explicit representations of sexual behavior that,* in the words of the Commission on Obscenity and Pornography, *have as a distinguishing characteristic "the degrading and demeaning portrayal of the role and status of the human female. . . as a mere sexual object to be exploited and manipulated sexually."* [3] In pornographic books, magazines, and films, women are represented as passive and as slavishily dependent upon men. The role of female characters is limited to the provision of sexual services to men. To the extent that women's sexual pleasure is represented at all, it is subordinated to that of men and is never an end in itself as is the sexual pleasure of men. What pleases women is the use of their bodies to satisfy male desires. While the sexual objectification of women is common to all pornography, women are the recipients of even worse treatment in violent pornography, in which women characters are killed, tortured, gang-raped, mutilated, bound, and otherwise abused, as a means of providing sexual stimulation or pleasure to the male characters. It is this development which has attracted the attention of feminists and been the stimulus to an analysis of pornography in general. [4]

Not all sexually explicit material is pornography, nor is all material which contains representations of sexual abuse and degradation pornography.

A representation of a sexual encounter between adult persons which is characterized by mutual respect is, once we have disentangled sexuality and morality, not morally objectionable. Such a representation would be one in which the desires and experiences of each participant were regarded by the other participants as having a validity and a subjective importance equal to those of the individual's own desire and experiences. In such an encounter, each participant acknowledges the other participant's basic human dignity and personhood. Similarly, a representation of a nude human body (in whole or in part) in such a manner that the person shown maintains self-respect—e.g., is not

---

[3]*Report of the Commission on Obscenity and Pornography* (New York: Bantam Books, 1970), p. 239. The Commission, of course, concluded that the demeaning content of pornography did not adversely affect male attitudes toward women.

[4]Among recent feminist discussions are Diana Russell, "Pornography: A Feminist Perspective" and Susan Griffin, "On Pornography," *Chrysalis,* Vol. I, No. 4, 1978; and Ann Garry, "Pornography and Respect for Women," *Social Theory and Practice,* Vol. 4, Spring 1978, pp. 395–421.

portrayed in a degrading position—would not be morally objectionable. The educational films of the National Sex Forum, as well as a certain amount of erotic literature and art, fall into this category. While some erotic materials are beyond the standards of modesty held by some individuals, they are not for this reason immoral.

A representation of a sexual encounter which is not characterized by mutual respect, in which at least one of the parties is treated in a manner beneath her or his dignity as a human being, is no longer simple erotica. That a representation is of degrading behavior does not in itself, however, make it pornographic. Whether or not it is pornographic is a function of contextual features. Books and films may contain descriptions or representations of a rape in order to explore the consequences of such an assault upon its victim. What is being shown is abusive or degrading behavior which attempts to deny the humanity and dignity of the person assaulted, yet the context surrounding the representation, through its exploration of the consequences of the act, acknowledges and reaffirms her dignity. Such books and films, far from being pornographic, are (or can be) highly moral, and fall into the category of moral realism.

What makes a work a work of pornography, then, is not simply its representation of degrading and abusive sexual encounters, but its implicit, if not explicit, approval and recommendation of sexual behavior that is immoral, i.e., that physically or psychologically violates the personhood of one of the participants. Pornography, then, is verbal or pictorial material which represents or describes sexual behavior that is degrading or abusive to one or more of the participants *in such a way as to endorse the degradation*. The participants so treated in virtually all heterosexual pornography are women or children, so heterosexual pornography is, as a matter of fact, material which endorses sexual behavior that is degrading and/or abusive to women and children. As I use the term "sexual behavior," this includes sexual encounters between persons, behavior which produces sexual stimulation or pleasure for one of the participants, and behavior which is preparatory to or invites sexual activity. Behavior that is degrading or abusive includes physical harm or abuse, and physical or psychological coercion. In addition, behavior which ignores or devalues the real interests, desires, and experiences of one or more participants in any way is degrading. Finally, that a person has chosen or consented to be harmed, abused, or subjected to coercion does not alter the degrading character of such behavior.

Pornography communicates its endorsement of the behavior it represents by various features of the pornographic context: the degradation of the female characters is represented as providing pleasure to the participant males and, even worse, to the participant females, and there is no suggestion that this sort of treatment of others is inappropriate to their status as human beings. These two features are together sufficient to constitute endorsement of the represented behavior. The contextual features which make material pornographic are intrinsic to the material. In addition to these, extrinsic features, such as the purpose for which the material is presented—i.e., the sexual arousal/pleasure/satisfaction of its (mostly) male consumers—or an accompanying text, may reinforce or make explicit the endorsement. Representations which in and of themselves do not show or endorse degrading behavior may be put into a pornographic context by juxtaposition with others that are degrading, or by a text which invites or recommends degrading behavior toward the subject represented. In such a case the whole complex—the series of representations or representations with text—is pornographic.

The distinction I have sketched is one that applies most clearly to sequential material—a verbal or pictorial (filmed) story—which represents an action and provides a temporal context for it. In showing the before and after, a narrator or film-maker has plenty of opportunity to acknowledge the dignity of the person violated or clearly to refuse to do so. It is somewhat more difficult to apply the distinction to single still representations. The contextual features cited above, however, are clearly present in still photographs or pictures that glamorize degradaton and sexual violence. Phonograph album covers and advertisements offer some prime examples of such glamorization. Their representations of women in chains (the Ohio Players), or bound by ropes and black and blue (the Rolling Stones) are considered high-quality commercial "art" and glossily prettify the violence they represent. Since the standard function of prettification and glamorization is the communication of desirability, these albums and ads are communicating the desirability of violence against women. Representations of women bound or chained, particularly those of women bound in such a way as to make their breasts, or genital or anal areas vulnerable to any passerby, endorse the scene they represent by the absence of any indication that this treatment of women is in any way inappropriate.

To summarize: Pornography is not just the explicit representation or description of sexual behavior, nor even the explicit representation or description of sexual behavior which is degrading and/or abusive to women. Rather, it is material that explicitly represents or describes degrading and abusive sexual behavior so as to endorse and/or recommend the behavior as described. The contextual features, moreover, which communicate such endorsement are intrinsic to the material; that is, they are features whose removal or alteration would change the representation or description.

This account of pornography is underlined by the etymology and original meaning of the word "pornography." *The Oxford English Dictionary* defines pornography as "Description of the life, manners, etc. of prostitutes and their patrons [from πόρνη (porne) meaning "harlot" and γράφειν (graphein) meaning "to write"]; hence the expression or suggestion of obscene or unchaste subjects in literature or art."[5]

Let us consider the first part of the definition for a moment. In the transactions between prostitutes and their clients, prostitutes are paid, directly or indirectly, for the use of their bodies by the client for sexual pleasure.[6] Traditionally males have obtained from female prostitutes what they could not or did not wish to get from their wives or women friends, who, because of the character of their relation to the male, must be accorded some measure of human respect. While there are limits to what treatment is seen as appropriate toward women as wives or women friends, the prostitute as prostitute exists to provide sexual pleasure to males. The female characters of contemporary pornography also exist to provide pleasure to males, but in the pornographic context no pretense is made to regard them as parties to a contractual arrange-

---

[5]*The Oxford English Dictionary*, Compact Edition (London: Oxford University Press, 1971), p. 2242.

[6]In talking of prostitution here, I refer to the concept of, rather than the reality of, prostitution. The same is true of my remarks about relationships between women and their husbands or men friends.

ment. Rather, the anonymity of these characters makes each one Everywoman, thus suggesting not only that all women are appropriate subjects for the enactment of the most bizarre and demeaning male sexual fantasies, but also that this is their primary purpose. The recent escalation of violence in pornography—the presentation of scenes of bondage, rape, and torture of women for the sexual stimulation of the male characters or male viewers—while shocking in itself, is from this point of view merely a more vicious extension of a genre whose success depends on treating women in a manner beneath their dignity as human beings.

III PORNOGRAPHY: LIES AND VIOLENCE AGAINST WOMEN

What is wrong with pornography, then, is its degrading and dehumanizing portrayal of women (and *not* its sexual content). Pornography, by its very nature, requires that women be subordinate to men and mere instruments for the fulfillment of male fantasies. To accomplish this, pornography must lie. Pornography lies when it says that our sexual life is or ought to be subordinate to the service of men, that our pleasure consists in pleasing men and not ourselves, that we are depraved, that we are fit subjects for rape, bondage, torture, and murder. Pornography lies explicitly about women's sexuality, and through such lies fosters more lies about our humanity, our dignity, and our personhood.

Moreover, since nothing is alleged to justify the treatment of the female characters of pornography save their womanhood, pornography depicts all women as fit objects of violence by virtue of their sex alone. Because it is simply being female that, in the pornographic vision, justifies being violated, the lies of pornography are lies about all women. Each work of pornography is on its own libelous and defamatory, yet gains power through being reinforced by every other pornographic work. The sheer number of pornographic productions expands the moral issue to include not only assessing the morality or immorality of individual works, but also the meaning and force of the mass production of pornography.

The pornographic view of women is thoroughly entrenched in a booming portion of the publishing, film, and recording industries, reaching and affecting not only all who look to such sources for sexual stimulation, but also those of us who are forced into an awareness of it as we peruse magazines at newsstands and record albums in record stores, as we check the entertainment sections of city newspapers, or even as we approach a counter to pay for groceries. It is not necessary to spend a great deal of time reading or viewing pornographic material to absorb its male-centered definition of women. No longer confined within plain brown wrappers, it jumps out from billboards that proclaim "Live X-rated Girls!" or "Angels in Pain" or "Hot and Wild," and from magazine covers displaying a woman's genital area being spread open to the viewer by her own fingers.[7] Thus, even men who do not frequent pornographic shops and movie houses are supported in the sexist objectification of women by their environment. Women, too, are crippled by internalizing as self-images those that are

---

[7]This was a full-color magazine cover seen in a rack at the check-out counter of a corner delicatessen.

presented to us by pornographers. Isolated from one another and with no source of support for an alternative view of female sexuality, we may not always find the strength to resist a message that dominates the common cultural media.

The entrenchment of pornography in our culture also gives it a significance quite beyond its explicit sexual messages. To suggest, as pornography does, that the primary purpose of women is to provide sexual pleasure to men is to deny that women are independently human or have a status equal to that of men. It is, moreover, to deny our equality at one of the most intimate levels of human experience. This denial is especially powerful in a hierarchical, class society such as ours, in which individuals feel good about themselves by feeling superior to others. Men in our society have a vested interest in maintaining their belief in the inferiority of the female sex, so that no matter how oppressed and exploited by the society in which they live and work, they can feel that they are at least superior to someone or some category of individuals— a woman or women. Pornography, by presenting women as wanton, depraved, and made for the sexual use of men, caters directly to that interest.[8] The very intimate nature of sexuality which makes pornography so corrosive also protects it from explicit public discussion. The consequent lack of any explicit social disavowal of the pornographic image of women enables this image to continue fostering sexist attitudes even as the society publicly proclaims its (as yet timid) commitment to sexual equality.

In addition to finding a connection between the pornographic view of women and the denial to us of our full human rights, women are beginning to connect the consumption of pornography with commiting rape and other acts of sexual violence against women. Contrary to the findings of the Commission on Obscenity and Pornography a growing body of research is documenting (1) a correlation between exposure to representations of violence and the committing of violent acts generally, and (2) a correlation between exposure to pornographic materials and the committing of sexually abusive or violent acts against women.[9] While more study is needed to establish precisely what the causal relations are, clearly so-called hard-core pornography is not innocent.

From "snuff" films and miserable magazines in pornographic stores to *Hustler,* to phonograph album covers and advertisements, to *Vogue,* pornography has come to occupy its own niche in the communications and entertainment media and to acquire a quasi-institutional character (signaled by the use of diminutives such as "porn" or "porno" to refer to pornographic material, as though such familiar naming could take the hurt out). Its acceptance by the mass media, whatever the motivation, means a cultural endorsement of its message. As much as the materials themselves, the social

---

[8]Pornography thus becomes another tool of capitalism. One feature of some contemporary pornography— the use of Black and Asian women in both still photographs and films—exploits the racism as well as the sexism of its white consumers. For a discussion of the interplay between racism and sexism under capitalism as it relates to violent crimes against women, see Angela Y. Davis, "Rape, Racism, and the Capitalist Setting," *The Black Scholar,* Vol. 9, No. 7, April 1978.

[9]Urie Bronfenbrenner, *Two Worlds of Childhood* (New York: Russell Sage Foundation, 1970); H. J. Eysenck and D.K.B. Nias, *Sex, Violence and the Media* (New York: St. Martin's Press, 1978); and Michael Goldstein, Harold Kant, and John Hartman, *Pornography and Sexual Deviance* (Berkeley: University of California Press, 1973); and the papers by Diana Russell, Pauline Bart, and Irene Diamond included in [Laura Lederer, ed., *Take Back the Night* (New York: William Morrow, 1980)].

tolerance of these degrading and distorted images of women in such quantities is harmful to us, since it indicates a general willingness to see women in ways incompatible with our fundamental human dignity and thus to justify treating us in those ways.[10] The tolerance of pornographic representations of the rape, bondage, and torture of women helps to create and maintain a climate more tolerant of the actual physical abuse of women.[11] The tendency on the part of the legal system to view the victim of a rape as responsible for the crime against her is but one manifestation of this.

In sum, pornography is injurious to women in at least three distinct ways:

1 Pornography, especially violent pornography, is implicated in the committing of crimes of violence against women.

2 Pornography is the vehicle for the dissemination of a deep and vicious lie about women. It is defamatory and libelous.

3 The diffusion of such a distorted view of women's nature in our society as it exists today supports sexist (i.e., male-centered) attitudes, and thus reinforces the oppression and exploitation of women.

Society's tolerance of pornography, especially pornography on the contemporary massive scale, reinforces each of these modes of injury: By not disavowing the lie, it supports the male-centered myth that women are inferior and subordinate creatures. Thus, it contributes to the maintenance of a climate tolerant of both psychological and physical violence against women. . . .

CONCLUSION

I have defined pornography in such a way as to distinguish it from erotica and from moral realism, and have argued that it is defamatory and libelous toward women, that it condones crimes against women, and that it invites tolerance of the social, economic, and cultural oppression of women. The production and distribution of pornographic material is thus a social and moral wrong. Contrasting both the current volume of pornographic production and its growing infiltration of the communications media with the status of women in this culture makes clear the necessity for its control. . . .

Appeals for action against pornography are sometimes brushed aside with the claim that such action is a diversion from the primary task of feminists—the elimination of sexism and of sexual inequality. This approach focuses on the enjoyment rather than the manufacture of pornography, and sees it as merely a product of sexism which will disappear when the latter has been overcome and the sexes are socially and econom-

---

[10]This tolerance has a linguistic parallel in the growing acceptance and use of nonhuman nouns such as "chick," "bird," "filly," "fox," "doll," "babe," "skirt," etc., to refer to women, and of verbs of harm such as "fuck," "screw," "bang," to refer to sexual intercourse. See Robert Baker and Frederick Elliston, " 'Pricks' and 'Chicks': A Plea for Persons." *Philosophy and Sex* (Buffalo, N.Y.: Prometheus Books, 1975).

[11]This is supported by the fact that in Denmark the number of rapes committed has increased while the number of rapes reported to the authorities has decreased over the past twelve years. See *WAVPM Newspage*, Vol. II, No. 5, June, 1978, quoting M. Harry, "Denmark Today—The Causes and Effects of Sexual Liberty" (paper presented to The Responsible Society, London, England, 1976). See also Eysenck and Nias, *Sex, Violence and the Media* (New York: St. Martin's Press, 1978), pp. 120–124.

ically equal. Pornography cannot be separated from sexism in this way: Sexism is not just a set of attitudes regarding the inferiority of women but the behaviors and social and economic rules that manifest such attitudes. Both the manufacture and distribution of pornography and the enjoyment of it are instances of sexist behavior. The enjoyment of pornography on the part of individuals will presumably decline as such individuals begin to accord women their status as fully human. A cultural climate which tolerates the degrading representation of women is not a climate which facilitates the development of respect for women. Furthermore, the demand for pornography is stimulated not just by the sexism of individuals but by the pornography industry itself. Thus, both as a social phenomenon and in its effect on individuals, pornography, far from being a mere product, nourishes sexism. The campaign against it is an essential component of women's struggle for legal, economic, and social equality, one which requires the support of all feminists.[12]

QUESTIONS

1 Do you accept Longino's suggested definition of pornography? Is there a better definition?
2 Emphasizing the injurious impact of pornography on women, Longino concludes that "its control is necessary." What specific controls on the production and distribution of pornography would you endorse?

Feminism, Pornography, and Censorship
Mark R. Wicclair

Mark R. Wicclair is associate professor of philosophy at West Virginia University. His published articles include "The Abortion Controversy and the Claim that This Body is Mine," "Human Rights and Intervention," and "Is Prostitution Morally Wrong?"

Wicclair operates with the definition of pornography suggested by Longino. He argues, however, that censorship of pornography is not a legitimate means to achieve the aims of feminism, nor is it even the most effective means. In his view, there is a strong presumption against censorship; this presumption is based on the principle of freedom of expression as well as the likely negative side effects of censorship. In rejecting the argument that censorship of pornography is a legitimate means of preventing harm to women, he claims that the connection between

[12]Many women helped me to develop and crystallize the ideas presented in this paper. I would especially like to thank Michele Farrell, Laura Lederer, Pamela Miller, and Dianne Romain for their comments in conversation and on the first written draft. Portions of this material were presented orally to members of the Society for Women in Philosophy and to participants in the workshops on "What Is Pornography?" at the Conference on Feminist Perspectives on Pornography, San Francisco, November 17, 18, and 19, 1978. Their discussion was invaluable in helping me to see problems and to clarify the ideas presented here.

pornography and harm to women is too speculative to warrant incurring the costs of censorship. In addition to emphasizing the costs of censorship, Wicclair warns against overestimating its expected benefits. He concludes by presenting the pro-censorship feminist with a series of difficulties.

It is sometimes claimed that pornography is objectionable because it violates conventional standards of sexual morality. Although feminists tend to agree that pornography is objectionable, they reject this particular argument against it.[1] This argument is unacceptable to feminists because it is associated with an oppressive Puritanical sexual ethic that inhibits the sexual fulfillment of all people, but especially women. In order to understand why feminists find pornography objectionable, one has to keep in mind that they do not equate the terms "pornographic" and "sexually explicit." Rather, sexually explicit material is said to be "pornographic" only if it depicts and condones the exploitation, dehumanization, subordination, abuse, or denigration of women. By definition, then, all pornography is sexist and misogynistic. Some pornographic material has the additional feature of depicting and condoning acts of *violence* against women (e.g., rape, brutality, torture, sadism). Thus there is a world of difference between harmless "erotica" and pornography. Whereas erotica depicts sexual activity in a manner which is designed to produce sexual arousal and is therefore likely to be objectionable only to those who subscribe to a Puritanical sexual ethic, pornography is "material that explicitly represents or describes degrading and abusive sexual behavior so as to endorse and/or recommend the behavior as described."[2]

Despite the general agreement among feminists that pornography, understood in the way just described, is objectionable, they are sharply divided over the question of its *censorship*. Whereas some feminists find pornography to be so objectionable that they call for its censorship, others oppose this proposal.[3] I will argue that anyone who supports the aims of feminism and who seeks the liberation of all people should reject the censorship of pornography.[4]

When discussing censorship, it is important to keep in mind that there are very strong reasons to be wary of its use. In our society, the importance of the principle of freedom of expression—an anticensorship principle—is widely recognized. The ability to speak one's mind and to express ideas and feelings without the threat of legal penalties or government control is rightly perceived as an essential feature of a

[1] Just as the civil rights movement in the United States in the 1950's and 1960's included many people who were not black, so one does not have to be a woman to be a feminist. As I am using the term, a feminist is any person who supports the fundamental goal of feminism: the liberation of women.

[2] Helen E. Longino, "Pornography, Oppression, and Freedom: A Closer Look," in Laura Lederer, ed., *Take Back the Night* (New York: William Morrow and Company, Inc., 1980), p. 44. Longino also stipulates that the sexual activities depicted in pornography are degrading or abusive *to women*.

[3] In response to the generally pro-censorship Women Against Violence in Pornography and Media, other feminists have organized the Feminist Anti-Censorship Taskforce.

[4] Until recently, advocates of censorship have pressed for laws which prohibit or restrict the production, distribution, sale, and exhibition of pornographic material. However, pro-censorship feminists have hit upon a new strategy: Ordinances which stipulate that pornography is *sex discrimination*, enabling women to file sex discrimination lawsuits against producers, distributors, sellers, and exhibitors of pornography. Most of the criticisms of censorship which I discuss in this paper apply to both strategies.

truly free society. Moreover, an environment that tolerates the expression of differing views about politics, art, lifestyles, etc., encourages progress and aids in the search for truth and justice. In addition to the many important values associated with the principle of freedom of expression, it is also necessary to consider likely negative side effects of censorship. There is a serious risk that once any censorship is allowed, the power to censor will, over time, expand in unintended and undesirable directions (the "slippery slope"). This is not mere speculation, for such an expansion of the power to censor is to be expected in view of the fact that it is extremely difficult, if not impossible, to formulate unequivocal and unambiguous criteria of censorship. Then, too, the power to censor can all too easily be abused or misused. Even though it may arise in a genuine effort to promote the general welfare and to protect certain rights, officials and groups might use the power to censor as a means to advance their own interests and values and to suppress the rights, interests, and values of others. Thus, given the value of freedom of expression and the many dangers associated with censorship, there is a strong *prima facie* case against censorship. In other words, advocates of censorship have the burden of showing that there are sufficiently strong overriding reasons which would justify it in a specific area.

Like racist and antisemitic material, sexist and misogynistic films, books, and magazines surely deserve condemnation. But censorship is another matter. In view of the strength of the case against censorship in general, it is unwise to advocate it merely to prevent depicting morally objectionable practices in a favorable light. Fortunately, proponents of the censorship of pornography tend to recognize this, for they usually base their call for censorship on a claim about the *effects* of pornography. Pornography, it is held, is *injurious* or *harmful* to women because it fosters the objectionable practices that it depicts. Pornography generally is said to promote the exploitation, humiliation, denigration, subordination, etc., of women; and pornography that depicts acts of violence against women is said to cause murder, rape, assault, and other acts of violence. On the basis of the "harm principle"—a widely accepted principle that allows us to restrict someone's freedom in order to prevent harm to others—it would appear to be justified to override the principle of freedom of expression and to restrict the freedom of would-be producers, distributors, sellers, exhibitors, and consumers of pornography. In short it seems that censorship of pornography is a legitimate means of preventing harm to women.

However, there are a number of problems associated with this attempt to justify censorship. To begin with, it is essential to recognize the important difference between words and images, on the one hand, and actions, on the other hand. A would-be rapist poses a *direct* threat to his intended victim, and by stopping him, we prevent an act of violence. But if there is a connection between the depiction of a rape—even one which appears to condone it—and someone's committing an act of violence against a woman, the connection is relatively *indirect;* and stopping the production, distribution, sale, and exhibition of depictions of rape does not directly restrict the freedom of would-be rapists to commit acts of violence against women. In recognition of the important difference between restricting words and images and preventing harmful behavior, exceptions to the principle of freedom of expression are generally thought to be justified only if words or images present a "clear and present danger" of harm or injury. Thus, to cite a standard example, it is justified to stop someone from falsely shouting "Fire!" in a crowded theater, for this exclamation is likely to cause a panic that would result in serious injury and even death.

It is doubtful that pornography satisfies the "clear and present danger" condition. For there does not seem to be conclusive evidence that establishes its *causal* significance. Most studies are limited to violent pornography. And even though some of these studies do suggest a *temporary* impact on *attitudes* (e.g., those who view violent pornography may be more likely to express the view that women seek and "enjoy" violence), this does not show that viewing violent pornography causes violent *behavior*. Moreover, there is some evidence suggesting that the effect on attitudes is only temporary and that it can be effectively counteracted by additional information.[5]

But even if there is no conclusive evidence that pornography causes harm, is it not reasonable to "play it safe," and does this not require censorship? Unfortunately, the situation is not as simple as this question appears to suggest. For one thing, it is sometimes claimed that exposure to pornography has a "cathartic" effect and that it therefore produces a net *reduction* in harm to women. This claim is based upon two assumptions, neither of which has been proven to be false: (1) Men who are not already violence-prone are more likely to be "turned off" than to be "turned on" by depictions of rape, brutality, dismemberment, etc. (2) For men in the latter category, exposure to pornography can function as a substitute for actually causing harm. It is also necessary to recall that there are significant values associated with the principle of freedom of expression, and that a failure to observe it involves a number of serious dangers. Since censorship has costs which are substantial and not merely speculative, the more speculative the connection between pornography and harm to women, the less basis there is for incurring the costs associated with censorship.

Just as it is easy to overlook the negative side of censorship, it is also common to overplay its positive effects. Surely it would be foolish to think that outlawing anti-semitism in sexually explicit material would have halted the slaughter of Jews in Hitler Germany or that prohibiting racism in sexually explicit material would reduce the suffering of Blacks in South Africa. Similarly, in view of the violent nature of American society generally and the degree to which sexism persists to this day, it is unlikely that censorship of pornography by itself would produce any significant improvement in the condition of women in the United States. Fortunately, there are other, more effective and direct means of eliminating sexism than by censoring pornography. Passage and strict enforcement of the Equal Rights Amendment, electing feminists to local, state, and national political office, achieving genuine economic justice for women, and securing their reproductive freedom will do considerably more to foster the genuine liberation of women in the United States than will the censorship of pornography. With respect to rape and other acts of violence, it has often been noted that American society is extremely violent, and, sadly, there are no magic solutions to the problems of rape and violence. But the magnitude of the problem suggests that censoring pornography only addresses a symptom and not the underlying disease. Although there

---

[5]For a discussion of research on the effects of pornography, see Edward Donnerstein and Neil Malamuth, eds., *Pornography and Sexual Aggression* (New York: Academic Press, 1984).

is still much dispute about the causes of violence generally and rape in particular, it is unlikely that there will be a serious reduction in acts of violence against women until there are rather drastic changes in the socioeconomic environment and in the criminal justice system.

Those who remain concerned about the possible contribution of pornography to violence and sexism should keep in mind that it can be "neutralized" in ways that avoid the dangers of censorship. One important alternative to government censorship is to help people understand why pornography is objectionable and why it and its message should be rejected. This can be accomplished by means of educational campaigns, discussions of pornography on radio and television and at public forums, letter writing, and educational picketing. In addition, attempts might be made to prevent or restrict the production, distribution, display, sale, and consumption of pornographic material by means of organized pickets, boycotts, and the like. Such direct measures by private citizens raise some troubling questions, but the dangers and risks which they pose are considerably less than those associated with government censorship.

There are several other reasons for questioning the view that the sexist and misogynistic nature of pornography justifies its censorship. Some of the more important of these include the following:

1 Although pornography depicts some practices that are both morally objectionable and illegal (e.g., rape, assault, torture), many of the practices depicted are morally repugnant *but do not break any law*. Thus, for example, our legal system does not explicitly prohibit men from treating women in a degrading or humiliating manner; and with some exceptions, it is not a crime to treat women exclusively as sex objects or to use them exclusively as means and not ends. But is it not odd to recommend making illegal the production, distribution, sale, and exhibition of materials that depict practices that are not themselves illegal?

2 It is essential that laws be clearly formulated and that vagueness be avoided. Vague laws can have a "chilling effect" on unobjectionable activities, and they tend to undermine the fair and effective enforcement of the law by giving police, prosecutors, and judges too much discretionary power. But those who call for the censorship of pornography on the grounds that it is sexist and misogynistic fail to recognize the difficulty of formulating laws which would have an acceptable degree of clarity and specificity. Proponents of censorship use terms like "degrading," "humiliating," "debasing," "exploitative," and "subordination of women." But these terms are far from unambiguous. In fact, they are highly subjective in the sense that different people have different criteria for deciding when something is degrading, humiliating, etc. For example, someone might think that the depiction of an unmarried female or a lesbian couple having and enjoying sex is "demeaning" or "debasing." Thus, in order to prevent censorship from being applied in unintended and undesirable ways, it is necessary to offer clear and unambiguous operational criteria for terms like "demeaning," "humiliating," etc. But the feasibility of articulating generally acceptable criteria of this sort remains highly doubtful.

3 Sexually explicit material that depicts violence against women or that depicts sexist practices is said to be subject to censorship only if it *condones* the objectionable practices. Thus, for example, news films, documentaries, and works which take a critical stance toward those practices are not to be censored. But it is exceedingly difficult in many cases to determine the "point of view" of films, books, photographs, etc.[6] If scholars who have advanced degrees in film, literature, and art can come to no general consensus about the "meaning" or "message" of certain works, is it plausible to think that prosecutors, judges, and juries are likely to fare any better?

4 Why call for the censorship of sexist and misognistic books, magazines, films, and photographs only if they include an explicit depiction of *sexual activity*? There is no conclusive evidence showing that material that includes a depiction of sexual activity has a greater causal impact on attitudes and behavior.[7] Moreover, it will not do to claim that such material is not worthy of protection under the principle of freedom of expression. Surely, many works which include explicit depictions of sex are not totally devoid of significant and challenging ideas. Consequently, advocates of censorship are faced with a dilemma: Either they can call for the censorship of *all* material that contains objectionable images of women; or they can call for censorship only in the case of sexually explicit materials of that nature. If the first alternative is chosen, then given the pervasiveness of objectionable portrayals of women in art, literature, and the mass media, very little would be immune from censorship. But in view of the strong *prima facie* case against censorship, this seems unacceptable. On the other hand, if the second alternative is chosen, this invites the suspicion that the restriction to sexual material is based upon the very same Puritanical sexual ethic which feminists rightly tend to reject. I am not suggesting that feminists who call for censorship wish to champion sexual oppression. But it is noteworthy that many conservatives who generally do not support the aims of feminism align themselves with feminists who advocate censoring pornography.

5 Why call for censorship of materials only if they depict violence or other objectionable practices in relation to *women*? Wouldn't consistency require censoring *all* violence and material that portrays *anyone* in a derogatory light? But this is clearly unacceptable. For so much of our culture is permeated with images of violence and morally distasteful treatment of people that it is hard to think of many films, television programs, books, or magazines which would be totally immune from censorship. Censorship would be the rule rather than an exception, and such pervasive censorship is incompatible with a truly free society. It also won't do to limit censorship to members of historically oppressed groups (e.g., women, Blacks, Jews). First, it is very unlikely that such "preferential censorship" would be accepted by the majority for too long. Sooner or later others would object and/or press for protection too. Second, in view of the significant costs of censorship, even if it were limited to the protection of historically oppressed groups, it would not be justified unless there were a demonstrable "clear and present danger;" and this remains doubtful. But what about the view that

---

[6]An informative illustration of how a film can resist unambiguous classification as either progressive or retrograde from a feminist perspective is provided in Lucy Fischer and Marcia Landy, *"The Eyes of Laura Mars:* A Binocular Critique," *Screen,* Vol. 23, Nos. 3–4 (September–October 1982).

[7]In fact some researchers claim that the impact of depictions of violence is *greater* in material which is *not* pornographic. See, for example, the contribution of Edward Donnerstein and Daniel Linz to a section on pornography, "Pornography: Love or Death?" in *Film Comment,* vol. 20, No. 6 (December 1984), pp. 34–35.

only pornography should be subject to censorship because *women need special protection*? This position is also unacceptable. For since men are victimized by acts of racism, antisemitism, and violence, and since there is no evidence to prove that depictions of objectionable practices have a greater effect on behavior in pornographic material than they do in nonpornographic material, this position seems to be based on the sexist assumption that women need greater protection than men because they are "naturally" more fragile and vulnerable.

I have tried to show that censorship of pornography is neither the most effective nor a legitimate means to achieve the aims of feminism. Much pornographic material is morally repugnant, but there are less costly ways to express one's moral outrage and to attempt to "neutralize" pornography than by censorship. Moreover, pornography is only a relatively minor manifestation of the sexist practices and institutions that still pervade our society. Hence, the genuine liberation of women—and men—is best served by directly attacking those oppressive practices and institutions. It may be easier to identify and attack pornography—and to win some battles—but the payoff would be slight, and the negative side effects would be substantial.

QUESTIONS

1 Does the easy availability of pornography pose a "clear and present danger" to women?
2 Considering the aims of feminism, are feminists well-advised to endorse the censorship of pornography?

Liberalism and Pornography

Lorenne M. G. Clark

Lorenne M. G. Clark, barrister and solicitor, is in private practice in Digby, Nova Scotia. A former professor of philosophy and criminology at the University of Toronto, she is coauthor of Rape: The Price of Coercive Sexuality *(1977) and coeditor of* The Sexism of Social and Political Theory *(1979). Among her published articles is "Privacy, Property, Freedom and the Family."*

Clark interprets pornography as a species of hate literature against women, functioning as a method of socialization to maintain traditional male advantages. She contends that the standard liberal argument against censorship (i.e., that it inhibits social progress) is not applicable with regard to pornography because pornography itself inhibits desirable social progress, by reinforcing the disadvantaged position of women. In Clark's view, pornography ought to be prohibited simply because it is an affront to the dignity of women, but she also

Reprinted with permission of the author from David Copp and Susan Wendell, eds., *Pornography and Censorship* (Buffalo, N.Y.: Prometheus, 1983), pp. 52–57. An earlier version of this material was published by Resources for Feminist Research, Toronto.

maintains that the harm to women that is produced by pornography is sufficiently *direct* to warrant its censorship.

Feminists and civil libertarians are now at complete loggerheads over [the issue of pornography]. The trend among feminists is clear. More and more of them are coming to see pornography as a species of hate literature.[1] Hate literature seeks to make one dislike and despise the people depicted, to make those persons seem inferior and unworthy of our respect. It seeks to set them apart and to show them as relevantly different from "us" in a way which justifies "us" in treating them differently, or it shows them as deserving to be treated badly because they have no respect for "us" or "our" values. What it must do to succeed is enforce a radical sense of their difference, their non-identity, with "us," a difference which is either utterly distasteful to "us," or one utterly opposed to "our" shared goals and values. It may also revel in their misery in an attempt to encourage feelings of wishing to contribute to that misery by doing things to them we would not think of doing to those we perceive to be relevantly similar to ourselves. So too with pornography. To achieve its impact, it relies on depicting women in humiliating, degrading, and violently abusive situations. To make matters worse, it frequently depicts them willingly, even avidly, suffering and inviting such treatment. As is obvious to even the naivest of eyes, such re-creations of heterosexual behavior and relationships feed traditional male phantasies about both themselves and women, and glorify the traditional advantages men have enjoyed in relation to exploitation of female sexuality.

Pornography is a method of socialization; it is the tangible, palpable embodiment of the imposition of the dominant sexual system which is a part of the dominant sex-class system. It is a vivid depiction of how to deploy male sexuality in just the way that will achieve maximum effect in maintaining the *status quo*. Pornography would be neither desired nor tolerated within any system other than one which sprang from the differential attribution of rights of ownership in which women and children are forms of sexual property, and in which they must either like it or quite literally lump it. It is a morality which stresses female passivity and submissiveness, and it encourages the actualization of such states through active aggression and violence. Pornography has very little to do with sex, certainly with any conception of egalitarian sexual relations between the sexes, but it has everything to do with showing how to use sexuality as an instrument of active oppression, and that is why it is wrong. Some allege that it also feeds female phantasies about themselves and men, but that is certainly being questioned, at least in so far as it can be said that there is any hard empirical data to support it.

That there should be no laws prohibiting the manufacture, sale, and distribution of pornography has traditionally and increasingly been defended as a freedom of speech, and freedom of press, issue. It is alleged that the reading or viewing of such material does not cause any harm, or that if it does, it is harm only to those who willingly consent to it. The premise that it doesn't cause harm is defended by arguing that it relates only to the phantasy level and does not translate itself into interpersonal behavior. And it goes further than this to argue that, indeed, it provides a healthy outlet, a cathartic effect, for those who might otherwise be tempted to act out their phantasies. Those who oppose pornography, particularly those who advocate its prohibition, are treated as Victorian prudes with sexual hangups. Women who object to it are seen as up-tight, unliberated, and just not "with it," sexually speaking.

The general principle underlying the liberal view is of course that expressed by Mill in "On Liberty," who argued against any form of censorship on the ground that it was only through the free flow of information that the true and the false could be separated. Prohibitions against the dissemination of any form of information function to preserve the *status quo* and to prevent the development of a critically reflective morality which is itself necessary to pave the way for needed social change. The principle has much to be said for it. But that cannot change the fact that when it is uncritically made to apply within a domain characterized by inequality and by frankly abusive behavior, a domain which is fundamentally shaped by a framework of social relations and institutions which makes all sexual relationships between men and women fundamentally coercive in nature,[2] it is bound to produce results which will be unacceptable because harmful to those who are in the preexisting inferior position and who stand to be most affected by the attitudes and beliefs, as well as the practices, of those who use it.

The liberal argument has been that such material isn't harmful at all, and certainly cannot be seen as harmful because it functions merely to inflame male sexual desire. What is the harm if all it does is give a guy a bit of a rush? And it is right here that we must begin our critique. Surely we must acknowledge at least two things. First, it is not "normal" to get one's rushes from just anything. Secondly, if one gets desirable reactions from things which create a clear and substantial risk to others, then one can justifiably be prohibited from getting them that way. Persons who get their sexual stimulation from watching the atrocities perpetrated against the Jews during the holocaust are not regarded as "normal," and rightly so. Furthermore, we do not feel that we are infringing any legitimate rights of others in preventing them access to material designed to provide sexual stimulation by this means. And the reasons for that are at least two-fold. First, as history has made all too clear, actions of this particular species do not remain at the level of mere phantasy. They have been acted out on the grand scale, so grand as to make any rational and reflective person aware that the possibility of a correlation between thought and action is at least strong enough to justify the imposition of prohibitions against material of this sort. Second, it stems from recognizing that even if the actual actions themselves are not acted out, the attitudes and beliefs of the persons enjoying it reflect attitudes toward the objects of the actions which are bad in themselves and which are bound to produce practical effects in real life, if only to be expressed in bigoted and racist attitudes. All of the same arguments apply to material which depicts black people in degrading, humiliating, and abusive circumstances. Such material is, in itself, an affront to the dignity of the objects depicted, not least because they *are* being depicted purely as objects, dehumanized and depersonalized instruments for the satisfaction of someone else's perverted tastes.

The same case can be made with respect to heterosexual pornography.[3] As Camille Le Grand puts it, "pornography teaches society to view women as less than human. It is this view which keeps women as victims."[4] The typical way in which women are depicted in pornography certainly reflects a view of them as inferior to men, as inherently masochistic, and as primarily of value as instruments for the satisfaction of male lust. That is, in itself, offensive to women, and is a straightforward objective affront to their dignity as equal persons. So on that ground alone, pornography ought to be prohibited, just as we prohibit material depicting other social groups in such a fashion.

Of course, we could hardly argue within the parameters of our present culture that it is abnormal for males to react as they do to pornography. It is, unfortunately, all too normal, at least where we have any notion of statistical normality in mind. But neither is it unusual for rape victims to feel shamed, humiliated, and degraded by being raped; this is "normal" in the culture, but from any more rational perspective, it certainly is not "normal" in any normative sense. Much of recent efforts around the issue of rape have been designed specifically to change the perspective which rape victims have on that experience. Rape victims can come to see the assaultive behavior perpetrated against them as legitimizing the anger which is appropriate to the nature of the attack. In short, it is possible both to identify the specific effects of socialization within a male supremacist and sexually coercive society, and to offset these effects with appropriate reconceptualization of the event. Women can come to identify the masochism and victimization into which they have been socialized, and can then act both to counteract it, and to be sublimely angry at a culture which socialized them into that mode. So, too, it should be possible for men to identify the sadism and attitudes of sexual aggressivity into which they are socialized and so act both to counteract them, and to be angry at a social system that produced that response. In short, *it is not a mark of personal depravity or immorality to be aroused by such material*. Given the cultural pattern of which it is a manifestation, that is not at all surprising. Indeed, it is just what we would expect. But what must be recognized is that it *is* a socialized response, and that it is a response about which men as well as women should be both concerned and angry. And certainly, once its cultural roots are exposed, it is a response which should not be seen as needing or justifying the sale and distribution of the material which elicited it. Women must object to pornography because it both reflects and reinforces the patterns of socialization appropriate to a system based on the unequal status of the sexes, in which women are consistently regarded and treated as the inferiors, and the sexual property, of men. The socialization it brings about is *in itself* a limitation of the autonomy of women. Men ought to object to it for the same reason, and they ought to recognize that the socialization it brings about in terms of their self-images and internalized standards of conduct is also undesirable, given any commitment to the notion of sexual equality.

To the extent that men are able to internalize the conviction that women and men are equal persons, and that men are not justified in using physical coercion to force women into sexual servitude, they must recognize that the pleasurable responses they get from pornography are inappropriate to that conviction and are destructive to their ability to form self-images consistent with it. But that does not entail that they are in any sense to blame for those responses: they had as little choice about that as they did about their names. But we have, then, given strong arguments in support of the view that the eliciting of a pleasurable response is not in itself any reason to condone the sale and distribution of pornography, and that a proper understanding of the nature and causes of that response gives men as well as women solid grounds for objecting to the material which occasioned it. I believe that many more men would be able to understand and accept the feminist perspective on pornography if they could come to realize that they are not responsible for their sexual responses to it given the pattern of socialization which exists to mould us all into a set of social relations which institutionalizes male aggression and female passivity.

Thus, pornography is harmful, both to women and to men, because it encourages men to combat feelings of inadequacy and low self-esteem by being aggressive and sadistic and women to feel shamed and humiliated just for being women. It encourages just that radical difference between men and women which allows men to see women as deserving of treatment they would refrain from subjecting someone to whom they perceived to be like themselves. To the extent that it also encourages women to combat insecurity and low self-esteem by becoming passive and masochistic, it presents even clearer dangers to them than it does to men, since it creates the conditions for their own victimization, but the damage it does to men who do not identify themselves as aggressive and superior to women cannot be underestimated either. However, that does not end the argument with defenders of liberalism, because their argument then moves on to the assertion that the harm to women is not direct enough to justify the legal prohibition of pornography. Frankly, I think that the argument that pornography is intrinsically offensive to the dignity of women ought to carry the day, but in the interests of completeness I want to go on to consider the other arguments that are brought to pornography's defence.

Apart from this notion of being intrinsically offensive and an infringement of the rights of women, it will be argued that even if pornography is harmful to the user, it does not lead to direct harm to women, because the phantasies it supports remain phantasies, and it in fact prevents direct harm to women through its cathartic effect. I may say at the outset that I'm not at all impressed with either of these arguments. So far as the first is concerned, there is plenty of hard evidence available which supports the contention that role modeling has a powerful effect on human behavior. Studies of wife and child abuse consistently attest to the fact that there is a strong correlation between those who are abusers and those who come from family situations which were themselves abusive. The battered child becomes the battering parent; the son who witnessed his father battering his mother, and who was himself battered, becomes a battering husband.[5] Also, the evidence about the effect of violence depicted on television on the behavior of children also points strongly in this direction.[6] People tend to act out and operationalize the behavior that they see typically acted out around them. And surely that is hardly surprising. It is what has kept civilization going. If we weren't able to perpetuate the patterns of behavior developed through cultural organization we wouldn't have come very far. So far as I know, however, there is no hard data to support the catharsis theory. It is a theory espoused by those who are looking for a rationale, though doubtless it has its roots in their awareness that they read pornography but don't rape and brutalize women. But raping and brutalizing women isn't the only harm that can be perpetrated against women. But so far there is little empirical support offered for the view that pornography feeds only the phantasy.

Most psychiatric literature dealing with the "perversions" asserts that some people remain content with the phantasy while others do not.[7] But no one knows what differentiates the one who does actualize it from the one who doesn't. If this argument is going to be effective, it must be empirically demonstrated that this is so, and surely we cannot predict until the data is in that those who don't so outnumber those who do that we should, in the interests of an open society, tolerate the risk that some will. And since we are all imprisoned by the cultural stereotypes and the patterns of socialization appropriate to a society based on the sexual coercion of one sex by the other, how can those who do read it assert with certainty that they do not cause harm to women? They are hardly the best judges. As rape makes clear again, there is nowhere greater difference in perception than there is in the confusion surrounding rape and seduction. The men believe they are merely seducing, but the women perceive it as rape. And who is to judge? Certainly it is unfair to permit only those who are the perpetrators of such behavior to have a say in its interpretation.

While the liberal principle behind opposition to censorship is based on a recognition that desirable social change requires public access to information which challenges the beliefs and practices of the *status quo,* what it does not acknowledge is that information which supports the *status quo* through providing role models which advocate the use or threat of coercion as a technique of social control directed at a clearly identifiable group depicted as inferior, subordinate, and subhuman, works against the interest both of desirable social change and of the members of the subgroup so identified. This has been clearly acknowledged in the case of violently antisemitic and other forms of racist literature. The same principles apply with respect to violently anti-female literature, and the same conclusion should follow. But this cannot come about until it is recognized and acknowledged that the dissemination of such material is itself a harm to the members of the group involved. . . .

NOTES

1 Among the articles that spring readily to mind are Morgan, Robin, "Theory and Practice: Pornography and Rape," *Going Too Far,* Random House, N.Y., 1977, Ch. IV, pp. 163–69; Russell, Diana, "Pornography: A Feminist Perspective," unpublished paper; Brownmiller, Susan, *Against Our Will,* Simon & Schuster, N.Y., 1975, pp. 394–6; and Shear, Marie, "Free Meat Talks Back," *J. of Communication,* Vol. 26, No. 1, Winter, 1976, pp. 38–9.
2 Clark, Lorenne M. G., and Lewis, Debra J., *Rape: The Price of Coercive Sexuality,* Canadian Women's Educational Press, Toronto, 1977, Chs. 7 and 8 in particular.
3 Indeed, it is true of male homosexual pornography as well. But in the interest of not legislating in the interest of others, I am not advocating that we should prohibit this species of pornography. If men object to it, as in my view they should, whether homo- or heterosexual, it is up to them to express their opposition. Certainly I do not wish to infringe the rights homosexuals have to look at what they like, even though I cannot say with certainty that I am not adversely affected by it.
4 Quoted in Russell, Diana, "Pornography: A Feminist Perspective," *op. cit.,* p. 7, no reference given.
5 See, for example, Martin, Del, *Battered Wives,* Glide Publications, San Francisco, 1976, pp. 22–3; Pizzey, Erin, *Scream Quietly or the Neighbours Will Hear,* Penguin Books, Eng-

land, 1974, Ch. 4; Van Stolk, Mary, *The Battered Child in Canada*, McClelland & Stewart, Toronto, 1972, pp. 23–7.

6 Bandura, A., Ross, D., and Ross, S. A., "Transmission of Aggression Through Imitation of Aggressive Models," *J. Abnormal and Social Psychology*, 63, No. 3, 575–82.

7 Kraft-Ebbing, Richard von, *Psychopathia Sexualis*, 11th ed. rev. and enlarged, Stuttgard, 1901, pp. 94–5; Freud, S., *Introductory Lectures on Psycho-Analysis*, Standard Edition, 16:306.

QUESTIONS

1 Is pornography correctly understood as a species of hate literature against women?

2 Would the censorship of pornography, on balance, tend more to inhibit or enhance social progress?

SUGGESTED ADDITIONAL READINGS FOR CHAPTER 7

BERGER, FRED R.: *Freedom of Expression*. Belmont, Calif.: Wadsworth, 1980. This anthology, which addresses a number of issues related to freedom of expression, includes two notable selections relevant to the problem of pornography and censorship. The first selection, "The Moral Theory of Free Speech and Obscenity Law" (pp. 99–127), is by David A. J. Richards. The second selection, "Women Fight Back" (pp. 128–133), is an excerpt from Susan Brownmiller's *Against Our Will: Men, Women and Rape* (1975).

COPP, DAVID and SUSAN WENDELL: *Pornography and Censorship*. Buffalo, N.Y.: Prometheus, 1983. Part I of this anthology contains a number of excellent philosophical essays. Part II contains essays by social scientists on the question of whether the wide availability of pornography has harmful consequences. Part III contains judicial essays.

DECEW, JUDITH WAGNER: "Violent Pornography: Censorship, Morality and Social Alternatives." *Journal of Applied Philosophy*, vol. 1, March 1984, pp. 79–93. DeCew discusses the morality of violent pornography. She does not endorse its censorship but also finds other suggested social responses to be unsatisfactory.

DEVLIN, PATRICK: *The Enforcement of Morals*. New York: Oxford University Press, 1965. Lord Devlin, a prominent English judge, is the foremost contemporary spokesperson for the legitimacy of the principle of legal moralism. This short book contains seven of his essays.

DYAL, ROBERT: "Is Pornography Good for You?" *Southwestern Journal of Philosophy*, vol. 7, Fall 1976, pp. 95–118. Dyal argues that pornographic materials ought not to be subject to censorship. He also encourages individuals to loosen "autonomous controls" so as "to explore the aesthetic possibilities, cultural dimensions, and existential depths opened up by pornography."

FEINBERG, JOEL: *Social Philosophy*. Englewood Cliffs, N.J.: Prentice-Hall, 1973. Chapters 2 and 3 of this book provide a very helpful discussion of liberty-limiting principles.

HOLBROOK, DAVID, ed.: *The Case against Pornography*. New York: Library Press, 1973. In this anthology, Holbrook has collected nearly thirty selections, all of which develop (from various points of view) the case against pornography.

LEDERER, LAURA, ed.: *Take Back the Night: Women on Pornography*. New York: Morrow, 1980. This anthology provides an overall indictment of pornography from a feminist point of view.

LEISER, BURTON M.: *Liberty, Justice and Morals,* 2d ed. New York: Macmillan, 1979. Part I of this book features a broad-based discussion of the enforcement of morals. Chapter 1 critiques the views of Lord Devlin. Successive chapters center on homosexuality, contraception and abortion, freedom of the press and censorship, and obscenity and pornography.

The Report of the Commission on Obscenity and Pornography. Washington, D.C.: U.S. Government Printing Office, 1970. This famous report, whose findings are frequently referred to in contemporary discussions of censorship, contains a wealth of valuable material. Part Three, Section II centers on the effects of erotic material.

CHAPTER 8

ECONOMIC JUSTICE AND WELFARE

Should everyone in an affluent society be guaranteed a minimum income? Should people be required to work for that income even if they do not want to work? Should they even be required to work at menial jobs they dislike? Is it morally correct to tax the income of those who work to provide incomes for those who do not? Questions such as these fall in the domain of economic justice. Answering them requires theorizing about what constitutes an economically just society. And this in turn involves us with questions about the part that a just government ought to play in the economic sphere and about the justifiable limits of government interference with individual liberty.

AN ECONOMICALLY JUST SOCIETY

In a short story called "The Babylon Lottery," Jorge Luis Borges describes a society in which all societal benefits and obligations are distributed solely on the basis of a periodic lottery. Simply as the result of chance, an individual may be a slave at one period, an influential government official the following period, and a person sentenced to jail the third one. When the temporary social and economic status of the individual is determined, no account is taken of the actual contribution the individual has made to society during a preceding period or of the individual's merit, effort, or need.[1] Such a situation strikes us as capricious. We are accustomed to think that there are some valid principles according to which a society's economic goods are distributed, even

---

[1]Jorge Luis Borges, "The Babylon Lottery," in *Ficciones* (New York: Grove Press, 1956).

if we disagree about what principles ought to be operative in an economically just society. In the United States, for example, aid to families with dependent children is sometimes said to be distributed on the basis of need; promotions in government offices and business firms are supposedly awarded on the basis of merit and achievement; and the high incomes of physicians and lawyers are assumed to be due them on the basis of either the contribution they make to society or the effort they exert in preparing for their professions.

Whether, and to what extent, merit and achievement, need, effort, or productive contribution ought to be taken into account in the distribution of society's benefits are basic questions of economic justice. In responding to these questions, philosophers propose and defend various principles of economic justice. According to their proposals, the wealth of society ought to be distributed on the basis of one or more of the following sorts of principles.

1 To each individual an equal share
2 To each individual according to that individual's needs
3 To each individual according to that individual's ability, merit, or achievement
4 To each individual according to that individual's effort
5 To each individual according to that individual's actual productive contribution

We will briefly discuss the first two principles since they are especially relevant to the readings in the chapter.

1 To Each Individual an Equal Share

On the strict equalitarian view, each individual in a society is entitled to the same portion of goods as every other individual. All human beings, just because they are human beings, have a right to an equal share in the wealth of their society. This strict equalitarian approach to economic justice leads to the paradoxical view that individual differences are to be ignored when society's resources are allocated. Since these resources include food, shelter, and health care, as well as money, it appears absurd to maintain that each individual in society ought to receive a share identical to that of every other individual. Distribution strictly on the basis of the principle of equal sharing would seem to result in an unjust situation in which the 200-pound man receives the same amount of food as the 140-pound one and the diabetic and paraplegic receive no more health care than the healthy individual who needs neither insulin nor physical therapy. Since there are differences between individuals, it is apparently more equalitarian to distribute according to the principle of need. Equal distribution would then require not identical distribution but the equal satisfaction of needs.

2 To Each Individual According to That Individual's Needs

If distribution is to be made on the basis of needs, it is necessary to determine just what "needs" are to be considered. Are we to consider only essential or basic needs, such as the needs for food, clothing, shelter, and health care? Or are we to consider other human needs as well, such as the needs for aesthetic satisfaction and intellectual stimulation? Whether the principle of need is accepted as the sole determinant of a just economic distribution within the society or as only one of those determinants, we need to select some way of ranking needs. If, on the one hand, the principle of need is the sole determinant of economic justice, we must first determine which needs take precedence—which needs must be satisfied before the satisfaction of other less important needs is even considered. Then, if our society has the means to meet not only these basic needs but other less essential ones, we should find some way of ranking the latter. (For example, does an artist's need for subsidy take precedence over a scientist's need to satisfy his or her intellectual curiosity about the existence of life on Mars?) If, on the other hand, the principle of need is to be taken as only one of the determinants of economic justice, we ought to determine which needs must be satisfied before some other principle can be used as the basis for distributing the rest of society's wealth.

Note that if either or both of the first two principles are held to be the determinants of economic justice, the individual's own efforts, achievements, abilities, or productive contribution to society are not taken into account in determining that individual's benefits. When the claim is made, for example, that each family in a society ought to be guaranteed a minimum yearly income, the moral justification for this claim is often given either in terms of the principle of need or in terms of the conjunction of that principle and the principle of equal sharing: All human beings, just because they are human beings, are entitled to equal treatment in some important respects; they are entitled, for example, to have at least their most basic needs met by the society to which they belong.

Philosophers, economists, and others vehemently disagree about whether the principle of need (or the principle of need in conjunction with the principle of equal sharing) is a morally acceptable principle of economic justice. Their disagreements stem in large measure from their different conceptions of the moral ideal around which the institutions of any just society ought to be organized. To understand three of the major positions on the relation between need and economic justice, it is necessary to understand the part played by certain moral ideals in theories about (1) the morally correct role of the government in economic activity and (2) the justifiable limits of government interference with individual liberty.

LIBERTY, EQUALITY, NEED, AND GOVERNMENT INTERFERENCE

Two moral ideals, liberty and equality, are of key importance in conceptions of justice in general, and economic justice in particular. A *libertarian* or *individualist* conception of justice, for example, holds *liberty* to be the ultimate moral ideal. A *socialist* conception of justice takes *social equality* to be the ultimate ideal; and a *liberal* conception of justice tries to combine both equality and liberty into one ultimate moral ideal.

The Libertarian Conception of Justice

For the libertarian, a society is just when individual liberty is maximized. To understand the libertarian position on liberty, it is necessary to see that liberty is not synonymous with freedom. Freedom is the broader category; liberty is one aspect of freedom. If freedom is understood as the overall absence of constraint, liberty can be understood as the absence of a specific kind of constraint—*coercion,* the forceful and deliberate interference by human beings in the affairs of other human beings. Coercion can take two forms—either the direct use of physical force or the threat of harm, backed up by enforcement power. An example will illustrate why liberty is not synonymous with freedom. In some countries, citizens need a government permit to live and work in certain cities. Thus their freedom, more specifically their liberty, to go to live and work in those cities is restricted by coercion, the threat of harm should they disobey the rules. In the United States, citizens do not need such permits. There are no laws that threaten them with harm should they choose to move to New York City or Los Angeles. But not everyone who wants to do so is free to go to live and work in either city. All kinds of constraints may prevent it. Individuals may not have the money for transportation, for example, and this lack may limit their freedom to do what they wish to do. The jobs they are capable of doing may not be available and this lack, too, may prevent them from moving to the city of their choice. So individual freedom may be limited in many different ways. It is important to see that when libertarians advocate the maximization of liberty, they are not concerned with maximizing freedom in general. Their focus is on minimizing coercion, especially on minimizing the coercive interferences of governments.

On a libertarian view, individuals have certain *moral rights* to life, liberty, and property that any just society must recognize and respect. These rights are sometimes described as *warnings against interference:* If A has a right to X, no one should prevent A from pursuing X or deprive A of X, since A is entitled to it. According to a libertarian, the sole function of the government is to protect the individual's life, liberty, and property against force and fraud. Everything else in society is a matter of individual responsibility, decision, and action. Providing for the welfare of those who cannot or will not provide for themselves is not a morally justifiable function of government. To make such provisions, the government would have to take from some against their will in order to give to others. This is perceived as an unjustifiable coercive limitation on individual liberty. Individuals own their own bodies (or lives) and, therefore, the labor they exert. It follows, for the libertarian, that individuals have the right to whatever income or wealth their labor can earn in a free marketplace. Taxing some to give to others is analogous to robbery. John Hospers, who defends a libertarian position in this chapter, argues that laws requiring people to help one another (e.g., via welfare payments) rob Peter to pay Paul.

The Socialist Conception of Justice

A direct challenge to libertarians comes from those who defend a socialist conception of justice. Although there are many varieties of socialism, one common element in socialist thought is a commitment to social equality and to government or collective measures furthering that equality. These measures include the collective ownership of productive property. Since social equality is the ultimate ideal, limitations on individual liberty that are necessary to promote equality are seen as justified. Socialists attack libertarian views on the primacy of liberty, in at least three ways. *First,* they offer defenses of their ideal of social equality. These take various forms and will not concern us here. *Second,* they point out the meaninglessness of libertarian rights to those who lack adequate food, shelter, health care, etc. For those who lack the money to buy the food and health care needed to sustain life, the libertarian right to life is an empty sham. The rights of liberty, such as the right to freedom of speech, are a joke to those who cannot exercise them because of economic considerations. *Third,* some defenders of socialism, as reflected in the selection by Carl Cohen in this chapter, argue that most people will have much more freedom in a socialist system than in a libertarian one because they will have more control over their economic lives. The freedom that the socialist wants to maximize, however, requires a society in which individuals have the greatest possible range of choices and not simply one in which government interference is minimal. Defenders of socialism may use the word "liberty" in discussing the freedom that they believe a socialist system will maximize, but it is important to recognize the difference between the way they use "liberty" and the notion of liberty explicated above. Thus where libertarians stress liberty, understood as freedom from coercion, especially from government interference, socialists stress freedom from want. Where libertarians stress *negative* rights (rights not to be interfered with), socialists stress *positive rights*—rights *to* food, health care, productive work, etc. Where libertarians criticize socialism for the limitations it imposes on liberty, socialists criticize libertarianism for allowing gross inequalities among those who are "equally human."

The Liberal Conception of Justice

Like the socialist, the liberal rejects the libertarian conception of justice since that conception does not include what liberals perceive as a fundamental moral concern. Any purported conception of justice that does not require those who have more than enough to help those in need is morally unacceptable to liberals. Socialists and liberals also agree in recognizing the extent to which economic constraints in an industrial society effectively limit the exercise of libertarian rights by those lacking economic power. Unlike many socialists, however, liberals consider some of the libertarian's negative rights extremely important and advocate social institutions that do two important things—ensure certain basic liberties for all (e.g., freedom of speech) and yet provide for the economic needs of the disadvantaged members of society. Liberals also differ from socialists insofar as they do not advocate the communal ownership of the means of production. Nor do liberals oppose all social and economic inequalities. Liberals disagree among themselves, however, concerning both the morally acceptable extent of such inequalities and their correct justification. A utilitarian committed to a liberal position might hold that inequalities are justified to the extent that allowing them maximizes the total amount of good in a society. If, for example, increased productivity depends on giving workers a significantly higher income than that given to those collecting welfare,[2] and if such incentive-stimulated productivity increases the total amount of good in a society, then the inequalities between the assembly-line worker and the welfare recipient would be justified for the utilitarian. A different approach, argued for by John Rawls,[3] maintains that only those inequalities of social goods are justified that will contribute to raising the position of the *least*-advantaged groups in the society. Here the concern is not with the total amount of good in a society but with the good of the least advantaged. In this view, income inequalities necessary for productivity gains are justified only if the productivity gains function to benefit those in the lowest economic strata.

Libertarianism, Liberalism, and Welfare

Some of the practical ramifications of the libertarian and liberal conceptions of justice are brought out in Trudy Govier's article in this chapter. Govier is concerned with the question, "Should the needy have a legal right to welfare benefits?" Criticizing the libertarian (individualist) position on welfare, she argues for a legal right to welfare based on both utilitarian and justice considerations. Underlying some of her arguments for the superiority of a particular approach to welfare is the liberal conception of justice.

Marxist-Socialism and Welfare

A different position regarding welfare programs, worthy of consideration but not explicitly discussed in the readings in this chapter, is based on a Marxist-socialist analysis of the role that welfare programs play in a capitalist society. A Marxist-socialist, like the socialists discussed above, is committed to the ideal of equality. The Marxist-socialist criticism of capitalist societies, however, does not center primarily on their social and economic inequalities. Rather, Marxist-socialists criticize what they perceive as capitalism's failure to pay the worker in accordance with productive contribution. Workers under capitalism, on a Marxist analysis, receive only a part of the value of what they have produced. The rest, the *surplus value,* goes to capitalists who are then able to use it to support institutions that function to maintain the status quo

---

[2]Just what constitutes *welfare* or a welfare program is a matter of dispute. Many would include a number of very different programs under this heading, e.g., unemployment benefits paid out of a fund supported by a mandatory payroll tax paid by employers, social security benefits paid out of a fund supported by a mandatory payroll tax on both employers and employees, Medicaid programs paid out of state and federal funds, and Aid to Families with Dependent Children paid out of state and federal funds. Usually, when what is at issue is a contrast between the incomes of workers and welfare recipients, the welfare in question includes such payments as aid to Families with Dependent Children, food stamps, and Medicaid.

[3]John Rawls, *A Theory of Justice* (Cambridge, Mass: Harvard University Press, 1971).

and work against the interests of the worker. On a Marxist analysis, the political, legal, and social institutions in a capitalist society operate in the interests of the capitalist class. These interests include the maintenance of a reserve industrial army which can be pulled into and pushed out of the work force in response to the capitalist's needs. On this analysis, welfare programs in capitalist societies provide one of the mechanisms for the maintenance of this army. As T. R. Young, a Marxist sociologist, puts it,

> In the United States, the surplus value of labor is used to make political donations by large corporations. These donations, in turn, are used to create the myth of the happy America, the prosperous America, the beneficent America by advertising agencies working on behalf of middle-class politicians. Such is the view of Marx concerning the use of labor against the body of men who engage in productive work. Under this analysis, in such society the more one works, the stronger grows the apparatus of oppression. In some societies the technology of oppression centers around force, terror, and prison; in other societies, the technology of repression depends upon the smooth, sophisticated tactics of professional managers using what they know of psychology, of organizational theory, and of dramaturgy to control dissent and resistance. . . .
>
> . . . In the United States, the social welfare solution to poverty is to fashion a docile pool of surplus labor maintained at brute animal levels while large-scale organizations are heavily subsidized. American social welfare also fashions a set of rules which humiliate and infantilize the poor. . . . [S]ocial welfare practices in the U.S. provide industry with a well-managed group of poor people. In times of political unrest, welfare rolls are expanded and the rules relaxed. In times of economic trouble, the rolls are reduced and the rules stringently enforced. The poor are thereby depoliticized and deprived where they should be supplied in order to establish the preconditions for humanity: all this in the most affluent nation in history.[4]

Jane S. Zembaty

What Libertarianism Is

John Hospers

John Hospers is professor of philosophy at the University of Southern California and past editor of Pacific Philosophical Quarterly. *His books include* Human Conduct: Problems of Ethics *(1972),* Libertarianism: A Political Philosophy for Tomorrow *(1971), and* Understanding the Arts *(1982).*

Hospers defends two ideas central to libertarianism: (1) Individuals own their own lives. They, therefore, have the right to act as they choose unless their actions interfere with the liberty of others to act as they choose; (2) The only appropriate

---

[4]T. R. Young, "The Contributions of Karl Marx to Social Psychology," a paper in the Transforming Sociology Series (Red Feather, Colo.: Red Feather Institute for Advanced Studies in Sociology), pp. 2, 6.

Reprinted with permission of Nelson-Hall Inc., Publishers from Tibor R. Machan, ed., *The Libertarian Alternative* (1974).

function of government is to protect human rights, understood as negative rights (i.e., rights of noninterference).

The political philosophy that is called libertarianism (from the Latin *libertas,* liberty) is the doctrine that every person is the owner of his own life, and that no one is the owner of anyone else's life; and that consequently every human being has the right to act in accordance with his own choices, unless those actions infringe on the equal liberty of other human beings to act in accordance with *their* choices.

There are several other ways of stating the same libertarian thesis:

1   *No one is anyone else's master, and no one is anyone else's slave.* Since I am the one to decide how my life is to be conducted, just as you decide about yours, I have no right (even if I had the power) to make you my slave and be your master, nor have you the right to become the master by enslaving me. Slavery is *forced* servitude, and since no one owns the life of anyone else, no one has the right to enslave another. Political theories past and present have traditionally been concerned with who should be the master (usually the king, the dictator, or government bureaucracy) and who should be the slaves, and what the extent of the slavery should be. Libertarianism holds that no one has the right to use force to enslave the life of another, or any portion or aspect of that life.

2   *Other men's lives are not yours to dispose of.* I enjoy seeing operas; but operas are expensive to produce. Opera-lovers often say, "The state (or the city, etc.) should subsidize opera, so that we can all see it. Also it would be for people's betterment, cultural benefit, etc." But what they are advocating is nothing more or less than legalized plunder. They can't pay for the productions themselves, and yet they want to see opera, which involves a large number of people and their labor; so what they are saying in effect is, "Get the money through legalized force. Take a little bit more out of every worker's paycheck every week to pay for the operas we want to see." But I have no right to take by force from the workers' pockets to pay for what I want.

Perhaps it would be better if he *did* go to see opera—then I should try to convince him to go voluntarily. But to take the money from him forcibly, because in my opinion it would be good for *him,* is still seizure of his earnings, which is plunder.

Besides, if I have the right to force him to help pay for my pet projects, hasn't he equally the right to force me to help pay for his? Perhaps he in turn wants the government to subsidize rock-and-roll, or his new car, or a house in the country? If I have the right to milk him, why hasn't he the right to milk me? If I can be a moral cannibal, why can't he too?

We should beware of the inventors of utopias. They would remake the world according to their vision—with the lives and fruits of the labor of *other* human beings. Is it someone's utopian vision that others should build pyramids to beautify the landscape? Very well, then other men should provide the labor; and if he is in a position of political power, and he can't get men to do it voluntarily, then he must *compel* them to "cooperate"—i.e. he must enslave them.

A hundred men might gain great pleasure from beating up or killing just one insignificant human being; but other men's lives are not theirs to dispose of. "In order to achieve the worthy goals of the next five-year-plan, we must forcibly collectivize the peasants . . ."; but other men's lives are not theirs to dispose of. Do you want to occupy, rent-free, the mansion that another man has worked for twenty years to buy? But other men's lives are not yours to dispose of. Do you want operas so badly that everyone is forced to work harder to pay for their subsidization through taxes? But other men's lives are not yours to dispose of. Do you want to have free medical care at the expense of other people, whether they wish to provide it or not? But this would require them to work longer for you whether they want to or not, and other men's lives are not yours to dispose of.

The freedom to engage in any type of enterprise, to produce, to own and control property, to buy and sell on the free market, is derived from the rights to life, liberty, and property . . . which are stated in the Declaration of Independence . . . [but] when a government guarantees a "right" to an education or parity on farm products or a guaranteed annual income, it is staking a claim on the property of one group of citizens for the sake of another group. In short, it is violating one of the fundamental rights it was instituted to protect.[1]

3 *No human being should be a nonvoluntary mortgage on the life of another.* I cannot claim your life, your work, or the products of your effort as mine. The fruit of one man's labor should not be fair game for every freeloader who comes along and demands it as his own. The orchard that has been carefully grown, nurtured, and harvested by its owner should not be ripe for the plucking for any bypasser who has a yen for the ripe fruit. The wealth that some men have produced should not be fair game for looting by government, to be used for whatever purposes its representatives determine, no matter what their motives in so doing may be. The theft of your money by a robber is not justified by the fact that he used it to help his injured mother.

It will already be evident that libertarian doctrine is embedded in a view of the rights of man. Each human being has the right to live his life as he chooses, compatibly with the equal right of all other human beings to live their lives as they choose.

All man's rights are implicit in the above statement. Each man has the right to life: any attempt by others to take it away from him, or even to injure him, violates this right, through the use of coercion against him. Each man has the right to liberty: to conduct his life in accordance with the alternatives open to him without coercive action by others. And every man has the right to property: to work to sustain his life (and the lives of whichever others he chooses to sustain, such as his family) and to retain the fruits of his labor.

People often defend the rights of life and liberty but denigrate property rights, and yet the right to property is as basic as the other two; indeed, without property rights no other rights are possible. Depriving you of property is depriving you of the means by which you live.

---

[1]William W. Bayes, "What Is Property?" *The Freeman*, July 1970, p. 348.

. . . All that which an individual possesses by right (including his life and property) are morally his to use, dispose of and even destroy, as he sees fit. If I own my life, then it follows that I am free to associate with whom I please and not to associate with whom I please. If I own my knowledge and services, it follows that I may ask any compensation I wish for providing them for another, or I may abstain from providing them at all, if I so choose. If I own my house, it follows that I may decorate it as I please and live in it with whom I please. If I control my own business, it follows that I may charge what I please for my products or services, hire whom I please and not hire whom I please. All that which I own in fact, I may dispose of as I choose to in reality. For anyone to attempt to limit my freedom to do so is to violate my rights.

Where do my rights end? Where yours begin. I may do anything I wish with my own life, liberty and property without your consent; but I may do nothing with your life, liberty and property without your consent. If we recognize the principle of man's rights, it follows that the individual is sovereign of the domain of his own life and property, and is sovereign of no other domain. To attempt to interfere forcibly with another's use, disposal or destruction of his own property is to initiate force against him and to violate his rights.

I have no right to decide how *you* should spend your time or your money. I can make that decision for myself, but not for you, my neighbor. I may deplore your choice of life-style, and I may talk with you about it provided you are willing to listen to me. But I have no right to use force to change it. Nor have I the right to decide how you should spend the money you have earned. I may appeal to you to give it to the Red Cross, and you may prefer to go to prizefights. But that is your decision, and however much I may chafe about it I do not have the right to interfere forcibly with it, for example by robbing you in order to use the money in accordance with *my* choices. (If I have the right to rob you, have you also the right to rob me?)

When I claim a right, I carve out a niche, as it were, in my life, saying in effect, "This activity I must be able to perform without interference from others. For you and everyone else, this is off limits." And so I put up a "no trespassing" sign, which marks off the area of my right. Each individual's right is his "no trespassing" sign in relation to me and others. I may not encroach upon his domain any more than he upon mine, without my consent. Every right entails a duty, true—but the duty is only that of *forbearance*—that is, of *refraining* from violating the other person's right. If you have a right to life, I have no right to take your life; if you have a right to the products of your labor (property), I have no right to take it from you without your consent. The non-violation of these rights will not guarantee you protection against natural catastrophes such as floods and earthquakes, but it will protect you against the aggressive activities *of other men*. And rights, after all, have to do with one's relations to other human beings, not with one's relations to physical nature.

Nor were these rights created by government; governments—some governments, obviously not all—*recognize* and *protect* the rights that individuals already have. Governments regularly forbid homicide and theft; and, at a more advanced stage, protect individuals against such things as libel and breach of contract. . . .

Government is the most dangerous institution known to man. Throughout history it has violated the rights of men more than any individual or group of individuals could do: it has killed people, enslaved them, sent them to forced labor and concentration camps, and regularly robbed and pillaged them of the fruits of their expended labor. Unlike individual criminals, government has the power to arrest and try; unlike individual criminals, it can surround and encompass a person totally, dominating every aspect of one's life, so that one has no recourse from it but to leave the country (and in totalitarian nations even that is prohibited). Government throughout history has a much sorrier record than any individual, even that of a ruthless mass murderer. The signs we see on bumper stickers are chillingly accurate: "Beware: the Government is Armed and Dangerous."

The only proper role of government, according to libertarians, is that of the protector of the citizen against aggression by other individuals. The government, of course, should never initiate aggression; its proper role is as the embodiment of the *retaliatory* use of force against anyone who initiates its use.

If each individual had constantly to defend himself against possible aggressors, he would have to spend a considerable portion of his life in target practice, karate exercises, and other means of self-defenses, and even so he would probably be helpless against groups of individuals who might try to kill, maim, or rob him. He would have little time for cultivating those qualities which are essential to civilized life, nor would improvements in science, medicine, and the arts be likely to occur. The function of government is to take this responsibility off his shoulders: the government undertakes to defend him against aggressors and to punish them if they attack him. When the government is effective in doing this, it enables the citizen to go about his business unmolested and without constant fear for his life. To do this, of course, government must have physical power—the police, to protect the citizen from aggression within its borders, and the armed forces, to protect him from aggressors outside. Beyond that, the government should not intrude upon his life, either to run his business, or adjust his daily activities, or prescribe his personal moral code.

Government, then, undertakes to be the individual's protector; but historically governments have gone far beyond this function. Since they already have the physical power, they have not hesitated to use it for purposes far beyond that which was entrusted to them in the first place. Undertaking initially to protect its citizens against aggression, it has often itself become an aggressor—a far greater aggressor, indeed, than the criminals against whom it was supposed to protect its citizens. Governments have done what no private citizens can do: arrest and imprison individuals without a trial and send them to slave labor camps. Government must have power in order to be effective—and yet the very means by which alone it can be effective make it vulnerable to the abuse of power, leading to managing the lives of individuals and even inflicting terror upon them.

What then should be the function of government? In a word, the *protection of human rights*.

1 *The right to life:* libertarians support all such legislation as will protect human beings against the use of force by others, for example, laws against killing, attempted killing, maiming, beating, and all kinds of physical violence.

2 *The right to liberty:* there should be no laws compromising in any way freedom of speech, of the press, and of peaceable assembly. There should be no censorship of ideas, books, films, or of anything else by government.

3 *The right to property:* libertarians support legislation that protects the property rights of individuals against confiscation, nationalization, eminent domain, robbery, trespass, fraud and misrepresentation, patent and copyright, libel and slander.

Someone has violently assaulted you. Should he be legally liable? Of course. He has violated one of your rights. He has knowingly injured you, and since he has initiated aggression against you he should be made to expiate.

Someone has negligently left his bicycle on the sidewalk where you trip over it in the dark and injure yourself. He didn't do it intentionally; he didn't mean you any harm. Should he be legally liable? Of course; he has, however unwittingly, injured you, and since the injury is caused by him and you are the victim, he should pay.

Someone across the street is unemployed. Should you be taxed extra to pay for his expenses? Not at all. You have not injured him, you are not responsible for the fact that he is unemployed (unless you are a senator or bureaucrat who agitated for further curtailing of business, which legislation passed, with the result that your neighbor was laid off by the curtailed business). You may voluntarily wish to help him out, or better still, try to get him a job to put him on his feet again; but since you have initiated no aggressive act against him, and neither purposely nor accidentally injured him in any way, you should not be legally penalized for the fact of his unemployment. (Actually, it is just such penalties that increase unemployment.)

One man, A, works hard for years and finally earns a high salary as a professional man. A second man, B, prefers not to work at all, and to spend wastefully what money he has (through inheritance), so that after a year or two he has nothing left. At the end of this time he has a long siege of illness and lots of medical bills to pay. He demands that the bills be paid by the government—that is, by the taxpayers of the land, including Mr. A.

But of course B has no such right. He chose to lead his life in a certain way—that was his voluntary decision. One consequence of that choice is that he must depend on charity in case of later need. Mr. A chose not to live that way. (And if everyone lived like Mr. B, on whom would he depend in case of later need?) Each has a right to live in the way he pleases, but each must live with the consequences of his own decision (which, as always, fall primarily on himself). He cannot, in time of need, claim A's beneficence as his right. . . .

Laws may be classified into three types: (1) laws protecting individuals against themselves, such as laws against fornication and other sexual behavior, alcohol, and drugs; (2) laws protecting individuals against aggressions by other individuals, such as laws against murder, robbery, and fraud; (3) laws requiring people to help one another; for example, all laws which rob Peter to pay Paul, such as welfare.

Libertarians reject the first class of laws totally. Behavior which harms no one else is strictly the individual's own affair. Thus, there should be no laws against becoming intoxicated, since whether or not to become intoxicated is the individual's own decision; but there should be laws against driving while intoxicated, since the drunken driver is a threat to every other motorist on the highway (drunken driving falls into type 2). Similarly, there should be no laws against drugs (except the prohibition of sale of drugs to minors) as long as the taking of these drugs poses no threat to anyone else. Drug addiction is a psychological problem to which no present solution exists. Most of the social harm caused by addicts, other than to themselves, is the result of thefts which they perform in order to continue their habit—and then the *legal* crime is the theft, not the addiction. The actual cost of heroin is about ten cents a shot; if it were legalized, the enormous traffic in illegal sale and purchase of it would stop, as well as the accompanying proselytization to get new addicts (to make more money for the pusher) and the thefts performed by addicts who often require eighty dollars a day just to keep up the habit. Addiction would not stop, but the crimes would: it is estimated that 75 percent of the burglaries in New York City today are performed by addicts, and all these crimes could be wiped out at one stroke through the legalization of drugs. (Only when the taking of drugs could be shown to constitute a threat to *others,* should it be prohibited by law. It is only laws protecting people against *themselves* that libertarians oppose.)

Laws should be limited to the second class only: aggression by individuals against other individuals. These are laws whose function is to protect human beings against encroachment by others; and this, as we have seen, is (according to libertarianism) the sole function of government.

Libertarians also reject the third class of laws totally: no one should be forced by law to help others, not even to tell them the time of day if requested, and certainly not to give them a portion of one's weekly paycheck. Governments, in the guise of humanitarianism, have given to some by taking from others (charging a "handling fee" in the process, which, because of the government's waste and inefficiency, sometimes is several hundred percent). And in so doing they have decreased incentive, violated the rights of individuals, and lowered the standard of living of almost everyone.

All such laws constitute what libertarians call *moral cannibalism.* A cannibal in the physical sense is a person who lives off the flesh of other human beings. A *moral* cannibal is one who believes he has a right to live off the "spirit" of other human beings—who believes that he has a moral claim on the productive capacity, time, and effort expended by others.

It has become fashionable to claim virtually everything that one needs or desires as one's *right.* Thus, many people claim that they have a right to a job, the right to free medical care, to free food and clothing, to a decent home, and so on. Now if one asks, apart from any specific context, whether it would be desirable if everyone had these things, one might well say yes. But there is a gimmick attached to each of them: *At whose expense?* Jobs, medical care, education, and so on, don't grow on trees. These are goods and services *produced only by men.* Who, then, is to provide them, and under what conditions?

If you have a right to a job, who is to supply it? Must an employer supply it even if he doesn't want to hire you? What if you are unemployable, or incurably lazy? (If you say "the government must supply it," does that mean that a job must be created for you which no employer needs done, and that you must be kept in it regardless of how much or little you work?) If the employer is forced to supply it at his expense even if he doesn't need you, then isn't *he* being enslaved to that extent? What ever happened to *his* right to conduct his life and his affairs in accordance with his choices?

If you have a right to free medical care, then, since medical care doesn't exist in nature as wild apples do, some people will have to supply it to you for free: that is, they will have to spend their time and money and energy taking care of you whether they want to or not. What ever happened to *their* right to conduct their lives as they see fit? Or do you have a right to violate theirs? Can there be a right to violate rights?

All those who demand this or that as a "free service" are consciously or unconsciously evading the fact that there is in reality no such thing as free services. All man-made goods and services are the result of human expenditure of time and effort. There is no such thing as "something for nothing" in this world. If you demand something free, you are demanding that other men give their time and effort to you without compensation. If they voluntarily choose to do this, there is no problem; but if you demand that they be *forced* to do it, you are interfering with their right not to do it if they so choose. "Swimming in this pool ought to be free!" says the indignant passerby. What he means is that others should build a pool, others should provide the materials, and still others should run it and keep it in functioning order, so that *he* can use it without fee. But what right has he to the expenditure of *their* time and effort? To expect something "for free" is to expect it *to be paid for by others* whether they choose to or not.

Many questions, particularly about economic matters, will be generated by the libertarian account of human rights and the role of government. Should government have no role in assisting the needy, in providing social security, in legislating minimum wages, in fixing prices and putting a ceiling on rents, in curbing monopolies, in erecting tariffs, in guaranteeing jobs, in managing the money supply? To these and all similar questions the libertarian answers with an unequivocal no.

"But then you'd let people go hungry!" comes the rejoinder. This, the libertarian insists, is precisely what would not happen; with the restrictions removed, the economy would flourish as never before. With the controls taken off business, existing enterprises would expand and new ones would spring into existence satisfying more and more consumer needs; millions more people would be gainfully employed instead of subsisting on welfare, and all kinds of research and production, released from the stranglehold of government, would proliferate, fulfilling man's needs and desires as never before. It has always been so whenever government has permitted men to be free traders on a free market. But *why* this is so, and how the free market is the best solution to all problems relating to the material aspect of man's life, is another and far longer story. . . .

QUESTIONS

1 Some libertarians argue that from a moral standpoint there is no difference between the actions of an ordinary thief and those of a government when it seizes money from some in order to support others. They assume that if the former are wrong, then so are the latter. Are they correct?

2 Do you agree that the government should have no role in assisting the needy? What reasons can you advance to defend your answer?

Socialist Democracy

Carl Cohen

Carl Cohen is professor of philosophy at the University of Michigan. He specializes in social and political philosophy. Cohen is the author of Civil Disobedience: Conscience, Tactics, and the Law *(1971) and* Four Systems *(1982). He is also editor of* Communism, Fascism, and Democracy *(1972) and* Democracy *(1971). His many articles include "Race and the Constitution" and "Medical Experimentation on Prisoners."*

In this excerpt from Cohen's *Four Systems, socialist democracy* is defended from the standpoint of an advocate strongly committed to both the democratic process and socialism, understood here as the democratic control of *all* resources in the community by society as a *whole*. It should be noted that the position espoused is not Cohen's. Rather, as *Four Systems* is constructed, the defense of each system is presented as if it were written by a staunch advocate of the system. Here, the advocate of socialist democracy attacks the "free enterprise system" seeing it as incompatible with economic justice for most people. *Political rights* (e.g., negative rights such as the freedom of speech and assembly) are contrasted with *economic* rights (e.g., positive rights such as the right to sufficient food or the right to employment). The advocate then contends that only a socialist democracy will protect both sorts of rights. On this account, a socialist democracy also maximizes liberty. But as the word "liberty" is used by the advocate of socialism, it is synonymous with the word "freedom," understood as the maximization of the range of choices available to citizens.

DEMOCRACY FULFILLED

We socialists agree that democracy is necessary and absolutely right. But it is not enough. Democracy is completed, fulfilled, by socialism—which is simply the democratic control of *all* resources in the community by society *as a whole*.

Socialism makes democratic ideals concrete. In it the collective will of the people is put to the service of the people in their daily lives. Through socialism the common interests of all the citizens are protected, their common needs met.

The name "socialism" has—at least to many American ears—a negative, even a threatening, connotation. Yet most ordinary people warmly support—under a different name—many activities that are truly socialist in nature. We all know that some things must be done for the community as a whole. And some things can be undertaken *for* the community only *by* the community, acting *as* a community. Constructive collective action in this spirit is socialism.

How, for example, do we "provide for the common defense"? Why, through social action, of course. Armies and warships cannot be maintained by private groups or individuals. National defense, undertaken jointly with democratic consent, is only one of many socialist enterprises that no one seriously questions.

How do we make and enforce the criminal law? Collectively, of course. Citizens can neither establish criminal codes and courts as individuals, nor punish as individuals. That would be the war of each against all, in which the lives of people would indeed prove nasty, poor, brutish, and short. The adoption of laws, and their enforcement, is an essentially *social* activity. Nothing else would be feasible or sane. Everyone grants that; to this extent we are all socialists.

Is not the same true of national foreign policy? We may differ as individuals, but do we not agree upon the need for one community position? And of health regulations? Do we allow the meat packers or the drug manufacturers to decide for themselves what is fit to eat or prescribe? And everyone now agrees on the need for community policies, collective undertakings to protect the environment, our forests and fish, animals and birds. Shall we not have public parks or seashores? Shall we not join to protect our historical treasures and the beauties of our land? Absurd even to ask. To do these things we must, of course, act as a society, because as individuals we are relatively helpless and ineffective. We will succeed, if we succeed at all, cooperatively, because there is absolutely no other way to have successful armies, just courts, or beautiful parks. All democratic experience teaches the need for collective action. Real democracy *is* social democracy, democratic socialism.

While we all practice socialism in many spheres, its applicability to other spheres in which it is equally necessary is widely denied. Sometimes manipulated by the rich and powerful, sometimes blinded by our own slogans, sometimes dreading unreal philosophical ghosts, we fear to take social action where we ought. We fail to complete our democracy.

How can we complete it? Where would collective action have greatest impact on daily life? In the economy, of course. Action as a society is needed most of all in producing and distributing the necessities and comforts of ordinary human life. Socialism is democracy extended to the world of work and money.

SOCIALISM AND POPULAR WILL

All the wealth of the world—the houses and food, the land and lumber and luxuries—is somehow divided and distributed. How is that done? And how should it be done? We socialists try to rethink such fundamental questions: Who gets what? And why?

Satisfactory answers to these questions must, of course, prove acceptable to the masses. Being democrats above all, we trust the judgment of the people. Their choices, when fully informed, will be rational and fair. We lay it down as a restriction upon ourselves, therefore, that the great changes socialism requires must come only as the honest expression of the will of the citizens, through action by their freely elected representatives. An organic transformation of society can succeed only when genuinely willed by its members. True socialists—unlike some who falsely parade under that banner—never have and never will force their solutions on an unwilling community. Democracies around the world, from India to Sweden, have enthusiastically applied socialist theory to their problems, devising socialist solutions specially suitable to their circumstances. The same basic theory can be applied successfully, with American ingenuity, to American circumstances. Confident that we can prove this to the satisfaction of the citizens concerned, we commit ourselves without reservations to abide by the judgment of the people after the case has been put fairly before them. We compel no one; our socialism is democratic, through and through.

RICH AND POOR

How the wealth of most of the world is now divided is very plain to see. A few people get a great deal, and most people get just barely enough, or a little less than enough, to live decently. Rich and poor are the great classes of society, and everyone knows it well. Early democracies accepted these stark inequities as natural and inevitable. We do not. Some democrats still accept them. Material success (they say) is open to everyone in a system of private enterprise, and rewards properly go to the industrious and the able, those ambitious enough to pull themselves out of poverty by effort and wit. Some succeed, some do not, and most (they conclude) receive their just deserts.

It isn't so. That picture of "free enterprise" is a myth and always has been. In fact, by putting control of industry and finance into private hands, free enterprise results in the ownership of more and more by fewer and fewer, making economic justice unattainable for most. For centuries, wherever capitalism has prevailed, the great body of wealth has rested in the pockets of a tiny fraction of the citizens, while the masses are divided between those who just get by on their wages, and those who are unemployed and poor, inadequately housed, and often hungry. That great division, between those who have and those who have not, is the leading feature of a private enterprise economy, even when democratic. Those who have get more, because money and property are instruments for the accumulation of more money and more property. Economic freedom in such a system, for the vast majority, is only the freedom to work for another. Working men and women are free to sweat for paychecks, free to look for another job, and maybe—if their needs are desperate—free to go on welfare. These are false freedoms, not deserving the name.

Why does it work out that way? Will the poor always be with us? Ought each person to look out only for himself or herself and devil take the hindmost? We deny that this is the spirit of a decent society. We do not accept the inevitability of poverty;

we do not think a democracy need be a cutthroat enterprise, and we know that cooperative action by the members of a society in their joint interests can protect both the essential freedoms of each individual and the economic well-being of all. That rational cooperation is called socialism.

PARKS AND INDUSTRIES

Consider this vivid contrast. No one questions the appropriateness of public parks—places for play and the enjoyment of nature, owned by the people, and operated by their elected representatives (and those they hire) in everyone's interest. Our parks (national, state, and municipal) are among our proudest possessions. Yes, possessions; we own them, each of us, and though some abuse them thoughtlessly, most of us love them and take satisfaction in their beauty. We do not begrudge the need to tax ourselves to maintain them. We could sell the forests and the land, reduce our tax burden thereby, and leave all citizens to take care of their own recreational needs as well as they can. If unable to pay for access to private parks or clubs, or to afford a private lake or a canyon—well, that would be their lookout. Simply to formulate this attitude is to exhibit its absurdity. Natural beauty and opportunity for relaxation and play for ourselves and our children are deep human needs; we fully understand how vital it is that the limited resources of nature, the lakes and forests, streams and wildlife, be preserved, in part at least, for our common and perpetual enjoyment.

Compare with this the condition of the steel industry. Virtually all of the steel in the United States is produced by three companies: U.S. Steel, Republic Steel, Inland Steel. The private owners of these three companies—a tiny fraction of our citizens—literally possess, own as their private property, the foundries, mills, and other facilities that constitute the literal foundation of almost all other industry. Virtually nothing works without steel. Steel mills are not as pretty as parks, true, but are they any less necessary to the well-being of a people? Can any of us do without steel? Not for a day. Cars, trucks, ships, and trains are made of it. Housing and communication depend utterly upon it. Kitchens and radios, elevators and pens—practically all tools and all conveniences require it. Hardly any activity, public or private, goes on without some use of iron or steel. Then why not exhibit the same community concern for steel that we exhibit for our parks? Why let a few capitalists charge us as they please (since we cannot control them) for what we must have? Why suppose that a fair price for steel includes an enormous profit—over and above all the costs of making and shipping the steel—for the private owners of the mills?

What explains so blind an infatuation with "private enterprise"? Under its spell we allow ourselves to be manipulated by the private owners of the steel foundries, gouged (even in our own homes!) by the private owners of the telephone wires. Oil wells and forests, precious resources from our common earth, are exploited by giant corporations whose ultimate object is profit alone. We must wake to see that productive industry, vital to the life of a society, is properly the possession of that society as a whole, not of private individuals or companies. The principles we apply unhesitatingly to parks apply with equal force to factories. Production as well as recreation can be a source of public pride and satisfaction—when socialized. Socialism is nothing more than the *general* application of collective intelligence.

Every democracy, socialist or not, will seek to protect citizens' political rights—but only socialist democracies protect citizens' *economic* rights. Freedom of speech and assembly are priceless; are not freedom from unemployment and hunger equally so? We think so. The same collective action needed to defend the citizens against aggression from without is needed to organize production rationally and to distribute wealth justly within our own borders. In the economic sphere as much as any other, cooperation and foresight are central. The public ownership of industry is the only way to achieve them.

THE UNFAIRNESS OF PRIVATE OWNERSHIP

History confirms this. The private ownership of productive industry has always resulted in deprivation for most, luxury for a few. The owners of factories and mines are forced, by competition, to exploit both workers and resources. Where private interests have been the foundation of the system, they have always been advanced at the expense of public interests. Why not build a power project in the heart of the Hudson River valley or on the seashores of Maine? It is not a concern for beauty but for bookkeeping that pays off. Drill for oil wherever it can be found—in the last of the forests, on the beaches, on the lawn of the state capitol. Business is business. The great redwoods of California, each hundreds of years old and a monument to nature's grandeur, fall by the thousands; the forests are clear-cut, left as ugly, muddy hillsides. The drive for profit is the sharpest of all saws.

The system of private ownership encourages, even demands, selfishness at every turn. Let buyers, employees, the general public beware! Cornering the market in computing equipment, controlling access to the telephone system, delaying the marketing of steers in order to raise the price of beef, steadily increasing the price of gasoline when petroleum is in short supply—all such maneuvers are within the rules of the capitalist game. Sharp play and toughness yield riches; generosity yields bankruptcy; and no one may refuse to play.

To limit the injustices done in the name of private enterprise, some have tried to adjust the rules of the game. It does not work. Fair business practice codes, antitrust legislation, minimum-wage laws, and the like, do restrain some of the excesses of the capitalists. But such changes are no more than cosmetics, mitigating but not eliminating the real evil. Injustice flows not merely from the excesses of capitalism but from the essence of the system of private ownership itself.

Changing the rules cannot eliminate exploitation and gross inequality; only changing the entire game can. If everyone is to be free from economic need, everyone must have the right to participate in planning production and controlling distribution. That can be only when industrial production and distribution is entirely in public hands. Just as those who are not represented in parliament will suffer politically, those not represented in economic decision making will surely suffer in the market. The very argument that justifies democracy in the political sphere justifies democracy in the economic sphere as well. Economic injustice in a private enterprise system is not an accident but a necessary outcome. To eliminate that injustice we must end the disproportion in the powers of its elements, just as the disproportionate powers of political elements were finally ended by giving the vote to all citizens. The case for socialism is the case for economic democracy.

THE INHUMANITY OF THE MARKET

Socialism is simply economic good sense. The long-term fruits of capitalism have become too bitter: cycles of boom and bust, unemployment and welfare, personal dissatisfaction and business failure. Inflation steals from everyone (except those who can raise prices and rents quickly); depression demoralizes everyone. Disorder and distress are widespread. Our land itself is abused, our water poisoned, and our air fouled. When everything is left "up for grabs," the grabbing will be vicious and the outcome chaotic. There can be no intelligent planning for future needs, no rational distribution of products or materials in short supply, no reasonable deployment of human energies, in an economy in which the fundamental rule is dog-eat-dog. Legislation designed to blunt the fangs can do no more than reduce the depth of a serious wound.

Capitalism relies upon the so-called "market economy." The prices asked or offered for raw materials and finished products it leaves entirely to private parties, individuals or business firms, who enter a supposedly open market. This free market, it is argued, will be self-regulating; supply and demand will rationalize prices, fairness and productivity will be ensured by competition, enterprise encouraged by the hope of profit.

None of this actually works in the way capitalist mythology depicts it. The system relies upon the wisdom and power of economic fairies that never did exist. Nothing in the market is dependable, since everything within it fluctuates in response to unpredictable and uncontrollable factors: the tastes of buyers, the moods of sellers, the special circumstances of either, accidents causing short supply, or fashions transforming reasonable supply into glut.

Rationality and fairness through competiton? No claim could be more fraudulent. In a capitalist market prices depend largely upon the relative strengths (or weaknesses) of the traders. If I own all the orchards, and am therefore the seller of all the cherries in the market, you, dear buyer, will pay my price or eat no cherries. Steel, timber, farm machinery are for sale in the market. Go, dear friend, and bargain with the sellers. Anyone tempted to believe capitalist propaganda about the give and take in the market should put it to the test. Reflect upon your own recent experiences as a shopper: You were told the price of the item you looked at—a TV set or a can of beans—and you paid that price or left without. That is how the market works for ordinary folks. Giant firms, manufacturers or chain retailers, may bargain with suppliers on occasion—but even then the stronger get the better deals. Those who control resources and money control the market, manipulating it in their own interests. Those who enter the market (either as buyer or seller) with great needs but little power are squeezed and exploited. The weak get twisted, the strong do the twisting. That's free enterprise.

Fairness? Markets do not know the meaning of the word. All's fair in war—and market competition is perpetual war, through guile and threat, on a thousand fronts. Rewards go to the aggressive; the keys to victory are accumulation, possession, control. And rules for fair dealing? They will be evaded, broken surreptitiously, even ignored— just like the rules of war—when it profits the combatants.

Private enterprise is worse than unfair. It is no-fair; it does not recognize justice as any concern for *homo economicus*. The only things that count, for it, are the things that can be counted. Such a system is by its nature, explicitly *inhumane*. To render it humane it is necessary to transform it into an instrument for humans. Socialism makes human concerns the fundamental concerns in the design, manufacture, and distribution of material goods. Only thus can an economic system achieve justice. What should appear in that holiest of capitalist places, "the bottom line"? A record of increased human satisfactions? Or a record of profit?

THE CRUELTY OF CAPITALISM

"Ah, but that callous system you attack," replies the capitalist, "is the most wonderfully productive in all the world. We do not, it is true, share everything and share alike— but by rewarding personal ambition and intellect, we encourage and tap the productivity of all. Capitalist societies may not be perfectly equitable, but they are rich—and that, in the end, is what we all want."

The true colors of the beast begin to show. Riches, material acquisition, is for it— but not for us—the paramount objective. Socialists think of human life in broader and deeper terms. For us money and goods are servants, not masters. General human well-being, we say, is the mark of a good society. Material wealth is only our tool.

Even on their own ground, however—measuring everything by prosperity—the case for capitalism fails. That private ownership leads to greater productivity is also myth. Enormous growth there has been, of course, in all modern economies; but that growth came with invention and discovery, with technological advance, with mass production and automation. It comes in capitalist countries *and* socialist countries, when relatively primitive methods of production are replaced by more efficient systems. Human intelligence, not capitalism, should get credit for that. There is no reason to believe that human intelligence must be less energetic, or less inventive, when put to common service than when serving private ends.

The ironic consequence of that private service is *deprivation*, the hidden *lack* of that very prosperity capitalism claims. In a system of private ownership the factories and mines must produce at a profit or not at all. Most steel foundries—under capitalism—operate well below capacity most of the time. Produce too much steel and the price will drop; what profit, after all, is there in that? Houses and apartments are needed by tens of millions of Americans; we have the capacity to build that housing, but it goes largely unused. Carpenters and masons wait impatiently in union halls for work; lumber yards and designers lay off workers; contractors and salesmen search desperately for buyers who can afford loans at high interest rates; banks wait cautiously for safe borrowers. The entire system permits even needed construction only when a profit is to be made. If there is no money in it, those in need of housing will simply wait. You cannot make a buck by being a nice guy. What does get built is outrageously expensive, affordable only by the rich. Building slows to a crawl while housing needs soar. The human need for housing plays second fiddle to the demand for profit, and the building industry floats like a chip on the waves of a capricious economic ocean.

So it is with every industry. Production within the plant may be organized and efficient in the highest degree—but the "free market" to which skills and products are brought is madness itself. Again and again capitalism carries itself, now with unbridled enthusiasm, now with unrelieved desperation, to the brink of dissolution. "Business cycles"—the euphemistic name for the manic booms and depressing busts of the capitalist market—are the inevitable consequence of stupid inaction, leaving to pure chance and private avarice the control of our essential common business. The resulting human misery has been incalculable. After a chain of depressions through the nineteenth and early twentieth centuries, capitalism produced the super depression of the 1930s— a slough of despair, fathomless in depth and a decade in length. It was cut short, at last, only by the productive impetus of a terrible war.

In that great depression the true face of capitalism showed itself. Hunger was rampant in the midst of plenty. While humiliated citizens waited in soup lines for a dole, food in warehouses could find no profitable market! Food there was, in great quantities, but because it could not be sold profitably it had to be destroyed. Destroyed! To hold up prices for the rest! We Americans actually burnt huge stores of wheat; we killed and buried great numbers of pigs; we milked the cows and literally poured out the milk onto the ground—because, in the free market, it yielded no profit.

Madness, you say? Yes, the madness of the market economy. A sane economy is a human economy, directed by human intelligence, to serve humans. It will not leave the fate of citizens to chance, or the supply of industrial goods to unpredictable market forces, or the control of essential foodstuffs to private greed. The market cannot be sane, because sanity is a human quality and the market has no humanity whatever. . . .

PUBLIC OWNERSHIP

Reasonable human beings can end all this. Production and distribution can be designed for human service. Cooperation is the key. Society must be organized with mutual service and mutual benefit as its fundamental theme. That theme is not alien to us; it lies at the core of our highest moral and religious ideals. We must realize these ideals in practice.

Economic cooperation entails two practical principles: (1) productive property must be publicly owned; and (2) production and distribution must be planned for the common good. *Public ownership* and *planning*—acting upon both we can readily achieve the substance of democratic socialism.

Public ownership is the base. Public ownership of what? Of the means by which goods are produced and work is carried on. Private persons are not entitled to own the instruments of our common good. A system enabling some to exact profit from the work of others, to wax rich while the glaring needs of others go unmet, is fundamentally corrupt. We would end that corruption by bringing all the elements of the productive economy—the electric utilities and the mines, agriculture and transport, the production of metals and paper and drugs, the airlines and the food chains and the telephone system—under public ownership.

We do not propose to confiscate anything. The capital now held by private owners we would have the community pay for, at a fair price. But we would end the surreptitious confiscation by a few of the common wealth. The people have a right to advance their own general welfare through state action. They have that right in the economic sphere as in every other. Individuals will not be deprived of their personal effects, their houses or cars, their books or boots. Indeed, we seek the enlargement of such private goods for individual satisfaction. Individual human beings, after all, are what government is created to serve. But productive property is our common good, our collective concern. We will move it—justly—from private to public hands.

THE ELIMINATION OF PRIVATE PROFIT

The nationalization of all industry will have two consequences. First, *profit* for some from the work of others will be no more. If there is surplus produced by the operation of the utility companies, or the design of computers, or the distribution of any manufactured goods, let that surplus return to the treasury of the entire community. Let all productive systems be used, we say, not for private enrichment but for public benefit, and for continuing investment in the components of public production themselves. Workers should know that they labor each for all, and that any value they produce beyond what they receive in wages will not be taken from them but returned to them in some form of general benefit. One of those benefits will be the reduction of prices; when profits do not need to be squeezed from an enterprise, the consumer need only be charged the actual cost of that product or service. Goods and services will at last be fairly priced. . . .

SOCIAL PLANNING

Two practical principles, we said earlier, comprise the substance of democratic socialism. Public ownership is the first, the foundation of socialism. Planning production and distribution for the common good is the second, and the fruit of socialism. When all members of the community have equal voice in the management of the economy, the elected representatives of those voices will naturally seek to deploy productive powers rationally. The community, then fully in command of its own affairs, will deliberate carefully in choosing its economic goals and in devising the means to attain them. It will make plans.

All intelligent humans plan. Preparing for the future is the mark of rational beings. Capitalists plan thoughtfully for their own advancement, plan cautiously for the security of their families, plan assiduously for the growth of their businesses. Yet they bitterly attack us for advocating the same foresight in the larger community! In matters close to them they do not cease to think ahead. But they insist that the community as a whole should entrust its future to an "invisible hand" that is somehow to ensure social health and prosperity. Sophisticated in private affairs, their handling of public affairs is simply immature, primitive.

Critics of socialism (it should be noted in fairness) often do recognize the need to plan in some particular sphere of the economy. Doing so, of course, such critics implicitly abandon their devotion to "free" markets. They plan the supplies of oil or gas, the road system, the storage of grain, and the money supply. But if the use of careful planning is appropriate in any single sphere of the economy, it is no less appropriate for the economy as a whole. Capitalists who plan, but are infuriated by planning, are blinded by an ideology from which they cannot free their own minds.

A few wealthy critics of socialism, on the other hand, are more perceptive but less forthright. They recognize the inconsistencies of capitalism, but they reject large-scale planning in their own interests. They know that in a system without rational direction, the private owners of productive capacity are in the best position when stormy times come. They will be able to capitalize on every fortuitous turn of events. That is how they got rich and will get richer. Economic planning will equalize opportunities in ways they do not like. It will deprive them of opportunities to exploit. Planning— from their selfish perspective—is a threat. . . .

PLANNING AND DEMOCRACY

[One] major objection to economic planning is the claim that it will cost us our freedom. This is as false as the claim that it does not work, and more pernicious.

Here lies the nub of the conflict between democratic socialists and our private enterprise critics. Freedom, says the critic, is the paramount social value. The freedom of each individual as an economic agent must be curtailed, they argue, by any large-scale economic plan. Once the goals are set, and the role of each economic element fixed, every private person must be sharply restricted in the use of his own resources. What can be bought and what can be sold or invested will be determined by the plan. The individual will be forced to work where, and when, and as the socialist bureaucrats have decided. Economic planning, they conclude, is but a pretty name for economic slavery.

The complaint is entirely unfounded. It is plausible only because it supposes, falsely, that economic planning under socialism will be imposed from above, by arbitrary authorities over whom we will have no control. Not so. Democratic socialism brings *democratic* planning. In an economy that is publicly owned and managed, *we* are the planners. Long-range designs for the allocation of resources, decisions about what is to be produced and how it is to be distributed, will come not from a secret, all-powerful elite but from *public* bodies, publicly selected, acting publicly, and answerable to the general public.

This genuine public accountability is absent, we agree, in some countries calling themselves "socialist." We despise that economic czarism as bitterly as do our capitalist friends. That is a false socialism which betrays the democratic spirit to which we are committed. Free citizens, accustomed to governing their own affairs, jealous of their own ultimate authority, will not be fooled by deceitful talk. They—we!—will know when our most important business is truly under our own control, and we will not stand for any other state of affairs. We will give up none of our freedom to do our own planning for our own needs. To the contrary, real freedom of action will be magnified in a truly *democratic* socialism by its increase of economic security for individuals and economic rationality in the whole society.

The critics' picture of socialist planning is a caricature of the real thing. They picture each citizen as a mindless cog in a great machine that grinds on unfeelingly, insensitive to mistakes or changing conditions. But the truly insensitive economy is the *un*-planned one, the economy that cannot respond to human needs because it responds to nothing human at all. In that disordered economy the individual is indeed helpless, a bobbing cork on uncontrolled currents. Those currents are brought under control only by giving each citizen a voice in the control of economic as well as political affairs. Democratic planning ensures that voice. The plans will be ours. We can adjust them as we make errors and learn from them; we can refine them as circumstances change. We can scrap bad plans and devise new ones as we develop new needs or new capacities. A planned economy, *honestly* socialized, will not be our master but our servant. Let our critics not forget that our first principle throughout is *self*-government, democracy.

PLANNING AND LIBERTY

For self-governed citizens liberty is, indeed, a paramount concern. And what is liberty, after all? It consists of the ability and the right of individuals to make choices in determining their own conduct. The greater the range of their choices, the greater their freedom. No one supposes that liberty is absolute, that individuals can be free to do entirely as they please without restriction. Even the best of our laws limit each person's freedom to do some sorts of things in order that all of us may be genuinely free to do many other, more valuable sorts of things. The more complex a society, the more essential are some kinds of self-restriction for the extension of real freedom within it.

We witness this rational trade-off everywhere. Primary education is made compulsory in order that all may enjoy the freedom possible only for those who can read and write. Social security taxation ensures freedom from want in old age. We may resort to a military draft, reluctantly, to keep the country free. And so on. Having to send our children to school, being deprived of some of our income by taxation—these and other sound policies clearly limit us. We accept such limitations in the interest of the greater liberties they promote.

In the economic sphere such trade-offs are essential. Even advocates of "free enterprise" readily admit the necessity of legislation that hinders private monopolies, obliges honest business reports, forbids the sale of untested drugs or spoiled foods, and so on. Such restrictions are justified by their benefits in safeguarding other more essential economic goods.

Limits on the absolute freedom of private economic agents will be entailed by socialized planning; we make no bones about that. Some of these limits—on the freedom to own, buy, and sell productive resources like factories and farms—will be painful to some, just as universal taxation or compulsory schooling are burdensome now to many. The freedoms gained, from economic insecurity and injustice, will be vastly greater than those given up, and vastly more important.

Socialist restrictions will be felt most keenly by a relatively small number of persons who now enjoy luxury and great economic power. Those who never had investment capital at their disposal, who never were the owners of profit-making wealth, are deprived of nothing in losing economic license. Socialist gains, on the other hand, will be felt directly by every citizen, experiencing steady improvement in the quality of his or her own life, and satisfaction in the increased well-being of others. Never was a wiser bargain struck. . . .

QUESTIONS

1 Is a socialist system morally preferable to a free enterprise system? If yes, why? If not, why not?
2 Critics of socialism frequently contend that under a socialist system political rights (e.g., negative rights such as freedom of speech) cannot long endure. Do you agree with this criticism? What reasons underlie your answer?

Majority Opinion in *Goldberg v. Kelly*

Justice William Brennan

A biographical sketch of Justice William Brennan is found on page 292.

A suit was brought against Jack R. Goldberg, Commissioner of Social Services of the City of New York, by residents of that city who were receiving financial aid under the federally assisted programs of Aid to Families with Dependent Children or under New York State's general Home Relief program. At issue was the right of the officials administering these programs to terminate aid without prior notice and

United States Supreme Court. 397 U.S. 254 (1970).

hearing. Such termination, the plaintiffs charged, denied them due process of law. According to the Fourteenth Amendment to the Constitution, states are prohibited from depriving any person of life, liberty, or property without "due process of law." In using this clause in the amendment to attack the "right" of the officials to deny welfare recipients pretermination hearings, the claim is made that welfare payments are not "gratuities" charitably given, but more like "property" of which an individual cannot be deprived without due process of law. The lower court ruled in favor of the plaintiffs, and the United States Supreme Court upheld that decision. In this majority opinion, Justice Brennan argues that procedural process requires that pretermination evidentiary hearings be held before welfare payments are stopped. He stresses the fact that welfare payments are entitlements and not simply gratuities. For the purposes of this chapter, the case is interesting primarily because it involves a case where need alone is held to *entitle* the members of a society to at least a portion of the goods of that society.

The constitutional issue to be decided . . . is the narrow one whether the Due Process Clause requires that the recipient be afforded an evidentiary hearing before the termination of benefits. The District Court held that only a pre-termination evidentiary hearing would satisfy the constitutional command, and rejected the argument of the state and city officials that the combination of the post-termination "fair hearing" with the informal pre-termination review disposed of all due process claims. The court said: "While post-termination review is relevant, there is one overpowering fact which controls here. By hypothesis, a welfare recipient is destitute, without funds or assets. . . . Suffice it to say that to cut off a welfare recipient in the face of . . . 'brutal need' without a prior hearing of some sort is unconscionable, unless overwhelming considerations justify it.". . . The court rejected the argument that the need to protect the public's tax revenues supplied the requisite "overwhelming consideration." "Against the justified desire to protect public funds must be weighed the individual's overpowering need in this unique situation not to be wrongfully deprived of assistance. . . . While the problem of additional expense must be kept in mind, it does not justify denying a hearing meeting the ordinary standards of due process. Under all the circumstances, we hold that due process requires an adequate hearing before termination of welfare benefits, and the fact that there is a later constitutionally fair proceeding does not alter the result." . . .

Appellant does not contend that procedural due process is not applicable to the termination of welfare benefits. Such benefits are a matter of statutory entitlement for persons qualified to receive them.[1] Their termination involves state action that adju-

---

[1] It may be realistic today to regard welfare entitlements as more like "property" than a "gratuity". Much of the existing wealth in this country takes the form of rights that do not fall within traditional common-law concepts of property. It has been aptly noted that

"Society today is built around entitlement. The automobile dealer has his franchise, the doctor and lawyer their professional licenses, the worker his union membership, contract, and pension rights, the executive his contract and stock options; all are devices to aid security and independence. Many of the most important of these entitlements now flow from government: subsidies to farmers and busi-

dicates important rights. The constitutional challenge cannot be answered by an argument that public assistance benefits are "a 'privilege' and not a 'right'."... Relevant constitutional restraints apply as much to the withdrawal of public assistance benefits as to disqualification for unemployment compensation; ... or to denial of a tax exemption; ... or to discharge from public employment. The extent to which procedural due process must be afforded the recipient is influenced by the extent to which he may be "condemned to suffer grievous loss," ... and depends upon whether the recipient's interest in avoiding that loss outweighs the governmental interest in summary adjudication. Accordingly, as we said in *Cafeteria & Restaurant Workers Union, etc. v. McElroy* (1961), ... "consideration of what procedures due process may require under any given set of circumstances must begin with a determination of the precise nature of the government function involved as well as of the private interest that has been affected by governmental action." ...

It is true of course, that some governmental benefits may be administratively terminated without affording the recipient a pre-termination evidentiary hearing.[2] But we agree with the District Court that when welfare is discontinued, only a pre-termination evidentiary hearing provides the recipient with procedural due process. ... Thus the crucial factor in this context—a factor not present in the case of the blacklisted government contractor, the discharged government employee, the taxpayer denied a tax exemption, or virtually anyone else whose governmental entitlements are ended—is that termination of aid pending resolution of a controversy over eligibility may deprive an eligible recipient of the very means by which to live while he waits. Since he lacks independent resources, his situation becomes immediately desperate. His need to concentrate upon finding the means for daily subsistence, in turn, adversely affects his ability to seek redress from the welfare bureaucracy.

Moreover, important governmental interests are promoted by affording recipients a pre-termination evidentiary hearing. From its founding the Nation's basic commitment has been to foster the dignity and well-being of all persons within its borders. We have come to recognize that forces not within the control of the poor contribute to their poverty. This perception, against the background of our traditions, has significantly influenced the development of the contemporary public assistance system.

---

nessmen, routes for airlines and channels for television stations; long term contracts for defense, space, and education; social security pensions for individuals. Such sources of security, whether private or public, are no longer regarded as luxuries or gratuities; to the recipients they are essentials, fully deserved, and in no sense a form of charity. It is only the poor whose entitlements, although recognized by public policy, have not been effectively enforced."

Reich, *Individual Rights and Social Welfare: The Emerging Legal Issues,* 74 Yale L. J. 1245, 1255 (1965). See also Reich, *The New Property,* 73 Yale L. J. 733 (1964).

[2]One Court of Appeals has stated: "In a wide variety of situations, it has long been recognized that where harm to the public is threatened, and the private interest infringed is reasonably deemed to be of less importance, an official body can take summary action pending a later hearing."

Welfare, by meeting the basic demands of subsistence, can help bring within the reach of the poor the same opportunities that are available to others to participate meaningfully in the life of the community. At the same time, welfare guards against the societal malaise that may flow from a widespread sense of unjustified frustration and insecurity. Public assistance, then, is not mere charity, but a means to "promote the general Welfare, and secure the Blessings of Liberty to ourselves and our Posterity." The same governmental interests that counsel the provision of welfare, counsel as well its uninterrupted provision to those eligible to receive it; pre-termination evidentiary hearings are indispensable to that end.

Appellant does not challenge the force of these considerations but argues that they are outweighed by countervailing governmental interests in conserving fiscal and administrative resources. These interests, the argument goes, justify the delay of any evidentiary hearing until after discontinuance of the grants. Summary adjudication protects the public fisc by stopping payments promptly upon discovery of reason to believe that a recipient is no longer eligible. Since most terminations are accepted without challenge, summary adjudication also conserves both the fisc and administrative time and energy by reducing the number of evidentiary hearings actually held.

We agree with the District Court, however, that these governmental interests are not overriding in the welfare context. The requirement of a prior hearing doubtless involves some greater expense, and the benefits paid to ineligible recipients pending decision at the hearing probably cannot be recouped, since these recipients are likely to be judgment-proof. But the State is not without weapons to minimize these increased costs. Much of the drain on fiscal and administrative resources can be reduced by developing procedures for prompt pre-termination hearings and by skillful use of personnel and facilities. Indeed, the very provision for a post-termination evidentiary hearing in New York's Home Relief program is itself cogent evidence that the State recognizes the primacy of the public interest in correct eligibility determinations and therefore in the provision of procedural safeguards. Thus, the interest of the eligible recipient in uninterrupted receipt of public assistance, coupled with the State's interest that his payments not be erroneously terminated, clearly outweighs the State's competing concern to prevent any increase in its fiscal and administrative burdens. As the District Court correctly concluded, "the stakes are simply too high for the welfare recipient, and the possibility for honest error or irritable misjudgment too great, to allow termination of aid without giving the recipient a chance, if he so desires, to be fully informed of the case against him so that he may contest its basis and produce evidence in rebuttal."

QUESTIONS

1 In an affluent society such as ours, do all individuals who are unable to support themselves have a *moral* right to welfare?

2 Are welfare payments a form of charity?

Majority Opinion in *Wyman v. James*

Justice Harry A. Blackmun

A biographical sketch of Justice Harry A. Blackmun is found on page 38.

This case centers on the question, "Can a beneficiary of the Aid to Families with Dependent Children program (AFDC) refuse a home visit by a caseworker without risking the termination of benefits?" One such beneficiary, Barbara James, refused such a visit. When notified that refusal meant the termination of benefits, she brought a suit against the commissioner of the New York department of social services (Wyman) and others. James argued that a caseworker's visit constitutes a search and thereby violates Fourth and Fourteenth Amendment rights. (The Fourth Amendment asserts "the right of the people to be secure in their persons, houses, papers, and effects." The Fourteenth Amendment prohibits states from depriving any person of life, liberty, or property "without due process of law.") The District Court of New York ruled in favor of James. The case was appealed to the United States Supreme Court, which reversed the lower court's decision.

In ruling against James, the Court held that the home visitation in question is a *reasonable* administrative tool and does not violate any Fourth or Fourteenth Amendment rights. In presenting the factors which make it a reasonable tool, Justice Blackmun describes such payments as a form of charity. He stresses the public interest (1) in seeing that the money is utilized as those who supply the funds intend it to be and (2) in assisting and rehabilitating the beneficiary.

I

Plaintiff Barbara James is the mother of a son, Maurice, who was born in May 1967. They reside in New York City. Mrs. James first applied for AFDC assistance shortly before Maurice's birth. A caseworker made a visit to her apartment at that time without objection. The assistance was authorized.

Two years later, on May 8, 1969, a caseworker wrote Mrs. James that she would visit her home on May 14. Upon receipt of this advice, Mrs. James telephoned the worker that, although she was willing to supply information "reasonable and relevant" to her need for public assistance, any discussion was not to take place at her home. The worker told Mrs. James that she was required by law to visit in her home and that refusal to permit the visit would result in the termination of assistance. Permission was still denied.

On May 13 the City Department of Social Services sent Mrs. James a notice of intent to discontinue assistance because of the visitation refusal. The notice advised

United States Supreme Court. 400 U.S. 309 (1971).

the beneficiary of her right to a hearing before a review officer. The hearing was requested and was held on May 27. Mrs. James appeared with an attorney at that hearing. They continued to refuse permission for a worker to visit the James home, but again expressed willingness to cooperate and to permit visits elsewhere. The review officer ruled that the refusal was a proper ground for the termination of assistance. His written decision stated:

> "The home visit which Mrs. James refuses to permit is for the purpose of determining if there are any changes in her situation that might affect her eligibility to continue to receive Public Assistance, or that might affect the amount of such assistance, and to see if there are any social services which the Department of Social Services can provide to the family."

A notice of termination was issued on June 2.

Thereupon, without seeking a hearing at the state level, Mrs. James, individually and on behalf of Maurice, and purporting to act on behalf of all other persons similarly situated, instituted the present civil rights suit. She alleged the denial of rights guaranteed to her under the First, Third, Fourth, Fifth, Sixth, Ninth, Tenth, and Fourteenth Amendments, and under Subchapters IV and XVI of the Social Security Act and regulations issued thereunder. She further alleged that she and her son have no income, resources, or support other than the benefits received under the AFDC program. . . .

II

When a case involves a home and some type of official intrusion into that home, as this case appears to do, an immediate and natural reaction is one of concern about Fourth Amendment rights and the protection which that Amendment is intended to afford. Its emphasis indeed is upon one of the most precious aspects of personal security in the home: "The right of the people to be secure in their persons, houses, papers, and effects. . . . " This Court has characterized that right as "basic to a free society." And over the years the Court consistently has been most protective of the privacy of the dwelling. . . .

III

This natural and quite proper protective attitude, however, is not a factor in this case, for the seemingly obvious and simple reason that we are not concerned here with any search by the New York social service agency in the Fourth Amendment meaning of that term. It is true that the governing statute and regulations appear to make mandatory the initial home visit and the subsequent periodic "contacts" (which may include home visits) for the inception and continuance of aid. It is also true that the caseworker's posture in the home visit is perhaps, in a sense, both rehabilitative and investigative. But this latter aspect, we think, is given too broad a character and far more emphasis than it deserves if it is equated with a search in the traditional criminal law context.

We note, too, that the visitation in itself is not forced or compelled, and that the beneficiary's denial of permission is not a criminal act. If consent to the visitation is withheld, no visitation takes place. The aid then never begins or merely ceases, as the case may be. There is no entry of the home and there is no search.

IV

If however, we were to assume that a caseworker's home visit, before or subsequent to the beneficiary's initial qualification for benefits, somehow (perhaps because the average beneficiary might feel she is in no position to refuse consent to the visit), and despite its interview nature, does possess some of the characteristics of a search in the traditional sense, we nevertheless conclude that the visit does not fall within the Fourth Amendment's proscription. This is because it does not descend to the level of unreasonableness. It is unreasonableness which is the Fourth Amendment's standard. . . .

There are a number of factors that compel us to conclude that the home visit proposed for Mrs. James is not unreasonable:

1 The public's interest in this particular segment of the area of assistance to the unfortunate is protection and aid for the dependent child whose family requires such aid for that child. The focus is on the *child* and, further, it is on the child who is *dependent*. There is no more worthy object of the public's concern. The dependent child's needs are paramount, and only with hesitancy would we relegate those needs, in the scale of comparative values, to a position secondary to what the mother claims as her rights.

2 The agency, with tax funds provided from federal as well as from state sources, is fulfilling a public trust. The State, working through its qualified welfare agency, has appropriate and paramount interest and concern in seeing and assuring that the intended and proper objects of that tax-produced assistance are the ones who benefit from the aid it dispenses. Surely it is not unreasonable, in the Fourth Amendment sense or in any other sense of that term, that the State have at its command a gentle means, of limited extent and of practical and considerate application, of achieving that assurance.

3 One who dispenses purely private charity naturally has an interest in and expects to know how his charitable funds are utilized and put to work. The public, when it is the provider, rightly expects the same. It might well expect more, because of the trust aspect of public funds, and the recipient, as well as the caseworker, has not only an interest but an obligation.

4 The emphasis of the New York statutes and regulations is upon the home, upon "close contact" with the beneficiary, upon restoring the aid recipient "to a condition of self-support," and upon the relief of his distress. The federal emphasis is no different. It is upon "assistance and rehabilitation," upon maintaining and strengthening family life, and upon "maximum self-support and personal independence consistent with the maintenance of continuing parental care and protection. . . . " It requires cooperation from the state agency upon specified standards and in specified ways. . . .

5 The means employed by the New York agency are significant. Mrs. James received written notice several days in advance of the intended home visit.[1] . . .

6 Mrs. James, in fact, on this record presents no specific complaint of any unreasonable intrusion of her home. . . . She alleges only, in general and nonspecific terms, that on previous visits and, on information and belief, on visitation at the home of other aid recipients, "questions concerning personal relationships, beliefs and behavior are raised and pressed which are unnecessary for a determination of continuing eligibility.". . . What Mrs. James appears to want from the agency that provides her and her infant son with the necessities for life is the right to receive those necessities upon her own informational terms, to utilize the Fourth Amendment as a wedge for imposing those terms, and to avoid questions of any kind. . . .

V

Our holding today does not mean, of course, that a termination of benefits upon refusal of a home visit is to be upheld against constitutional challenge under all conceivable circumstances. The early morning mass raid upon homes of welfare recipients is not unknown. But that is not this case. Facts of that kind present another case for another day.

We therefore conclude that the home visitation as structured by the New York statutes and regulations is a reasonable administrative tool; that it serves a valid and proper administrative purpose for the dispensation of the AFDC program; that it is not an unwarranted invasion of personal privacy; and that it violates no right guaranteed by the Fourth Amendment. . . .

QUESTIONS

1 Justice Blackmun sees private dispensation of charity as analogous to government dispensation of welfare monies. Is this a good analogy? Explain.

2 Are people like Barbara James expected to sacrifice certain important political rights for economic reasons? If yes, is this morally acceptable?

---

[1]It is true that the record contains 12 affidavits, all essentially identical, of aid recipients (other than Mrs. James) which recite that a caseworker "most often" comes without notice; that when he does, the plans the recipient had for that time cannot be carried out; that the visit is "very embarrassing to me if the caseworker comes when I have company"; and that the caseworker "sometimes asks very personal questions" in front of children.

Dissenting Opinion in *Wyman v. James*

Justice William O. Douglas

William O. Douglas (1898–1980), who received his law degree from the Yale University Law School and taught law for a number of years, served as associate justice of the United States Supreme Court from 1939 to 1975. Justice Douglas is the author of many books, including The Right of the People *(1958),* The Anatomy of Liberty *(1963), and* The Court Years: The Autobiography of William O. Douglas *(1980).*

Justice Douglas asks whether "the government by force of its largesse has the power to 'buy up rights' guaranteed by the Constitution." Citing various forms of government payments, Douglas sees it as inconsistent that the recipients of some of these payments are not subjected to "searches without warrant," but that the recipients of aid to families with dependent children are. He criticizes the view that the latter kind of aid is a form of charity whose recipients are rightfully subject to policing activities which deny them their constitutional rights.

We are living in a society where one of the most important forms of property is government largesse which some call the "new property." The payrolls of government are but one aspect of that "new property." Defense contracts, highway contracts, and the other multifarious forms of contracts are another part. So are subsidies to air, rail, and other carriers. So are disbursements by government for scientific research. So are TV and radio licenses to use the air space which of course is part of the public domain. Our concern here is not with those subsidies but with grants that directly or indirectly implicate the *home life* of the recipients.

In 1969 roughly 127 billion dollars were spent by the federal, state, and local governments on "social welfare." To farmers alone almost four billion dollars were paid, in part for not growing certain crops. Almost 129,000 farmers received $5,000 or more, their total benefits exceeding $1,450,000,000. Those payments were in some instances very large, a few running a million or more a year. But the majority were payments under $5,000 each.

Yet almost every beneficiary whether rich or poor, rural or urban, has a "house"— one of the places protected by the Fourth Amendment against "unreasonable searches and seizures." The question in this case is whether receipt of largesse from the government makes the *home* of the beneficiary subject to access by an inspector of the agency of oversight, even though the beneficiary objects to the intrusion and even though the Fourth Amendment's procedure for access to one's *house* or *home* is not followed. The penalty here is not, of course, invasion of the privacy of Barbara James, only her loss of federal or state largesse. That, however, is merely rephrasing the

United States Supreme Court. 400 U.S. 309 (1971).

problem. Whatever the semantics, the central question is whether the government by force of its largesse has the power to "buy up" rights guaranteed by the Constitution. But for the assertion of her constitutional right, Barbara James in this case would have received the welfare benefit. . . .

. . . In *See v. City of Seattle* (1967) we [decided] that the "businessman, like the occupant of a residence, has a constitutional right to go about his business free from unreasonable official entries upon his private commercial property." There is not the slightest hint in *See* that the Government could condition a business license on the "consent" of the licensee to the administrative searches we held violated the Fourth Amendment. It is a strange jurisprudence indeed which safeguards the businessman at his place of work from warrantless searches but will not do the same for a mother in her *home*.

Is a search of her home without a warrant made "reasonable" merely because she is dependent on government largesse?

Judge Skelly Wright has stated the problem succinctly:

"Welfare has long been considered the equivalent of charity and its recipients have been subjected to all kinds of dehumanizing experiences in the government's effort to police its welfare payments. In fact, over half a billion dollars are expended annually for administration and policing in connection with the Aid to Families with Dependent Children program. Why such large sums are necessary for administration and policing has never been adequately explained. No such sums are spent policing the government subsidies granted to farmers, airlines, steamship companies, and junk mail dealers, to name but a few. The truth is that in this subsidy area society has simply adopted a double standard, one for aid to business and the farmer and a different one for welfare." Poverty, Minorities, and Respect For Law, 1970 Duke L. J. 425, 437-438.

If the welfare recipient was not Barbara James but a prominent, affluent cotton or wheat farmer receiving benefit payments for not growing crops, would not the approach be different? Welfare in aid of dependent children, like social security and unemployment benefits, has an aura of suspicion. There doubtless are frauds in every sector of public welfare whether the recipient be a Barbara James or someone who is prominent or influential. But constitutional rights—here the privacy of the *home*—are obviously not dependent on the poverty or on the affluence of the beneficiary. It is the precincts of the *home* that the Fourth Amendment protects; and their privacy is as important to the lowly as to the mighty. . . .

I would place the same restrictions on inspectors entering the *homes* of welfare beneficiaries as are on inspectors entering the *homes* of those on the payroll of government, or the *homes* of those who contract with the government, or the *homes* of those who work for those having government contracts. The values of the *home* protected by the Fourth Amendment are not peculiar to capitalism as we have known it; they are equally relevant to the new form of socialism which we are entering. Moreover, as the numbers of functionaries and inspectors multiply, the need for protection of the individual becomes indeed more essential if the values of a free society are to remain. . . .

QUESTIONS

1 At the beginning of his opinion, Justice Douglas lists various subsidy programs as examples of government largesse. Are the programs he lists analogous to the welfare program under which Barbara James received funds? What are the similarities? What are the differences?

2 Is it morally correct for those who receive what is traditionally called "welfare" (e.g., aid to families with dependent children) to be subjected to attempts to "reform" their lives and to checkups by government caseworkers?

The Right to Eat and the Duty to Work

Trudy Govier

Trudy Govier is a philosopher who has taught at Trent University, Ontario. Her areas of specialization are moral philosophy and logic. Govier's articles include "What Should We Do About Future People?," "Nuclear Illusions and Individual Obligations," and "Thoughts From Under the Nuclear Umbrella."

Govier focuses on issues arising out of the question, "Should the needy have a legal right to welfare benefits?" She first examines three positions that could be adopted in response: (1) the individualist (libertarian) position; (2) the permissive position; and (3) the puritan position. She proceeds to evaluate the three positions' policies regarding welfare on the basis of both utilitarian considerations and considerations of social justice. Govier concludes that permissivism is superior from both standpoints.

Although the topic of welfare is not one with which philosophers have often concerned themselves, it is a topic which gives rise to many complex and fascinating questions— some in the area of political philosophy, some in the area of ethics, and some of a more practical kind. The variety of issues related to the subject of welfare makes it particularly necessary to be clear just which issue one is examining in a discussion of welfare. In a recent book on the subject, Nicholas Rescher asks:

> In what respects and to what extent is society, working through the instrumentality of the state, responsible for the welfare of its members? What demands for the promotion of his welfare can an individual reasonably make upon his society? These are questions to which no answer can be given in terms of some *a priori* approach with reference to universal ultimates. Whatever answer can appropriately be given will depend, in the final analysis, on what the society decides it should be.[1]

Reprinted with permission of the publisher from *Philosophy of the Social Sciences*, vol. 5 (1975), pp. 125–143.

[1]Nichols Rescher, *Welfare: Social Issues in Philosophical Perspective,* p. 114.

Rescher raises this question only to avoid it. His response to his own question is that a society has all and only those responsibilities for its members that it thinks it has. Although this claim is trivially true as regards legal responsibilities, it is inadequate from a moral perspective. If one imagines the case of an affluent society which leaves the blind, the disabled, and the needy to die of starvation, the incompleteness of Rescher's account becomes obvious. In this imagined case one is naturally led to raise the question as to whether those in power ought to supply those in need with the necessities of life. Though the needy have no legal right to welfare benefits of any kind, one might very well say that they ought to have such a right. It is this claim which I propose to discuss here.[2]

I shall approach this issue by examining three positions which may be adopted in response to it. These are:

1 *The Individualist Position:* Even in an affluent society, one ought not to have any legal right to state-supplied welfare benefits.

2 *The Permissive Position:* In a society with sufficient resources, one ought to have an unconditional legal right to receive state supplied welfare benefits. (That is, one's right to receive such benefits ought not to depend on one's behaviour; it should be guaranteed).

3 *The Puritan Position:* In a society with sufficient resources one ought to have a legal right to state-supplied welfare benefits; this right ought to be conditional, however, on one's willingness to work.

But before we examine these positions, some preliminary clarification must be attempted. . . .

Welfare systems are state-supported systems which supply benefits, usually in the form of cash income, to those who are in need. Welfare systems thus exist in the sort of social context where there is some private ownership of property. If no one owned anything individually (except possibly his own body), and all goods were considered to be the joint property of everyone, then this type of welfare system could not exist. A state might take on the responsibility for the welfare of its citizens, but it could not meet this responsibility by distributing a level of cash income which such citizens would spend to purchase the goods essential for life. The welfare systems which exist in the western world do exist against the background of extensive private ownership of property. It is in this context that I propose to discuss moral questions about having

[2]One might wish to discuss moral questions concerning welfare in the context of natural rights doctrines. Indeed, Article 22 of the United Nations Declaration of Human Rights states, "Everyone, as a member of society, has the right to social security and is entitled, through national effort and international cooperation and in accordance with the organization and resources of each State, to the economic, social and cultural rights indispensable for his dignity and the free development of his personality." I make no attempt to defend the right to welfare as a natural right. Granting that rights imply responsibilities or duties and that "ought" implies "can," it would only be intelligible to regard the right to social security as a natural right if all states were able to ensure the minimum well-being of their citizens. This is not the case. And a natural right is one which is by definition supposed to belong to all human beings simply in virtue of their status as human beings. The analysis given here in the permissive view is compatible with the claim that all human beings have a *prima facie* natural right to social security. It is not, however, compatible with the claim that all human beings have a natural right to social security if this right is regarded as one which is so absolute as to be inviolable under any and all conditions.

a right to welfare benefits. By setting out my questions in this way, I do not intend to endorse the institution of private property, but only to discuss questions which many people find real and difficult in the context of the social organization which they actually do experience. The present analysis of welfare is intended to apply to societies which (a) have the institution of private property, if not for means of production, at least for some basic good; and (b) possess sufficient resources so that it is at least possible for every member of the society to be supplied with the necessities of life.

1 The Individualist View

It might be maintained that a person in need has no legitimate moral claim on those around him and that the hypothetical inattentive society which left its blind citizens to beg or starve cannot rightly be censured for doing so. This view, which is dramatically at odds with most of contemporary social thinking, lives on in the writings of Ayn Rand and her followers.[3] The Individualist sets a high value on uncoerced personal choice. He sees each person as a responsible agent who is able to make his own decisions and to plan his own life. He insists that with the freedom to make decisions goes responsibility for the consequences of those decisions. A person has every right, for example, to spend ten years of his life studying Sanskrit—but if, as a result of this choice, he is unemployable, he ought not to expect others to labour on his behalf. No one has a proper claim on the labour of another, or on the income ensuing from that labour, unless he can repay the labourer in a way acceptable to that labourer himself. Government welfare schemes provide benefits from funds gained largely by taxing earned income. One cannot "opt out" of such schemes. To the Individualist, this means that a person is forced to work part of his time for others.

Suppose that a man works forty hours and earns two hundred dollars. Under modern-day taxation, it may well be that he can spend only two-thirds of that money as he chooses. The rest is taken by government and goes to support programmes which the working individual may not himself endorse. The beneficiaries of such programmes—those beneficiaries who do not work themselves—are as though they have slaves working for them. Backed by the force which government authorities can command, they are able to exist on the earnings of others. Those who support them do not do so voluntarily, out of charity; they do so on government command.

> Someone across the street is unemployed. Should you be taxed extra to pay for his expenses? Not at all. You have not injured him, you are not responsible for the fact that he is unemployed (unless you are a senator or bureaucrat who agitated for further curtailing of business which legislation passed, with the result that your neighbour was laid off by the curtailed business). You may voluntarily wish to help him out, or better still, try to get him a job to put him on his feet again; but since you have initiated no aggressive act against him, and neither purposefully nor accidentally injured him in any way, you should not be legally penalized for the fact of his unemployment.[4]

[3]See, for example, Ayn Rand's *Atlas Shrugged, The Virtue of Selfishness,* and *Capitalism: the Unknown Ideal.*

[4]John Hospers, *Libertarianism: A Political Philosophy for Tomorrow,* p. 67.

The Individualist need not lack concern for those in need. He may give generously to charity; he might give more generously still, if his whole income were his to use, as he would like it to be. He may also believe that, as a matter of empirical fact, existing government programmes do not actually help the poor. They support a cumbersome bureaucracy and they use financial resources which, if untaxed, might be used by those with initiative to pursue job-creating endeavours. The thrust of the Individualist's position is that each person owns his own body and his own labour; thus each person is taken to have a virtually unconditional right to the income which that labour can earn him in a free market place.[5] For anyone to pre-empt part of a worker's earnings without that worker's voluntary consent is tantamount to robbery. And the fact that the government is the intermediary through which this deed is committed does not change its moral status one iota.

On an Individualist's view, those in need should be cared for by charities or through other schemes to which contributions are voluntary. Many people may wish to insure themselves against unforeseen calamities and they should be free to do so. But there is no justification for non-optional government schemes financed by taxpayers' money. . . .

2 The Permissive View

Directly contrary to the Individualist view of welfare is what I have termed the Permissive view. According to this view, in a society which has sufficient resources so that everyone could be supplied with the necessities of life, every individual ought to be given the legal right to social security, and this right ought not to be conditional in any way upon an individual's behavior. *Ex hypothesi* the society which we are discussing has sufficient goods to provide everyone with food, clothing, shelter and other necessities. Someone who does without these basic goods is scarcely living at all, and a society which takes no steps to change this state of affairs implies by its inaction that the life of such a person is without value. It does not execute him; but it may allow him to die. It does not put him in prison; but it may leave him with a life of lower quality than that of some prison inmates. A society which can rectify these circumstances and does not can justly be accused of imposing upon the needy either death or lifelong deprivation. And those characteristics which make a person needy—whether they be illness, old age, insanity, feeblemindedness, inability to find paid work, or even poor moral character—are insufficient to make him deserve the fate to which an inactive society would in effect condemn him. One would not be executed for inability or failure to find paid work; neither should one be allowed to die for this misfortune or failing.

A person who cannot or does not find his own means of social security does not thereby forfeit his status as a human being. If other human beings, with physical,

[5]I say virtually unconditional, because an Individualist such as John Hospers sees a legitimate moral role for government in preventing the use of force by some citizens against others. Since this is the case, I presume that he would also regard as legitimate such taxation as was necessary to support this function. Presumably that taxation would be seen as consented to by all, on the grounds that all "really want" government protection.

mental and moral qualities different from his, are regarded as having the right to life and to the means of life, then so too should he be regarded. A society which does not accept the responsibility for supplying such a person with the basic necessities of life is, in effect, endorsing a difference between its members which is without moral justification. . . .

The adoption of a Permissive view of welfare would have significant practical implications. If there were a legal right, unconditional upon behaviour, to a specified level of state-supplied benefits, then state investigation of the prospective welfare recipient could be kept to a minimum. Why he is in need, whether he can work, whether he is willing to work, and what he does while receiving welfare benefits are on this view quite irrelevant to his right to receive those benefits. A welfare recipient is a person who claims from his society that to which he is legally entitled under a morally based welfare scheme. The fact that he makes this claim licenses no special state or societal interference with his behaviour. If the Permissive view of welfare were widely believed, then there would be no social stigma attached to being on welfare. There is such a stigma, and many long-term welfare recipients are considerably demoralized by their dependent status.[6] These facts suggest that the Permissive view of welfare is not widely held in our society.

3 The Puritan View

This view of welfare rather naturally emerges when we consider that no one can have a right to something without someone else's, or some group of other persons', having responsibilities correlative to this right. In the case in which the right in question is a legal right to social security, the correlative responsibilities may be rather extensive. They have been deemed responsibilities of "the state." The state will require resources and funds to meet these responsibilities, and these do not emerge from the sky miraculously, or zip into existence as a consequence of virtually effortless acts of will. They are taken by the state from its citizens, often in the form of taxation on earned income. The funds given to the welfare recipient and many of the goods which he purchases with these funds are produced by other members of society, many of whom give a considerable portion of their time and their energy to this end. If a state has the moral responsibility to ensure the social security of its citizens then all the citizens of that state have the responsibility to provide state agencies with the means to carry out their duties. This responsibility, in our present contingent circumstances, seems to generate an obligation to *work*.

A person who works helps to produce the goods which all use in daily living and, when paid, contributes through taxation to government endeavours. The person who does not work, even though able to work, does not make his contribution to social efforts towards obtaining the means of life. He is not entitled to a share of the goods produced by others if he chooses not to take part in their labours. Unless he can show that there is a moral justification for his not making the sacrifice of time and energy which others make, he has no legitimate claim to welfare benefits. If he is disabled

---

[6]Ian Adams, William Cameron, Brian Hill, and Peter Penz, *The Real Poverty Report,* pp. 167–187.

or unable to obtain work, he cannot work; hence he has no need to justify his failure to work. But if he does choose not to work, he would have to justify his choice by saying "others should sacrifice their time and energy for me; I have no need to sacrifice time and energy for them." This principle, a version of what Rawls refers to as a free-rider's principle, simply will not stand up to criticism.[7] To deliberately avoid working and benefit from the labours of others is morally indefensible.

Within a welfare system erected on these principles, the right to welfare is conditional upon one's satisfactorily accounting for his failure to obtain the necessities of life by his own efforts. Someone who is severely disabled mentally or physically, or who for some other reason cannot work, is morally entitled to receive welfare benefits. Someone who chooses not to work is not. The Puritan view of welfare is a kind of compromise between the Individualist view and the Permissive view. . . .

The Puritan view of welfare, based as it is on the inter-relation between welfare and work, provides a rationale for two connected principles which those establishing welfare schemes in Canada and in the United States seem to endorse. First of all, those on welfare should never receive a higher income than the working poor. Secondly, a welfare scheme should, in some way or other, incorporate incentives to work. These principles, which presuppose that it is better to work than not to work, emerge rather naturally from the contingency which is at the basis of the Puritan view: the goods essential for social security are products of the labour of some members of society. If we wish to have a continued supply of such goods, we must encourage those who work to produce them. . . .

APPRAISAL OF POLICIES: SOCIAL CONSEQUENCES AND SOCIAL JUSTICE

In approaching the appraisal of prospective welfare policies under these two aspects I am, of course, making some assumptions about the moral appraisal of suggested social policies. Although these cannot possibly be justified here, it may be helpful to articulate them, at least in a rough way.

Appraisal of social policies is in part teleological. To the extent that a policy, P, increases the total human welfare more than does an alternative policy, P', P is a better social policy then P'. Or, if P leaves the total human welfare as it is, while P' diminishes it, then to that extent, P is a better social policy than P'. Even this skeletal formulation of the teleological aspect of appraisal reveals why appraisal cannot be entirely teleological. We consider total consequences—effects upon the total of "human well-being" in a society. But this total is a summation of consequences on different individuals. It includes no judgements as to how far we allow one individual's well-being to decrease while another's increases, under the same policy. Judgements relating to the latter problems are judgements about social justice.

In appraising social policies we have to weigh up considerations of total well-being

---

[7]See *A Theory of Justice*, pp. 124, 136. Rawls defines the free-rider as one who relies on the principle "everyone is to act justly except for myself, if I choose not to," and says that his position is a version of egoism which is eliminated as a morally acceptable principle by formal constraints. This conclusion regarding the tenability of egoism is one which I accept and which is taken for granted in the present context.

against considerations of justice. Just how this is to be done, precisely, I would not pretend to know. However, the absence of precise methods does not mean that we should relinquish attempts at appraisal: some problems are already with us, and thought which is necessarily tentative and imprecise is still preferable to no thought at all.

1 Consequences of Welfare Schemes

First, let us consider the consequences of the non-scheme advocated by the Individualist. He would have us abolish all non-optional government programmes which have as their goal the improvement of anyone's personal welfare. This rejection extends to health schemes, pension plans and education, as well as to welfare and unemployment insurance. So following the Individualist would lead to very sweeping changes.

The Individualist will claim (as do Hospers and Ayn Rand) that on the whole his non-scheme will bring beneficial consequences. He will admit, as he must, that there are people who would suffer tremendously if welfare and other social security programmes were simply terminated. Some would even die as a result. We cannot assume that spontaneously developing charities would cover every case of dire need. Nevertheless the Individualist wants to point to benefits which would accrue to businessmen and to working people and their families if taxation were drastically cut. It is his claim that consumption would rise, hence production would rise, job opportunities would be extended, and there would be an economic boom, if people could only spend all their earned income as they wished. This boom would benefit both rich and poor.

There are significant omissions which are necessary in order to render the Individualist's optimism plausible. Either workers and businessmen would have insurance of various kinds, or they would be insecure in their prosperity. If they did have insurance to cover health problems, old age and possible job loss, then they would pay for it; hence they would not be spending their whole earned income on consumer goods. Those who run the insurance schemes could, of course, put this money back into the economy—but government schemes already do this. The economic boom under Individualism would not be as loud as originally expected. Furthermore the goal of increased consumption-increased productivity must be questioned from an ecological viewpoint: many necessary materials are available only in limited quantities.

Finally, a word about charity. It is not to be expected that those who are at the mercy of charities will benefit from this state, either materially or psychologically. Those who prosper will be able to choose between giving a great deal to charity and suffering from the very real insecurity and guilt which would accompany the existence of starvation and grim poverty outside their padlocked doors. It is to be hoped that they would opt for the first alternative. But, if they did, this might be every bit as expensive for them as government-supported benefit schemes are now. If they did not give generously to charity, violence might result. However one looks at it, the consequences of Individualism are unlikely to be good.

Welfare schemes operating in Canada today are almost without exception based upon the principles of the Puritan view. To see the consequences of that type of welfare scheme we have only to look at the results of our own welfare programmes. Taxation to support such schemes is high, though not so intolerably so as to have led to widescale resentment among taxpayers. Canadian welfare programmes are attended by complicated and often cumbersome bureaucracy, some of which results from the interlocking of municipal, provincial and federal governments in the administration and financing of welfare programmes. The cost of the programmes is no doubt increased by this bureaucracy; not all the tax money directed to welfare programmes goes to those in need. Puritan welfare schemes do not result in social catastrophe or in significant business stagnation—this much we know, because we already live with such schemes. Their adverse consequences, if any, are felt primarily not by society generally nor by businessmen and the working segment of the public, but rather by recipients of welfare.

Both the Special Senate Committee Report on Poverty and the Real Poverty Report criticize our present system of welfare for its demoralization of recipients, who often must deal with several levels of government and are vulnerable to arbitrary interference on the part of administering officials. Welfare officials have the power to check on welfare recipients and cut off or limit their benefits under a large number of circumstances. The dangers to welfare recipients in terms of anxiety, threats to privacy and loss of dignity are obvious. According to the Senate Report, the single aspect shared by all Canada's welfare systems is "a record of failure and insufficiency, of bureaucratic rigidities that often result in the degradation, humiliation and alienation of recipients."[8] The writers of this report cite many instances of humiliation, leaving the impression that these are too easily found to be "incidental aberrations."[9] Concern that a welfare recipient either be unable to work or be willing to work (if unemployed) can easily turn into concern about how he spends the income supplied him, what his plans for the future are, where he lives, how many children he has. And the rationale underlying the Puritan scheme makes the degradation of welfare recipients a natural consequence of welfare institutions. Work is valued and only he who works is thought to contribute to society. Welfare recipients are regarded as parasites and spongers—so when they are treated as such, this is only what we should have expected. Being on welfare in a society which thinks and acts in this fashion can be psychologically debilitating. Welfare recipients who are demoralized by their downgraded status and relative lack of personal freedom can be expected to be made less capable of self-sufficiency. To the extent that this is so, welfare systems erected on Puritan principles may defeat their own purposes.

In fairness, it must be noted here that bureaucratic checks and controls are not a feature only of Puritan welfare systems. To a limited extent, Permissive systems would have to incorporate them too. Within those systems, welfare benefits would be given only to those whose income was inadequate to meet basic needs. However, there would be no checks on "willingness to work," and there would be no need for welfare workers to evaluate the merits of the daily activities of recipients. If a Permissive guaranteed

---

[8]*Senate Report on Poverty*, p. 73.

[9]The Hamilton Public Welfare Department takes automobile licence plates from recipients, making them available again only to those whose needs meet with the Department's approval. (*Real Poverty Report*, p. 186.) The *Globe and Mail* for 12 January 1974 reported that welfare recipients in the city of Toronto are to be subjected to computerized budgeting. In the summer of 1973, the two young daughters of an Alabama man on welfare were sterilized against their own wishes and without their parents' informed consent. (See *Time*, 23 July 1973.)

income system were administered through income tax returns, everyone receiving the basic income and those not needing it paying it back in taxes, then the special status of welfare recipients would fade. They would no longer be singled out as a special group within the population. It is to be expected that living solely on government-supplied benefits would be psychologically easier in that type of situation.

Thus it can be argued that for the recipients of welfare, a Permissive scheme has more advantages than a Puritan one. This is not a very surprising conclusion. The Puritan scheme is relatively disadvantageous to recipients, and Puritans would acknowledge this point; they will argue that the overall consequences of Permissive schemes are negative in that these schemes benefit some at too great a cost to others. (Remember, we are not yet concerned with the *justice* of welfare policies, but solely with their consequences as regards *total* human well-being within the society in question.) The concern which most people have regarding the Permissive scheme relates to its costs and its dangers to the "work ethic." It is commonly thought that people work only because they have to work to survive in a tolerable style. If a guaranteed income scheme were adopted by the government, this incentive to work would disappear. No one would be faced with the choice between a nasty and boring job and starvation. Who would do the nasty and boring jobs then? Many of them are not eliminable and they have to be done somehow, by someone. Puritans fear that a great many people—even some with relatively pleasant jobs—might simply cease to work if they could receive non-stigmatized government money to live on. If this were to happen, the permissive society would simply grind to a halt.

In addressing these anxieties about the consequences of Permissive welfare schemes, we must recall that welfare benefits are set to ensure only that those who do not work have a bearable existence, with an income sufficient for basic needs, and that they have this income regardless of why they fail to work. Welfare benefits will not finance luxury living for a family of five! If jobs are adequately paid so that workers receive more than the minimum welfare income in an earned salary, then there will still be a financial incentive to take jobs. What guaranteed income schemes will do is to raise the salary floor. This change will benefit the many non-unionized workers in service and clerical occupations.

Furthermore it is unlikely that people work solely due to (i) the desire for money and the things it can buy and (ii) belief in the Puritan work ethic. There are many other reasons for working, some of which would persist in a society which had adopted a Permissive welfare system. Most people are happier when their time is structured in some way, when they are active outside their own homes, when they feel themselves part of an endeavour whose purposes transcend their particular egoistic ones. Women often choose to work outside the home for these reasons as much as for financial ones. With these and other factors operating I cannot see that the adoption of a Permissive welfare scheme would be followed by a level of slothfulness which would jeopardize human well-being.

Another worry about the Permissive scheme concerns cost. It is difficult to comment on this in a general way, since it would vary so much from case to case. Of Canada at the present it has been said that a guaranteed income scheme administered through income tax would cost less than social security payments administered through the present bureaucracies. It is thought that this saving would result from a drastic cut in administrative costs. The matter of the work ethic is also relevant to the question of costs. Within a Puritan framework it is very important to have a high level of employment and there is a tendency to resist any reorganization which results in there being fewer jobs available. Some of these proposed reorganizations would save money; strictly speaking we should count the cost of keeping jobs which are objectively unnecessary as part of the cost of Puritanism regarding welfare.

In summary, we can appraise Individualism, Puritanism and Permissivism with respect to their anticipated consequences, as follows: Individualism is unacceptable; Puritanism is tolerable, but has some undesirable consequences for welfare recipients; Permissivism appears to be the winner. Worries about bad effects which Permissive welfare schemes might have due to high costs and (alleged) reduced work-incentives appear to be without solid basis.

2   Social Justice under Proposed Welfare Schemes

We must now try to consider the merits of Individualism, Puritanism and Permissivism with regard to their impact on the distribution of the goods necessary for well-being. [Robert] Nozick has argued against the whole conception of a distributive justice on the grounds that it presupposes that goods are like manna from heaven: we simply get them and then have a problem—to whom to give them. According to Nozick we know where things come from and we do not have the problem of to whom to give them. There is not really a problem of distributive justice, for there is no central distributor giving out manna from heaven! It is necessary to counter Nozick on this point since his reaction to the (purported) problems of distributive justice would undercut much of what follows.[10]

There is a level at which Nozick's point is obviously valid. If A discovers a cure for cancer, then it is A and not B or C who is responsible for this discovery. On Nozick's view this is taken to imply that A should reap any monetary profits which are forthcoming; other people will benefit from the cure itself. Now although it cannot be doubted that A is a bright and hardworking person, neither can it be denied that A and his circumstances are the product of many co-operative endeavours: schools and laboratories, for instance. Because this is so, I find Nozick's claim that "we know where things come from" unconvincing at a deeper level. Since achievements like A's presuppose extensive social co-operation, it is morally permissible to regard even the monetary profits accruing from them as shareable by the "owner" and society at large.

Laws support existing income levels in many ways. Governments specify taxation so as to further determine net income. Property ownership is a legal matter. In all these ways people's incomes and possibilities for obtaining income are affected by deliberate state action. It is always possible to raise questions about the moral desirability of actual conventional arrangements. Should university professors earn less than lawyers? More than waitresses? Why? Why not? Anyone who gives an account of distributive justice is trying to specify principles which will make it possible to

---

[10]Robert Nozick, "Distributive Justice," *Philosophy and Public Affairs*, Fall 1973.

answer questions such as these, and nothing in Nozick's argument suffices to show that the questions are meaningless or unimportant.

Any human distribution of anything is unjust insofar as differences exist for no good reason. If goods did come like manna from heaven and the Central Distributor gave A ten times more than B, we should want to know why. The skewed distribution might be deemed a just one if A's needs were objectively ten times greater than B's, or if B refused to accept more than his small portion of goods. But if no reason at all could be given for it, or if only an irrelevant reason could be given (e.g., A is blue-eyed and B is not), then it is an unjust distribution. All the views we have expounded concerning welfare permit differences in income level. Some philosophers would say that such differences are never just, although they may be necessary, for historical or utilitarian reasons. Whether or not this is so, it is admittedly very difficult to say just what would constitute a good reason for giving A a higher income than B. Level of need, degree of responsibility, amount of training, unpleasantness of work—all these have been proposed and all have some plausibility. We do not need to tackle all this larger problem in order to consider justice under proposed welfare systems. For we can deal here solely with the question of whether everyone should receive a floor level of income; decisions on this matter are independent of decisions on overall equality or principles of variation among incomes above the floor. The Permissivist contends that all should receive at least the floor income; the Individualist and the Puritan deny this. All would claim justice for their side.

The Individualist attempts to justify extreme variations in income, with some people below the level where they can fulfill their basic needs, with reference to the fact of people's actual accomplishments. This approach to the question is open to the same objections as those which have already been raised against Nozick's non-manna-from-heaven argument, and I shall not repeat them here. Let us move on to the Puritan account. It is because goods emerge from human efforts that the Puritan advances his view of welfare. He stresses the unfairness of a system which would permit some people to take advantage of others. A Permissive welfare system would do this, as it makes no attempt to distinguish between those who choose not to work and those who cannot work. No one should be able to take advantage of another under the auspices of a government institution. The Puritan scheme seeks to eliminate this possibility, and for that reason, Puritans would allege, it is a more just scheme than the Permissive one.

Permissivists can best reply to this contention by acknowledging that any instance of free-riding would be an instance where those working were done an injustice, but by showing that any justice which the Puritan preserves by eliminating free-riding is outweighed by *injustice* perpetrated elsewhere. Consider the children of the Puritan's free-riders. They will suffer greatly for the "sins" of their parents. Within the institution of the family, the Puritan cannot suitably hurt the guilty without cruelly depriving the innocent. There is a sense, too, in which Puritanism does injustice to the many people on welfare who are not free-riders. It perpetuates the opinion that they are non-contributors to society and this doctrine, which is over-simplified if not downright false, has a harmful effect upon welfare recipients.

Social justice is not simply a matter of the distribution of goods, or the income with which goods are to be purchased. It is also a matter of the protection of rights. Western societies claim to give their citizens equal rights in political and legal contexts; they also claim to endorse the larger conception of a right to life. Now it is possible to interpret these rights in a limited and formalistic way, so that the duties correlative to them are minimal. On the limited, or negative, interpretation, to say that A has a right to life is simply to say that others have a duty not to interfere with A's attempts to keep himself alive. This interpretation of the right to life is compatible with Individualism as well as with Puritanism. But it is an inadequate interpretation of the right to life and of other rights. A right to vote is meaningless if one is starving and unable to get to the polls; a right to equality before the law is meaningless if one cannot afford to hire a lawyer. And so on.

Even a Permissive welfare scheme will go only a very small way towards protecting people's rights. It will amount to a meaningful acknowledgement of a right to life, by ensuring income adequate to purchase food, clothing and shelter—at the very least. These minimum necessities are presupposed by all other rights a society may endorse in that their possession is a precondition of being able to exercise these other rights. Because it protects the rights of all within a society better than do Puritanism and Individualism, the Permissive view can rightly claim superiority over the others with regard to justice.

QUESTIONS

1 Which of the three approaches to welfare described by Govier (individualist, permissive, puritan) is found in our society?
2 Govier finds the permissive position superior to the others on the basis of both utilitarian and justice considerations. What arguments could an individualist offer to rebut Govier's arguments? What arguments could an advocate of the puritan position offer to counter Govier's?

SUGGESTED ADDITIONAL READINGS FOR CHAPTER 8

ARTHUR, JOHN, and WILLIAM SHAW, eds.: *Justice and Economic Distribution*. Englewood Cliffs, N.J.: Prentice-Hall, 1978. This collection of articles epitomizes the dominant current approach to distributive justice. That approach is highly abstract, pays little attention to practical applications, and is usually restricted to the intranational level. The theories which dominate current discussion are those of John Rawls, Robert Nozick, and utilitarianism. The first part of the book presents selections by Rawls, Nozick, and utilitarians. The second part consists of selections which present positions offered in opposition to the dominant theories.

BROWN, PETER G., CONRAD JOHNSON, and PAUL VERNIER, eds.: *Income Support: Conceptual and Policy Issues*. Totowa, N.J.: Rowman and Littlefield, 1981. The articles in this collection examine some of the basic moral and conceptual issues underlying both the welfare reform efforts in the late 1970s and any future attempts to evaluate or change income support policies in the United States. Authors include philosophers, economists, and various policy makers.

FRIEDMAN, MILTON: *Capitalism and Freedom*. Chicago: University of Chicago Press, 1962. For Friedman, an economist and libertarian, the ethical principle governing the distribution of income in a free society is "to each according to what he or the instruments he owns produces." He sees economic freedom as a necessary condition for political freedom.

HARRINGTON, MICHAEL: *Socialism*. New York: Saturday Review Press, 1970, 1972. Harrington explores various "socialisms"—positions which he considers antisocialist. He presents his account of socialism as a possible alternative to both communism and the welfare state.

HAYEK, F. A.: *Law, Legislation and Liberty*. Vol. 2, *The Mirage of Social Justice*. Chicago: University of Chicago Press, 1976. Hayek, a libertarian, considers and criticizes the concept of "social justice." On Hayek's view the ideal of social justice (1) has no meaning, (2) is the harmful and dangerous cause of the misdirection of well-meant efforts, and (3) is a remnant of a closed society and incompatible with the individual freedom promised by an open society.

HELD, VIRGINIA, ed.: *Property, Profits, and Economic Justice*. Belmont, Calif.: Wadsworth, 1980. This is an excellent collection of readings centering on questions about our rights and interests in acquiring and holding property and in increasing or limiting profits.

MACHAN, TIBOR R., ed.: *The Libertarian Alternative: Essays in Social and Political Philosophy*. The writers anthologized in this volume represent a wide spectrum of views although they can all be characterized as "individualist" or "libertarian."

NOZICK, ROBERT: *Anarchy, State, and Utopia*. New York: Basic books, 1974. This book has engendered a great deal of discussion among philosophers concerned with distributive justice. Nozick, who endorses the libertarian conception of justice, holds the libertarian ideal to be exemplified by the principle, "from each as he chooses, to each as he is chosen."

RAWLS, JOHN: "Justice as Fairness." *Philosophical Review*, vol. 67, April 1958, pp. 164–194. In this article, Rawls offers a definition of justice in terms of two principles, which he maintains all rational, self-interested persons would agree are in the equal interests of all. He argues (1) that everyone has the right to equal liberty, and (2) that differences of wealth and privilege are justified only if everyone is free to compete for them and if everyone benefits from them.

————: *A Theory of Justice*. Cambridge, Mass.: Harvard University Press, 1971. This is a more developed discussion of the position Rawls presents in the above article. It is a seminal work that has stimulated a great deal of discussion among philosophers.

SHUE, HENRY: *Basic Rights: Subsistence, Affluence, and U.S. Foreign Policy*. Princeton, N.J.: Princeton University Press, 1980. Shue argues that there is at least one small set of economic rights, subsistence rights, that have equal priority with the highest ranked political rights.

THUROW, LESTER: *The Zero Sum Society*. New York: Basic Books, 1980. Thurow, a professor of economics and management, analyzes the unprecedented economic predicament presently confronting the United States and discusses various policy prescriptions designed to solve our economic problems. In Thurow's view, the government must be willing to make equity decisions designed to achieve and maintain a just distribution of income.

CHAPTER 9

WORLD HUNGER

Widespread world hunger is an undeniable fact. Famines in Africa and Southeast Asia are commonplace. For many in places like Zaire, Haiti, Colombia, and Nigeria malnutrition is an everyday fact of life. Very few of the victims of famine and malnutrition actually "die of hunger"; but they die of illnesses, such as flu and intestinal problems, which they could have survived if they had not been weakened by hunger. The victims are often very old or very young. Aftereffects for those who survive are often tragic and long-lasting. A large number of children are stunted in growth and suffer incapacitating brain damage as a result of malnutrition. Whole populations are permanently weakened, listless, and lethargic, lacking the energy for any economic advances which might help prevent future famines. What does morality dictate that affluent countries (or their people) *should* do to prevent such devastating hunger and malnutrition? What *can* they do? This chapter presents some recent attempts to answer these two inseparable questions. As the readings show, answers concerning the moral *obligations* of more affluent individuals and nations in regard to world hunger are intertwined with answers concerning the *causes of world hunger* and *effective ways of eliminating those causes*.

NEO-MALTHUSIANISM

One answer regarding the causes of world hunger is offered by people labeled "Neo-Malthusians." Following Thomas Robert Malthus (1766–1834), they identify the cause as *overpopulation*. For Malthus, unrestricted population growth necessarily outstrips economic growth, especially the growth in food supplies. This, in turn, *necessarily* results in famines. Uncontrolled fertility is the cause of poverty, and poverty is the cause of the miseries of the poor, including starvation. It has been shown that Malthus was wrong in certain respects, since in many countries the economic growth rate, including the growth in food supplies, has far outstripped the population growth rate.

But contemporary Neo-Malthusians hold that the economic growth rate cannot be sustained. They offer different reasons in support of this view (e.g., political or technical ones), but they all agree that continued economic growth is impossible. Having identified overpopulation as *the cause* of scarcity, Neo-Malthusians locate the solution to problems of world hunger in population control. Optimistic Neo-Malthusians hold that birth-control measures can eventually succeed in curbing population growth sufficiently to avert future famines. Pessimistic Neo-Malthusians hold that serious political and psychological obstacles to planned population-control measures make famines inevitable in some countries. They predict that these famines will in turn effectively curb unmaintainable population growth unless those in more affluent countries intervene. Some pessimistic Neo-Malthusians, including Garrett Hardin in this chapter, use their Malthusian analyses of world hunger to support claims about what more affluent individuals and nations *ought* to do regarding the needs of potential famine victims. The expressions "ethics of triage" and "lifeboat ethics" are often applied to the ethical approaches advocated by pessimistic Neo-Malthusians.

The expression "method of triage" was first used to describe the French approach to their wounded in the First World War. The wounded were sorted into three categories. Those with the slightest injuries were given quick first aid. Those who could not be helped were simply allowed to die. Those in between received the most intensive medical care. Analogously, applying the method of triage to world food problems involves a three-way classification of countries/societies: (1) those which will survive even without aid; (2) those with serious food and population problems which will nevertheless survive if given enough aid because they are prepared to take the measures necessary to bring their food resources and populations into line—these ought to be given the necessary aid; (3) those whose problems are insoluble in the long run because they are not willing to adopt the necessary population-control measures—according to the ethics of triage, this last group should receive no help. Thus, the proponents of the ethics of triage argue that the affluent should help only those potential victims of famine and malnutrition who reside in countries which are effectively trying to bring population size into line with the country's food supply.[1]

The argument for the moral correctness of the ethics of triage is a consequentialist one and depends on the correctness of the following factual claim: Economic aid to countries with long-run "insoluble" problems is only a stopgap measure which in the long run will have highly undesirable consequences. Aid to societies in group 3, it is said, may alleviate current suffering, but it will cause more long-term suffering for the members of both the needy and affluent countries. Suffering will increase because economic aid will enable more people to survive and reproduce. If no real attempt is made to control population growth, the ever-increasing population will make ever-increasing demands on the world food supply. These demands will have a strong adverse effect on the quality of the life led by future members of today's more affluent societies. In time, it will be impossible even for the members of the once affluent countries to survive. If help is withheld from the countries in group 3, however, one of two things will follow. Either the needy countries will instigate measures to limit

---

[1]See especially Paul and William Paddock, *Famine—1975!* (Boston: Little, Brown, 1968).

their populations in keeping with their own resources, or else nature itself through famine and disease will decimate the population to the appropriate level. In effect, those who argue in this way maintain that responsibilities and rights go hand in hand. People in the afflicted societies cause their own problems by having too many children. They are entitled to have their most basic needs met by more affluent individuals and societies only if they accept a crucial responsibility—the responsibility for limiting their fertility sufficiently so that they do not continue to place an ever-growing burden on the world's food resources.

Garrett Hardin's lifeboat-ethics argument echoes some of the major contentions of the ethics of triage. Comparing nations to boats, Hardin maintains that many countries have outstripped their "carrying capacity." He advances a consequentialist argument to support his claim that the affluent *ought not* to help those in the overpopulating countries. In Hardin's view, the long-range effects of food aid will not only be harmful but disastrous for everyone. They will be disastrous for countries whose fertility rates remain uncontrolled by either human planning or nature, since future generations in these countries will suffer massive starvation and profound misery. They will be disastrous for the human species as a whole, since the eventual outcome may be the elimination of the species. Hardin sees no real need to use the method of triage in making decisions about which countries should be given aid. If giving food to *any* overpopulated country does more harm than good, he argues, that food should not be given. For Hardin, "the question of triage does not even arise."[2]

NON-MALTHUSIAN ALTERNATIVES

Criticisms of Neo-Malthusianism take many forms. Some critics, for example, attack the *moral* claims of pessimistic Neo-Malthusians. Rejecting the consequentialist approach to the moral dilemma, they maintain that no matter what the long-term consequences might be, we have an obligation to meet the most basic need of *existing* persons—the need for food. The most prominent attacks against Malthusianism, however, center around rejections of some or all of the Malthusian claims regarding the causes and/or the inevitability of famine and malnutrition in needy, developing countries. The counteranalyses offered reject the Neo-Malthusian contention that the necessary economic growth is impossible. On these analyses, economic growth in the developing countries *themselves* is both possible and an essential part of the solution to problems of world hunger. Two major lines of argument emerge in these counteranalyses.

The first counteranalysis, exemplified by some of the arguments offered by William Murdoch and Allan Oaten in this chapter, focuses on identifying the causes of high fertility rates among the poor in developing countries. Only if we understand why the poor have high rates of reproduction can we help to instigate and support social practices which will tend to end the cycle of poverty, high birth rates, and starvation which Neo-Malthusians see as inevitable. Against the pessimistic Neo-Malthusians, proponents of this analysis argue that famines and malnutrition are not inevitable. Against

[2]Garrett Hardin, "Carrying Capacity as an Ethical Concept," in George R. Lucas, Jr., and Thomas W. Ogletree, eds., *Lifeboat Ethics* (New York: Harper & Row, 1976), p. 131.

the optimistic Neo-Malthusians, they argue that planned birth-control practices backed by government policies are not the solution. Ironically, the major factors influencing high fertility rates are identified as hunger and poverty. The Presidential Commission on World Hunger makes the point succinctly:

> Where hunger and poverty prevail, the population growth rate is more likely to increase than to decrease. Under inequitable social and economic conditions, a poor couple's desire for many children is a response to high infant mortality, the need for extra hands to help earn the family's daily bread, and the hope of support in old age. The key to reducing family size is to improve the social conditions which make large families a reasonable option.[3]

On this analysis, eradicating famine and malnutrition requires social and economic changes in the developing countries themselves, changes which would eliminate some of the gross inequalities of wealth and property in these countries. Without the recommended changes, it is argued, economic growth, including growth in the food supply, will not take place, population growth will not be slowed, and the tragic cycle will be repeated indefinitely.

Some of those who utilize this first approach against Neo-Malthusians argue that the practices of members of more affluent nations prevent some of the poorest countries from increasing their own food supply. The identified culprits include multinational agribusinesses based in Western societies. It is charged that these multinationals have shifted the production of luxury items for the Western market from the highly industrialized countries to underdeveloped ones where cheap land and labor are available. As a result, the land in needy, underdeveloped countries is used to produce goods for members of the more affluent countries, while the food that is needed for the home market remains unproduced. In addition, it is argued that the international economic order favors the affluent, industrialized nations and is shaped by their needs. It is the affluent, industrialized societies which largely determine the prices for both the manufactured goods which developing nations must import and the agricultural products which the needy countries export. To the extent that the practices of those in affluent societies work against the potential self-sufficiency and real economic growth of the developing countries, they help create and perpetuate the cycle of poverty, high fertility rates, and hunger.

The second counteranalysis against Neo-Malthusianism comes from Marxist-socialists and incorporates some of the elements of the first counteranalysis. Marxist-socialists reject both the contention that overpopulation is the cause of scarcity in the world and the contention that the requisite economic growth is impossible. They identify capitalism as the major cause of worldwide scarcity. Agreeing with the kinds of claims just discussed concerning the negative impact of multinational corporations on the economic growth of developing countries, they see a Marxist-socialist economic system as the only solution to the problem of world hunger. Howard L. Parsons's article in this chapter exemplifies the Marxist-socialist position.

---

[3]The Presidential Commission on World Hunger, *Overcoming World Hunger: The Challenge Ahead* (1980), p. 26.

WHAT OUGHT WE TO DO?

What responsibilities do we as individuals have toward potential and actual famine victims? As the above discussion shows, our answers may depend on what we take to be a correct analysis of the causes of famine and malnutrition in the world. But if we put aside the kind of factual questions discussed above, we can still ask questions about the basis of *any* possible moral obligation that we as individuals might have to prevent starvation and malnutrition among the needy. Peter Singer in this chapter attempts to establish a foundation for such a moral obligation on the general principle, "Persons are morally required to prevent something bad from happening if they can do so without sacrificing anything of comparable moral significance." In his view, even a weaker version of this principle is sufficient to establish a moral obligation to aid the victims of severe famines. Other ethicists rely on one or more of the principles of economic justice discussed in the introduction to Chapter 8. Some, for example, extend claims based on the principle of need in conjunction with the principle of equal sharing to the international level. They maintain that all human beings, just because they are human beings, are entitled to equal treatment in some important respects; they are entitled, for example, to have at least their most basic needs, such as their need for food, met by other human beings who have more than enough to meet their own needs.

Jane S. Zembaty

Why Should the United States Be Concerned?

The Presidential Commission on World Hunger

In 1978 President Jimmy Carter appointed a Presidential Commission on World Hunger, chaired by Ambassador Sol Linowitz. It included Dr. Jean Mayer, Dr. Stephen Muller, Dr. Norman Borlaug, David W. Brooks, Harry Chapin, John Denver, Senator Robert Dole, Dr. Walter P. Falcon, Orville Freeman, Representative Benjamin Gilman, Senator Patrick Leahy, Bess Myerson, Representative Richard Nolan, Dr. Howard A. Schneider, Dr. Adele Smith Simmons, Raymond Singletary Jr., Dr. Eugene L. Stockwell, Dr. Clifford Wharton, Mr. Thomas H. Wyman, and Daniel E. Shaughnessy. The Commission was charged with the following tasks: (1) to identify the basic causes of domestic and international hunger and malnutrition; (2) to assess past and present national programs and policies that affect hunger and malnutrition; (3) to review existing studies and research on hunger; (4) to recommend to the President and Congress specific actions to create a coherent national food and hunger policy; and (5) to help implement those recommendations and focus public attention on food and hunger issues. The selection appearing here is excerpted from the Commission's final report, Overcoming World Hunger: The Challenge Ahead.

Reprinted from *Overcoming World Hunger: The Challenge Ahead* (Washington, D.C.: Government Printing Office, 1980).

The Commission's major recommendation is that the elimination of hunger should be the primary focus of the United States Government in its relationship with developing countries. To support its recommendations the Commission offers the following reasons: (1) The moral obligation to overcome hunger, based on two universal values—respect for human dignity and social justice; (2) the dependence of national security on the economic well-being of the developing countries; and (3) the dependence of the economic vitality of the United States on a healthy international economy.

The major recommendation of the Presidential Commission on World Hunger is that the United States make the elimination of hunger the primary focus of its relations with the developing world—with all that implies for U.S. policy toward development assistance, trade, foreign investment and foreign affairs. In the Commission's view, there are significant reasons for the United States to place the elimination of hunger at the top of its list of global concerns.

MORAL OBLIGATION AND RESPONSIBILITY

Moral obligation alone would justify giving highest priority to the task of overcoming hunger. Even now, millions of human beings live on the edge of starvation—in conditions of subhuman poverty that, if we think about them at all, must fill us with shame and horror. We see this now most poignantly in famine conditions, but it is a fact of life every day for half a billion people. At least one out of every eight men, women and children on earth suffers malnutrition severe enough to shorten life, stunt physical growth, and dull mental ability.

Whether one speaks of human rights or basic human needs, the right to food is the most basic of all. Unless that right is first fulfilled, the protection of other human rights becomes a mockery for those who must spend all their energy merely to maintain life itself. The correct moral and ethical position on hunger is beyond debate. The major world religions and philosophical systems share two universal values: respect for human dignity and a sense of social justice. Hunger is the ultimate affront to both. Unless all governments begin now to act upon their rhetorical commitments to ending hunger, the principle that human life is sacred, which forms the very underpinnings of human society, will gradually but relentlessly erode. By concentrating its international efforts on the elimination of hunger, the United States would provide the strongest possible demonstration of its renewed dedication to the cause of human rights.

Moral obligation includes responsibility. In the Commission's view, the United States has a special capability and hence a special responsibility to lead the campaign against world hunger. The United States is by far the most powerful member of the world's increasingly interdependent food system. It harvests more than half the grain that crosses international borders. Its corporations dominate world grain trade. Its grain reserves are the largest on earth. Because of its agricultural productivity, its advanced food technology, and its market power, the United States inevitably exerts a major influence on all aspects of the international food system.

Global interdependence in food means that two straight years of bad harvests in any of the major grain-producing nations of the world could precipitate another global food crisis like the one that occurred in 1972–74. Recurrent crises of this nature could bring widespread famine and political disorder to the developing countries and would severely disrupt a fragile world economy already weakened by energy shortages and rampant inflation. U.S. policies will have a major role in determining whether or not this scenario will be played out.

American policies and resources also hold the key to solving that continuing world food crisis embodied in the swelling ranks of the chronically malnourished. To these hungry millions, it makes no difference whether such policies are made by choice or inertia, by acts of commission or acts of omission. In view of the undeniable influence that this nation's actions will have on world hunger, the Commission urges immediate yet careful long-range planning to assure that U.S. policy truly helps rather than harms the world's hungry people. Delay will only make the same ends more difficult and expensive to accomplish, and will not lift responsibility from the United States.

The Commission does not mean to imply that the United States alone can solve the world hunger problem. All nations, including those of the developing world, must make the conquest of hunger a common cause. However, the Commission is persuaded that unless the United States plays a major role by increasing its own commitment and action toward this goal, no effective and comprehensive global program to combat hunger is likely to be undertaken in the foreseeable future. Moreover, once its own commitment is clear, the United States will be in a particularly strong position to encourage others to do more. The Commission believes that the United States is uniquely situated to influence the fate of millions who do not get enough to eat.

NATIONAL SECURITY

The Commission believes that promoting economic development in general, and overcoming hunger in particular, are tasks far more critical to the U.S. national security than most policymakers acknowledge or even believe. Since the advent of nuclear weapons most Americans have been conditioned to equate national security with the strength of strategic military forces. The Commission considers this prevailing belief to be a simplistic illusion. Armed might represents merely the physical aspect of national security. Military force is ultimately useless in the absence of the global security that only coordinated international progress toward social justice can bring. . . .

ECONOMIC INTEREST

The Commission also finds compelling economic reasons for the United States to focus on the elimination of hunger. The United States can maintain its own economic vitality only within a healthy international economy whose overall strength will increase as each of its component parts becomes more productive, more equitable and more internationally competitive. To sustain a healthy global economy, the purchasing power of today's poor people must rise substantially, in order to set in motion that mutually reinforcing exchange of goods, services and commodities which provides the foundation for viable economic partnership and growth. . . .

[Thus we conclude that there] are compelling moral, economic and national security reasons for the United States Government to make the elimination of hunger the central focus of its relations with the developing world. . . .

QUESTIONS

1 According to the Commission, there are compelling *economic* reasons for the United States to focus on the elimination of hunger in its relations with developing countries. If this is correct, what evidence can be given to support it?
2 It has been said that the United States cannot solve the problem of world hunger; it *is* the problem. What reasons could be offered to support such a contention?

Famine, Affluence, and Morality

Peter Singer

Peter Singer is a member of the philosophy department at La Trobe University, Victoria, Australia. His books include Animal Liberation *(1975),* Practical Ethics *(1980),* The Expanding Circle: Ethics and Sociobiology *(1981) and* Hegel *(1983).*

Singer expresses concern over the fact that while members of the more affluent nations spend money on trivia, people in the needier nations are starving. He argues that it is morally wrong not to prevent suffering whenever one can do so without sacrificing anything morally significant. Giving aid to the victims of famine can prevent such suffering. Even if giving requires a drastic reduction in the standard of living of the members of the more affluent societies, the latter are morally required to meet at least the basic need for food of people who will otherwise starve to death.

As I write this, in November 1971, people are dying in East Bengal from lack of food, shelter, and medical care. The suffering and death that are occurring there now are not inevitable, not unavoidable in any fatalistic sense of the term. Constant poverty, a cyclone, and a civil war have turned at least nine million people into destitute refugees; nevertheless, it is not beyond the capacity of the richer nations to give enough assistance to reduce any further suffering to very small proportions. The decisions and actions of human beings can prevent this kind of suffering. Unfortunately, human beings have not made the necessary decisions. At the individual level, people have, with very few exceptions, not responded to the situation in any significant way.

Peter Singer, "Famine, Affluence, and Morality," *Philosophy & Public Affairs* 1, no. 3 (Spring 1972). Copyright © 1972 by Princeton University Press. Reprinted by permission.

Generally speaking, people have not given large sums to relief funds; they have not written to their parliamentary representatives demanding increased government assistance; they have not demonstrated in the streets, held symbolic fasts, or done anything else directed toward providing the refugees with the means to satisfy their essential needs. At the government level, no government has given the sort of massive aid that would enable the refugees to survive for more than a few days. Britain, for instance, has given rather more than most countries. It has, to date, given £14,750,000. For comparative purposes, Britain's share of the nonrecoverable development costs of the Anglo-French Concorde project is already in excess of £275,000,000, and on present estimates will reach £440,000,000. The implication is that the British government values a supersonic transport more than thirty times as highly as it values the lives of the nine million refugees. Australia is another country which, on a per capita basis, is well up in the "aid to Bengal" table. Australia's aid, however, amounts to less than one-twelfth of the cost of Sydney's new opera house. The total amount given, from all sources, now stands at about £65,000,000. The estimated cost of keeping the refugees alive for one year is £464,000,000. Most of the refugees have now been in the camps for more than six months. The World Bank has said that India needs a minimum of £300,000,000 in assistance from other countries before the end of the year. It seems obvious that assistance on this scale will not be forthcoming. India will be forced to choose between letting the refugees starve or diverting funds from her own development program, which will mean that more of her own people will starve in the future.[1]

These are the essential facts about the present situation in Bengal. So far as it concerns us here, there is nothing unique about this situation except its magnitude. The Bengal emergency is just the latest and most acute of a series of major emergencies in various parts of the world, arising both from natural and from man-made causes. There are also many parts of the world in which people die from malnutrition and lack of food independent of any special emergency. I take Bengal as my example only because it is the present concern, and because the size of the problem has ensured that is has been given adequate publicity. Neither individuals nor governments can claim to be unaware of what is happening there.

What are the moral implications of a situation like this? In what follows, I shall argue that the way people in relatively affluent countries react to a situation like that in Bengal cannot be justified; indeed, the whole way we look at moral issues—our moral conceptual scheme—needs to be altered, and with it, the way of life that has come to be taken for granted in our society.

In arguing for this conclusion I will not, of course, claim to be morally neutral. I shall, however, try to argue for the moral position that I take, so that anyone who accepts certain assumptions, to be made explicit, will, I hope, accept my conclusion.

I begin with the assumption that suffering and death from lack of food, shelter, and medical care are bad. I think most people will agree about this, although one may

[1]There was also a third possibility: that India would go to war to enable the refugees to return to their lands. Since I wrote this paper, India has taken this way out. The situation is no longer that described above, but this does not affect my argument, as the next paragraph indicates.

reach the same view by different routes. I shall not argue for this view. People can hold all sorts of eccentric positions, and perhaps from some of them it would not follow that death by starvation is in itself bad. It is difficult, perhaps impossible, to refute such positions, and so for brevity I will henceforth take this assumption as accepted. Those who disagree need read no further.

My next point is this: if it is in our power to prevent something bad from happening, without thereby sacrificing anything of comparable moral importance, we ought, morally, to do it. By "without sacrificing anything of comparable moral importance" I mean without causing anything else comparably bad to happen, or doing something that is wrong in itself, or failing to promote some moral good, comparable in significance to the bad thing that we can prevent. This principle seems almost as uncontroversial as the last one. It requires us only to prevent what is bad, and not to promote what is good, and it requires this of us only when we can do it without sacrificing anything that is, from the moral point of view, comparably important. I could even, as far as the application of my argument to the Bengal emergency is concerned, qualify the point so as to make it: if it is in our power to prevent something very bad from happening, without thereby sacrificing anything morally significant, we ought, morally, to do it. An application of this principle would be as follows: if I am walking past a shallow pond and see a child drowning in it, I ought to wade in and pull the child out. This will mean getting my clothes muddy, but this is insignificant, while the death of the child would presumably be a very bad thing.

The uncontroversial appearance of the principle just stated is deceptive. If it were acted upon, even in its qualified form, our lives, our society, and our world would be fundamentally changed. For the principle takes, firstly, no account of proximity or distance. It makes no moral difference whether the person I can help is a neighbor's child ten yards from me or a Bengali whose name I shall never know, ten thousand miles away. Secondly, the principle makes no distinction between cases in which I am the only person who could possibly do anything and cases in which I am just one among millions in the same position.

I do not think I need to say much in defense of the refusal to take proximity and distance into account. The fact that a person is physically near to us, so that we have personal contact with him, may make it more likely that we *shall* assist him, but this does not show that we *ought* to help him rather than another who happens to be further away. If we accept any principle of impartiality, universalizability, equality, or whatever, we cannot discriminate against someone merely because he is far away from us (or we are far away from him). Admittedly, it is possible that we are in a better position to judge what needs to be done to help a person near to us than one far away, and perhaps also to provide the assistance we judge to be necessary. If this were the case, it would be a reason for helping those near to us first. This may once have been a justification for being more concerned with the poor in one's own town than with famine victims in India. Unfortunately for those who like to keep their moral responsibilities limited, instant communication and swift transportation have changed the situation. From the moral point of view, the development of the world into a "global village" has made an important, though still unrecognized, difference to our moral situation. Expert observers and supervisors, sent out by famine relief organizations or permanently stationed in famine-prone areas, can direct our aid to a refugee in Bengal almost as effectively as we could get it to someone in our own block. There would seem, therefore, to be no possible justification for discriminating on geographical grounds.

There may be a greater need to defend the second implication of my principle— that the fact that there are millions of other people in the same position, in respect to the Bengali refugees, as I am, does not make the situation significantly different from a situation in which I am the only person who can prevent something very bad from occurring. Again, of course, I admit that there is a psychological difference between the cases; one feels less guilty about doing nothing if one can point to others, similarly placed, who have also done nothing. Yet this can make no real difference to our moral obligations. Should I consider that I am less obliged to pull the drowning child out of the pond if on looking around I see other people, no further away than I am, who have also noticed the child but are doing nothing? One has only to ask this question to see the absurdity of the view that numbers lessen obligation. It is a view that is an ideal excuse for inactivity; unfortunately most of the major evils—poverty, overpopulation, pollution—are problems in which everyone is almost equally involved.

The view that numbers do make a difference can be made plausible if stated in this way: if everyone in circumstances like mine gave £5 to the Bengal Relief Fund, there would be enough to provide food, shelter, and medical care for the refugees; there is no reason why I should give more than anyone else in the same circumstances as I am; therefore I have no obligation to give more than £5. Each premise in this argument is true, and the argument looks sound. It may convince us, unless we notice that it is based on a hypothetical premise, although the conclusion is not stated hypothetically. The argument would be sound if the conclusion were: if everyone in circumstances like mine were to give £5, I would have no obligation to give more than £5. If the conclusion were so stated, however, it would be obvious that the argument has no bearing on a situation in which it is not the case that everyone else gives £5. This, of course, is the actual situation. It is more or less certain that not everyone in circumstances like mine will give £5. So there will not be enough to provide the needed food, shelter, and medical care. Therefore by giving more than £5 I will prevent more suffering than I would if I gave just £5.

It might be thought that this argument has an absurd consequence. Since the situation appears to be that very few people are likely to give substantial amounts, it follows that I and everyone else in similar circumstances ought to give as much as possible, that is, at least up to the point at which by giving more one would begin to cause serious suffering for oneself and one's dependents—perhaps even beyond this point to the point of marginal utility, at which by giving more one would cause oneself and one's dependents as much suffering as one would prevent in Bengal. If everyone does this, however, there will be more than can be used for the benefit of the refugees, and some of the sacrifice will have been unnecessary. Thus, if everyone does what he ought to do, the result will not be as good as it would be if everyone did a little less than he ought to do, or if only some do all that they ought to do.

The paradox here arises only if we assume that the actions in question—sending money to the relief funds—are performed more or less simultaneously, and are also unexpected. For if it is to be expected that everyone is going to contribute something, then clearly each is not obliged to give as much as he would have been obliged to had others not been giving too. And if everyone is not acting more or less simultaneously, then those giving later will know how much more is needed, and will have no obligation to give more than is necessary to reach this amount. To say this is not to deny the principle that people in the same circumstances have the same obligations, but to point out that the fact that others have given, or may be expected to give, is a relevant circumstance: those giving after it has become known that many others are giving and those giving before are not in the same circumstances. So the seemingly absurd consequence of the principle I have put forward can occur only if people are in error about the actual circumstances—that is, if they think they are giving when others are not, but in fact they are giving when others are. The result of everyone doing what he really ought to do cannot be worse than the result of everyone doing less than he ought to do, although the result of everyone doing what he reasonably believes he ought to do could be.

If my argument so far has been sound, neither our distance from a preventable evil nor the number of other people who, in respect to that evil, are in the same situation as we are, lessens our obligation to mitigate or prevent that evil. I shall therefore take as established the principle I asserted earlier. As I have already said, I need to assert it only in its qualified form: if it is in our power to prevent something very bad from happening, without thereby sacrificing anything else morally significant, we ought, morally, to do it.

The outcome of this argument is that our traditional moral categories are upset. The traditional distinction between duty and charity cannot be drawn, or at least, not in the place we normally draw it. Giving money to the Bengal Relief Fund is regarded as an act of charity in our society. The bodies which collect money are known as "charities." These organizations see themselves in this way—if you send them a check, you will be thanked for your "generosity." Because giving money is regarded as an act of charity, it is not thought that there is anything wrong with not giving. The charitable man may be praised, but the man who is not charitable is not condemned. People do not feel in any way ashamed or guilty about spending money on new clothes or a new car instead of giving it to famine relief. (Indeed, the alternative does not occur to them.) This way of looking at the matter cannot be justified. When we buy new clothes not to keep ourselves warm but to look "well-dressed" we are not providing for any important need. We would not be sacrificing anything significant if we were to continue to wear our old clothes, and give the money to famine relief. By doing so, we would be preventing another person from starving. It follows from what I have said earlier that we ought to give money away, rather than spend it on clothes which we do not need to keep us warm. To do so is not charitable, or generous. Nor is it the kind of act which philosophers and theologians have called "supererogatory"—an act which it would be good to do, but not wrong not to do. On the contrary, we ought to give the money away, and it is wrong not to do so.

I am not maintaining that there are no acts which are charitable, or that there are no acts which it would be good to do but not wrong not to do. It may be possible to redraw the distinction between duty and charity in some other place. All I am arguing here is that the present way of drawing the distinction, which makes it an act of charity for a man living at the level of affluence which most people in the "developed nations" enjoy to give money to save someone else from starvation, cannot be supported. It is beyond the scope of my argument to consider whether the distinction should be redrawn or abolished altogether. There would be many other possible ways of drawing the distinction—for instance, one might decide that it is good to make other people as happy as possible, but not wrong not to do so.

Despite the limited nature of the revision in our moral conceptual scheme which I am proposing, the revision would, given the extent of both affluence and famine in the world today, have radical implications. These implications may lead to further objections, distinct from those I have already considered. I shall discuss two of these.

One objection to the position I have taken might be simply that it is too drastic a revision of our moral scheme. People do not ordinarily judge in the way I have suggested they should. Most people reserve their moral condemnation for those who violate some moral norm, such as the norm against taking another person's property. They do not condemn those who indulge in luxury instead of giving to famine relief. But given that I did not set out to present a morally neutral description of the way people make moral judgments, the way people do in fact judge has nothing to do with the validity of my conclusion. My conclusion follows from the principle which I advanced earlier, and unless that principle is rejected, or the arguments shown to be unsound, I think the conclusion must stand, however strange it appears. . . .

The second objection to my attack on the present distinction between duty and charity is one which has from time to time been made against utilitarianism. It follows from some forms of utilitarian theory that we all ought, morally, to be working full time to increase the balance of happiness over misery. The position I have taken here would not lead to this conclusion in all circumstances, for if there were no bad occurrences that we could prevent without sacrificing something of comparable moral importance, my argument would have no application. Given the present conditions in many parts of the world, however, it does follow from my argument that we ought, morally, to be working full time to relieve great suffering of the sort that occurs as a result of famine or other disasters. Of course, mitigating circumstances can be adduced—for instance, that if we wear ourselves out through overwork, we shall be less effective than we would otherwise have been. Nevertheless, when all considerations of this sort have been taken into account, the conclusion remains: we ought to be preventing as much suffering as we can without sacrificing something else of comparable moral importance. This conclusion is one which we may be reluctant to face. I cannot see, though, why it should be regarded as a criticism of the position for which I have argued, rather than a criticism of our ordinary standards of behavior. Since most people are self-interested to some degree, very few of us are likely to do everything that we ought to do. It would, however, hardly be honest to take this as evidence that it is not the case that we ought to do it. . . .

The conclusion reached earlier [raises] the question of just how much we all ought to be giving away. One possibility, which has already been mentioned, is that we ought to give until we reach the level of marginal utility—that is, the level at which, by giving more, I would cause as much suffering to myself or my dependents as I would relieve by my gift. This would mean, of course, that one would reduce oneself to very near the material circumstances of a Bengali refugee. It will be recalled that earlier I put forward both a strong and a moderate version of the principle of preventing bad occurrences. The strong version, which required us to prevent bad things from happening unless in doing so we would be sacrificing something of a comparable moral significance, does seem to require reducing ourselves to the level of marginal utility. I should also say that the strong version seems to me to be the correct one. I proposed the more moderate version—that we should prevent bad occurrences unless, to do so, we had to sacrifice something morally significant—only in order to show that even on this surely undeniable principle a great change in our way of life is required. On the more moderate principle, it may not follow that we ought to reduce ourselves to the level of marginal utility, for one might hold that to reduce oneself and one's family to this level is to cause something significantly bad to happen. Whether this is so I shall not discuss, since, as I have said, I can see no good reason for holding the moderate version of the principle rather than the strong version. Even if we accepted the principle only in its moderate form, however, it should be clear that we would have to give away enough to ensure that the consumer society, dependent as it is on people spending on trivia rather than giving to famine relief, would slow down and perhaps disappear entirely. There are several reasons why this would be desirable in itself. The value and necessity of economic growth are now being questioned not only by conservationists, but by economists as well.[2] There is no doubt, too, that the consumer society has had a distorting effect on the goals and purposes of its members. Yet looking at the matter purely from the point of view of overseas aid, there must be a limit to the extent to which we should deliberately slow down our economy; for it might be the case that if we gave away, say, forty percent of our Gross National Product, we would slow down the economy so much that in absolute terms we would be giving less than if we gave twenty-five percent of the much larger GNP that we would have if we limited our contribution to this smaller percentage.

I mention this only as an indication of the sort of factor that one would have to take into account in working out an ideal. Since Western societies generally consider one percent of the GNP an acceptable level for overseas aid, the matter is entirely academic. Nor does it affect the question of how much an individual should give in a society in which very few are giving substantial amounts.

It is sometimes said, though less often now than it used to be, that philosophers have no special role to play in public affairs, since most public issues depend primarily on an assessment of facts. On questions of fact, it is said, philosophers as such have no special expertise, and so it has been possible to engage in philosophy without committing oneself to any position on major public issues. No doubt there are some issues of social policy and foreign policy about which it can truly be said that a really expert assessment of the facts is required before taking sides or acting, but the issue of famine is surely not one of these. The facts about the existence of suffering are beyond dispute. Nor, I think, is it disputed that we can do something about it, either

---

[2]See, for instance, John Kenneth Galbraith, *The New Industrial State* (Boston, 1967); and E. J. Mishan, *The Costs of Economic Growth* (London, 1967).

through orthodox methods of famine relief or through population control or both. This is therefore an issue on which philosophers are competent to take a position. The issue is one which faces everyone who has more money than he needs to support himself and his dependents, or who is in a position to take some sort of political action. These categories must include practically every teacher and student of philosophy in the universities of the Western world. If philosophy is to deal with matters that are relevant to both teachers and students, this is an issue that philosophers should discuss.

Discussion, though, is not enough. What is the point of relating philosophy to public (and personal) affairs if we do not take our conclusions seriously? In this instance, taking our conclusion seriously means acting upon it. The philosopher will not find it any easier than anyone else to alter his attitudes and way of life to the extent that, if I am right, is involved in doing everything that we ought to be doing. At the very least, though, one can make a start. The philosopher who does so will have to sacrifice some of the benefits of the consumer society, but he can find compensation in the satisfaction of a way of life in which theory and practice, if not yet in harmony, are at least coming together.

QUESTIONS

1 Think about the following claim: Contributing to famine relief is not a moral obligation which we must perform if we are to act in a morally correct way, but an act of charity which we may or may not perform. Can you offer any arguments to defend it?

2 Singer says, "We ought to be preventing as much suffering as we can without sacrificing something else of comparable moral importance." What moral considerations would outweigh the obligation Singer claims we have to aid famine victims?

Living on a Lifeboat

Garrett Hardin

Garrett Hardin is professor of biology at the University of California at Santa Barbara. He is the author of many books, including Population, Evolution, and Birth Control *(1969),* Exploring New Ethics for Survival *(1972),* The Limits of Altruism: An Ecologist's View of Survival *(1977), and* Promethean Ethics: Living with Death, Competition, and Triage *(1980).*

Using the metaphor of a lifeboat, Hardin argues that the time may have come to refuse aid in the form of food to needy countries which do not accept the responsibility for limiting their population growth. He maintains that adherence to the principle "From each according to his ability; to each according to his need" will have strong adverse effects. Bolstered by our aid, needy countries will continue their irresponsible policies in regard to food production and population growth. Furthermore, the food we supply will enable these populations to continue to increase. This in the long run will jeopardize the survival of the human species.

No generation has viewed the problem of the survival of the human species as seriously as we have. Inevitably, we have entered this world of concern through the door of metaphor. Environmentalists have emphasized the image of the earth as a spaceship—Spaceship Earth. Kenneth Boulding (1966) is the principal architect of this metaphor. It is time, he says, that we replace the wasteful "cowboy economy" of the past with the frugal "spaceship economy" required for continued survival in the limited world we now see ours to be. The metaphor is notably useful in justifying pollution control measures.

Unfortunately, the image of a spaceship is also used to promote measures that are suicidal. One of these is a generous immigration policy, which is only a particular instance of a class of policies that are in error because they lead to the tragedy of the commons (Hardin 1968). These suicidal policies are attractive because they mesh with what we unthinkingly take to be the ideals of "the best people." What is missing in the idealistic view is an insistence that rights and responsibilities must go together. The "generous" attitude of all too many people results in asserting inalienable rights while ignoring or denying matching responsibilities.

For the metaphor of a spaceship to be correct the aggregate of people on board would have to be under unitary sovereign control (Ophuls 1974). A true ship always has a captain. It is conceivable that a ship could be run by a committee. But it could not possibly survive if its course were determined by bickering tribes that claimed rights without responsibilities.

What about Spaceship Earth? It certainly has no captain, and no executive committee. The United Nations is a toothless tiger, because the signatories of its charter wanted it that way. The spaceship metaphor is used only to justify spaceship demands on common resources without acknowledging corresponding spaceship responsibilities.

An understandable fear of decisive action leads people to embrace "incrementalism"—moving toward reform in tiny stages. As we shall see, this strategy is counterproductive in the area discussed here if it means accepting rights before responsibilities. Where human survival is at stake, the acceptance of responsibilities is a precondition to the acceptance of rights, if the two cannot be introduced simultaneously.

LIFEBOAT ETHICS

Before taking up certain substantive issues let us look at an alternative metaphor, that of a lifeboat. In developing some relevant examples the following numerical values are assumed. Approximately two-thirds of the world is desperately poor, and only one-third is comparatively rich. The people in poor countries have an average per capita GNP (Gross National Product) of about $200 per year; the rich, of about $3,000. (For the United States it is nearly $5,000 per year.) Metaphorically, each rich nation amounts to a lifeboat full of comparatively rich people. The poor of the world are in other, much more crowded lifeboats. Continuously, so to speak, the poor fall out of their lifeboats and swim for a while in the water outside, hoping to be admitted to a rich lifeboat, or in some other way to benefit from the "goodies" on board. What should the passengers on a rich lifeboat do? This is the central problem of "the ethics of a lifeboat."

First we must acknowledge that each lifeboat is effectively limited in capacity. The land of every nation has a limited carrying capacity. The exact limit is a matter for argument, but the energy crunch is convincing more people every day that we have already exceeded the carrying capacity of the land. We have been living on "capital"—stored petroleum and coal—and soon we must live on income alone.

Let us look at only one lifeboat—ours. The ethical problem is the same for all, and is as follows. Here we sit, say 50 people in a lifeboat. To be generous, let us assume our boat has a capacity of 10 more, making 60. (This, however, is to violate the engineering principle of the "safety factor." A new plant disease or a bad change in the weather may decimate our population if we don't preserve some excess capacity as a safety factor.)

The 50 of us in the lifeboat see 100 others swimming in the water outside, asking for admission to the boat, or for handouts. How shall we respond to their calls? There are several possibilities.

One. We may be tempted to try to live by the Christian ideal of being "our brother's keeper," or by the Marxian ideal (Marx 1875) of "from each according to his abilities, to each according to his needs." Since the needs of all are the same, we take all the needy into our boat, making a total of 150 in a boat with a capacity of 60. The boat is swamped, and everyone drowns. Complete justice, complete catastrophe.

Two. Since the boat has an unused excess capacity of 10, we admit just 10 more to it. This has the disadvantage of getting rid of the safety factor, for which action we will sooner or later pay dearly. Moreover, *which* 10 do we let in? "First come, first served?" The best 10? The neediest 10? How do we *discriminate?* And what do we say to the 90 who are excluded?

Three. Admit no more to the boat and preserve the small safety factor. Survival of the people in the lifeboat is then possible (though we shall have to be on our guard against boarding parties).

The last solution is abhorrent to many people. It is unjust, they say. Let us grant that it is.

"I feel guilty about my good luck," say some. The reply to this is simple: *Get out and yield your place to others*. Such a selfless action might satisfy the conscience of those who are addicted to guilt but it would not change the ethics of the lifeboat. The needy person to whom a guilt-addict yields his place will not himself feel guilty about his sudden good luck. (If he did he would not climb aboard.) The net result of conscience-stricken people relinquishing their unjustly held positions is the elimination of their kind of conscience from the lifeboat. The lifeboat, as it were, purifies itself of guilt. The ethics of the lifeboat persist, unchanged by such momentary aberrations.

This then is the basic metaphor within which we must work out our solutions. Let us enrich the image step by step with substantive additions from the real world.

REPRODUCTION

The harsh characteristics of lifeboat ethics are heightened by reproduction, particularly by reproductive differences. The people inside the lifeboats of the wealthy nations are doubling in numbers every 87 years; those outside are doubling every 35 years, on the average. And the relative difference in prosperity is becoming greater.

Let us, for a while, think primarily of the U.S. lifeboat. As of 1973 the United States had a population of 210 million people, who were increasing by 0.8% per year, that is, doubling in number every 87 years.

Although the citizens of rich nations are outnumbered two to one by the poor, let us imagine an equal number of poor people outside our lifeboat—a mere 210 million poor people reproducing at a quite different rate. If we imagine these to be the combined populations of Colombia, Venezuela, Ecuador, Morocco, Thailand, Pakistan, and the Philippines, the average rate of increase of the people "outside" is 3.3% per year. The doubling time of this population is 21 years.

Suppose that all these countries, and the United States, agreed to live by the Marxian ideal, "to each according to his needs," the ideal of most Christians as well. Needs, of course, are determined by population size, which is affected by reproduction. Every nation regards its rate of reproduction as a sovereign right. If our lifeboat were big enough in the beginning it might be possible to live *for a while* by Christian-Marxian ideals. *Might.*

Initially, in the model given, the ratio of non-Americans to Americans would be one to one. But consider what the ratio would be 87 years later. By this time Americans would have doubled to a population of 420 million. The other group (doubling every 21 years) would now have swollen to 3,540 million. Each American would have more than eight people to share with. How could the lifeboat possibly keep afloat?

All this involves extrapolation of current trends into the future, and is consequently suspect. Trends may change. Granted: but the change will not necessarily be favorable. If—as seems likely—the rate of population increase falls faster in the ethnic group presently inside the lifeboat than it does among those now outside, the future will turn out to be even worse than mathematics predicts, and sharing will be even more suicidal.

RUIN IN THE COMMONS

The fundamental error of the sharing ethics is that it leads to the tragedy of the commons. Under a system of private property the man (or group of men) who own property recognize their responsibility to care for it, for if they don't they will eventually suffer. A farmer, for instance, if he is intelligent, will allow no more cattle in a pasture than its carrying capacity justifies. If he overloads the pasture, weeds take over, erosion sets in, and the owner loses in the long run.

But if a pasture is run as a commons open to all, the right of each to use it is not matched by an operational responsibility to take care of it. It is no use asking independent herdsmen in a commons to act responsibly, for they dare not. The considerate herdsman who refrains from overloading the commons suffers more than a selfish one who says his needs are greater. (As Leo Durocher says, "Nice guys finish last.")

Christian-Marxian idealism is counterproductive. That it *sounds* nice is no excuse. With distribution systems, as with individual morality, good intentions are no substitute for good performance.

A social system is stable only if it is insensitive to errors. To the Christian-Marxian idealist a selfish person is a sort of "error." Prosperity in the system of the commons cannot survive errors. If *everyone* would only restrain himself, all would be well; but it takes *only one less than everyone* to ruin a system of voluntary restraint. In a crowded world of less than perfect human beings—and we will never know any other—mutual ruin is inevitable in the commons. This is the core of the tragedy of the commons. . . .

WORLD FOOD BANKS

In the international arena we have recently heard a proposal to create a new commons, namely an international depository of food reserves to which nations will contribute according to their abilities, and from which nations may draw according to their needs. Nobel laureate Norman Borlaug has lent the prestige of his name to this proposal.

A world food bank appeals powerfully to our humanitarian impulses. We remember John Donne's celebrated line, "Any man's death diminishes me." But before we rush out to see for whom the bell tolls let us recognize where the greatest political push for international granaries comes from, lest we be disillusioned later. Our experience with Public Law 480 clearly reveals the answer. This was the law that moved billions of dollars worth of U.S. grain to food-short, population-long countries during the past two decades. When P.L. 480 first came into being, a headline in the business magazine *Forbes* (Paddock 1970) revealed the power behind it: "Feeding the World's Hungry Millions: How it will mean billions for U.S. business."

And indeed it did. In the years 1960 to 1970 a total of $7.9 billion was spent on the "Food for Peace" program, as P.L. 480 was called. During the years of 1948 to 1970 an additional $49.9 billion were extracted from American taxpayers to pay for other economic aid programs, some of which went for food and food-producing machinery. (This figure does *not* include military aid.) That P.L. 480 was a give-away program was concealed. Recipient countries went through the motions of paying for P.L. 480 food—with IOU's. In December 1973 the charade was brought to an end as far as India was concerned when the United States "forgave" India's $3.2 billion debt (Anonymous 1974). Public announcement of the cancellation of the debt was delayed for two months: one wonders why. . . .

What happens if some organizations budget for emergencies and others do not? If each organization is solely responsible for its own well-being, poorly managed ones will suffer. But they should be able to learn from experience. They have a chance to mend their ways and learn to budget for infrequent but certain emergencies. The weather, for instance, always varies and periodic crop failures are certain. A wise and competent government saves out of the production of the good years in anticipation of bad years that are sure to come. This is not a new idea. The Bible tells us that Joseph taught this policy to Pharaoh in Egypt more than 2,000 years ago. Yet it is literally true that the vast majority of the governments of the world today have no such policy. They lack either the wisdom or the competence, or both. Far more difficult than the transfer of wealth from one country to another is the transfer of wisdom between sovereign powers or between generations.

"But it isn't their fault! How can we blame the poor people who are caught in an emergency? Why must we punish them?" The concepts of blame and punishment are irrelevant. The question is, what are the operational consequences of establishing a world food bank? If it is open to every country every time a need develops, slovenly rulers will not be motivated to take Joseph's advice. Why should they? Others will bail them out whenever they are in trouble.

Some countries will make deposits in the world food bank and others will withdraw from it: there will be almost no overlap. Calling such a depository-transfer unit a "bank" is stretching the metaphor of *bank* beyond its elastic limits. The proposers, of course, never call attention to the metaphorical nature of the word they use.

THE RATCHET EFFECT

An "international food bank" is really, then, not a true bank but a disguised oneway transfer device for moving wealth from rich countries to poor. In the absence of such a bank, in a world inhabited by individually responsible sovereign nations, the population of each nation would repeatedly go through a cycle of the sort shown in Figure 1. P_2 is greater than P_1, either in absolute numbers or because a deterioration of the food supply has removed the safety factor and produced a dangerously low ratio of resources to population. P_2 may be said to represent a state of overpopulation, which becomes obvious upon the appearance of an "accident," e.g., a crop failure. If the "emergency" is not met by outside help, the population drops back to the "normal" level—the "carrying capacity" of the environment—or even below. In the absence of population control by a sovereign, sooner or later the population grows to P_2 again and the cycle repeats. The long-term population curve (Hardin 1966) is an irregularly fluctuating one, equilibrating more or less about the carrying capacity.

A demographic cycle of this sort obviously involves great suffering in the restrictive phase, but such a cycle is normal to any independent country with inadequate population control. The third century theologian Tertullian (Hardin 1969) expressed what must

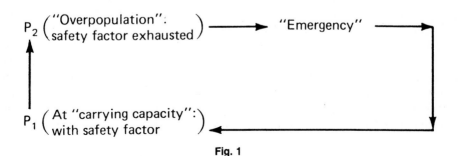

Fig. 1

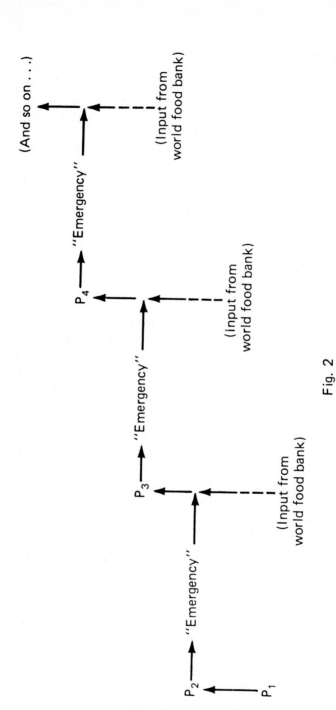

Fig. 2

have been the recognition of many wise men when he wrote: "The scourges of pestilence, famine, wars, and earthquakes have come to be regarded as a blessing to overcrowded nations, since they serve to prune away the luxuriant growth of the human race."

Only under a strong and farsighted sovereign—which theoretically could be the people themselves, democratically organized—can a population equilibrate at some set point below the carrying capacity, thus avoiding the pains normally caused by periodic and unavoidable disasters. For this happy state to be achieved it is necessary that those in power be able to contemplate with equanimity the "waste" of surplus food in times of bountiful harvests. It is essential that those in power resist the temptation to convert extra food into extra babies. On the public relations level it is necessary that the phrase "surplus food" be replaced by "safety factor."

But wise sovereigns seem not to exist in the poor world today. The most anguishing problems are created by poor countries that are governed by rulers insufficiently wise and powerful. If such countries can draw on a world food bank in times of "emergency," the population *cycle* of Figure 1 will be replaced by the population *escalator* of Figure 2. The input of food from a food bank acts as the pawl of a ratchet, preventing the population from retracing its steps to a lower level. Reproduction pushes the population upward, inputs from the world bank prevent its moving downward. Population size escalates, as does the absolute magnitude of "accidents" and "emergencies." The process is brought to an end only by the total collapse of the whole system, producing a catastrophe of scarcely imaginable proportions.

Such are the implications of the well-meant sharing of food in a world of irresponsible reproduction. . . .

To be generous with one's own possessions is one thing; to be generous with posterity's is quite another. This, I think, is the point that must be gotten across to those who would, from a commendable love of distributive justice, institute a ruinous system of the commons. . . .

If the argument of this essay is correct, so long as there is no true world government to control reproduction everywhere it is impossible to survive in dignity if we are to be guided by Spaceship ethics. Without a world government that is sovereign in reproductive matters mankind lives, in fact, on a number of sovereign lifeboats. For the foreseeable future survival demands that we govern our actions by the ethics of a lifeboat. Posterity will be ill served if we do not.

REFERENCES

1 Anonymous. 1974. *Wall Street Journal* 19 Feb.
2 Boulding, K. 1966. The economics of the coming spaceship earth. In H. Jarrett, ed. *Environmental Quality in a Growing Economy*. Johns Hopkins Press, Baltimore.
3 Hardin, G. 1966. Chap. 9 in *Biology: Its Principles and Implications*, 2nd ed. Freeman, San Francisco.
4 ———. 1968. The tragedy of the commons. *Science* 162: 1243–1248.
5 ———. 1969. Page 18 in *Population, Evolution, and Birth Control*, 2nd ed. Freeman, San Francisco.

6 Marx, K. 1875. *Critique of the Gotha program.* Page 388 in R. C. Tucker, ed. *The Marx-Engels Reader,* Norton, N.Y., 1972.
7 Ophuls, W. 1974. The scarcity society. *Harpers* 248 (1487): 47–52.
8 Paddock, W. C. 1970. How green is the green revolution? *Bioscience* 20: 897–902.

QUESTIONS

1 What evidence is available to support the claim that the resources of the world will not be able to save all the poor countries? If it cannot be conclusively proved that all the poor countries cannot be saved, can a moral justification be given for refusing to aid famine victims in all those countries?

2 Suppose that it is highly unlikely that all the nations in the world can be saved. Which would be the better moral choice:

   a to deliberately cut off aid to those least likely to survive in order to ensure the survival of the others or

   b to continue our aid despite our awareness of the consequences which will probably follow?

Population and Food: Metaphors and the Reality

William W. Murdoch
and Allan Oaten

William W. Murdoch is professor of biological science at the University of California at Santa Barbara. His research centers on population and community dynamics of organisms. He is the editor of Environment: Resources, Pollution and Society *(2d ed., 1975) and the author of* The Poverty of Nations: The Political Economy of Hunger and Population *(1981). Allan Oaten is also a biologist who has taught at the University of California at Santa Barbara. His areas of specialization are mathematical biology and statistics.*

Murdoch and Oaten begin by pointing out several weaknesses in Garrett Hardin's lifeboat, commons, and ratchet metaphors. They then bring out various factors other than food supply which affect population growth. These factors include parental confidence about the future, low infant mortality rates, literacy, widely available rudimentary health care, increased income and employment, and an adequate diet above subsistence levels. For Murdoch and Oaten, if the bulk of a population does not share in the increased social and economic benefits which result from significant national progress, fertility rates in poor and relatively poor countries are unlikely to fall.

Reprinted with permission, from the September 9, 1975 issue of *BioScience,* © American Institute of Biological Sciences.

MISLEADING METAPHORS

[Hardin's] "lifeboat" article actually has two messages. The first is that our immigration policy is too generous. This will not concern us here. The second, and more important, is that by helping poor nations we will bring disaster to rich and poor alike:

> Metaphorically, each rich nation amounts to a lifeboat full of comparatively rich people. The poor of the world are in other, much more crowded lifeboats. Continuously, so to speak, the poor fall out of their lifeboats and swim for a while in the water outside, hoping to be admitted to a rich lifeboat, or in some other way to benefit from the "goodies" on board. What should the passengers on a rich lifeboat do? This is the central problem of "the ethics of a lifeboat." (Hardin, 1974, p. 561)

Among these so-called "goodies" are food supplies and technical aid such as that which led to the Green Revolution. Hardin argues that we should withhold such resources from poor nations on the grounds that they help to maintain high rates of population increase, thereby making the problem worse. He foresees the continued supplying and increasing production of food as a process that will be "brought to an end only by the total collapse of the whole system, producing a catastrophe of scarcely imaginable proportions" (p. 564).

Turning to one particular mechanism for distributing these resources, Hardin claims that a world food bank is a commons—people have more motivation to draw from it than to add to it; it will have a ratchet or escalator effect on population because inputs from it will prevent population declines in over-populated countries. Thus "wealth can be steadily moved in one direction only, from the slowly-breeding rich to the rapidly-breeding poor, the process finally coming to a halt only when all countries are equally and miserably poor" (p. 565). Thus our help will not only bring ultimate disaster to poor countries, but it will also be suicidal for us.

As for the "benign demographic transition" to low birth rates, which some aid supporters have predicted, Hardin states flatly that the weight of evidence is against this possibility.

Finally, Hardin claims that the plight of poor nations is partly their own fault: "wise sovereigns seem not to exist in the poor world today. The most anguishing problems are created by poor countries that are governed by rulers insufficiently wise and powerful." Establishing a world food bank will exacerbate this problem: "slovenly rulers" will escape the consequences of their incompetence—"Others will bail them out whenever they are in trouble"; "Far more difficult than the transfer of wealth from one country to another is the transfer of wisdom between sovereign powers or between generations" (p. 563).

What arguments does Hardin present in support of these opinions? Many involve metaphors: lifeboat, commons, and ratchet or escalator. These metaphors are crucial to his thesis, and it is, therefore, important for us to examine them critically.

The lifeboat is the major metaphor. It seems attractively simple, but it is in fact simplistic and obscures important issues. As soon as we try to use it to compare various policies, we find that most relevant details of the actual situation are either missing or distorted in the lifeboat metaphor. Let us list some of these details.

Most important, perhaps, Hardin's lifeboats barely interact. The rich lifeboats may drop some handouts over the side and perhaps repel a boarding party now and then, but generally they live their own lives. In the real world, nations interact a great deal, in ways that affect food supply and population size and growth, and the effect of rich nations on poor nations has been strong and not always benevolent.

First, by colonization and actual wars of commerce, and through the international marketplace, rich nations have arranged an exchange of goods that has maintained and even increased the economic imbalance between rich and poor nations. Until recently we have taken or otherwise obtained cheap raw material from poor nations and sold them expensive manufactured goods that they cannot make themselves. In the United States, the structure of tariffs and internal subsidies discriminates selectively against poor nations. In poor countries, the concentration on cash crops rather than on food crops, a legacy of colonial times, is now actively encouraged by western multinational corporations (Barraclough 1975). Indeed, it is claimed that in famine-stricken Sahelian Africa, multinational agribusiness has recently taken land out of food production for cash crops (Transnational Institute 1974). Although we often self-righteously take the "blame" for lowering the death rates of poor nations during the 1940s and 1950s, we are less inclined to accept responsibility for the effects of actions that help maintain poverty and hunger. Yet poverty directly contributes to the high birth rates that Hardin views with such alarm.

Second, U.S. foreign policy, including foreign aid programs, has favored "pro-Western" regimes, many of which govern in the interests of a wealthy elite and some of which are savagely repressive. Thus, it has often subsidized a gross maldistribution of income and has supported political leaders who have opposed most of the social changes that can lead to reduced birth rates. In this light, Hardin's pronouncements on the alleged wisdom gap between poor leaders and our own, and the difficulty of filling it, appear as a grim joke: our response to leaders with the power and wisdom Hardin yearns for has often been to try to replace them or their policies as soon as possible. Selective giving and withholding of both military and nonmilitary aid has been an important ingredient of our efforts to maintain political leaders we like and to remove those we do not. Brown (1974b), after noting that the withholding of U.S. food aid in 1973 contributed to the downfall of the Allende government in Chile, comments that "although Americans decry the use of petroleum as a political weapon, calling it 'political blackmail,' the United States has been using food aid for political purposes for twenty years—and describing this as 'enlightened diplomacy.' "

Both the quantity and the nature of the supplies on a lifeboat are fixed. In the real world, the quantity has strict limits, but these are far from having been reached (University of California Food Task Force 1974). Nor are we forced to devote fixed proportions of our efforts and energy to automobile travel, pet food, packaging, advertising, corn-fed beef, "defense" and other diversions, many of which cost far more than foreign aid does. The fact is that enough food is now produced to feed the world's population adequately. That people are malnourished is due to distribution and to economics, not to agricultural limits (United Nations Economic and Social Council 1974).

Hardin's lifeboats are divided merely into rich and poor, and it is difficult to talk about birth rates on either. In the real world, however, there are striking differences among the birth rates of the poor countries and even among the birth rates of different parts of single countries. These differences appear to be related to social conditions (also absent from lifeboats) and may guide us to effective aid policies.

Hardin's lifeboat metaphor not only conceals facts, but misleads about the effects of his proposals. The rich lifeboat can raise the ladder and sail away. But in real life, the problem will not necessarily go away just because it is ignored. In the real world, there are armies, raw materials in poor nations, and even outraged domestic dissidents prepared to sacrifice their own and others' lives to oppose policies they regard as immoral.

No doubt there are other objections. But even this list shows the lifeboat metaphor to be dangerously inappropriate for serious policy making because it obscures far more than it reveals. Lifeboats and "lifeboat ethics" may be useful topics for those who are shipwrecked; we believe they are worthless—indeed detrimental—in discussions of food-population questions.

The ratchet metaphor is equally flawed. It, too, ignores complex interactions between birth rates and social conditions (including diets), implying as it does that more food will simply mean more babies. Also, it obscures the fact that the decrease in death rates has been caused at least as much by developments such as DDT, improved sanitation, and medical advances, as by increased food supplies, so that cutting out food aid will not necessarily lead to population declines.

The lifeboat article is strangely inadequate in other ways. For example, it shows an astonishing disregard for recent literature. The claim that we can expect no "benign demographic transition" is based on a review written more than a decade ago (Davis 1963). Yet, events and attitudes are changing rapidly in poor countries: for the first time in history, most poor people live in countries with birth control programs; with few exceptions, poor nations are somewhere on the demographic transition to lower birth rates (Demeny 1974); the population-food squeeze is now widely recognized, and governments of poor nations are aware of the relationship. Again, there is a considerable amount of evidence that birth rates can fall rapidly in poor countries given the proper social conditions (as we will discuss later); consequently, crude projections of current population growth rates are quite inadequate for policy making.

THE TRAGEDY OF THE COMMONS

Throughout the lifeboat article, Hardin bolsters his assertions by reference to the "commons" (Hardin 1968). The thesis of the commons, therefore, needs critical evaluation.

Suppose several privately owned flocks, comprising 100 sheep altogether, are grazing on a public commons. They bring in an annual income of $1.00 per sheep. Fred, a herdsman, owns only one sheep. He decides to add another. But 101 is too many: the commons is overgrazed and produces less food. The sheep lose quality and income drops to 90¢ per sheep. Total income is now $90.90 instead of $100.00. Adding the sheep has brought an overall loss. But Fred has gained: *his* income is $1.80 instead of $1.00. The gain from the additional sheep, which is his alone, outweighs the loss from overgrazing, which he shares. Thus he promotes his interest at the expense of the community.

This is the problem of the commons, which seems on the way to becoming an archetype. Hardin, in particular, is not inclined to underrate its importance: "One of the major tasks of education today is to create such an awareness of the dangers of the commons that people will be able to recognize its many varieties, however disguised" (Hardin 1974, p. 562) and "All this is terribly obvious once we are acutely aware of the pervasiveness and danger of the commons. But many people still lack this awareness . . ." (p. 565).

The "commons" affords a handy way of classifying problems: the lifeboat article reveals that sharing, a generous immigration policy, world food banks, air, water, the fish populations of the ocean, and the western range lands are, or produce, a commons. It is also handy to be able to dispose of policies one does not like and "only a particular instance of a class of policies that are in error because they lead to the tragedy of the commons" (p. 561).

But no metaphor, even one as useful as this, should be treated with such awe. Such shorthand can be useful, but it can also mislead by discouraging thought and obscuring important detail. To dismiss a proposal by suggesting that "all you need to know about this proposal is that it institutes a commons and is, therefore, bad" is to assert that the proposed commons is worse than the original problem. This might be so if the problem of the commons were, indeed, a tragedy—that is, if it were insoluble. But it is not.

Hardin favors private ownership as the solution (either through private property or the selling of pollution rights). But, of course, there are solutions other than private ownership; and private ownership itself is no guarantee of carefully husbanded resources.

One alternative to private ownership of the commons is communal ownership of the sheep—or, in general, of the mechanisms and industries that exploit the resource—combined with communal planning for management. (Note, again, how the metaphor favors one solution: perhaps the "tragedy" lay not in the commons but in the sheep. "The Tragedy of the Privately Owned Sheep" lacks zing, unfortunately.) Public ownership of a commons has been tried in Peru to the benefit of the previously privately owned anchoveta fishery (Gulland 1975). The communally owned agriculture of China does not seem to have suffered any greater over-exploitation than that of other Asian nations.

Another alternative is cooperation combined with regulation. For example, Gulland (1975) has shown that Antarctic whale stocks (perhaps the epitome of a commons since they are internationally exploited and no one owns them) are now being properly managed, and stocks are increasing. This has been achieved through cooperation in the International Whaling Commission, which has by agreement set limits to the catch of each nation.

In passing, Hardin's private ownership argument is not generally applicable to nonrenewable resources. Given discount rates, technology substitutes, and no more than an average regard for posterity, privately owned nonrenewable resources, like oil, coal and minerals, are mined at rates that produce maximum profits, rather than at those rates that preserve them for future generations. . . .

BIRTH RATES: AN ALTERNATIVE VIEW

Is the food-population spiral inevitable? A more optimistic, if less comfortable, hypothesis, presented by Rich (1973) and Brown (1974a), is increasingly tenable: contrary to the "ratchet" projection, population growth rates are affected by many complex conditions beside food supply. In particular, a set of socioeconomic conditions can be identified that motivate parents to have fewer children; under these conditions, birth rates can fall quite rapidly, sometimes even before birth control technology is available. Thus, population growth can be controlled more effectively by intelligent human intervention that sets up the appropriate conditions than by doing nothing and trusting to "natural population cycles."

These conditions are: parental confidence about the future, an improved status of women, and literacy. They require low infant mortality rates, widely available rudimentary health care, increased income and employment, and an adequate diet above subsistence levels. Expenditure on schools (especially elementary schools), appropriate health services (especially rural paramedical services), and agricultural reform (especially aid to small farmers) will be needed, and foreign aid can help here. It is essential that these improvements be spread across the population; aid can help here, too, by concentrating on the poor nations' poorest people, encouraging necessary institutional and social reforms, and making it easier for poor nations to use their own resources and initiative to help themselves. It is *not* necessary that per capita GNP be very high, certainly not as high as that of the rich countries during their gradual demographic transition. In other words, low birth rates in poor countries are achievable long before the conditions exist that were present in the rich countries in the late 19th and early 20th centuries.

Twenty or thirty years is not long to discover and assess the factors affecting birth rates, but a body of evidence is now accumulating in favor of this hypothesis. Rich (1973) and Brown (1974a) show that at least 10 developing countries have managed to reduce their birth rates by an average of more than one birth per 1,000 population per year for periods of 5 to 16 years. A reduction of one birth per 1,000 per year would bring birth rates in poor countries to a rough replacement level of about 16/1,000 by the turn of the century, though age distribution effects would prevent a smooth population decline. We have listed these countries in Table 1, together with three other nations, including China, that are poor and yet have brought their birth rates down to 30 or less, presumably from rates of over 40 a decade or so ago.

These data show that rapid reduction in birth rates is possible in the developing world. No doubt it can be argued that each of these cases is in some way special. Hong Kong and Singapore are relatively rich; they, Barbados, and Mauritius are also tiny. China is able to exert great social pressure on its citizens; but China is particularly significant. It is enormous; its per capita GNP is almost as low as India's; and it started out in 1949 with a terrible health system. Also, Egypt, Chile, Taiwan, Cuba, South

TABLE 1
DECLINING BIRTH RATES AND PER CAPITA INCOME IN SELECTED DEVELOPING
COUNTRIES. (These are crude birth rates, uncorrected for age distribution.)

		Births/1,000/Year		
Country	Time span	Avg. annual decline in crude birth rate	Crude birth rate 1972	$ per capita per year 1973
Barbados	1960–69	1.5	22	570
Taiwan	1955–71	1.2	24	390
Tunisia	1966–71	1.8	35	250
Mauritius	1961–71	1.5	25	240
Hong Kong	1960–72	1.4	19	970
Singapore	1955–72	1.2	23	920
Costa Rica	1963–72	1.5	32	560
South Korea	1960–70	1.2	29	250
Egypt	1966–70	1.7	37	210
Chile	1963–70	1.2	25	720
China			30	160
Cuba			27	530
Sri Lanka			30	110

Korea, and Sri Lanka are quite large, and they are poor or very poor (Table 1). In fact, these examples represent an enormous range of religion, political systems, and geography and suggest that such rates of decline in the birth rate can be achieved whenever the appropriate conditions are met. "The common factor in these countries is that the *majority* of the population has shared in the economic and social benefits of significant national progress. . . . [M]aking health, education and jobs more broadly available to lower income groups in poor countries contribute[s] significantly toward the motivation for smaller families that is the prerequisite of a major reduction in birth rates" (Rich 1973).

The converse is also true. In Latin America, Cuba (annual per capita income $530), Chile ($720), Uruguay ($820), and Argentina ($1,160) have moderate to truly equitable distribution of goods and services and relatively low birth rates (27, 26, 23, and 22, respectively). In contrast, Brazil ($420), Mexico ($670), and Venezuela ($980) have very unequal distribution of goods and services and high birth rates (38, 42, and 41, respectively). Fertility rates in poor and relatively poor nations seem unlikely to fall as long as the bulk of the population does not share in increased benefits. . . .

. . . As a disillusioning quarter-century of aid giving has shown, the obstacles of getting aid to those segments of the population most in need of it are enormous. Aid has typically benefitted a small rich segment of society, partly because of the way aid programs have been designed but also because of human and institutional factors in the poor nations themselves (Owens and Shaw 1972). With some notable exceptions, the distribution of income and services in poor nations is extremely skewed—much more uneven than in rich countries. Indeed, much of the population is essentially outside the economic system. Breaking this pattern will be extremely difficult. It will require not only aid that is designed specifically to benefit the rural poor, but also important institutional changes such as decentralization of decision making and the development of greater autonomy and stronger links to regional and national markets for local groups and industries such as cooperative farms.

Thus, two things are being asked of rich nations and of the United States in particular: to increase nonmilitary foreign aid, including food aid, and to give it in ways, and to governments, that will deliver it to the poorest people and will improve their access to national economic institutions. These are not easy tasks, particularly the second, and there is no guarantee that birth rates will come down quickly in all countries. Still, many poor countries have, in varying degrees, begun the process of reform, and recent evidence suggests that aid and reform together can do much to solve the twin problems of high birth rates and economic underdevelopment. The tasks are far from impossible. Based on the evidence, the policies dictated by a sense of decency are also the most realistic and rational.

REFERENCES

1 Barraclough, G. 1975. The great world crisis I. *The N.Y. Rev. Books* **21:** 20–29.
2 Brown, L. R. 1974a. In the Human Interest. W. W. Norton & Co., Inc., New York. 190 pp.
3 ———. 1974b. By Bread Alone. Praeger, New York. 272 pp.
4 Davis, K. 1963. Population. *Sci. Amer.* **209**(3): 62–71.
5 Demeny, P. 1974. The populations of the underdeveloped countries. *Sci. Amer.* **231**(3): 149–159.
6 Gulland, J. 1975. The harvest of the sea. Pages 167–189 in W. W. Murdoch, ed. Environment: Resources, Pollution and Society, 2nd ed. Sinauer Assoc., Sunderland, Mass.
7 Hardin, G. 1968. The tragedy of the commons. *Science* **162:** 1243–1248.
8 ———. 1974. Living on a lifeboat. *BioScience* **24**(10): 561–568.
9 Owens, E., and R. Shaw. 1972. Development Reconsidered. D. C. Heath & Co., Lexington, Mass. 190 pp.
10 Rich, W. 1973. Smaller families through social and economic progress. Overseas Development Council, Monograph #7, Washington, D.C. 73 pp.
11 Teitelbaum, M. S. 1975. Relevance of demographic transition theory for developing countries. *Science* **188:** 420–425.
12 Transnational Institute. 1974. World Hunger: Causes and Remedies. Institute for Policy Studies, 1520 New Hampshire Ave., NW, Washington, D.C.
13 United Nations Economic and Social Council. 1974. Assessment present food situation and dimensions and causes of hunger and malnutrition in the world. E/Conf. 65/Prep/6, 8 May 1974.
14 University of California Food Task Force. 1974. A hungry world: the challenge to agriculture. University of California, Division of Agricultural Sciences. 303 pp.

QUESTIONS

1 Suppose that Murdoch and Oaten are correct in their analysis of the causes of high fertility rates. What changes should our government make in its treatment of those developing countries that have the most serious food problems?

2 Murdoch and Oaten hold that there are solutions other than private ownership to the "problems of the commons." They suggest a possible alternative—the communal ownership of the mechanisms and industries that exploit the resource, combined with communal planning for management. Just what would this alternative require from the United States? From you?

Malthusianism and Socialism

Howard L. Parsons

Howard L. Parsons is professor of philosophy at the University of Bridgeport. He is a founding sponsor of the American Institute for Marxist Studies. Parsons's books include Ethics in the Soviet Union Today *(1967),* Man East and West: Essays in East-West Philosophy *(1975), and* Marx and Engels on Ecology *(1977). He is also coeditor of* Marxism, Revolution and Peace *(1977).*

Parsons rejects the analysis of the causes of scarcity offered by Neo-Malthusians such as Garrett Hardin. For Parsons, the primary cause of scarcity lies in the private ownership, management, and direction of the means of production and reproduction. Capitalism, and the multinational corporations it has spawned, are responsible for world scarcities. In Parsons's view, those who offer a Neo-Malthusian analysis of the problems are interested in preserving capitalism and the privileges of those who benefit from it, and not in the satisfaction of the human needs of all people, including those of the Third World. Parsons sees Marxist-socialism as the best Third World response to the problems of scarcity.

Like their mentor, Neo-Malthusians write as if the blind forces of natural and political economy determine the destiny of mankind. What they mean but hide by humanitarian computer language is that capitalism does and ought to determine that destiny and that a no-growth policy is capitalism's only way to survive. Modern Malthusians, armed with a computer, take, from the viewpoint of needs, a conservative, timid attitude toward natural and social economy. They do not challenge it with humankind's collective imagination, ingenuity, and effort. They emphasize limitation and restraint. They take scarcity to be a consequence of impersonal forces like technology (while population is, as Malthus argued, the "responsibility" of individual persons). But when they speak of scarcity they mean continued scarcity for large masses of people and continued exploitation and affluence for the ruling groups. They do not intend to save mankind. They intend to save themselves. While they are busy gobbling up the world's resources, they call on the world's people to stop propagating.

Capitalism cannot solve the scarcity problem. It limits production according to profit and market standards. It generates a surplus product that it cannot dispose of. It creates

Reprinted with permission of the publisher from *Revolutionary World*, Special Issue, "Self, Global Issues, and Ethics," vols. 21/22 (1977).

chronic unemployment. It is fearful of established communist economies and imminent Third World socialism. Therefore it cries out to the masses: We have enough people! Stop reproducing! Control your appetites for sex, food, fuel, etc.!

NEO-MALTHUSIAN CAPITALISM AND SOCIALISM

The philosophical views of Neo-Malthusian capitalism on nature, man, and political economy, in opposition to Marxist-socialist views, may be summarized as follows:

1 Nature is *severely limited* (scarce) in its resources for man and the laws it imposes on man, vs.: nature is *not so severely limited*.

2 Man is *either over nature or under nature,* vs.: man is *with nature*.

3 Man has *relatively little freedom* to control nature, vs.: man has *relatively much freedom* to control nature.

4 The limits of nature and man's freedom require *scarcity economics,* vs.: the potentialities of nature and man's freedom make possible *abundance economics*.

5 Nature should be controlled primarily by and for a *ruling class,* vs.: nature should be controlled by and for *the people*.

6 The growth of population and production should be *arrested* in accordance with the demands of the preservation of *capitalism* and its ruling class, vs.: population and production should be *developed* in accordance with the demands of a system serving human need, i.e., *socialism*.

7 There ought to be a *class division* between the capitalists who control the resources of nature and society and the people who control their sex and propagation, vs.: there ought to be a *classless society* in which all the people collectively control their lives in their social and natural environment.

The primary cause of scarcity in the modern world centers in the private ownership, management, and direction of the means of production and reproduction. Where industrial factories and techniques, machines, tools, and money are owned by a capitalist class, managed by their hirelings, and directed to the maximizing of profit for the owners, then the class of wage earners working for that class will live in absolute and relative scarcity, and those not working will be bordering on or in a state of starvation. An industrial capitalist enterprise if it is successful produces goods for consumption but also a certain portion of wealth which is returned to the enterprise in the form of investment in new means of production. The result is increased production, hence increased investment, and so on. This is industrial growth—in contemporary parlance, a positive feedback loop. Marx called it accumulation, a basic feature of capitalism. Accumulation is made possible because the capitalist appropriates the "free gifts" of nature[1]—the soil, the raw materials, the water, the wind and water power, etc.—and then the surplus product of laborers after they are paid a wage. . . .

[Such exploitation] generates wealth, but it also concentrates the wealth and the control of the wealth-creating process in the hands of a few. Nature and labor create

---

[1]Karl Marx, *Capital, A Critique of Political Economy,* Vol. III. Ed. by Frederick Engels. Translated from the first German edition by Ernest Untermann. Chicago: Charles H. Kerr, 1909, p. 865.

wealth or value; a capitalist class organizes nature and labor so as to expand wealth and simultaneously restrict its expansion. The restriction occurs because the capitalist does not return to nature the soil-nutrients and vegetation that it strips from nature, defiling it with pollutants;[2] because the laborer is not paid enough to buy back his product; and because the growth and centralization of capital and the improvement of technology and labor-power produce a growing "industrial reserve army." A few become rich, most become poor. The accumulation of wealth is also the accumulation of misery. Capitalism engenders the "paradox" of "overproduction" and "underconsumption." The creativity of the laboring masses is both released and inhibited. This contradiction shows itself in the periodic rhythm of the boom and bust of capitalism.

Scarcity, which is an insufficiency of goods and services to meet the generic human needs of all the people, is a function of both the means of production and the size of the population. In what it produces capitalism is restricted in both quantity and kind because its obsessive drive is toward the greatest amount of surplus-value, accumulation, profitable production, and market expansion.[3] For example, U.S. capitalism does not use one-fourth of its industrial machinery. Capitalism is not organized primarily to produce goods and services directed to the fulfillment of generic human needs—food, clothing, housing, fuel, safety, medical care, family life, education, vocational skill, recreation, play, art, a fit ecological environment, love, creativity, old age security, etc. U.S. capitalism devotes much capital to the technology of war, the petroleum and automotive industries, banking, junk merchandise, and sales. In 1970 $44 billion were spent on public education, $77 billion on the military establishment. Advertising consumed $20 billion in 1971. Between 10 and 20 million U.S. people are chronically hungry.

This economy is anarchic and arbitrary with respect to its ends. In 1968, 100 of the biggest industrial firms owned about half of the total assets of the nation's 1.5 million corporations.[4] These monopolies exercise a tight control over investment, production, price, employment, competition, and innovation. Moreover, the system is very inefficient and wasteful on its own grounds, i.e., in the misemployment and underemployment of natural and human resources; the shunting of human energies, skills, and talents into profitable but humanly unproductive activities; the distribution of goods and services by means of commerce, competition, production, employment, wage, and demand; the distribution of income by ownership of the means of production; and the employment of parasitic, unproductive labor. Examples of unproductive laborers (as given by Paul A. Baran) are those engaged in armament manufacture, and in the making of items of luxury, conspicuous display, and social distinction; government officials; members of the military; clergymen; lawyers; tax evasion specialists; public relations experts; advertising agents; brokers; merchants; speculators.[5] An econ-

---

[2]Thus the prime cause of pollution is not individuals but corporations. See Gus Hall, *Ecology: Can We Survive Under Capitalism?* New York: International, 1972.

[3]Paul A. Baran and Paul M. Sweezy have emphasized the giant corporation's problem of utilizing rising surplus by private consumption and investment, sales, civilian government, militarism, and imperialism. *Monopoly Capital.* New York: Monthly Review, 1966.

[4]Robert L. Heilbroner et al., *In the Name of Profit.* New York: Doubleday, 1972.

[5]*The Political Economy of Growth.* New York: Monthly Review, 1957, pp. 32–33.

omy organized to serve humanistic ends by rational means would eliminate millions of such unproductive workers, and the scarcity which they now perpetuate would be overcome by productive employment directed to the fulfillment of generic human needs. Such workers now live off the surplus product of capital; they do not contribute to the production of wealth but serve to facilitate and solidify a system whose main ingredient is scarcity. . . .

A primary cause of the scarcity in the capitalist world is U.S. multinational corporations. The U.S. economy accounts for nearly half of the world capitalist industrial output and for 60 percent of the global total of foreign investment.[6] In 1968 the investments in Asia and Africa yielded more than 40 percent of all direct private foreign investment.[7] From 1961 to 1971 U.S. direct investors extracted a net balance of $30 billion from foreign countries.[8] During the decade of the 1950s, when they controlled 40 percent of the total GNP of Latin America, they invested more than $6 billion and took home more than $11 billion.[9] In manufacturing in Latin America, 78 percent of multinational foreign investments are financed from domestic savings; more than half of the profits made from these monies leave the country.[10] So there is a parasitic draining of the resources of these poor countries to the rich ones, pre-eminently the United States.

It is now public knowledge that these multinational investments have been protected on a world scale by intelligence agencies of the U.S. government, in collaboration with the Armed Forces and other official agencies. They have, in foreign countries, assisted in the overthrow of governments, initiated or sided in efforts at the kidnapping and assassination of government leaders in the Congo, Cuba, the Dominican Republic, and Chile,[11] bribed officials, blown up refineries, bridges, and railroads, bribed newspaper employees, corrupted scientists and Christian missionaries, and counterfeited currencies. (I omit here comparable crimes committed by these agencies at home.) The democratic governments overthrown—in Iran, Guatemala, Brazil, Uruguay, Chile— were replaced by fascistic, repressive, murderous regimes protecting multinational corporations[12] in collusion with local capitalists.

The principal perpetrators and perpetuators of scarcity and poverty, of oppression and suffering among the peoples of the world, are these multinational capitalists, their

---

[6]*Multinational Corporations*. A compendium of Papers Submitted to the Subcommittee on International Trade of the Committee on Finance of the United States Senate. Washington, D.C.: U.S. Government Printing Office, 1973, p. 44.

[7]Gus Hall, *Imperialism Today*. New York: International, 1972, p. 56.

[8]*Multinational Corporations*, p. 112.

[9]William Appleman Williams, *The Great Evasion*. Chicago: Quandrangle, 1964, p. 63.

[10]Ronald Müller, "The Multinational Corporation and the Underdevelopment of the Third World," in Charles K. Wilber, ed., *The Political Economy of Development*. New York: Random House, 1973, pp. 138–139.

[11]*Alleged Assassination Plots Involving Foreign Leaders*. An Interim Report of the Select Committee to Study Governmental Operations with Respect to Intelligence Activities United States Senate. Washington, D.C.: U.S. Government Printing Office, 1975.

[12]The subversion of these governments has now been established by sworn testimony. See Herbert Aptheker, "U.S. Imperialism and Its Intelligence Agencies," *Political Affairs*, Vol. LIV, No. 11 (November, 1975), pp. 54–55.

government agents, and their reactionary ideologues, who strive to block the people's progress, abundance, democracy, and socialism at every turn.

The new Malthusianism of our time gets support from two groups both of whom side with capitalism and oppose socialism: (1) the liberals, who for partially humanitarian reasons are distressed about the "excess" population and "scarce" means of subsistence in the world and want to moderate the scarcity; and (2) the conservatives, who are openly partisan toward the preservation of capitalism and against communism and the rising Third World. . . .

QUESTIONS

1 Is Marxist-socialism the solution to problems of scarcity?
2 Is capitalism the cause of the problems of world hunger and overpopulation? Explain.

SUGGESTED ADDITIONAL READINGS FOR CHAPTER 9

AIKEN, WILLIAM, and HUGH LAFOLLETTE, eds.: *World Hunger and Moral Obligation.* Englewood Cliffs, N.J.: Prentice-Hall, 1977. With the exception of Joseph Fletcher, a theologian, and Garrett Hardin, a biologist, all the authors in this collection are philosophers. The writers examine various issues raised by the central question, "What moral responsibility do affluent nations (or the people in them) have to the starving masses?" The article by Peter Singer which is reprinted in this chapter is also reprinted in this volume and is followed by a postscript in which Singer (1) presents some later thoughts on the topic and (2) responds to some critics.

BERELSON, BERNARD: "Beyond Family Planning." *Science,* vol. 163, February 7, 1969, pp. 533–543. Berelson wrote this article while he was president of the Population Council. He provides an exhaustive categorization of proposals that go "beyond family planning" for the sake of "solving" the population problem. He then appraises these proposals in terms of technological readiness, political viability, administrative feasibility, economic capability, ethical acceptability, and presumed effectiveness.

BROWN, PETER G., and HENRY SHUE, eds.: *Food Policy.* New York: Free Press, 1977. This book is designed to provide a foundation for a reflective appraisal of questions about the moral obligation of the agriculturally affluent in regard to world hunger. The articles, which were all written specifically for this volume, are divided into four sections: (1) "Needs and Obligations"; (2) "Responsibilities in the Public Sector"; (3) "Responsibilities in the Private Sector"; and (4) "Reducing Dependence."

EBERSTADT, NICK: "Myths of the Food Crisis." *New York Review of Books,* February 19, 1976, pp. 32–37. Eberstadt attacks the myths about world hunger which distort our perception of the problems and lead to the pessimism exemplified by Garrett Hardin.

GUSSOW, JOAN DYE: *The Feeding Web: Issues in Nutritional Ecology.* Palo Alto, Calif.: Bull Publishing Co., 1978. Gussow, a nutritionist, provides a collection of readings accompanied by her interpretations of those readings. She is concerned with "what the facts about the present state of the world" imply for "living human organisms completely dependent on complex foodstuffs for survival." The readings examine the biological, technical, social, scientific, and commercial matrices in which the production, purchasing, and consumption of food are embedded.

KUTZNER, PATRICIA L., CHRISTIAN MILLER, and MARK LEWY: *Who's Involved with Hunger: An Organizational Guide*. World Hunger Education Service, 1979. This is a list of various organizations which are concerned with hunger. The list includes government organizations and private agencies. The private agencies are subdivided according to their focus—global, national, and regional.

LAPPÉ, FRANCES MOORE, and JOSEPH COLLINS: *Food First: Beyond the Myth of Scarcity*, rev. ed. New York: Ballantine Books, 1978. Lappé and Collins reject the Neo-Malthusianism represented by Garrett Hardin. They try to dispel the "myths" which surround the world hunger issue and argue that the obstacles to overcoming world hunger are put up in our name, using our tax money, by corporations based in our economy.

LUCAS, GEORGE R., JR., and THOMAS OGLETREE, eds.: *Lifeboat Ethics*. New York: Harper & Row, 1976. Most of the articles in this anthology appeared initially in *Soundings*. The articles are written by ethicists (many of whom are theologians) and scientists and grew out of concerns stemming from the advocacy of triage as a methodological response to world hunger.

RACHELS, JAMES: "Killing and Starving to Death." *Philosophy*, vol. 54, April 1979, pp. 159–171. Rachels, attacking the view that killing is worse than letting die, argues that letting die is just as bad as killing. For Rachels our duty not to let people die from starvation is as strong as our duty not to kill them.

WATTS, MICHAEL: *Silent Violence: Food, Famine & Peasantry in Northern Nigeria*. Berkeley, Calif.: University of California Press, 1983. Watts, whose discipline is geography, looks at the current food crisis in Africa from a historical perspective. He traces the varying character of food systems among Hausa peasants in northern Nigeria, examining the relationship among food crises, climate, and society.

WOGAMAN, J. PHILIP, ed.: *The Population Crisis and Moral Responsibility*. Washington, D.C.: Public Affairs Press, 1973. This anthology emphasizes theological perspectives but contains articles by ethicists and population experts as well. The various articles are collected in four separate sections: (1) the moral basis of policy objectives; (2) the moral responsibility of government; (3) moral analysis of policy proposals; (4) moral responsibility of religious communities.

CHAPTER 10

WAR AND NUCLEAR DETERRENCE

It is difficult and painful to think about nuclear weapons, nuclear strategies, and nuclear war. The possibilities are horrendous—massive destruction of life, agony for countless survivors, and potential changes to the earth and to the human genetic structure that make a human postnuclear-war future uncertain. Yet nuclear weapons continue to be built and positioned, military game plans incorporating their use continue to be developed, and supporters of nuclear deterrence continue to defend their strategies as the best way of preventing nuclear war and ensuring world peace. This chapter focuses on some of the moral issues raised by nuclear weapons. This requires raising questions about (1) the morality of *using* nuclear weapons and (2) the morality of *building and deploying* them in order to deter potential aggressors from either launching a nuclear offensive or beginning a war using conventional weapons. In order to understand the moral debate concerning nuclear war and nuclear deterrence, it is necessary to first understand the lines of reasoning advanced about the morality of war in general.

MORALITY AND WAR

Writers on the morality of war fall roughly into four major groups: (1) pacifists, (2) those writing from the standpoint of traditional just-war doctrine, (3) those advancing utilitarian reasoning, and (4) realists.

Pacifism

Pacifism is sometimes described as the view that war, by its very nature, is wrong because it necessarily involves the intentional killing of human beings. What is sometimes labeled "absolutist pacifism" holds that it is impossible in principle to justify any use of violence against people. For absolutist pacifists, human life has absolute value and no other value (e.g., freedom) can supercede it. Pacifism is not synonymous with passivism or passivity. A commitment to pacifism is also a commitment to cooperative social conduct, among both individuals and nations, based on agreement and general moral opposition to war. Recent forms of pacifism, all of which might be labeled "limited pacifism," do not reject all lethal uses of violence and do not condemn all past wars as immoral. One version of limited pacifism rejects as immoral, however, any war that involves the slaughter of innocent bystanders and sees contemporary wars as necessarily involving such slaughter. Another version of limited pacifism, sometimes called "nuclear pacifism," will be discussed later.

Just-War Doctrine

There are close affinities between limited pacifists and just-war theorists. Both have a strong commitment to the value of human life but grant that taking it may not always be wrong. Rather than condemning the violence of war absolutely, just-war theorists seek to restrict the use of violence by specifying the conditions under which it could be justified. Just-war theory focuses on two questions. (1) When does one nation have a moral right to wage war against another? (2) What restrictions, if any, does morality place on the legitimate means used in fighting a war? In answering the first question, just-war doctrine lays out a set of conditions that must hold if a nation is to have a moral right to engage in war. In answering the second, it lays out a set of conditions that place moral limits on the conduct of those engaged in war.

The Right to Go to War   Just-war theorists have given different accounts of the conditions that must hold before a nation has a right to go to war. The following statement, however, is one way of capturing their central concerns. One nation (A) is justified in engaging in war with another nation (B) if and only if:

1 A is attacked by B, or is attempting to help another nation (C) that has been attacked by B, or A or C are about to be attacked by B (*the just cause requirement*).[1]

2 The individuals in A who declare war on B are those members of A who have the legitimate authority to do so (*the legitimate authority requirement*).

3 A's intentions in waging war are limited to repelling B's attack and establishing a fair peace (*the good intentions requirement*).

4 A has a reasonable hope of successfully achieving the good it intends (*the reasonable hope of success requirement*).

5 The good A can reasonably hope to achieve is proportional to the evils that can reasonably be expected to result from waging war (*proportionality of just cause to means requirement*).

6 A has exhausted all peaceful alternatives and fighting the war is the last resort (*the last resort requirement*).

[1]Many proponents of just-war doctrine reject the view that it can be justifiable to attack one's opponent first. On their position, there is just cause for A to go to war only if B attacks first. Thus the nation launching the first attack is always considered the aggressor.

7 *A* does not use or anticipate using immoral means in waging war (*the moral means requirement*).

In light of these requirements, an aggressor nation is never justified in fighting a war. Given condition (1), however, the nation which launches the first attack is not necessarily considered the aggressor. If *B* is posed to attack *A* and all the advances *A* makes to *B* in order to avert war are rejected, *B* is still considered the aggressor even if *A* strikes first to prevent some of the losses *B* intends to inflict. At the same time, even fighting a war in self-defense is not justified if the other conditions are not met. Although these requirements come into play primarily when decisions about going to war are made, just-war theorists argue that a periodic reassessment while the war is being waged is also essential, especially in regards to requirements (4) and (5).

Just Conduct in War In just-war doctrine, two principles are central in determining what types of action are morally permissible in warfare:

1 The level of force employed must be proportional to the good that the action is intended to achieve (*the principle of proportionality*).

2 Force should be used in a way that respects the distinction (discriminates) between combatants and noncombatants (*the principle of discrimination*).

The principle of proportionality requires that the good that the action is intended to achieve will outweigh any bad consequences caused by the action. An example will illustrate the requirements of this principle. At the end of World War II, many German soldiers surrendered to the Allied forces. Suppose that the Allies had adopted the policy of not taking prisoners and instead had killed all those who tried to surrender. The evils caused by the policy (the deaths of thousands of Germans) would have been disproportionate to the result achieved—the neutralizing of enemy combatants. Note that both the decision to go to war (and remain at war) and decisions made in conducting the war require the weighing of probable good against probable evil. In the first case, as requirement (5) specifies, the probable evils of the war must be outweighed by the probable good to be achieved by fighting the war. In the second case, as the principle of proportionality specifies, any particular use of force must be proportional to the intended legitimate military end. "Legitimate military end" here can be understood as either (a) the overall military end of winning the war or (b) the immediate end of a particular use of force (e.g., the forced surrender of a battalion, the giving up of a specific piece of a contested battlefield, etc.).

The principle of discrimination is usually understood as prohibiting the direct *intentional* killing of *noncombatants*. Disagreement then centers on the meaning of "noncombatants" and "direct intentional killing." Richard Wasserstrom in this chapter discusses the various ways in which the combatant-noncombatant distinction is understood and presents his own views on the topic. Regarding the meaning of the prohibition against the direct *intentional* killing of noncombatants, three interpretations are found in contemporary discussions of the morality of war. The second interpretation discussed below, however, is the one found in traditional just-war doctrine. On the first interpretation, the principle of discrimination prohibits any military action whose *foreseen* results include the deaths of noncombatants. This interpretation is found in the thinking of some limited pacifists. Understood in this way, the principle of discrimination would prohibit the use of most modern weapons—conventional as well as nuclear—in any environment that included both combatants and noncombatants. If the foreseeable consequences of bombing military targets included the deaths of any noncombatants, for example, the bombing would be immoral. Definitely prohibited would be the World War II saturation bombing of cities and the atomic-bomb destruction of Hiroshima and Nagasaki.

The second interpretation, a necessary component of traditional just-war doctrine, incorporates the *doctrine of double effect*. According to this doctrine, an act that would have good and bad effects, *both of which can be foreseen,* is morally permissible despite its bad effects, if it meets the following restrictions.

1 The act itself (considered apart from the bad effect it produces) is not impermissible.
2 The good but not the bad effect is intended.
3 The bad effect is not the means to the good effect.
4 The good effect is commensurate with the bad effect.

Two ideas are basic to understanding these restrictions. The first idea is that in acting we can *intend* a certain effect, which is the *direct* object of our act. Although certain bad effects can also be foreseen and cannot be avoided, they are the *indirect, unintended* results of the act. The second idea is that some result may be the inevitable concomitant of another one without being its cause. Two examples will illustrate the doctrine.

Suppose that *A* is engaged in fighting a just war against *B*. *A*'s generals decide that if *B* is to be forced to end the war, it is essential to destroy two of *B*'s strongest military bases. The generals know that some children live on these bases and that their deaths are inevitable if the total destruction intended is achieved. Thinking in terms of the doctrine of double effect, the principle of discrimination would not be violated because (1) the bombing destruction of strategic military targets by those waging a just war is not morally impermissible; (2) the direct, intended result is the destruction of the bases; (3) the death of the children is not the means to this destruction; and (4) although some children will die, the good result intended—the destruction of the bases and the end of the war—is at least commensurate with the evil of their deaths. In contrast, the World War II bombing of Dresden is frequently cited as an example of a military action that would be forbidden according to the double-effect interpretation of the principle of discrimination. Dresden, which had no military value, was bombed and destroyed purportedly to sap the will of the German people. Strategists thought that the destruction of this city would spark a revolt against the Nazi regime, thus ending the war.[2] Even if the bombing of Dresden is seen as consistent with (1) and (4), problems arise in light of (2) and (3). Here the bad effects, including massive death and suffering for noncombatants, were *intended* as the *means* to the good effect.

---

[2]This is a simplified version of the reasons that led to the bombing of Dresden. For a more detailed account see Alexander McKee, *Dresden 1945: The Devil's Tinderbox* (New York: E. P. Dutton, 1982, 1984), especially Chapter 5.

The third interpretation of the principle of discrimination is adopted by some contemporary just-war theorists who reject the doctrine of double effect. They question the distinction between intended or direct effects and unintended or indirect effects. At the same time, they reject the view that any use of force in war whose foreseen consequences will include the killing of noncombatants is morally prohibited. On their approach, the principle of discrimination does not absolutely prohibit acts whose foreseen results include the killing of noncombatants. Rather, it requires those engaged in war to concentrate on military targets, to minimize the destruction of civilian targets and noncombatants, and to engage in acts which destroy the latter only if the destruction of a critical military target justifies a proportionate collateral destruction of noncombatants and civilian targets. The death of civilians who live or work near a nuclear missile site might be justified on their view, for example, if destroying the site is crucial to ending the war and the death of the noncombatants is a necessary concomitant of the destruction.

The Utilitarian Approach

Utilitarian reasoning on the morality of war involves assessments of the potential good and bad consequences of alternative policies. On the international level, as in other sorts of cases, the utilitarian considers conceivable alternatives. The morally preferable policy is the one that on balance will tend to produce the best consequences when the interests of everyone affected are counted equally. A utilitarian might conclude, for example, that the scale of violence involved in war is such an immense evil that no good consequences could possibly outweigh it. Such a conclusion would lead the utilitarian to advocate some form of pacifism. A utilitarian might also adopt a pacifist stance if convinced that in the long run a consistently followed policy of never resorting to military force would result in less harm than a policy of deciding each case on utilitarian grounds. In contrast, a utilitarian might also argue that a blanket approach of this type would cause more harm than good on balance. On this view, questions about the morality of using military force to resolve an international dispute would have to be handled on a case-by-case basis. Some wars might then be seen as moral, others not. Regarding the conduct of war, similar approaches could be adopted. Utilitarians might argue, for example, that those engaged in war should adhere to the principle of discrimination (understood, perhaps, in the third way discussed above) if adhering to it were seen as tending to produce better consequences on balance than adopting a policy that made no distinction between combatants and noncombatants. It is obvious then that different assessments of potential good and bad consequences may lead utilitarians to very different conclusions regarding both the morality of engaging in war in the first place and the morality of the means used in conducting the war.

The Realist Approach

In literature dealing with international relations, individuals who hold that questions of morality do not apply to relations among nations are often called "realists" or "Hobbesians," after the seventeenth-century philosopher, Thomas Hobbes. On Hobbes's account, there are no binding moral obligations among nations. Rather, relations among nations are relations of *power,* unconstrained by moral rules. As the realist position is understood here, the only considerations that have moral relevance for the leaders of a nation-state are those relating to the welfare and interest of that state. In evaluating the alternative international policies open to the nation-states of which they are a part, realists, like utilitarians, concentrate on their probable consequences. Unlike utilitarians, however, they do not take into account the policies' effects on the well-being of everyone who will be affected. Rather, their concern is with maximizing the well-being of their own nation-state and its allies. War, for realists, is simply another way of settling a dispute, to be engaged in when no other way of resolving the dispute promises to be as advantageous.

MORALITY AND THE USE OF NUCLEAR WEAPONS

Discussions of the use of nuclear weapons raise questions about (1) the morality of an all-out nuclear war and (2) the morality of a limited use of nuclear weapons. Two types of scenarios are envisioned. The first involves the kind of massive destruction of cities and military installations expressed in the notion of a nuclear holocaust. The second involves a more limited use of nuclear weapons, perhaps to counter setbacks in military battles fought with conventional weapons. A possible scenario of the latter type, envisioned by the United States and its European allies runs as follows. The Soviets attack West Germany using conventional military forces. NATO's conventional forces are overrun. At this point, NATO leaders might use tactical or intermediate-range nuclear weapons to destroy the attacking Soviet forces.

Morality and All-Out Nuclear War

The various positions taken on the morality of all-out nuclear war should be apparent given our earlier discussion on the morality of war in general. Absolutist pacifists reject all wars as immoral. Those limited pacifists who are sometimes called "nuclear pacifists" reject all use of nuclear weapons as immoral because of their belief that even their limited use in warfare will spark off a nuclear holocaust. Just-war theorists see the destruction inflicted by an all-out nuclear war as grossly incompatible with just-war criteria, especially with the principles of proportionality and discrimination. In this chapter, the U.S. Catholic Bishops' statement exemplifies the just-war approach to nuclear war. Utilitarians, given the devastation resulting from an all-out nuclear war, would be hard-pressed to come up with any probable good consequences that could outweigh the massive killing and destruction. Realists, it would seem, could support such a war only in the unlikely event that it could be seen as serving national self-interest.

The Limited Use of Nuclear Weapons

Two major questions arise regarding the limited use of nuclear weapons. The first question is an empirical one: Would a limited nuclear war or nuclear exchange inevitably escalate into an all-out nuclear war? This question is discussed in the Bishops' statement. After raising numerous, perhaps unanswerable questions about limited exchanges, the Bishops adopt a sceptical stance regarding the possibility of nonescalation. The second question is a moral one: Can even a limited nuclear war be justified? Nuclear pacifists reply no, rejecting all uses of nuclear weapons as immoral, although they do not necessarily condemn the use of all conventional weapons. Just-war theorists differ in their answers, depending on their interpretations of the principle of discrimination and on their assessments of the extent of the destruction that would result from the limited use of nuclear weapons. Utilitarians and realists, or course, offer various answers depending on their assessments of the consequences of various alternatives, including the use of nuclear weapons. In assessing alternatives, however, utilitarians give equal weight to the interests of everyone considered, and realists focus on the interests of their own nation and its allies.

MORALITY AND NUCLEAR DETERRENCE

Nuclear deterrence policies are adopted and implemented to deter potential enemies from launching nuclear attacks or from using their military strength to threaten and conquer other nation-states. An excerpt from a U.S. Department of Defense statement in this chapter, for example, asserts the need for a military buildup sufficient to deter the Soviet Union from attacking the United States or its allies or from exploiting its military strength to coerce and subjugate others. Nuclear deterrence policies take several forms depending on what kind of nuclear weapons are built and how they are deployed. The deterrence policy that dominates current United States–Soviet Union relations is sometimes called "MAD." It threatens massive nuclear strikes against both civilian and military populations. MAD incorporates what is called *countervalue* or *countercity* targeting, which threatens retaliation by making the opponent lose "value" for "value." The central idea here is that each nuclear power will develop the capacity to destroy the other, targeting its opponent's cities as well as its military installations. Should one nation, then, launch a nuclear first strike against the other, the latter would immediately launch a retaliatory strike. The result would be *mutual assured destruction* (MAD). The threat of mutual devastation is supposed to ensure that neither nation will launch a nuclear first strike. Thus, a nuclear war will never occur. In contrast to MAD, other deterrence policies, sometimes called minimalist nuclear deterrence policies, threaten a more limited nuclear exchange. Minimalist approaches frequently involve *counterforce* targeting only—the targeting of military targets.

The position of some just-war theorists regarding nuclear deterrence is grounded in their moral condemnation of any use of nuclear weapons. Their discussion centers on the following questions: (1) If the use of nuclear weapons is morally prohibited, can a policy which threatens such use be moral? (2) Is it morally permissible to *risk* doing that which it would be morally impermissible to do? Some just-war theorists, including nuclear pacifists, answer both questions in the negative. Other just-war theorists develop different positions which follow from their not holding that *all* nuclear use is immoral. Thus, for example, the U.S. Catholic Bishops hold for minimalist nuclear deterrence based on the position that under some circumstances some use of nuclear weapons might be morally acceptable. Still other just-war theorists, convinced that only strong deterrence policies such as MAD can keep the Soviet Union in check, argue that, at this point, the criteria of just war can legitimately be set aside in the interest of *preventing* a greater evil—either nuclear blackmail and domination by the Soviet Union or nuclear destruction by the Soviets. While granting that the deterrence policy is an evil, such thinkers maintain that in this case one must choose the lesser evil over the much greater one.

Articles on nuclear deterrence incorporating utilitarian reasoning, exemplified by Douglas P. Lackey's in this chapter, focus of course on the probable consequences of deterrence policies. Lackey argues for unilateral nuclear disarmament on the part of the United States based on his assessment of the probable consequences of alternative policies. In another reading in this chapter, Gregory S. Kavka challenges Lackey's conclusions, raising doubts about the latter's assessment of the effect of unilateral nuclear disarmament on subsequent U.S.S.R. behavior.

Realists hold that nuclear deterrence is necessary, but they disagree about which nuclear deterrence policy is morally correct insofar as they disagree about which one will be most effective in preventing nuclear war. Some realists argue, for example, that moving away from MAD toward counterforce targeting only could be destabilizing. A different approach to the question of the morality of MAD from a modified realist standpoint is advanced by Christopher W. Morris in this chapter. Morris is concerned with responding to the following claim. Since the massive destruction envisioned by deterrence policies incorporating countervalue targeting is morally impermissible, so, too, is threatening that destruction. In contrast to the realists, Morris offers a modified Hobbesian position. When nations are engaged in mutually advantageous interactions, he maintains, moral rules do apply. When one nation launches a nuclear attack against another, however, mutually advantageous interaction has ended and moral rules, including the principle of discrimination, no longer apply. On Morris's analysis, under those conditions, massive retaliatory nuclear strikes are not morally impermissible. It follows, for Morris, that policies, such as MAD, whose intent is to deter aggression and prevent nuclear war are not morally prohibited.

AN ALTERNATIVE TO NUCLEAR DETERRENCE?

One possible tactic suggested as an alternative to MAD was signalled by President Ronald Reagan in a speech sometimes called the "star wars speech." Reagan declared his intent to direct U.S. scientists to explore the technical feasibility of developing a defense against nuclear-armed ballistic missiles. Subsequently, an organization called the Strategic Defense Initiative Office (SDI) was formed to implement Reagan's policy. Its task was to develop defensive systems that would drastically reduce the military effectiveness of nuclear weapons and make them unreliable for modern warfare.

Supporters of SDI see it as morally superior to MAD and cite the following advantages. First, SDI would replace weapons involving the threat of retaliatory massive destruction by defensive systems that could destroy launched missiles. This would prevent the loss of both American and enemy lives since there would be no need for massive retaliatory destruction. Second, the "neutralization" of an opponent's weapons would offer a real promise of a major bilateral nuclear disarmament. Third, SDI would lessen the risk of nuclear war since any possible advantages to be gained by launching nuclear strikes would be drastically reduced.

In rebuttal, numerous reservations are expressed about the morality of SDI and the advantages promised by its proponents. First, the technical feasibility of such defensive systems is seen as highly doubtful. Second, only ballistic missiles shot above the atmosphere are potentially defendable by the SDI system. Various other weapons are not covered. Third, SDI might adversely affect the stability of the Western Alliance since Europe, unlike the United States, is protected mostly by tactical weapons not covered by SDI. Fourth, the costs of SDI promise to be staggering, with projections running from around one hundred billion to half a trillion dollars. Questions are raised about the impact of these costs on programs filling social needs. Fifth, there is good reason to think that the offensive nuclear system required by MAD would continue to be maintained, not only because SDI's defenses would have no effect on a lot of the enemy's weapons, but also because the MAD system would be seen as providing a backup should the defensive system fail. Thus SDI would simply be a shield behind which the buildup of offensive arms would continue. Sixth, SDI is seen as destabilizing if the Soviets *perceive* it as being coupled with a buildup of offensive weapons in order to destroy them. The result could be another arms race and/or a preemptive attack by the Soviets and the nuclear holocaust that deterrence policies are supposed to prevent.

Jane S. Zembaty

Security and Stability through Military Buildup

U.S. Department of Defense

This excerpt from *Soviet Military Power* exemplifies the reasoning of those who hold the following related beliefs: (1) The Soviet Union will exploit every foreign policy opportunity open to it to expand its formidable power; (2) To deter the Soviet Union from attacking the United States or its allies, the United States must continue to strengthen its strategic nuclear forces as well as its conventional forces.

Military power continues to be the principal instrument of Soviet expansionist policy. Year in and year out, for the past two decades, the Soviet Armed Forces have been accorded an inordinately large share of the national resources. The capabilities of those forces—relative to our own and those of our allies—have been steadily augmented in every dimension; and there is no sign of abatement of the scope of buildup. They have been readied for war at any level and at any time. Doctrine, structure and offensive posture combine to constitute a threat of direct military action that is of unprecedented

Reprinted from *Soviet Military Power* (Washington, D.C.: U.S. Government Printing Office, 1983).

proportions. However, the Politburo's grand strategy is to win, if possible, without wholesale shedding of more Russian blood save as necessary to complete the subjugation of Afghanistan. Thus, the main operative role of that formidable war machine is to undergird, by its very presence, the step by step extension of Soviet influence and control by instilling fear and promoting paralysis, by sapping the vitality of collective security arrangements, by subversion, by coercive political actions of every genre.

The lengthening shadow of Soviet military power cannot be wished away or ignored. But neither does it provide the slightest basis for despair. We have the capacity to restore a stable balance and to do so without jeopardizing our other national goals. The combined resources of the United States and its Allies dwarf those of the Soviet orbit. More to the point, we have reservoirs of strength without counterpart in the Soviet Union: the concepts and values of the great civilizations which are our priceless legacy.

We must—and we can—invalidate the Soviet strategy. In conjunction with our Allies, we must—and we can—convince the Soviet Union that it cannot profit from the use of force or the threat of force in the international arena. We must stay the course our predecessors had the wisdom to plot in forging the North Atlantic Treaty, the Rio Treaty, the ANZUS Treaty and the bilateral pacts with our Asian Allies to provide for the common defense.

Deterrence of direct attack on US interests and those of our Allies must command our priority attention and shape our defense programs. The capabilities needed to prevent war—war which we will never initiate—are fundamentally different from those that drive Soviet force development and deployment. Given these asymmetries, there is no requirement to match the Soviets unit for unit, weapons systems for weapons systems. What is required is a nuclear and conventional posture that makes any Soviet military option too uncertain of outcome and too high of cost to be pursued. That posture is in part military sinew and in part national resolve. The combination must convince the aggressor that we have the stamina to withstand an initial onslaught and the will to respond in a manner that denies attainment of the objective of aggression.

Apart from the deterrence of direct attack, we must prevent the Soviet Union from exploiting its growing military strength—on and off the Eurasian land mass—to further its objectives through coercion and other indirect means. Our collective security arrangements—strengthened by the mutually supporting assets of our Allies, our forward deployment and our rapid reinforcement capabilities—provide the barrier against such threats. Our alliance structures must continue to make evident to the entire world that we stand together against all threats to the territorial integrity or internal security of any members.

The defense programs we have set in train will help to redress the adverse trends in the military balance and assure that the Soviet Union cannot capitalize on the power of its armed forces for political advantage. Our programs thus promote the security and stability of the world community.

Those programs reflect difficult choices. Given the immediacy of the threat and the inherited deficiencies of our force structure, first priority has been placed on the modernization of all three components of our strategic nuclear forces and associated command and control systems, and the readiness upgrade of our conventional forces. But we have also recognized that defense is a longterm effort, unless and until the Soviet Union becomes a fully cooperating member of a world community of nations functioning under the rule of law. Thus, we and our Allies have also begun to modernize our conventional forces, increase their staying power and expand their numbers to be able to cope with the continuing growth of Soviet military power.

We must demonstrate a constancy in our own programs. Of equal importance, we must have the resolve to work unceasingly for the security of all free nations. Only then will the Soviets be convinced that their military buildup is futile and the way be paved for restoring peace at the lowest level of armaments.

QUESTIONS

1 Suppose that a similar statement was being written by policy makers in the Soviet Union. Would it differ in any important ways from this statement?
2 What moral principles, if any, are implicit in the statement?

Noncombatants, Indiscriminate Killing, and the Immorality of Nuclear War

Richard Wasserstrom

A biographical sketch of Richard Wasserstrom is found on page 213.

Wasserstrom rejects as morally impermissible any use of nuclear weapons that would result in the indiscriminate killing of massive numbers of wholly innocent persons. He focuses on two questions dealing with the distinction between combatants and noncombatants: (1) Are there differences, even in total wars, that make it possible to distinguish between combatants and noncombatants? (2) If yes, do these differences support a defensible moral position concerning things that it is wrong to do to noncombatants even in time of war? On Wassesrstrom's analysis, such differences exist and young children provide the paradigm example. Even if wars of national self-defense are justified, he maintains, there are limits to what may justifiably be done under the legitimate claim of self-defense. In particular, he claims, the intentional massive destruction of innocent lives cannot be justified on the grounds of self-defense.

The idea that even in time of war there are certain things it is wrong to do is neither an unintelligible nor an unfamiliar one. Even in the more total, quite unrestrained armed conflicts of this century, certain limits on the conduct of the wars, on the ways

Reprinted with permission of the publisher from Michael Allen Fox and Leo Groarke, eds., *Nuclear War: Philosophical Perspectives* (New York: Peter Lang, 1985), pp. 39–48.

they were fought, were both acknowledged and adhered to. Members of armed forces who surrendered were taken prisoner rather than killed, the neutrality of certain countries was recognized and respected, and weapons, such as poison gas, were not employed (at least in World War II). In addition, of course, after the end of World War II, the victorious Allied powers conducted trials based in part upon the idea that some individuals had in the course of the conduct of the war violated important norms and principles prohibiting certain kinds of wartime conduct—violations of the laws of war. And members of the armed forces of the United States, as well as many other countries, are taught that there are certain specifiable things they may not do in war; some, though not very many, have been disciplined and punished for having done them.

Those who have sought to make moral as well as intellectual sense out of the idea that even in time of war there are some ways of fighting it which are impermissible and wrong have proceeded along several distinct lines of analysis and argument. One approach takes the existing conventions, treaties and practice which establish prohibitions upon the forms and kinds of warfare and weapons as providing the exhaustive content of what it is impermissible to do in the conduct of war. A second, potentially more fruitful approach is the view that such prohibitions' having been accepted and agreed to is evidence that they reflect or embody those moral considerations and values that continue to have place and application in time of war. I have on other occasions endeavored to indicate and explain what I take to be the problems with both approaches, and I will not pursue such questions here. Rather, I will assume, what I take to be in fact the case, that the existing laws of war do not clearly prohibit nuclear weapons from being used in war. At the very least, if it would always be wrong to use them it is not because the Hague or Geneva Conventions or the principles accepted and applied after World War II expressly govern and prohibit their use. Hence, my aim is to try to develop a plausible theory about what considerations matter most in time of war, about what it is wrong to do in time of war and why, and about why nuclear weapons are impermissible to use.

The distinction that is a central part of the tradition of moral thought about the laws of war and that is, I think, still the central distinction that properly holds in time of war is the one expressed in and through the ideas that even in time of war there are differences between combatants and noncombatants, that these differences give rise to, explain, or justify the different moral status of each, and make it wrong to do to noncombatants what it may not, in wartime, be wrong to do to combatants. Sometimes this gets expressed in terms of the innocence of noncombatants and in terms of principles or considerations having to do with the claims they have and with things that it is wrong to do to or with them. But, without explication, the sense of "innocence" which is relevant here is neither clear nor obvious, and without further thought and argument the relevant principles or considerations concerning the innocent are neither apparent nor manifestly correct. So, there are at least two questions that must be investigated: (1) Are there differences, even in wars that are total, that in fact make it possible to identify and distinguish the combatants from the noncombatants?; and (2) If there are, do these give rise to a defensible moral position concerning things that it is wrong to do to noncombatants, even in time of war?

If the combatants in question were only those individuals who were members of the armed forces and if all members of the armed forces were to wear distinctive uniforms, then we could identify them accordingly and distinguish them from the noncombatants who were not so garbed and not so specially engaged in conducting (i.e. fighting) the war. And we could then also develop an account of their differences in moral standing or status and of the reasons why things it would be permissible to do to combatants would be wrong to do to noncombatants. For in war the armed forces of each side are at least prepared, under a claim of right, to subdue the opposing armed forces. Under such circumstances it seems surely appropriate that members of the armed forces of each side view and regard members of the armed forces of the other side as their prospective killers. They are *armed* with weapons of deadly force and the arms are the means by which armed forces fight, and battles and wars are won and lost. So it seems quite reasonable to think and to argue that once it is a war that is going on, it is not wrong, for reasons that borrow upon familiar ideas of self-defense, that members of the armed forces of either side should either intentionally or knowingly seek to kill those similarly situated on the other side—at least, surely, unless and until they have surrendered and laid down their arms, so that they no longer possess the ability, as well as the intention (which they still may, of course, possess), to kill or otherwise subdue them. As long as they have that ability and that intention constitutive of membership in the armed forces the use and employment of weapons of deadly force against them seems a part of the internal logic and morality of war.

Noncombatants are different. Because they are not armed they cannot kill and are not committed to killing in the same way. They do not constitute the same kind of danger, and therefore the case, if there is one, for justifiably, intentionally, or knowingly killing them in time of war must be different and not founded in the same relatively secure fashion upon relatively familiar ideas concerning the permissible use of deadly force in self-defense.

It can, though, be argued that the distinction between noncombatants and combatants is not so easily made out nor the difference in moral status so easily established. One might hold that wars, especially total wars, require the organized support, energies, and activities of large numbers of persons not themselves members of the armed forces. Weapons and armaments need to be designed, manufactured, and supplied to the armed forces. The members of the armed forces need to be clothed, fed, and housed. And even their morale is an important component of how effectively and well they will fight. It is the so-called "noncombatants" of the country who can be and are engaged in doing all of these kinds of things. If they were not supporting the armed forces in all sorts of ways, both material and ideological, by and through their own intentional and knowing actions, the war would be a short and unsuccessful one because of the failure of the effort required to sustain it. The point is that the causal chains which lead to the wielding and employment of the weapons of war by the members of the armed forces are longer, more complex, and less clear than appeared at first, and it is no longer either obvious or right that the targets of these weapons be only those who are most immediately or distinctively in the position to employ them, and hence to constitute a deadly danger.

What is more, just as it does not and cannot matter, once a war is underway, whether the members of the armed forces volunteered or were conscripted under circumstances that left them no real choice, so too it does not and cannot matter much whether the noncombatants working in the factories or the fields are enthusiastic supporters of the war or are there because they have no real choice. If they are there, they are doing things, acting in ways that aid, help, contribute to, and are parts of the causal chains that go to make up the fighting and the waging of war. And if they are not there, but in their beds asleep, they will be there the next day. They are still tightly connected to the war and the war effort, just as are members of the armed forces when they are asleep at night. In war, especially in total war, the distinction between combatants and noncombatants, so this line of argument concludes, is not a clear-cut or coherent one; nor is it one that can or should have moral weight; nor is it one that could possibly be maintained in practice, even if there were theoretical distinctions that could, in the abstract, be identified and defended. That is why, for example, there was nothing wrong *per se* with the saturation bombing of cities in World War II. The war effort was at work in Dresden as well as in the battlefield, and there was no way to identify and destroy the factories and the factory workers effectively, except in this way.

Nor is this the only argument that could be advanced. Even if there are noncombatants in the sense so far considered, there are other things to take into account. Any number of noncombatants may have opted for the war in the first place and it will of course be impossible to tell which ones. They may have supported it and helped to bring it about. They may support it still. If so, then there are different causal chains within which they are enmeshed and a different moral dimension since it was or is their actions that played a role in bringing about the situation in which the weapons of war are what they now confront. And if the war that they favored and helped to bring into being is a wrongful or unjust one, then they are, still more clearly, morally culpable for their places in these causal chains and what they produced. If they are culpable in this way, their special moral status as noncombatants is undermined further. Bearing some responsibility for the war and its unusual dangers, it is permissible that the dangers and risks so created be borne by them rather than by those on the opposing side. In the imperfect moral world of war, killing them, even if they are noncombatants, is permissible as the only kind of punishment they are likely to receive and do deserve. In all these ways persons can be and are noncombatants without being morally innocent, and for that reason distinct from the rest who may not permissibly be killed in time of war.

And finally, there is just the matter of practicality. Even if there were theoretical distinctions that in the abstract could be made, they could not possibly be maintained in practice. Innocent noncombatants, if there are any, do not wear special uniforms or keep to special places. If a war is to be waged at all effectively, perhaps it is wrong to try deliberately to kill them if we do know who and where they are, but that is all that morality in war can or should require.

I do not think these lines of argument are right, despite their apparent plausibility and despite the difficulties and complexities which provide that plausibility. One of the guiding ideas is that of self-defense *in* war, extended, as we have seen, to the peculiar and special circumstances of what is and must be true of war. But the extension goes too far and in ways that morality does not licence. No matter how extensively and complexly the causal chains are extended back from the actual possessors and employers of the weapons of war, they do not and cannot reasonably be thought to include all persons living within a country at war, or even all activities in which persons within a country may be engaged. There are differences of degree as well as kind, and both matter when the case for intentional and knowing killing rests upon the permissible use of deadly force as a matter of self-defense *in* war. If persons are not causing, producing, or constituting in any way a threat to life it is hard to see how killing them on grounds of self-defense, no matter how that notion be relaxed or loosened, can itself be maintained or defended.

If the things that link noncombatants to the war and to armed combatants are matters that have to do with their causal relationship to the war, with ideas having to do with assumption of risk, perhaps, or just with a fair and reasonable redistribution of risk in the light of the dangers they helped to create or favored, then these are ties and connections which must in fact exist and must not merely be asserted. I do not know how loose the ties and connections can be in reasoning about these matters when the relationships are between individual action, acquiescence, or enthusiasm, on the one hand, and the behavior of groups and collective action and conduct, on the other. Nor do I know how and to what extent that relationship, if and when it holds, properly shifts or imposes liability to being deliberately killed on the individuals tied and connected in these more tenuous, but still real and intelligible ways. But it cannot be correct that just because they are *there,* in a country at war, they are sufficiently tied and hence permissibly killed. There must be some basis in fact for the assertion of a further connection before this way of reasoning becomes plausible.

To regard the intentional or knowing killing of noncombatants as justifiable as a kind of summary capital punishment requires, surely, a stronger, tighter connection. It is one that has to do, at the very least, with the moral culpability of the individuals executed in this way for their wrongdoing. Perhaps in war and in the absence of enforceable municipal laws and courts, our ideas about the conditions for permissible punishment can be appreciably loosened and relaxed here too. But there must be here, as well, some basis in fact for the assertion of an actual culpability before this way of reasoning can assert a legitimate claim to be considered.

If these very general and only partially explicated considerations and conclusions are correct, then there are, I believe, real and deep problems with all of the lines of argument offered in support of the permissibility of the deliberate killing of noncombatants, especially in indiscriminate fashion. For among the classes of noncombatants that we might identify as those possessing none of the characteristics that might affect or alter their moral status, children, of whom there are many in all countries, are fully noncombatants in all of the senses challenged, and clearly so. They are innocent in each and every one of the senses in which a lack of innocence might be relevant to the permissibility of acting to kill those who are not. They exist in large numbers, they are alive and most if not all of them are, just as fully as adults, persons whose lives are as valuable as those of any other persons. It is as wrong to kill them, intentionally or knowingly, as it is to kill other persons. More so, I am inclined to think, in part because they have most of their lives still before them, and in part because they are defenseless and even more unable to protect themselves from dangers, especially from the dangers of war when it occurs.

If they are reasonably young children, they literally cannot fight and in that way be a danger to others, nor do they engage in any of the other activities that might be thought to have the requisite causal connection with the more direct activities of making war. Their lives, their continued existences, even given the duration of wars such as World War II, are not (in any reasonably extended sense of "now") *now* a threat to the lives of any of those on the other side. To kill them intentionally or knowingly is not to kill them within the context of justifiable self-defense no matter how relaxed the standards may be thought to become, given the inner dictates and morality of war and the justifiability of such killing in war. Typically, too, they had no hand or choice whatsoever in being wherever they happened to be once war begins, or as it continues. And given the way social, institutional, and political life is organized in all countries, they played no role at all in bringing about the occurrence of war. A large and indeterminate number of them are fully noncombatants and wholly innocent in each and every one of the relevant senses. Children are the clearest kind of case, I think, but there are surely many other individuals in all countries to whom these descriptions and accounts apply. Perhaps, though, the problem is with the indeterminacy of the numbers and the identification of the individuals.

To be sure, given the features of urban life, or even those of contemporary societies more generally, those who possess the characteristics I have just described and which seem to me to have the moral significance I have indicated, are not individually identifiable or distinguishable so that one can tell at a distance exactly who or where they are. But when it can most surely be known that they are at a place, and there in numbers, as children are in the cities and towns of every country, then to kill them deliberately along with others who may more rightly be killed is to do something wrong, and seriously so. To intend to destroy a populated city, particularly if there is no warning and no shelter, is to intend to kill its inhabitants. If the answer is that that is what bombs do and what is involved, in, say, the adoption and pursuit of the tactic of the saturation bombing of cities, then this seems to me not to settle things at all but rather to call quite directly into question whether that is not the wrong, rather than the permissible way to fight a war. And if such a tactic is not impermissible under the existing laws and conventions of war, that may be one reason to think there is something morally unsatisfactory and wrong about such standards.

A nuclear "war" is the limiting case of all this, if it is a war at all in any proper or meaningful sense. It would, I believe, be clearly wrong to act so as to cause such an event in virtue of the absolutely indiscriminate, massive killing that everyone must know would occur. Were the nuclear missiles and bombs of the USSR and those of the US to be launched and detonated there would not be, nor could there be, a differentiation either intended or expected among the individuals who would be killed by the explosions, the fires, and the radiation. Nuclear "weapons" are surely among the very small number of weapons least capable of being used, no matter where aimed and how targeted, in a way by which any person or group might claim to distinguish between combatants, in any of the meaningful though extended senses, and noncombatants. As they are deployed and aimed at present, they embody neither the intention, desire, nor capability in any way to do so. I do not therefore see how their use in such circumstances could be anything but the deliberate wrongful killing, the murder, of vast numbers of wholly innocent persons on a scale and in a fashion that is barely comprehensible. I do not see how it could possibly be thought other than absolutely wrong to use them, and the choice to engage in nuclear "war" of the sort I have described seems to me to be the morally worst and most despicable act conceivable.

If what I have said so far is plausible or right, I do not think that the cause for which a war is fought, the justness of going to war, matters as much as is often supposed in the contexts that are now relevant. Let us grant that the clearest, most justifiable case in which it is right to go to war is that of national self-defense. Let us grant, too, that it is self-defense in the sense that if the country against which war is being made does not go to war in order to keep the aggressor from being successful, its citizens will be killed wrongly by the aggressor country, acting through its armed forces using weapons of mass destruction, or acting with and through some other means and other individuals in order to accomplish its murderous aims. Let us suppose further, although I think it somewhat more problematic, that wars of national self-defense are sometimes justifiably pursued for reasons other than to prevent the wrongful killing of the individuals in the country being aggressed against. And let us suppose, finally, that when it is self-defense (individual or national) which is at stake, deadly force may be used to prevent death (or permanent or very serious injury, or enslavement) from occurring without requiring that the aggressor be morally culpable in any of the usual senses.

There is still, I believe, the problem of what may justifiably be done under the legitimate claim of self-defense, either in the individual or the national case. In the individual case the circumstances and conditions under which lethal force may permissibly be used in self-defense (or in defense of others under attack) are, surely, appropriately more restrictive than those which apply in the case of national self-defense—and for the kinds of reasons suggested earlier: there is no background of international criminal law, of international police and of international courts (of the right analogous sort). And because countries act, aggressively or otherwise, through the complex, coordinated actions of many individuals, both the causal networks and the networks of culpability relating individual actions to the collective actions of countries are different, and looser, than those which must reasonably be thought to hold in the individual case before the use of lethal force in self-defense legitimately comes into play. Yet even in the case of national self-defense there must be *some causal or analogous connections* that are reasonably thought to hold, and some defensible theory about why these are the sufficient connections that do in fact hold, between the individuals against whom deadly force is used in self-defense and the danger which that use of deadly force seeks to prevent. If our ideas about national self-defense and the permissible use of deadly force on its behalf are to have any connection with our ideas about individual self-defense, the individuals against whom such force is used in the case of a war of self-defense must have some causal or closely analogous connection with the danger at hand before they are intentionally or knowingly killed by the weapons used in a war of self-defense. And if, as I think is surely the case for the reasons I gave before, there are many such individuals in any country, no matter what its character as an aggressor, who have no such connections, then the deliberate use of weapons of indiscriminate mass destruction against them is not and cannot be a part of an intelligible or defensible recourse to ideas of legitimate national self-defense.

Perhaps there is an account of permissible national self-defense which can be constructed, developed, and defended and which can make a place for the actual use of weapons of indiscriminate mass destruction in wars of self-defense; and if there is such an account, then it is of course possible that it would also be able to explain how it is permissible, rather than wrong, actually to *use* nuclear "weapons" indiscriminately to kill the inhabitants of an aggressor country as a matter of national self-defense. I, however, am unable to construct such an account, or even to anticipate at all clearly what the plausible lines of argument might be. I certainly do not understand in what sense it could be right—that it would be better and not wrong—for us all literally "to be dead, not red," or even better, that tens or hundreds or millions of the inhabitants of the USSR, the children as well as the adults, the farmers as well as the Commissars, should be killed so that those of us in the US and in other countries should not be "red" if that is in fact the only choice at hand.

The only other possible lines of argument I can think of are the three which follow, and while (c) might possess certain merits, neither of the other two seems to me to be at all plausible or ultimately defensible and creditable.

(a) In war, as well perhaps as in other contexts, the nation-state is essentially a unitary entity composed of, in part, but neither morally nor in other ways reducible to, the individuals who are its members or who reside within its borders. In war it is this entity which makes war and fights it, and it is this entity against which another nation-state, at war with it, uses deadly force in order to defend itself. As long as such force is used against the aggressor country (and, perhaps, as long as only reasonable deadly force is used), there is no further issue. Countries, so conceived, are the only relevant entities which act, and no reductions to the more micro-level of individual actions, interests, claims, or places in the causal and analogous chains have central meaning or moral significance.

(b) Because children are tied and connected to their parents in various and obvious ways, they are necessarily tied and connected, regrettably perhaps, in other ways as well. If the parents chose to go to war, or if they are involved in waging it, then it is their fault and their problem if their children get killed in war. The parents are more the cause of their children's deaths than are their opponents, especially if the war is not a war of self-defense. Moreover, putting issues of causality and assumptions of risk to one side, the connections between parents and children are simply such that children's good and bad prospects and chances cannot be separated from those of their parents. Simply because the children are *theirs,* the children are linked to the parents in ways that make it closer to and more like injuring or killing the parents to kill their children than to kill others who are not so connected. Somehow this matters morally because in killing the children the injury is being inflicted upon a part, an extension or a possession of the adult parents whom, in self-defense, it would be right or permissible to kill.

(c) In cases of very great, extraordinary emergency or peril, on either the individual or the international level, it is sometimes permissible to do wrong or to treat persons unjustly in order to prevent a still greater wrong or injustice. If the differential magnitudes of loss of life, say, are great enough, that may itself make the moral difference, while still giving sense to the idea that something seriously wrong and regrettable was done. It is hard, and morally not very plausible, whatever one's worries about utilitarianism, not to allow consequences at least to matter mightily in this way in circumstances such as these—especially when the calculations are concerned with magnitudes all having to do with innocent lives and their preservation. And all of this is to say nothing about how, even if such is not justifiable, it may come very close to being so because it is so easily and so understandably excusable. If the stakes are really high enough and the options really bleak enough, we can understand why otherwise innocent persons do act so as to save themselves rather than suffer death, even if other innocent persons must be killed to do so.

I think that there is something plausible here, and that the plausibility increases as the differential magnitudes become greater, the danger more imminent and the choice genuinely this bleak and limited. I do not see, however, how the unleashing of massive nuclear devastation of the sort described could possibly satisfy these conditions.

QUESTIONS

1 Has Wasserstrom successfully brought out the crucial distinction between combatants and noncombatants? Explain the distinction as you understand it.

2 Do you agree with Wasserstrom that any use of nuclear weapons that deliberately and indiscriminately kills and maims millions of children cannot be morally justified?

Nuclear Weapons and Nuclear Deterrence

The National Conference of Catholic Bishops

In 1980, following a general meeting of the National Conference of Catholic Bishops, a committee of Bishops was appointed to draft a pastoral letter on war and peace. In 1983, during a plenary assembly, the body of Bishops approved the letter from which this selection is excerpted.

The Bishops condemn any use of weapons—either nuclear or conventional—that would result in the indiscriminate taking of many innocent lives. In regard to nuclear weapons, they reject as morally impermissible (1) any "first use" policy and (2) any nuclear response to either conventional or nuclear attacks that causes destruction going far beyond "legitimate defense." Expressing scepticism about the possibility of limited nuclear war, the Bishops maintain that our first imperative is to prevent *any* use of nuclear arms. In regard to nuclear deterrence policies, the Bishops express a "strictly conditioned moral acceptance" of some deterrence policies, but emphasize that nuclear deterrence is inadequate as a long-term basis for peace. They then evaluate current nuclear deterrence policies and make specific recommendations for arms control.

THE USE OF NUCLEAR WEAPONS

Establishing moral guidelines in the nuclear debate means addressing first the question of the use of nuclear weapons. That question has several dimensions.

It is clear that those in the Church who interpret the gospel teaching as forbidding all use of violence would oppose any use of nuclear weapons under any conditions. In a sense the existence of these weapons simply confirms and reinforces one of the initial insights of the non-violent position, namely, that Christians should not use lethal force since the hope of using it selectively and restrictively is so often an illusion. Nuclear weapons seem to prove this point in a way heretofore unknown.

For the tradition which acknowledges some legitimate use of force, some important elements of contemporary nuclear strategies move beyond the limits of moral justification. A justifiable use of force must be both discriminatory and proportionate. Certain aspects of both U.S. and Soviet strategies fail both tests as we shall discuss below. The technical literature and the personal testimony of public officials who have been closely associated with U.S. nuclear strategy have both convinced us of the overwhelming probability that major nuclear exchange would have no limits.

On the more complicated issue of "limited" nuclear war, we are aware of the extensive literature and discussion which this topic has generated. As a general statement, it seems to us that public officials would be unable to refute the following conclusion of the study made by the Pontifical Academy of Sciences:

> Even a nuclear attack directed only at military facilities would be devastating to the country as a whole. This is because military facilities are widespread rather than concentrated at only a few points. Thus, many nuclear weapons would be exploded.
>
> Furthermore, the spread of radiation due to the natural winds and atmospheric mixing would kill vast numbers of people and contaminate large areas. The medical facilities of any nation would be inadequate to care for the survivors. An objective examination of the medical situation that would follow a nuclear war leads to but one conclusion: prevention is our only recourse.[1]

MORAL PRINCIPLES AND POLICY CHOICES

In light of these perspectives we address three questions more explicitly: (1) counter population warfare; (2) initiation of nuclear war; and (3) limited nuclear war.

1 Counter Population Warfare

Under no circumstances may nuclear weapons or other instruments of mass slaughter be used for the purpose of destroying population centers or other predominantly civilian targets. Popes have repeatedly condemned "total war" which implies such use. For example, as early as 1954 Pope Pius XII condemned nuclear warfare "when it entirely escapes the control of man," and results in "the pure and simple annihilation of all

[1]Pontifical Academy of Sciences, "Statement on the Consequences of the Use of Nuclear Weapons," in *Peace and Disarmament: Documents of the World Council of Churches and the Roman Catholic Church* (Geneva and Rome: 1982), p. 243.

human life within the radius of action."[2] The condemnation was repeated by the Second Vatican Council:

> Any act of war aimed indiscriminately at the destruction of entire cities or of extensive areas along with their population is a crime against God and man itself. It merits unequivocal and unhesitating condemnation.[3]

Retaliatory action whether nuclear or conventional which would indiscriminately take many wholly innocent lives, lives of people who are in no way responsible for reckless actions of their government, must also be condemned. This condemnation, in our judgment, applies even to the retaliatory use of weapons striking enemy cities after our own have already been struck. No Christian can rightfully carry out orders or policies deliberately aimed at killing non-combatants.[4]

We make this judgment at the beginning of our treatment of nuclear strategy precisely because the defense of the principle of noncombatant immunity is so important for an ethic of war and because the nuclear age has posed such extreme problems for the principle. Later in this letter we shall discuss specific aspects of U.S. policy in light of this principle and in light of recent U.S. policy statements stressing the determination not to target directly or strike directly against civilian populations. Our concern about protecting the moral value of noncombatant immunity, however, requires that we make a clear reassertion of the principle our first word on this matter.

2 The Initiation of Nuclear War

We do not perceive any situation in which the deliberate initiation of nuclear warfare, on however restricted a scale, can be morally justified. Non-nuclear attacks by another state must be resisted by other than nuclear means. Therefore, a serious moral obligation exists to develop non-nuclear defensive strategies as rapidly as possible. . . .

At the same time we recognize the responsibility the United States has had and continues to have in assisting allied nations in their defense against either a conventional or a nuclear attack. Especially in the European theater, the deterrence of a *nuclear* attack may require nuclear weapons for a time, even though their possession and deployment must be subject to rigid restrictions.

The need to defend against a conventional attack in Europe imposes the political and moral burden of developing adequate, alternative modes of defense to present reliance on nuclear weapons. Even with the best coordinated effort—hardly likely in view of contemporary political division on this question—development of an alternative defense position will still take time.

In the interim, deterrence against a conventional attack relies upon two factors: the not inconsiderable conventional forces at the disposal of NATO and the recognition by a potential attacker that the outbreak of large scale conventional war could escalate to the nuclear level through accident or miscalculation by either side. We are aware

---

[2]Pius XII, "Address to the VIII Congress of the World Medical Association," ibid., p. 131.
[3]Vatican II, the *Pastoral Constitution on the Church in the Modern World* (hereafter cited: *Pastoral Constitution*), #80. Papal and conciliar texts will be referred to by title with paragraph number.
[4]Ibid.

that NATO's refusal to adopt a "no first use" pledge is to some extent linked to the deterrent effect of this inherent ambiguity. Nonetheless, in light of the probable effects of initiating nuclear war, we urge NATO to move rapidly toward the adoption of a "no first use" policy, but doing so in tandem with development of an adequate alternative defense posture.

3 Limited Nuclear War

It would be possible to agree with our first two conclusions and still not be sure about retaliatory use of nuclear weapons in what is called a "limited exchange." The issue at stake is the *real* as opposed to the *theoretical* possibility of a "limited nuclear exchange."

We recognize that the policy debate on this question is inconclusive and that all participants are left with hypothetical projections about probable reactions in a nuclear exchange. While not trying to adjudicate the technical debate, we are aware of it and wish to raise a series of questions which challenge the actual meaning of "limited" in this discussion.

• Would leaders have sufficient information to know what is happening in a nuclear exchange?

• Would they be able under the conditions of stress, time pressures, and fragmentary information to make the extraordinarily precise decision needed to keep the exchange limited if this were technically possible?

• Would military commanders be able, in the midst of the destruction and confusion of a nuclear exchange, to maintain a policy of "discriminate targeting"? Can this be done in modern warfare, waged across great distances by aircraft and missiles?

• Given the accidents we know about in peacetime conditions, what assurances are there that computer errors could be avoided in the midst of a nuclear exchange?

• Would not the casualties, even in a war defined as limited by strategists, still run in the millions?

• How "limited" would be the long-term effects of radiation, famine, social fragmentation, and economic dislocation?

Unless these questions can be answered satisfactorily, we will continue to be highly skeptical about the real meaning of "limited." One of the criteria of the just-war tradition is a reasonable hope of success in bringing about justice and peace. We must ask whether such a reasonable hope can exist once nuclear weapons have been exchanged. The burden of proof remains on those who assert that meaningful limitation is possible.

A nuclear response to either conventional or nuclear attack can cause destruction which goes far beyond "legitimate defense." Such use of nuclear weapons would not be justified.

In the face of this frightening and highly speculative debate on a matter involving millions of human lives, we believe the most effective contribution or moral judgment is to introduce perspectives by which we can assess the empirical debate. Moral perspective should be sensitive not only to the quantitative dimensions of a question but to its psychological, human, and religious characteristics as well. The issue of limited war is not simply the size of weapons contemplated or the strategies projected. The debate should include the psychological and political significance of crossing the boundary from the conventional to the nuclear arena in any form. To cross this divide is to enter a world where we have no experience of control, much testimony against its possibility, and therefore no moral justification for submitting the human community to this risk. We therefore express our view that the first imperative is to prevent any use of nuclear weapons and our hope that leaders will resist the notion that nuclear conflict can be limited, contained, or won in any traditional sense.

DETERRENCE IN PRINCIPLE AND PRACTICE

The moral challenge posed by nuclear weapons is not exhausted by an analysis of their possible uses. Much of the political and moral debate of the nuclear age has concerned the strategy of deterrence. Deterrence is at the heart of the U.S.–Soviet relationship, currently the most dangerous dimension of the nuclear arms race. . . .

1   The Moral Assessment of Deterrence

The distinctively new dimensions of nuclear deterrence were recognized by policy-makers and strategists only after much reflection. Similarly, the moral challenge posed by nuclear deterrence was grasped only after careful deliberation. The moral and political paradox posed by deterrence was concisely stated by Vatican II:

> Undoubtedly, armaments are not amassed merely for use in wartime. Since the defensive strength of any nation is thought to depend on its capacity for immediate retaliation, the stockpiling of arms which grows from year to year serves, in a way hitherto unthought of, as a deterrent to potential attackers. Many people look upon this as the most effective way known at the present time for maintaining some sort of peace among nations. Whatever one may think of this form of deterrent, people are convinced that the arms race, which quite a few countries have entered, is no infallible way of maintaining real peace and that the resulting so-called balance of power is no sure genuine path to achieving it. Rather than eliminate the causes of war, the arms race serves only to aggravate the position. As long as extravagant sums of money are poured into the development of new weapons, it is impossible to devote adequate aid in tackling the misery which prevails at the present day in the world. Instead of eradicating international conflict once and for all, the contagion is spreading to other parts of the world. New approaches, based on reformed attitudes, will have to be chosen in order to remove this stumbling block, to free the earth from its pressing anxieties, and give back to the world a genuine peace.[5]

Without making a specific moral judgment on deterrence, the council clearly designated the elements of the arms race: the tension between "peace of a sort" preserved by deterrence and "genuine peace" required for a stable international life; the contradiction between what is spent for destructive capacity and what is needed for constructive development.

In the post-conciliar assessment of war and peace, and specifically of deterrence,

---

[5]*Pastoral Constitution,* #81.

different parties to the political-moral debate within the Church and in civil society have focused on one aspect or another of the problem. For some, the fact that nuclear weapons have not been used since 1945 means that deterrence has worked, and this fact satisfies the demands of both the political and the moral order. Others contest this assessment by highlighting the risk of failure involved in continued reliance on deterrence and pointing out how politically and morally catastrophic even a single failure would be. Still others note that the absence of nuclear war is not necessarily proof that the policy of deterrence has prevented it. Indeed, some would find in the policy of deterrence the driving force in the superpower arms race. Still other observers, many of them Catholic moralists, have stressed that deterrence may not morally include the intention of deliberately attacking civilian populations or non-combatants. . . .

In June 1982, Pope John Paul II provided new impetus and insight to the moral analysis with his statement to the United Nations Second Special Session on Disarmament. The pope first situated the problem of deterrence within the context of world politics. No power, he observes, will admit to wishing to start a war, but each distrusts others and considers it necessary to mount a strong defense against attack. He then discusses the notion of deterrence:

> Many even think that such preparations constitute the way—even the only way—to safeguard peace in some fashion or at least to impede to the utmost in an efficacious way the outbreak of wars, especially major conflicts which might lead to the ultimate holocaust of humanity and the destruction of the civilization that man has constructed so laboriously over the centuries.
>
> In this approach one can see the "philosophy of peace" which was proclaimed in the ancient Roman principle: *Si vis pacem, para bellum*. Put in modern terms, this "philosophy" has the label of "deterrence" and one can find it in various guises of the search for a "balance of forces" which sometimes has been called, and not without reason, the "balance of terror."[6]

Having offered this analysis of the general concept of deterrence, the Holy Father introduces his considerations on disarmament, especially, but not only, nuclear disarmament. Pope John Paul II makes this statement about the morality of deterrence:

> In current conditions "deterrence" based on balance, certainly not as an end in itself but as a step on the way toward a progressive disarmament, may still be judged morally acceptable. Nonetheless in order to ensure peace, it is indispensable not to be satisfied with this minimum which is always susceptible to the real danger of explosion.[7]

In Pope John Paul II's assessment we perceive two dimensions of the contemporary dilemma of deterrence. One dimension is the danger of nuclear war, with its human and moral costs. The possession of nuclear weapons, the continuing quantitative growth of the arms race, and the danger of nuclear proliferation all point to the grave danger of basing "peace of a sort" on deterrence. The other dimension is the independence and freedom of nations and entire peoples, including the need to protect smaller nations from threats to their independence and integrity. Deterrence reflects the radical distrust

---

[6]John Paul II, "Message to the Second Special Session of the United Nations General Assembly Devoted to Disarmament" (June 1982) (hereafter cited: "Message U.N. Special Session 1982"), #3.

[7]Ibid., #8.

which marks international politics, a condition identified as a major problem by Pope John XIII in *Peace on Earth* and reaffirmed by Pope Paul VI and Pope John Paul II. Thus a balance of forces, preventing either side from achieving superiority, can be seen as a means of safeguarding both dimensions.

The moral duty today is to prevent nuclear war from ever occurring *and* to protect and preserve those key values of justice, freedom and independence which are necessary for personal dignity and national integrity. In reference to these issues, Pope John Paul II judges that deterrence may still be judged morally acceptable, "certainly not as an end in itself but as a step on the way toward a progressive disarmament." . . .

In preparing this letter we have tried, through a number of sources, to determine as precisely as possible the factual character of U.S. deterrence strategy. Two questions have particularly concerned us: 1) the targeting doctrine and strategic plans for the use of the deterrent, particularly their impact on civilian casualties; and 2) the relationship of deterrence strategy and nuclear war-fighting capability to the likelihood that war will in fact be prevented.

MORAL PRINCIPLES AND POLICY CHOICES

Targeting doctrine raises significant moral questions because it is a significant determinant of what would occur if nuclear weapons were ever to be used. Although we acknowledge the need for deterrent, not all forms of deterrence are morally acceptable. There are moral limits to deterrence policy as well as to policy regarding use. Specifically, it is not morally acceptable to intend to kill the innocent as part of a strategy of deterring nuclear war. The question of whether U.S. policy involves an intention to strike civilian centers (directly targeting civilian populations) has been one of our factual concerns.

This complex question has always produced a variety of responses, official and unofficial in character. The NCCB Committee has received a series of statements of clarification of policy from U.S. government officials. Essentially these statements declare that it is not U.S. strategic policy to target the Soviet civilian population as such or to use nuclear weapons deliberately for the purpose of destroying population centers. These statements respond, in principle at least, to one moral criterion for assessing deterrence policy: the immunity of non-combatants from direct attack either by conventional or nuclear weapons.

These statements do not address or resolve another very troublesome moral problem, namely, that an attack on military targets or militarily significant industrial targets could involve "indirect" (i.e., unintended) but massive civilian casualties. We are advised, for example, that the United States strategic nuclear targeting plan (SIOP—Single Integrated Operational Plan) has identified 60 "military" targets within the city of Moscow alone, and that 40,000 "military" targets for nuclear weapons have been identified in the whole of the Soviet Union. It is important to recognize that Soviet policy is subject to the same moral judgment; attacks on several "industrial targets" or politically significant targets in the United States could produce massive civilian casualties. The number of civilians who would necessarily be killed by such strikes is horrendous. This problem is unavoidable because of the way modern military facilities and production centers are so thoroughly interspersed with civilian living and working areas. It is aggravated if one side deliberately positions military targets in the midst of a civilian population. In our consultations, administration officials readily admitted that, while they hoped any nuclear exchange could be kept limited, they were prepared to retaliate in a massive way if necessary. They also agreed that once any substantial numbers of weapons were used, the civilian casualty levels would quickly become truly catastrophic, and that even with attacks limited to "military" targets, the number of deaths in a substantial exchange would be almost indistinguishable from what might occur if civilian centers had been deliberately and directly struck. These possibilities pose a different moral question and are to be judged by a different moral criterion: the principle of proportionality.

While any judgment of proportionality is always open to differing evaluations, there are actions which can be decisively judged to be disproportionate. A narrow adherence exclusively to the principle of noncombatant immunity as a criterion for policy is an inadequate moral posture for it ignores some evil and unacceptable consequences. Hence, we cannot be satisfied that the assertion of an intention not to strike civilians directly, or even the most honest effort to implement that intention, by itself constitutes a "moral policy" for the use of nuclear weapons.

The location of industrial or militarily significant economic targets within heavily populated areas or in those areas affected by radioactive fallout could well involve such massive civilian casualties that, in our judgment, such a strike would be deemed morally disproportionate, even though not intentionally indiscriminate.

The problem is not simply one of producing highly accurate weapons that might minimize civilian casualties in any single explosion, but one of increasing the likelihood of escalation at a level where many, even "discriminating," weapons would cumulatively kill very large numbers of civilians. Those civilian deaths would occur both immediately and from the long-term effects of social and economic devastation.

A second issue of concern to us is the relationship of deterrence doctrine to warfighting strategies. We are aware of the argument that war-fighting capabilities enhance the credibility of the deterrent, particularly the strategy of extended deterrence. But the development of such capabilities raises other strategic and moral questions. The relationship of war-fighting capabilities and targeting doctrine exemplifies the difficult choices in this area of policy. Targeting civilian populations would violate the principle of discrimination—one of the central moral principles of a Christian ethic of war. But "counterforce targeting," while preferable from the perspective of protecting civilians, is often joined with a declaratory policy which conveys the notion that nuclear war is subject to precise rational and moral limits. We have already expressed our severe doubts about such a concept. Furthermore, a purely counterforce strategy may seem to threaten the viability of other nations' retaliatory forces, making deterrence unstable in a crisis and war more likely.

While we welcome any effort to protect civilian populations, we do not want to legitimize or encourage moves which extend deterrence beyond the specific objective of preventing the use of nuclear weapons or other actions which could lead directly to a nuclear exchange.

These considerations of concrete elements of nuclear deterrence policy, made in

light of John Paul II's evaluation, but applying it through our own prudential judgments, lead us to a strictly conditioned moral acceptance of nuclear deterrence. We
cannot consider it adequate as a long-term basis for peace.

This strictly conditioned judgment yields *criteria* for morally assessing the elements of deterrence strategy. Clearly, these criteria demonstrate that we cannot approve
of every weapons system, strategic doctrine, or policy initiative advanced in the name
of strengthening deterrence. On the contrary, these criteria require continual public
scrutiny of what our government proposes to do with the deterrent.

On the basis of these criteria we wish now to make some specific evaluations:

1 If nuclear deterrence exists only to prevent the *use* of nuclear weapons by others,
then proposals to go beyond this to planning for prolonged periods of repeated nuclear
strikes and counterstrikes, or "prevailing" in nuclear war, are not acceptable. They
encourage notions that nuclear war can be engaged in with tolerable human and moral
consequences. Rather, we must continually say "no" to the idea of nuclear war.

2 If nuclear deterrence is our goal, "sufficiency" to deter is an adequate strategy;
the quest for nuclear superiority must be rejected.

3 Nuclear deterrence should be used as a step on the way toward progressive
disarmament. Each proposed addition to our strategic system or change in strategic
doctrine must be assessed precisely in light of whether it will render steps toward
"progressive disarmament" more or less likely.

Moreover, these criteria provide us with the means to make some judgments and
recommendations about the present direction of U.S. strategic policy. Progress toward
a world freed of dependence on nuclear deterrence must be carefully carried out. But
it must not be delayed. There is an urgent moral and political responsibility to use the
"peace of a sort" we have as a framework to move toward authentic peace through
nuclear arms control, reductions, and disarmament. Of primary importance in this
process is the need to prevent the development and deployment of destabilizing weapons systems on either side; a second requirement is to insure that the more sophisticated
command and control systems do not become mere hair triggers for automatic launch
on warning; a third is the need to prevent the proliferation of nuclear weapons in the
international system.

In light of these general judgments *we oppose* some specific proposals in respect
to our present deterrence posture:

1 The addition of weapons which are likely to be vulnerable to attack, yet also
possess a "prompt hard-target kill" capability that threatens to make the other side's
retaliatory forces vulnerable. Such weapons may seem to be useful primarily in a first
strike; we resist such weapons for this reason and we oppose Soviet deployment of
such weapons which generate fear of a first strike against U.S. forces.

2 The willingness to foster strategic planning which seeks a nuclear war-fighting
capability that goes beyond the limited function of deterrence outlined in this letter.

3 Proposals which have the effect of lowering the nuclear threshold and blurring
the difference between nuclear and conventional weapons.

In support of the concept of "sufficiency" as an adequate deterrent, and in light of the present size and composition of both the U.S. and Soviet strategic arsenals, *we recommend:*

1 Support for immediate, bilateral, verifiable agreements to halt the testing, production, and deployment of new nuclear weapons systems.

2 Support for negotiated bilateral deep cuts in the arsenals of both superpowers, particularly those weapons systems which have destabilizing characteristics; U.S. proposals like those for START (Strategic Arms Reduction Talks) and INF (Intermediate-range Nuclear Forces) negotiations in Geneva are said to be designed to achieve deep cuts; our hope is that they will be pursued in a manner which will realize these goals.

3 Support for early and successful conclusion of negotiations of a comprehensive test ban treaty.

4 Removal by all parties of short-range nuclear weapons which multiply dangers disproportionate to their deterrent value.

5 Removal by all parties of nuclear weapons from areas where they are likely to be overrun in the early stages of war, thus forcing rapid and uncontrollable decisions on their use.

6 Strengthening of command and control over nuclear weapons to prevent inadvertent and unauthorized use.

These judgments are meant to exemplify how a lack of unequivocal condemnation of deterrence is meant only to be an attempt to acknowledge the role attributed to deterrence, but not to support its extension beyond the limited purpose discussed above. Some have urged us to condemn all aspects of nuclear deterrence. This urging has been based on a variety of reasons, but has emphasized particularly the high and terrible risks that either deliberate use or accidental detonation of nuclear weapons could quickly escalate to something utterly disproportionate to any acceptable moral purpose. That determination requires highly technical judgments about hypothetical events. Although reasons exist which move some to condemn reliance on nuclear weapons for deterrence, we have not reached this conclusion for the reasons outlined in this letter.

Nevertheless, there must be no misunderstanding of our profound skepticism about the moral acceptability of any use of nuclear weapons. It is obvious that the use of any weapons which violate the principle of discrimination merits unequivocal condemnation. We are told that some weapons are designed for purely "counterforce" use against military forces and targets. The moral issue, however, is not resolved by the design of weapons or the planned intention for use; there are also consequences which must be assessed. It would be a perverted political policy or moral casuistry which tried to justify using a weapon which "indirectly" or "unintentionally" killed a million innocent people because they happened to live near a "militarily significant target."

Even the "indirect effects" of initiating nuclear war are sufficient to make it an unjustifiable moral risk in any form. It is not sufficient, for example, to contend that "our" side has plans for "limited" or "discriminate" use. Modern warfare is not readily contained by good intentions or technological designs. The psychological climate of the world is such that mention of the term "nuclear" generates uneasiness. Many contend that the use of one tactical nuclear weapon could produce panic, with completely unpredictable consequences. It is precisely this mix of political, psychological, and technological uncertainty which has moved us in this letter to reinforce with moral prohibitions and prescriptions the prevailing political barrier against resort to nuclear weapons. Our support for enhanced command and control facilities, for major reductions in strategic and tactical nuclear forces, and for a "no first use" policy (as set forth in this letter) is meant to be seen as a complement to our desire to draw a moral line against nuclear war.

Any claim by any government that it is pursuing a morally acceptable policy of deterrence must be scrutinized with the greatest care. We are prepared and eager to participate in our country in the ongoing public debate on moral grounds.

The need to rethink the deterrence policy of our nation, to make the revisions necessary to reduce the possibility of nuclear war, and to move toward a more stable system of national and international security will demand a substantial intellectual, political, and moral effort. It also will require, we believe, the willingness to open ourselves to the providential care, power and word of God, which call us to recognize our common humanity and the bonds of mutual responsibility which exist in the international community in spite of political differences and nuclear arsenals. . . .

QUESTIONS

1 On what moral principles does the Bishops' reasoning rely? Do you believe that these are morally binding principles? If yes, why? If not, why not?

2 Is a nuclear deterrence policy that includes targeting civilian centers morally acceptable? What reasons can you offer to support your answer?

3 Is it ever morally acceptable to intend to kill the innocent?

Missiles and Morals: A Utilitarian Look at Nuclear Deterrence

Douglas P. Lackey

Douglas P. Lackey is professor of philosophy at Baruch College of the City University of New York where he teaches courses in philosophy and business policy. He has written several articles on nuclear deterrence including "The Moral Case for Unilateral Nuclear Disarmament" and "Ethics and Nuclear Deterrence." Lackey is also the author of Moral Principles and Nuclear Weapons *(1984).*

Lackey identifies three strategies at the center of debates about nuclear armaments: the Superiority Strategy, the Equivalence Strategy, and the Nuclear Disarmament Strategy. He assesses the possible consequences of adopting each of these strategies and argues that unilateral nuclear disarmament by the United States is preferable both morally and prudentially. Lackey concludes by arguing that, for utilitarians,

Douglas P. Lackey, "Missiles and Morals: A Utilitarian Look at Nuclear Deterrence," *Philosophy & Public Affairs* 11, no. 3 (Summer 1982). Copyright © 1982 by Princeton University Press. Excerpts reprinted with permission of Princeton University Press.

not only is unilateral nuclear deterrence the morally right strategy but that advocating its adoption is also morally correct.

Though there are many strategies for nuclear armament, these three have been at the center of the strategic debate at least since the late 1950s:

S: Maintain second strike capacity; seek first strike capacity; threaten first and second strikes ("Superiority").

E: Maintain second strike capacity; do not seek first strike capacity; threaten second strikes only ("Equivalence").

ND: Do not seek to maintain second strike capacity ("Nuclear Disarmament").

In the statement of these strategies the terminology is standard: Nation A is presumed to have *first-strike capacity* against B if A can launch a nuclear attack on B without fear of suffering unacceptable damage from B's subsequent counterstrike; nation A is said to have *second-strike capacity* against B if A is capable of inflicting unacceptable damage on B after having suffered a nuclear first strike by B.

Strategy S has been the favored strategy of hard-line anticommunists ever since the early 1950s. In its original form, as we find it in John Foster Dulles, the Superiority Strategy called for threats of American first strikes against Russian cities in retaliation for what American policy defined as Soviet acts of aggression. In its present form, as it is developed by Paul Nitze, Colin Gray, and others, the Superiority Strategy calls for threats, or implied threats, of American first strikes against Soviet military forces, combined with large-scale increases in American strategic arms.[1]

The Superiority Strategy, however, is not the exclusive property of doctrinaire anticommunists or hard-line "forward" strategists. Since aiming one's missiles at enemy missiles implies a desire to destroy those missiles before they are launched, that is, a desire to launch a first strike, all retargeting of American missiles from Soviet cities to Soviet missiles, up to and including President Carter's Directive 59 in the summer of 1980, imply partial endorsement of Strategy S. Such "counterforce" as opposed to "countervalue" targetings are entailed by Strategy S even if they do not in fact bring first strike capacity; Strategy S as defined implies that the United States will *seek* first strike capacity, not that it will in fact obtain it. Strategy S advocates steps which will produce first strike capacity unless new countermeasures are developed by the Soviet Union to cancel them out.

Strategy E, the "equivalence" strategy, enshrines Robert McNamara's doctrine of Assured Destruction, and includes both massive retaliations against massive strikes and flexible responses against lesser strikes.[2] The possibility and permanence of Strategy E seemed assured by SALT I in 1972, since negotiated restrictions on the deployment of antiballistic missiles seemed to guarantee permanent second-strike capac-

---

[1] On "massive retaliation" see John Foster Dulles, Dept. of State Bulletin 30, 791, 25 Jan. 1954. For Superiority policy in the 1960s see, for example, Barry Goldwater, *Why Not Victory?* (New York: McGraw-Hill, 1962), p. 162. . . .

For a recent interpretation of Superiority see Colin Gray and Keith Payne, "Victory Is Possible," *Foreign Policy* 39 (Summer 1980): 14–27, and Colin Gray, "Nuclear Strategy: The Case for a Theory of Victory," *International Security* 4 (Summer 1979): 54–87.

[2] Robert McNamara, *The Essence of Security* (London: Hodder and Stoughton, 1968).

ity to both sides. Unfortunately, SALT I did not limit the development and deployment of MIRVs (multiple independently targeted reentry vehicles), and the deployment of MIRVs through the 1970s has led to cries on both sides that mutual second-strike capacity is dissolving and mutual first-strike capacity is emerging.

Notice that although Strategy E permits bilateral arms control, it actually prohibits substantial reductions in nuclear arms. The delicate balance of mutual second-strike capacity becomes increasingly unstable as arms levels are lowered, and sooner or later, mutual disarmament brings a loss of second-strike capacity on one side and the emergence of first-strike capacity on the other, contrary to E.

Strategy ND calls for a unilateral halt in the development of American nuclear weapons and delivery systems, even if such a halt eventuates in Soviet first strike capacity. Strategy ND is a policy of *nuclear* disarmament; it does *not* call for the abandonment of conventional weapons and should not be equated with pacifism or confused with general and complete disarmament. In fact, increases in conventional weapons levels are compatible with Strategy ND. . . .

EXPECTED VALUE

Perhaps the most natural of all responses to the problem of uncertainty is to discount the weight of consequences by whatever chance there is that they will not occur. To compute the "expected value" of a policy, then, we should consider each possible outcome of the policy, multiply the utility of that outcome by the probability that it will occur, and take the sum of all these products. In the area of nuclear strategy we cannot supply precise numbers for the probabilities of the outcomes, nor can we attempt to supply precise figures for the corresponding utilities. Nevertheless, we *do* have much more information about these subjects than [an ordering] of probabilities . . . and what imprecision there is in our information can be respected by stating the information in the form of approximations. For example, we can classify the probability of outcomes as "negligible," "small but substantial," "fifty-fifty," "very likely," and "almost certain," and we can classify outcomes as "extremely bad," "bad," "neutral," and so forth. In considering the products of utilities and outcomes, we can neglect all outcomes of negligible probability, and all outcomes of small but substantial probability *except* those classified as extremely good or extremely bad. In many cases, use of such estimates will yield surprisingly definite results.

Now, what are the "outcomes" the probabilities of which we ought to consider? Given the traditionally assumed goals of deterrence, we should certainly consider the effects of each policy on the probability of nuclear war, the probability of Soviet nonnuclear aggression, and the probability of Soviet nuclear blackmail. . . . In considering the probability of nuclear war, it is essential to distinguish the probability of a one-sided nuclear strike from the probability of all-out nuclear war. Among other outcomes, we will consider only the effects of nuclear strategies on military spending, since the impact of policies on spending can be determined with little controversy. Since we have four outcomes and three policies to consider, the probabilities can be represented on a three-by-four grid (see table 1). Each probability assessment will be defended in turn.

TABLE I

	One-sided strike*	All-out nuclear war	Soviet aggression	Very high military spending
Superiority	Fifty-fifty [a]	Fifty-fifty [b]	Small [c]	Certain [d]
Equivalence	Small [e]	Small [f]	Small [g]	Fifty-fifty [h]
Nuclear Disarmament	Small [i]	Zero [j]	Small [k]	Small [l]

*A "one-sided strike" is a first strike that may or may not be answered by a second strike. A comparison of the probability of one-sided strikes and two-sided strikes in a given row indicates that a first strike will lead to an all-out nuclear war.

Value of the Superiority Strategy

[a] Strategists disagree about the probability of Soviet or American first strike under the Superiority Strategy. All students of the subject rate it as having at least a small but substantial probability. I believe that it is more reasonable to rate the probability as fifty-fifty within a time frame of about fifty years, since (1) every real or presumed step towards first strike capacity by either side raises the chance of a preemptive first strike by the side falling behind; (2) the concentration on technological development prompted by the Superiority Strategy raises that chance of a technological break-through that might destabilize the balance of power; (3) the increasing technological complexity of weapons required by the Superiority Strategy raises the chance of a first strike as a result of accident or mistake; (4) the constant changes of weaponry required by the Superiority Strategy creates pressure for proliferation, either because obsolete weapons are constantly disposed of on the international arms market or because wealthy developing countries, dazzled by new weapons, make buys to keep up with appearances.

[b] Under Superiority, the chance of an American second strike—given a Soviet first strike—is practically the same as the chance of a Soviet first strike. Though it is always possible that the President or his survivor will not respond to a Soviet first strike, the military and technological systems installed under the Superiority Strategy are geared for belligerence. Accordingly the chance of an American failure to respond is negligible.

[c] Even in the face of the Superiority Strategy, the chance of Soviet nonnuclear aggression (an invasion of West Germany or Iran, for example) must be rated as small but not negligible. The prospect of an American first strike in response to a Soviet conventional attack may not be taken seriously by the Soviets, especially if Soviet military personnel think that they can deter any American first strike with the prospect of a massive Soviet second strike.

[d] The sums of money required to sustain the Superiority Strategy are staggering. The Reagan administration's rejection of SALT and its apparent acceptance of the Superiority Strategy will produce an increase in the fraction of the American gross national product devoted to defense from five to six and one-half percent: an increase of over $150 billion per year over the Carter projections, which were largely keyed to the Equivalence Strategy.

Value of the Equivalence Strategy

[e] Most students of strategy agree that the chance of an American or Soviet first strike under the Equivalence Strategy is small but substantial. The peculiar pressures for a first strike listed under the Superiority Strategy are absent, but there is still the chance of a first strike through accident, mistake, human folly, or a suicidal leadership.

[f] Since the chance of a first strike is less under Equivalence than under Superiority, there is less chance of an all-out nuclear war under Equivalence than under Superiority. The chance of a first strike under Equivalence is small, and the chance of all-out war following a first strike is smaller still. Since the primary aim of the Equivalence Strategy is not to "defeat" the Soviet Union or to develop a first-strike capacity, but to deter a Soviet first strike, it may be obvious to the President or his survivor that once a Soviet first strike is actually launched, there is no point whatsoever in proceeding with an American second strike. If the chance that the President will fail to respond is substantial, the chance of an all-out war under Equivalence is considerably less than the chance of a first strike under Equivalence. On the other hand, the credibility of the American deterrent to a first strike depends on the perception by Soviet planners that an American second strike is inevitable once a Soviet first strike is launched, and the President and his defense strategists may decide that the only convincing way to create this perception is to make the American second strike a *semi-automatic* response. Thus it might be difficult to stop an American second strike even if the President wished to forgo it. On balance, it seems reasonable to rate the chance of the second strike as greater than one-half the chance that the Soviet first strike will be launched. This would make the chance small but still substantial.

[g] Over the years two arguments have been proposed to show that Superiority provides a more effective deterrent against Soviet aggression than does Equivalence.

(1) The Superiority Strategy requires constant technological innovation, and technological innovation is an area in which the United States possesses a relative advantage. If the United States presses forward with strategic weapons development, the Soviet Union will be so exhausted from the strain of keeping up with the United States that it will have little money or energy left over for nonnuclear aggression. In the end, the strain such competition will exert on the Soviet economy might produce food riots like those in Poland in 1970, and might even bring down the Soviet socioeconomic system.

But since "the strain of keeping up" did not stop the Soviets from invading Hungary, Czechoslovakia, and Afghanistan, the level of expenditure needed to produce truly effective strain is unknown. Furthermore, the assumption of *relative* economic stress is undemonstrated: at least one economist who has seriously studied the subject has argued on various grounds that a unit of military spending by the United States disrupts the American economy far more than the equivalent military spending by the Soviet Union.[3]

(2) It is occasionally argued that the Soviets will take the possibility of an American second strike more seriously under the Superiority Strategy than under the Equivalence Strategy, since the Superiority Strategy gives the United States something closer to first-strike capacity and therefore something less to fear from a Soviet second strike.

But in the game of nuclear strategy one cannot "almost" have first strike capacity; one either has it or one doesn't. There is no reason to think that the Superiority Strategy will ever yield first-strike capacity, since the Soviet Union will feel forced to match the United States step for step. The Soviets know that the President will never be confident enough in American striking capacity to risk the survival of the United States on a nuclear response to Soviet nonnuclear aggression. Consequently, there is no reason to think that Superiority provides a better deterrent against Soviet aggression than does Equivalence. The chance of serious nonnuclear Soviet aggression under Equivalence is small.

[h] In the presence of serious efforts at arms control, expenditures for strategic weapons will be much less under Equivalence than under Superiority. If efforts at arms control fail, then expenditures will remain very high. The chance of very high expenditures under Equivalence would best be put at about fifty-fifty.

Value of the Nuclear Disarmament Strategy

[i] Most strategists are agreed that the chance of a Soviet first strike under the Equivalence Strategy is small. I believe that the chance of a Soviet first strike is small even under the strategy of Nuclear Disarmament.

(1) Since under Nuclear Disarmament at most one side retains nuclear arms, the chance of nuclear war occurring by accident is reduced at least by one half, relative to the Equivalence Strategy. Since only half the technology is deployed, there is only half the chance of a mechanical malfunction leading to war.

(2) Since at most one side remains armed, there is considerably less chance under Nuclear Disarmament that a nuclear war will occur by mistake. The principal mistake that might cause a nuclear war is the mistake of erroneously thinking that the other side is about to launch a nuclear attack. Such mistakes create enormous pressure for the launching of preemptive strikes, in order to get one's weapons in the air before they are destroyed on the ground. There is no chance that this mistake can occur under Nuclear Disarmament. The side that remains armed (if any) need not fear that the other side will launch a nuclear attack. The side that chooses to disarm cannot be tempted to launch a preemptive strike no matter what it believes the other side is doing, since it has no weapons with which to launch the strike.

(3) Even the opponents of Nuclear Disarmament describe the main peril of nuclear disarmament as nuclear blackmail by the Soviet Union. Opponents of disarmament

---

[3]See Seymour Melman, *Our Depleted Society* (New York: Holt, Rinehart & Winston, 1965), and *Pentagon Capitalism* (New York: McGraw-Hill, 1970).

apparently feel that after nuclear disarmament, nuclear threats are far more probable than nuclear disasters.

(4) Though nuclear weapons are not inherently more destructive than other sorts of weapons, conceived or actual (the napalm raids on Tokyo in March 1945 caused more deaths than Hiroshima or Nagasaki), nuclear weapons are universally *perceived* as different in kind from nonnuclear weapons. The diplomatic losses a nation would incur upon using even tactical nuclear weapons would be immense.

(5) A large scale nuclear attack by the Soviet Union against the United States might contaminate the American and Canadian Great Plains, a major source of Soviet grain imports. The Soviets could still turn to Argentina, but the price of grain after the attack would skyrocket, and no combination of Argentinean, Australian, or other grain sources could possibly compensate for American or Canadian losses.

(6) The Soviets will find it difficult to find actual military situations in which it will be practical to use atomic weapons against the United States, or against anyone else. Nuclear weapons proved superfluous in the Soviet invasions of Hungary and Czechoslovakia, and they do not seem to be practicable in Afghanistan, where the human costs of the Soviet attempt to regain control are high. If the Soviets did not use nuclear weapons against China between 1960 and 1964 in order to prevent the development of Chinese nuclear capacity, it is hardly likely that they could use them against a nonnuclear United States. Of course it is always *possible* that the Soviet Union might launch a nuclear attack against a nonnuclear United States, perhaps as an escalatory step in a conventional conflict, but it is also *possible* that the Soviet Union will launch a nuclear attack on the United States *right now,* despite the present situation of Equivalence. The point is that there is no such thing as a guarantee against nuclear attack, but the probability of an actual attack is small under either strategy.

[j] The chance of all-out nuclear war under the Equivalence Strategy is slight, but the chance of all-out nuclear war under Nuclear Disarmament is zero. There cannot be a two-sided nuclear war if only one side possesses nuclear arms.

[k] In considering the threat of Soviet nonnuclear aggression under Nuclear Disarmament, we must consider Soviet nuclear threats—usually called "nuclear blackmail"—as well as possible uses of conventional arms by the Soviets.

(1) Suppose that the United States unilaterally gives up second-strike capacity. What are the odds that the Soviet Union would attempt to influence American behavior through nuclear threats? Obviously, one's views about the chances for successful nuclear blackmail depend on one's views about the chances of a Soviet first strike against a nonnuclear United States. If the chances of a Soviet first strike are slight, then the chances of successful blackmail will also be slight. We have already argued on a variety of grounds that chances of a Soviet first strike under ND are small. I would suggest that the ability of the Soviet Union to manipulate a nonnuclear United States would be the same as the ability of the United States to manipulate the Soviet Union from 1945 to 1949, when strategic conditions were reversed. Anyone who reflects on events from 1945 to 1949 will conclude that nuclear threats have little effect on nations capable of acting with resolve.

There is always the chance that the Soviet Union will carry out its nuclear threats, but there is always the chance that the Soviet Union will carry out its threats even if the United States retains nuclear weapons. There is no device that provides a guarantee against nuclear blackmail. Consequently it cannot be argued that Equivalence provides a guarantee against blackmail that Nuclear Disarmament does not.

The foregoing dismissal of nuclear blackmail violates conventional strategic wisdom, which is concerned with nuclear blackmail almost to obsession. Numerous authors, for example, cite the swift fall of Japan after Hiroshima as evidence of the strategic usefulness of nuclear weapons and nuclear threats. The case of Japan is worth considering. Contrary to the canonical view certified by Secretary Stimson in his famous (and self-serving) *Harper's* article in 1947,[4] I believe that the bombings of Hiroshima and Nagasaki had almost no effect on events leading to the surrender of Japan. If so, the force of the Japanese precedent, which still influences strategic thought, is greatly attenuated.

Obviously the bombings of Hiroshima and Nagasaki had no effect on the popular desire for peace in Japan, since the Japanese public did not know of the atomic bombings until the war was over. What is more surprising is that the bombings do not seem to have influenced either the Emperor or the military command in making the decision to sue for peace. The Emperor, as is now well known, had decided for peace as early as January 1945, and if he was set on peace in January, he did not need the bombings of August to make up his mind. The military, on the other hand, do not seem to have desired peace even after the bombs were dropped; the record shows that the military (a) correctly surmised that the United States had a small supply of these bombs, (b) debated improved antiaircraft measures to prevent any further bombs from being delivered, and (c) correctly inferred that bombs of this type could not be used to support a ground invasion, which they felt they could repulse with sufficient success to secure a conditional surrender. What tipped the political scales so that the Emperor could find his way to peace was not the bombing of Nagasaki on 9 August, but the Russian declaration of war on 8 August. Unaware of Stalin's commitment at Yalta to enter the war against Japan, the Japanese had hoped through the spring and summer of 1945 that the Soviets would mediate a negotiated settlement between the United States and Japan rather than send the Red Army into a new theater of war. When the Russians invaded Manchuria on 9 August, Premier Suzuki, according to reports, cried, "The game is over," and when the Emperor demanded surrender from the Council of Elders on 10 August, he never mentioned atomic bombs as the occasion of his demand for peace.[5] Little can be inferred from such evidence about the effectiveness of nuclear threats.

(2) The strategy of Nuclear Disarmament does not forbid uses of conventional arms in response to acts of aggression. Since there is no reason to believe that adoption of

[4]Stimson's "The Decision to Use the Atomic Bomb" appeared in the February 1947 *Harper's Magazine*, pp. 97–107. Typical of Stimson's *post hoc ergo propter hoc* is:
We believed that our attacks struck cities which must certainly be important to the Japanese military leaders, both Army and Navy, and we waited for a result. We waited one day.

[5]For the Emperor's active attempts to obtain peace see Herbert Feis, *The Atomic Bomb and the End of World War II* (Princeton: Princeton University Press, 1966), p. 66. For the military response to the atomic bombings see Hanson Baldwin, *Great Mistakes of the War* (New York: Collins-Knowlton-Wing, 1950), pp. 87–107. For Suzuki's remark that "The game is over" see W. Craig, *The Fall of Japan* (New York: Dial, 1967), p. 107. . . .

the strategy of Nuclear Disarmament by the United States will make acts of Soviet aggression any more palatable than they are at present, in all probability the American government under ND will appropriate funds for conventional arms sufficient to provide a deterrent to Soviet aggression roughly comparable to the deterrent provided by nuclear arms under S and E. This argument assumes that the deterrent effects of the American strategic nuclear arsenal (whatever they are) can be obtained with a developed arsenal of modern conventional weapons. A review of the difficulties involved in the use of strategic nuclear weapons in concrete situations may convince the reader that conventional weapons can match the deterrent effect of nuclear weapons. Indeed, the whole development of "flexible response" systems during the McNamara era testifies to the widespread recognition that strategic nuclear weapons provide little leverage to nations who would seek to control the flow of world events.

[1] Since it is impossible to predict how much money must be spent on conventional forces in order to supply a deterrent equal to the present (nuclear) deterrent against Soviet nonnuclear aggression, it is possible that levels of military spending under ND will be greater than levels under E. But it is also possible that the levels of spending will be much less. The technical equipment needed to maintain E is fantastically expensive, but the labor costs of training and improving conventional forces can also be staggering. All things considered, it is still likely that spending will be less under ND than under E, especially if the draft is revived.

Comparison of Superiority and Equivalence

The chance of a Soviet first strike is greater under Superiority than under Equivalence, and the chance of all-out nuclear war is greater under Superiority than under Equivalence. The ability of Equivalence to deter Soviet nonnuclear aggression is equal to the ability of Superiority to deter such aggression, and the Equivalence strategy costs less. Thus Equivalence is preferable to Superiority from both the prudential and the moral point of view.

Comparison of Equivalence and Nuclear Disarmament

We have argued that Nuclear Disarmament and Equivalence are equal in their ability to deter Soviet nonnuclear aggression. In the category of military spending Nuclear Disarmament is preferable to Equivalence. In the category of "all-out war" ND is clearly superior to E, and in the category of "first strikes," ND seems to be about equal to E. Thus we have what seems to be a decisive prudential and moral argument in favor of Nuclear Disarmament: in every category, ND is either equal to or superior to E. . . . Furthermore, since there is the possibility of *two* first strikes under E and *at most* the possibility of one first strike under ND, there is considerable reason to conclude that the probability of a first strike under ND is less than the probability of a first strike under E.

On the other hand, the chance that the Soviet Union will start a nuclear war through calculation of presumed advantage is greater under ND than under E. Certainly the fact that the Soviet Union could use nuclear weapons against the United States without fear of American nuclear reprisal might tempt them to use these weapons, especially if the United States and the Soviet Union were involved in a large-scale war using conventional weapons. After all, that was the way nuclear weapons came to be used the first time around. But such a strike would have difficulties and costs, which we have already enumerated, and in general the Soviet Union might be disinclined to use nuclear weapons against a nation it does not perceive as a source of nuclear threats. Though aggression studies have been among the most lavishly funded of recent psychological projects, we still do not have anything like a set of rules which tell us whether aggression is more or less likely between two parties who fear each other than it is between two parties, one of whom has nothing to fear from the other.

Considering the military awkwardness and diplomatic costs of using nuclear weapons, I find it quite incredible that the majority of official statements on this subject consider the chance of a calculated Soviet attack on a nonnuclear United States as greater than the chance under Equivalence of a Soviet attack by accident *or* a Soviet attack by mistake *or* an American attack by accident *or* an American attack by mistake. . . .

FROM MORALS TO POLITICS

Nuclear Disarmament, Superiority, and Equivalence are the nuclear strategies most discussed by theorists, and other strategies are largely variants or specifications of these three. If utilitarianism favors Nuclear Disarmament over Superiority and Equivalence, it favors Nuclear Disarmament *tout court*. For utilitarians, ND is morally right, and ought to be adopted.

It remains to consider whether it is also morally right to *advocate* or *support* Nuclear Disarmament. Support is logically distinct from adoption, and acts of support have their own sets of consequences. It is possible, and by no means paradoxical, that within the utilitarian framework support for the morally right policy may be morally wrong.

The commonest situation where support for the right leads to the wrong is a three-way election in which support for the best candidate will elect the worst, while support for the second best outcome will defeat the worst. Moderate liberals whose support for Charles Goodell over Richard Ottinger led to the election of James Buckley in 1972 and whose support for Jacob Javits over Elisabeth Holtzman led to the election of Al d'Amato in 1980 found themselves in each case with their least preferred candidate. In such situations utilitarianism joins hands with a Weberian ethic of responsibility and calls on moral agents to support the second best.

It is often alleged that the competition between S, E, and ND is rather like the Senate race in New York in 1972 and 1980, and many who agree that ND is morally superior to E fear that open advocacy of ND will drain support from E and lead to victory for the Superiority Strategy. The flaw in this reasoning is to compare a three-way election with winners determined by votes to a three-way policy choice with winners determined by the ultimate vector of political pressure. With candidates and votes, support for the extreme steals votes from the center. With policies and pressures, pressure from one extreme helps support the center against pressure from the other. In choosing platforms and policies, Americans have traditionally shied away from extremes, and a three-way race between S, E, and ND places E in the central position historically favored by the American people. A two-way race, which places the "center" between Equivalence and Superiority, allows the supporters of Superiority to argue that their strategy is no more extreme than Equivalence. If the moral principle which evaluates support of strategic policies (as opposed to the policies themselves) determines that support should be exercised in the way most likely to defeat Superiority, there is as much a case for public support of Nuclear Disarmament as there is for Nuclear Disarmament itself.[6]

QUESTIONS

1 Is unilateral nuclear disarmament by the United States the morally best strategy? Is it the prudentially best strategy?

2 What response do you think Lackey would give to the Bishops' "strictly conditioned" acceptance of nuclear deterrence policies?

Doubts about Unilateral Nuclear Disarmament

Gregory S. Kavka

Gregory S. Kavka is professor of philosophy at the University of California, Irvine. He specializes in political philosophy and ethics. Kavka's articles include "Nuclear Deterrence: Some Moral Perplexities" and "Space War Ethics."

Kavka criticizes Lackey's assessment of the possible consequences of U.S. unilateral nuclear disarmament. Lackey, he argues, seriously underestimates the probability of nuclear attack or nuclear blackmail should the United States give up nuclear arms. Thus, on Kavka's view, Lackey is wrong to conclude that unilateral nuclear disarmament "would involve a *smaller* risk of producing a *lesser* disaster" than continued U.S. nuclear deterrence policies. Kavka concludes by rejecting Lackey's claim that public advocacy of U.S. unilateral disarmament will maximize the chances for peace.

The practice of nuclear deterrence by the United States poses an apparent dilemma when examined from a utilitarian point of view. Continuation of this practice risks the gravest of disasters for humankind—a large-scale nuclear war with the Soviet Union. But its abandonment would appear to risk, with greater (combined) probability,

[6]The author would like to thank the National Endowment for the Humanities for fellowship support during the period of time in which this article was written. Thanks are also due to Mrs. Esther Gutenberg for her help and patience.

the lesser utilitarian disasters of a Soviet nuclear strike or Soviet world-domination by means of nuclear blackmail. Further, an expected value calculation will not solve this problem. For reliable estimates of the probabilities and utilities of the relevant possible outcomes are not available. Hence, in comparing nuclear deterrence and unilateral nuclear disarmament, the utilitarian seems trapped between the Scylla of a smaller risk of a worse disaster (that is, full-scale nuclear war) and the Charybdis of a greater risk of a smaller disaster (that is, a nuclear strike or Soviet domination via blackmail).[1]

In a recent article,[2] Douglas Lackey seeks to extricate us from this utilitarian dilemma by denying one of the factual presuppositions that underlies it. He claims that the probability, P, of a Soviet nuclear strike or domination via nuclear blackmail, given U.S. unilateral nuclear disarmament, is actually *less* than the probability of a U.S.–Soviet nuclear war, given a continued policy of deterrence by the United States (pp. 204–5, 221–22). If this is so, unilateral nuclear disarmament by the United States would involve a *smaller* risk of producing a *lesser* disaster, compared to continued U.S. deterrence. The utilitarian problem is then solved, or dissolved, with an obvious verdict for unilateral nuclear disarmament emerging.

Unfortunately, however, Lackey's solution to this important problem is a pseudosolution based on an implausibly optimistic estimate of P. Lackey describes the probability of continued deterrence leading to nuclear war as "small, but substantial" (p. 208), yet he believes that P is smaller still.[3] A more common view is that P is high, perhaps even close to one. For throughout history nations have been quite inclined to use their power to unilateral advantage, and there is little in the history of the Soviet state to indicate that it is abnormal in this respect. What evidence does Lackey offer to counteract this common view?

He lays much emphasis on the fact that the United States did not use its early atomic monopoly for blackmail or attack (pp. 205 and 212). But there are too many differences between that situation and the one the Soviets would be in now after U.S. unilateral nuclear disarmament, to rely on this precedent. The United States was a democratic nation whose people had just experienced a substantial war, and which was recently allied to the nation it might have employed its weapons against—the U.S.S.R. Technologically, nuclear weapons were much smaller, many fewer, and much less well-tested than they are at present, and the instruments for delivering them were more vulnerable to defensive measures. Militarily, the Soviets had a massive, mobilized, and well-positioned land army that could have readily been used to conquer Europe. This to some degree counterbalanced the military power of early nuclear weapons. Nor was there sufficient appreciation of the power of nuclear weapons to allow leaders to use them most effectively as political-strategic weapons. None of these political,

---

[1]See my "Deterrence, Utility, and Rational Choice," *Theory and Decision* **12** (March 1980): 41–60.

[2]Douglas Lackey, "Missiles and Morals: A Utilitarian Look at Nuclear Deterrence," *Philosophy & Public Affairs* **11** (Summer 1982): 189–231. Page references in the text are to this article. Though my comments explicitly address only Lackey's utilitarian analysis of deterrence, they apply to his prudential analysis as well.

[3]In addition to the pages cited above in the text, see Lackey, "Missiles," pp. 191, 197–98, 206, 210–12, 215, and 218 on the improbability of Soviet attack; and pp. 205, 206, 212, and 215 on the improbability of nuclear blackmail.

technological, military, and intellectual constraints would apply in the same way to the Soviet Union now, if the United States dismantled its nuclear arsenal.

Might the Soviets' generally cautious military behavior (for example, directly invading only nations on their geographic periphery) be taken as evidence they would not exploit nuclear predominance if they had it? Lackey suggests so with regard to at least one instance—the Soviets' failure to attack Chinese nuclear facilities (p. 211). But the moral of that story is not what Lackey takes it to be. Memoirs from the Nixon administration suggest that the Soviets may well have refrained from such an attack only out of concern about the response of the United States, its only equal in nuclear power.[4] From this—and other instances of relatively cautious international behavior—we may not infer how the Soviets would act in the absence of any nuclear equal (or near equal). To do so would be to follow the lead of the apocryphal banker who, upon observing that the bank had never been robbed, did away with locks and guards as unnecessary.

Lackey fails to fully appreciate the force of this point. He writes,

> the Soviet Union has never made the conquest of the United States or a change in its form of government an announced policy goal, and . . . there is no scenario short of fantasy in which it could become a Soviet policy goal. (p. 222)

This may be true, as there is no scenario short of fantasy in which the United States will adopt unilateral nuclear disarmament. But it does not follow that we *would be* safe from Soviet conquest if we practiced unilateral nuclear disarmament, as Lackey seems to suppose. Compare a potential robber's side of our bank case. Lefty may want money and be willing to rob to get it. But as the bank is well guarded and well locked, he never adopts robbing the bank as a goal.[5] But should our banker unlock and unguard, we can predict that Lefty will be there with his hands in the till.

Perhaps Lackey believes Soviet leaders are unlikely to attack a nuclearly disarmed United States because they would not have any reason to attack in the absence of a U.S. nuclear threat (p. 221). But, notoriously, the mere expansion of one's power has seemed to numerous political leaders throughout history a good enough reason to undertake aggressive military action. And the Soviets might conceivably attack or employ nuclear blackmail out of loftier motives—to impose lasting peace through world government and to prevent later U.S. nuclear rearmament and possible two-sided nuclear war. After all, even so peaceloving and rational an individual as Bertrand Russell advocated, during the time of the U.S. nuclear monopoly, that it adopt such a course toward the Soviet Union for essentially these very reasons.[6]

Much ado is made by Lackey about conventional armament as an effective substitute for nuclear deterrence (pp. 196, 205, and 214). This may well have been so in the

---

[4]H. R. Haldeman, *The Ends of Power* (New York: Dell, 1978), pp. 128–35. Also see Marvin Kalb and Bernard Kalb, *Kissinger* (Boston: Little, Brown & Co., 1974), pp. 226–28.

[5]Not expecting the bank to unlock and unguard, Lefty never even adopts the conditional goal of robbing it if it does. Like busy Soviet leaders, he does not make contingency plans for fantastical contingencies.

[6]See Ronald Clark, *The Life of Bertrand Russell* (London: Jonathan Cape, 1975), chap. 19, which includes a number of relevant quotations from articles, speeches, and letters by Russell. See also Bertrand Russell, "The Future of Mankind," in his *Unpopular Essays* (New York: Simon & Schuster, 1950), pp. 34–44.

early days of atomic weaponry, but not today, given the enormous nuclear arsenals of the superpowers. If a modern superpower were willing to use nuclear attack on a nuclearly disarmed foe to obtain concessions or capitulation, resistance with conventional forces would be quite ineffectual. If these forces massed for defense, or attack, they could be destroyed with tactical nuclear weapons. And they could not defend cities or military bases from nuclear destruction ordered to force compliance with political demands.

There is much reason then to doubt Lackey's sanguine estimate of P. So far, however, we have largely ignored the fact that there are other nuclear powers besides the United States and the Soviet Union. When we take this into account, our estimate of P must increase substantially. For if the United States adopted unilateral nuclear disarmament, it is unlikely that all other nuclear powers—especially China—would follow suit. Their nuclear arsenals would then be tempting targets for Soviet preemptive attack, especially if these countries began to expand their nuclear weaponry to compensate for the removal of the American nuclear umbrella. Lackey, citing a theoretical result of Lewis Richardson, suggests that the fewer the nations armed with nuclear weapons, the smaller the chance of nuclear war (p. 230). But it seems reasonable to give more weight to the specific historical evidence which suggests, as noted above, that America's nuclear power may be all that has prevented the Soviets from striking the Chinese. Are we not safer relying on our recent experience that mutual deterrence by nearly equal nuclear powers works, than laying humankind open to the uncertainties and instabilities of a world of vastly unequal nuclear powers, with the Soviets having nuclear forces much greater than all the others combined?

In sum, a number of considerations indicate that Lackey has seriously underestimated the probability of nuclear attack or nuclear blackmail if the United States should adopt unilateral nuclear disarmament: (1) the general historical tendency of great powers and their leaders to exploit military advantages, (2) disanalogies between past U.S. nuclear dominance and (hypothetical) future Soviet nuclear dominance, (3) the significance of the distinction between current Soviet policy and behavior and what that policy and behavior might become after U.S. unilateral nuclear disarmament, (4) the existence of plausible prudential and "moral" motives for Soviet use of nuclear weapons in such circumstances, (5) the ineffectiveness of conventional defense against a vast nuclear arsenal, and (6) the instabilities of a world with multiple unequal nuclear powers. In light of these considerations, it seems clear that the probability, P, of Soviet nuclear attack or blackmail following U.S. unilateral nuclear disarmament exceeds the "small, but substantial" probability of continued U.S. deterrence leading to nuclear war. And the utilitarian dilemma concerning deterrence sketched in the opening paragraph of this paper remains in force.

Two final points should be briefly noted. First, even if the risks of continued deterrence *in the form Lackey discusses* were so grave as to make unilateral nuclear disarmament a better option, it does not follow that such disarmament is our best option. For there are a range of policies that retain deterrence but might well reduce the risks of nuclear war which Lackey mentions: initiation by accident, mistake, or escalation (pp. 216–18 and 221). These include significant unilateral peaceful steps that invite Soviet reciprocation; more reasonable negotiation postures on mutual disarmament; willingness to compromise on political differences; a no first use declaration; abrogation of launch on warning procedures, and so on. Adopting such policies might allow us to continue deterrence while greatly reducing the already small (but surely nonnegligible) risk of nuclear war, and it might even eventually lead toward the most desirable of outcomes, mutual (or even multilateral) nuclear disarmament.[7]

Second, and finally, I cannot accept at Lackey's judgment that public advocacy of U.S. unilateral nuclear disarmament serves the cause of peace (pp. 230–31). I fear it is more likely to facilitate the ready dismissal and discrediting of the nuclear disarmament movement, both by its foes and by the uncommitted. This movement will flourish more if it avoids excesses of wishful thinking and sticks to the path of reason and moral commitment tempered by realism.[8]

QUESTIONS

1 Do you agree with Kavka that Lackey has erred in his assessment of the probable Soviet reaction to unilateral nuclear disarmament by the United States?

2 What utilitarian arguments can you advance for or against nuclear deterrence strategies?

3 As a citizen of the United States, what role should you play regarding U.S. nuclear deterrence policies? Should you, for example, be a public advocate of unilateral nuclear disarmament? Support policies designed to lead to bilateral nuclear disarmament?

The Ethics of Nuclear Deterrence: A Contractarian Account

Christopher W. Morris

Christopher W. Morris is visiting assistant professor of philosophy at the University of California, Riverside. His published articles include "The Hart-Rawls Principle of Fairness Amended" and "Human Anatomy and the Natural Right to be Free." Morris is currently working on a rational-choice and contractarian account of the liberal state.

Morris argues that it is not immoral to adopt nuclear deterrence policies that threaten potential enemies with nuclear destruction. He rejects (1) unilateral nuclear disarmament, (2) the view that nuclear deterrence is morally impermissible, and (3)

---

[7]Lackey faces a dilemma here. If he admits the Soviets are too unreasonable to mutually disarm on fair or generous terms, he casts doubt on his claim that they are reasonable enough not to attack or blackmail us if we practice unilateral nuclear disarmament. But if the Soviets will disarm on reasonable terms, isn't offering such terms the optimal utilitarian policy?

[8]This paper was written while I was supported by a fellowship for independent study and research from the National Endowment for the Humanities.

Reprinted with permission of the author from Manuel Velasquez and Cynthia Rostankowski, eds., *Ethics: Theory and Practice* (Englewood Cliffs, N.J.: Prentice-Hall, 1985), pp. 203–213. Copyright © 1983 Christopher W. Morris.

the view that the retaliatory use of nuclear weapons is morally impermissible because it would result in the massive direct killing of innocents. On Morris's analysis, basic moral principles are binding only on parties interacting in a cooperative and mutually beneficial manner. When one nation launches a nuclear attack against another, cooperative mutual interaction has ended. Thus, although the principle that prohibits directly killing the innocent is a basic moral principle binding on moral agents engaged in cooperative interaction, it is inapplicable when two nations are engaged in a nuclear war. Since the use of nuclear weapons is not morally impermissible, he concludes, neither are nuclear deterrence policies whose intent is to prevent nuclear war by threatening massive countervalue retaliatory destruction.

It is a widely accepted moral principle that it is wrong to kill the innocent. Yet this is precisely what we threaten to do in the event of a nuclear attack. In fact, it is an essential part of nuclear deterrence. Is nuclear deterrence then immoral? Many people, both of the left and the right, believe this to be so.

However, the principle prohibiting the killing of the innocent as stated above is implausible since it does not make allowances for accidental and unintended killings. Thus, many moral philosophers distinguish between direct and indirect killings and argue that indirect killings are not always wrong. One very influential way of making this distinction involves the traditional doctrine of double effect, according to which only acts of direct killing are morally prohibited, while acts of indirect killing may be morally permissible. The doctrine is usually stated as follows: in distinguishing between the good and the bad effects of an act of killing, the act is indirect and morally permissible if

1 the act in itself is not impermissible,
2 the bad effect is not the means to the good effect,
3 the good but not the bad effect is intended, and
4 the good effect is not outweighed by the bad effect.

Killing some civilians while bombing an enemy military installation might thus be permissible if the bad effect (killing the civilians) was neither intended nor the means to the good effect (destroying the installation) and if, say, the number of lives saved by the bombing is greater than the number of civilian casualties. The doctrine would justify such killings where the deaths were the unintended side effects of permissible acts.

An appeal to the doctrine of double effect may not, however, help the defender of nuclear deterrence, for the innocent civilians who are slaughtered by nuclear retaliation surely would not be killed indirectly. Consider what is called "countervalue" retaliation, the nuclear targeting of enemy centers of population. Such retaliation clearly would involve acts of direct killing since conditions 2 and 3 of the doctrine of double effect would not be satisfied. The bad effect (killing massive numbers of innocent civilians) would be both intended and a means to the good effect ("punishing" enemy aggression, deterring future aggression, or whatever).

In view of this, some moral philosophers counsel that we use only "counterforce" strategies, that is, strategies that aim our missiles solely at military targets and not at innocent civilians. However, given the huge numbers of Soviet casualties to be expected from counterforce retaliatory strikes, condition 4 of the doctrine of double effect surely is not satisfied. In terms of numbers of lives, the good effect is outweighed by the bad.

Threatening to kill, however, is not the same as actually killing. Perhaps we are justified in *threatening* nuclear retaliation, so long as we do not intend to carry out our threat. That is, perhaps the morally appropriate deterrent strategy is bluffing. Naturally, we should not expect such an insincere threat to be credible once our moral reluctance became known to our adversary. The effectiveness of such a bluff depends on our adversary's belief that we would (or might) launch a retaliatory second strike in the event of nuclear attack. I do not believe that a policy based on such a bluff is acceptable. First, it would depend on deception—or at least dissimulation—for its effectiveness, and this may be impossible to achieve in an open society. Second, a deceptive policy is inconsistent with the values of an open society like ours. Third, it seems incredible that the most effective means of national defense should depend on such deception. Thus it is my belief that this approach will not salvage our deterrence practices.

Faced with the apparent choice between interpreting P as absolute (as recommended by many natural law and natural rights theories) and the demand to accord equal weight to the welfare of the enemy (as recommended by utilitarianism), some moral philosophers counsel retreat into moral nihilism: in war, anything goes; nothing is prohibited. In the social sciences and in politics, such a position often goes under the name of "realism." But such talk is dubious, as well as dangerous. For one, it contradicts seemingly entrenched patterns of ordinary discourse. In war, as well as at other times, most people attempt to justify their actions by reference to moral standards. It is extremely difficult to talk about war without using moral language; even slogans such as "war is hell" do not usually allow us to dispense with moral categories.

Given the unacceptability of unilateral nuclear disarmament, how can we justify nuclear deterrence? Nuclear deterrence involves threatening to kill directly massive numbers of innocents in the event of an enemy nuclear attack, an act not justified by the traditional doctrine of double effect. Is nuclear deterrence then morally impermissible? I shall argue that this is not the case.

Let me begin by stating clearly the moral principle that is involved in this issue. Nuclear deterrence involves threatening to kill directly massive numbers of innocents. Directly killing the innocent is thought to be morally wrong, at least in normal circumstances. The relevant moral principle would thus seem to be the following, which I will call principle P: It is wrong directly to kill innocent persons.

The terms involved in this principle should be understood as follows. An act of direct killing is one that is not an act of indirect killing as defined by the doctrine of double effect. A person is any creature that is owed some moral consideration. An innocent person is a person who is not threatening another. (Sometimes this is called the "causal" sense of innocence, in contrast to the "moral" or "juridical" sense, according to which innocence is equivalent to absence of guilt.) Thus, principle P prohibits the killing of nonthreatening persons except in those cases of indirect or unintentional killing justified by the doctrine of double effect.

According to the natural law tradition, killing the innocent directly is absolutely wrong, that is, it is impermissible whatever the consequences. But I reject the interpretation of P as absolute. Interpreting P as absolute commits us to refrain from using (or threatening to use) nuclear weapons. Given what I have said above, interpreting the principle in this manner would commit us to bluffing or, more likely, to unilateral nuclear disarmament and that, I am assuming, is unacceptable in the present circumstances. Further, given that some deterrent strategies reduce considerably the likelihood of nuclear conflict and that absolutist interpretations of P commit us to rejecting such strategies, then surely that is at least a partial reason for rejecting such interpretations.

Does my rejection of the absolute interpretation of P commit me to interpreting P as *defeasible?* A moral principle is defeasible when it may be overridden by other moral considerations. Utilitarianism, for example, supposes that all of our duties are derived from the principle of maximizing the total quantity of the good, where the good is identified with happiness, well-being, or utility. According to such a view, all of our duties are defeasible, since whatever maximizes happiness in one situation may very well not do so in another.

Utilitarian interpretations of P are, of course, only one way of rendering the principle defeasible; other moral theories may do this as well. But understanding the inappropriateness of utilitarian accounts will set the stage for the interpretation of P that I wish to defend.

Utilitarianism would have us consider in our moral deliberations the welfare of all individuals that could be affected by our actions. Further, not only are we to do this, we are also to count their well-being equally with ours. Utilitarianism has often been criticized as too flexible a moral theory; depending on the circumstances, it can be said to justify too much that we think is wrong. It is not always clear that such criticisms are correct, but they seem beside the point here. Rather, what is striking about utilitarianism as it is applied to matters of conflict and war is not how flexible but how demanding a theory it is. After all, it requires us to count our enemy's welfare equally with our own.

Utilitarianism, as has often been noted, is a moral theory that takes a certain ideal that is at best suited for close friends or family and applies it to all persons. Countless critics have remarked on the inappropriateness of this transference. However, another point needs to be emphasized, and that is that utilitarianism is very irrational when applied to situations of major conflict, such as nuclear war. While most wars are not zero sum—that is, both sides have some interests in common—it is doubtful that any argument could be given for the rationality of accepting the principle of utility in all such situations, at least if we understand rationality as not requiring total self-sacrifice. After all, the interests in conflict may be too important to be compromised or abandoned so easily. It is one thing to commit oneself to the principle of utility in situations when others are themselves willing to accept the same principle, but it is entirely another matter to commit oneself to the principle of utility in a nonutilitarian world. I conclude, therefore, that the utilitarian interpretation of principle P as defeasible is not acceptable.

Normally, in moral theory it is thought that "absolute" and "defeasible" are contradictory terms. That is, it is assumed that if a principle is not absolute, then it must be defeasible, and vice versa. However, I want to argue that there are circumstances in which P is neither defeasible nor absolute.

The position I wish to defend is this: In certain circumstances respecting P would be irrational. In such circumstances, P (and other principles of justice) is no longer rationally binding.[1] Thus, in such circumstances directly killing the innocent would not be unjust because nothing would be unjust.[2] These circumstances, which I shall call Hobbesian states of nature, are, I believe, exceedingly rare in the modern world, the behavior of nation-states to the contrary. However, an enemy nuclear attack would bring about such circumstances, or so I shall argue. Therefore, massive nuclear retaliation would not, in those circumstances, be unjust because during an enemy nuclear attack nothing would be unjust. P, on this account, would not be absolute, for it would not be wrong to do what P prohibits. But neither would P be defeasible: since considerations of justice would no longer be binding, there would be no considerations of justice that could override it. Let me now turn to defending these claims.

Faced with the apparent choice between interpreting P as absolute (as recommended by many natural law and natural rights theories) and the demand to accord equal weight to the welfare of the enemy (as recommended by utilitarianism), some moral philosophers counsel retreat into moral nihilism: in war, anything goes; nothing is prohibited. In the social sciences and in politics, such a position often goes under the name of "realism." But such talk is dubious, as well as dangerous. For one, it contradicts seemingly entrenched patterns of ordinary discourse. In war, as well as at other times, most people attempt to justify their actions by reference to moral standards. It is extremely difficult to talk about war without using moral language; even slogans such as "war is hell" do not usually allow us to dispense with moral categories.

Equally important, however, is the danger of destabilization that comes from nihilism. Obviously, such a position reinforces mutual suspicion. At present the United States and the Soviet Union greatly distrust each other. Each appears to believe that the other is acquiring or already possesses offensive nuclear weapons. Should either party come to believe, or be reinforced in its belief, that the other thinks nothing is forbidden, then that party would find it difficult to trust the other to refrain from seeking a first-strike advantage. Assurance that the other side is capable and willing to impose constraints on its behavior is crucial to stabilization. Since abstaining from first-strike advantage is stabilizing, it is clear that a retreat to nihilism may have a significant destabilizing effect. In this context, the suspicion that the other side seeks to use allegedly defensive weapons for offensive, first-strike ends can only increase.

Nonetheless, the retreat to nihilism has an important grain of truth to it, and this is the truth expressed in Thomas Hobbes' account of the relations between nations. According to Hobbes, nations find themselves in a "state of nature" in which there

---

[1]The notion of rationality I am using here is basically that widely used in the social sciences, especially in economics and game theory, i.e., a person is rational insofar as he maximizes the satisfaction of his preferences. I would want, however, to amend this conception in the manner suggested by David P. Gauthier in "Reason and Maximization," *Canadian Journal of Philosophy*, vol. 4 (1975), pp. 411–33, so as to handle certain types of problems of strategic interaction (namely, prisoners' dilemmas, for those readers familiar with these issues).

[2]The "nothing" will be qualified later, with regard to uninvolved third parties.

are no binding moral obligations. Relations between nations thus are relations of power, unconstrained by moral rules. In a similar fashion, relations between individuals in a state of nature are also mere relations of power, unconstrained by moral considerations. The difference for Hobbes is that individuals have the possibility of establishing an enforcer or sovereign and thus of escaping from their plight, while no such escape is possible in the world of nations.[3]

But Hobbes' account may be defective in two ways. First, it may be possible to accept his analysis of the problem facing rational individuals in a state of nature without accepting his solution of absolute and unconstrained sovereignty, that is, without accepting his view that only the establishment of an all-powerful and indivisible ruler can end the state of nature. Second, it is not clear that Hobbes' account of international relations must be accepted. I shall not pronounce on the accuracy of Hobbes' account in terms of the nations with which he was familiar in the seventeenth century, but nations today are interdependent in ways that transform their situation. Let me explain these two points.

According to contractarian ethics, relations of justice obtain only between parties that find themselves in certain situations. Following John Rawls, we may call these "circumstances of justice."[4] In this view, relations of justice exist only between parties that are interdependent in certain ways. Individuals in the circumstances of justice are roughly equal in physical and mental powers, and thus are unable to dominate one another and are vulnerable to attack; resources are moderately scarce (relative to needs and wants); needs and wants, although in conflict to some degree, are such as to allow for mutually beneficial interaction. The most important condition here for our purposes is that of mutual advantage: individuals find themselves in the circumstances of justice only if there exists the possibility of mutually beneficial interaction. But in the absence of possible mutual advantage, there is no place for justice since individuals have no reason to constrain their self-interested activity.

Cooperative interaction, as I shall define it, is mutually beneficial interaction made possible by constraints on self-interested behavior. Between interdependent nations today there appears to be at least some room for such interaction. Thus, contrary to Hobbes' account of international relations, modern nations meet one of the most important conditions for cooperative interaction. Assuming the remaining circumstances of justice obtain between nations, norms of cooperation such as Hobbes' first few laws of nature would be rationally binding on them.[5]

Such norms, however, would be binding on nations only insofar as others are willing to abide by them.[6] The problem in international relations, of course, is to obtain assurances that others are willing to abide by these norms of cooperation.

---

[3]Thomas Hobbes, *The Leviathan* (Harmondsworth: Penguin Books, 1968; 1651); see especially chapter 13.

[4]See David Hume, "Enquiry Concerning the Principles of Morals," section 3, in *Enquiries,* 3rd ed., rev. by P. H. Nidditch (Oxford: Clarendon Press, 1975), and John Rawls, *A Theory of Justice* (Cambridge: Harvard University Press, 1971), pp. 126ff.

[5]These laws require that one pursue peace, be willing to give up an equal amount of natural liberty on the condition that others do so as well, and keep one's agreements. Hobbes believed that the laws of nature are summarized in the counsel "Do not that to another, which thou wouldest not have done to thy selfe." Hobbes, *Leviathan,* chapters 14–15.

[6]"Be willing when others are too. . . ." Hobbes, *Leviathan,* chapter 14.

Between nations, there is no absolute sovereign capable of impartial enforcement of agreements and some system of enforcement is necessary if cooperation is to be rational.

Hobbes assumed that the requisite international mechanism would have to be a supranational sovereign. Since no such international sovereign exists, he concluded that norms of cooperation could not be enforced between nations. But this is a mistake. In many relations between individuals where police protection is unavailable, norms of cooperation are often adequately enforced by the parties themselves. Indeed, the threat to retaliate can often provide adequate enforcement without recourse to other measures. In the same way, we may suppose that threats to retaliate when leveled among nations can also provide the requisite enforcement mechanism that makes cooperation possible. If such threats are morally permissible, then we need not search for an international sovereign to ensure international cooperation.

What strategies promise to stabilize the current situation and provide an enforcement mechanism that can make cooperative interaction between nations possible? Let us suppose that

> [i]n the long run, insofar as nuclear weapons are concerned, what each superpower needs for the deterrence of nuclear and conventional attacks on itself and its main allies is the capacity for assured destruction . . . and a limited capacity for actual warfare. A complete counter-force capability would be disastrous for crisis stability if it consisted of vulnerable forces; and even a complete invulnerable counter-force capability might incite the opponent to strike first in order to use his vulnerable weapons.[7]

Thus, we might suppose that the United States should renounce a first strike on the condition that the Soviet Union does so as well. Adoption of the recommendations quoted above—maintaining the capacity for assured destruction—would convince each party that the other renounces striking first and would provide the threat that makes cooperative interaction possible.

But a threat to retaliate with massive strikes is an acceptable means of deterrence only if it does not violate a basic norm of justice like principle P. Such threats will not violate basic norms of justice when norms of justice no longer bind, i.e., when cooperation between the two parties no longer is possible. But in the event of an enemy nuclear attack, cooperative relations have in fact ended. In such circumstances the parties are back in a Hobbesian state of nature and norms of justice no longer bind.

In such a state of nature, the prohibition on the direct killing of the innocent, like all other principles of justice, becomes a mere counsel of nonmoral prudence. Threatening an adversary with countervalue retaliation in the event of a nuclear attack is therefore permissible because in the circumstances in which such a threat would be carried out it would not be impermissible to do so. I am assuming here, of course, that a *threat* to do X in circumstances C is morally permissible if *doing* X in those circumstances is not morally impermissible.[8]

---

[7]Albert Carnesale, Paul Doty, Stanley Hoffman, Samuel P. Huntington, Joseph S. Nye, Jr., and Scott Sagan, *Living with Nuclear Weapons* (New York: Bantam Books, 1983), p. 250.

[8]I am assuming merely that if an act is not impermissible, then neither is threatening that act. I also think that sincerely threatening an act is not impermissible if and only if the act itself is not impermissible. But this is a stronger and more controversial principle, and my argument in this paper does not require it. . . .

In the account above I have assumed that the prohibition against killing the innocent directly is part of an acceptable contractarian morality. Rational agents, in a contractarian choice situation, would find such a prohibition mutually advantageous. Further, I am supposing that this prohibition is a basic principle, one that binds as long as contractarian morality is in force. A morality is "in force," I shall say, when rational agents are in the "circumstances of justice" and are not forced back into a state of nature; in those situations, such a morality is binding on rational agents.

Principle P, then, binds rational agents up until the point at which they are forced back to a state of nature. It is never permissible, I shall assume, to return unilaterally to a state of nature since this would violate Hobbes' first law of nature, which is to seek peace and follow it. But should another nation unilaterally return to a state of nature, e.g., by launching a nuclear attack, then P (and all other principles of justice) become mere counsels of nonmoral prudence. Thus, massive retaliation is not, under such circumstances, morally impermissible, and by extension a threat to retaliate massively is also morally permissible.

Such an account of P would not justify the killing of the innocent in any situation of conflict. The account that I have developed shows how P is suspended in certain situations, namely when an adversary unilaterally returns to a Hobbesian state of nature. In the event, say, of an enemy nuclear attack, the United States (or the Soviet Union) would no longer be bound by P. This does not mean, however, that P is suspended in all conflicts. For surely not all wars involve the complete return to a Hobbesian state of nature. In most wars, there is an important residue of mutual interest, enough to generate binding rules of conduct—those prohibiting certain weapons, protecting noncombatants, governing the treatment of prisoners, and so on. Thus, this argument is not a justification of terror or obliteration bombing, to cite just two examples. For instance, it is doubtful that the Allies during the latter years of World War II were in a situation in which P was suspended. Certainly the American bombings of Tokyo and Hiroshima and Nagasaki could not be justified by the account I offer here; nothing has been said about suspending P in the pursuit of the unconditional surrender of an enemy state. Mere expediency in the conduct of war would not suffice to justify suspending P.

Nevertheless, an important objection deserves to be considered. In the event of an enemy attack, I have argued that massive countervalue retaliation is not prohibited because P (and other principles of justice) no longer would be in force. Thus killing the innocent would not be wrong (or right). Now someone might grant that we would be in a state of nature with regard to the Soviet leaders and other officials involved in the decision to attack, but demur at the idea that innocent Soviet citizens would be in a similar position. After all, the inhabitants of uninvolved third countries would not be placed in a state of nature by Soviet aggression against us, so we would not be relieved of the prohibition against attacking them. Why should Soviet children, for example, be different?

Such an objection to my argument is difficult to meet. I do not wish to argue that all persons are plunged back into a state of nature by enemy aggression and that we would not be acting wrongly were we to use the occasion to drop bombs on other peoples. Yet I do want to hold that we would not be acting wrongly to retaliate against innocent Soviet citizens in the event of a Soviet attack.

May we deter, for instance, an enemy nuclear attack by threatening some third party about which enemy leaders happen to care? Would the inhabitants of this otherwise uninvolved nation also be in a state of nature with respect to us in the event of an enemy nuclear attack?

According to my reasoning, members of society A are not prohibited from deterring attack by society B by threatening to kill innocent members of that society. Is A, however, not prohibited from deterring B by threatening to kill members of C, where C is an uninvolved third country? Should I agree, then am I not supposing that members of B are in some way collectively responsible for the aggressive acts of their leaders? It is hard to conceive of a plausible account of collective responsibility that could hold Soviet children responsible for the aggressive acts of Kremlin officials. Yet I must be able to distinguish between innocent Soviets and innocent third parties since I wish to hold that the latter are not placed in a state of nature by the aggressive actions of Soviet leaders. A reply to this objection requires further analysis of the nature of contractarian moral relations between individuals and groups.

Two individuals who find themselves in the contractarian circumstances of justice and who directly interact with one another are bound to one another by obligations of justice. This much is granted by all contractarian moral theories. What if the individuals are in the circumstances of justice yet do not directly interact with one another? Suppose two individuals, Ann and Boris, stand to benefit mutually from cooperative interaction yet do not interact directly because they live very far apart, Ann in the United States, Boris in the Soviet Union. Yet the two are in the circumstances of justice. While Ann and Boris do not stand to benefit mutually from direct cooperative interaction (until they directly interact), they do stand to benefit from indirect cooperative interaction as members of different societies.

Cooperative relations can be direct or indirect. Obligations of justice can thus bind individuals directly, as natural individuals, or indirectly, as members of a group. Ann and Boris each have obligations of the first sort to the individuals with which they directly interact, perhaps most members of their respective societies. They have only obligations of the second sort to one another. These latter obligations they have by virtue of their membership in societies that stand to benefit from cooperative interaction. Obligations of international justice thus bind individuals only as citizens of a society; obligations of individual justice bind natural individuals.

Suppose that cooperative relations between two countries break down due to a nuclear attack of one upon the other. Then Ann and Boris would find themselves in a Hobbesian state of nature with respect to one another. While it is possible that they could be able to return to civil society with greater ease than their aggressive leaders, nonetheless relations of justice no longer obtain between them.

Note, however, that if Boris were visiting Ann in the United States when his leaders launched an attack, then each would be bound by justice to one another as natural individuals, even though neither would be bound to one another as members of different societies. Ann, or any other American, would be bound by justice not to kill Boris, assuming that he is innocent in the relevant sense.

What distinguishes Soviet citizens from third parties is that we remain bound by justice to the latter even when our obligations to the former are dissolved. In the absence of aggressive behavior on their part, relations of justice continue between the United States and third party nations, thus rendering nuclear strikes against them morally impermissible.

I shall briefly note an implication of this reply to the objection just considered. If we remain bound by justice to uninvolved third parties, then the doctrine of double effect (which I accept) obligates us to minimize the adverse side effects of nuclear retaliation on third parties. Were a massive nuclear retaliation against the Soviet Union to destroy human life on the planet, then the fourth condition of the doctrine of double effect would prohibit it. Note, though, that our obligations, according to my account, would be to the third parties and not to the Soviet citizens. My argument thus places some moral restrictions on the nature of a permissible retaliatory strike against an enemy nuclear attack. Such retaliation could not directly kill innocent third parties.

I have sketched a contractarian account of the moral prohibition on the killing of the innocent. If my account should prove to be sound, then I shall have provided reason to believe that threatening massive slaughter of the innocent is not a morally prohibited response to an enemy nuclear threat. Insofar as such an account is necessary in order to justify nuclear deterrence, which is under attack from both the right and the left, then the argument may prove a useful contribution to current debates.[9]

QUESTIONS

1 Do you agree with Morris that utilitarianism as it applies to matters of conflict and war is too demanding insofar as it requires us to count the welfare of our enemy equally with our own?

2 If the leaders of one nation (A) refuse to abide by the principles of discrimination and proportionality in attacking another nation (B), is B then free of any obligation to abide by these principles in regard to everyone living in A?

3 What grounds, if any, could morally justify the nuclear holocaust resulting from all-out nuclear war?

SUGGESTED ADDITIONAL READINGS FOR CHAPTER 10

BLAKE, NIGEL and KAY POLE, eds.: *Objections to Nuclear Defence: Philosophers on Deterrence*. London: Routledge & Kegan Paul, 1984. The articles in this book focus on the morality of nuclear deterrence. They include " 'Better Dead than Red' " by Anthony Kenny. Kenny analyzes the various interpretations of the slogan "Better dead than red" and argues that a *nuclear* war against communism could never be just because waging such a war would require deserting precisely those values whose defense would be a justification for going to war.

COHEN, MARSHALL, THOMAS NAGEL, and THOMAS SCANLON, eds.: *War and Moral Responsibility*. Princeton, N.J.: Princeton University Press, 1974. The articles in this two-part volume are written by philosophers, lawyers, and political scientists. Part I examines

---

[9]This essay is essentially a simplified version of the position developed in "A Contractarian Defense of Nuclear Deterrence," *Ethics*, 95 (April 1985), pp. 479–496. Readers interested in the details of the position are referred to the *Ethics* version.

both the legal and ethical restrictions on military aims and methods. Part II deals with issues arising out of the Vietnam War and World War II.

Ethics, vol. 95, April 1985. This issue contains papers first given at a conference on ethics and nuclear deterrence at Aspen, Colorado in 1984. The authors include both philosophers and strategists. The introduction written by Russell Hardin and John J. Mearsheimer is especially useful in bringing out the differences between the approaches of the two groups.

FOX, MICHAEL ALLEN and LEO GROARKE, eds.: *Nuclear War: Philosophical Perspectives.* New York: Peter Lang Publishing, 1985. The majority of the articles in this collection were written for this volume. The book is divided into five sections: Nuclear Delusions, The Individual and the State, The Environment, Conceptual and Psychological Dilemmas, and the Pursuit of Peace. Each section contains both articles and commentaries on the articles.

HARDIN, RUSSELL: "Unilateral Versus Mutual Disarmament." *Philosophy and Public Affairs,* vol. 12, 1983, pp. 236–254. Hardin assesses Douglas Lackey's utilitarian analysis, rejects his contention that utilitarian morality recommends unilateral nuclear disarmament, and offers prudential arguments in support of mutual disarmament.

MACLEAN, DOUGLAS, ed.: *The Security Gamble: Deterrence Dilemmas in the Nuclear Age.* Totowa, N.J.: Rowman & Allanheld, 1984. The papers and responses in this collection were originally written for a conference on nuclear deterrence held at the University of Maryland in 1983. Two of the articles focus on the U.S. Catholic Bishops' position on nuclear deterrence. Several others, including David Gauthier's "Deterrence, Maximization, and Rationality," discuss the rationality of nuclear deterrence policies.

O'BRIEN, WILLIAM V.: "Just-War Doctrine in a Nuclear Context." *Theological Studies,* vol. 44, 1983, pp. 191–220. O'Brien offers his position as an alternative to that promulgated in the U.S. Catholic Bishops' letter. His analysis is based on a different assessment of both the relevant facts and just-war doctrine as it applies to nuclear deterrence, defense, and arms control.

Philosophy and Social Criticism, vol. 10, Winter 1984. This special issue is edited by William C. Gay and titled "Philosophy and the Debate on Nuclear Weapons Systems and Policies." Included are articles on the immorality of deterrence and the prospects and means for obtaining peace.

SHAW, WILLIAM H.: "Nuclear Deterrence and Deontology." *Ethics,* vol. 94, 1984, pp. 248–260. Shaw examines various critiques of nuclear deterrence policies and defends the moral legitimacy of nuclear deterrence.

CHAPTER 11

ANIMALS AND THE ENVIRONMENT

Humankind is not alone on this planet. We live among a multitude of animals, plants, and natural (inanimate) objects. Our interactions with these nonhuman forms of life and with the environment as a whole raise a number of moral problems. Some of the most prominent of these problems are explored in this chapter.

OUR TREATMENT OF ANIMALS

In a now well-known book, *Animal Liberation* (1975), Peter Singer forcefully calls attention to the suffering that humankind routinely inflicts on (nonhuman) animals.[1] For one thing, to ensure a steady supply of meat at our tables, we raise animals in such a way (the intensive rearing methods of "factory farming") that their short lives are dominated by pain and suffering. For another, to obtain scientific information whose value is often questionable, we devise experiments which entail the infliction of intense pain on animals, our experimental subjects. Because Singer finds humankind so willing to subordinate important animal interests to much less important human interests, he charges the human community with "speciesism." "Experimenting on animals, and eating their flesh, are perhaps the two major forms of speciesism in our society."[2]

Singer employs the term "speciesism" in order to emphasize similarities with racism and sexism. Just as black liberation entails the eradication of racism and women's liberation entails the eradication of sexism, animal liberation entails the eradication of speciesism. According to Singer,

---

[1]Peter Singer, *Animal Liberation* (New York: New York Review, 1975).
[2]Peter Singer, "All Animals are Equal," *Philosophic Exchange,* vol. 1 (Summer 1974), p. 111.

> The racist . . . [gives] greater weight to the interests of members of his own race, when
> there is a clash between their interests and the interests of another race. Similarly the speciest
> allows the interests of his own species to override the greater interests of members of other
> species.[3]

We share a common moral conviction that it is wrong to treat a human being "like a
guinea pig." In the face of Singer's attack on speciesism, we are encouraged to wonder
if it might be wrong to treat a guinea pig "like a guinea pig."

It seems clear that we do, by and large, treat animals as means to our own ends.
Is our underlying attitude toward animals justifiable? As soon as reflection begins on
this topic, the questions seem to multiply rapidly. What is the difference between
human life and animal life? To what extent, and on what grounds, is human life of
greater worth than animal life? Do animals have rights, perhaps even a right to life?
Are animal interests rightly accorded equal consideration with human interests, as
Singer believes? Or, perhaps, are animal interests rightly subordinated, at least to
some extent, to human interests? In one of this chapter's selections, Martin Benjamin
suggests that the difference between human beings and animals is essentially the
difference between beings who possess reflective consciousness (persons) and those
who possess only simple consciousness. Since he considers the former to have greater
worth than the latter, he believes that it is not wrong to attribute more weight to human
interests than animal interests. In his view, however, animal interests must not be
disregarded. They may not be sacrificed for the sake of "trivial (human) tastes or
desires," but they may be sacrificed in order to meet "important (human) needs."

Is the human interest in eating meat sufficiently important to justify our practice of
raising and slaughtering animals? Intertwined with this question is the issue of a
vegetarian diet. Advocates of vegetarianism offer diverse arguments to support their
position. Some advocate a vegetarian diet simply because they believe it to be superior
in terms of health benefits. If a vegetarian diet does offer special health advantages
(a controversial claim), then each individual, as a matter of personal prudence, would
be well advised to adopt it. Apart from this *prudential argument,* many vegetarians
advance *moral arguments* in defense of their diet. One common moral argument,
closely related to the considerations developed in Chapter 9, is based on the fact that
hunger, malnutrition, and starvation seriously threaten many people in our world. It
is morally indefensible, the argument goes, to waste desperately needed protein by
feeding our grain to animals whom we then eat. Eight pounds of protein in the form
of grain are necessary on the average to produce one pound of protein in the form of
meat. Since this process is so inefficient, we are morally obliged to adopt a vegetarian
diet so that our protein resources in the form of grain can be shared with those who
desperately need help. Though this particular moral argument is not without force, it
would seem that it does not establish a need for a completely vegetarian diet. It may
well be that world hunger could effectively be alleviated if people in affluent countries
simply consumed *less* meat.

The most important moral arguments advanced in defense of a vegetarian diet are
those which take account of the impact of meat production on the animals themselves.

[3]Ibid., p. 108.

Two lines of argument in this category may be distinguished. (1) Though it is not necessarily wrong to kill animals for food (assuming the killing is painless), it is morally indefensible to subject them to the cruelty of "factory farming." Since the meat available in our society is produced in just this way, we are morally obliged not to eat it. (2) It is morally wrong to kill animals for food, however painless the killing; animals, like human beings, have a right to life. In the opening selection of this chapter, James Rachels explicitly advances the first line of argument and is strongly inclined to accept the second as well.

THE ENVIRONMENT AND THE HUMAN COMMUNITY

We live now in a time not infrequently called the "age of ecology." There is an increasing awareness of and dissatisfaction with a number of tendencies in our society: (1) the tendency to produce material goods with little regard for the extent to which the by-products of industrial technology serve to pollute and degrade the environment; (2) the tendency to "develop" the land with little regard for the preservation of wilderness areas as well as endangered plant and animal species; (3) the tendency to exploit natural resources with little regard for conservation.

What moral obligations do we have with regard to the environment? In the rest of this section, we will consider only those moral obligations which are related to and predicated on human needs and interests. As will be made clear in the following section, however, it is a controversial matter whether an adequate "environmental ethic" can be predicated solely on a consideration of *human* interests.

The Duty Not to Pollute the Environment

It seems clear, by reference to human needs and interests, that we can make out a prima facie duty not to pollute the environment. That is, in the absence of overriding moral considerations, we are morally obliged not to pollute. Human welfare, in fact human life, crucially depends on such necessities as breathable air, drinkable water, and eatable food. Thus, in the absence of overriding moral considerations, pollution is morally unacceptable precisely because it is damaging to the public welfare. On an alternative construal, the prima facie duty not to pollute may be understood as based on a basic human right, the right to a livable environment. Still, however confident we are in positing a prima facie duty not to pollute, we are left with the problem of weighing the collective human interest in a nonpolluted environment against competing human interests, often economic in nature.

The following schematic example illustrates some of the complexities that confront us when environmental interests clash with economic interests. An industrial plant, representing a (small, large, massive) financial investment, producing a product that is (unessential, very desirable, essential) to society, and providing a (small, large, enormous) number of jobs, pollutes the environment in a (minor, substantial, major) way. In which of these several cases is the continued operation of the plant morally unacceptable? Certainly the general public interest in the quality of the environment must be recognized. But what of the economic interests of the owner, the employees, and potential consumers? In sum, how is the collective human interest in a nonpolluted environment to be equitably weighed against competing economic interests? At this point, many are inclined to appeal to the kind of cost/benefit analyses that are characteristic of utilitarian thinking.

The Duty to Preserve the Environment

If human interests provide a viable foundation for a moral obligation not to pollute, it may also be possible to recruit them in support of a more generalized moral obligation to preserve our natural environment. Ecology teaches us that human life is crucially intertwined with the ecosystem as a whole, yet ecologists frequently emphasize how little we actually know about the complicated multileveled interaction of life forms. If we destroy one part of the ecosystem, we may unwittingly trigger a chain of events that ultimately culminates in substantial detriment to human well-being. Hence, a serious regard for human welfare seems to necessitate our making every effort to preserve our natural environment.

The Duty to Preserve Endangered Species and Wilderness Areas

Are we morally obliged to preserve endangered animal and plant species? Are we morally obliged to preserve (at least some) wilderness areas? In many ways the continued existence of endangered species and wilderness areas brings enjoyment to or has utility for people. Hence, it can be argued, a moral obligation to preserve both endangered species and wilderness areas can be firmly based on the interests of the human community. In one of this chapter's selections, Joel Feinberg emphasizes the interests of future generations and argues that we have a duty to future generations to preserve endangered species.

Duties to Future Generations

In speaking of duties *to* future generations, we imply that future generations have rights which we are morally obligated to respect. Yet some philosophers contend that it does not make sense to speak of future generations as having rights: How can something that does not even exist have rights? Feinberg defends the view that it makes sense to speak of future generations as having rights. In providing such a defense, he enters on a difficult but enlightening analysis of the concept of a right. Along the way, he draws conclusions as to whether or not individual animals, individual plants, and whole species (of plants and animals) may be said to have rights. Such conclusions are relevant in assessing whether or not, with regard to environmental matters, we have moral obligations *to* nonhuman forms of life.

Both the presently existing generation and future generations, it would seem, have a serious interest in the minimization of pollution, the preservation of the environment in general, and the preservation of endangered species and wilderness areas in particular. With regard to the conservation of natural resources, however, our interests (i.e., those of the present generation) may very well conflict with those of posterity. Thus we find John Passmore in this chapter concerned with the following question: To what extent, if at all, do we have a duty to future generations to conserve natural resources?

Broadly speaking, two approaches to this important question may be distinguished.

1 Approaches Minimizing the Duty to Future Generations Here the optimistic argument is made that science and technology will develop to the point that future generations will easily find substitutes for natural resources that we find essential. At any rate, the needs of future generations are so uncertain and unforeseeable that we ought not to bother about conservation at all.

2 Approaches Maximizing the Duty to Future Generations Here it is contended that, despite inevitable uncertainties about the needs of future generations, we are relatively certain of some of these needs. At any rate, we must act responsibly on the facts as we see them. Thus it is our duty to future generations to conserve the planet's natural resources, to cut excess consumption, and to recycle as effectively as possible.

DO WE NEED A NONANTHROPOCENTRIC ETHIC?

Our morality can be called *anthropocentric* in that we ordinarily presume that moral obligation is essentially a function of *human* interests. In recent years, however, it has frequently been suggested that an anthropocentric morality cannot provide an adequate foundation for an understanding of our moral obligations with regard to the environment. In this spirit, we have heard proposals for the development of a "new ethic," an "ecological ethic," an "environmental ethic." The extension of moral consideration to the nonhuman community is the thread that links all such proposals. Aldo Leopold (1887–1948), whose essay "The Land Ethic" has encouraged many to take seriously the possibility of developing a nonanthropocentric ethic, writes:

> The land ethic simply enlarges the boundaries of the community to include soils, waters, plants, and animals, or collectively, the land. . . . In short, a land ethic changes the role of *Homo sapiens* from conqueror of the land-community to plain member and citizen of it. It implies respect for his fellow-members, and also respect for the community as such. . . . A thing is right when it tends to preserve the integrity, stability, and beauty of the biotic community. It is wrong when it tends otherwise.[4]

In one of this chapter's selections, William Godfrey-Smith considers the value of wilderness. He maintains that wilderness has substantial *instrumental* value (for humankind) but insists that it has *intrinsic* value as well. In the spirit of Leopold, Godfrey-Smith calls for the development of a nonanthropocentic ethic and briefly explores its possibilities.

Thomas A. Mappes

[4]Aldo Leopold, "The Land Ethic," in *A Sand County Almanac* (New York: Oxford University Press, 1966), pp. 219, 220, 240.

Vegetarianism

James Rachels

A biographical sketch of James Rachels is found on page 60.

The primary reason why cruelty to animals is wrong, Rachels argues, is that
tortured animals *suffer,* just as tortured humans suffer. Inflicting pain on animals
can sometimes be justified, he maintains, but we must have a sufficiently good
reason for doing so. The fact that we enjoy the way meat tastes is a reason that
"will not even come close to justifying the cruelty" that is part and parcel of
contemporary meat production. Moreover, he contends, since humanely produced
meat would be prohibitively expensive for most of us, a vegetarian diet is, for all
practical purposes, a moral demand. Rachels considers the theoretical possibility of
obtaining meat by painlessly killing humanely raised animals. In his view, even
this option is morally problematic. Reluctant to dismiss the view that animals have
a "right to life," he insists that we must abandon "the Kantian attitude that animals
are nothing more than things to be used for our purposes."

. . . One of my conclusions will be that it is morally wrong for us to eat meat. Many
readers will find this implausible and even faintly ridiculous, as I once did. After all,
meat eating is a normal, well-established part of our daily routines; people have always
eaten meat; and many find it difficult even to conceive of what an alternate diet would
be like. So it is not easy to take seriously the possibility that it might be wrong.
Moreover, vegetarianism is commonly associated with Eastern religions whose tenets
we do not accept, and with extravagant, unfounded claims about health. A quick
perusal of vegetarian literature might confirm the impression that it is all a crackpot
business: tracts have titles like "Victory Through Vegetables" and promise that if one
will only keep to a meatless diet one will have perfect health and be filled with wisdom.
Of course we can ignore this kind of nonsense. However, there are other arguments
for vegetarianism that must be taken seriously. . . .

I

The wrongness of cruelty to animals is often explained in terms of its effects on human
beings. The idea seems to be that the animals' interests are not *themselves* morally
important or worthy of protection, but, since cruelty to animals often has bad consequences for *humans,* it is wrong to make animals suffer. In legal writing, for example,
cruelty to animals is included among the "victimless crimes," and the problem of
justifying legal prohibitions is seen as comparable to justifying the prohibition of other
behavior, such as homosexuality or the distribution of pornography, where no one (no

Reprinted with permission of the author from "Vegetarianism and 'The Other Weight Problem'," in
World Hunger and Moral Obligation, edited by William Aiken and Hugh LaFollette (Englewood Cliffs,
N.J.: Prentice-Hall, 1977), pp. 180–193. Copyright © by James Rachels.

human) is obviously hurt. Thus, Louis Schwartz says that, in prohibiting the torturing of animals:

> It is not the mistreated dog who is the ultimate object of concern. . . . Our concern is for the feelings of other human beings, a large proportion of whom, although accustomed to the slaughter of animals for food, readily identify themselves with a tortured dog or horse and respond with great sensitivity to its sufferings.[1]

Philosophers also adopt this attitude. Kant, for example, held that we have no direct duties to nonhuman animals. "The Categorical Imperative," the ultimate principle of morality, applies only to our dealings with humans:

> The practical imperative, therefore, is the following: Act so that you treat humanity, whether in your own person or in that of another, always as an end and never as a means only.[2]

And of other animals, Kant says:

> But so far as animals are concerned, we have no direct duties. Animals are not self-conscious, and are there merely as means to an end. That end is man.[3]

He adds that we should not be cruel to animals only because "He who is cruel to animals becomes hard also in his dealings with men."[4]

Surely this is unacceptable. Cruelty to animals ought to be opposed, not only because of the ancillary effects on humans, but because of the direct effects on the animals themselves. Animals that are tortured *suffer,* just as tortured humans suffer, and *that* is the primary reason why it is wrong. We object to torturing humans on a number of grounds, but the main one is that the victims suffer so. Insofar as nonhuman animals also suffer, we have the *same* reason to oppose torturing them, and it is indefensible to take the one suffering but not the other as grounds for objection.

Although cruelty to animals is wrong, it does not follow that we are never justified in inflicting pain on an animal. Sometimes we are justified in doing this, just as we are sometimes justified in inflicting pain on humans. It does follow, however, that there must be a *good reason* for causing the suffering, and if the suffering is great, the justyfing reason must be correspondingly powerful. As an example, consider the treatment of the civet cat, a highly intelligent and sociable animal. Civet cats are trapped and placed in small cages inside darkened sheds, where the temperature is kept up to 110°F by fires.[5] They are confined in this way until they finally die. What justifies this extraordinary mistreatment? These animals have the misfortune to produce a substance that is useful in the manufacture of perfume. Musk, which is scraped

---

[1]Louis B. Schwartz, "Morals Offenses and the Model Penal Code," *Columbia Law Review,* 63 (1963); reprinted in Joel Feinberg and Hyman Gross, eds., *Philosophy of Law* (Encino, Calif.: Dickenson Publishing Company, Inc., 1975), p. 156.

[2]Immanuel Kant, *Foundations of the Metaphysics of Morals,* trans. Lewis White Beck (Indianapolis: The Bobbs-Merrill Co., Inc., 1959), p. 47.

[3]Immanual Kant, *Lectures on Ethics,* trans. Louis Infield (New York: Harper Torchbooks, 1963), p. 239.

[4]Ibid., p. 240.

[5]Muriel the Lady Dowding, "Furs and Cosmetics: Too High a Price?" in Stanley and Rosling Godlovitch and John Harris, eds., *Animals, Men and Morals* (New York: Taplinger Publishing Co., Inc., 1972), p. 36.

from their genitals once a day for as long as they can survive, makes the scent of perfume last a bit longer after each application. (The heat increases their "production" of musk.) Here Kant's rule—"Animals are merely means to an end; that end is man"—is applied with a vengeance. To promote one of the most trivial interests we have, thousands of animals are tormented for their whole lives.

It is usually easy to persuade people that this use of animals is not justified, and that we have a moral duty not to support such cruelties by consuming their products. The argument is simple: Causing suffering is not justified unless there is a good reason; the production of perfume made with musk causes considerable suffering; our enjoyment of this product is not a good enough reason to justify causing that suffering; therefore, the use of animals in this way is wrong. At least my experience has been that, once people learn the facts about musk production, they come to regard using such products as morally objectionable. They are surprised to discover, however, that an exactly analogous argument can be given in connection with the use of animals as food. Animals that are raised and slaughtered for food also suffer, and our enjoyment of the way they taste is not a sufficient justification for mistreating them.

Most people radically underestimate the amount of suffering that is caused to animals who are raised and slaughtered for food.[6] They think, in a vague way, that slaughterhouses are cruel, and perhaps even that methods of slaughter ought to be made more humane. But after all, the visit to the slaughterhouse is a relatively brief episode in the animal's life; and beyond that, people imagine that the animals are treated well enough. Nothing could be further from the truth. Today the production of meat is Big Business, and the helpless animals are treated more as machines in a factory than as living creatures.

Veal calves, for example, spend their lives in pens too small to allow them to turn around or even to lie down comfortably—exercise toughens the muscles, which reduces the "quality" of the meat, and besides, allowing the animals adequate living space would be prohibitively expensive. In these pens the calves cannot perform such basic actions as grooming thmselves, which they naturally desire to do, because there is not room for them to twist their heads around. It is clear that the calves miss their mothers, and like human infants they want something to suck: they can be seen trying vainly to suck the sides of their stalls. In order to keep their meat pale and tasty, they are fed a liquid diet deficient in both iron and roughage. Naturally they develop cravings for these things, because they need them. The calf's craving for iron is so strong that, if it is allowed to turn around, it will lick at its own urine, although calves normally find this repugnant. The tiny stall, which prevents the animal from turning, solves this "problem." The craving for roughage is especially strong since without it the animal cannot form a cud to chew. It cannot be given any straw for bedding, since the animal would be driven to eat it, and that would spoil the meat. For these animals the slaughterhouse is not an unpleasant end to an otherwise contented life. As terrifying

[6]By far the best account of these cruelties is to be found in Chapter 3 of Peter Singer's *Animal Liberation* (New York: New York Review of Books, 1975). I have drawn on Singer's work for the factual material in the following two paragraphs. *Animal Liberation* should be consulted for a thorough treatment of matters to which I can refer here only sketchily.

as the process of slaughter is, for them it may actually be regarded as a merciful release.

Similar stories can be told about the treatment of other animals on which we dine. In order to "produce" animals by the millions, it is necessary to keep them crowded together in small spaces. Chickens are commonly kept eight or ten to a space smaller than a newspaper page. Unable to walk around or even stretch their wings—much less build a nest—the birds become vicious and attack one another. The problem is sometimes exacerbated because the birds are so crowded that, unable to move, their feet literally grow around the wire floors of the cages anchoring them to the spot. An "anchored" bird cannot escape attack no matter how desperate it becomes. Mutilation of the animals is an efficient solution. To minimize the damage they can do to one another, the birds' beaks are cut off. The mutilation is painful, but probably not as painful as other sorts of mutilations that are routinely practiced. Cows are castrated, not to prevent the unnatural "vices" to which overcrowded chickens are prone, but because castrated cows put on more weight, and there is less danger of meat being "tainted" by male hormones.

> In Britain an anesthetic must be used, unless the animal is very young, but in America anesthetics are not in general use. The procedure is to pin the animal down, take a knife and slit the scrotum, exposing the testicles. You then grab each testicle in turn and pull on it, breaking the cord that attaches it; on older animals it may be necessary to cut the cord.[7]

It must be emphasized that the treatment I am describing—and I have hardly scratched the surface here—is not out of the ordinary. It is typical of the way that animals raised for food are treated, now that meat production is Big Business. As Peter Singer puts it, these are the sorts of things that happened to your dinner when it was still an animal.

What accounts for such cruelties? As for the meat producers, there is no reason to think they are unusually cruel men. They simply accept the common attitude expressed by Kant: "Animals are merely means to an end; that end is man." The cruel practices are adopted not because they are cruel but because they are efficient, given that one's only concern is to produce meat (and eggs) for humans as cheaply as possible. But clearly this use of animals is immoral if anything is. Since we can nourish ourselves very well without eating them, our *only reason* for doing all this to the animals is our enjoyment of the way they taste. And this will not even come close to justifying the cruelty.

II

Does this mean that we should stop eating meat? Such a conclusion will be hard for many people to accept. It is tempting to say: "What is objectionable is not *eating* the animals, but only making them suffer. Perhaps we ought to protest the way they are treated, and even work for better treatment of them. But it doesn't follow that we must stop eating them." This sounds plausible until you realize that it would be

---

[7]Singer, *Animal Liberation,* p. 152.

impossible to treat the animals decently and still produce meat in sufficient quantities to make it a normal part of our diets. As I have already remarked, cruel methods are used in the meat-production industry because such methods are economical; they enable the producers to market a product that people can afford. Humanely produced chicken, beef, and pork would be so expensive that only the very rich could afford them. (*Some* of the cruelties could be eliminated without too much expense—the cows could be given an anesthetic before castration, for example, even though this alone would mean a slight increase in the cost of beef. But others, such as overcrowding, could not be eliminated without really prohibitive cost.) So to work for better treatments for the animals would be to work for a situation in which most of us would *have* to adopt a vegetarian diet.

Still, there remains the interesting theoretical question: *If* meat could be produced humanely, without mistreating the animals prior to killing them painlessly, would there be anything wrong with it? The question is only of theoretical interest because the actual choice we face in the supermarket is whether to buy the remains of animals that are *not* treated humanely. Still, the question has some interest, and I want to make two comments about it.

First, it is a vexing issue whether animals have a "right to life" that is violated when we kill them for trivial purposes; but we should not simply assume until proven otherwise that they *don't* have such a right.[8] We assume that humans have a right to life—it would be wrong to murder a normal, healthy human even if it were done painlessly—and it is hard to think of any plausible rationale for granting this right to humans that does not also apply to other animals. Other animals live in communities, as do humans; they communicate with one another, and have ongoing social relationships, killing them disrupts lives that are perhaps not as complex, emotionally and intellectually, as our own, but that are nevertheless quite complicated. They suffer, and are capable of happiness as well as fear and distress, as we are. So what could be the rational basis for saying that we have a right to life, but that they don't? Or even more pointedly, what could be the rational basis for saying that a severely retarded human, who is inferior in every important respect to an intelligent animal, has a right to life but that the animal doesn't? Philosophers often treat such questions as "puzzles," assuming that there must be answers even if we are not clever enough to find them. I am suggesting that, on the contrary, there may not be any acceptable answers to these questions. If it seems, intuitively, that there *must* be some difference between us and the other animals which confers on us, but not them, a right to life, perhaps this intuition is mistaken. At the very least, the difficulty of answering such questions should make us hesitant about asserting that it is all right to kill animals, as long as we don't make them suffer, unless we are also willing to take seriously the possibility that it is all right to kill people, so long as we don't make them suffer.

---

[8]It is controversial among philosophers whether animals can have any rights at all. See various essays collected in Part IV of Tom Regan and Peter Singer, eds., *Animal Rights and Human Obligations* (Englewood Cliffs, N.J.: Prentice-Hall, 1976). My own defense of animal rights is given in "Do Animals Have a Right to Liberty?" pp. 205–223, and in "A Reply to VanDeVeer," pp. 230–32.

Second, it is important to see the slaughter of animals for food as part of a larger pattern that characterizes our whole relationship with the nonhuman world. Animals are wrenched from their natural homes to be made objects of our entertainment in zoos, circuses, and rodeos. They are used in laboratories, not only for experiments that are themselves morally questionable,[9] but also in testing everything from shampoo to chemical weapons. They are killed so that their heads can be used as wall decorations, or their skins as ornamental clothing or rugs. Indeed, simply killing them for the fun of it is thought to be "sport."[10] This pattern of cruel exploitation flows naturally from the Kantian attitude that animals are nothing more than things to be used for our purposes. It is this whole attitude that must be opposed, and not merely its manifestation in our willingness to hurt the animals we eat. Once one rejects this attitude, and no longer regards the animals as disposable at one's whim, one ceases to think it all right to kill them, even painlessly, just for a snack.

But now let me return to the more immediate practical issue. The meat at the supermarket was not produced by humane methods. The animals whose flesh this meat once was were abused in ways similar to the ones I have described. Millions of other animals are being treated in these ways now, and their flesh will soon appear in the markets. Should one support such practices by purchasing and consuming its products?

It is discouraging to realize that no animals will actually be helped simply by one person ceasing to eat meat. One consumer's behavior, by itself, cannot have a noticeable impact on an industry as vast as the meat business. However, it is important to see one's behavior in a wider context. There are already millions of vegetarians, and because they don't eat meat there *is* less cruelty than there otherwise would be. The question is whether one ought to side with that group, or with the carnivores whose practices cause the suffering. Compare the position of someone thinking about whether to buy slaves in the year 1820. He might reason as follows: "The whole practice of slavery is immoral, but I cannot help any of the poor slaves by keeping clear of it. If I don't buy these slaves, someone else will. One person's decision just can't by itself have any impact on such a vast business. So I may as well use slaves like everyone else." The first thing we notice is that this fellow was too pessimistic about the possibilities of a successful movement; but beyond that, there is something else wrong with his reasoning. If one really thinks that a social practice is immoral, that *in itself* is sufficient grounds for a refusal to participate. In 1848 Thoreau remarked that even if someone did not want to devote himself to the abolition movement, and actively oppose slavery, ". . . it is his duty, at least, to wash his hands of it, and, if he gives it no thought longer, not to give it practically his support."[11] In the case of slavery, this seems clear. If it seems less clear in the case of the cruel exploitation of nonhuman animals, perhaps it is because the Kantian attitude is so deeply entrenched in us. . . .

---

[9]See Singer, *Animal Liberation,* Chap. 2.

[10]It is sometimes said, in defense of "non-slob" hunting: "Killing for pleasure is wrong, but killing for food is all right." This won't do, since for those of us who are able to nourish ourselves without killing animals, killing them for food *is* a form of killing for pleasure, namely, the pleasures of the palate.

[11]Henry David Thoreau, *Civil Disobedience* (1848).

QUESTIONS

1 Are we morally obligated to adopt a vegetarian diet?
2 Do animals have a right to life?
3 Is hunting a morally justifiable practice?

Ethics and Animal Consciousness

Martin Benjamin

*Martin Benjamin is professor of philosophy at Michigan State University. He is especially
interested in the application of philosophical analysis and theory to questions of social policy.
He is the coauthor of* Ethics and Nursing *(1981) and the author of such articles as* "Pacifism
for Pragmatists," "Moral Agency and Negative Acts in Medicine," *and* "Can Moral Responsibility be Collective and Non-Distributive?"

Benjamin focuses attention on three historically important philosophical positions
regarding the "nature and extent of ethical restrictions on the human use and
treatment of nonhuman animals"—"indirect obligation" theories, "no obligation"
theories, and "direct obligation" theories. Rejecting each of these positions as
inadequate, he nevertheless identifies in each a "kernel of truth" which he
incorporates into a fourth position. According to this alternative position, it is
important to distinguish beings possessing reflective-consciousness from those
possessing only simple consciousness. The former (identified as persons) may
justifiably be thought to have a higher status or greater worth than the latter. By
virtue of the higher status or greater worth of persons, their important needs (but
not their "trivial tastes or desires") are considered sufficient to justify the infliction
of pain and suffering on beings possessing only simple consciousness.

INTRODUCTION

Are there any ethical restrictions on the ways in which human beings may use and
treat nonhuman animals? If so, what are they and how are they to be justified? In what
follows, I will first review three standard responses to these questions and briefly
indicate why none of them is entirely satisfactory. Next I will identify what I take to
be the kernel of truth in each of the three responses and then I will attempt to blend
them into a fourth, more adequate, position. In so doing, I hope to suggest the
importance, from an ethical point of view, of further inquiry into the nature and extent
of consciousness in nonhuman animals.

THREE STANDARD POSITIONS

Historically, Western philosophers have responded to questions about the nature and extent of ethical restrictions on the human use and treatment of nonhuman animals in three ways. First, those who hold what I label "Indirect Obligation" theories maintain that ethical restrictions on the use and treatment of animals can be justified *only* if they can be derived from direct obligations to human beings. The second type of response, which I label "No Obligation" theories, holds that there are no restrictions whatever on what humans may do to other animals. And the third type of response, which I label "Direct Obligation" theories, maintains that ethical restrictions on the use and treatment of animals can sometimes be justified solely for the sake of animals themselves. I will now elaborate each of these positions.

1 Indirect Obligation

Among the most noted philosophers in the Western tradition, St. Thomas Aquinas (1225–1274) and Immanuel Kant (1724–1804) have acknowledged restrictions on human conduct with regard to the use and treatment of nonhuman animals, but these restrictions are, in their view, ultimately grounded upon obligations to other human beings. Blending views that can be traced both to the Bible and Aristotle, Aquinas held a hierarchial or means-end view of the relationship between plants, animals, and humans, respectively:

> There is no sin in using a thing for the purpose for which it is. Now the order of things is such that the imperfect are for the perfect . . . things, like plants which merely have life, are all alike for animals, and all animals are for man. Wherefore it is not unlawful if men use plants for the good of animals, and animals for the good of man, as the Philosopher states (*Politics,* i, 3).
>
> Now the most necessary use would seem to consist in the fact that animals use plants, and men use animals, for food, and this cannot be done unless these be deprived of life, wherefore it is lawful both to take life fron plants for the use of animals, and from animals for the use of men. In fact this is in keeping with the commandment of God himself (*Genesis,* i, 29, 30 and *Genesis* ix, 3).[1]

Nevertheless, it does not follow, for Aquinas, that one can do anything to an animal. For example, one is still prohibited from killing another person's ox: "He that kills another's ox, sins, not through killing the ox, but through injuring another man in his property. Wherefore this is not a species of the sin of murder but of the sin of theft or robbery." And there may even be similarly *indirect* grounds for not harming animals who are no one's property. Thus, Aquinas explains,

> if any passages of Holy Writ seem to forbid us to be cruel to dumb animals, for instance to kill a bird with its young: this is either to remove man's thoughts from being cruel to other

---

[1]St. Thomas Aquinas, *Summa Theologica,* literally translated by the English Dominican Fathers (Benziger Brothers, 1918), Part II, Question 64, Article 1. Reprinted in Tom Regan and Peter Singer, eds., *Animals Rights and Human Obligations* (Prentice-Hall, 1976), p. 119.

men, and lest through being cruel to animals one become cruel to human beings; or because injury to an animal leads to the temporal hurt of man, either of the doer of the deed, or of another.[2]

Kant, too, held that insofar as humans are obligated to restrain themselves in their dealings with animals, it is due to their obligations to other humans. Thus,

> so far as animals are concerned, we have no direct duties. Animals are not self-conscious and are there merely as a means to an end. That end is man. . . . Our duties towards animals are merely indirect duties towards humanity. Animal nature has analogies to human nature, and by doing our duties to animals in respect of manifestations of human nature, we indirectly do our duty to humanity. . . . If . . . any acts of animals are analogous to human acts and spring from the same principles, we have duties towards the animals because thus we cultivate the same duties towards human beings. If a man shoots his dog because the animal is no longer capable of service, he does not fail in his duty to the dog, for the dog cannot judge, but his act is inhuman and damages in itself that humanity which it is his duty to show towards mankind. If he is not to stifle his human feelings, he must practice kindness towards animals, for he who is cruel to animals becomes hard also in his dealings with men.[3]

Thus Aquinas and Kant both hold what I have labeled "Indirect Obligation" theories with regard to ethical restrictions on the use and treatment of animals. Although they agree that we have obligations *with* regard to animals, these obligations are *not,* at bottom, *owed to* the animals themselves but rather they are owed to other human beings.

There are, nonetheless, significant problems with Aquinas's and Kant's positions, at least in their present forms. First, insofar as Aquinas assumes that it is necessary for humans to use animals for food and thus to deprive them of life, his position must be reconsidered in the light of modern knowledge about nutrition. It has been maintained, for example, that a perfectly nutritious diet may require little or no deprivation of animal life and, even if it does, that the average American consumes twice as much animal protein as his or her body can possibly use.[4] Insofar as we continue to consume large quantities of animal foodstuff requiring pain and the deprivation of life, then, we do so, not so much to serve vital nutritional demands, but rather to indulge our acquired tastes. Secondly, insofar as Aquinas's view is based upon a hierarchial worldview and assumes that those lower in the order or less perfect are to serve the good of those higher or more perfect, it is open to a serious theoretical objection. It is, unfortunately, not difficult to imagine a group of beings—perhaps from another part of the universe—who are more rational and more powerful than we. Assuming that such beings are more perfect than we are, it seems to follow, if we adopt the principles underlying Aquinas's view, that we ought to acquiesce in their using us for whichever of their purposes they fancy we would serve. But do we want to agree with the rightness of this? And if we take Aquinas's view, would we have any grounds on which to disagree?

[2]St. Thomas Aquinas, *Summa Contra Gentiles,* literally translated by the English Dominican Fathers (Benziger Brothers, 1928), Third Book, Part II, Chap. CXII. Reprinted in Regan and Singer, p. 59.

[3]Immanual Kant, "Duties to Animals and Spirits," in *Lectures on Ethics,* translated by Louis Infield (Harper and Row, 1963). Reprinted in Regan and Singer, p. 122.

[4]Francis Moore Lappé, "Fantasies of Famine," *Harper's,* 250 (February 1975), p. 53.

As for Kant's view, the main difficulties have to do first with his emphasis on self-consciousness as a condition for being the object of a direct obligation, and second with his assumption that all and only human beings are self-conscious. I will postpone consideration of the first difficulty until later. For the moment, let me simply develop the second. Even supposing that being self-conscious is a necessary condition for being the object of a direct obligation, it does not follow either that *all* human beings are the objects of direct obligations or that *no* animal can be the object of such an obligation. First, advances in medical knowledge, techniques, and technology have, among other things, preserved and prolonged the lives of a number of human beings who are severely retarded or otherwise mentally impaired due to illness or accident and the irreversibly comatose (e.g., Karen Ann Quinlan). In our day, then, if not in Kant's, one cannot assume that all human beings are self-conscious. Second, some contemporary researchers have suggested that at least some nonhuman animals have a capacity for becoming self-conscious that has, until recently, been undetected or ignored by humans. Thus, even if we follow Kant and accept self-consciousness as a condition for being the object of direct obligations, it does not follow that *all* and *only* humans satisfy this condition. Some humans, it may turn out, will not be the objects of direct obligations and some animals will.

2 No Obligation

If animals are not conscious—that is, if they are not sentient and have no capacity for pleasure, pain, or any other mental states—they may not even be the objects of indirect obligations. Insofar as Aquinas says that it is possible to be "cruel to dumb animals" and Kant says that "he who is cruel to animals becomes hard in his dealings with men," each presupposes that animals, unlike plants and machines, are sentient and are therefore capable of sensation and consciousness. Thus it is surprising to find René Descartes (1596–1650), a renowned philosopher, mathematician, and scientist, comparing animals to machines. Nonetheless, this is just what he did in his influential *Discourse on Method* when he compared machines made by the hand of man with human and nonhuman animal bodies made by the hand of God: "From this aspect the body is regarded as a machine which, having been made by the hands of God, is incomparably better arranged, and possesses in itself movements which are much more admirable than any of those which can be invented by man."[5] Living *human* bodies were, for Descartes, distinguished from living *animal* bodies by the presence of an immortal soul which was a necessary condition for mental experiences. Without a soul, a living biological body was a natural automation, "much more splendid," but in kind no different from those produced by humans.

For Descartes, the criterion for distinguishing those living bodies which were ensouled from those which were not was the capacity to use language. The former, he believed, included all and only human beings. Among humans, he maintained,

---

[5]René Descartes, *Discourse on Method*, in *Philosophical Works of Descartes*, translated by E. S. Haldane and G. R. T. Ross (Cambridge University Press), Vol. I. Reprinted in Regan and Singer, p. 61.

there are none so depraved and stupid, without even exempting idiots, that they cannot arrange different words together, forming of them a statement by which they make known their thoughts; while on the other hand, there is no other animal, however perfect and fortunately circumstanced it may be, which can do the same.[6]

Insofar as nonhuman animals do appear to do some things better than we do, Descartes added, "it is nature which acts in them according to the disposition of their organs, just as a clock, which is only composed of wheels and weights is able to tell the hours and measure the time more correctly than we can do with all our wisdom."[7] As for the ethical implications of his view, Descartes, in a letter to Henry More, noted that his "opinion is not so much cruel to animals as indulgent to men . . . since it absolves them from the suspicion of crime when they eat or kill animals."[8]

Insofar as Descartes's position presupposes that all and only human beings have the capacity to use language, it is open to the same sort of criticisms and objections that we raised against Kant. That is, advances in medicine are providing more non-linguistic humans and advances in science are suggesting that at least some nonhuman animals have more linguistic facility or capacity than we previously supposed. More-over, even if Descartes were correct in believing that the capacity to use language is uniquely human, why should this, rather than the capacity to feel pain and experience distress, be the principal criterion for determining the nature and extent of ethical restrictions on the use and treatment of animals? It is this objection which sets the stage for positions which hold that humans have direct obligations to at least some animals.

3 Direct Obligation

Jeremy Bentham (1748–1832), the father of modern utilitarianism, held that pain and pleasure were what governed behavior and that any ethical system which was founded on anything but maximizing the net balance of pleasure over pain, dealt in "sounds instead of sense, in caprice instead of reason, in darkness instead of light." Every action, for Bentham was to be assessed in terms of its likelihood of maximizing the net balance of happiness. But, he noted, if the capacity to experience pleasure and pain was what qualified one to be taken into account in estimating the effects of various courses of action, then nonhuman as well as human animals would have to be taken into account insofar as they, too, had the capacity to experience pleasure and pain. Thus, for Bentham, it is sentience, or the capacity for pleasure and pain, that determines whether a being qualifies for moral consideration.

> What else is it that should trace the insuperable line? Is it the faculty of reason, or perhaps the faculty of discourse? But a full-grown horse or dog is beyond comparison a more rational, as well as a more conversable animal than an infant of a day or a week or even a month

---

[6]*Ibid.*

[7]*Ibid*, p. 62.

[8]René Descartes, Letter to Henry More, in *Descartes: Philosophical Letters,* translated and edited by Anthony Kenny (Oxford University Press, 1970). Reprinted in Regan and Singer, p. 66.

old. But suppose they were otherwise, what would it avail? The question is not, Can they *reason* nor Can they *talk?* but, *Can they suffer?*[9]

The question now is, what grounds do we have to believe that animals *can* suffer, can feel pain, or can experience distress? If a being lacks the capacity to convey his suffering, pain, or distress linguistically how do we know that it actually has such experiences and isn't a rather splendid automaton going through the motions?

In response to such skepticism, one holding a utilitarian direct obligation theory must show why he or she believes that nonhuman animals are conscious. There are a number of ways one might go about this. First, one could stress behavioral similarities between human and nonhuman animals in their respective responses to certain standard pain- and pleasure-producing stimuli. Comparing the behavior of nonhuman animals with human infants would be especially forceful here. Second, we could stress relevant neurophysiological similarities between humans and nonhumans. After making these comparisons we may then be inclined to agree with Richard Sergeant when he claims that:

> Every particle of factual evidence supports the contention that the higher mammalian vertebrates experience pain sensations at least as acute as our own. To say that they feel less because they are lower animals is an absurdity; it can easily be shown that many of their senses are far more acute than ours—visual acuity in certain birds, hearing in most wild animals, and touch in others; these animals depend more than we do on the sharpest possible awareness of a hostile environment.[10]

So, if Sergeant is correct in this, at least some animals are conscious and hence, on utilitarian grounds, qualify as the objects of direct obligation.

There are, nonetheless, significant limitations to this view. First, although utilitarianism takes nonhuman animals directly into account in determining ethical obligations, there is no guarantee that animals will, in fact, fare better on this view than they will on an Indirect Obligation view like that of Aquinas or Kant. Contemporary animal welfare advocates who find utilitarianism hospitable to their position have not fully appreciated utilitarianism's indifference to any outcome apart from the maximization of happiness. Thus, for example, on utilitarian grounds, a policy which causes a great amount of pain to animals which also causes an even greater amount of offsetting pleasure to humans, would appear to be ethically justified. Second, one who adopts utilitarianism because it takes direct account of animal suffering, must recognize all of its implications. One of the standard objections to utilitarianism is that it seems, on the face of it, more suited to animals than it is to human beings. Thus Bentham's version was initially caricatured as philosophy for swine because it seemed to imply that it was better to be a satisfied pig than a dissatisfied human; or better to be a fool satisfied than Socrates dissatisfied.

---

[9]Jeremy Bentham, *The Principles of Morals and Legislation* (1789), Chapter XVII, Section 1. Reprinted in Regan and Singer, p. 129.

[10]Richard Sergeant, *The Spectrum of Pain* (London, Hart-Davis, 1969), p. 72. Cited by Peter Singer in Tom Regan, ed., *Matters of Life and Death* (Random House, 1980), p. 225.

A FOURTH POSITION

Although none of the positions we have examined is entirely satisfactory, each, I believe, has something to recommend it. *Indirect Obligation* theories are correct to stress the difference between what I will call "simple consciousness" and "reflective-consciousness," but they have not adequately characterized the difference nor have they fully appreciated its ethical significance. *No Obligation* theories, at least that of Descartes, are correct in emphasizing the relationship between the use of language and the development of reflective-consciousness. And, finally, *Direct Obligation* theories are correct in noting that the possession of simple consciousness (or sentience) in human or nonhuman animals is, by itself, sufficient to give them independent standing in the ethical deliberations of beings who are reflectively-conscious. I will now, very briefly, outline each of these fundamental insights and suggest how they may be integrated into a fourth, more adequate position.

The fundamental insight of *Indirect Obligation* theories is their recognition of a difference between simple and reflective consciousness. Beings having only simple consciousness can experience pain, have desires, and make choices. But they are not capable of reflecting upon their experiences, desires, and choices and altering their behavior as a result of such self-conscious evaluation and deliberation. Beings who can do this I will, following John Locke (1632–1704), label "persons." A person, in Locke's view, is "A thinking intelligent being that has reason and reflection and can consider itself as itself, the same thinking thing, in different times and places."[11] Although they were mistaken in believing that the class of persons fully coincided with the class of human beings, *Indirect Obligation* theorists were correct to emphasize the special status of persons. For only persons are capable of tracing the consequences and implications of various courses of action and then deliberating and deciding to embark on one rather than another on grounds other than self-interest. To do this is part of what it means to have a morality, and it is the capacity for taking the moral point of view (that is, voluntarily restricting one's appetite or desires for the sake of others) that gives the persons their special worth.

The fundamental insight of Descartes's *No Obligation* theory was to recognize the connection between the development and exercise of personhood and the development and exercise of language. As Stuart Hampshire has recently pointed out, although people often associate the use of language primarily with communication, "language's more distinctive and far-reaching power is to bring possibilities before the mind. Culture has its principal source in the use of the word 'if,' in counterfactual speculation."[12] Only language, then, gives us the power to entertain complex unrealized possibilities. "The other principal gift of language to culture," Hampshire continues, "is the power to date, and hence to make arrangements for tomorrow and to regret yesterday."[13] Thus a being cannot become a person and, in Locke's words, "consider itself as itself, the same thinking thing, in different times and places," without the use of language.

[11]John Locke, *Essay Concerning Human Understanding*, ed. by John Yolton (J. M. Dent & Sons, 1961), Vol. One, Book II, Ch. XXVII, p. 281.
[12]Stuart Hampshire, *"Human Nature,"* New York Review of Books, XXVI (December 6, 1979), Special Supplement, p. d.
[13]*Ibid.*

Finally, the fundamental insight of *Direct Obligation* theories was to note that one needn't be a person to be the object of a moral obligation. Simple consciousness or sentience is sufficient to entitle a being to be considered *for its own sake* in the ethical deliberations of persons. If, for example, the capacity to feel pain is sufficient ground for a *prima facie* obligation not to cause gratuitous pain to persons, why is it not also a sufficient ground for a similar obligation not to cause pain to beings having simple consciousness? With regard to the evil of avoidable and unjustifiable pain, the question is, as Bentham emphasized, not "Can they reason nor Can they talk? but, Can they suffer?"

Putting all of this together, we may say that persons, who are characterized as possessing reflective consciousness, may have a higher status than beings having only simple consciousness. Their special worth is a function of the extent to which they use language "to bring possibilities before the mind" and then restrain their more trivial desires for the sake of not harming others whom they recognize, from the moral point of view, as their equals in certain respects. Among the beings whose interests must be taken into account *for their own sake* in the moral deliberations of persons are beings possessing only simple consciousness. To the extent that persons reluctantly cause pain, suffering, and even death to beings possessing simple consciousness in order to meet *important needs,* what they do may be justified by appeal to their higher status or greater worth. But, to the extent that persons inflict avoidable pain and suffering on such beings merely to satisfy certain *trivial tastes or desires,* they pervert their greater capacities. In so doing, they ironically undermine their claim to higher status or worth and thereby weaken any justifiction they may have had for sacrificing beings having only simple consciousness for important ends.

Whether something is to be classified as an "important need" or a "trivial taste or desire" will frequently be a matter of debate and uncertainty. Yet we should not allow disputes over difficult cases to blind us to the existence of relatively easy cases. There is, for example, little doubt that well-designed, nonduplicative research on animals aimed at preventing or treating disease serves an important need. And it seems just as certain that causing pain to animals in order to test the toxicity of "new and improved" floor polishes or cosmetics serves trivial tastes or desires. And even cases that are not so immediately clear may be resolved by a bit of thoughtful investigation. Thus I suspect that most people who care to learn something about human nutrition and the treatment of animals on modern "factory farms" will be strongly inclined to conclude that factory farming causes pain and suffering to animals for the sake of trivial tastes and desires.[14]

FURTHER INQUIRY

The foregoing is at best a sketch or outline of a position on the ethical significance of animal awareness. A number of refinements need to be made and a number of questions need to be answered before we can confidently use it to make particular

---

[14]See, for example, Peter Singer, *Animal Liberation* (New York: New York Review of Books, 1975); and Jim Mason and Peter Singer, *Animal Factories* (New York: Crown Publishers, 1980).

judgments and decisions about the use and treatment of nonhuman animals. First, we must do more in the way of spelling out the crucial distinction between simple consciousness and reflective consciousness. In addition, we must determine the extent to which *various degrees* of both types of consciousness are distributed or realized within members of various classes of human and nonhuman animals. It is important to note here that since there is nothing in the distinction between simple and reflective consciousness that requires it to follow species lines, the investigations in question will involve infants and severely retarded and severely brain-damaged human beings, as well as nonhuman animals.

Among the important questions we must ask is whether, and if so, to what extent, beings who lack reflective consciousness can experience things other than pain and pleasure. For example, can chimps, dogs, pigs, or chickens experience sadness, boredom, loneliness, frustration, apprehensiveness, disappointment, anxiety, and other states that are not as closely identified with determinate behavioral responses as is pain? If so, how would we know? Questions of this kind will, I hope, be soon addressed by philosophers of mind, ethologists, psychologists, neurophysiologists, and others. My principal aim has been to show why, from an ethical point of view, they are important questions.

QUESTIONS

1 Benjamin rejects the "indirect obligation" theories of both Aquinas and Kant, the "no obligation" theory of Descartes, and the "direct obligation" theory of Bentham. Is any of these theories essentially defensible?
2 Does human life have greater worth than animal life? If so, on what grounds?
3 What human needs, if any, are sufficiently important to warrant the infliction of pain and suffering on animals?

The Rights of Animals and Unborn Generations

Joel Feinberg

Joel Feinberg is professor of philosophy at the University of Arizona. He has published many articles in the fields of ethics, philosophy of law, and social philosophy. He is also the author of Doing and Deserving *(1970) and* Social Philosophy *(1973), the editor of* Reason and Responsibility *(1965) and* Moral Concepts *(1969), and the coeditor of* Philosophy of Law *(1975).*

Feinberg provides a detailed analysis of the concept of a right. He undertakes such an analysis for the *proximate purpose* of showing that it is conceptually possible to ascribe rights to unborn generations and for the *ultimate purpose* of providing support for the view that unborn generations have rights against us—rights which

Reprinted with permission of the publisher from *Philosophy & Environmental Crisis,* edited by William T. Blackstone, pp. 43–68. Copyright © 1974 by the University of Georgia Press.

entail the moral demand that those of us now living protect the environment. On Feinberg's analysis, only the sorts of beings who are capable of having interests can meaningfully be said to have rights. In the light of this principle, he argues that individual animals may be said to have rights but individual plants may not be said to have rights. Likewise, he contends, a *species* of animals (or plants) cannot be said to have rights. (Feinberg interprets the duty to protect a threatened species as a duty to future human beings rather than as a duty to the threatened species itself.) With regard to unborn generations, he contends, it is clear that they will have interests when they eventually come to exist. Feinberg argues that the rights of unborn generations are *contingent*; he denies that they have a right to be born, but given the fact that some persons will in fact be born, they have the right to be born into a world which is not "a used up garbage heap."

Every philosophical paper must begin with an unproved assumption. Mine is the assumption that there will still be a world five hundred years from now, and that it will contain human beings who are very much like us. We have it within our power now, clearly, to affect the lives of these creatures for better or worse by contributing to the conservation or corruption of the environment in which they must live. I shall assume furthermore that it is psychologically possible for us to care about our remote descendants, that many of us in fact do care, and indeed that we ought to care. My main concern then will be to show that it makes sense to speak of the rights of unborn generations against us, and that given the moral judgment that we ought to conserve our environmental inheritance for them, and its grounds, we might well say that future generations *do* have rights correlative to our present duties toward them. Protecting our environment now is also a matter of elementary prudence, and insofar as we do it for the next generation already here in the persons of our children, it is a matter of love. But from the perspective of our remote descendants it is basically a matter of justice, of respect for their rights. My main concern here will be to examine the concept of a right to better understand how that can be.

THE PROBLEM

To have a right is to have a claim[1] *to* something and *against* someone, the recognition of which is called for by legal rules or, in the case of moral rights, by the principles of an enlightened conscience. In the familiar cases of rights, the claimant is a competent adult human being, and the claimee is an officeholder in an institution or else a private individual, in either case, another competent adult human being. Normal adult human beings, then, are obviously the sorts of beings of whom rights can meaningfully be predicated. Everyone would agree to that, even extreme misanthropes who deny that anyone in fact has rights. On the other hand, it is absurd to say that rocks can have rights, not because rocks are morally inferior things unworthy of rights (that statement makes no sense either), but because rocks belong to a category of entities of whom

---

[1]I shall leave the concept of a claim unanalyzed here, but for a detailed discussion, see my "The Nature and Value of Rights," *Journal of Value Inquiry* 4 (Winter 1971): 263–277.

rights cannot be meaningfully predicated. That is not to say that there are no circumstances in which we ought to treat rocks carefully, but only that the rocks themselves cannot validly claim good treatment from us. In between the clear cases of rocks and normal human beings, however, is a spectrum of less obvious cases, including some bewildering borderline ones. Is it meaningful or conceptually possible to ascribe rights to our dead ancestors? to individual animals? to whole species of animals? to plants? to idiots and madmen? to fetuses? to generations yet unborn? Until we know how to settle these puzzling cases, we cannot claim fully to grasp the concept of a right, or to know the shape of its logical boundaries.

One way to approach these riddles is to turn one's attention first to the most familiar and unproblematic instances of rights, note their most salient characteristics, and then compare the borderline cases with them, measuring as closely as possible the points of similarity and difference. In the end, the way we classify the borderline cases may depend on whether we are more impressed with the similarities or the differences between them and the cases in which we have the most confidence.

It will be useful to consider the problem of individual animals first because their case is the one that has already been debated with the most thoroughness by philosophers so that the dialectic of claim and rejoinder has now unfolded to the point where disputants can get to the end game quickly and isolate the crucial point at issue. When we understand precisely what *is* at issue in the debate over animal rights, I think we will have the key to the solution of all the other riddles about rights.

INDIVIDUAL ANIMALS

Almost all modern writers agree that we ought to be kind to animals, but that is quite another thing from holding that animals can claim kind treatment from us as their due. Statutes making cruelty to animals a crime are now very common, and these, of course, impose legal duties on people not to mistreat animals; but that still leaves open the question whether the animals, as beneficiaries of those duties, possess rights correlative to them. We may very well have duties *regarding* animals that are not at the same time duties *to* animals, just as we may have duties regarding rocks, or buildings, or lawns, that are not duties *to* the rocks, buildings, or lawns. Some legal writers have taken the still more extreme position that animals themselves are not even the directly intended beneficiaries of statutes prohibiting cruelty to animals. During the nineteenth century, for example, it was commonly said that such statutes were designed to protect human beings by preventing the growth of cruel habits that could later threaten human beings with harm too. Prof. Louis B. Schwartz finds the rationale of the cruelty-to-animals prohibition in its protection of animal lovers from affronts to their sensibilities. "It is not the mistreated dog who is the ultimate object of concern," he writes. "Our concern is for the feelings of other human beings, a large proportion of whom, although accustomed to the slaughter of animals for food, readily identify themselves with a tortured dog or horse and respond with great sensitivity to its sufferings."[2] This seems

---

[2]Louis B. Schwartz, "Morals, Offenses and the Model Penal Code," *Columbia Law Review* 63 (1963): 673.

to me to be factitious. How much more natural it is to say with John Chipman Gray that the true purpose of cruelty-to-animals statutes is "to preserve the dumb brutes from suffering."[3] The very people whose sensibilities are invoked in the alternative explanation, a group that no doubt now includes most of us, are precisely those who would insist that the protection belongs primarily to the animals themselves, not merely to their own tender feelings. Indeed, it would be difficult even to account for the existence of such feelings in the absence of a belief that the animals deserve the protection in their own right and for their own sakes.

Even if we allow, as I think we must, that animals are the intended direct beneficiaries of legislation forbidding cruelty to animals, it does not follow directly that animals have legal rights, and Gray himself, for one,[4] refused to draw this further inference. Animals cannot have rights, he thought, for the same reason they cannot have duties, namely, that they are not genuine "moral agents." Now, it is relatively easy to see why animals cannot have duties, and this matter is largely beyond controversy. Animals cannot be "reasoned with" or instructed in their responsibilities; they are inflexible and unadaptable to future contingencies; they are subject to fits of instinctive passion which they are incapable of repressing or controlling, postponing or sublimating. Hence, they cannot enter into contractual agreements, or make promises; they cannot be trusted; and they cannot (except within very narrow limits and for purposes of conditioning) be blamed for what would be called "moral failures" in a human being. They are therefore incapable of being moral subjects, of acting rightly or wrongly in the moral sense, of having, discharging, or breeching duties and obligations.

But what is there about the intellectual incompetence of animals (which admittedly disqualifies them for duties) that makes them logically unsuitable for rights? The most common reply to this question is that animals are incapable of *claiming* rights on their own. They cannot make motion, on their own, to courts to have their claims recognized or enforced; they cannot initiate, on their own, any kind of legal proceedings; nor are they capable of even understanding when their rights are being violated, of distinguishing harm from wrongful injury, and responding with indignation and an outraged sense of justice instead of mere anger or fear.

No one can deny any of these allegations, but to the claim that they are the grounds for disqualification of rights of animals, philosophers on the other side of this controversy have made convincing rejoinders. It is simply not true, says W. D. Lamont,[5] that the ability to understand what a right is and the ability to set legal machinery in motion by one's own initiative are necessary for the possession of rights. If that were the case, then neither human idiots nor wee babies would have any legal rights at all. Yet it is manifest that both of these classes of intellectual incompetents have legal rights recognized and easily enforced by the courts. Children and idiots start legal

---

[3]John Chipman Gray, *The Nature and Sources of the Law,* 2d ed. (Boston: Beacon Press, 1963), p. 43.

[4]And W. D. Ross for another. See *The Right and The Good* (Oxford: Clarendon Press, 1930), app. 1, pp. 48–56.

[5]W. D. Lamont, *Principles of Moral Judgment* (Oxford: Clarendon Press, 1946), pp. 83–85.

proceedings, not on their own direct initiative, but rather through the actions of proxies or attorneys who are empowered to speak in their names. If there is no conceptual absurdity in this situation, why should there be in the case where a proxy makes a claim on behalf of an animal? People commonly enough make wills leaving money to trustees for the care of animals. Is it not natural to speak of the animal's right to his inheritance in cases of this kind? If a trustee embezzles money from the animal's account,[6] a proxy speaking in the dumb brute's behalf presses the animal's claim, can he not be described as asserting the animal's *rights?* More exactly, the animal itself claims its right through the vicarious actions of a human proxy speaking in its name and in its behalf. There appears to be no reason why we should require the animal to understand what is going on (so the argument concludes) as a condition for regarding it as a possessor of rights.

Some writers protest at this point that the legal relation between a principal and an agent cannot hold between animals and human beings. Between humans, the relation of agency can take two different forms, depending upon the degree of discretion granted to the agent, and there is a continuum of combinations between the extremes. On the one hand, there is the agent who is the mere "mouthpiece" of his principal. He is a "tool" in much the same sense as is a typewriter or telephone; he simply transmits the instructions of his principal. Human beings could hardly be the agents or representatives of animals in this sense, since the dumb brutes could no more use human "tools" than mechanical ones. On the other hand, an agent may be some sort of expert hired to exercise his professional judgment on behalf of, and in the name of, the principal. He may be given, within some limited area of expertise, complete independence to act as he deems best, binding his principal to all the beneficial or detrimental consequences. This is the role played by trustees, lawyers, and ghost-writers. This type of representation requires that the agent have great skill, but makes little or no demand upon the principal, who may leave everything to the judgment of his agent. Hence, there appears, at first, to be no reason why an animal cannot be a totally passive principal in this second kind of agency relationship.

There are still some important dissimilarities, however. In the typical instance of representation by an agent, even of the second, highly discretionary kind, the agent is hired by a principal who enters into an agreement or contract with him; the principal tells his agent that within certain carefully specified boundaries "You may speak for me," subject always to the principal's approval, his right to give new directions, or to cancel the whole arrangement. No dog or cat could possibly do any of those things. Moreover, if it is the assigned task of the agent to defend the principal's rights, the principal may often decide to release his claimee, or to waive his own rights, and instruct his agent accordingly. Again, no mute cow or horse can do that. But although the possibility of hiring, agreeing, contracting, approving, directing, canceling, releasing, waiving, and instructing is present in the typical (all-human) case of agency representation, there appears to be no reason of a logical or conceptual kind why that *must* be so, and indeed there are some special examples involving human principals where it is not in fact so. I have in mind legal rules, for example, that require that a

---

[6]Cf. H. J. McCloskey, "Rights," *Philosophical Quarterly* 15 (1965): 121, 124.

defendant be represented at his trial by an attorney, and impose a state-appointed attorney upon reluctant defendants, or upon those tried *in absentia,* whether they like it or not. Moreover, small children and mentally deficient and deranged adults are commonly represented by trustees and attorneys, even though they are incapable of granting their own consent to the representation, or of entering into contracts, of giving directions, or waiving their rights. It may be that it is unwise to permit agents to represent principals without the latters' knowledge or consent. If so, then no one should ever be permitted to speak for an animal, at least in a legally binding way. But that is quite another thing than saying that such representation is logically incoherent or conceptually incongruous—the contention that is at issue.

H. J. McCloskey,[7] I believe, accepts the argument up to this point, but he presents a new and different reason for denying that animals can have legal rights. The ability to make claims, whether directly or through a representative, he implies, is essential to the possession of rights. Animals obviously cannot press their claims on their own, and so if they have rights, these rights must be assertable by agents. Animals, however, cannot be represented, McCloskey contends, not for any of the reasons already discussed, but rather because representation, in the requisite sense, is always of interest, and animals (he says) are incapable of having interests.

Now, there is a very important insight expressed in the requirement that a being have interests if he is to be a logically proper subject of rights. This can be appreciated if we consider just why it is that mere things cannot have rights. Consider a very precious "mere thing"—a beautiful natural wilderness, or a complex and ornamental artifact, like the Taj Mahal. Such things ought to be cared for, because they would sink into decay if neglected, depriving some human beings, or perhaps even all human beings, of something of great value. Certain persons may even have as their own special job the care and protection of these valuable objects. But we are not tempted in these cases to speak of "thing-rights" correlative to custodial duties, because, try as we might, we cannot think of mere things as possessing interests of their own. Some people may have a duty to preserve, maintain, or improve the Taj Mahal, but they can hardly have a duty to help or hurt it, benefit or aid it, succor or relieve it. Custodians may protect it for the sake of a nation's pride and art lovers' fancy; but they don't keep it in good repair for "its own sake," or for "its own true welfare," or "well-being." A mere thing, however valuable to others, has no good of its own. The explanation of that fact, I suspect, consists in the fact that mere things have no conative life: no conscious wishes, desires, and hopes; or urges and impulses; or unconscious drives, aims, and goals; or latent tendencies, direction of growth, and natural fulfillments. Interests must be compounded somehow out of conations; hence mere things have no interests. *A fortiori,* they have no interests to be protected by legal or moral rules. Without interests a creature can have no "good" of its own, the achievement of which can be its due. Mere things are not loci of value in their own right, but rather their value consists entirely in their being objects of other beings' interests.

So far McCloskey is on solid ground, but one can quarrel with his denial that any animals but humans have interests. I should think that the trustee of funds willed to

---

[7]Ibid.

a dog or cat is more than a mere custodian of the animal he protects. Rather his job is to look out for the interests of the animal and make sure no one denies it its due. The animal itself is the beneficiary of his dutiful services. Many of the higher animals at least have appetites, conative urges, and rudimentary purposes, the integrated satisfaction of which constitutes their welfare or good. We can, of course, with consistency treat animals as mere pests and deny that they have any rights; for most animals, especially those of the lower orders, we have no choice but to do so. But it seems to me, nevertheless, that in general, animals *are* among the sorts of beings of whom rights can meaningfully be predicated and denied.

Now, if a person agrees with the conclusion of the argument thus far, that animals are the sorts of beings that *can* have rights, and further, if he accepts the moral judgment that we ought to be kind to animals, only one further premise is needed to yield the conclusion that some animals do in fact have rights. We must now ask ourselves for whose sake ought we to treat (some) animals with consideration and humaneness? If we conceive our duty to be one of obedience to authority, or to one's own conscience merely, or one of consideration for tender human sensibilities only, then we might still deny that animals have rights, even though we admit that they are the kinds of beings that *can* have rights. But if we hold not only that we ought to treat animals humanely but also that we should do so for the animals' own sake, that such treatment is something we owe animals as their due, something that can be claimed for them, something the withholding of which would be an injustice and a wrong, and not merely a harm, then it follows that we do ascribe rights to animals. I suspect that the moral judgments most of us make about animals do pass these phenomenological tests, so that most of us do believe that animals have rights, but are reluctant to say so because of the conceptual confusions about the notion of a right that I have attempted to dispel above.

Now we can extract from our discussion of animal rights a crucial principle for tentative use in the resolution of the other riddles about the applicability of the concept of a right, namely, that the sorts of beings who *can* have rights are precisely those who have (or can have) interests. I have come to this tentative conclusion for two reasons: (1) because a right holder must be capable of being represented and it is impossible to represent a being that has no interest, and (2) because a right holder must be capable of being a beneficiary in his own person, and a being without interests is a being that is incapable of being harmed or benefitted, having no good or "sake" of its own. Thus, a being without interests has no "behalf" to act in, and no "sake" to act for. My strategy now will be to apply the "interest principle," as we can call it, to the other puzzles about rights, while being prepared to modify it where necessary (but as little as possible), in the hope of separating in a consistent and intuitively satisfactory fashion the beings who can have rights from those which cannot.

VEGETABLES

It is clear that we ought not to mistreat certain plants, and indeed there are rules and regulations imposing duties on persons not to misbehave in respect to certain members of the vegetable kingdom. It is forbidden, for example, to pick wildflowers in the mountainous tundra areas of national parks, or to endanger trees by starting fires in dry forest areas. Members of Congress introduce bills designed, as they say, to "protect" rare redwood trees from commercial pillage. Given this background, it is surprising that no one[8] speaks of plants as having rights. Plants, after all, are not "mere things"; they are vital objects with inherited biological propensities determining their natural growth. Moreover, we do say that certain conditions are "good" or "bad" for plants, thereby suggesting that plants, unlike rocks, are capable of having a "good." (This is a case, however, where "what we say" should not be taken seriously: we also say that certain kinds of paint are good or bad for the internal walls of a house, and this does not commit us to a conception of walls as beings possessed of a good or welfare of their own.) Finally, we are capable of feeling a kind of affection for particular plants, though we rarely personalize them, as we do in the case of animals, by giving them proper names.

Still, all are agreed that plants are not the kinds of beings that can have rights. Plants are never plausibly understood to be the direct intended beneficiaries of rules designed to "protect" them. We wish to keep redwood groves in existence for the sake of human beings who can enjoy their serene beauty, and for the sake of generations of human beings yet unborn. Trees are not the sorts of beings who have their "own sakes," despite the fact that they have biological propensities. Having no conscious wants or goals of their own, trees cannot know satisfaction or frustration, pleasure or pain. Hence, there is no possibility of kind or cruel treatment of trees. In these morally crucial respects, trees differ from the higher species of animals.

Yet trees are not mere things like rocks. They grow and develop according to the laws of their own nature. Aristotle and Aquinas both took trees to have their own "natural ends." Why then do I deny them the status of beings with interests of their own? The reason is that an interest, however the concept is finally to be analyzed, presupposes at least rudimentary cognitive equipment. Interests are compounded out of *desires* and *aims,* both of which presuppose something like *belief,* or cognitive awareness. . . .

WHOLE SPECIES

The topic of whole species, whether of plants or animals, can be treated in much the same way as that of individual plants. A whole collection, as such, cannot have beliefs, expectations, wants, or desires, and can flourish or languish only in the human interest-related sense in which individual plants thrive and decay. Individual elephants can have interests, but the species elephant cannot. Even where individual elephants are not granted rights, human beings may have an interest—economic, scientific, or sentimental—in keeping the species from dying out, and *that* interest may be protected in various ways by law. But that is quite another matter from recognizing a right to survival belonging to the species itself. Still, the preservation of a whole species may quite properly seem to be a morally more important matter than the preservation of an individual animal. Individual animals can have rights but it is implausible to ascribe

[8]Outside of Samuel Butler's *Erewhon.*

to them a right to life on the human model. Nor do we normally have duties to keep individual animals alive or even to abstain from killing them provided we do it humanely and nonwantonly in the promotion of legitimate human interests. On the other hand, we do have duties to protect threatened species, not duties to the species themselves as such, but rather duties to future human beings, duties derived from our housekeeping role as temporary inhabitants of this planet. . . .

FUTURE GENERATIONS

We have it in our power now to make the world a much less pleasant place for our descendants than the world we inherited from our ancestors. We can continue to proliferate in ever greater numbers, using up fertile soil at an even greater rate, dumping our wastes into rivers, lakes and oceans, cutting down our forests, and polluting the atmosphere with noxious gases. All thoughtful people agree that we ought not to do these things. Most would say we have a duty not to do these things, meaning not merely that conservation is morally required (as opposed to merely desirable) but also that it is something due our descendants, something to be done for their sakes. Surely we owe it to future generations to pass on a world that is not a used up garbage heap. Our remote descendants are not yet present to claim a livable world as their right, but there are plenty of proxies to speak now in their behalf. These spokesmen, far from being mere custodians, are genuine representatives of future interests.

Why then deny that the human beings of the future have rights which can be claimed against us now in their behalf? Some are inclined to deny them present rights out of a fear of falling into obscure metaphysics, by granting rights to remote and unidentifiable beings who are not yet even in existence. Our unborn great-great-grandchildren are in some sense "potential" persons, but they are far more remotely potential, it may seem, than fetuses. This, however, is not the real difficulty. Unborn generations are more remotely potential than fetuses in one sense, but not in another. A much greater period of time with a far greater number of causally necessary and important events must pass before their potentiality can be actualized, it is true; but our collective posterity is just as certain to come into existence "in the normal course of events" as is any given fetus now in its mother's womb. In that sense the existence of the distant human future is no more remotely potential than that of a particular child already on its way.

The real difficulty is not that we doubt whether our descendants will ever be actual, but rather that we don't know who they will be. It is not their temporal remoteness that troubles us so much as their indeterminacy—their present facelessness and namelessness. Five centuries from now men and women will be living where we live now. Any given one of them will have an interest in living space, fertile soil, fresh air, and the like, but that arbitrarily selected one has no other qualities we can presently envision very clearly. We don't even know who his parents, grandparents, or great-grandparents are, or even whether he is related to us. Still, whoever these human beings may turn out to be, and whatever they might reasonably be expected to be like, they will have interests that we can affect, for better or worse, right now. That much we can and do know about them. The identity of the owners of these interests is now necessarily obscure, but the fact of their interest-ownership is crystal clear, and that is all that is necessary to certify the coherence of present talk about their rights. We can tell, sometimes, that shadowy forms in the spatial distance belongs to human beings, though we know not who or how many they are; and this imposes a duty on us not to throw bombs, for example, in their direction. In like manner, the vagueness of the human future does not weaken its claim on us in light of the nearly certain knowledge that it will, after all, be human.

Doubts about the existence of a right to be born transfer neatly to the question of a similar right to come into existence ascribed to future generations. The rights that future generations certainly have against us are contingent rights: the interests they are sure to have when they come into being (assuming of course that they will come into being) cry out for protection from invasions that can take place now. Yet there are no actual interests, presently existent, that future generations, presently nonexistent, have now. Hence, there is no actual interest that they have in simply coming into being, and I am at a loss to think of any other reason for claiming that they have a right to come into existence (though there may well be such a reason). Suppose then that all human beings at a given time voluntarily form a compact never again to produce children, thus leading within a few decades to the end of our species. This of course is a wildly improbable hypothetical example but a rather crucial one for the position I have been tentatively considering. And we can imagine, say, that the whole world is converted to a strange ascetic religion which absolutely requires sexual abstinence for everyone. Would this arrangement violate the rights of anyone? No one can complain on behalf of presently nonexistent future generations that their future interests which give them a contingent right of protection have been violated since they will never come into existence to be wronged. My inclination then is to conclude that the suicide of our species would be deplorable, lamentable, and a deeply moving tragedy, but that it would violate no one's rights. Indeed if, contrary to fact, all human beings could ever agree to such a thing, that very agreement would be a symptom of our species' biological unsuitability for survival anyway.

CONCLUSION

For several centuries now human beings have run roughshod over the lands of our planet, just as if the animals who do live there and the generations of humans who will live there had no claims on them whatever. Philosophers have not helped matters by arguing that animals and future generations are not the kinds of beings who can have rights now, that they don't presently qualify for membership, even "auxiliary membership," in our moral community. I have tried in this essay to dispel the conceptual confusions that make such conclusions possible. To acknowledge their rights is the very least we can do for members of endangered species (including our own). But that is something.

QUESTIONS

1 What rights, if any, do animals have? Do all animals have the same rights? (For example, do mosquitos have the same rights as chimpanzees? Do pets perhaps have special rights?)

2 What rights, if any, do future generations have? In particular, do future generations have a right to come into existence?

3 Do we have a moral obligation to protect an animal or plant species threatened with extinction? If so, on what grounds?

Conservation and Posterity

John Passmore

John Passmore is professor of philosophy at Australian National University (Canberra, Australia). His published works include Hume's Intentions *(1952),* A Hundred Years of Philosophy *(1957),* Philosophical Reasoning *(1961), and* Science and Its Critics *(1978).* Man's Responsibility for Nature *(1974), from which this selection is excerpted, is a book dedicated entirely to ecological themes.*

Passmore reviews the question of the extent to which we can be certain that our successors will need certain natural resources. He concludes that uncertainties in this regard are difficult to eradicate. Yet, he argues, to the extent that there is a reasonable certainty that our successors will need certain resources, we are obliged not to waste them. On Passmore's view, we ought to be prepared to sacrifice certain forms of enjoyment for the sake of conservation, but we ought not to sacrifice the continued development of our cultural heritage. To allow human "loves" (art, science, friendship, etc.) to languish in the name of conservation, he argues, is not in the true interest of posterity.

The conservationist programme confronts us with a fundamental moral issue: ought we to pay any attention to the needs of posterity? To answer this question affirmatively is to make two assumptions: first, that posterity will suffer unless we do so; secondly that if it will suffer, it is our duty so to act as to prevent or mitigate its sufferings. Both assumptions can be, and have been, denied. To accept them does not, of course, do anything to solve the problem of conservation, but to reject them is to deny that there is any such problem, to deny that our society would be a better one—morally better—if it were to halt the rate at which it is at present exhausting its resources. Or it is to deny this, at least, in so far as the arguments in favour of slowing-down are purely conservationist in character—ignoring for the moment, that is, such facts as that the lowering of the consumption-rate is one way of reducing the incidence of pollution and that a high rate of consumption of metals and fossil fuels makes it impossible to preserve untouched the wildernesses in which they are so often located.

   To begin with the assumption that posterity will suffer unless we alter our ways, it is still often suggested that, on the contrary, posterity can safely be left to look after itself, provided only that science and technology continue to flourish. This optimistic interpretation of the situation comes especially from economists and from nuclear physicists. . . . If these scientists, these economists, are right, there simply is no "problem of conservation."

Very many scientists, of course, take the opposite view, especially if they are biologists. Expert committees set up by such scientific bodies as the American National Academy of Sciences have, in fact, been prepared to commit themselves to definite estimates of the dates at which this resource or that will be exhausted. This is always, however, on certain assumptions. It makes a considerable difference whether one supposes or denies that rates of consumption will continue to increase exponentially as they have done since 1960; it makes a very great—in many cases an overwhelming—difference whether one supposes or denies that substitutes will be discovered for our major resources. The Academy's extrapolations are best read as a *reductio ad absurdum* of the supposition that our present patterns of resource consumption can continue even over the next century.

The possibility that substitutes will be discovered introduces a note of uncertainty into the whole discussion, an uncertainty which cannot be simply set aside as irrelevant to our moral and political decisions about conservation, which it inevitably and properly influences. At the moment, for example, the prospect of developing a fuel-cell to serve as a substitute for petrol is anything but bright; confident predictions that by 1972 nuclear fusion would be available as an energy source have proved to be unrealistic. But who can say what the situation will be in twenty years time? The now commonplace comparison of earth to a space-ship is thus far misleading: the space-ship astronaut does not have the facilities to invent new techniques, nor can he fundamentally modify his habits of consumption. Any adequate extrapolation would also have to extrapolate technological advances. But by the nature of the case—although technologists have a bad habit of trying to persuade us otherwise—we cannot be at all certain when and whether those advances will take place, or what form they will assume, especially when, unlike the moonshots, they involve fundamental technological innovations such as the containing of nuclear fusion within a magnetic field.

No doubt, the space-ship analogy is justified as a protest against the pronouncements of nineteenth-century rhetoricians that the earth's resources are "limitless" or "boundless." (It was often supposed, one must recall, that oil was being produced underground as fast as it was being consumed.) Fuel-cells, nuclear fusion reactors, machinery for harnessing solar energy all have to be built out of materials, including, as often as not, extremely rare metals. Men can learn to substitute one source of energy or one metallic alloy for another, the more plentiful for the less plentiful. But that is the most they can do. They cannot harness energy without machines, without radiating heat, without creating wastes. Nor can they safely presume that no source of energy, no metal, is indispensable; there is nothing either in the structure of nature or in the structure of human intelligence to ensure that new resources will *always* be available to replace old resources. Think how dependent we still are on the crops our remote agriculture-creating forefathers chose to cultivate; we have not found substitutes for wheat, or barley, or oats, or rice. Nor have we domesticated new animals as beasts or burden. So, quite properly, the conservationist points out.

The uncertainties, however, remain. We can be confident that some day our society will run out of resources, but we do not know when it will do so or what resources it will continue to demand. The Premier of Queensland recently swept aside the protests of conservationists by arguing that Queensland's oil and coal resources should be fully utilised now, since posterity may have no need for them. This is not a wholly irrational attitude. One can readily see the force of an argument which would run thus: we are entitled, given the uncertainty of the future, wholly to ignore the interests of posterity, a posterity whose very existence is hypothetical—granted the possibility of a nuclear disaster—and whose needs, except for such fundamentals as air and water, we cannot possibly anticipate. . . .

We are called upon not to waste those resources our successors will certainly need. But we ought not to act, out of concern for posterity's survival, in ways which are likely to destroy the civilised ideals we hope posterity will share with us. We should try so to act that our successors will not be wholly without electricity, but we need not, should not, close down our civilisation merely in the hope that a remote posterity will have some hope of surviving. . . .

But what sort of sacrifices ought we to make? It follows from what I have already said that we ought not to be prepared, in the supposed interests of posterity, to surrender our loves or the freedom which makes their exercise possible, to give up art, or philosophy, or science, or personal relationships, in order to conserve resources for posterity. Posterity will need our loves as much as we need them; it needs chains of love running to and through it. . . . Those who urge us to surrender our freedom and to abandon our loves so that posterity can enjoy a "true freedom" and a "true love" ought never to be trusted. No doubt, as individuals, we might sometimes have to sacrifice our freedom or certain of our loves. But only to ensure their maintenance and development by others. And this is true, I should argue, even if they can be maintained only at the cost of human suffering—although there is in fact no evidence to suggest that we shall save posterity from suffering by surrendering our freedoms.

The surrender of forms of enjoyment is a different matter. What we would be called upon to do, at this level, is to reduce the consumption of certain goods—those which depend on raw materials which cannot be effectively recycled—and to recycle whenever that is possible, even although the costs of doing so would involve the sacrifice of other goods. That is the kind of sacrifice we ought to be prepared to make, if there is a real risk that it is essential for the continued existence of a posterity able to carry on the activities we love. . . .

QUESTIONS

1 To what extent can we be certain about the needs of posterity for natural resources?

2 Do we have any significant moral obligations to posterity with regard to the conservation of natural resources?

The Value of Wilderness

William Godfrey-Smith

William Godfrey-Smith is an Australian philosopher whose major philosophical interests include environmental philosophy and the metaphysics of time. These interests are reflected in such articles as "The Rights of Non-Humans and Intrinsic Values," "Beginning and Ceasing to Exist," and "Special Relativity and the Present."

Godfrey-Smith investigates the kinds of justification that might come into play in making a case for the preservation of wilderness. He begins by calling attention to a characteristic assumption of Western moral thought: "Value can be ascribed to the nonhuman world only insofar as it is good for the sake of the well-being of human beings." In the light of this "decidedly anthropocentric bias," he contends, only *instrumental* justifications for preserving wilderness are deemed acceptable. Though Godfrey-Smith maintains that a powerful case for the preservation of wilderness can be founded on its instrumental value (i.e., its value for humankind), he believes that we must develop an ecologically based morality which recognizes natural systems as possessing their own intrinsic value. In the spirit of Aldo Leopold, Godfrey-Smith argues that the boundaries of the moral community should be extended. In his view, we must learn to extend moral consideration to "items treated heretofore as matters of expediency."

Wilderness is the raw material out of which man has hammered the artifact called civilization.

Aldo Leopold[1]

The framework which I examine is the framework of *Western* attitudes toward our natural environment, and wilderness in particular. The philosophical task to which I shall address myself is an exploration of attitudes toward wilderness, especially the sorts of justification to which we might legitimately appeal for the preservation of wilderness: what grounds can we advance in support of the claim that wilderness is something which we should *value?*

There are two different ways of appraising something as valuable. It may be that the thing in question is good or valuable *for the sake* of something which we hold to be valuable. In this case the thing is not considered to be good in itself; value in this sense is ascribed in virtue of the thing's being a *means* to some valued end, and not as an *end in itself.* Such values are standardly designated *instrumental* values. Not

---

Reprinted, as a shortened version prepared by the author, from "The Value of Wilderness," *Environmental Ethics,* vol. 1 (Winter 1979), pp. 309–319. Copyright © by William Godfrey-Smith.

[1]Aldo Leopold, *A Sand County Almanac* (New York: Oxford University Press, 1949), p. 188.

everything which we hold to be good or valuable can be good for the sake of something else: our values must ultimately be *grounded* in something which is held to be good or valuable in itself. Such things are said to be *intrinsically* valuable. As a matter of historical fact, those things which have been held to be instrinsically valuable, within our Western traditions of thought, have nearly always been taken to be states or conditions of *persons*, e.g., happiness, pleasure, knowledge, or self-realization, to name but a few.

It follows from this that a very central assumption of Western moral thought is that value can be ascribed to the nonhuman world only insofar as it is good for the sake of the well-being of human beings.[2] Our entire attitude toward the natural environment, therefore, has a decidedly anthropocentric bias, and this fact is reflected in the sorts of justification which are standardly provided for the preservation of the natural environment.

A number of thinkers, however, are becoming increasingly persuaded that our anthropocentric morality is in fact inadequate to provide a satisfactory basis for a moral philosophy of ecological obligation. It is for this reason that we hear not infrequently the claim that we need a "new morality." A new moral framework—that is, a network of recognized obligations and duties—is not, however, something that can be casually conjured up in order to satisfy some vaguely felt need. The task of developing a sound biologically based moral philosophy, a philosophy which is not anthropocentrically based, and which provides a satisfactory justification for ecololgical obligation and concern, is, I think, one of the most urgent tasks confronting moral philosophers at the present. It will entail a radical reworking of accepted attitudes—attitudes which we currently accept as "self-evident"—and this is not something which can emerge suddenly. Indeed, I think the seminal work remains largely to be done.

In the absence of a comprehensive and convincing ecologically based morality we naturally fall back on *instrumental* justifications for concern for our natural surroundings, and for preserving wilderness areas and animal species. We can, I think, detect at least four main lines of instrumental justification for the preservation of wilderness. By *wilderness* I understand any reasonably large tract of the Earth, together with its plant and animal communities, which is substantially unmodified by humans and in particular by human technology. The natural contrast to *wilderness* and *nature* is an *artificial* or *domesticated* environment. The fact that there are borderline cases which are difficult to classify does not, of course, vitiate this distinction.

The first attitude toward wilderness espoused by conservationists to which I wish to draw attention is what I shall call the "cathedral" view. This is the view that wilderness areas provide a vital opportunity for spiritual revival, moral regeneration, and aesthetic delight. The enjoyment of wilderness is often compared in this respect with religious or mystical experience. Preservation of magnificent wilderness areas for those who subscribe to this view is essential for human well-being, and its destruction is conceived as something akin to an act of vandalism, perhaps comparable

---

[2]Other cultures have certainly included the idea that nature should be valued for its own sake in their moral codes, e.g., the American Indians, the Chinese, and the Australian Aborigines.

to—some may regard it as more serious than[3]—the destruction of a magnificent and moving human edifice, such as the Parthenon, the Taj Mahal, or the Palace of Versailles.

Insofar as the "cathedral" view holds that value derives solely from human satisfactions gained from its contemplation it is clearly an instrumentalist attitude. It does, however, frequently approach an *intrinsic value* attitude, insofar as the feeling arises that there is importance in the fact that it is there to be contemplated, whether or not anyone actually takes advantage of this fact. Suppose for example, that some wilderness was so precariously balanced that *any* human intervention or contact would inevitably bring about its destruction. Those who maintained that the area should, nevertheless, be preserved, unexperienced and unenjoyed, would certainly be ascribing to it an intrinsic value.

The "cathedral" view with respect to wilderness in fact is a fairly recent innovation in Western thought. The predominant Graeco-Christian attitude, which generally speaking was the predominant Western attitude prior to eighteenth- and nineteenth-century romanticism, had been to view wilderness as threatening or alarming, an attitude still reflected in the figurative uses of the expression *wilderness,* clearly connoting a degenerate state to be avoided. Christianity, in general, has enjoined "the transformation of wilderness, those dreaded haunts of demons, the ancient nature-gods, into farm and pasture,"[4] that is, to a domesticated environment.

The second instrumental justification of the value of wilderness is what we might call the "laboratory" argument. This is the argument that wilderness areas provide vital subject matter for scientific inquiry which provides us with an understanding of the intricate interdependencies of biological systems, their modes of change and development, their energy cycles, and the source of their stabilities. If we are to understand our own biological dependencies, we require natural systems as a norm, to inform us of the biological laws which we transgress at our peril.

The third instrumentalist justification is the "silo" argument which points out that one excellent reason for preserving reasonable areas of the natural environment intact is that we thereby preserve a stockpile of genetic diversity, which it is certainly prudent to maintain as a backup in case something should suddenly go wrong with the simplified biological systems which, in general, constitute agriculture. Further, there is the related point that there is no way of anticipating our future needs, or the undiscovered applications of apparently useless plants, which might turn out to be, for example, the source of some pharmacologically valuable drug—a cure, say, for leukemia. This might be called, perhaps, the "rare herb" argument, and it provides another persuasive instrumental justification for the preservation of wilderness.

The final instrumental justification which I think should be mentioned is the "gymnasium" argument, which regards the preservation of wilderness as important for athletic or recreational activities.

---

[3]We can after all *replace* human artifacts such as buildings with something closely similar, but the destruction of a wilderness or a biological species is irreversible.

[4]John Passmore, *Man's Responsibility for Nature* (London: Duckworth, 1974; New York: Charles Scribner's Sons, 1974), p. 17; cf. chap. 5.

An obvious problem which arises from these instrumental arguments is that the various activities which they seek to justify are not always possible to reconcile with one another. The interests of the wilderness lover who subscribes to the "cathedral" view are not always reconcilable with those of the ordinary vacationist. Still more obvious is the conflict between the recreational use of wilderness and the interests of the miner, the farmer, and the timber merchant.

The conflict of interest which we encounter here is one which it is natural to try and settle through the economic calculus of cost-benefit considerations. So long as the worth of natural systems is believed to depend entirely on instrumental values, it is natural to suppose that we can sort out the conflict of interests within an objective frame of reference, by estimating the human satisfactions to be gained from the preservation of wilderness, and by weighing these against the satisfactions which are to be gained from those activities which may lead to its substantial modification, domestication, and possibly even, destruction.

Many thinkers are liable to encounter here a feeling of resistance to the suggestion that we can apply purely economic considerations to settle such conflicts of interest. The assumption behind economic patterns of thought, which underlie policy formulation and planning, is that the values which we attach to natural systems and to productive activities are commensurable; and this is an assumption which may be called into question. It is not simply a question of the difficulty of quantifying what value should be attached to the preservation of the natural environment. The feeling is more that economic considerations are simply out of place. This feeling is one which is often too lightly dismissed by tough-minded economists as being obscurely mystical or superstitious; but it is a view worth examining. What it amounts to, I suggest, is the belief that there is something *morally* objectionable in the destruction of natural systems, or at least in their wholesale elimination, and this is precisely the belief that natural systems, or economically "useless" species, do possess an *intrinsic* value. That is, it is an attempt to articulate the rejection of the anthropocentric view that all value, ultimately, resides in *human* interest and concerns.

A feeling persists that cost-benefit analyses tend to overlook important values. One consideration which tends to be discounted from policy deliberations is that which concerns *economically* unimportant species of animals or plants. A familiar subterfuge which we frequently encounter is the attempt to invest such species with spurious economic value, as illustrated in the rare herb argument. A typical example of this, cited by Leopold, is the reaction of ornithologists to the threatened disappearance of certain species of songbirds: they at once came forward with some distinctly shaky evidence that they played an essential role in the control of insects.[5] The dominance of economic modes of thinking is again obvious: the evidence has to be economic in order to be acceptable. This exemplifies the way in which we turn to instrumentalist justifications for the maintenance of biotic diversity.

The alternative to such instrumentalist justifications, the alternative which Leopold advocated with great insight and eloquence, is to widen the boundary of the moral community to include animals, plants, the soil, or collectively *the land*.[6] This involves

---

[5]Aldo Leopold, "The Land Ethic," in *Sand County Almanac*, p. 210.
[6]Cf. Aldo Leopold, "The Conservation Ethic," *Journal of Forestry* 31 (1933): 634–43, and "The Land Ethic," *Sand County Almanac*.

a radical shift in our conception of nature, so that land is recognized not simply as property, to be dealt with or disposed of as a matter of expediency: land in Leopold's view is not a commodity which belongs to us, but a community to which we belong. This change in conception is far-reaching and profound. It involves a shift in our metaphysical conception of nature—that is, a change in what sort of thing we take our natural surroundings to *be*.

The predominant Western conception of the natural world is largely a legacy of the philosophy of Descartes. This philosophy has alienated man from the natural world through its sharp ontological division between conscious minds and mechanically arranged substances which, for Descartes, constitute the rest of nature. An adequate environmental ethic must, *inter alia,* replace the world-view which emerges from Cartesian metaphysics.

This will involve a shift from the piecemeal reductive conception of natural items, to a *holistic* or systemic view in which we come to appreciate the symbiotic interdependencies of the natural world. On the holistic or total-field view, organisms—including man—are conceived as nodes in a biotic web of intrinsically related parts.[7] That is, our understanding of biological organisms requires more than just an understanding of their structure and properties; we also have to attend seriously to their interrelations. Holistic or systemic thinking does not deny that organisms are complex physicochemical systems, but it affirms that the methods employed in establishing the high-level functional relationships expressed by physical laws are often of very limited importance in understanding the nature of biological systems.

The holistic conception of the natural world contains, I think, the possibility of extending the idea of community beyond human society. And in this way biological wisdom does, I think, carry implications for ethics. Just as Copernicus showed us that man does not occupy the physical center of the universe, Darwin and his successors have shown us that man occupies no *biologically* privileged position. We still have to assimilate the implications which this biological knowledge has for morality.

Can we regard man and the natural environment as constituting a community in any morally significant sense? Passmore, in particular, has claimed that this extended sense of community is entirely spurious.[8] Leopold, on the other hand, found the biological extension of community entirely natural.[9] If we regard a community as a collection of individuals who engage in cooperative behavior, Leopold's extension seems to me entirely legitimate. An ethic is no more than a code of conduct designed to ensure cooperative behavior among the members of a community. Such cooperative behavior is required to underpin the health of the community, in this biologically extended sense, *health* being understood as the biological capacity for self-renewal,[10] and *ill-health* as the degeneration or loss of this capacity.

Man, of course, cannot be placed on "all fours" with his biologically fellow creatures in all respects. In particular, man is the only creature who can act as a full-fledged

---

[7]Cf. Arne Naess, "The Shallow and the Deep, Long-Range Ecology Movement," *Inquiry* 16 (1973): 95–100.

[8]Passmore, *Man's Responsibility for Nature,* chap. 6; "Attitudes to Nature," in R. S. Peters, ed., *Nature and Conduct* (London: Macmillan, 1975), p. 262.

[9]Leopold, "The Land Ethic."

[10]*Ibid.,* p. 221.

moral agent, i.e., an individual capable of exercising reflective rational choice on the basis of principles. What distinguishes man from his fellow creatures is not the capacity to *act,* but the fact that his actions are, to a great extent, free from programming. This capacity to modify our own behavior is closely bound up with the capacity to acquire knowledge of the natural world, a capacity which has enabled us, to an unprecedented extent, to manipulate the environment, and—especially in the recent past—to alter it rapidly, violently, and globally. Our hope must be that the capacity for knowledge, which has made ecologically hazardous activities possible, will lead to a more profound understanding of the delicate biological interdependencies which some of these actions now threaten, and thereby generate the wisdom for restraint.

To those who are skeptical of the possibility of extending moral principles, in the manner of Leopold, to include items treated heretofore as matters of expediency, it can be pointed out that extensions have, to a limited extent, already taken place. One clear—if partial—instance, is in the treatment of animals. It is now generally accepted, and this is a comparatively recent innovation,[11] that we have at least a *prima facie* obligation not to treat animals cruelly or sadistically. And this certainly constitutes a shift in moral attitudes. If—as seems to be the case—cruelty to animals is accepted as intrinsically wrong, then there *is* at least one instance in which it is *not* a matter of moral indifference how we behave toward the nonhuman world.

More familiar perhaps are the moral revolutions which have occurred within the specific domain of human society—witness the progressive elimination of the "right" to racial, class, and sex exploitation. Each of these shifts involves the acceptance, on the part of some individuals, of new obligations, rights, and values which, to a previous generation, would have been considered unthinkable.[12] The essential step in recognizing an enlarged community involves coming to see, feel, and understand what was previously preceived as alien and apart: it is the evolution of the capacity of *empathy.*

We can, however, provide—and it is important that we can provide—an answer to the question: "What is the *use* of wilderness?" We certainly ought to preserve and protect wilderness areas as gymnasiums, as laboratories, as stockpiles of genetic diversity, and as cathedrals. Each of these reasons provides a powerful and sufficient instrumental justification for their preservation. But note how the very posing of this question about the *utility* of wilderness reflects an anthropocentric system of values. From a genuinely ecocentric point of view the question "What is the *use* of wilderness?" would be as absurd as the question "What is the *use* of happiness?"

The philosophical task is to try to provide adequate justification, or at least clear the way, for a scheme of values according to which concern and sympathy for our environment is immediate and natural, and the desirability of protecting and preserving wilderness self-evident. When once controversial propositions become platitudes, the philosophical task will have been successful.

I will conclude, nevertheless, on a deflationary note. It seems to me (at least much of the time) that the shift in attitudes which I think is required for promoting genuinely

---

[11]Cf. Passmore, "The Treatment of Animals," *Journal of the History of Ideas* 36 (1975): 195–218.

[12]Cf. Christopher D. Stone, "Should Trees Have Standing? Toward Legal Rights for Natural Objects," *Southern California Law Review* 45 (1972): 450–501.

harmonious relations with nature is too drastic, too "unthinkable," to be very persuasive for most people. If this is so, then it will be more expedient to justify the preservation of wilderness in terms of instrumentalist considerations; and I have argued that there *are* powerful arguments for preservation which can be derived from the purely anthropocentric considerations of human self-interest. I hope, however, that there will be some who feel that such anthropocentric considerations are not wholly satisfying, i.e., that they do not really do justice to our intuitions. But at a time when *human* rights are being treated in some quarters with a great deal of skepticism it is perhaps unrealistic to expect the rights of nonhumans to receive sympathetic attention. Perhaps, though, we should not be too abashed by this: extensions in ethics have seldom followed the path of political expediency.

QUESTIONS

1 Does wilderness have only instrumental value?
2 Is it true, as Godfrey-Smith maintains, that our anthropocentric morality is "inadequate to provide a satisfactory basis for a moral philosophy of ecological obligations"?

Dissenting Opinion in *Sierra Club v. Morton*

Justice William O. Douglas

A biographical sketch of Justice William O. Douglas is found on page 361.

This case developed when Walt Disney Enterprises, Inc., was awarded a permit from the U.S. Forest Service to construct a $35 million recreational complex in the Mineral King Valley, a wilderness area in the Sierra Nevada Mountains of California. The Sierra Club, an organization with a well-known interest in environmental preservation, opposed the "development" of Mineral King Valley and brought suit against the Secretary of the Interior (Rogers C. B. Morton) in an effort to block it. Though the Sierra Club was successful in obtaining a preliminary injunction from the District Court, the Ninth Circuit Court of Appeals reversed. The United States Supreme Court, by a four-to-three margin (two justices not participating), upheld the reversal. The Court's decision was predicated entirely upon the contention that the Sierra Club lacked *standing* to bring suit in such a case. For an organization to have standing to bring suit, the Court said, it is necessary that it be "adversely affected" or "aggrieved"; it is not sufficient that it simply have a special "interest in a problem."

Justice Douglas, in his dissenting opinion, directly addresses the issue of standing. He argues that environmental objects themselves must be granted legal standing, thereby becoming capable of suing for their own preservation. "Those

United States Supreme Court, 405 U.S. 727 (1972).

who have an intimate relation with the inanimate object about to be injured, polluted, or otherwise despoiled are its legitimate spokesmen." Thus, he suggests, the Sierra Club should be recognized as speaking in the name of Mineral King Valley.

. . . The critical question of "standing" would be simplified and also put neatly in focus if we fashioned a federal rule that allowed environmental issues to be litigated before federal agencies or federal courts in the name of the inanimate object about to be despoiled, defaced, or invaded by roads and bulldozers and where injury is the subject of public outrage. Contemporary public concern for protecting nature's ecological equilibrium should lead to the conferral of standing upon environmental objects to sue for their own preservation.[1] This suit would therefore be more properly labeled as *Mineral King v. Morton.*

Inanimate objects are sometimes parties in litigation. A ship has a legal personality, a fiction found useful for maritime purposes. The corporation sole—a creature of ecclesiastical law—is an acceptable adversary and large fortunes ride on its cases.[2] The ordinary corporation is a "person" for purposes of the adjudicatory processes, whether it represents proprietary, spiritual, aesthetic, or charitable causes.[3]

So it should be as respects valleys, alpine meadows, rivers, lakes, estuaries, beaches, ridges, groves of trees, swampland, or even air that feels the destructive pressures of modern technology and modern life. The river, for example, is the living symbol of all the life it sustains or nourishes—fish, aquatic insects, water ouzels, otter, fisher, deer, elk, bear, and all other animals, including man, who are dependent on it or who enjoy it for its sight, its sound, or its life. The river as plaintiff speaks for the ecological unit of life that is part of it. Those people who have a meaningful relation to that body of water—whether it be a fisherman, a canoeist, a zoologist, or a logger—must be able to speak for the values which the river represents and which are threatened with destruction.

I do not know Mineral King. I have never seen it nor travelled it, though I have seen articles describing its proposed "development.". . . The Sierra Club in its complaint alleges that "One of the principal purposes of the Sierra Club is to protect and conserve the national resources of the Sierra Nevada Mountains." The District Court held that this uncontested allegation made the Sierra Club "sufficiently aggrieved" to have "standing" to sue on behalf of Mineral King.

Mineral King is doubtless like other wonders of the Sierra Nevada such as Tuolumne Meadows and the John Muir Trail. Those who hike it, fish it, hunt it, camp in it, or

---

[1]See Stone, "Should Trees have Standing? Toward Legal Rights for Natural Objects," 45 S. Cal. L. Rev. 450 (1972).

[2]At common law, an office holder, such as a priest or the King, and his successors constituted a corporation sole, a legal entity distinct from the personality which managed it. Rights and duties were deemed to adhere to this device rather than to the office holder in order to provide continuity after the latter retired. The notion is occasionally revived by American courts.

[3]Early jurists considered the conventional corporation to be a highly artificial entity. Lord Coke opined that a corporation's creation "rests only in intendment and consideration of the law." Mr. Chief Justice Marshall added that the device is "an artificial being, invisible, intangible, and existing only in contemplation of law." Today suits in the names of corporations are taken for granted.

frequent it, or visit it merely to sit in solitude and wonderment are legitimate spokesmen for it, whether they may be a few or many. Those who have intimate relation with the inanimate object about to be injured, polluted, or otherwise despoiled are its legitimate spokesmen.

The Solicitor General . . . takes a wholly different approach. He considers the problem in terms of "government by the Judiciary." With all respect, the problem is to make certain that the inanimate objects, which are the very core of America's beauty, have spokesmen before they are destroyed. It is, of course, true that most of them are under the control of a federal or state agency. The standards given those agencies are usually expressed in terms of the "public interest." Yet "public interest" has so many differing shades of meaning as to be quite meaningless on the environmental front. Congress accordingly has adopted ecological standards . . . and guidelines for agency action have been provided by the Council on Environmental Quality of which Russell E. Train is Chairman.

Yet the pressures on agencies for favorable action one way or the other are enormous. The suggestion that Congress can stop action which is undesirable is true in theory; yet even Congress is too remote to give meaningful direction and its machinery is too ponderous to use very often. The federal agencies of which I speak are not venal or corrupt. But they are notoriously under the control of powerful interests who manipulate them through advisory committees, or friendly working relations, or who have that natural affinity with the agency which in time develops between the regulator and the regulated. As early as 1894, Attorney General Olney predicted that regulatory agencies might become "industry-minded," as illustrated by his forecast concerning the Interstate Commerce Commission:

"The Commission is or can be made of great use to the railroads. It satisfies the public clamor for supervision of the railroads, at the same time that supervision is almost entirely nominal. Moreover, the older the Commission gets to be, the more likely it is to take a business and railroad view of things." M. Josephson, The Politicos 526 (1938).

Years later a court of appeals observed, "the recurring question which has plagued public regulation of industry [is] whether the regulatory agency is unduly oriented toward the interest of the industry it is designed to regulate, rather than the public interest it is supposed to protect."

The Forest Service—one of the federal agencies behind the scheme to despoil Mineral King—has been notorious for its alignment with lumber companies, although its mandate from Congress directs it to consider the various aspects of multiple use in its supervision of the national forests.

The voice of the inanimate object, therefore, should not be stilled. That does not mean that the judiciary takes over the managerial functions from the federal agency. It merely means that before these priceless bits of Americana (such as a valley, an alpine meadow, a river, or a lake) are forever lost or are so transformed as to be reduced to the eventual rubble of our urban environment, the voice of the existing beneficiaries of these environmental wonders should be heard.

Perhaps they will not win. Perhaps the bulldozers of "progress" will plow under all the aesthetic wonders of this beautiful land. That is not the present question. The sole question is, who has standing to be heard?

Those who hike the Appalachian Trail into Sunfish Pond, New Jersey, and camp or sleep there, or run the Allagash in Maine, or climb the Guadalupes in West Texas, or who canoe and portage the Quetico Superior in Minnesota, certainly should have standing to defend those natural wonders before courts or agencies, though they live 3,000 miles away. Those who merely are caught up in environmental news or propaganda and flock to defend these waters or areas may be treated differently. That is why these environmental issues should be tendered by the inanimate object itself. Then there will be assurances that all of the forms of life which it represents will stand before the court—the pileated woodpecker as well as the coyote and bear, the lemmings as well as the trout in the streams. Those inarticulate members of the ecological group cannot speak. But those people who have so frequented the place as to know its values and wonders will be able to speak for the entire ecological community.

Ecology reflects the land ethic; and Aldo Leopold wrote in A Sand County Almanac 204 (1949), "The land ethic simply enlarges the boundaries of the community to include soils, waters, plants, and animals, or collectively, the land."

That, as I see it, is the issue of "standing" in the present case and controversy.

QUESTIONS

1 Suppose someone made the following objection to Justice Douglas: "Since an inanimate object has no interests of its own, it is simply impossible for anyone to 'speak in its name.' " Would this be a justifiable criticism?

2 Does the wilderness have a moral right to exist?

SUGGESTED ADDITIONAL READINGS FOR CHAPTER 11

Environmental Ethics. This journal, identifying itself as "An Interdisciplinary Journal Dedicated to the Philosophical Aspects of Environmental Problems," began publication in 1979. It is an invaluable source of material relevant to the issues under discussion in this chapter.

FREY, R. G.: *Interests and Rights: The Case Against Animals.* Oxford: The Clarendon Press, 1980. In Frey's view, animals do not have *interests* and thus they do not have moral rights. Accordingly, he contends, arguments for vegetarianism that are based on the claim that animals have moral rights are unsound.

LEOPOLD, ALDO: "The Land Ethic." In *A Sand County Almanac.* New York: Oxford University Press, 1966, pp. 217–241. In this essay, a frequent reference point of contemporary discussions, Leopold calls for an extension of the ethical community beyond its traditional anthropocentric limits.

REGAN, TOM, ed.: *Earthbound: New Introductory Essays in Environmental Ethics.* New York: Random House, 1984. In this collection of original essays, a wide range of issues in environmental ethics is addressed.

———: *The Case for Animal Rights.* Berkeley, Calif.: University of California Press, 1983. Regan argues that animals have a basic moral right to respectful treatment. He derives the following conclusions: (1) vegetarianism is obligatory; (2) hunting and trapping are wrong; (3) the use of animals in science is impermissible.

———, and PETER SINGER, eds.: *Animal Rights and Human Obligations.* Englewood Cliffs, N.J.: Prentice-Hall, 1976. This very useful anthology provides readings organized in four categories: (1) "Contemporary Realities," (II) "Animal and Human Nature," (III) "Do Humans Have Obligations to Other Animals?" and (IV) "Do Animals Have Rights?"

ROLLIN, BERNARD E.: *Animal Rights and Human Morality*. Buffalo, N.Y.: Prometheus, 1981. Rollin suggests an overall account of the rights of animals. He also provides an extensive discussion of both animals as research subjects and animals as pets.

ROLSTON, HOLMES, III: "Is There an Ecological Ethic?" *Ethics,* vol. 85, January 1975, pp. 93–109. In analyzing the notion of an ecological ethic, Rolston distinguishes between a *secondary* ecological ethic (in which an underlying classical moral principle or system is simply applied to generate moral conclusions about the environment) and a *primary* ecological ethic (in which a basic moral principle or system itself emerges from ecological considerations). He finds the latter, the more radically ecological ethic, to be the more attractive option.

SCHERER, DONALD, and THOMAS ATTIG, eds.: *Ethics and the Environment*. Englewood Cliffs, N.J.: Prentice-Hall, 1983. Part One of this anthology organizes material under the heading of "Defining an Environmental Ethic." Part Two deals with "Specific Environmental Problems."

SINGER, PETER: *Animal Liberation*. New York: New York Review, 1975. Singer advances a vigorous critique of our present attitudes toward animals and our dealings with them. He also provides a wealth of relevant factual material.

STONE, CHRISTOPHER: *Should Trees Have Standing?* Los Altos, Calif.: Kaufman, 1974. This short book bears the subtitle, "Toward Legal Rights for Natural Objects." Stone develops in great depth the line of argument relied on by Justice Douglas in *Sierra Club v. Morton* (1972).

DATE DUE

NOV 3 0 1998		
DEC 15 2000		
MAY 0 2 2000		
SEP 25		
APR 1 9 2010		

Demco, Inc. 38-293